A SPECIAL NOTE TO STUDENTS

My goal in writing this book is to create the foundation for you to learn about the important issues and concepts in labor relations in an engaging and enjoyable fashion. Studying labor relations can be both intellectually stimulating and fun! Labor relations have been influenced by everything from violent strikes to religious writings, from libertarians to Marxists, from radical union leaders to great industrialists. You will encounter two characters named Big Bill, the brazen yet grandmotherly Mother Jones, and the still-missing Jimmy Hoffa—not to mention the colorful language of labor relations, which includes yellow dog contracts, the blue flu, hot cargo, whipsawing, and a narcotic effect. You can enrich your studies by listening to union folk songs and watching *Norma Rae, On the Waterfront, Matewan, Billy Elliot, Pride*, and other films. Studying labor relations draws on scholarship in industrial relations, management, economics, history, psychology, sociology, political science, law, working class and women's studies, and philosophy, and I hope you find this diversity both stimulating and interesting.

At the same time, labor relations can be controversial, and many people have strongly formed opinions about labor unions even if they've had little or no firsthand experience with them. I encourage you to approach this book and your labor relations course with an open mind. As you will see, whether labor unions are good or bad depends largely on how one thinks the employment relationship works, especially the extent to which one believes that labor markets are competitive. You do not need to change your beliefs about the employment relationship (and by extension, labor unions), but you do need to understand other perspectives and respect those with other views—just as they must respect your viewpoint. Try to learn from your classmates with different perspectives and engage them in reasoned and respectful discussions with an open mind. I've worked hard to include diverse materials in this textbook to help you understand labor relations from multiple perspectives and to foster lively classroom exercises and discussions. Be an active yet respectful learner in your classroom.

U.S. labor relations are often equated to negotiating thick contracts full of detailed work rules. This is undeniably an important part of labor relations, and it will receive the necessary attention in this book; but do not sell labor relations short by limiting your expectations to this narrow view. I wrote this book so you can learn not only *how* the traditional labor relations processes (like negotiating contracts) work but also *why* these processes exist. Ultimately, labor relations are not about negotiating work rules—they are about trying to balance the economic and human needs of a democratic society and foster broadly shared prosperity. As you learn about the existing processes, continually ask yourself how they contribute (or not) to balancing these needs, and whether there are better ways of achieving these objectives—with traditional unions, with new types of unions, or without any unions at all—in the 21st century world of work. Even if you are a current or future manager or union leader with practical concerns, understanding the pros and cons of the labor relations processes—not just simply grasping how things currently work—is necessary because the labor relations system is in flux. Designing new policies, practices, and strategies that are effective hinges on a deep understanding of the employment relationship and the past, present, and future of labor relations.

Enjoy your stimulating journey through the fascinating world of labor relations!

John W. Budd

To my students and my colleagues

Labor Relations: Striking a Balance

Fifth Edition

John W. Budd
University of Minnesota

LABOR RELATIONS: STRIKING A BALANCE, FIFTH EDITION

This book is printed on acid-free paper.

1 2 3 4 5 6 7 8 9 LWI 21 20 19 18 17

ISBN 978-1-259-41238-7
MHID 1-259-41238-5

Chief Product Officer, SVP Products & Markets: *G. Scott Virkler*
Vice President, General Manager, Products & Markets: *Michael Ryan*
Vice President, Content Design & Delivery: *Betsy Whalen*
Managing Director: *Susan Gouijnstook*
Director, Product Development: *Meghan Campbell*
Product Developer: *Laura Hurst Spell*
Marketing Manager: *Necco McKinley*
Director, Content Design & Delivery: *Terri Schiesl*
Program Manager: *Marianne Musni*
Content Project Managers: *Kelly Hart, Keri Johnson, Karen Jozefowicz*
Buyer: *Jennifer Pickel*
Cover Design: *Studio Montage, St. Louis, MO*
Content Licensing Specialists: *Shannon Manderscheid*
Cover Image: *Sophian Rosly/EyeEm/Getty Images*
Compositor: *Lumina Datamatics, Inc.*
Printer: *LSC Communications*

All credits appearing on page or at the end of the book are considered to be an extension of the copyright page.

Library of Congress Cataloging-in-Publication Data

Names: Budd, John W., author.
Title: Labor relations : striking a balance / John W. Budd, University of Minnesota.
Description: Fifth Edition. | Dubuque, IA : McGraw-Hill Education, [2017] | Revised edition of the author's Labor relations, c2013. | Includes bibliographical references and indexes.
Identifiers: LCCN 2016050775 | ISBN 9781259412387 (pbk. : alk. paper) | ISBN 9781259865107 (ebook)
Subjects: LCSH: Industrial relations—United States.
Classification: LCC HD8066 .B83 2017 | DDC 331.880973—dc23
LC record available at https://lccn.loc.gov/2016050775

mheducation.com/highered

About the Author

John W. Budd is a professor in the Center for Human Resources and Labor Studies at the University of Minnesota's Carlson School of Management, where he holds the Industrial Relations Land Grant Chair. He is a Phi Beta Kappa graduate of Colgate University and received M.A. and Ph.D. degrees from Princeton University. Professor Budd has taught labor relations to undergraduates, professional master's students, and Ph.D. candidates and has received multiple departmental teaching awards as well as an excellence in education award from the Labor and Employment Relations Association (LERA). He has served on LERA's education committee and executive board and has published journal articles about teaching labor relations. Professor Budd's main research interests are in industrial relations, especially labor relations. He is the author of *The Thought of Work* (Cornell University Press) *Employment with a Human Face: Balancing Efficiency, Equity, and Voice* (Cornell University Press), and *Invisible Hands, Invisible Objectives: Bringing Workplace Law and Public Policy into Focus* (with Stephen Befort, Stanford University Press) and the coeditor of *The Ethics of Human Resources and Industrial Relations* (with James Scoville, Labor and Employment Relations Association). He has also published numerous articles in *Industrial and Labor Relations Review, Industrial Relations*, the *Journal of Labor Economics*, the *British Journal of Industrial Relations*, the *Journal of Industrial Relations, Labor Studies Journal*, and other journals and edited volumes. He is the recipient of a LERA Outstanding Young Scholar Award and serves on the editorial boards of the *British Journal of Industrial Relations* and *Industrial and Labor Relations Review*. Professor Budd is director of the University of Minnesota's Center for Human Resources and Labor Studies and has also served as director of graduate studies for Minnesota's graduate program in human resources and industrial relations, one of the oldest and largest such graduate programs in the United States. He also has a monthly blog called "Whither Work?"

Preface

The traditional approach to studying U.S. labor relations focuses on an uncritical exploration of how the existing labor processes work: how unions are organized, how contracts are negotiated, and how disputes and grievances are resolved. And because U.S. unions have typically used these processes to win detailed work rules, there is a tendency to equate labor relations with work rules and therefore to structure labor relations courses and textbooks around examination of these work rules. In other words, traditional labor relations textbooks are dominated by rich descriptions of the *how, what,* and *where* of the major labor relations processes. But what's missing is the *why.* Labor relations are not about work rules. Labor relations processes and work rules are simply a means to more fundamental ends or objectives. What are these objectives? Under what conditions are collectively bargained work rules a desirable or undesirable method for achieving these objectives? In the 21st century world of work, are there better ways of pursuing these objectives? These are the central and engaging questions of labor relations—questions ignored by textbooks that narrowly focus on how the existing labor relations processes and detailed work rules operate in practice.

The importance of moving beyond a process-based focus in studying labor relations is underscored by the fact that today's labor relations processes are under attack from all directions. Business professionals, labor leaders, and diverse academics frequently criticize the operation of contemporary U.S. labor relations, albeit usually for different reasons. Analyzing whether the labor relations system needs updating and evaluating alternative options for reform requires an intellectual framework that is rooted in the objectives of the employment relationship. A description of how the current processes work without any discussion of what the processes are trying to achieve fails to provide the basis for determining whether the processes are working and fails to supply metrics for judging alternative strategies, policies, and processes.

This textbook presents labor relations as a system for striking a balance between the employment relationship goals of efficiency, equity, and voice and between the rights of labor and management. It is important to examine these goals to discover what motivates contemporary U.S. labor relations processes and to evaluate whether these processes remain effective in the 21st century. What are the differing assumptions (such as whether labor markets are competitive) that underlie alternative mechanisms for achieving efficiency, equity, and voice? Why is a balance important? These questions provide the framework for analyzing the existing processes—especially organizing, bargaining, dispute resolution, and contract administration—as well as the major issues facing these processes—particularly the need for workplace flexibility, employee empowerment, and labor–management partnerships in the context of globalization and financialization. Another recurring theme is that the current processes are one option for balancing workplace objectives and rights, but that this system is under fire from many directions. The book therefore concludes with chapters to promote reflection on the strengths and weaknesses of the current system and the possibilities for reform. This material includes a comparative examination of labor relations systems in other countries and a consideration of varied U.S. reform proposals that include changes in union and corporate behavior as well as public policies.

This textbook thus replaces the tired paradigm of "labor relations equal detailed work rules" with the dynamic paradigm of "labor relations equal balancing workplace goals and rights." This is *not* to say that the existing processes are unimportant. Labor law, union organizing, bargaining, dispute resolution, and contract administration are central topics that are thoroughly covered in the heart of this book using diverse historical and contemporary examples. Current and future labor relations practitioners will certainly learn the ins and outs of the traditional labor relations processes. But this is no longer sufficient for effective practice because labor relations practices are in flux. Indeed, recent movements in various states to change public sector labor relations or implement right-to-work laws, sometimes punctuated by large-scale protests such as those we witnessed in Wisconsin, as well as the new dynamism around fast food strikes, highlight the unsettled nature of contemporary labor relations. As such, the labor relations processes are not presented in this textbook as self-evidently good; they are placed in the broader context of the nature of the employment relationship to foster a deep understanding of labor relations. The logic and relevance of the existing labor relations processes are more readily understood when explicitly linked to the beliefs about the employment relationship that underlie these processes. This deep understanding further provides the foundation for critically evaluating future directions for labor relations and labor policy—what labor relations strategies, policies, and practices can most effectively balance the workplace goals and rights of workers and employers in the environment of the 21st century?

ORGANIZATION

Labor Relations: Striking a Balance has four parts and is written for upper-level undergraduates and professional-level graduate students. Part One provides the intellectual framework for studying labor relations. Chapter 1 sketches the major concerns in labor relations within a context explicitly rooted in the objectives of the employment relationship (efficiency, equity, and voice) and of labor relations (striking a balance). In Chapter 2 four different views of labor unions in the employment relationship are presented from the perspectives of mainstream economics, human resource management, industrial relations, and critical (or radical or Marxist) industrial relations. The industrial relations viewpoint shapes the existing U.S. policies on collective bargaining, so a thorough understanding of this school of thought is essential, and this understanding is best achieved through contrasts with the other three schools.

Part Two focuses on the New Deal industrial relations system—today's U.S. labor relations system: its historical development (Chapter 3), labor law (Chapter 4), the strategies and organizational structures used by labor and management and the environmental constraints they face (Chapter 5), how new unions are organized (Chapter 6), how contracts are negotiated (Chapter 7), how bargaining disputes are resolved (Chapter 8), and how grievances over contract administration are resolved (Chapter 9). Part Two provides a thorough understanding of these processes to help develop effective management professionals and labor advocates, as well as for thinking more critically about future directions for U.S. labor relations. Part Three focuses on four issues that are putting particular strain on the New Deal industrial relations system in the 21st century: workplace flexibility, employee empowerment, and labor–management partnerships (Chapter 10) as well as globalization and financialization (Chapter 11). These are important issues for business, policymakers, and labor unions and also reflect struggles with efficiency, equity, and voice and trying to balance labor rights and property rights. Consequently, these issues are critical for both policy and practice.

The goals of Parts One, Two, and Three are to develop a deep understanding of the current state of U.S. labor relations—its goals, major processes, and current pressures. But many individuals from nearly every viewpoint—pro-business or pro-union, liberal or conservative, Republican or Democrat, academic or practitioner—have called for reform of the existing U.S. labor relations system. Thus, Part Four reflects on the current state of U.S. labor relations and options for reform. Other countries wrestle with the same goal of balancing efficiency, equity, and voice, and Chapter 12 presents some comparative examples of different labor relations systems. In a global economy it is important to understand how things work in other countries to be a better manager or labor leader, but there are also lessons for reflection and reform. The concluding chapter returns to the starting questions: What should labor relations do? What should labor relations seek to accomplish? And in light of the material in the rest of the book, what reforms are needed—in union strategies, corporate governance and social responsibility, and labor law? Chapter 13 therefore integrates the past lessons with directions for the future. Throughout the chapters, engaging historical and contemporary examples are combined with concrete issues for both practice and policy to develop a deep understanding of the past, present, and future of U.S. labor relations for managers, unionists, workers, and anyone concerned with the employment relationship. Much of the material has important implications for nonunion managers, too.

The first four editions of *Labor Relations: Striking a Balance* were well received by instructors and students alike. In fact, the first edition was recognized with a Texty excellence award from the Textbook and Academic Authors Association for the best textbook in accounting, business, economics, and management in 2005. This fifth edition continues to refine and update rather than overhaul the successful approach of the earlier editions. The particular emphases of the revisions for this fifth edition are engagement with new events, pressures, and ideas as well as removal of unnecessary details and additional clarity of specific topics identified by the reviewers. In various places in this new edition, issues raised by the Fight for $15 movement, alt-labor initiatives, protests over proposals to change public sector bargaining laws, debates over right-to-work laws, and new NLRB policies and rulings are incorporated. Every chapter now includes an explicit nonunion application element as well as two online exploration exercises in the flow of the text. And Chapter 11 has been significantly re-written to more efficiently focus on the labor relations relevance of globalization while adding a brand new section on financialization which many scholars now recognize as another very important pressure on labor relations. Updated statistics and references appear throughout the text.

KEY FEATURES

- Extensive supporting pedagogical materials (discussed below).
- A rich intellectual framework for understanding both the current labor relations system and possible alternatives. This framework focuses on three conceptual elements: the objectives of the employment relationship (efficiency, equity, and voice), the objectives of labor relations (striking a balance), and differing views of labor markets and conflict.
- Comprehensive, even-handed coverage of the New Deal industrial relations system—including history, law, and all the major labor relations processes—as well as current issues (workplace flexibility, employee empowerment, labor–management partnerships, globalization, and financialization) and multiple alternative directions for union strategies, corporate behavior, and labor law. Engaging historical and contemporary examples illustrate many issues; these examples are drawn from a wide variety of industries, occupations, and demographic groups.
- Discussion of whether workers' rights are human rights. Moreover, the clash between property rights and labor rights is highlighted as a central conflict in labor relations. This theme is used to increase the understanding of the legal doctrines that underlie the labor relations processes by seeking to balance these competing rights.
- A serious treatment of ethics integrated throughout the text. Unlike any other labor relations textbook, major ethical theories and principles are discussed (Chapter 5). Many chapters ask students to apply these principles to important labor relations issues.
- Contemporary management and union strategic issues integrated throughout the text, including integrative bargaining, workplace flexibility, work teams, reengineering, leadership, change management, the organizing model of union representation, and social movement unionism.

- Separate chapters on globalization/financialization and comparative labor relations systems. The comparative chapter discusses labor relations in representative industrialized countries (Canada, Great Britain, Ireland, France, Germany, Sweden, Australia, and Japan) as well as in Mexico, eastern Europe, China, and other Asian developing countries, along with the debate over convergence of policies and practices. The globalization and financialization chapter is unique among labor relations textbooks and explores the pros and cons of globalization, debates over free or fair trade, the use of corporate codes of conduct and the International Labor Organization to promote workers' rights, transnational union collaboration, issues for international managers, multiple dimensions of financialization, and ethical concerns.
- Issues specific to public sector labor relations integrated throughout the text rather than relegated to a special topics chapter. Nonunion applications appear in every chapter, too.
- Explicit discussions of four schools of thought about the employment relationship—mainstream economics, human resource management, pluralist industrial relations, and critical industrial relations—and the importance of these different perspectives in understanding conflicting views of labor unions and labor policies.
- Inclusion of diverse scholarship on labor relations incorporated throughout the text to promote a broad understanding of the subject and to create an engaging, interesting book for the reader that draws on many disciplines and perspectives.
- Appendixes including the full text of the National Labor Relations Act, the United Nations' Universal Declaration of Human Rights, and a sample NLRB decision.
- The Zinnia and Service Workers Local H-56: An accompanying online bargaining simulation for students to experience the collective bargaining process by renegotiating a hotel's union contract. The simulation is structured around websites for the hotel and the union, and all the necessary materials are online at *www.thezinnia.com*.

LEARNING AIDS

Labor Relations: Striking a Balance combines a rich intellectual framework and the latest issues and debates in labor relations with extensive pedagogical aids. My teaching philosophy embraces contemporary developments in learning theory by using active learning strategies that are responsive to diverse learning styles. In my own teaching of labor relations, this approach has resulted in a stimulating classroom environment as well as multiple teaching awards. Helping instructors create similar learning environments to facilitate enriched student learning is an important objective of this textbook. Significant learning aids in this textbook include the following:

- Numerous case studies to promote classroom discussion appear throughout each chapter. Tables and figures also summarize and reinforce important elements of each chapter.
- Varied active learning exercises to foster an active learning approach and increase student participation are included in the text and supplementary materials.
- Each chapter begins with an advance organizer, list of learning objectives, and outline to prepare students for the chapter's material. Each chapter concludes with a list of key terms (boldfaced in the chapter) and reflection questions.
- Visual learning aids such as diagrams, pictures, cartoons, time lines, and charts help students with diverse learning styles connect with the material. Each chapter also includes two online exploration exercises integrated into the flow of the text to help learners engage with the material.
- Ten labor law discussion cases in Chapters 4, 6, 7, 8, 10, and 11 help students apply important legal concepts. An additional 10 grievance discussion cases in Chapter 9 help

students wrestle with the central elements of contract administration. A sample NLRB decision is also included in Appendix C.

- The accompanying web-based bargaining simulation at *www.thezinnia.com* also promotes active learning. Rather than reading a spoon-fed narrative, students must explore the websites of a fictitious employer and union to learn about the bargaining environment.

TEACHING AIDS

Labor Relations: Striking a Balance includes and with a variety of teaching aids to help instructors create a dynamic learning environment.

McGraw-Hill Connect®: connect.mheducation.com

Continually evolving, McGraw-Hill Connect® has been redesigned to provide the only true adaptive learning experience delivered within a simple and easy-to-navigate environment, placing students at the very center.

- Performance Analytics–Now available for both instructors and students, easy-to-decipher data illuminates course performance. Students always know how they're doing in class, while instructors can view student and section performance at-a-glance.
- Personalized Learning–Squeezing the most out of study time, the adaptive engine within Connect creates a highly personalized learning path for each student by identifying areas of weakness and providing learning resources to assist in the moment of need.

This seamless integration of reading, practice, and assessment ensures that the focus is on the most important content for that individual.

Instructor Library

The Connect Management Instructor Library is your repository for additional resources to improve student engagement in and out of class. You can select and use any asset that enhances your lecture.

The Library for the fifth edition includes the following resources:

- The detailed instructor's manual contains
  - Chapter outlines, learning objectives, lecture ideas, teaching tips, active learning exercises, ideas for using technology in the classroom, and suggestions for videos and other supplementary materials, along with a glossary of key terms and answers to the end-of-chapter questions.
  - Detailed teaching notes for all of the text's 20 labor law and grievance cases that appear in Chapters 4, 6, 7, 8, 9, 10, and 11.
  - Tips and hints for using the accompanying online collective bargaining simulation, The Zinnia and Service Workers Local H-56 (available at *www.thezinnia.com*).
  - A unique "Pedagogical Introduction to Teaching Labor Relations" that discusses the use of active learning techniques and other best practices to help instructors engage students with diverse learning styles.
- The revised test bank contains approximately 100 questions per chapter and consists of multiple-choice, true/false, and essay questions; correct answers are accompanied by page references and tags indicating level of difficulty.
- PowerPoint presentations outline the important concepts of each chapter and reference relevant text exhibits.

Acknowledgments

I am indebted to numerous individuals for their direct and indirect assistance in the creation of all three editions of *Labor Relations: Striking a Balance*. I must first thank my family—Gwen, Gregory, Cecily, and Elizabeth for their continued support, patience, good humor, stress relief, and occasional proofreading. We all miss Bert and his stress relief contributions. For the first edition, my colleague John Fossum was instrumental in helping me get started; since then, John Weimeister, Laura Hurst Spell, and the rest of the McGraw-Hill Education team have encouraged me to be innovative while providing the editorial support to improve and refine my ideas. The editorial coordinators—Trina Hauger on the first edition, Heather Darr on the second, Jane Beck on the third, and Robin Bonner on the fourth—were especially helpful, supportive, and responsive. I continue to be indebted to the University of Minnesota human resources and industrial relations students who over the years have tolerated my classroom experimentation and provided feedback for improvements. I am similarly grateful to many professors at Minnesota and elsewhere, as well as numerous human resources professionals, union leaders, and neutrals for sharing their experiences, expertise, and encouragement. The staff members of the Georgianna Herman Library deserve special thanks for their helpfulness in identifying references and sources.

Each edition has been greatly improved by the careful feedback I have received from the reviewers. For the first edition, I thank Alexander J.S. Colvin (Cornell University), Victor Devinatz (Illinois State University), Richard Hannah (Middle Tennessee State University), Michael LeRoy (University of Illinois), Barbara Rau (University of Wisconsin–Oshkosh), William Ross (University of Wisconsin–LaCrosse), Howard Stanger (Canisius College), and James E. Wanek (Boise State University). For the second edition, I thank Matthew M. Bodah (University of Rhode Island), Phillip Ettman (Westfield State College), Robert A. Figler (The University of Akron), James Randall Nutter (Geneva College), and James E. Wanek (Boise State University). For the third edition, I thank Diane Galbraith (Slippery Rock University), Toni Knechtges (Eastern Michigan University), Jonathan Monat (California State University–Long Beach), Barbara Rau (University of Wisconsin–Oshkosh), and Elizabeth Welsh (University of Minnesota). Helpful comments were also provided by Greg Saltzman (Albion College) and John Remington (University of Minnesota). For the fourth edition, I am grateful to David Nye (Athens State University), Barbara Rau (University of Wisconsin–Oshkosh), Decateur Reed (Boise State University), and Martin St. John (Westmoreland County Community College). For the fifth edition, thank you to Anne M. Fiedler (Nova Southeastern University), Bryan Kennedy (Athens State University), Roger Kubler (Embry-Riddle Aeronautical University), and Kimberly A. LaFevor (Athens State University).

John W. Budd
Minneapolis, Minnesota
July 2016

Brief Contents

Contents

Foundations

It is tempting to study labor relations by focusing on how the key processes work, such as how union contracts are negotiated. But we cannot effectively understand these processes unless we know both what they are trying to achieve and how they fit with the employment relationship. The first two chapters therefore provide a foundation for studying labor relations by introducing the key issues and problems in contemporary labor relations within a context that emphasizes the objectives of labor relations and alternative models of the employment relationship.

Chapter One

Contemporary Labor Relations: Objectives, Practices, and Challenges

Advance Organizer

You probably have preconceived notions about labor relations and labor unions—perhaps from your parents, from the news media, or from personal experiences. Now it is time to think more carefully about labor relations in an open-minded way. The starting point for studying labor relations is consideration of the objectives of a labor relations system. Specifically, the U.S. labor relations system attempts to balance the objectives of employees, employers, and society; but this system faces significant pressures and continues to be criticized from many directions.

Learning Objectives

By the end of this chapter, you should be able to

1. **Understand** why studying labor relations is important and how the subject can be fascinating.
2. **Define** the objectives of the employment relationship (efficiency, equity, and voice) and of labor relations (striking a balance).
3. **Describe** the basic features of the contemporary U.S. labor relations system—collective bargaining, detailed union contracts, and private sector union density decline.
4. **Discuss** the current pressures on the U.S. labor relations system—on the corporate side, workplace flexibility and employment involvement (stemming at least partly from globalization); on the labor side, low union density, a representation gap, and difficulties in organizing new workers.

Contents

On April 14, 2016, fast-food workers walked off the job or didn't report to work in New Orleans. And Milwaukee. And Atlanta, Denver, Boston, Minneapolis, and Seattle. And in Chile, Thailand, and France. In fact, thousands of workers in over 300 cities demonstrated for higher minimum wages and better working conditions for low-paid workers as part of the ongoing "Fight for $15" movement. These protesters were supported by many others through tweets, re-tweets, online petitions, Facebook pages, and other social media actions. Indeed, throughout history individuals have used collective action to voice dissatisfaction and to seek change. It is for these reasons that millions of people in all kinds of occupations—perhaps your parents, your grandparents, or even you—have joined and been represented by labor unions around the world.

Although many labor unions today are large, bureaucratic organizations, the essence of a **labor union** is a group of workers who join together to influence the nature of their employment. Perhaps they are seeking improved wages and benefits, protection against arbitrary treatment and discharge, or a greater voice in workplace decision making. Even retired managers and executives turn to collective action to redress perceived injustices, as with the formation of the Association of BellTel Retirees and other retiree organizations to challenge unilateral corporate reductions in pension cost-of-living increases and health care benefits for retirees. From the worker's perspective, this is fundamentally what labor relations are about: collective work-related protection, influence, and voice.

For employers, in contrast, labor relations are about managing relationships with employees and labor unions in ways that promote organizational goals such as profitability (in the private sector) or cost-effective service delivery (in the public sector). Nonunion employers typically pursue these goals by trying to remain union-free through preventive labor relations strategies (see the "Ethics in Action" case at the end of this chapter). These strategies can range from aggressive union-busting tactics that scare workers away from unions to progressive human resource management tactics that seek to make unions unnecessary. Unionized employers might also try to undermine labor unions by using these same strategies, but most deal with their unions constructively, primarily through collective bargaining, adhering to the resulting union contracts, and resolving disputes through grievance procedures. Competitive pressures are thereby transferred to the bargaining table, where managers try to keep their wage and benefit costs in line with those of their competitors, and try to negotiate for work rule changes when additional flexibility is needed.

Society, too, has an important stake in labor relations. The Occupy movement's slogan "We are the 99 percent" has raised awareness about the dramatic increase in income inequality that has occurred since 1980.[1] At least part of the cause of this increase has been the weakening of labor unions, and these inequalities burden taxpayers and can destabilize society.[2] Strikes and other forms of labor–management conflict can deprive consumers of goods and services and can even jeopardize safety: for example, hospital strikes increase mortality rates, and defective Firestone tires that caused numerous deaths were significantly more likely to have been produced during two critical periods of labor–management conflict when managers demanded concessions and when permanent strike replacements were used.[3] At the other end of the spectrum, labor–management relationships that produce well-trained and motivated unionized employees produce clear benefits for society, such as the thousands of police, firefighters, and other unionized rescue workers who performed heroically after the 9/11/2001 terrorist attacks, or the unionized nurses and other health care professionals who work all hours of the day providing compassionate care. Labor relations can also serve democracy by allowing labor unions to promote the decent working and living conditions that free and equal citizens deserve, and to provide a voice for workers in the political arena.[4]

Employees, employers, labor unions, the public, and policymakers therefore are affected by the major processes of labor relations. Consequently, studying labor relations frequently emphasizes these processes—the union organizing process (how unions are formed), the collective-bargaining process (how contracts are negotiated), the dispute resolution process (how bargaining impasses are prevented or resolved), and the contract administration process (how grievances over the application of the contract are managed). These are important processes in U.S. labor relations, and they are the focus of the middle part of this book (for a road map to the entire book, see the "Organization" section of the preface). But these processes are only means to deeper objectives. This book therefore also emphasizes the importance of understanding what the labor relations processes try to achieve.

THE OBJECTIVES OF LABOR RELATIONS

The foundation of studying any work-related subject is the objectives of the employment relationship. When you work, what do you want to get out of it? Money? Health insurance? A feeling of accomplishment? A sense of self-worth? Other things? When you work, how would you like to be treated? Like a machine? Or with dignity and respect? Would you be satisfied to always have someone else telling you how your job should be done, or would you like to have input into the nature of your job? What does your employer want? Now think about society at large. From this perspective, what should be the goals of work?

This book is based on three objectives of the employment relationship: **efficiency, equity, and voice.**[5] Efficiency is the productive, profit-maximizing use of labor to promote economic prosperity; equity is fairness in the distribution of economic rewards, the administration of employment policies, and the provision of employee security; and voice is the ability of employees to have meaningful input into workplace decisions. Efficiency is a standard of economic or business performance; equity is a standard of fair treatment for employees; and voice is a standard of employee participation. In the public sector, efficiency can be seen as including cost-effective service delivery and other indicators of an efficient government agency. Workplace policies that promote flexibility and productivity are examples of how efficiency might be achieved; decent wage and benefit packages or policies that dismiss workers only for valid, performance-related reasons are examples of providing equity; and employee autonomy and representation by labor unions are examples of ways to pursue the voice dimension (see Figure 1.1).[6]

Sometimes these three objectives work together, such as when equitable treatment and employee voice increase commitment, reduce turnover, and therefore improve productivity and quality (efficiency). Unfortunately these goals often conflict: Equitable treatment might reduce flexibility and therefore efficiency, or employee voice might make decision making more cumbersome and therefore less efficient. The sharpest conflicts are typically between efficiency on one hand and equity and voice on the other. But equity and voice can also clash, such as when unions centralize their power to better achieve equity but in the process become less responsive to individual needs and voices. Labor relations, therefore,

FIGURE 1.1
Aspects of Efficiency, Equity, and Voice in the Employment Relationship

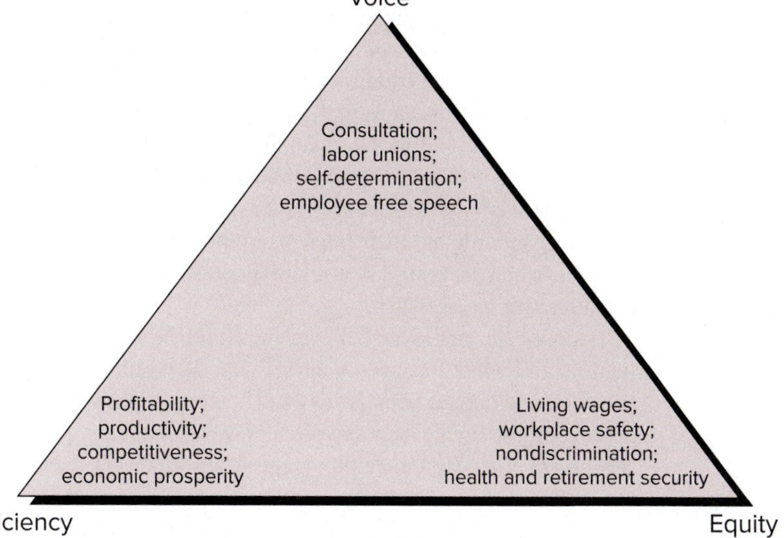

must strike a balance between these three sometimes conflicting goals.[7] As a result, studying labor relations involves analyzing how employee representation through independent labor unions contributes to achieving a balance among efficiency, equity, and voice. This is the first major theme of this book.

Furthermore, it is the official policy of the United States to "encourag[e] the practice and procedure of collective bargaining" and to protect workers' rights to join together for "negotiating the terms and conditions of their employment" and for "other mutual aid or protection."[8] U.S. policy, at least as written in law, is not to *tolerate* collective bargaining but to *encourage* it. And according to the United Nations' Universal Declaration of Human Rights, "Everyone has the right to form and to join trade unions for the protection of his interests." But why should society encourage or discourage the formation of labor unions? This is the second major theme of this book.

Finally, what do labor unions do? U.S. unions are stereotypically associated with inflated wages and restrictive work rules.[9] However, an alternative perspective sees unions as securing better wages to provide decent living standards for their members and as negotiating extensive work rules to protect their members against unfair treatment by management. Moreover, unions can provide voice and representation to individual workers while the labor movement can advocate for working people in the social and political arenas. Based on these and other activities, why do some workers support unions while others oppose them? Why do employers typically oppose unions? And *if* labor unions are a good thing, how should they be structured and promoted in the 21st-century world of work? This is the third theme of this book.

Isn't Efficiency Enough?

For business leaders, business schools, the business press, and business-friendly politicians, the primary objective of the employment relationship is efficiency. Business is seen as best promoting economic prosperity through free-market competition. Profits, not wages, are seen as the critical barometer of economic health, and shareholder interests trump the interests of other stakeholders. In the American social imagination, we are a nation of consumers, not workers.[10] Debates over labor unions, minimum wage laws, and paid family or sick leave are thereby reduced to debates over their effects on labor costs and competitiveness. The old saying "What's good for General Motors is good for the country" is perhaps more widely believed than ever, especially if it is updated to "What's good for Walmart is good for the world." Individuals who defraud shareholders can be sentenced to 25 years in jail, but someone who willfully violates federal workplace safety standards that results in a worker's death faces maximum jail time of only six months—even lower than the prison sentence for harassing a wild burro. Concerns like equity and voice are seen as social issues that interfere with business. Companies, it is argued, have no obligation to provide personal and moral development, and business is not designed to be a "training ground for democracy."[11] And public sector agencies should be focused on cost-effective service delivery. Managers are responsible to investors or taxpayers while workers freely choose to subordinate their interests to managerial directives in return for wages and benefits. So when studying labor relations or other work-related topics, isn't it enough to just consider efficiency issues?

Suppose an employer believed it would be efficient to hire only African American janitors and white managers—or vice versa. Would this be acceptable? If not, there must be social and human boundaries on efficiency.[12] These boundaries are equity and voice. In practice, these boundaries can often be weak. For example, the U.S. employment relationship is governed by the employment-at-will doctrine.[13] Although employees typically do not realize it, this means that employers can fire workers for many reasons—or no reason at all. In fact, the United States is unique among industrialized countries in the lack of just

Labor Relations Application Take the Employment-at-Will Quiz

Instructions: For each of the following scenarios, indicate whether you believe a court of law would find the termination to be lawful or unlawful, *not* what you would like the result to be. In each case, the employee is *not* represented by a union and was *not* fired because of his or her race, sex, national origin, religion, age, or disability. Except for scenario 7, there is no formal written or oral agreement between the employee and employer stating the terms of employment.

	Lawful	Unlawful
1. An organization fires an employee with satisfactory job performance in order to hire another person to do the same job at a lower wage. This termination is	______	______
2. An organization fires someone because their job performance is unsatisfactory. This termination is	______	______
3. An employee with satisfactory job performance is fired because their manager thought they had stolen money. In court, the employee is able to prove that they did not steal and that the manager was mistaken. This termination is	______	______
4. An employee is terminated because there is no longer enough work. This termination is	______	______
5. A worker with satisfactory job performance is accused of being dishonest. Their manager knows that this is untrue, but fires the employee anyway because the manager personally dislikes the employee. This termination is	______	______
6. An organization is violating the law by billing customers for services not performed. Upon finding out about this scheme, an employee refuses to illegally overcharge customers. As a result of this refusal, the employee is fired. This termination is	______	______
7. An organization's employee handbook includes the following: "Employees will be dismissed only for just and sufficient cause." Because of this, an employee quits their current job to work for this organization. After several years, this person is fired and is replaced by someone doing the same work for lower pay. The employee's job performance was satisfactory during their entire time with the organization. This termination is	______	______

Answers: The termination is lawful in questions 1–5 (unless you live in Montana). The termination in question 6 is unlawful. The termination in question 7 is lawful in states that have adopted broad public policy exceptions to at-will employment. Pauline T. Kim, "Bargaining with Imperfect Information: A Study of Worker Perceptions of Legal Protection in an At-Will World" *Cornell Law Review* 83 (November 1997), pp. 105–60, reports the results of a survey in which less than 20% of individuals correctly answered questions similar to numbers 1, 3, 5, and 7. So workers believe they have greater protections than they actually do.

cause discharge protections that provide safeguards against being arbitrarily fired for reasons not related to job performance or business need.[14] There are a few exceptions to the employment-at-will doctrine in the United States, but these are limited to several legislative restrictions (especially antidiscrimination laws), contractual restrictions (most widely associated with union contracts), and a patchwork of state-by-state judicial exceptions (such as firing someone for refusing to break the law); otherwise, U.S. employers do not need a good reason to fire someone.

Labor Relations Application Workplace Cybervoice

In what must be one of the first instances of employee voice being facilitated by communications technology, hundreds of telegraph operators conducted an online meeting in the mid-1800s. The employees were from 33 offices along 700 miles of telegraph lines stretching from Boston to the Canadian border with Maine. They conducted the meeting, and even passed resolutions, electronically using Morse code. Today, modern information technologies and social media tools are greatly enhancing workplace voice in both nonunion and unionized settings.

A large, nonunion technology company, for example, established a companywide electronic bulletin board for employees to discuss issues. Case study evidence shows that this enabled management to better share information with the employees. But more important for issues of employee voice, this electronic communication provided a forum for employees to express their concerns to management and to discuss issues with other employees. In response to a proposed change in the company's profit-sharing plan, hundreds of messages were posted on the electronic bulletin board; and after a number of electronic conversations among employees and management, the plan was revised.

Numerous blogs also address employment-related issues. Some blogs are forums for workers to exchange technical information; others are a way for individuals to vent work-related frustrations. Union-run blogs can be used to build support for specific organizing campaigns, contract negotiations, or public policy debates; many individuals express support for and criticism of labor unions in their own blogs. Social media campaigns are also popular among union activists around the globe, and the LabourStart website (*www.labourstart.org*) regularly lists active campaigns in support of workers who have been fired or jailed for trying to form unions. Work-related cybervoice is now an important aspect of labor relations, and no Morse code is required.

References: Tom Standage, *The Victorian Internet: The Remarkable Story of the Telegraph and the Nineteenth Century's Online Pioneers* (New York: Walker, 1998), p. 133; Libby Bishop and David I. Levine, "Computer-Mediated Communication as Employee Voice: A Case Study," *Industrial and Labor Relations Review* 52 (January 1999), pp. 213–33; Rafael Gely and Leonard Bierman, "Workplace Blogs and Workers' Privacy," *Louisiana Law Review* 66 (Summer 2006), pp. 1079–110.

Although the employment-at-will doctrine treats workers as if they are nothing more than economic commodities exchanged in the marketplace, the fact that workers are human beings forces us to pay attention to equity and voice in addition to efficiency. In earlier agrarian and crafts-based societies, the quality of life for you and your family was critically linked to your property such as your farm or workshop; but in today's industrial or postindustrial society, modern workers and their families are often completely dependent on *jobs*, not property. Moreover, working adults spend much of their lives at work, and "the workplace is the single most important site of cooperative interactivity and sociability among adult citizens outside the family."[15] The quality of employment and the nature of the workplace are therefore important for individuals, families, and society.

Work is not simply an economic transaction; work is a fully human activity such that employees are entitled to fair treatment and opportunities to have input into decisions that affect their daily lives. The lack of at least minimal standards and nondiscriminatory treatment (equity) contradicts the basic ideals of democracy with free and equal citizens, and it violates religious and moral views on the sanctity of human life and human dignity.[16] Employee voice has similar justifications, ranging from moral, religious, and psychological beliefs about the importance of human self-determination to political views of liberty and democracy.[17] From this latter perspective, employee voice is essential for **industrial democracy,** a term that captures the belief that workers in a democratic society are entitled to the same democratic principles of participation in the workplace:

> It is a fundamental doctrine of political democracy that one should have some voice in regard to matters that vitally affect him. . . . [A worker's] life is a factory life; and it is the incidents of factory life over which he needs some control. If there is an argument for giving him a vote, even more is there an argument for giving him a voice in the conditions of shop and factory.[18]

FIGURE 1.2
AFL–CIO Palm Card Emphasizing Voice

Source: AFL–CIO

For some, then, work is not only about wages and other material benefits, it also involves dignity, voice, and freedom.

If we see work as more than an economic transaction, equity and voice along with efficiency must be the key objectives of the employment relationship.[19] Efficiency alone is not enough. This is also reflected in what workers want. It is easy to imagine that workers want decent wages and fair treatment (equity). But many workers also want a voice.[20] A survey of American workers revealed that 63 percent want more influence over "company decisions that affect your job or work life."[21] Individuals indicated they would enjoy their jobs more, and their businesses would be more competitive, if they had a greater voice in the workplace. The survey also showed an important dichotomy between managers and employees: Managers prefer to deal with workers one-on-one, but half of workers prefer to deal with management as a group. A majority of workers also indicated that they would like representation that is independent of management.

The centrality of voice in contemporary labor relations is further underscored by the frequency of this theme in union literature and campaigns. The American Federation of Labor–Congress of Industrial Organizations (AFL–CIO), the umbrella federation for most U.S. labor unions, emphasizes themes such as "A Voice for America's Working Families" and "Together We Can Make Our Voice Heard" (see Figure 1.2). Thus a number of social commentators, labor leaders, and workers themselves want workplaces that provide fairly distributed outcomes (equity) and participation in decision making (voice), in addition to the profitable and effective production of goods and services (efficiency). Whether unionized or not, each business organization must consider how to respond to these sometimes conflicting desires.

CONFLICTING GOALS MEAN BALANCING RIGHTS

While remembering that labor and management have many common goals, we know that the greatest challenges in labor relations arise from conflicting goals. Conceptually we can think of these clashes as conflicts between the business pursuit of efficiency and workers' pursuit of equity and voice. All else equal, companies prefer paying lower wages, but employees desire higher wages. Employees want security, but managers want flexibility.

These conflicts are generally resolved privately by individuals, unions, and companies through bargaining and other means.

But at a more fundamental level, society sets the ground rules for how corporations can make profits, and therefore establishes rights and obligations for corporations, unions, and workers. A key challenge when establishing these rights is wrestling with conflicts between the property rights of employers and the workers' rights of employees. Can property rights be used by employers to restrict union organizers and therefore potentially interfere with workers' rights to organize unions? Can workers' rights be used by employees to force employers to bargain over work design issues, plant closings, or other questions related to controlling a business? Does recording a video of picketing workers support property rights by protecting the employer's property, or does it violate workers' rights by intimidating workers who are exercising their voice? Can companies restrict the use of social media in their workplaces, or does this violate freedom of speech or other individual rights?

All labor relations systems must resolve these conflicts. Proponents of voluntary, market-based economic transactions (i.e., the "neoliberal market ideology") privilege property rights over workers' rights because basic economic theory shows that competitive markets and well-defined property rights are optimal for achieving efficiency. From this perspective, the key right of workers is the ability to quit jobs they do not like, and labor unions should not enjoy any special legal protections.[22] From the opposite perspective, workers' rights are seen as human rights; in this case workers' rights should trump property rights (see the "Digging Deeper" feature at the end of this chapter).[23] Most of the world's labor relations systems, however, are based on a compromise position: a pluralist perspective that sees the employment relationship as analogous to a pluralist political society in which multiple parties (such as employers and employees) have legitimate but sometimes conflicting interests and rights.[24] From this perspective, property rights and workers' rights should be balanced.

The U.S. labor relations system is therefore based on the belief that labor and management should freely interact and resolve their conflicts within a framework that appropriately respects the rights of each party involved. Operationally, U.S. labor law tries to balance property rights and workers' rights, thereby balancing efficiency, equity, and voice. This is a critical theme to remember throughout this book. When trying to understand and evaluate labor law or union contracts, ask how property rights conflict with workers' rights. Do seniority-based promotion policies strike a good balance between property rights and workers' rights? When thinking about whether the U.S. labor relations system needs to be reformed, ask whether property rights and workers' rights could be better balanced in a different system. Outside of the labor relations arena, the Occupy protests, the Fight for $15, and many other protest movements ultimately reflect deep frustration with perceived imbalances in the promotion of corporate property rights over individual (and environmental) rights and welfare, and a belief that these imbalances lead to significant economic and social inequality.[25] Understanding the conflicts between property rights and workers' rights and the desire to balance them is therefore vital for understanding not only labor relations but also key societal challenges.

CONTEMPORARY U.S. LABOR RELATIONS

The three objectives of efficiency, equity, and voice provide a rich framework for understanding labor relations. Why might society want to encourage some type of unionism, and why might workers support unionization? Because labor unions can help strike a balance between efficiency, equity, and voice. Others oppose unionization because they believe that there are better ways to achieve the desired objectives, but labor relations systems around the world are premised on the belief that the "invisible hand" of markets and the visible hands of human resource managers cannot balance efficiency, equity, and voice by themselves. Each labor law regime assumes that corporations have significantly greater bargaining power than individual, nonunion workers that can result in substandard wages and benefits, discriminatory treatment, autocratic supervision, long hours, and dangerous working conditions. These outcomes do not fulfill the desired objectives:

- Low pay and worker unrest can cause inefficiencies through lack of consumer purchasing power and economic disruptions because of strikes and other disputes.
- Long hours at low pay under dangerous and discriminatory conditions violate equity.
- Employer dictation of employment conditions as well as autocratic supervision fail to provide employee voice and are counter to democratic standards.

The specific institutional approaches to striking a balance between efficiency, equity, and voice vary widely between countries. The legal regulation of labor unions and other forms of worker representation, the scope of bargaining, and the specific nature of union contracts are therefore quite different, as we will see when we compare labor relations in North America to those in Europe and Asia in Chapter 12. But all labor relations systems strive to balance efficiency, equity, and voice in a dynamic global economy.

Compared to the labor relations systems of many other countries, U.S. labor relations processes are tightly regulated by the legal system. U.S. labor law specifies that if a majority of workers in a specific workplace want union representation, their employer has a legal obligation to bargain with the union over wages, hours, and other terms and conditions of employment. Workers cannot be fired or otherwise discriminated against because of their support for a union. Employers cannot threaten employees or undertake other actions for the sole purpose of preventing unionization. The rationale for these legal protections is to allow workers to unionize to equalize bargaining power between employees and employers and thereby strike a balance between efficiency, equity, and voice by:

- Increasing the purchasing power of workers and reducing disruptive strike activity (efficiency).
- Achieving fair labor standards and protection against worker exploitation (equity).
- Providing democracy in the workplace (voice).

These outcomes are not directly legislated, however. Rather, the legal emphasis is on regulating the processes to maintain fairness. For example, U.S. labor law specifies how the parties must act during bargaining but does not concern itself with the outcome of the bargaining process.

Contemporary Pressures: The Management Perspective

When the U.S. labor relations system works effectively, efficiency, equity, and voice are achieved through **collective bargaining.** In collective bargaining, representatives of the employer and the employees negotiate the terms and conditions of employment that will apply to the employees. These are the major subjects of bargaining:

- *Compensation:* wages, benefits, vacations and holidays, shift premiums, profit sharing.
- *Personnel policies and procedures:* layoff, promotion, and transfer policies, overtime and vacation rules.
- *Employee rights and responsibilities:* seniority rights, job standards, workplace rules.
- *Employer rights and responsibilities:* management rights, just cause discipline and discharge, subcontracting, safety standards.

- *Union rights and responsibilities:* recognition as bargaining agent, bulletin board, union security, dues checkoff, shop stewards, no strike clauses.
- *Dispute resolution and ongoing decision making:* grievance procedures, committees, consultation, renegotiation procedures.

Note that this list includes much more than basic compensation (often called economic items) and covers a number of issues related to personnel policies and work rules (often called language issues). For all these items, the crucial feature of collective bargaining is that management's traditional authority to unilaterally establish terms and conditions of employment is replaced by bilateral negotiations. Employers cannot singlehandedly dictate compensation, policies, and work rules; rather, workers have a collective voice when employment conditions are being determined.

In the United States, when the collective-bargaining process results in terms that are approved by both upper management and union members, the provisions are written down and bound into a legally enforceable collective-bargaining agreement, also called a union contract. Traditionally these contracts have been detailed and legalistic, and over the last few decades they have grown thick. As an extreme example, the first contract between the United Automobile Workers (UAW) and General Motors in 1937 was only a page long, whereas recent UAW–General Motors contracts have been hundreds of pages long and divided into several volumes.

Since the 1980s business pressures for competitiveness, quality, and significant financial returns have pressured the collective-bargaining process in at least three major ways. First, the business need for flexibility (efficiency) clashes with lengthy contracts that spell out detailed work rules (equity). As a result, there has been experimentation with shorter, less detailed (less restrictive) contracts, such as the former UAW–Saturn agreement (see Figure 1.3). Flexible compensation systems to promote and reward highly performing employees can also clash with equity if these systems are perceived as overly subjective, competitive, or unfair. Second, the business need for cooperation and employee involvement clashes with the traditionally adversarial bargaining process in which labor and management use aggressive tactics to extract as many gains or concessions from the other side as their power allows. As a result, some advocate the mutual gains of integrative or "win–win" bargaining, which embraces a culture of joint problem solving rather than competition and conflict. Third, the need for both flexibility and involvement is not well served by a process in which contracts are renegotiated every three years or so with little productive communication (voice) between these formal negotiating periods. More bargaining relationships, therefore, are establishing mechanisms to foster ongoing communication, such as labor–management partnerships. Because of these challenges, it is imperative that students of labor relations not only study the existing processes but also consider reform possibilities.

FIGURE 1.3
The Thickness of U.S. Union Contracts

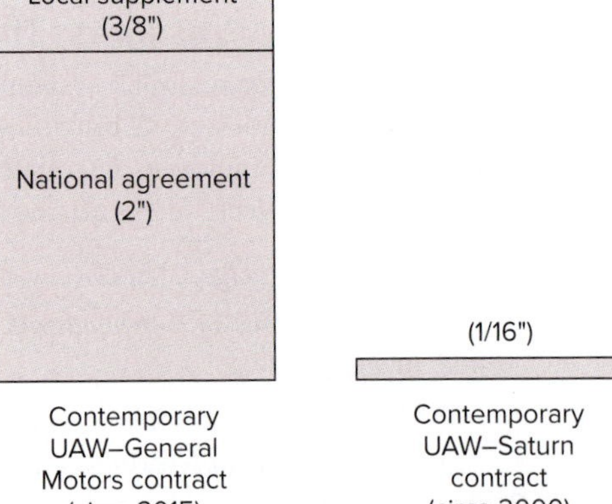

Online Exploration Exercise: Search online to find a union contract (or get a copy of a contract from a friend or acquaintance). What provisions increase efficiency? Decrease efficiency? Provide equity? Provide voice?

The current legal framework in the U.S. private sector dates back to the Wagner Act (the National Labor Relations Act or NLRA) in 1935—hence the label "New Deal industrial relations system" because of its genesis during President Franklin Roosevelt's New Deal during the Great Depression. That this framework is more than 75 years old further reinforces the pressures for reform. The decades around the Depression, and especially immediately after World War II, were characterized by mass manufacturing, sharp distinctions between manual (blue-collar) and managerial (white-collar) workers, and American domination of world markets. Many argue that labor law is outdated because few of these business features remain true. Rather, the business climate of the 21st century is characterized by flexible production methods, the rise of knowledge workers, the blurring of traditional distinctions between brawn and brains, and intense global competition. In the 2010s, there have also been sharp attacks on labor law in the public sector, particularly by conservative political groups and politicians who see strong public sector unions not only as political opponents but also as obstacles to reducing the size of government.[26] This altered environment cannot be ignored in any study of labor relations.

Contemporary Pressures: The Labor Union Perspective

U.S. labor law is also criticized by union supporters—not so much for being outdated but rather for being too weak. This is directly related to another significant trend, which also points toward the need for reform: the weak health of the U.S. labor movement. In 2015 there were an estimated 14.8 million union members and another 1.6 million workers were covered by union contracts but were not union members.[27] Figure 1.4 reveals several important features of labor union membership in the postwar period. First, while the overall number of union members grew into the 1970s, it has declined since then. Moreover, much of the growth after the 1950s was in the public sector. The private sector had roughly the same number of union members in 1965 and 1980, whereas the public sector had twice as many union members in 1980 as in 1965. In recent years total union membership has been more stable because a continued decline in private sector membership has been offset by an increase in public sector membership.

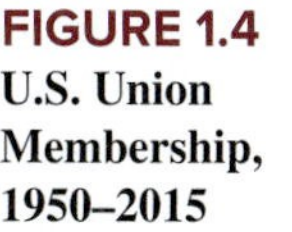

FIGURE 1.4
U.S. Union Membership, 1950–2015

Source: U.S. Department of Labor.

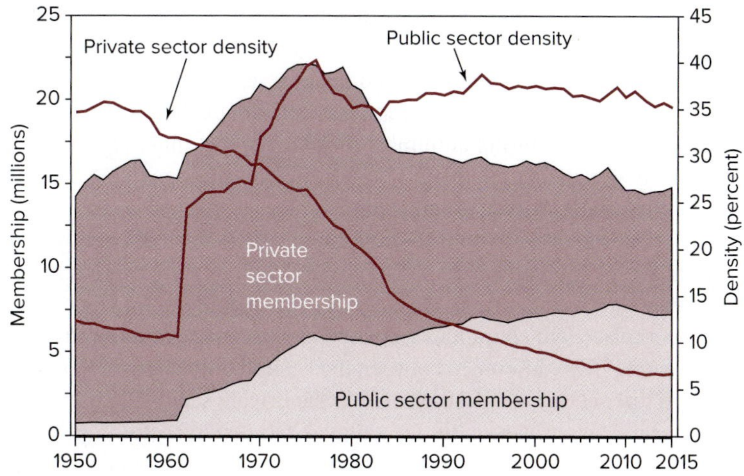

The key measure of the state of organized labor is **union density**—the percentage of workers who are union members. Overall, union density in 2015 was 11.1 percent. But private sector union density in the United States has declined since 1955 from about 35 percent to only 6.7 percent of the workforce in 2015. In sharp contrast, public sector union density jumped in the early 1960s (when the first laws protecting public sector unionizing efforts were enacted), increased steadily for 15 years, and after a slight decline has leveled off at around 35 percent.

The reasons for the 60-year decline of private sector U.S. union density are controversial. One possible explanation is that employment has declined in traditionally unionized industries such as manufacturing while employment has increased in nonunion industries such as services. Related structural, or compositional, changes include regional and demographic shifts, such as faster employment growth in southern states, more women in the labor force, and increases in education and skill levels.[28] These structural factors may explain part of the decline, but they also beg important questions about why certain industries, occupations, regions, or workers are more or less receptive to unionization. Similarly, it has been argued that the inability of unionized workplaces to compete in dynamic economy is a reason for the decline in private sector unionization.[29] But this still leaves *unanswered* questions of why and under what conditions.

A second possibility is that demand for union services has declined.[30] This explanation has three components. (1) Demand can decline because unions are not doing a good job of responding to the desires of a changing workforce and overcoming the negative stereotypes of unions that are so common in American culture.[31] Related to this dimension, U.S. unions have traditionally devoted few resources toward organizing new workers, though some unions are trying to change this practice.[32] (2) If employers have improved their responsiveness to employees' needs, this can reduce demand for union protection and advocacy. (3) Increased protective legislation may have provided a substitute for unions.[33] Examples include the Civil Rights Act and Equal Pay Act (and related laws pertaining to age and disability discrimination) forbidding discriminatory employment practices; the Occupational Safety and Health Act governing workplace safety standards; the Family and Medical Leave Act, which requires employers to provide unpaid leave for parental, family, and medical reasons; and the Affordable Care Act (Obamacare) expanding the availability of health insurance. In short, perhaps workers no longer need unions to win these basic protections and benefits.

The third, and most controversial, possible reason for the decline in U.S. union density is employer resistance or opposition. Compared to businesses in other industrialized countries, U.S. businesses are exceptionally hostile toward labor unions and have developed a wide range of union avoidance tactics.[34] For example, rather than investing in unionized plants or workplaces, U.S. companies often invest in their nonunion operations.[35] Moreover, it is argued that many companies actively fight union organizing drives by firing union supporters, interrogating workers about their support for a union, making threats and promises, hiring antiunion consultants, manipulating the legal system to frustrate and delay organizing campaigns, and in unionized companies, forcing strikes and then hiring replacement workers to bust unions.[36]

One factor that seems to support the significance of employer opposition is the existence of a **representation gap:** Employees say they want more representation in the workplace than they have.[37] Approximately one-third of nonunion workers would like a union in their workplace, which implies a desired union density rate of roughly 40 percent in the private sector.[38] The difference between the desired union density rate of 40 percent and the actual private sector rate of 10 percent is the private sector representation gap. Interestingly, this desired figure is roughly the same as the public sector density rate of 35 percent. This is thought-provoking because the scope for fighting unionization by public sector employers

Labor Relations Application Continuing Pressures on the New Deal Industrial Relations System

Management's Perspective

- Adversarial negotiations create distrust and acrimony rather than trust and cooperation.
- Need to supplement high-level, periodic negotiations with ongoing low-level communication and problem-solving mechanisms.
- Lengthy, detailed contracts inhibit flexibility and involvement.
- Labor law is outdated; bureaucratic production, American domination of world markets, and management versus labor attitudes are things of the past.

Labor's Perspective

- Labor law is weak: penalties are minimal, delays are frequent, employers can use captive audience speeches and permanent strike replacements, and secondary boycotts are prohibited.
- Private sector union density is less than 10 percent.
- Workers need protection more than ever in the global economy.

has traditionally been lesser than in the private sector—the local board of education cannot threaten to close a school and move it to Mexico or some other low-wage area in response to a union organizing drive, though some states have recently tried to remove bargaining rights for public sector workers. Perhaps private sector union density would also be close to 40 percent if managerial opposition were more limited. This evidence regarding the importance of private sector employer opposition to unionization attempts is only suggestive, but the representation gap is a significant feature of U.S. labor relations.

Union membership trends might also be caught in a downward spiral. The fraction of workers who have never been unionized is increasing so there are fewer opportunities for nonunion workers to experience unionization.[39] Like some consumer products, however, union membership might be fully appreciated only after it is experienced.[40] So if workers are increasingly less likely to experience unionization, they are less likely to develop an appreciation for unions; and union membership will continue to decline. Then even fewer workers will experience unionization, and the cycle of low union experience and low union demand will build on itself. On the other hand, significantly more people experience unionism at some point in their working lives than the low union density figures at any one time might suggest. But those who do experience unionism are likely to first do so at a young age (maybe you had a teen job in a unionized grocery store), so there is an opportunity for unions to do a better job of making this experience a good one.[41]

The decline in private sector union density and recent attacks on public sector unionization are central features of contemporary U.S. labor relations and serve as important backdrops to the study of labor relations. The private sector decline is likely the result of all the discussed factors, though their relative importance is debated. Remember these different factors when considering the need for labor relations reform. The explanations based on structural changes and declining demand for unionization due to improved corporate policies and employment laws imply that little reform is warranted. On the other hand, if union density has declined because of unresponsive union behavior, labor relations reform must look at transforming unions. If employer opposition is key, labor law should be reformed to close the representation gap.

THE CONTINUED RELEVANCE OF LABOR RELATIONS

Some people are tempted to dismiss labor unions as relics from a bygone era and to consider studying labor relations unimportant for business careers in the 21st century. Yes, unions represent less than 12 percent of the U.S. workforce, but this is still a large number of workers in many of the country's leading companies. Contrary to popular stereotypes, unions are relevant not only to blue-collar occupations; doctors, nurses, lawyers, teachers, writers, professional athletes, college professors, and even graduate students are represented by unions. Pick up a newspaper or browse online news sources and you will be surprised by the number of union-related current events, ranging from struggling phone companies renegotiating union contracts and retiree health benefits, to legislative proposals to suspend bargaining rights for public employees to reduce budget deficits, to debates over pay for performance for unionized teachers or whether college athletes or teaching assistants should be allowed to unionize. Some local businesses—a Starbucks, a Target or Walmart, or a local hotel, for example—might have some employees who are thinking about unionizing, or at least some managers who are worrying about this possibility. Labor relations are therefore a relevant and dynamic area of study and practice.[42]

Online Exploration Exercise: The National College Players Association was formed by college athletes "to provide the means for college athletes to voice their concerns and change NCAA rules." Find their website and research their goals, strategies, and campaigns. How is this association like a labor union? How is it different from a union? What advantages does it have over a union? What disadvantages? Alternatively, find a website for an association of retirees and explore these same issues and questions. Some of these associations can be found on the website of the National Retiree Legislative Network.

All managers and business professionals—not just human resource managers—can benefit from learning about labor relations, whether or not they plan to work in companies where unions are present. Consider the four scenarios in the Nonunion Application "In a Nonunion Workplace, Can Managers . . . ?" Each scenario is something that a nonunion manager might do. But whether intentional or not, all these actions undermine unionlike activities and therefore are illegal under U.S. labor law—even in a nonunion workplace. This is because a union does not have to be a large, formal, bureaucratic organization; a union is simply a group of workers acting together to influence their working conditions. Wage and benefit packages in union contracts can also influence nonunion compensation through a threat effect: The threat that dissatisfied workers will unionize sometimes causes nonunion firms to at least partially match union wage and benefit terms.[43] Studying labor relations also reveals the consequences of poorly managing a workforce. Thus an understanding of labor relations is important for all current and future managers.

Studying labor relations can also help business leaders appreciate the broader historical, social, and political influences on business and better deal with the realities of managing a business in a complex world. Stylized economic models conveniently assume a tidy world of rational agents interacting in perfectly competitive economic markets; most business courses consider only the objectives of businesses and consumers. In contrast, the study of labor relations considers the goals of workers and society and does not shy away from the conflicts that can arise between competing groups, especially in a real world characterized by imperfect competition. Labor relations can therefore help everyone understand and resolve conflict—in the workplace, in business relationships, and in everyday personal interactions. Studying labor relations also reveals how work and business are embedded in a complex environment—at various points in this book we will consider market forces,

Nonunion Application In a Nonunion Workplace, Can Managers. . . ?

Scenario one: You implement a new pay-for-performance program, and five employees together decide to refuse to work until the program is withdrawn. Can you fire the employees?

Scenario two: You are interviewing applicants for a web designer position in your organization. One applicant has a Graphic Communications International Union day planner and pen. Can you refuse to hire this qualified individual because you don't want any union troublemakers in your organization?

Scenario three: You overhear two employees discussing a union during a break in the employee cafeteria. Can you stop their conversation?

Scenario four: You want to change your company's health care insurance provider, but only if the employees feel that this is a positive change. Can you handpick an employee committee to represent the other employees in discussions about new health insurance options?

individual emotions, managerial strategies, forms of work organization, constitutional and legal issues, history, questions of human rights, negotiation and conflict resolution strategies, debates over globalization, pressures of financialization, ethical challenges, and much more. These topics contain important lessons for all business leaders because the principles apply to many business and social issues, not just those pertaining to labor relations. For others who are interested in work and workers, labor relations offer an engaging subject for thinking about the world of work—what we want to gain from work, how work should be structured, the rights of labor, and other questions that greatly affect the type of society we live in.[44]

The study of labor relations is not confined to a business analysis of problems or to a description of how existing processes work. U.S. labor relations are a system in flux. Business, unions, and employees are confronted with diversity and experimentation in both business and human resource practices. As a result, a deeper understanding of the underlying issues—the goals of the employment relationship, how the employment relationship and labor markets operate in practice, major environmental pressures—is required to devise new business practices, union strategies, and public policies in a turbulent world with weak processes and institutions. This book examines current U.S. labor relations processes but also provides a rich foundation for understanding the logic of these processes and for critically evaluating them to consider possible reforms. This approach also raises vital questions about how workers should be treated and valued in society—questions dramatically illustrated by the financial crisis of 2008, in which bank executives laid off tens of thousands of workers while accepting billions of dollars in federal bailout money and paying themselves millions of dollars in bonuses. A deeper analysis of the employment relationship provides the basis for questioning whether such behavior is appropriate or whether reforms are needed.

Even though workers are better off than in the previous recession, many problems remain. Millions of workers fail to earn enough to support a family.[45] Sweatshops and forms of modern slavery continue to exist, even in the United States.[46] The "gloves-off economy," in which some employers avoid established labor standards and undermine more responsible employers, is growing.[47] Appalling behavior that recalls the foreman's empire of 100 years ago continues today in the form of quid pro quo sexual harassment—demands for sexual conduct in return for job-related benefits.[48] Workers also continue to be fired for numerous reasons unrelated to job performance: trying to form a union, their race or age, refusing to falsify medical records, and even because of whom they date or what they blog about.[49] Some employers have rules against using the bathroom "on company time" more than once a week.[50] Even some professional work has been labeled a "white-collar sweatshop" as smartphones and other technologies combine to create pressure for continuous access, leading to overwork, stress, and burnout.[51] Although it is unfair to characterize all employers, coworkers, or jobs in such terms, it is equally inaccurate to wish away contemporary abuses. Rather, institutional checks and balances are needed. Labor relations are ultimately concerned with the analysis of such problems. Labor relations are about striking a balance between efficiency, equity, and voice.

Key Terms

labor union, *4*
efficiency, equity, and voice, *5*
industrial democracy, *8*
collective bargaining, *11*
union density, *14*
representation gap, *14*

Reflection Questions

1. In a concise paragraph, paraphrase what you have learned about labor relations to explain to a potential employer why studying labor relations will make you a stronger job candidate.
2. Interview workers, union officials, and managers who have been involved in a union organizing drive (or look in a newspaper or online). What issues were emphasized in the organizing drive? Are the issues examples of efficiency, equity, or voice?
3. Summarize the major facts about U.S. union density. Why has union density declined so sharply in the private sector? Is this good or bad?
4. As an employee, what kind of voice would you like on a job? Would this make you more productive? Should whether you are more productive be the only criterion for whether you should have this voice in the workplace?

Ethics in Action Honda's Restrictive Hiring Policy in Indiana

While frequently unionized in their home countries, foreign multinationals often try to remain union-free when opening factories in the United States. The auto industry offers such a case. There are more than 30 automobile assembly, engine, and transmission plants in the United States that are wholly owned by foreign auto companies, but not one is unionized. New factories are strategically located in rural and southern locations where unions are traditionally weaker. These factories are often subsidized by state and local governments trying to attract new jobs.

A new Honda plant opened in 2008 in Greensburg in southeastern Indiana with the help of $140 million in tax breaks and other subsidies. To staff the factory, Honda considered job applications only from individuals living in the 20 counties within an hour's drive; individuals from the 72 other counties in Indiana were not allowed to apply for positions, even if they were willing to move closer to the plant if hired. Thousands of laid-off Indiana autoworkers from unionized General Motors plants were thus prohibited from applying for the jobs at Honda because they lived outside the restricted hiring zone. In 19 of the 20 counties within the hiring zone, the population is 96 percent white.[52]

QUESTIONS

1. Why do foreign auto companies focus on being union-free in the United States?
2. Why do you think Honda implemented its restrictive hiring policy? Is it an antiunion tactic? Is it discriminatory?
3. Should Honda's restrictive hiring policy be illegal? Is it ethical?

Digging Deeper Are Workers' Rights Human Rights?

The strongest advocates for workers' rights are increasingly asserting that workers' rights are human rights. The foundation of human rights thought is the belief that everyone is entitled to basic rights simply by being human.[53] These rights are "essential to the adequate functioning of a human being" and do not depend on "varying social circumstances and degrees of merit."[54] Visions of human rights can be traced back to various early religious and moral philosophy traditions, including all major religions, which "share a universal interest in addressing the integrity, worth, and dignity of all persons, and, consequently, the duty toward other people."[55] The roots of human rights are therefore both religious and moral, Western and non-Western (see Table 1.1). What are these rights to which everyone is entitled?

At the time of the Declaration of Independence in 1776, the focus was on first-generation human rights: civil and political rights. These include private property rights, freedom of speech, religion, and assembly, and the right to due process. Agitation for these rights continued through the 19th century. First there was the fight against slavery, which also raised questions about the oppression of women.[56] The worldwide attention to slavery also provided the opportunity for reformers to expand awareness of other forms of economic exploitation, such as sweatshop conditions in the mills and mines of mid-19th-century Europe:

> What good were civil rights such as freedom of speech or political rights for voting, asked those who suffered, to people like themselves who had no food, no home, no clothing, no medical care, or no prospect of an education? What were the benefits of freedom from slavery or serfdom if the alternative was destitution?[57]

From this movement grew a second generation of human rights—positive economic and social rights in which governments are responsible for ensuring adequate standards of living, including employment opportunities, income, housing, medical care, safety, and education. Workers' rights received further attention at the end of World War I, partly because of labor's sacrifices during the war and partly as a strategy to further continued peace, which led to the creation of the International Labor Organization (ILO) in 1919. The ILO is based on the following principles:

1. Labor is not a commodity.
2. Freedom of expression and of association are essential to sustained progress.
3. Poverty anywhere constitutes a danger to prosperity everywhere.
4. The war against want must be carried on with unrelenting vigor within each nation, and by continuous and concerted international effort in which the representatives of workers and employers, enjoying equal status with those of governments, join with them in free discussion and democratic decision with a view to the promotion of the common welfare.[58]

The ILO is now a specialized agency of the United Nations and is the chief international authority on, and promoter of, labor standards pertaining to union organizing and collective bargaining, forced labor, discrimination, and other conditions of work.

The Great Depression in the 1930s increased calls for economic and social rights.[59] In response to the devastation of World War II and to Hitler's assertion of national sovereignty over Nazi Germany's right to commit incredible atrocities in the Holocaust, the United Nations was formed in 1945 "to save succeeding generations from the scourge of war" and to "reaffirm faith in fundamental human rights, in the dignity and worth of the human person, in the equal rights of men and women of nations large and small" (United Nations Charter). The Universal Declaration of Human Rights was adopted and proclaimed by the United Nations' General Assembly in 1948 and integrates second-generation economic and social rights with first-generation civil and political rights. The entire text of the Universal Declaration is reproduced in Appendix B at the end of this book.

With respect to workers' rights, the Universal Declaration proclaims that everyone has the right to just and favorable conditions of work, including pay sufficient for an existence worthy of human dignity, equal pay for equal work, reasonable working hours, periodic paid holidays, unemployment and disability insurance, and the ability to form labor unions. The importance of labor unions in this platform of work-related human rights is reinforced by the ILO. Specifically, of the eight ILO conventions that have been identified as fundamental to the rights of human beings at work, two pertain to the ability to organize unions and engage in collective bargaining.[60]

Consequently, a number of scholars and activists now argue that workers' rights are human rights.[61] Human dignity and freedom, it is argued, are violated if people cannot maintain a minimal standard of living and are subjected to onerous working hours in dangerous or unsanitary conditions. Due process protections against arbitrary and discriminatory discipline and discharge are essential for

Continued

TABLE 1.1
Human Rights Timeline

Adapted from Paul Gordon Lauren, *The Evolution of International Human Rights: Visions Seen* (Philadelphia, PA: University of Pennsylvania Press, 1998); James MacGregor Burns and Stewart Burns, *A People's Charter: The Pursuit of Rights in America* (New York: Alfred A. Knopf, 1991); and Alan S. Rosenbaum (ed.), *The Philosophy of Human Rights: International Perspectives* (Westport, CT: Greenwood Press, 1980).

First generation: Civil and political rights.	1500 BC	Birth of Hinduism: sanctity of human life and noninjury to others.
	1300 BC	Birth of Judaism: sacredness of human life and equality of all.
	500 BC	Birth of Confucianism and Buddhism: harmony, compassion, and duty.
	400 BC	Greek Philosophy (Plato, Aristotle): principles of a just society.
	100 BC	Roman Philosophy (Cicero): universal, egalitarian natural law.
	AD 30	Birth of Christianity: sacredness of human life and compassion.
	600	Birth of Islam: sanctity of human life, equality, and charity.
	1215	Magna Carta: liberties of citizens, limits on rulers.
	1270	St. Thomas Aquinas: Catholic analysis of moral life and natural law.
	1690	John Locke: natural rights to preserve life, liberty, and property.
	1776	Declaration of Independence (United States): inalienable rights to life, liberty, and the pursuit of happiness.
	1780	Immanuel Kant: universal moral law of treating people as ends in themselves, not as means; also advocated a federation of nations to punish aggressor nations.
	1789	Declaration of the Rights of Man and Citizen (France): universal natural rights to liberty, property, security, and resistance to oppression.
	1791	Bill of Rights (United States): freedom of speech, religion, assembly, from unreasonable search and seizure, and right to due process.
Second generation: Economic and social rights.	1800s	Industrial Revolution: rise of wage work and factories.
	1833	Abolition Act (Great Britain): end of slavery in the British Empire.
	1841	Treaty of London (Russia, France, Prussia, Austria, and Great Britain): abolished slavery.
	1848	Seneca Falls Declaration: launched the women's rights movement.
	1864	Geneva Convention: formed the Red Cross and protected the rights of wounded and captured soldiers.
	1865	13th Amendment to the Constitution (United States): freed slaves.
	1891	*Rerum Novarum* (Pope Leo XIII): rights and justice for wage earners.
	1914–1918	World War I: 8 million killed, 20 million wounded; all were equal in death, why not in life?
	1919	Founding of the International Labor Organization (ILO): promotion of workers' rights and peace through social justice.
	1920	19th Amendment to the Constitution (United States): gave women the right to vote.
	1929–1939	Great Depression: in 1933, U.S. unemployment rate was 25 percent.
	1939–1945	World War II: 25 million military and 30 million civilian casualties (not including the Holocaust victims).
	1941–1945	Holocaust: killing of 6 million Jewish people in Nazi Germany.
	1941	President Franklin Roosevelt issues call for four freedoms worldwide—freedom of speech, of religion, from want, and from fear.
	1944	President Franklin Roosevelt calls for an economic bill of rights—rights to a useful job, earnings to obtain adequate food, clothing, shelter, and recreation, medical care, education, and protection against insecurity from old age, sickness, accidents, and unemployment.
	1944	Declaration of Philadelphia: reaffirmation of ILO principles and workers' rights to material well-being and dignity.
Third generation: Environmental, cultural, and developmental rights	1945	Founding of the United Nations by 51 countries: to promote peace, justice, social progress, and human rights.
	1948	United Nations Universal Declaration of Human Rights: statement of civil, political, social, and economic rights for all because of inherent human dignity.
	1950–1960	Decolonization of Asia and Africa.
	1964	Civil Rights Act (United States): forbade racial, gender, and religious discrimination.
	1976	The United Nations International Covenants on Civil and Political Rights and on Economic, Social, and Cultural Rights enter into force: parties to the treaties must comply with international human rights standards.
	1998	ILO Declaration of Fundamental Principles and Rights at Work: all countries have an obligation to promote freedom of association and collective bargaining, equality and nondiscrimination, and the abolition of forced and child labor.
	2003	United Nations issues "Norms on the Responsibilities of Transnational Corporations and Other Business Enterprises with Regard to Human Rights": business has an obligation to respect human rights, including collective-bargaining rights.
	2015	ILO launches the 50 for Freedom campaign to end modern slavery.

Continued

human dignity, as is freedom of speech. Denying workers the freedom of association "denies individuals what they need to live a fully human life"—human dignity and freedom.[62]

But this perspective has critics. Conservative critics emphasize the importance of individual sovereignty enshrined in classical civil and political rights, and they see legislated labor standards as a coercive violation of someone else's liberty.[63] Others who support the need for workers' rights prefer to see workers' rights as citizenship rights rather than as human rights.[64] Although the differences can be subtle, citizenship rights stem from membership in a human community such as a nation, rather than from being part of overall humanity, and thereby more clearly place obligations on the nation to provide citizenship rights.[65] Whereas human rights are seen as universal, citizens have obligations as well as rights; so characterizing workers' rights as citizenship rights rather than human rights makes it easier to allow for workers' interests such as equity and voice to be balanced with other objectives such as efficiency. Still others who support workers' rights are wary of the individualism embedded within human rights discourse that has eroded recognition of and support for the collective action needed to counter corporate power.[66] From this perspective, active social movements and other community-building activities, not "rights talk," are necessary for changing social norms and labor laws and thereby achieving dignity for workers. In this way, seeing workers' rights as human rights can show the rich justifications for the importance of dignity for workers; but it is not nearly as helpful as determining how to make this a reality.

End Notes

1. Thomas Piketty, *Capital in the Twenty-First Century*, trans. Arthur Goldhammer (Cambridge, MA: Harvard University Press, 2014); David Rolf, *The Fight for Fifteen: The Right Wage for a Working America* (New York: The New Press, 2016).
2. Bruce Western and Jake Rosenfeld, "Unions, Norms, and the Rise in US Wage Inequality," *American Sociological Review* 76 (August 2011), pp. 513–37; Jonas Pontusson, "Unionization, Inequality, and Redistribution," *British Journal of Industrial Relations* 51 (December 2013), pp. 797–825; Martin Behrens (ed.), *Unions Matter: Advancing Democracy, Economic Equality, and Social Justice* (Toronto: Canadian Foundation for Labour Rights, 2014).
3. Jonathan Gruber and Samuel A. Kleiner, "Do Strikes Kill? Evidence from New York State," *American Economic Journal: Economic Policy* 4 (February 2012), pp. 127–57; Alan B. Krueger and Alexandre Mas, "Strikes, Scabs, and Tread Separations: Labor Strife and the Production of Defective Bridgestone/Firestone Tires," *Journal of Political Economy* 112 (April 2004), pp. 253–89.
4. Rick Fantasia and Kim Voss, *Hard Work: Remaking the American Labor Movement* (Berkeley, MA: University of California Press, 2004); Nelson Lichtenstein, *State of the Union: A Century of American Labor* (Princeton, NJ: Princeton University Press, 2013); Emmanuel Teitelbaum, *Mobilizing Restraint: Democracy and Industrial Conflict in Post-Reform South Asia* (Ithaca, NY: Cornell University Press, 2011); Behrens, *Unions Matter*.
5. Stephen F. Befort and John W. Budd, *Invisible Hands, Invisible Objectives: Bringing Workplace Law and Public Policy into Focus* (Stanford, CA: Stanford University Press, 2009); John W. Budd, *Employment with a Human Face: Balancing Efficiency, Equity, and Voice* (Ithaca, NY: Cornell University Press, 2004).
6. Befort and Budd, *Invisible Hands, Invisible Objectives*.
7. Jack Barbash, *The Elements of Industrial Relations* (Madison, WI: University of Wisconsin Press, 1984); Befort and Budd, *Invisible Hands, Invisible Objectives;* Budd, *Employment with a Human Face;* John R. Commons, *Industrial Goodwill* (New York: McGraw-Hill, 1919); Sidney Webb and Beatrice Webb, *Industrial Democracy* (London: Longmans, Green, and Co., 1897).
8. National Labor Relations Act (1935), section 1.
9. William J. Puette, *Through Jaundiced Eyes: How the Media View Organized Labor* (Ithaca, NY: ILR Press, 1992).
10. Fantasia and Voss, *Hard Work;* Christopher R. Martin, *Framed! Labor and the Corporate Media* (Ithaca, NY: Cornell University Press, 2004).
11. Stephen M. Bainbridge, "Corporate Decision Making and the Moral Rights of Employees: Participatory Management and Natural Law," *Villanova Law Review* 43 (1998), pp. 741–828.
12. I am grateful to Alex Colvin for suggesting this example.
13. Richard A. Bales, "Explaining the Spread of At-Will Employment as an Inter-Jurisdictional Race-to-the-Bottom of Employment Standards," *Tennessee Law Review* 75 (Spring 2008), pp. 453–71.
14. Hoyt N. Wheeler, Brian S. Klaas, and Douglas M. Mahony, *Workplace Justice without Unions* (Kalamazoo, MI: W.E. Upjohn Institute for Employment Research, 2004); Joseph E. Slater, "The 'American Rule' That Swallows the Exceptions," *Employee Rights and Employment Policy Journal* 11 (2007), pp. 53–110.
15. Cynthia Estlund, *Working Together: How Workplace Bonds Strengthen a Diverse Democracy* (Oxford: Oxford University Press, 2003), p. 7.
16. Budd, *Employment with a Human Face;* John Rawls, *Justice as Fairness: A Restatement* (Cambridge, MA: Harvard University Press, 2001); Dominique Peccoud (ed.), *Philosophical and Spiritual Perspectives on Decent Work* (Geneva: International Labour Office, 2004).
17. Budd, *Employment with a Human Face;* Edward L. Deci and Richard M. Ryan, *Intrinsic Motivation and Self-Determination in Human Behavior* (New York: Plenum Press, 1985); Michael J. Naughton, "Participation in the Organization: An Ethical Analysis from the Papal Social Tradition," *Journal of Business Ethics* 14 (November 1995), pp. 923–35; Marshall Sashkin, "Participative Management Is an Ethical Imperative," *Organizational Dynamics* 12 (Spring 1984), pp. 5–22.
18. J.A. Estey, *The Labor Problem* (New York: McGraw-Hill, 1928), p. 208; Milton Derber, *The American Idea of Industrial Democracy, 1865–1965* (Urbana, IL: University of Illinois Press, 1970); Nelson Lichtenstein and Howell John Harris (eds.), *Industrial Democracy in America: The Ambiguous Promise* (Washington, DC: Woodrow Wilson Center Press, 1993).
19. Befort and Budd, *Invisible Hands, Invisible Objectives;* Budd, *Employment with a Human Face.*
20. Richard B. Freeman, Peter Boxall, and Peter Haynes (eds.), *What Workers Say: Employee Voice in the Anglo-American World* (Ithaca, NY: Cornell University Press, 2007).

21. Richard B. Freeman and Joel Rogers, *What Workers Want,* updated ed. (Ithaca, NY: Cornell University Press, 2006).
22. Richard A. Epstein, "A Common Law for Labor Relations: A Critique of the New Deal Labor Legislation," *Yale Law Journal* 92 (July 1983), pp. 1357–408; Richard Epstein, "The Deserved Demise of EFCA (and Why the NLRA Should Share its Fate)," in Cynthia L. Estlund and Michael L. Wachter (eds.), *Research Handbook on the Economics of Labor and Employment Law* (Northampton, MA: Edward Elgar, 2012), pp. 177–208.
23. James A. Gross, *A Shameful Business: The Case for Human Rights in the American Workplace* (Ithaca, NY: Cornell University Press, 2010); Hoyt N. Wheeler, "Globalization and Business Ethics in Employment Relations," in John W. Budd and James G. Scoville (eds.), *The Ethics of Human Resources and Industrial Relations* (Champaign, IL: Labor and Employment Relations Association, 2005), pp. 115–40.
24. H.A. Clegg, "Pluralism in Industrial Relations," *British Journal of Industrial Relations* 13 (November 1975), pp. 309–16; John W. Budd, Rafael Gomez, and Noah M. Meltz, "Why a Balance Is Best: The Pluralist Industrial Relations Paradigm of Balancing Competing Interests," in Bruce E. Kaufman (ed.), *Theoretical Perspectives on Work and the Employment Relationship* (Champaign, IL: Industrial Relations Research Association, 2004), pp. 195–227.
25. Marjorie Cohn, "The World Trade Organization: Elevating Property Interests above Human Rights," *Georgia Journal of International and Comparative Law* 29 (Summer 2001), pp. 427–40.
26. Lichtenstein, *State of the Union*; Richard B. Freeman and Eunice Han, "The War Against Public Sector Collective Bargaining in the US," *Journal of Industrial Relations* 54 (June 2012), pp. 386–408; Robert Hebdon, Joseph E. Slater, and Marick F. Masters, "Public Sector Collective Bargaining: Tumultuous Times," in Howard R. Stanger, Paul F. Clark, and Ann C. Frost (eds.), *Collective Bargaining under Duress: Case Studies of Major North American Industries* (Champaign, IL: Labor and Employment Relations Association, 2013), pp. 255–95.
27. U.S. Bureau of Labor Statistics, "Union Members in 2015" (Washington, DC: U.S. Department of Labor, 2016), www.bls.gov/news.release/union2.nr0.htm, June 14, 2016.
28. Gary N. Chaison and Joseph B. Rose, "The Macrodeterminants of Union Growth and Decline," in George Strauss, Daniel G. Gallagher, and Jack Fiorito (eds.), *The State of the Unions* (Madison, WI: Industrial Relations Research Association, 1991), pp. 3–46.
29. Barry T. Hirsch, "Unions, Dynamism, and Economic Performance," in Cynthia L. Estlund and Michael I. Wachter (eds.), *Research Handbook on the Economics of Labor and Employment Law* (Northampton, MA: Edward Elgar, 2012), pp. 107–145.
30. Henry S. Farber and Alan B. Krueger, "Union Membership in the United States: The Decline Continues," in Bruce E. Kaufman and Morris M. Kleiner (eds.), *Employee Representation: Alternatives and Future Directions* (Madison, WI: Industrial Relations Research Association, 1993), pp. 105–34; Robert Flanagan, "Has Management Strangled U.S. Unions?" in James T. Bennett and Bruce E. Kaufman (eds.), *What Do Unions Do? A Twenty-Year Perspective* (New Brunswick, NJ: Transaction Publishers, 2007), pp. 459–91.
31. Lawrence Richards, *Union-Free America: Workers and Antiunion Culture* (Urbana, IL: University of Illinois Press, 2008); Jane McAlevey with Bob Ostertag, *Raising Expectations (and Raising Hell): My Decade Fighting for the Labor Movement* (London: Verso, 2012).
32. Jack Fiorito and Paul Jarley, "Union Organizing and Union Revitalization in the United States," *Proceedings of the Sixtieth Annual Meeting* (Champaign, IL: Labor and Employment Relations Association, 2008), pp. 92–100.
33. James T. Bennett and Jason E. Taylor, "Labor Unions: Victims of Their Political Success?" *Journal of Labor Research* 22 (Spring 2001), pp. 261–73.
34. Sanford M. Jacoby, "American Exceptionalism Revisited: The Importance of Management," in Sanford M. Jacoby (ed.), *Masters to Managers: Historical and Comparative Perspectives on American Employers* (New York: Columbia University Press, 1991), pp. 173–200; Daphne Gottlieb Taras, "Collective Bargaining Regulation in Canada and the United States: Divergent Cultures, Divergent Outcomes," in Bruce E. Kaufman (ed.), *Government Regulation of the Employment Relationship* (Madison, WI: Industrial Relations Research Association, 1997), pp. 295–341; Fantasia and Voss, *Hard Work.*
35. Thomas A. Kochan, Harry C. Katz, and Robert B. McKersie, *The Transformation of American Industrial Relations* (New York: Basic Books, 1986).
36. John J. Lawler, *Unionization and Deunionization: Strategy, Tactics, and Outcomes* (Columbia, SC: University of South Carolina Press, 1990); Fantasia and Voss, *Hard Work;* John Logan, "The Union Avoidance Industry in the United States," *British Journal of Industrial Relations* 44 (December 2006), pp. 651–75.

37. Freeman and Rogers, *What Workers Want;* Richard B. Freeman and Joel Rogers, "Who Speaks for Us? Employee Representation in a Nonunion Labor Market," in Bruce E. Kaufman and Morris M. Kleiner (eds.), *Employee Representation: Alternatives and Future Directions* (Madison, WI: Industrial Relations Research Association, 1993), pp. 13–80; Seymour Martin Lipset and Noah M. Meltz, with Rafael Gomez and Ivan Katchanovski, *The Paradox of American Unionism: Why Americans Like Unions More Than Canadians Do but Join Much Less* (Ithaca, NY: Cornell University Press, 2004).
38. Freeman and Rogers, *What Workers Want;* Freeman and Rogers, "Who Speaks for Us?"
39. Jonathan E. Booth, John W. Budd, and Kristen M. Munday, "Never Say Never? Uncovering the Never-Unionized in the United States," *British Journal of Industrial Relations* 48 (March 2010), pp. 26–52; Alex Bryson and Rafael Gomez, "Why Have Workers Stopped Joining Unions? The Rise in Never-Membership in Britain," *British Journal of Industrial Relations* 43 (March 2005), pp. 67–92.
40. Rafael Gomez and Morley Gunderson, "The Experience Good Model of Trade Union Membership," in Phanindra V. Wunnava (ed.), *The Changing Role of Unions: New Forms of Representation* (Armonk, NY: M. E. Sharpe, 2004), pp. 92–112.
41. Jonathan E. Booth, John W. Budd, and Kristen M. Munday, "First-Timers and Late-Bloomers: Youth-Adult Unionization Differences in a Cohort of the U.S. Labor Force," *Industrial and Labor Relations Review* 64 (October 2010), pp. 53–73; John W. Budd, "When Do U.S. Workers First Experience Unionization? Implications for Revitalizing the Labor Movement," *Industrial Relations* 49 (April 2010), pp. 209–225.
42. Philip M. Dine, State of the Unions: How Labor Can Strengthen the Middle Class, Improve Our Economy, and Regain Political Influence (New York: McGraw-Hill, 2008); Jake Rosenfeld, *What Unions No Longer Do* (Cambridge, MA: Harvard University Press, 2014).
43. Henry S. Farber, "Nonunion Wage Rates and the Threat of Unionization," *Industrial and Labor Relations Review* 58 (April 2005), pp. 335–52.
44. John W. Budd, *The Thought of Work* (Ithaca, NY: Cornell University Press, 2011).
45. Steven Greenhouse, *The Big Squeeze: Tough Times for the American Worker* (New York: Random House, 2008); Beth Shulman, *The Betrayal of Work: How Low-Wage Jobs Fail 30 Million Americans and Their Families* (New York: The New Press, 2003); David K. Shipler, *The Working Poor: Invisible in America* (New York: Alfred A. Knopf, 2004).
46. Edna Bonacich and Richard P. Appelbaum, *Behind the Label: Inequality in the Los Angeles Apparel Industry* (Berkeley, CA: University of California Press, 2000); Kevin Bales, *Disposable People: New Slavery in the Global Economy,* rev. ed. (Berkeley, CA: University of California Press, 2004).
47. Annette Bernhardt et al. (eds.), *The Gloves-Off Economy: Workplace Standards at the Bottom of America's Labor Market* (Champaign, IL: Labor and Employment Relations Association, 2008).
48. Ann Juliano and Stewart J. Schwab, "The Sweep of Sexual Harassment Cases," *Cornell Law Review* 86 (March 2001), pp. 548–602; Linda LeMoncheck and James P. Sterba (eds.), *Sexual Harassment: Issues and Answers* (New York: Oxford University Press, 2001).
49. Lewis Maltby, *Can They Do That? Retaking Our Fundamental Rights in the Workplace* (New York: Portfolio, 2009); Rafael Gely and Leonard Bierman, "Social Isolation and American Workers: Employee Blogging and Legal Reform," *Harvard Journal of Law and Technology* 20 (Spring 2007), pp. 288–331.
50. Marc Linder and Ingrid Nygaard, *Void Where Prohibited: Rest Breaks and the Right to Urinate on Company Time* (Ithaca, NY: ILR Press, 1998), p. 2.
51. Jill Andresky Fraser, *White-Collar Sweatshop: The Deterioration of Work and Its Rewards in Corporate America* (New York: W.W. Norton, 2001).
52. Neal E. Boudette, "Honda and UAW Clash over Factory Jobs," *The Wall Street Journal* (October 10, 2007).
53. Jack Donnelly, *Universal Human Rights in Theory and Practice,* 2nd ed. (Ithaca, NY: Cornell University Press, 2003).
54. Michael Freeden, *Rights* (Minneapolis: University of Minnesota Press, 1991), p. 7; Jerome J. Shestack, "The Jurisprudence of Human Rights," in Theodor Meron (ed.), *Human Rights in International Law: Legal and Policy Issues* (Oxford: Oxford University Press, 1984), pp. 69–113 at 74.
55. Paul Gordon Lauren, *The Evolution of International Human Rights: Visions Seen* (Philadelphia, PA: University of Pennsylvania Press, 1998), p. 5; Michael J. Perry, *The Idea of Human Rights: Four Inquiries* (New York: Oxford University Press, 1998); Shestack, "The Jurisprudence of Human Rights."
56. Lauren, *The Evolution of International Human Rights;* James MacGregor Burns and Stewart Burns, *A People's Charter: The Pursuit of Rights in America* (New York: Alfred A. Knopf, 1991).
57. Lauren, *The Evolution of International Human Rights,* p. 54.

58. International Labor Organization, "Declaration of Philadelphia" (1944); Gerry Rodgers et al., *The International Labour Organization and the Quest for Social Justice, 1919–2009* (Ithaca, NY: Cornell University Press, 2009).

59. Cass R. Sunstein, *The Second Bill of Rights: FDR's Unfinished Revolution and Why We Need It More Than Ever* (New York: Basic Books, 2004).

60. Lance A. Compa, "Workers' Freedom of Association in the United States: The Gap between Ideals and Practice," in James A. Gross (ed.), *Workers' Rights as Human Rights* (Ithaca, NY: Cornell University Press, 2003), pp. 23–52.

61. Gross, *A Shameful Business*; Roy J. Adams, *Labour Left Out: Canada's Failure to Protect and Promote Collective Bargaining as a Human Right* (Ottawa, Canadian Centre for Policy Alternatives, 2006); Human Rights Watch, Unfair Advantage: Workers' Freedom of Association in the United States under International Human Rights Standards (Washington, DC, 2000); Richard D. Kahlenberg and Moshe Z. Marvit, *Why Labor Organizing Should Be a Civil Right: Re-Building a Middle-Class Democracy by Enhancing Worker Voice* (New York: The Century Foundation, 2012).

62. Gross, *A Shameful Business*, p. 100.

63. Tibor R. Machan, *Private Rights and Public Illusions* (New Brunswick, NJ: Transaction Publishers, 1995).

64. Colin Crouch, "The Globalized Economy: An End to the Age of Industrial Citizenship?"in Ton Wilthagen (ed.), *Advancing Theory in Labour Law and Industrial Relations in a Global Context* (Amsterdam: North-Holland, 1998), pp. 151–64.

65. Guy Mundlak, "Industrial Citizenship, Social Citizenship, Corporate Citizenship: I Just Want My Wages," *Theoretical Inquiries in Law* 8 (July 2007), pp. 719–48.

66. Richard P. McIntyre, *Are Worker Rights Human Rights?* (Ann Arbor: University of Michigan Press, 2008).

Chapter Two

Labor Unions: Good or Bad?

Advance Organizer

Stereotypes of unions are pervasive; what are yours? Understanding labor relations requires replacing these stereotypes with informed views. Employee representation through labor unions and collective bargaining is one way to pursue a balance among efficiency, equity, and voice. But how labor union representation compares to other possible ways of structuring the employment relationship—in short, whether unions are good or bad—depends on how one thinks labor markets and the employment relationship work, not on stereotypes.

Learning Objectives

By the end of this chapter, you should be able to

1. **Explain** the four distinct schools of thought about the employment relationship—mainstream economics, human resource management, industrial relations, and critical or Marxist industrial relations.
2. **Understand** how different views of labor unions are fundamentally rooted in the basic assumptions of these four schools of thought.
3. **Discuss** various roles of labor unions in the employment relationship and in society.
4. **Identify** alternative methods for making workplace rules.
5. **Compare** employee representation through labor unions to other methods of workplace governance.

Contents

It is not hard to find passionately held views of labor unions. Search for labor union blogs in Google, for example, and you will easily find exchanges such as the following:

> *Posted by J.*: Forty years of proud union membership, excellent wages, terrific benefits, wonderful retirement, all brought to me by my union.
>
> *Posted by R.*: J, I'm glad you have enjoyed those benefits and high wages all these years—no one's denying that a union is generally very good for its members—the problem is that they are generally very bad for everyone else. Here's how. . .
>
> - Unions shift the extra cost of those wages and benefits to the consumer. . . .
> - They drive whole industries out of business and overseas, ultimately lessening the number of jobs in this country. . . .
> - They promote laziness and a sense of entitlement, which is a very dangerous thing. . . .[1]

The common sentiment among Americans that unions are outdated is also often repeated in blogs and online comments:

> *Posted by C.*: Hopefully no one is behind the unions anymore, unless they are pushing them the rest of the way over the cliff. They served a very good purpose 50–100 years ago when they helped push labor issues and worker treatment to the forefront. Now their bloated wage/benefit packages and refusal to compromise threaten hundreds of thousands of jobs at UAW plants and in the airline industry.[2]

The major TV networks and newspapers, which are themselves corporations concerned with making profits, reinforce important stereotypes of labor unions.[3] In general terms, the mainstream media report on issues from a consumer rather than worker perspective while emphasizing the accomplishments of business leaders and entrepreneurs. As representatives of producers rather than consumers and as proponents of collective rather than individual actions, unions are therefore devalued. Even though strikes are rare, they are the most frequent union news story in the media, and such stories often convey images of worker greed, inflation, consumer inconvenience, and violence.

Other elements of popular culture can reinforce similar stereotypes.[4] TV sitcoms and dramas rarely include labor unions; when such issues arise, they are often references to union corruption, strikes, or work rules. The characters on the TV shows *Monk; Married with Children; Spin City; WKRP in Cincinnati; ER; Trapper John, MD; Fraggle Rock;* and *Mona the Vampire* all had to deal with garbage strikes; on *All in the Family*, Archie Bunker was on strike for four episodes and was portrayed at the conclusion of the strike as being no better off than before the strike. In an episode of *Seinfeld*, when George wonders about becoming a movie projectionist, Jerry says, "But you gotta know how to work the projector. . . . And it's probably a union thing." George then scoffs, "Those unions," and gives up being a projectionist because he figures that he won't be able to break the union's alleged stranglehold on the occupation. Stereotypes about restrictive union work rules or the protection of lazy workers are also reinforced through jokes on sitcoms or in comic strips. One *Dilbert* comic portrays a union steward as wanting to add laptops to the list of things that employees should not be able to move because "that's union work." Such stereotypes perpetuate America's antiunion culture.[5]

It is important for students of labor relations to recognize their own stereotypes of labor unions and to replace them with an informed understanding of the central issues in labor relations and to appreciate multiple perspectives on labor relations and labor unions. Thus,

A Comical Portrayal of Restrictive Union Work Rules Stereotypes

Source: www.CartoonStock.com.

this chapter presents four different schools of thought about labor unions. This provides the foundation for accurately assessing what unions do and whether they are good or bad. These schools of thought are essential for understanding, and therefore practicing, labor relations.

THE LABOR PROBLEM

Because there is more agreement that unions were once useful, this section considers the historical example of the labor conditions of the early 20th century, which were labeled the "labor problem." Turning then to the question of how to solve this labor problem provides the opportunity to consider four different schools of thought about the employment relationship. Understanding these four intellectual perspectives is the basis for a reasoned rather than stereotypical or naïve consideration of labor unions and labor–management relations. It is easier to tackle these perspectives in a historical context because we have fewer preconceived ideas; but at the end of the discussion, the strong relevance for contemporary labor relations should also be clear.

Today's critical issues in human resources and industrial relations are perhaps familiar to you:

- Significant labor market disparities.
- Problems of low-wage workers trying to move out of poverty and support families.
- Corporate pressures for cost control, quality, and flexibility to compete in a global, information-rich economy.
- The need to educate individuals as lifelong learners because of ever-changing technologies.
- Problems of work–life balance, especially for working mothers.

But what about at the start of the previous century? The critical human resources and industrial relations issue in the early 1900s was the labor problem: undesirable outcomes that stem from an inequitable and contentious, or perhaps even oppressive and exploitative, employment relationship.[6] Many important dimensions of the labor problem are captured, in the observers' and participants' own words, in the testimony from around 1900 reported in Table 2.1.

The first entry in Table 2.1 highlights the long hours that were often the norm. Workweeks of between 54 and 57 hours were common. In the iron and steel industry, over 40 percent of laborers worked more than 72 hours per week and about 20 percent worked more than 84 hours per week.[7] These long hours were often for low pay (see the second entry in Table 2.1). At least half of working-class families had annual incomes below the $800 that was estimated "as a reasonable minimum for healthful, efficient, and decent living."[8] Households were therefore forced to resort to a patchwork of methods for earning income to survive—renting rooms to boarders, sewing garments or doing other tasks as home-based subcontractors, using children to earn wages—and yet poor living conditions were widespread (see the third entry in Table 2.1).

Conditions in the workplace were also unsanitary, if not downright dangerous. In March 1911 a fire at the Triangle Shirtwaist Company in New York City killed 146 workers because of inadequate and locked fire exits. A 1915 study in New York City found shocking rates of tuberculosis among low-paid garment workers. One source estimates that industrial accidents resulted in 25,000 deaths, 25,000 permanent disability cases, and 2,000,000 temporary disability cases per year—which implies that U.S. casualties during World War I were greater in the workplace than on the battlefield.[9]

Workers' Lives circa 1900 as Reported to the U.S. Industrial Commission

Table 2.1

TESTIMONY OF NATIONAL ASSOCIATION OF MANUFACTURERS PRESIDENT

Ten hours [of work] has been fixed as the legal day in [Pennsylvania], and it has been very satisfactory. Many of our trades are now working 57 hours a week. More of our factory force is employed only 54 hours a week, yet in the same branches where we employ them 54 some other manufacturers keep them 60. . . .

TESTIMONY OF INTERNATIONAL TYPOGRAPHICAL UNION PRESIDENT

The capitalist who owns the factory in Massachusetts has been transferring his industry nearer to the cotton fields; and we find that, in the State of Georgia, where industrial conditions are not as good as in the State of Massachusetts, the man who has been subject in the State of Massachusetts to all these [labor, inspection, and compulsory education] laws has been living under them, has been putting rails around his machinery, has been boxing in his belting, has been refusing to employ in his factory a child under the age of 14 years, and has been putting on every floor of his factory separate closets for male and female labor, has been giving Saturday half holidays for his employees, and abolishing the company store and complying with the law of the State of Massachusetts—when he goes to the State of Georgia and transfers his business there he does not put any railing around his machinery; he does not box in his belting; he employs children 9, 10, or 12 years of age at wages as low as 15 or 20 cents per day, and works them from the time the light shines in the morning until it is dark at night; and in his factory he has no closets, no sanitary conditions, such as are required in the State of Massachusetts; he simply does as he pleases and acts in a most tyrannical and unchristian-like manner.

TESTIMONY OF HEAD OF SOUTH END HOUSE, BOSTON

In this district there is a great lack of sanitary facilities on account of the increase of inhabitants per house; that is, these old houses which formerly were used as residences of well-to-do citizens and formerly accommodated one family, now accommodate a number of families, and accommodate two or three or four times as many people as they were intended for; so that the bathing facilities and water closet facilities and all that are very inadequate to the present number of inhabitants. Where there are houses that have been specially built as tenement houses there appears the evil of the ventilating shaft and the dark inside rooms. . . . Of course this state of things means dampness, darkness, and bad air. The crowding of the houses puts immorality and uncleanliness at a premium.

TESTIMONY OF OHIO STATE BOARD OF ARBITRATION SECRETARY

Wages did not at any time enter into [the causes of the streetcar strike in Cleveland]. There was no question of wages, no dispute whatever on that subject between the company and the men. The men claimed that for a long time the company had established unjust rules; that they were arbitrary in their dealings with the men. They would refuse men a hearing; men were suspended for very trifling causes and frequently discharged. . . . They were not allowed sufficient times for meals . . . in fact, they were not even allowed time for the necessaries of nature.

TESTIMONY OF BOOT AND SHOE WORKERS' UNION SECRETARY–TREASURER

There are about 100 subdivisions of labor in the manufacture of a shoe, varying more or less according to the factory and methods and the kind of shoe made. . . .

Question: The workman only knows how to perform the labor of one particular department?

Answer: That is all, and he becomes a mere machine. . . . Now, take the proposition of a man operating a machine to nail on 40 to 60 pairs cases of heels in a day. That is 2,400 pairs, 4,800 shoes, in a day. One not accustomed to it would wonder how a man could pick up and lay down 4,800 shoes in a day, to say nothing of putting them on a jack into a machine and having them nailed on. That is the driving method of the manufacture of shoes under the minute subdivisions.

Source: United States Industrial Commission, *Report of the Industrial Commission on the Relations and Conditions of Capital and Labor Employed in Manufactures and General Business* [multiple volumes] (Washington, DC: Government Printing Office, 1901).

The long hours at low pay in dangerous and unsanitary conditions were also marked by great insecurity. Many lived with constant fear of injury and unemployment. Companies might hire workers on a short-term basis, perhaps for only one day at a time with the foreman selecting the day's employees each morning from among those massed outside the factory gate. A 1909 government investigation found that only 37 percent of male workers did not have any time lost from work during a full year; half of the workers lost four or more months. And in the foreman's empire system of complete management control, there was the fear of arbitrary dismissal (see the fourth entry in Table 2.1).[10] Workers could be—and were—fired for any reason: poor performance, absenteeism, ethnicity, union sympathies, age, failing to provide the foreman with extra services (such as raking his leaves . . . or worse), or simply as a demonstration to others of the foreman's absolute power. Discrimination was also widespread with foremen forcing workers into segregated occupations based on biases about what races or ethnic groups were suited for particular types of work.[11]

These important dimensions of the labor problem—long hours, low wages, unsafe conditions, and insecurity—were reinforced and worsened by the managerial mindset of "workers as machines." Labor was frequently viewed as just another production input no different from machines or raw materials. With mass manufacturing methods emphasizing repetitive, narrowly defined tasks by individual workers to achieve high output, workers had no contact with the final product and minimal control over the content of their jobs. The final entry in Table 2.1 describes how the production of a shoe was divided into 100 specialized operations; the worker who, for example, nailed heels to 4,800 shoes in a single day was "a mere machine." In modern human resource management terms, employees had no ownership in their work. And if workers are simply machines, they are not entitled to equity or voice; the sole concern of the owner of a machine is efficiency.

These labor problems were widespread and not limited to manufacturing industries in urban areas.[12] Thousands of Mexican Americans and Mexican immigrants migrated through the Southwest and Midwest following agricultural planting and harvesting seasons, earning perhaps $1 a day and living in appalling conditions. In the public sector, police officers regularly worked more than 70 hours per week out of vermin-infested stations.

Across the private and public sectors, the poor conditions of the labor problem were a problem for two broad reasons. First is the societal or human perspective. Put simply, people should have better lives than this. This is partly an economic issue—workers should be able to afford decent housing, clothing, food, and the like; in other words, equity is important. But as emphasized by employee voice, the labor problem is more than a material concern. In particular, one should question whether treating workers as commodities, even as valuable ones, in an autocratic relationship, even if benevolent, fulfills the standards of a democratic society.[13]

There is also the business perspective on the labor problem. Are the workers motivated? Loyal? Productive? Absenteeism and turnover were costly. At Ford the absenteeism rate in 1913 was 10 percent, and the annual turnover rate was 370 percent; Henry Ford offered the then-large sum of $5 a day in 1914 as an attempt to tackle these problems.[14] Also, with significant numbers living below the poverty line, a second business problem was that they lacked consumer purchasing power. In the words of one union president in 1899, "as the workingman is himself the consumer, he can not purchase unless he has that with which to purchase."[15] The unskilled workers at Ford, for example, couldn't afford to buy the cars they produced until the $5-a-day plan was implemented. Finally, strikes and other forms of industrial conflict that resulted from the labor problem in both the private and public sectors were costly to business and to society more generally.

FOUR SCHOOLS OF THOUGHT ABOUT THE EMPLOYMENT RELATIONSHIP

The labor problem embodies the ultimate human resources and industrial relations problem: balancing efficiency, equity, and voice. To understand how to solve a problem, we need to analyze its underlying causes. But beliefs about the cause of the labor problem differ among four schools of thought: the mainstream economics school, the human resource management school, the industrial relations school, and the critical industrial relations school. Understanding and appreciating the basic assumptions of these four schools are essential for understanding not only labor relations but also the entire field of human resources and industrial relations—past, present, and future.[16]

The Mainstream Economics School

First let's consider the **mainstream economics school** of thought. This school focuses on the economic activity of self-interested agents, such as firms and workers, who interact in competitive markets.[17] In mainstream economic thought, efficiency, equity, and voice are achieved through free-market competition. Under some assumptions (such as perfect information), competition results in the optimal allocation and pricing of resources. Prices in a competitive market reflect the value of what's being purchased, so outcomes are efficient. No one can be made better off without making someone else worse off. In the labor market, competitive outcomes are also seen as fair because the price of labor equals the value that labor contributes to the production process. In the words of a Nobel Prize–winning economist, low-paid labor is poorly paid "not because it gets less than it is worth, but because it is worth so appallingly little."[18] And voice is expressed through freely participating or abstaining from transactions—if you do not like your working conditions, vote with your feet and quit, and find an employer who treats workers better.[19]

From the perspective of the mainstream economics school, then, the conditions of the labor problem are not seen as exploitation if there is sufficient labor market competition. Employees are paid their economic value and are free to quit if they feel they are being exploited. But if market failures prevent competitive markets from working properly, what should be done? Ensure competition. In the mainstream economics school, the best protection an employee has against his or her current employer is not the government, a lawyer, or a union, but rather other employers.[20] If there is insufficient labor market competition because of excess unemployment, the appropriate policy response is a macroeconomic policy to stimulate the economy and thus reduce unemployment. Or if competition is prevented because of a barrier such as government regulation, the appropriate policy response is to remove this barrier. As long as there is enough competition, employment outcomes are not seen as a "problem" (with its negative connotations) in this school of thought. Outcomes are value-free, so there may be a labor *situation* (which simply describes the outcomes) but not a labor *problem* (which implies that the outcomes are undesirable).

What is the role of labor unions in the mainstream economics school of thought? Unions are seen as labor market monopolies that restrict individual freedom to decide terms and conditions of employment and interfere with the invisible hand of free-market competition.[21] By threatening to strike, unions use their monopoly power to raise wages above their competitive levels and thereby distort employment and output levels throughout the economic system. Moreover, the economics view of work is that it is a lousy activity endured only to earn money. As such, companies rely on the threat of unemployment to motivate otherwise disinterested workers. Unions are seen as interfering with the discipline of the market by protecting lazy workers. To those who believe in perfect competition, then, labor unions are bad because their monopoly power interferes with the efficient operation

FIGURE 2.1
"King Debs," drawing from *Harper's Weekly* (July 14, 1894)

© Fotosearch/Getty Images

of the economy. This mainstream economics view is graphically captured by the drawing from 1894 in Figure 2.1. The drawing portrays union leader Eugene Debs as a powerful king who is able to use a strike to control the railroads and therefore shut down shipments of food, passengers, mail, coal, and freight, and by extension to close factories. In other words, labor unions are powerful monopolies that harm the economy and the public.

This mainstream economics view of labor unions rests on some strong assumptions about competitive markets, and relaxing these assumptions to make them more realistic results in a more nuanced economic model in which unions might not simply be harmful monopolies that always reduce aggregate economic welfare (see the "Digging Deeper" feature at the end of this chapter). Nevertheless, the mainstream view of monopoly labor unions is deeply ingrained in economic thought and continues to be the dominant view. Moreover, labor unions are not singled out; this dominant mainstream view applies the same reasoning to other government interventions in the labor market, such as minimum wage policies, and to monopolies in other sectors, such as corporate monopolies. The role of government is to promote competition, not to establish labor standards. The role of law is to protect individual freedoms that are necessary for competition.[22] This perspective is significant for understanding important arguments against labor unions and other labor market policies as solutions to historical and contemporary labor problems; but other contrasting perspectives must also be appreciated.

The Human Resource Management School

The second school of thought to consider is the **human resource management school,** which was formerly called the personnel management school.[23] In short, this school of thought believes that the labor problem stems from poor management. This is easy to remember: "PM" can stand for both personnel management and poor management.

Recall from our earlier discussion that in the early 1900s foremen used the drive system to motivate and manage workers through fear and intimidation.[24] This was an autocratic, authoritarian management system in which workers were viewed as a commodity

FIGURE 2.2
"Bringing Home the Turkey," drawing from *Forbes* (December 1, 1928)

Source: Forbes

or a machine, and thus were exploited. A common mind-set was to drive employees to get maximum production for the least cost, and when they broke down (from exertion, age, or injury), discard them and get fresh workers to replace them—as you would with a machine. Hence there was little concern with how low the wage rates might be, how long the hours, how dangerous the conditions, or how arbitrary the hiring and firing procedures. Moreover, scientific management and the movement to large-scale mass manufacturing and assembly lines tended to reduce workers' tasks to their simplest components; this emphasis on specialization led to monotony, boredom, and de-skilling.[25]

This school of thought, therefore, presents a different underlying cause of the labor problem than does the mainstream economics school: poor management. The resulting solution to the labor problem is simple: better management. This solution to the labor problem is reflected in today's human resource management philosophy: Align the interests of workers and the firm via better management. To create motivated and efficient workers, firms should design and implement better supervisory methods, selection procedures, training methods, compensation systems, and evaluation and promotion mechanisms. If workers want justice, security, respect, and opportunities for advancement, then design nondiscriminatory human resource management policies that are responsive to these needs because workers will then be motivated, engaged, and productive, proponents claim, and high levels of performance (efficiency) will be achieved. Because management policies are responsive to the needs of employees, equity will also be achieved. Voice is typically informal, such as in open-door dispute resolution procedures in which workers individually discuss complaints with their managers.

The human resource management philosophy is depicted in the drawing from 1928 shown in Figure 2.2. The pilgrim, representing business, brings home the Thanksgiving bounty to stockholders, workers, and the government. Business is clearly depicted as the provider, with passive roles for both labor and government. Note that the pilgrim's gun is labeled "new methods." The methods of the personnel management school, which were considered new in the 1920s, along with other newly improved business practices in accounting and other areas, are depicted as producing rewards for all stakeholders.[26]

To consider the role of unions in the human resource management school of thought, it is important to distinguish independent labor unions from nonindependent employee organizations. The term *union* in most Western societies today and throughout this text refers to independent labor unions—those that are legally and functionally independent of employers and governments. Independent labor unions have the power to elect their own leaders, collect and spend their own dues money, establish their organizational objectives and strategies, and lead strikes. Nonindependent employee organizations lack such authority and are controlled by employers (like the company unions in the United States in the 1920s) or by governments (as traditionally is the case for unions in China).

In the human resource management school, independent unions are seen as adversarial and inimical to cooperation.[27] A popular saying in human resource management circles is that "companies get the unions they deserve." If companies are following the human resource management school's ideas of effective management, workers will be satisfied and will not support a union. But if a company has bad managerial practices, workers will seek unionization to combat these poor practices. In other words, unions are a fever—a sign of unhealthy human resource practices—and a healthy company shouldn't have one. This reveals a significant irony and tension within human resource management: Human resource professionals have greater influence in companies when there is a threat of unionization, but an important objective is often to keep unions out.[28] In fact, critics see human resource management as nothing more than a sophisticated (albeit gentle) antiunion device.[29]

The human resource management school of thought also believes that independent unions are unnecessary "third parties" that prevent employers and employees from getting "closer together." This remains a popular theme today. It is interesting to note, however, that in the 1920s many in this school of thought felt that workers should have some type of voice and representation. Having representation, it was believed, would help companies treat employees with respect, create a cooperative, constructive relationship, and foster loyalty.[30] Companies therefore created "company unions," though a better label is "nonunion representation plans." Management would meet and confer with worker representatives; but there would be no bargaining, and the representation plans had no authority outside management. In China, unions are similarly controlled not only by managers but also by the government. They are generally not seen as independent bargaining agents for workers, but are instead viewed as promoters of the common good.

In sum, for adherents of the human resource management school of thought, labor problems are best solved with effective management practices. Part of this desired management strategy for creating a motivated, productive workforce might include structures that are called unions, such as the 1920s-style company unions or traditional Chinese unions. But these unions are not the independent unions of today's Western societies, which the human resource management school sees as adversarial and inimical to cooperation.

The Industrial Relations School

The third school of thought is the **industrial relations school,** formerly called the institutional labor economics school.[31] In this school the labor problem is believed to stem from unequal bargaining power between corporations and individual workers. Recall that at the turn of the century in 1900, the modern economic system was still emerging. The emergence of large corporations, which separated the owners of the production process from a new wage-earning class who did the manual work, was relatively new.[32] Institutional labor economists accepted this modern corporation as an efficient organization of mass production, but they rejected the mainstream economics belief in perfect competition. Rather, institutional labor economists saw many signs of market imperfections: persistent unemployment; company towns dominated by a single employer; lack of worker savings

FIGURE 2.3
Striking a Balance between Labor and Capital, *Survey* (February 7, 1914)

Source: Survey Magazine

and other safety nets; and large, monopolistic employers with undue influence in markets, politics, and the legal system. In other words, "often the invisible guiding hand of competition is all thumbs."[33]

As a result of these imperfections, individual wage earners have vastly inferior bargaining power relative to employers. With greater bargaining power, employers can pay low wages for working long hours under dangerous working conditions. This greater bargaining power also allows managers to be autocratic and authoritarian. In short, in the industrial relations school, unequal bargaining power is the primary cause of the labor problem.[34] The labor market is characterized not by competition but by bargaining, and society is worse off if either side has too much power. These problems are compounded by business cycles that create additional insecurities.

The struggle for a balance between labor and management is richly illustrated in Figure 2.3. The laborer, clad only in shorts and a headband, is struggling with the capitalist, complete with ruffled collar and puffy pantaloons, for power, as represented by the pendulum. When there is a balance of power in the middle of the spectrum labeled "equity," there is an abundant harvest for both to share. However, when capital has too much power, the result is despotism, and the cornucopia overflows with the weapons of dictators such as shackles. At the other end of the spectrum, when labor is too powerful, anarchy results, and the cornucopia is filled with the weapons of anarchists, such as daggers and bombs. This is a great characterization of the industrial relations school of thought—and for much of this book, and the study and practice of labor relations. This pendulum imagery will also be important in later chapters as labor law struggles to balance the rights of employers and labor.

Compared to the other schools of thought, in the industrial relations school the causes of the labor problem are very different, and so the solutions also differ. *Most important for labor relations, if the labor problem stems from unequal bargaining power, the solution is to increase workers' bargaining power by forming independent labor unions and pursuing collective bargaining.*[35]

The Critical Industrial Relations School

The fourth school of thought to consider is the **critical industrial relations school,** traditionally labeled "Marxist industrial relations" and also referred to as a radical perspective. The "critical" label comes from being critical of existing societal institutions and social orderings. The critical school emphasizes that capitalist institutions do not simply exist but are created by society (such as through laws governing market transactions or business incorporation, and through social norms governing acceptable behaviors). This school of thought focuses our attention on how dominant groups design and control institutions to serve their own interests, albeit imperfectly due to resistance from competing groups.[36] For example, in the 1880s railroad titan James J. Hill set up trust funds to create and manage a Catholic seminary to train local priests so that these priests could in turn Americanize Irish immigrants and preach to them about the importance of diligence and respect for authority—values that Hill wanted in his largely Irish-American Catholic workforce.[37] As a contemporary example, a program at George Mason University funded by corporations, wealthy individuals, and conservative foundations has provided free training for several thousand judges to help them see legal theory through the lens of mainstream economic thought that prioritizes commercial and corporate interests.[38] Even initiatives that appear to benefit workers can be seen as reflecting class interests. For example, a labor law that legally protects workers who try to unionize is seen through a critical lens as an attempt to mollify the working class and prevent it from agitating for deeper changes in the capitalist system.[39] Corporations can therefore shape the broader social context of labor relations to serve their own interests and, in the view of the critical school, perpetuate their control over labor.

Within their own organizations, employers are similarly seen as structuring the organization of work and human resource management practices to serve their interests at the expense of labor. The division of labor is viewed as a strategy to make labor easily replaceable and therefore weak.[40] Fair treatment through progressive human resources policies, the perception of input through nonunion voice mechanisms, and the creation of pro-company attitudes through the development of distinctive corporate cultures are interpreted as strategies to prevent workers from unionizing.[41] Race, gender, nationality, and other identities are similarly seen as being manipulated to foster managerial control by pitting, for example, white and African American workers against each other in a divide-and-rule strategy that weakened broad worker solidarity.[42] In the critical school, then, the cause of the labor problem is believed to be the control of society's institutions and the means of production by specific groups or classes. In this school of thought, the solution to the labor problem is therefore a significant restructuring of the nature of capitalism—such as replacing capitalism with socialism.

The critical perspective is illustrated by the drawing in Figure 2.4. Through the symbolism of a vampire attacking a worker, capitalism is portrayed as preying on and victimizing the working class. This highlights the centrality of sharply-conflicting goals between labor and capital in the critical perspective. Moreover, socialism is providing a clarion call to alert the working class to the dangers of capitalism. In contrast with Figure 2.3 and the industrial relations paradigm, it is not a balance that is sought, but rather a significant change in the capitalist system.

Labor unions can be important in critical industrial relations. Strong, militant unions can aid workers' struggles with capitalism by mobilizing and raising the consciousness of the working class and fighting for improved compensation, better working conditions, and greater control over workplace decision making. The anarcho-syndicalist perspective within the critical school also sees radical unions as the key revolutionary vehicle for overthrowing capitalism and creating a society managed by workers. In contrast, proponents of socialism envision a political rather than revolutionary movement away from capitalism; and under socialism, unions would no longer be needed as representatives of the working class (though they might still exist to help the state educate and mobilize workers). In spite of these differing views, many adherents to the various perspectives within critical industrial relations are critical of the pragmatic, collective-bargaining focus of U.S. unions which does not do enough to challenge capital's power in the workplace and which reinforces capitalism rather than educating and leading the working class toward worker control or socialism.[43]

FIGURE 2.4
Walter Crane, "The Capitalist Vampire" (1885)

The Fundamental Assumptions of Human Resources and Industrial Relations

The labor problem of the early 20th century—low wages for long hours of dangerous work under autocratic supervision and periods of insecurity—can be traced to four possible underlying causes: market failures, poor management, unequal bargaining power between employers and individual employees, or the domination of labor by the capitalist class. In turn, these lead to four different views of labor unions (see Table 2.2). Underlying these views are three fundamental assumptions about how markets work and the nature of employment:

1. Is labor just a commodity?
2. Are employers and employees equals in competitive labor markets?
3. What is the nature of conflict between employers and employees?[44]

Each of the four schools of thought answers these questions differently. First, what is the nature of labor? Mainstream economics views the purpose of the economic system as consumption. Work is an unpleasant activity that one endures only to earn money, which can then be used to buy things (including leisure), but it does not provide intrinsic rewards. Labor is just another commodity or machine in the production process. The other three schools (human resource management, industrial relations, and critical industrial relations)

TABLE 2.2
Four Schools of Thought about Labor Unions

In Each School of Thought. . .	Labor Unions Are. . .
Mainstream economics	*Bad:* Monopolies that benefit a few at the expense of everyone else.
Human resource management (formerly personnel management)	*Unnecessary:* Effective management policies are best. Also, unions add unproductive conflict.
Industrial relations (formerly institutional labor economics)	*Important:* Necessary to counter corporate bargaining power and to balance efficiency, equity, and voice in democratic, capitalist societies.
Critical industrial relations (formerly Marxist industrial relations)	*Important but inadequate:* One key vehicle for aiding labor's struggle against capitalists and for protecting workers; but because of capitalism's inherent imbalances, greater sociopolitical changes are needed for true reform.

reject the belief that labor is just a commodity and instead see labor as human beings with aspirations, feelings, and rights. Work fulfills important psychological and social needs and provides more than extrinsic, monetary rewards that support consumerism.[45]

Second, are employers and employees equals in the labor market and the legal arena? Yes, *if* the fundamental assumptions of mainstream economics, such as perfect information and no transaction costs, are fulfilled. The other schools of thought, however, assert that employers and employees are not equals, either in the labor market or in the legal arena. Imperfect information, mobility costs, and tilted benefit structures can give firms monopsony (single-buyer) power. Lack of worker savings and persistent unemployment can cause individual workers to have inferior bargaining power relative to employers. These factors can turn perfect competition into excessive or destructive competition that creates substandard wages and working conditions.[46] In the legal arena, too, individual workers can be at a disadvantage if they don't understand their rights or cannot afford legal representation.[47]

Third, what is the nature of conflict between employers and employees? Three different answers distinguish the human resource management, industrial relations, and critical industrial relations schools of thought—and are therefore important. The human resource management school has a **unitarist view of conflict** in the employment relationship.[48] Conflict is not seen as an inherent or a permanent feature of the employment relationship; conflict is seen as a manifestation of poor human resource management policies or interpersonal clashes such as personality conflicts. Fundamentally, employees and employers have a unity of interests, and therefore effective management policies can align these interests for the benefit of all—recall the imagery in Figure 2.2 of the pilgrim (business) bringing home plenty of turkey for all stakeholders to share when business uses effective management practices.

In contrast, the industrial relations school sees the workplace as characterized by multiple interests—that is, a plurality of legitimate interests akin to a pluralist political system—so this school embraces a **pluralist view of conflict** in the employment relationship. Some of these interests are shared—both employers and employees want their organizations to be successful—but for other issues there is an inherent conflict of interest between employers and employees. In its simplest form, employers' drive for higher profits conflicts with labor's desire for higher wages. To be clear, the pluralist belief in an inherent conflict of interest does not mean that all workplace issues involve conflict, but rather is a rejection of the unitarist view that all workplace issues can be structured as shared interests. In other words, the pluralist view is that employment relationship conflict features mixed motives; some issues are conflictual and some involve mutual interests.[49] Employees want their employers to be profitable, but their desires for higher wages, better benefits, increased security, favorable working conditions, and input into decision making (equity and voice) clash with employers' pressures for lower labor costs, flexibility, and high output (efficiency).

Believers in pluralist workplace conflict therefore see government laws and labor unions as important for lessening power imbalances so that conflict is resolved in ways that strike a balance among efficiency, equity, and voice (recall the image of a plentiful harvest in Figure 2.3 when bargaining power is balanced). Because some conflict is inherent, it is unwise to rely on managerial goodwill to protect workers and to rely on management-initiated programs to provide employee voice. When times get bad enough, even enlightened managers can be tempted to put their interests above those of the workers—"recessions, depressions, and major industrial downsizings are a mortal threat to advanced, mutual gain [human resource management] systems and can quickly transform employees from high-valued human resource assets to low-valued disposable commodities."[50] And unlike the mainstream economics school, the industrial relations school does not believe it is sufficient to rely on economic markets to fairly mediate the conflicting interests of employers and employees because market failures mean that markets unfairly favor one side. From a pluralist perspective, then, labor unions that are independent of managerial authority provide checks and balances in the private and public sector workplace and are therefore essential for protection *and* participation—equity *and* voice.[51]

A different view of employment relationship conflict distinguishes the critical industrial relations school from other perspectives. This school believes in an inherent conflict between employers and employees, but it is significantly broader than the limited economic conflict in the pluralist view. From a critical perspective, employment relationship conflict is not limited to higher wages or better benefits; it is a social conflict of unequal power relations or **class conflict.**[52] As such, the critical industrial relations school believes that the pluralist limitation of the concept of "power" to bargaining power, rather than greater social relations, is superficial.[53] Unequal social relations are believed to pervade all capitalist institutions, and it is therefore inadequate to think about *balancing* the conflict between labor and management because management always has the upper hand—their domination is built into the entire political, legal, economic, and social structure, as captured by the capitalist serpent strangling working families in Figure 2.4.

The power of these alternative perceptions of the true nature of the employment relationship is that they yield contrasting perspectives on the practice of human resource management, diversity initiatives, public policies on work, and of particular importance here, employee voice mechanisms.[54] Employee voice is an important component of many contemporary human resource strategies; and with a unitarist view of conflict, workplace voice can successfully be provided through policies that encourage individual voice or through a nonunion employee representation plan.[55] As the name suggests, an employee representation plan is like a labor union to the extent that employee representatives communicate employee interests to management, but it is not independent. Managers, not employees, typically control how the plans are structured, when meetings occur, and what topics are covered.[56] Company management can unilaterally create and disband nonunion employee representation committees.

In contrast, if employment relationship conflict is in fact pluralist (the industrial relations belief in the existence of some inherent conflicts of interest), it follows that industrial democracy can be achieved only by traditional labor unions that are independent of management.[57] Only independent unions can fight for the protection necessary for industrial democracy such as free speech and due process protections. Taking this one step further, if labor–management conflict is embedded throughout society and is not limited

HR Strategy Employee Voice

There are a number of reasons why human resource managers might want to develop a strategy for providing employee voice. Here are some possibilities:

- Learning about employee ideas for improved productivity, quality, and cost savings.
- Increasing employee satisfaction and loyalty (therefore improving productivity and reducing turnover).
- Decentralizing decision making to improve responsiveness and flexibility to changing business needs.
- Providing a substitute for a union. (Is this ethical?)
- Increasing employees' problem-solving, communication, and decision-making skills.
- Making work more democratic.

Choose a specific nonunion business situation (such as a hotel, automobile assembly line, retail food manufacturing marketing group, or insurance company sales force) and determine what type of employee voice mechanism should be implemented. Why? Outline the structure of the employee voice mechanism (voluntary or mandatory, individual or group, decision-making authority or just talk, and so on) and a strategy for making it successful.

Now consider the same business situation in the presence of a union. How might the voice mechanism you developed improve with a union? How might the voice mechanism be less effective with a union? Do your answers to these two questions reflect the perspective of the company or the employees?

to the employment relationship (as believed by the critical industrial relations school), then labor unions ultimately are inadequate for challenging the power of employers. The sometimes intense debates about nonunion employee representation plans, independent yet conservative labor unions (i.e., unions that focus on collective bargaining in a specific workplace rather than on a more general class struggle), and more militant unions continue to be an important issue in U.S. labor relations and will be addressed in later chapters.[58] Differing assumptions about employment relationship conflict underlie these debates. Understanding these assumptions is therefore critical for understanding labor relations.

THE CONTINUED RELEVANCE OF THE LABOR PROBLEM

Thinking about differing views of labor unions and the four models of the employment relationship that underlie them is usefully pursued in the historical context of the labor problem. Our views of today's employment relationship are powerfully shaped by our limited personal experiences, so it can be easier to acknowledge the poor working conditions of earlier eras and think more open mindedly about various causes and solutions. But this is not intended as a purely historical exercise; although conditions for many workers have improved over the last 100 years, the fundamental issues surrounding the four schools of thought about the employment relationship are timeless and apply to today's employment relationships as much as 100 years ago.

To understand labor unions and labor relations, it is imperative to understand the beliefs of the different schools of thought about the labor problem. These four intellectual frameworks provide the keys to a reasoned rather than stereotypical understanding of labor unions and to appreciating the basis for differing views about whether unions are good or bad (recall Table 2.2). More generally, these four schools of thought continue to be the key frameworks for analyzing all aspects of the employment relationship in the 21st century and for thinking about how to improve employment issues. In fact, how to balance the employment relationship goals of efficiency, equity, and voice is a critical question for all eras. The focus of this book is how employee representation and collective bargaining help and hinder the achievement of these goals, but there are other options for structuring the employment relationship that do not involve labor union representation. Some might argue that human resource management, government laws, or unregulated, competitive markets are better mechanisms for balancing efficiency, equity, and voice. To better understand labor unions, it is important to explicitly compare collective bargaining to these alternative methods for determining wages and other terms and conditions of employment.

Workplace Governance

All workplaces need rules. In addition to standard rules of behavior and performance, these rules also include compensation and benefits, as well as policies and procedures. Some of these rules might be, for example, written in an employee handbook or a union contract, or posted on a bulletin board. Others might be unwritten. Some might simply be "The workers must do whatever the boss says." But at a more fundamental level, who gets to make these rules? In other words, what are the rules for making the rules?[59] Are they dictated by the marketplace? Are they established unilaterally by management? Are they mandated by government laws? Or do they result from negotiations between employers and labor unions? Each of these represent a form of **workplace governance.,** which is to say a method of ruling the workplace.[60] The method of workplace governance used in practice determines the nature of the balance that is struck among efficiency, equity, and voice. And though it is called *workplace* governance because of the focus on how workplace rules are determined, note that the ramifications are much broader and determine the quality of life for retirees, spouses, dependents, and communities.

Analyzing workplace governance is particularly instructive for understanding labor relations because it provides the context for evaluating whether unions are good or bad. The statement that unions are good is really the belief that unions achieve a better balance among efficiency, equity, and voice than do alternative mechanisms. The assertion that unions are bad is actually the belief that alternative mechanisms strike a better balance. Moreover, analyzing workplace governance reveals that these evaluations are critically related to the underlying assumptions about the nature of markets and employment outlined earlier in this chapter. Supporters of free markets, human resource management, or labor unions have different fundamental beliefs about the value of work, how labor markets work, and the nature of conflict between employers and employees. Understanding these differing beliefs is essential for understanding the evolution of the U.S. labor relations systems, the operation of the processes in practice, and the possible need for reform.

There are five major possibilities for creating workplace rules—that is, for governing the workplace: competitive labor markets, human resource management, worker control, bargaining with independent employee representatives (labor unions), and statutory government regulation.[61] These five alternatives are summarized in Table 2.3.

Laissez faire reliance on competitive labor markets includes two central critical features: mainstream economic theories plus common-law legal rules that protect individual liberties with the freedom of contract (the right of individuals and organizations to freely enter into economic relationships of their own choosing). Workplace rules—broadly defined to include implicit and explicit rules governing compensation, benefits, working conditions, and performance standards—result from self-interested individuals and organizations interacting in competitive markets. Workplace rules will favor management (lower wages, less generous benefits, shorter vacations, and the like) when labor demand is low and/or labor supply is high; rules will favor employees (higher wages, good benefits, training opportunities, and the like) when labor demand is high and/or labor supply is low. But the rules always result from the invisible hand of market forces.

TABLE 2.3
Options for Workplace Governance

Governance Mechanism	Workplace Rules Determined By	Key Feature	Questions
1. Competitive labor markets	Competition among firms for employees; competition among individuals for jobs.	Competitive markets promote efficiency and provide protections against abuses.	What if markets are not competitive? Should humans be solely at the mercy of markets?
2. Human resource management	Human resource managers, perhaps in consultation with employees or by employees within parameters established by managers who have veto power.	Human resource policies and employee participation in decision making can align the interests of employers and employees and promote efficiency, equity, and voice.	What prevents managerial abuse of its authority and power? Is management-controlled voice meaningful?
3. Worker control	Workers or their representatives.	Workers' interests are served by having them in control.	What prevents exploitation of investors? How is efficiency achieved?
4. Independent employee representation	Jointly by employers and employees (especially via collective bargaining).	Collective bargaining can equalize power between employees and employers while involving both sides in decision making.	Are unions adversarial and harmful to efficiency? What if unions are weak or absent?
5. Government regulation	Legislatures or government agencies.	Laws can establish uniform standards for all that are not dependent on the vagaries of markets, managers, or worker power.	How can regulations be established and enforced for many diverse workplaces? Do regulations stifle efficiency?

This can be thought of as a system of individual representation—workers looking out for their own interests in competitive markets—in contrast to the union model of collective representation.[62]

In the human resource management model of workplace governance, managers establish employment conditions. They are perhaps constrained to a range of alternatives established by the marketplace, but within this range managers choose specific terms and conditions of employment. For example, salary surveys always indicate that wages are not equal, even for a single occupation in a single location; managers decide whether to set salaries below, at, or above the market average. The prime mover of workplace rules is therefore not markets but management. This option of workplace governance contains a variety of human resource management strategies or philosophies and may or may not include nonunion forms of voice. Any voice mechanisms, however, are established and directed by management. Regardless of the specific strategies used, the distinguishing feature of the human resource management model of workplace governance is that the policies, practices, and conditions are unilaterally determined by management.

The opposite possibility is worker control, such as in producer cooperatives or models of worker control and ownership under socialism. This is more than employee participation—it is employee control over organizational objectives and rule making.[63]

This is also more than many employee stock ownership plans in which employees have a financial stake, but not control rights.[64] Rather, workers instead of managers unilaterally establish the terms and conditions of employment. Perhaps the leading U.S. example of worker self-governance was the craft union model of the early 20th-century unions, before the dominance of mass manufacturing. These unions often unilaterally established work rules and enforced them by refusing to work on any other terms and by fining or expelling members who undermined these standards.[65] In industrial settings, worker-managed enterprises can be run by delegates elected to a workers' council. There are no managers; rather, decision making is done through this delegates system. There were multiple examples of workers' councils in Europe in the early 20th century, and contemporary examples include bankrupt South American factories that have been taken over and managed by the workers.[66]

Another possibility for governing the workplace is to replace the unilateral authority of the human resource management or worker control models with a system of shared, bilateral authority in which employee voice is independent of managerial authority.[67] The major example of this shared control mechanism is collective bargaining. Workplace rules are not determined by competitive markets or unilaterally by either managers or workers; they are determined via negotiations between two parties with broadly equal bargaining power.

Finally, workplace rules can be set by government regulation.[68] Major U.S. examples of governing the workplace include the Fair Labor Standards Act (to establish a minimum wage and maximum work hours), Title VII of the Civil Rights Act (to provide equal opportunity), and the Occupational Safety and Health Act (to establish minimum safety standards). Ideally this system protects everyone, and standards can be determined by rational debate rather than bargaining or market power. On the other hand, regulations are determined by a central authority, not the workplace participants—so it can be difficult to shape agreements to fit particular needs and situations, and enforcement can be inconsistent, lax, and expensive.[69]

What determines which system of workplace governance is best? To answer this question we need to put these governance alternatives together with the intellectual models outlined earlier in the chapter (see Figure 2.5). In other words, individual opinions about the preferred system of workplace governance are rooted in how one thinks the employment relationship works. If, as assumed in the mainstream economics school of thought, labor is simply an economic factor of production (in other words, just another commodity) and employers and employees are economic and legal equals, then the appropriate workplace governance mechanism is reliance on competitive markets. Similarly, the assumptions of the human resource management school of thought lead to a human resource management model of workplace governance, and the assumptions of the critical industrial relations school lead to worker control or socialism as the preferred workplace governance model.

Or if one believes that the employment relationship is characterized by unequal bargaining power as in the industrial relations school, there are two important governance mechanisms for balancing the goals of employers and employees: statutory government regulation and labor unions. Government regulation can try to establish labor standards, but it does not involve employee voice; labor unions can try to counter corporate bargaining power and also provide voice that is independent of managerial authority. Understanding the linkages among the key assumptions of human resources and industrial relations, the four schools of thought about the employment relationship, and the various alternatives for governing the workplace is the key to understanding all aspects of employment, evaluating and designing solutions to historical and contemporary labor problems, and considering whether labor unions are good or bad.

FIGURE 2.5
The Intellectual Foundations of the Options for Governing the Workplace

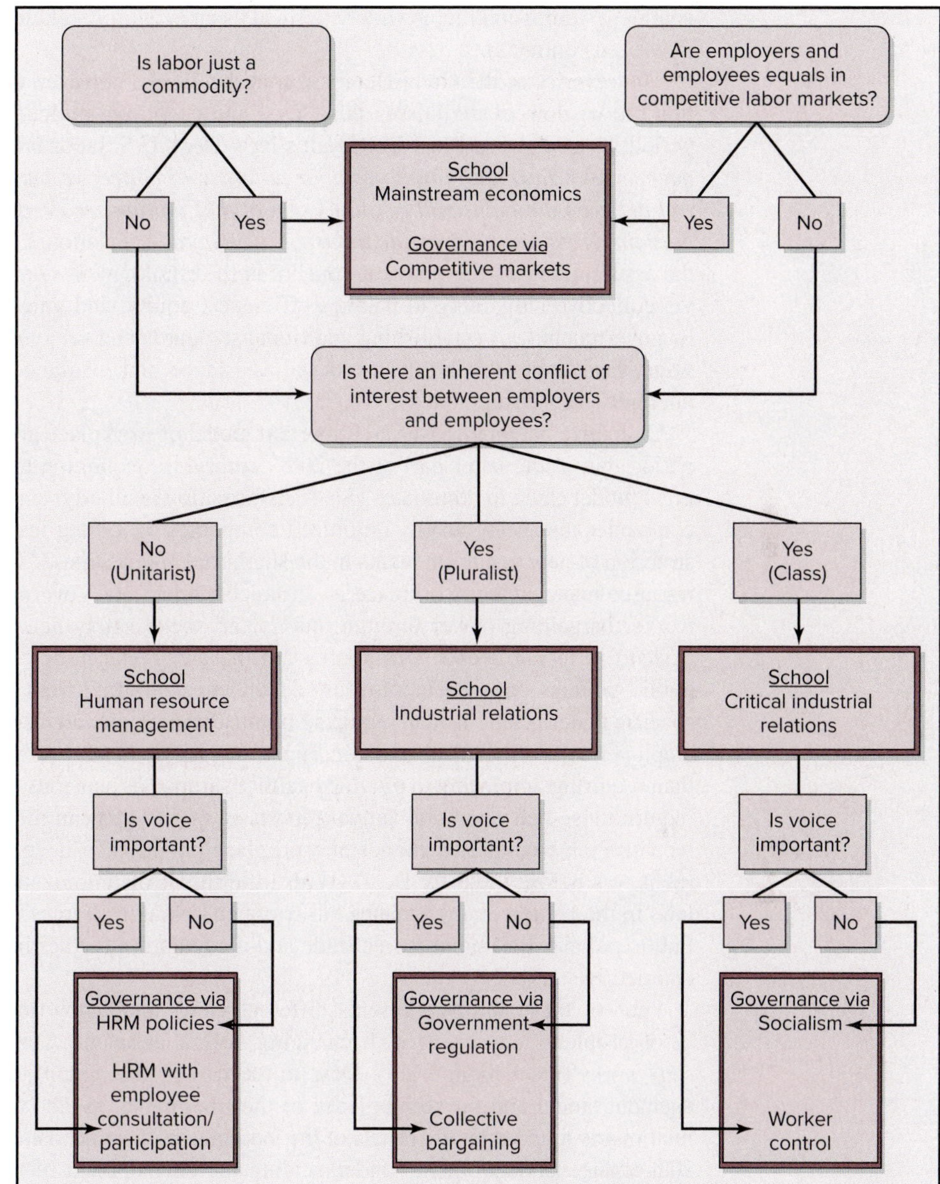

Solving Labor Problems

U.S. political and legal thought during the 1800s and early 1900s was dominated by laissez faire views consistent with the mainstream economics school, especially the supremacy of the freedom to enter any type of economic relationship—including employment—without government or union interference. Few laws were passed that set even minimal labor standards, and many of those enacted did not last long because they were ruled unconstitutional. For example, beginning in 1912 some states passed minimum wage laws for women and children only; but this ended in 1923 when the U.S. Supreme Court declared the District of Columbia's law unconstitutional because the law violated the rights of parties to freely enter economic relationships (generally referred to as the "freedom to contract," where contract is widely defined as an economic relationship and is not limited to written contracts).[70]

The severity of the Great Depression in the 1930s, however, called into serious question the wisdom of the laissez faire legal and economic philosophy.[71] During this time period, as part of President Roosevelt's New Deal, U.S. labor law was born. *As a consequence, U.S. laws pertaining to labor unions and collective bargaining reflect the central belief of the industrial relations school that unions are needed to counter corporate bargaining power and provide industrial democracy.*[72] National labor policy is based on the assumption that the pluralist conflict in the employment relationship is best resolved via collective bargaining to balance efficiency, equity, and voice. This is supplemented by government laws establishing additional standards and safety nets, such as a minimum wage, mandated overtime pay, old age assistance and insurance (Social Security), and unemployment insurance.

Collective bargaining was an important model of workplace governance in the postwar period, but in the latter part of the 20th century, the nonunion human resource management model came to dominate. This transformation resulted from the growth of nonunion companies and from heavily unionized companies becoming less unionized by the construction of new nonunion plants in the southern United States.[73] Consistent with a human resource management workplace governance model, new government laws to strengthen worker bargaining power through unions and social safety nets have been largely nonexistent in recent decades. In contrast to the New Deal policies of the 1930s, postwar public policies concede employees' dependence on employers by avoiding mandating specific benefits and instead requiring nondiscrimination and disclosure requirements for employer-controlled terms and conditions of employment.[74] As just one example, rather than requiring employers to provide health insurance or pensions, government regulations require those that do to file annual reports so employees can monitor these plans. More recently, the free-market model of workplace governance is again becoming dominant (as it was before the New Deal). With little threat of unionization or new employment laws in the United States, finance has trumped human resources in many organizations.[75] Public policies that support free trade and deregulation further increase the emphasis on competitive markets.

Each of these shifts represents different views about how to solve that generation's labor problems consistent with changing beliefs about how the employment relationship works (recall Figure 2.5). Despite the rise of the nonunion human resource management model and the reemergence of the free-market model, the U.S. system of labor relations is founded on the beliefs of the industrial relations school in the context of the early 20th-century labor problem. Understanding the development of the New Deal industrial relations system, therefore, grows out of an examination of the early 20th-century labor problem. Moreover, because contemporary labor relations continue to be dominated by laws rooted in the industrial relations school's principles, understanding the logic of current practices and strategies requires an appreciation of this school of thought.

But again, all four schools of thought continue to have great practical relevance (see the accompanying "Nonunion Application" box). The laissez faire emphasis of mainstream economics dominates national and international policy debates under the guise of the neoliberal market ideology; today's corporate human resource policies are rooted in the principles of the human resource management school of thought; the critical model underlies the movement to revitalize unions by transforming them into aggressive champions of the working class. And the principles of the industrial relations school continue to appear in practice in many places around the globe, such as in New Zealand's Employment Relations Act of 2000, which is based on the belief that "there is an inequality of bargaining power in many employment relationships" such that "employers and

Nonunion Application Perspectives on HRM

This chapter emphasizes the need to see the importance of four alternative schools of thought for understanding contrasting perspectives on labor unions. The usefulness of this framework, however, is not limited to the labor relations domain. Rather, students and professionals should use this framework to understand different perspectives on many work-related issues. Of particular note, consider human resource management (HRM). In the human resource management school of thought (and in HRM courses), well-designed, high-road HRM practices emphasizing engagement and alignment are embraced as the key managerial mechanism for creating profitable organizations because these practices are the way to unify the interests of employees and employers. But not everyone shares this HRM-as-critically-important perspective. The other schools of thought can help you understand the detractors and skeptics.

In mainstream economics theorizing, HRM practices are believed to be determined by the labor market—fall behind the market, and employees will quit; get too generous relative to the market, and the employer will be unable to sell products and services at a competitive price. Through the lens of the mainstream economics school, then, HRM is seen as an administrative mechanism for implementing what the labor market commands. So HRM is viewed as an administrative rather than a strategic value-creation business function by those who subscribe to an economics way of thinking, such as those in finance and accounting. Moreover, low-road HRM strategies that include low wages and managerial control are rooted in this way of thinking because they emphasize what the labor market will bear.

From a pluralist perspective that believes there are at least some conflicts of interest in the employment relationship, HRM is seen as beneficial for aligning those employee–employer interests that are shared. But pluralists are skeptical toward completely relying on manager-driven HRM practices to govern the workplace because some interests are not shared, and for those issues, some organizations are likely to use their power and authority to benefit themselves at the workers' expense. Those in the critical industrial relations camp are even more critical of HRM. Because of the socially rooted, ongoing conflict between employers and employees assumed in this school, HRM policies are not seen as methods for aligning interests, but rather as disguised rhetoric that quietly undermines labor power while perpetuating capital's control. For example, above-market compensation policies and informal dispute resolution procedures are viewed as union substitution strategies to prevent employees from gaining more power by unionizing.

As you can see, the four schools of thought presented in this chapter are useful not only for understanding labor relations but are also insightful in other areas.

employees share many common interests, but they also have separate interests"—which means that "productive employment relationships depend on . . . promoting areas of common interest and managing competing interests in a way that maintains and builds relationships."[76]

Finally, although some details may have changed, the United States and every other developed and developing country in the 21st century continue to struggle with the modern equivalent of the labor problem. All three dimensions of efficiency, equity, and voice are relevant to today's employment relationships. Modern sweatshops, in the United States and elsewhere, continue to exist and exploit workers. The Occupy and Fight for $15 movements have brought the problem of 21st-century economic and social inequality into the public consciousness. The arbitrary power of supervisors persists, as illustrated by the thousands of complaints of quid pro quo sexual harassment filed with the U.S. Equal Employment Opportunity Commission. Workers in many occupations want a stronger voice in the workplace, and by some accounts this should be a fundamental human right. At the same time, private and public sector organizations continue to struggle with issues of competitiveness, productivity, and quality. Efficiency, equity, and voice continue to be crucial themes for policy makers and practitioners, workers, and employers. The seemingly historical discussion of the labor problem continues to have great relevance for us in the 21st century both intellectually and practically.

How much has work changed? Compare these two photos.

Garment Factory Workers Sewing at Long Tables in New York City, 1900.

Garment Factory Workers Sewing at Long Tables, Los Angeles, 2011.

Online Exploration Exercise: Explore the online exhibit about the 1911 Triangle Shirtwaist Factory fire (*trianglefire.ilr.cornell.edu*). What were working conditions like? Search online for information on sweatshops in the 21st century. How do these compare to sweatshops of the early 20th century? If modern sweatshops are a problem, what should be done?

WHAT DO U.S. UNIONS DO?

So are unions good or bad? The four schools of thought and the labor problem discussion reveal that the evaluation of labor unions fundamentally depends on the nature of work, how labor markets operate, the nature of employment relationship conflict, and the importance of employee voice (recall Table 2.2 and Figure 2.5). In mainstream economics unions are harmful because they are monopolies that impair economic efficiency. Unions may exist, but they are bad. The preferred method of workplace governance is reliance on competitive markets. In the human resource management school, unions are an indication that management is not successfully creating motivated and efficient workers via firm-created human resource management policies. Unions may exist, but they are unnecessary. The preferred workplace governance method is human resource management. In critical industrial relations thought, unions are either management tools of worker suppression or worker tools of power and revolution, though neither of these are mainstream U.S. beliefs. The desired mechanisms for governing the workplace are worker control or socialism.

But within the intellectual framework of the industrial relations school, unions are a critical part of the solution to the labor problem because collective, not individual, bargaining is needed to match corporate bargaining power and because independent employee voice is important in a democratic society. Unions provide protection and participation, equity and voice. The preferred method of workplace governance is a combination of government standards and labor union representation. So one important method for answering the question of whether unions are good or bad is conceptual. A second approach to addressing this question is to look at the empirical research record about what unions do in practice, and whether, on balance, these things are beneficial or harmful and to whom.[77]

Evaluating the Effects of Unionism

The research on the effects of unions on U.S. workers and workplaces is summarized in Table 2.4. Unionized workers in the United States are generally estimated to have wages approximately 15 percent higher than comparable nonunion workers.[78] This is called the **union wage premium.** Unions also reduce wage inequality and CEO pay.[79] With respect to other terms and conditions of employment, research finds that unions increase the likelihood of employee benefits, seniority rights, and just cause discipline and discharge provisions.[80] For example, unionized workers are at least 15 percent more likely to have employer-provided health insurance and pensions than similar nonunion workers.[81]

In terms of efficiency, there is a lot of research on the effects of unions on productivity.[82] Unions can be hypothesized to lower productivity by using their power to negotiate restrictive work rules and by introducing time-consuming decision-making procedures. On the other hand, unions can potentially enhance productivity in several ways. The research evidence supports the presence of a **shock effect:** The presence of a union shocks managers out of complacency and forces them to develop better managerial practices and policies that improve workplace efficiency, including more formal human resource policies such as training programs, and objective rather than subjective selection tests.[83] Moreover, grievance procedures, seniority provisions, and other gains can increase morale, improve communication between managers and employees, and reduce turnover, which can all increase productivity. One study finds that the heart attack mortality rate is lower in hospitals with unionized nurses relative to similar nonunion hospitals, perhaps because of improved work climate, communication, and trust.[84] Overall, however, the results are mixed. Some research finds that unions are associated with increased productivity, but

TABLE 2.4
What Do Unions Do?

Dimension	Estimated Effect of U.S. Unions
Efficiency	
Job satisfaction	Union workers are less satisfied on average, but probably because their working conditions are different.
Turnover	Reduced turnover.
Productivity	Mixed evidence—controversial effects.
Profits	Reduced profitability.
Equity	
Wage levels	Higher wages (15 percent higher on average).
Wage distribution	Compressed (less unequal) wage structure.
Employee benefits	Increased likelihood of benefits being offered.
Just cause discipline and discharge	Nearly universal in union contracts; rare elsewhere.
Public policies	Assistance with exercising rights (e.g., workers' compensation).
Seniority	Increased importance of seniority provisions in personnel changes.
Voice	
Collective negotiations	Management is required to bargain with a certified union.
Grievance procedures	Nearly universal presence of formal grievance procedures in union contracts; few nonunion procedures with same level of due process and representation.

other studies find no or negative effects of unions on productivity and organizational effectiveness; these differences might be partly explained by whether managers react to unionization in productive or hostile ways.[85] In contrast to this mixed track record for productivity, the presence of a union is usually associated with lower profitability.[86] In other words, even when unions raise productivity, these gains do not offset the higher unionized labor costs. Research also finds that unions reduce employment growth but are not likely to drive firms out of business, perhaps because employers adjust by hiring fewer high-skilled workers.[87]

Unions have other important effects in the workplace. Union voice gives workers an alternative to quitting when they are dissatisfied with a job, and research finds that unionized workers are in fact less likely to quit than similar nonunion workers.[88] For many years this created a puzzle because early research indicated that unionized workers were less satisfied with their jobs—but if they were less satisfied, then why would they quit less often?[89] Later research, however, revealed that there do not appear to be significant union–nonunion differences in job satisfaction once one accounts for differences in working conditions and workplace climate.[90] Moreover, there shouldn't be a puzzle because quitting isn't necessarily the most frequent response to dissatisfaction; adaptation, for example, is often personally less costly.[91] Union-provided voice mechanisms can perhaps help unionized workers adapt as well as change their working conditions. Unions also facilitate the receipt of benefits to which workers are entitled. For example, unions can tell employees about benefit plans through union newsletters and can protect against retaliation for exercising their rights.[92] Consistent with this union facilitation effect, research finds that unions appear to improve employee awareness of employer-provided and government-mandated family friendly policies, help employees file valid unemployment insurance and workers' compensation claims, and increase employer compliance with nondiscrimination laws.[93]

Labor unions can also provide a sense of community in the workplace and counter some negative psychological effects of the lack of ownership in one's work.[94] And as we will discuss in the next chapter, the Knights of Labor in the 1800s emphasized moral and spiritual reform. In fact, the Catholic Church advocates for labor unions not only as a vehicle for improving working conditions but also for the spiritual improvements that can come when workers enjoy a better life. In the words of Pope John Paul II, "It is always to be hoped that, thanks to the work of their unions, workers will not only *have* more, but above all *be* more: in other words, that they will realize their humanity more fully in every respect."[95]

The empirical research on what unions do greatly contributes to our understanding of labor relations. But consideration of this research reinforces the need for a conceptual basis for interpreting the results. Is the fact that unions negotiate higher wages and reduce profits good or bad? It depends on the analytical lens we use. From a mainstream economics perspective, the union wage premium and reduced profitability are bad because they reflect the extent to which unions interfere with and distort optimal competitive outcomes (for a more complex treatment of this issue, see the "Digging Deeper" feature at the end of this chapter). From an industrial relations perspective, in contrast, higher wages and reduced profitability represent a socially beneficial redistribution of income that creates a more equitable distribution of economic property than the inequalities produced by imperfectly competitive labor markets and their inherent bargaining power imbalances. In fact, to address the social ills of the labor problem and to boost consumer purchasing power, U.S. labor law is explicitly intended to *help* unions *raise* wages! As such, the empirical evidence that unions raise wages, increase the probability of receiving health insurance and other employee benefits, facilitate the receipt of social insurance benefits, reduce income inequality, and negotiate for grievance procedures with just cause discipline and discharge provisions is interpreted in the industrial relations school of thought as evidence that unions promote economic and social justice. Through the lenses of other schools of thought, these things that unions do might be seen as distortionary or unnecessary. So the question of whether unions are good or bad does not have an easy answer.

Theories of the Labor Movement

In the United States, it is common to focus on the workplace when thinking about labor unions. To wit, the four views of labor unions revealed by the mainstream economics, human resource management, industrial relations, and critical industrial relations schools of thought capture the central debates over the workplace roles of unions. However, unions are not purely workplace institutions, and any discussion of what unions do should look beyond the workplace. At this point it is also useful to distinguish labor unions from the labor movement. A **labor movement** is a social movement in which workers and unions from multiple workplaces join together to pursue common interests, most frequently in the political and social arenas.

More specifically, the labor movement provides a voice for workers in the political arena.[96] Labor unions, or their associated political action committees, endorse candidates for political offices, mobilize get-out-the-vote efforts, campaign on behalf of candidates, and lobby and make donations to lawmakers. Under the Obama administration, the labor movement lobbied for health care and immigration reform as well as passage of the Employee Free Choice Act (see Chapters 4 and 6). European labor movements continue to lobby for European policies to combat unemployment and poverty, while labor movements around the world are allied in campaigns to include labor rights in free trade agreements. In many countries unions are closely intertwined with political parties, such as the Labour Party in Great Britain or the Workers' Party in Brazil.

As with the workplace role of labor unions, evaluating the political and social roles of labor movements depends on our frame of reference. From the perspective of mainstream economics in which labor unions are labor market monopolies, a labor movement's political activities are also seen as the use of power to benefit unionized workers at the expense of others. At the other end of the spectrum, the critical industrial relations model sees labor movements that are active in the political and social arenas as vital for countering the dominant power of employers. Taking this one step further, some labor movements see themselves as agents of radical reform, and outside North America, it is not uncommon to have unions aligned with socialist or communist political parties.

Finally, recall that the industrial relations school of thought is rooted in the belief that the workplace encompasses a plurality of employer and employee interests. Extending this perspective to the political and social arenas, a democratic society is seen as a pluralist society in which numerous groups have common and conflicting interests—corporations, consumers, farmers, workers, home owners, and the like. From this frame of reference, the labor movement represents workers in the political arena just as the Chamber of Commerce represents business and the American Association of Retired Persons (AARP) represents senior citizens. Unions are thus seen as balancing the economic power of employers in the workplace, and as balancing the political power of employers and their allies in the political arena. As another contribution to democracy, by engaging in conflict resolution in the workplace, taking advantage of union-provided training, and participating in the affairs of a local union, unionized workers can develop advocacy and leadership tools, become more politically aware, and even get elected to political office.[97] Labor unions can also be important organizations in civil society where individuals gather to socialize, discuss issues, pursue charitable goals, and form a sense of community, often with a much greater diversity of individuals than when people gather with friends and others outside of the workplace.[98] From a pluralist perspective then, the labor movement makes important contributions in the political and civil arenas in contemporary democratic societies; and the relationship between a vibrant, independent labor movement and a healthy, balanced democratic society must be remembered when evaluating labor unions.[99]

Online Exploration Exercise: The major union federations in the United States, Canada, and Great Britain are the American Federation of Labor–Congress of Industrial Organizations (AFL–CIO) (*www.aflcio.org*), Canadian Labour Congress (*canadianlabour.ca*), and the Trades Union Congress (*www.tuc.org.uk*), respectively. Explore their sites, or those of individual unions, and look for examples of the different types of union roles outlined in this chapter. Compare the sites of the three major federations to that of the Industrial Workers of the World (*www.iww.org* or *www.iww.org.uk*).

In sum, whether labor unions are good or bad is a difficult, complex question. There are undoubtedly specific examples in which most would agree that a certain labor union was either harmful (e.g., with a corrupt, predatory leadership) or beneficial (e.g., winning basic protections against an exploitative, sweatshop employer). On a broader scale, however, thinking about the labor problem and the question of workplace governance reveals the basis for evaluating labor unionism. As we have discussed, the four schools of thought on these questions—mainstream economics, human resource management, industrial relations, and critical industrial relations—have their own beliefs about the nature of markets and the employment relationship. Consequently, each school of thought has its own views about labor unions and labor movements—good, bad, or indifferent. Understanding these differing views, and where they come from, is essential for understanding labor relations and therefore for designing appropriate business practices, union strategies, and public policies. And appreciating these views is vital for thinking about both the past and the future.

In particular, it is difficult to understand U.S. labor law, and the U.S. system of labor relations, from the perspectives of the mainstream economics, human resource management, and critical industrial relations schools of thought. *The intellectual foundations of the U.S. system of labor relations come from the industrial relations school of thought.* Labor laws protecting employees' rights to form unions were passed because of the beliefs that labor market competition is not among equals, that it is not wise to rely on managerial benevolence, and that employee voice is important in a democratic society. One does not need to agree with this pluralist industrial relations philosophy, but it is imperative to remember this intellectual foundation when studying and practicing U.S. labor relations.

Key Terms

mainstream economics school, *32*
human resource management school, *33*
industrial relations school, *35*
critical industrial relations school, *36*
unitarist view of conflict, *39*
pluralist view of conflict, *39*
class conflict, *40*
workplace governance, *42*
union wage premium, *49*
shock effect, *49*
labor movement, *51*

Reflection Questions

1. Mother Jones, a colorful figure in U.S. labor history who will be introduced in Chapter 3, said in 1913, "The world is suffering, today, from an industrial yellow fever, not less fatal, but I am certain, as preventable."[100] Yellow fever was caused by mosquitoes, so Mother Jones continued, "Search for the mosquito! That ought to be a slogan with investigators on both sides of the labor question." What is the mosquito that causes the labor problem in each of the four schools of thought?
2. How are the major premises of the mainstream economics and industrial relations schools consistent with Figure 2.2? How would you change the label on the gun to make this into a mainstream economics drawing? An industrial relations drawing?
3. Review Figure 2.3. Sketch a similar diagram to capture the range of outcomes possible within the human resource management school. (*Hint*: Use a pendulum but not necessarily a power struggle between labor and management.)
4. Think of jobs you or someone you know has had. What was undesirable about these jobs? Was the pay too low? Hours too long? Were you treated poorly? Which of the four schools of thought best explains the causes of these undesirable aspects? What would you try to do to redress these undesirable features?
5. How should the workplace be governed? Why?

Digging Deeper The Two Economic Faces of Unionism

THREE KEY MAINSTREAM ECONOMICS ASSUMPTIONS AND THREE ALTERNATIVES

The mainstream economics view of labor unions as harmful monopolies relies on a set of fairly strong assumptions pertaining to perfectly competitive markets. First, the standard economic model assumes that goods and services are private—you consume only what you purchase. But an alternative assumption is that some aspects of the workplace are public goods. Safety provisions, heating, lighting, ventilation, just cause discipline and discharge provisions, and grievance procedures benefit everyone regardless of whether someone "pays" for it. With individual decision making there is a free-rider problem, and too few of these beneficial public goods will be provided (analogous to standard societal examples such as national defense). Second, in the standard economic model, mobility and transaction costs are assumed to be zero. Moreover, in competitive markets, compensation and employment conditions are determined by the intersection of supply and demand as shaped by what economists call the marginal worker (the individual who is on the margin of joining or leaving the company with small changes in compensation and employment conditions). For the firm to retain the optimal number of workers, employment conditions must satisfy the marginal worker. If mobility and transaction costs are zero, anyone who doesn't like these terms and conditions of employment and can get a better deal elsewhere is assumed to be able to easily quit and change jobs. But for workers with seniority, children, a mortgage, or doctors through a specific health insurance plan, quitting can be risky and costly. As such, a nonunion workplace might include a group of less mobile workers who are effectively locked into their jobs but who are also not satisfied by the compensation package that is tailored to younger, more mobile, marginal workers. Third, the standard economic model assumes that workers are purely rational. If we relax this assumption, then trust, communication, respect, and fairness become more important.

LABOR UNIONS WHEN THE ALTERNATIVE ASSUMPTIONS ARE ACCURATE

Weakening these assumptions results in a different economic perspective on labor unions.[101] First, having a collective voice mechanism such as a union in the workplace internalizes both the costs and benefits of workplace public goods and solves the free-rider problem. Workers likely respond positively to these workplace public goods, which can increase productivity and efficiency. Second, with a union, employment conditions are determined by bargaining, not the market and the marginal worker. As political organizations, unions are concerned with satisfying a majority of the workers. This is often referred to as the median voter model: If union leaders can satisfy the median worker, they will have satisfied at least 50 percent and will be reelected. Thus terms and conditions of employment that are determined by collective bargaining will reflect the preferences of a majority of the workers, who are likely to be older and less likely to leave the firm than the marginal workers. This can increase economic efficiency. Third, regular consultation between management and a union provides a visible avenue for sustained communication and a forum for employees to voice concerns or resolve grievances. This consultation can promote employee commitment by promoting a sense of dignity, respect, and procedural justice, which in turn can enhance economic efficiency.

More generally, note that standard economic models rely on exit for expressing displeasure. If you don't like your job, quit; if you feel a store is too expensive, shop elsewhere. But there is an alternative to exit: communication or voice.[102] Instead of quitting an undesirable job, you can communicate your displeasure to your boss, discuss the situation, and try to work out improvements. If the strong mainstream economics assumptions necessary for perfect competition are fulfilled, then exit is costless. But voice can be better than exit if exit is costly. By replacing exit with collective voice, unions can increase economic efficiency if real-world workplaces do not satisfy the simplifying assumptions of the standard mainstream economics model of perfect competition. *If there are workplace public goods, if quitting a job is costly for workers or employers, or if trust and fairness are important to workers, then collective voice in the workplace can be socially beneficial.*

THE TWO ECONOMIC FACES OF LABOR UNIONS

Unions therefore have two economic faces: a monopoly face and a collective voice/institutional response face.[103] The monopoly face is the dominant mainstream economics view of unions in which unions use their monopoly power in the labor market to raise wages for their members above the competitive level, which can be harmful for everyone else. The collective voice face is a second side of unions in which they add collective voice to the workplace and potentially improve outcomes for workers *and* employers. This face is based on the alternatives to the mainstream economics assumptions. In this face, unions do not raise compensation; rather they represent the collective voice of the workers to alter the mix of the compensation package

Continued

(e.g., more health insurance benefits in lieu of a wage increase, holding total costs constant) to better satisfy a majority of the workforce.

So which face dominates in practice? Research finds that unions exhibit a mixture of both faces.[104] As an example, consider employee benefits. In the monopoly face, unions increase the overall amount of employee benefits; whereas in the collective voice face, the composition of the benefits package is rearranged to better satisfy worker preferences. Empirical research finds that unions increase the total amount of spending on employer-provided benefits relative to comparable nonunion workers (consistent with the monopoly face), *and* that holding total compensation constant, unionized employees have a greater relative fraction of benefits in their overall compensation package (consistent with the voice face). The magnitudes of these two results further indicate that the overall effect of unions on benefits is split roughly equally between these two faces.[105]

The model of two economic faces of unionism undermines the single-mindedness of the mainstream economics tradition in which unions are seen as socially harmful monopolies, and thereby complicates the question of whether unions are good or bad. Even within the mainstream economics paradigm in which unions are traditionally viewed negatively, the collective voice face of unionism can improve both efficiency and social welfare. At the same time, it is important not to push the two faces of unionism model too far. The evidence in support of unions improving productivity, for example, is mixed, and it is difficult to make a case for unions on this basis. But one should not have to. The economic effects of unions—on workers, productivity, and competitiveness—are certainly important, but they should not be the *sole* basis for evaluating labor unions and employee representation (recall efficiency *and* equity *and* voice). Unions were not established as productivity-enhancing mechanisms and should not be evaluated only in this vein.

End Notes

1. www.nathannewman.org/laborblog/archive/003635.shtml
2. http://blog.washingtonpost.com/thefix/2005/12/aflcio_asks_whos_on_our_side.html
3. Robert Bruno, "Evidence of Bias in the Chicago Tribune Coverage of Organized Labor: A Quantitative Study from 1991 to 2001," *Labor Studies Journal* 34 (September 2009), pp. 385–407; Christopher R. Martin, *Framed! Labor and the Corporate Media* (Ithaca, NY: Cornell University Press, 2004).
4. Pepi Leistyna, *Class Dismissed: How TV Frames the Working Class* [DVD] (Northampton, MA: Media Education Foundation, 2005).
5. Lawrence Richards, *Union-Free America: Workers and Antiunion Culture* (Urbana, IL: University of Illinois Press, 2008).
6. Bruce E. Kaufman, *The Origins and Evolution of the Field of Industrial Relations in the United States* (Ithaca, NY: ILR Press, 1993); Bruce E. Kaufman, "Labor Markets and Employment Regulation: The View of the 'Old' Institutionalists," in Bruce E. Kaufman (ed.), *Government Regulation of the Employment Relationship* (Madison, WI: Industrial Relations Research Association, 1997), pp. 11–55; J.A. Estey, *The Labor Problem* (New York: McGraw-Hill, 1928); E.E. Cummins, *The Labor Problem in the United States* (New York: D. Van Nostrand, 1932); William E. Barns, *The Labor Problem: Plain Questions and Practical Answers* (New York: Harper and Brothers, 1886); Carroll R. Daugherty, *Labor Problems in American Industry* (Boston, MA: Houghton Mifflin, 1933); Warren B. Catlin, *The Labor Problem in the United States and Great Britain* (New York: Harper and Brothers, 1926).
7. W. Jett Lauck and Edgar Sydenstricker, *Conditions of Labor in American Industries: A Summarization of the Results of Recent Investigations* (New York: Funk and Wagnalls, 1917), pp. 185–86; Interchurch World Movement of North America, *Report on the Steel Strike of 1919* (New York: Harcourt, Brace and Howe, 1920).
8. Lauck and Sydenstricker, *Conditions of Labor in American Industries*, pp. 29, 376; Seth D. Harris, "Conceptions of Fairness and the Fair Labor Standards Act," *Hofstra Labor and Employment Law Journal* 18 (Fall 2000), pp. 19–166; Cummins, *The Labor Problem in the United States.*
9. Leon Stein, *The Triangle Fire* (Philadelphia, PA: Lippincott, 1962); Lauck and Sydenstricker, *Conditions of Labor in American Industries* , p. 347; Cummins, *The Labor Problem in the United States*, pp. 90–94; Ezekiel H. Downey, *Workmen's Compensation* (New York: Macmillan, 1924), p. 1.
10. Lauck and Sydenstricker, *Conditions of Labor in American Industries* , pp. 77, 157–60; Sanford M. Jacoby, *Employing Bureaucracy: Managers, Unions, and the Transformation of Work in American Industry, 1900–1945* (New York: Columbia University Press, 1985); Nelson Lichtenstein, "'The Man in the Middle': A Social History of Automobile Industry Foremen," in Nelson Lichtenstein and Stephen Meyer (eds.), *On the Line: Essays in the History of Auto Work* (Urbana, IL: University of Illinois Press, 1989), pp. 153–89; Lizabeth Cohen, *Making a New Deal: Industrial Workers in Chicago, 1919–1939* (Cambridge: Cambridge University Press, 1990); Susan A. Glenn, *Daughters of the Shtetl: Life and Labor in the Immigrant Generation* (Ithaca, NY: Cornell University Press, 1990); Nancy F. Gabin, *Feminism in the Labor Movement: Women and the United Auto Workers, 1935–1975* (Ithaca, NY: Cornell University Press, 1990); Meghan Cope, "'Working Steady': Gender, Ethnicity, and Change in Households, Communities, and Labor Markets in Lawrence, Massachusetts, 1930–1940," in Andrew Herod (ed.), *Organizing the Landscape: Geographical Perspectives on Labor Unionism* (Minneapolis, MN: University of Minnesota Press, 1998), pp. 297–323.
11. David Roediger and Elizabeth Esch, *The Production of Difference: Race and the Management of Labor in U.S. History* (New York: Oxford University Press, 2012).
12. Zaragosa Vargas, *Labor Rights Are Civil Rights: Mexican American Workers in Twentieth-Century America* (Princeton, NJ: Princeton University Press, 2005); Joseph E. Slater, *Public Workers: Government Employee Unions, the Law, and the State, 1900–1962* (Ithaca, NY: Cornell University Press, 2004).
13. John W. Budd, *Employment with a Human Face: Balancing Efficiency, Equity, and Voice* (Ithaca, NY: Cornell University Press, 2004); Bruce E. Kaufman, "The Social Welfare Objectives and Ethical Principles of Industrial Relations," in John W. Budd and James G. Scoville (eds.), *The Ethics of Human Resources and Industrial Relations* (Champaign, IL: Labor and Employment Relations Association, 2005), pp. 23-59.
14. Stephen Meyer, *The Five Dollar Day: Labor Management and Social Control in the Ford Motor Company, 1908–1921* (Albany, NY: State University of New York Press, 1981), p. 80.
15. United States Industrial Commission, *Report of the Industrial Commission on the Relations and Conditions of Capital and Labor Employed in Manufactures and General Business* [Volume 7] (Washington, DC: Government Printing Office, 1901), p. 397.

16. John W. Budd and Devasheesh Bhave, "Values, Ideologies, and Frames of Reference in Industrial Relations," in Paul Blyton et al. (eds.), *Sage Handbook of Industrial Relations* (London: Sage, 2008), pp. 92–112; John W. Budd and Devasheesh Bhave, "The Employment Relationship," in Adrian Wilkinson et al. (eds.), *Sage Handbook of Human Resource Management* (London: Sage, 2010), pp. 51–70.
17. Roger Backhouse, *A History of Modern Economic Analysis* (New York: Blackwell, 1985); George J. Borjas, *Labor Economics*, 4th ed. (Boston, MA: McGraw-Hill/Irwin, 2008); George R. Boyer and Robert S. Smith, "The Development of the Neoclassical Tradition in Labor Economics," *Industrial and Labor Relations Review* 54 (January 2001), pp. 199–223; Leo Troy, *Beyond Unions and Collective Bargaining* (Armonk, NY: M. E. Sharpe, 1999).
18. J.R. Hicks, *The Theory of Wages*, 2nd ed. (London: Macmillan, 1963), p. 82.
19. Troy, *Beyond Unions and Collective Bargaining*.
20. Milton Friedman and Rose Friedman, *Free to Choose: A Personal Statement* (New York: Harcourt Brace Jovanovich, 1980), p. 246; Paul C. Weiler, *Governing the Workplace: The Future of Labor and Employment Law* (Cambridge, MA: Harvard University Press, 1990).
21. Friedman and Friedman, *Free to Choose*; Morgan O. Reynolds, *Power and Privilege: Labor Unions in America* (New York: Universe Books, 1984); Dan C. Heldman, James T. Bennett, and Manuel H. Johnson, *Deregulating Labor Relations* (Dallas, TX: Fisher Institute, 1981); Richard Epstein, "The Deserved Demise of EFCA (and Why the NLRA Should Share its Fate)," in Cynthia L. Estlund and Michael L. Wachter (eds.), *Research Handbook on the Economics of Labor and Employment Law* (Northampton, MA: Edward Elgar, 2012), pp. 177–208; Cedric de Leon, *The Origins of Right to Work: Antilabor Democracy in Nineteenth-Century Chicago* (Ithaca, NY: Cornell University Press, 2015).
22. Richard A. Epstein, *Simple Rules for a Complex World* (Cambridge, MA: Harvard University Press, 1995); Richard A. Posner, *Economic Analysis of Law*, 3rd ed. (Boston, MA: Little, Brown, 1986).
23. Bruce E. Kaufman, *Managing the Human Factor: The Early Years of Human Resource Management in American Industry* (Ithaca, NY: Cornell University Press, 2008).
24. Jacoby, *Employing Bureaucracy*; Bruce E. Kaufman, *Hired Hands or Human Resources? Case Studies of HRM Programs and Practices in Early American Industry* (Ithaca, NY: Cornell University Press, 2010); Daniel Nelson, *Managers and Workers: Origins of the Twentieth-Century Factory System in the United States, 1880–1920* (Madison, WI: University of Wisconsin Press, 1995).
25. Meyer, *The Five Dollar Day*; Harry Braverman, *Labor and Monopoly Capital: The Degradation of Work in the Twentieth Century* (New York: Monthly Review Press, 1974).
26. Jacoby, *Employing Bureaucracy*; Kaufman, *Managing the Human Factor*.
27. Charles L. Hughes, *Making Unions Unnecessary* (Dallas, TX: Center for Values Research, 2000); Kaufman, *The Origins and Evolution of the Field of Industrial Relations in the United States*; Frank Koller, *Spark: How Old-Fashioned Values Drive a Twenty-First-Century Corporation* (New York: PublicAffairs, 2010).
28. Sanford M. Jacoby, *The Embedded Corporation: Corporate Governance and Employment Relations in Japan and the United States* (Princeton, NJ: Princeton University Press, 2005).
29. Tom Keenoy and Peter Anthony, "HRM: Metaphor, Meaning, and Morality," in Paul Blyton and Peter Turnbull (eds.), *Reassessing Human Resource Management* (London: Sage, 1992), pp. 233–55; Karen Legge, *Human Resource Management: Rhetorics and Realities* (Basingstoke: Macmillan Press, 1995).
30. Bruce E. Kaufman, "The Case for the Company Union," *Labor History* 41 (August 2000), pp. 321–50; Bruce E. Kaufman, "Accomplishments and Shortcomings of Nonunion Employee Representation in the Pre-Wagner Act Years: A Reassessment," in Bruce E. Kaufman and Daphne Gottlieb Taras (eds.), *Nonunion Employee Representation: History, Contemporary Practice, and Policy* (Armonk, NY: M. E. Sharpe, 2000), pp. 21–60.
31. Bruce E. Kaufman, *The Global Evolution of Industrial Relations: Events, Ideas, and the IIRA* (Geneva: International Labour Office, 2004); Kaufman, *The Origins and Evolution of the Field of Industrial Relations in the United States*; Kaufman, "Labor Markets and Employment Regulation"; Yuval P. Yonay, *The Struggle over the Soul of Economics: Institutionalist and Neoclassical Economists in America between the Wars* (Princeton, NJ: Princeton University Press, 1998); Boyer and Smith, "The Development of the Neoclassical Tradition in Labor Economics"; Stephen M. Hills, *Employment Relations and the Social Sciences* (Columbia, SC: University of South Carolina Press, 1995).
32. Nelson Lichtenstein et al., *Who Built America? Working People and the Nation's Economy, Politics, Culture, and Society,* Volume 2 (New York: Worth Publishing, 2000).
33. Garth Mangum and Peter Philips (eds.), *Three Worlds of Labor Economics* (Armonk, NY: M. E. Sharpe, 1988), pp. 4–5.

34. Kaufman, *The Origins and Evolution of the Field of Industrial Relations in the United States*; Kaufman, "Labor Markets and Employment Regulation"; John W. Budd, Rafael Gomez, and Noah M. Meltz, "Why a Balance Is Best: The Pluralist Industrial Relations Paradigm of Balancing Competing Interests," in Bruce E. Kaufman (ed.), *Theoretical Perspectives on Work and the Employment Relationship* (Champaign, IL: Industrial Relations Research Association, 2004), pp. 195–227.
35. Kaufman, *The Origins and Evolution of the Field of Industrial Relations in the United States*; Kaufman, "Labor Markets and Employment Regulation."
36. Anthony Giles and Gregor Murray, "Industrial Relations Theory and Critical Political Economy," in Jack Barbash and Noah M. Meltz (eds.), *Theorizing in Industrial Relations: Approaches and Applications* (Sydney: Australian Centre for Industrial Relations Research and Teaching, 1997), pp. 77–120; Richard Hyman, "Marxist Thought and the Analysis of Work," in Marek Korczynski, Randy Hodson, and Paul Edwards (eds.), *Social Theory at Work* (Oxford: Oxford University Press), pp. 26–55; Erik Olin Wright, "Foundations of a Neo-Marxist Class Analysis," in Erik Olin Wright (ed.), *Approaches to Class Analysis* (Cambridge: Cambridge University Press, 2005), pp. 4–30.
37. Mary Lethert Wingerd, *Claiming the City: Politics, Faith, and the Power of Place in St. Paul* (Ithaca, NY: Cornell University Press, 2001).
38. Sanford M. Jacoby, "Finance and Labor: Perspectives on Risk, Inequality, and Democracy," *Comparative Labor Law and Policy Journal 30* (Fall 2008), pp. 17–65.
39. Karl E. Klare, "Judicial Deradicalization of the Wagner Act and the Origins of Modern Legal Consciousness, 1937–1941," *Minnesota Law Review* 62 (March 1978), pp. 265–339; David Montgomery, *Workers' Control in America: Studies in the History of Work, Technology, and Labor Struggles* (Cambridge, England: Cambridge University Press, 1979).
40. Braverman, *Labor and Monopoly Capital*; Richard C. Edwards, *Contested Terrain: The Transformation of the Workplace in the Twentieth Century* (New York: Basic Books, 1979).
41. Keenoy and Anthony, "HRM"; Legge, *Human Resource Management*; and Tony Royle, "Just Vote No! Union Busting in the European Fast-Food Industry: The Case of McDonald's," *Industrial Relations Journal* 33 (August 2002), pp. 262–78.
42. Carolina Bank Muñoz, *Transnational Tortillas: Race, Gender and Shop Floor Politics in the United States and Mexico* (Ithaca, NY: Cornell University Press, 2008); Roediger and Esch, *The Production of Difference*.
43. Bill Fletcher, Jr., and Fernando Gapasin, *Solidarity Divided: The Crisis in Organized Labor and a New Path toward Social Justice* (Berkeley, CA: University of California Press, 2008); Ralph Darlington, "The Role of Trade Unions in Building Resistance: Theoretical, Historical and Comparative Perspectives," in Maurizio Atzeni (ed.), *Workers and Labour in a Globalised Capitalism* (Basingstoke: Palgrave Macmillan, 2014), pp. 111–138; Immanuel Ness (ed.), *New Forms of Worker Organization: The Syndicalist and Autonomist Restoration of Class-Struggle Unionism* (Oakland, CA: PM Press, 2014).
44. Budd, *Employment with a Human Face*
45. John W. Budd, *The Thought of Work* (Ithaca, NY: Cornell University Press, 2011).
46. Kaufman, "Labor Markets and Employment Regulation."
47. Weiler, *Governing the Workplace*.
48. Alan Fox, *Beyond Contract: Work, Power and Trust Relations* (London: Farber and Farber, 1974); David Lewin, "IR and HR Perspectives on Workplace Conflict: What Can Each Learn from the Other?" *Human Resource Management Review* 11 (Winter 2001), pp. 453–85; Budd and Bhave, "The Employment Relationship."
49. Thomas A. Kochan, "On the Paradigm Guiding Industrial Relations Theory and Research: Comment on John Godard and John T. Delaney, 'Reflections on the "High Performance" Paradigm's Implications for Industrial Relations as a Field,'" *Industrial and Labor Relations Review* 53 (July 2000), pp. 704–11; Richard E. Walton and Robert B. McKersie, *A Behavioral Theory of Labor Negotiations* (New York: McGraw-Hill, 1965); Budd and Bhave, "The Employment Relationship."
50. Kaufman, *Managing the Human Factor*, p. 278.
51. Philip M. Dine, *State of the Unions: How Labor Can Strengthen the Middle Class, Improve Our Economy, and Regain Political Influence* (New York: McGraw-Hill, 2008); Weiler, *Governing the Workplace*.
52. Giles and Murray, "Industrial Relations Theory and Critical Political Economy"; Wright, "Foundations of a Neo-Marxist Class Analysis."
53. Richard Hyman, *Industrial Relations: A Marxist Introduction* (London: Macmillan, 1975); Fletcher and Gapasin, *Solidarity Divided*.
54. Budd and Bhave, "The Employment Relationship."

55. Kaufman, "The Case for the Company Union"; John Leitch, *Man to Man: The Story of Industrial Democracy* (New York: Forbes, 1919); Bruce E. Kaufman, "Experience with Company Unions and their Treatment under the Wagner Act: A Four Frames of Reference Analysis," *Industrial Relations* 55 (January 2016), pp. 3–39.
56. Bruce E. Kaufman and Daphne Gottlieb Taras (eds.), *Nonunion Employee Representation: History, Contemporary Practice, and Policy* (Armonk, NY: M. E. Sharpe, 2000).
57. Patricia A. Greenfield and Robert J. Pleasure, "Representatives of Their Own Choosing: Finding Workers' Voice in the Legitimacy and Power of Their Unions," in Bruce E. Kaufman and Morris M. Kleiner (eds.), *Employee Representation: Alternatives and Future Directions* (Madison, WI: Industrial Relations Research Association, 1993), pp. 169–96; W. Jett Lauck, *Political and Industrial Democracy, 1776–1926* (New York: Funk and Wagnalls, 1926).
58. Kaufman and Taras, *Nonunion Employee Representation*; Kaufman and Kleiner, *Employee Representation*; Kaufman, "The Case for the Company Union"; Sheldon Friedman, Richard W. Hurd, and Rudolph A. Oswald (eds.), *Restoring the Promise of American Labor Law* (Ithaca, NY: ILR Press, 1994).
59. John T. Dunlop, *Industrial Relations Systems* (New York: Holt, 1958); Hugh Armstrong Clegg, *The Changing System of Industrial Relations in Great Britain* (Oxford, England: Basil Blackwell, 1979).
60. Weiler, *Governing the Workplace*; Kaufman, *The Origins and Evolution of the Field of Industrial Relations in the United States*; Thomas A. Kochan, "Labor Policy for the Twenty-First Century," *University of Pennsylvania Journal of Labor and Employment Law* 1 (Spring 1998), pp. 117–31; Estey, *The Labor Problem*; John R. Commons, *Industrial Goodwill* (New York: McGraw-Hill, 1919).
61. Budd, *Employment with a Human Face*.
62. Troy, *Beyond Unions and Collective Bargaining*.
63. Avner Ben-Ner and Derek C. Jones, "Employee Participation, Ownership, and Productivity: A Theoretical Framework," *Industrial Relations* 34 (October 1995), pp. 532–54.
64. John Godard, *Industrial Relations, the Economy, and Society,* 4th ed. (Concord, ON: Captus Press, 2011).
65. Montgomery, *Workers' Control in America*.
66. Immanuel Ness and Dario Azzellini (eds.), *Ours to Master and to Own: Workers' Control from the Commune to the Present* (Chicago, IL: Haymarket Books, 2011); Maurizio Atzeni (ed.), *Alternative Work Organizations* (Basingstoke: Palgrave Macmillan, 2012).
67. Weiler, *Governing the Workplace*; Cynthia Estlund, *Regoverning the Workplace: From Self-Regulation to Co-Regulation* (New Haven: Yale University Press, 2010).
68. Stephen F. Befort and John W. Budd, *Invisible Hands, Invisible Objectives: Bringing Workplace Law and Public Policy into Focus* (Stanford, CA: Stanford University Press, 2009).
69. Weiler, *Governing the Workplace*.
70. *Adkins v. Children's Hospital*, 261 U.S. 525 (1923); Harris, "Conceptions of Fairness and the Fair Labor Standards Act"; Elizabeth Brandeis, "Labor Legislation," in John R. Commons (ed.), *History of Labor in the United States, 1896–1932,* Volume 3 (New York: Macmillan, 1935), pp. 399–741.
71. Stanley Vittoz, *New Deal Labor Policy and the American Industrial Economy* (Chapel Hill, NC: University of North Carolina Press, 1987).
72. Melvyn Dubofsky, *The State and Labor in Modern America* (Chapel Hill, NC: University of North Carolina Press, 1994); Yonay, *The Struggle over the Soul of Economics*; Thomas A. Kochan, Harry C. Katz, and Robert B. McKersie, *The Transformation of American Industrial Relations* (New York: Basic Books, 1986); Budd, *Employment with a Human Face*.
73. Kochan, Katz, and McKersie, *The Transformation of American Industrial Relations*.
74. Befort and Budd, *Invisible Hands, Invisible Objectives*.
75. Jacoby, *The Embedded Corporation*.
76. "In Good Faith: Collective Bargaining under the Employment Relations Act 2000" (Wellington: New Zealand Department of Labour, 2001), p. 8. www.ers.dol.govt.nz/publications/pdfs/A5_good_faith_bargain.pdf
77. Richard B. Freeman and James L. Medoff, *What Do Unions Do?* (New York: Basic Books, 1984); James T. Bennett and Bruce E. Kaufman (eds.), *What Do Unions Do? A Twenty-Year Perspective* (New Brunswick, NJ: Transaction Publishers, 2007).
78. Alison L. Booth, *The Economics of the Trade Union* (Cambridge, England: Cambridge University Press, 1995); H. Gregg Lewis, *Union Relative Wage Effects: A Survey* (Chicago, IL: University of Chicago Press, 1986); Barry T. Hirsch, "Reconsidering Union Wage Effects: Surveying New Evidence

on an Old Topic," *Journal of Labor Research* 25 (Spring 2004), pp. 233–66; David G. Blanchflower and Alex Bryson, "What Effect Do Unions Have on Wages Now and Would Freeman and Medoff Be Surprised?" in James T. Bennett and Bruce E. Kaufman (eds.), *What Do Unions Do? A Twenty-Year Perspective* (New Brunswick, NJ: Transaction Publishers, 2007), pp. 79–113.

79. David Card, Thomas Lemieux, and W. Craig Riddell, "Unions and Wage Inequality," in James T. Bennett and Bruce E. Kaufman (eds.), *What Do Unions Do? A Twenty-Year Perspective* (New Brunswick, NJ: Transaction Publishers, 2007), pp. 114–59; Rafael Gomez and Konstantinos Tzioumis, "What Do Unions Do to CEO Compensation?" Centre for Economic Performance Discussion Paper No. 720, London School of Economics, 2007.

80. Richard B. Freeman and Morris M. Kleiner, "The Impact of New Unionization on Wages and Working Conditions," *Journal of Labor Economics* 8 (January 1990), pp. S8–25; Tom Juravich, Kate Bronfenbrenner, and Robert Hickey, "Significant Victories: An Analysis of Union First Contracts," in Richard N. Block et al. (eds.), *Justice on the Job: Perspectives on the Erosion of Collective Bargaining in the United States* (Kalamazoo, MI: Upjohn, 2006), pp. 87–114.

81. John W. Budd, "The Effect of Unions on Employee Benefits and Non-Wage Compensation: Monopoly Power, Collective Voice, and Facilitation," in James T. Bennett and Bruce E. Kaufman (eds.), *What Do Unions Do? A Twenty-Year Perspective* (New Brunswick, NJ: Transaction Publishers, 2007), pp. 160–92.

82. Freeman and Medoff, *What Do Unions Do?*; Barry T. Hirsch, "What Do Unions Do for Economic Performance?" in James T. Bennett and Bruce E. Kaufman (eds.), *What Do Unions Do? A Twenty-Year Perspective* (New Brunswick, NJ: Transaction Publishers, 2007), pp. 193–237; Christos Doucouliagos and Patrice LaRoche, "What Do Unions Do to Productivity? A Meta-Analysis," *Industrial Relations* 42 (October 2003), pp. 650–91.

83. Anil Verma, "What Do Unions Do to the Workplace? Union Effects on Management and HRM Policies," in James T. Bennett and Bruce E. Kaufman (eds.), *What Do Unions Do? A Twenty-Year Perspective* (New Brunswick, NJ: Transaction Publishers, 2007), pp. 275–312.

84. Michael Ash and Jean Ann Seago, "The Effect of Registered Nurses' Unions on Heart-Attack Mortality," *Industrial and Labor Relations Review* 57 (April 2004), pp. 422–42.

85. Hirsch, "What Do Unions Do for Economic Performance?"; Doucouliagos and LaRoche, "What Do Unions Do to Productivity?"; Verma, "What Do Unions Do to the Workplace?"; Aaron J. Sojourner et al., "Impacts of Unionization on Quality and Productivity: Regression Discontinuity Evidence from Nursing Homes," *Industrial and Labor Relations Review* 68 (August 2015), pp. 771–806; Cassandra M.D. Hart and Aaron J. Sojourner, "Unionization and Productivity: Evidence from Charter Schools," *Industrial Relations* 55 (July 2015), pp. 422–48; Dionne Pohler and Andrew Luchak, "Are Unions Good or Bad for Organizations? The Moderating Role of Management's Response," *British Journal of Industrial Relations* 53 (September 2015), pp. 423–59.

86. Hirsch, "What Do Unions Do for Economic Performance?"; Christos Doucouliagos and Patrice LaRoche, "Unions and Profits: A Meta-Analysis," *Industrial Relations* 48 (January 2009), pp. 146–84.

87. Hirsch, "What Do Unions Do for Economic Performance?"; Richard B. Freeman and Morris M. Kleiner, "Do Unions Make Enterprises Insolvent?" *Industrial and Labor Relations Review* 52 (July 1999), pp. 510–27; John DiNardo and David S. Lee, "Economic Impacts of New Unionization on Private Sector Employers: 1984–2001," *Quarterly Journal of Economics* 119 (November 2004), pp. 1383–441. Sojourner et al., "Impacts of Unionization on Quality and Productivity."

88. Richard B. Freeman, "The Exit–Voice Trade-Off in the Labor Market: Unionism, Job Tenure, Quits, and Separations," *Quarterly Journal of Economics* 94 (June 1980), pp. 643–73; Tove Helland Hammer and Ariel Avgar, "The Impact of Unions on Job Satisfaction, Organizational Commitment, and Turnover," in James T. Bennett and Bruce E. Kaufman (eds.), *What Do Unions Do? A Twenty-Year Perspective* (New Brunswick, NJ: Transaction Publishers, 2007), pp. 346–72.

89. Richard B. Freeman, "Job Satisfaction as an Economic Variable," *American Economic Review* 68 (May 1978), pp. 135–41; George J. Borjas, "Job Satisfaction, Wages, and Unions," *Journal of Human Resources* 14 (Spring 1979), pp. 21–40.

90. Jeffrey Pfeffer and Alison Davis-Blake, "Unions and Job Satisfaction: An Alternative View," *Work and Occupations* 17 (August 1990), pp. 259–83; Michael E. Gordon and Angelo S. DeNisi, "A Re-Examination of the Relationship between Union Membership and Job Satisfaction," *Industrial and Labor Relations Review* 48 (January 1995), pp. 226–36; Keith A. Bender and Peter J. Sloane, "Job Satisfaction, Trade Unions, and Exit–Voice Revisited," *Industrial and Labor Relations Review* 51 (January 1998), pp. 222–40; Alex Bryson, Lorenzo Cappellari, and Claudio Lucifora, "Does Union Membership Really Reduce Job Satisfaction?" *British Journal of Industrial Relations* 42 (September 2004), pp. 439–59.

91. Hammer and Avgar, "The Impact of Unions on Job Satisfaction, Organizational Commitment, and Turnover."
92. Budd, "The Effect of Unions on Employee Benefits and Non-Wage Compensation."
93. John W. Budd and Karen Mumford, "Trade Unions and Family-Friendly Policies in Britain," *Industrial and Labor Relations Review* 57 (January 2004), pp. 204–22; Amit Kramer, "Unions as Facilitators of Employment Rights: An Analysis of Individuals' Awareness of Parental Leave in the National Longitudinal Survey of Youth," *Industrial Relations* 47 (October 2008), pp. 651–58; John W. Budd and Brian P. McCall, "Unions and Unemployment Insurance Benefits Receipt: Evidence from the CPS," *Industrial Relations* 43 (April 2004), pp. 339–55; Barry T. Hirsch, David A. Macpherson, and J. Michael DuMond, "Workers' Compensation Recipiency in Union and Nonunion Workplaces," *Industrial and Labor Relations Review* 50 (January 1997), pp. 213–36; Mark Harcourt, Geoffrey Wood, and Sondra Harcourt, "Do Unions Affect Employer Compliance with the Law? New Zealand Evidence for Age Discrimination," *British Journal of Industrial Relations* 42 (September 2004), pp. 527–41.
94. Frank Tannenbaum, *A Philosophy of Labor* (New York: Alfred A. Knopf, 1951); Simeon Larson and Bruce Nissen (eds.), *Theories of the Labor Movement* (Detroit, MI: Wayne State University Press, 1987); Roland Zullo, "Organized Labor's Civic Niche," *Nonprofit and Voluntary Sector Quarterly* 42 (August 2013), pp. 781–802.
95. Pope John Paul II, *On Human Work: Encyclical Laborem Exercens* (1981), §20.
96. Taylor E. Dark, *The Unions and the Democrats: An Enduring Alliance* (Ithaca, NY: ILR Press, 2001); Marick F. Masters and John T. Delaney, "Organized Labor's Political Scorecard," in James T. Bennett and Bruce E. Kaufman (eds.), *What Do Unions Do? A Twenty-Year Perspective* (New Brunswick, NJ: Transaction Publishers, 2007), pp. 492–519.
97. Michael Wasser and J. Ryan Lamare, "Unions as Conduits of Democratic Voice for Non-Elites: Worker Politicization from the Shop Floor to the Halls of Congress," *Nevada Law Journal* 14 (Spring 2014), pp. 396–413; Aaron Sojourner, "Do Unions Promote Members' Electoral Office Holding? Evidence from Correlates of State Legislatures' Occupational Shares," *Industrial and Labor Relations Review* 66 (April 2013), pp. 467–86.
98. Zullo, "Organized Labor's Civic Niche"; Cynthia Estlund, *Working Together: How Workplace Bonds Strengthen a Diverse Democracy* (Oxford: Oxford University Press, 2003).
99. Nelson Lichtenstein, *State of the Union: A Century of American Labor* (Princeton, NJ: Princeton University Press, 2013); Emmanuel Teitelbaum, *Mobilizing Restraint: Democracy and Industrial Conflict in Post-reform South Asia* (Ithaca, NY: Cornell University Press, 2011); Jake Rosenfeld, *What Unions No Longer Do* (Cambridge: Harvard University Press, 2014).
100. Elliot J. Gorn, *Mother Jones: The Most Dangerous Woman in America* (New York: Hill and Wang, 2001), p. 195.
101. Richard B. Freeman and James L. Medoff, "The Two Faces of Unionism," *The Public Interest* (Fall 1979), pp. 69–93; Freeman and Medoff, *What Do Unions Do?*; Bruce E. Kaufman and David I. Levine, "An Economic Analysis of Employee Representation," in Bruce E. Kaufman and Daphne Gottlieb Taras (eds.), *Nonunion Employee Representation: History, Contemporary Practice, and Policy* (Armonk, NY: M. E. Sharpe, 2000), pp. 149–75; Alan Manning, *Monopsony in Motion: Imperfect Competition in Labor Markets* (Princeton, NJ: Princeton University Press, 2003); Tove Helland Hammer, "Nonunion Representational Forms: An Organizational Behavior Perspective," in Bruce E. Kaufman and Daphne Gottlieb Taras (eds.), *Nonunion Employee Representation: History, Contemporary Practice, and Policy* (Armonk, NY: M. E. Sharpe, 2000), pp. 176–95.
102. Albert O. Hirschman, *Exit, Voice, and Loyalty: Responses to Decline in Firms, Organizations, and States* (Cambridge, MA: Harvard University Press, 1970).
103. Freeman and Medoff, "The Two Faces of Unionism"; Freeman and Medoff, *What Do Unions Do?*; Bennett and Kaufman, *What Do Unions Do?*
104. Freeman and Medoff, *What Do Unions Do?*
105. Budd, "The Effect of Unions on Employee Benefits and Non-Wage Compensation."

Part **Two**

The U.S. New Deal Industrial Relations System

The New Deal industrial relations system is the set of labor relations policies and practices that grew out of the New Deal economic policies during the Great Depression in the 1930s and that attempts to balance efficiency, equity, and voice. Even though it is more than 75 years old, the New Deal industrial relations system still governs U.S. labor relations today. The next seven chapters therefore describe the development of this system and its current operation, especially with respect to how unions are organized, how contracts are negotiated, and how disputes are resolved.

Chapter Three

Historical Development

Advance Organizer

The contemporary U.S. labor relations system can be studied as it exists today without any reference to the past, but this is not satisfying. Today's laws, philosophies, processes, organizations, and strategies have evolved out of experiences from 10, 50, and even 150 years ago. To better understand the current system—and its future challenges—this chapter presents important events, organizations, and strategies from the history of U.S. labor relations.

Learning Objectives

By the end of this chapter, you should be able to

1. **Understand** why workers have tried to form unions throughout U.S. history and the influences on their successes and failures.
2. **Identify** the major events in U.S. labor history, including what happened and why each event is significant.
3. **Compare** the major organizations in labor history and their contrasting strategies, including labor strategies for promoting collective action among workers and business strategies for discouraging or repressing such action.
4. **Understand** how studying the historical record deepens our comprehension of the current labor relations system and alternatives for reform.

Contents

The current U.S. labor relations system is a product of history. Some of this history is relatively recent, such as the series of fast-food strikes that began in 2012, whereas other aspects might seem like ancient history, such as the Great Uprising of 1877; but it is all relevant to a richer understanding of labor relations. Workers' efforts to form unions are better appreciated against the backdrop of changes in the nature of work and the growth of corporate power. The continued emphasis on seniority rights in U.S. union contracts is more logical in the context of the abuses of all-powerful supervisors in the early 1900s. Union hostility toward nonunion forms of employee representation is rooted in corporate manipulation of company unions in the 1930s. U.S. labor laws that emphasize representation elections stem from the historical record of strike activity and labor–management conflict. Moreover, unions and their members tend to have longer memories than corporations and their leaders. Historical events are frequently an integral part of a union's culture, and history therefore continues to influence the perspectives and behaviors of today's union leaders. Consequently, a good manager must appreciate the historical context within which unions operate, make decisions, and form perceptions about management motives not only to better understand unions' roles in society but also to develop good working relationships with union leaders.

Two related yet distinct historical elements are emphasized throughout this chapter: events and organizational strategies. Every student of labor relations should be aware of the major events in U.S. labor history. These events often reveal the leading issues and conflicts of an era, and they altered the course of labor relations. It is thus difficult to understand labor relations without discussing these events. At the same time the history of labor relations contains a rich tapestry of organizations and strategies. Some of these organizations and strategies exist today; others have passed into the annals of history. A broad historical investigation therefore provides the opportunity to consider a wider range of organizational strategies than currently exists in 21st-century labor relations. This wider analysis sharpens our understanding of each organizational strategy while broadening our ideas for future options. As a key example, today's U.S. unions are dominated by a business unionism philosophy, but an investigation of several historical labor organizations reveals significantly different philosophies. Examination of these philosophies and their accompanying strategies enriches our understanding of business unionism and also provides potential ideas for future labor union strategies.

Consideration of major events and organizational strategies in the history of U.S. labor relations also illustrates the twin roles of the environment and individual choice that are so important for understanding outcomes. As this chapter unfolds, pay attention to how the external environment—the economic and political climate, technology, and the like—affects events and organizations, but do not reduce workers, unions, managers, and corporations to mere puppets of the environment. History reveals choices that are actively made by individuals and organizations. This history is more than just labor history—the study of workers and their unions. The historical development of U.S. labor relations also involves important components of social, business, economic, and legal history.[1] The historical development of U.S. labor law is discussed in Chapter 4; our concern for the rest of this chapter is the rich fabric of events, organizations, and strategies that weave together with social, economic, business, and labor history to show the historical development of the U.S. labor relations system.

FROM LOCAL TO NATIONAL ORGANIZATIONS

In the 21st century we see working for someone else as natural. Most workers today are *employees* selling their labor for a wage or a salary, and many work for large organizations with 500 or more employees. This situation is taken for granted because it has been true for a century or more; but it is essential to appreciate that this pattern is the result of tremendous, tumultuous economic and social changes that occurred in the 1800s—changes typically summarized as "industrialization." At the end of the 1700s, a large majority of free people were self-employed as farmers, shopkeepers, blacksmiths, shoemakers, and the like.[2] In major cities a few skilled workers might have worked as employees for a master craftsman, but these businesses were small and local. The early "large" businesses were in the iron industry and employed perhaps 25 employees.[3] Most individuals, then, controlled when, how, and how hard they worked. Slightly more than 100 years later, U.S. Steel employed 170,000 employees, Ford's Highland Park factory outside Detroit had 15,000 employees, and the era of self-employment was over.[4] Working for a paycheck became widespread; fixed working hours and days, punctuality, and constant work effort replaced autonomous work habits.[5] Business became "big business" characterized by hierarchical,

FIGURE 3.1
A Timeline of Labor History up to 1875

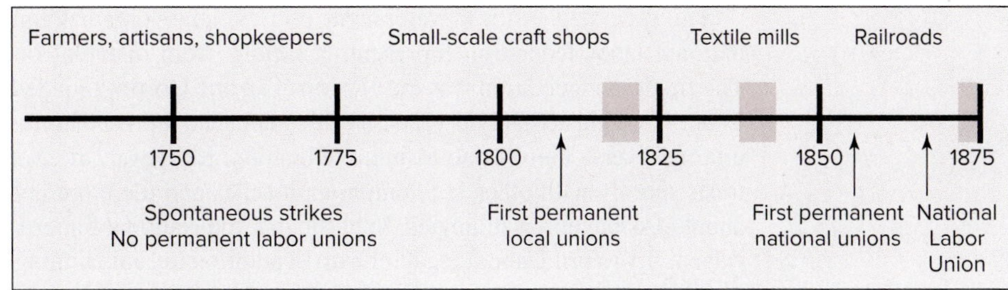

Note: Shading indicates economic recessions.

centralized control and concentrated wealth and power. And as emphasized in Chapter 2, the pay was often low, the hours were long and dull, the work effort was intense and dangerous, and supervision was frequently abusive (recall Table 2.1). The roots of the modern labor relations system lie in these massive changes in the nature of work and of industrial society.

Naturally, the forms and functions of labor unions paralleled these changes in work and business organization (see Figure 3.1). The earliest examples of unionlike activity in the United States were short-term actions triggered by specific complaints, such as a strike by fishermen on a Maine island in 1636 protesting the withholding of a year's wages or a strike by 20 journeymen tailors in 1768 in New York City protesting a reduction in wages.[6] Not until the 1790s did Philadelphia shoemakers form the first permanent union. The first organizations were local and focused on a single-skilled occupation such as shoemakers, printers, carpenters, and tailors. These local craft unions established work standards and a minimum wage rate; union members agreed not to work for any employer paying less.[7] Their existence, however, was tenuous. Some strikes were ruled to be illegal criminal conspiracies (see Chapter 4), and depressions in 1819 and 1837 severely crippled the early labor unions because union members were desperate for any work they could get.[8] This importance of the legal and economic environment for labor relations is a universal theme from the 18th to the 21st centuries.

As business organizations became larger and more national in scope, so too did labor unions. National unions began to develop in the 1850s—necessitated by the ability of manufactured goods to be shipped via railroads, and likely facilitated by the ability of union leaders to travel via railroads. While the budding national unions were mainly craft unions of pre-factory occupations such as printers, plumbers, and railroad engineers, some also included craft occupations in factory settings, especially iron molders and machinists.[9] The iron molders' experiences in stove foundries are illustrative of the 19th-century transformation of work and therefore labor unions: With the advent of the railroads, iron stove manufacturers tried to capture national market share through mass manufacturing methods. Previously each iron molder used skill and discretion to mold an entire stove; but with a mass manufacturing system, the parts of the stove were divided and each molder was relegated to repetitively making one part. The work became impersonal and subject to constant pressure to reduce labor costs—a common trend resulting in the widespread labor problem described in Chapter 2. In Philadelphia, for example, foundry owners tried imposing four pay cuts between 1847 and 1857. The National Molders Union was thus formed in 1859 in reaction to these changing conditions. One year later it had 44 locals ranging from St. Louis to New York to Toronto.[10] After the Civil War this union became the Iron Molders' International Union, which for a time was the strongest in the country; its features resembled today's unions—centralized and national control, a per capita tax on all union members, creation of a national strike fund to support striking workers, and an emphasis on strong collective bargaining.[11]

The next step in the development of U.S. labor organizations was the creation of a national labor federation representing unions from different occupations or industries. The first such federation was the **National Labor Union,** founded in 1866.[12] The National Labor Union lasted only 6 years, but it established a precedent for the labor movement by uniting diverse unions into a single federation. Moreover, the National Labor Union contrasts sharply with other U.S. union approaches and therefore helps broaden our thinking about possible union strategies. In particular, the National Labor Union emphasized political activity to bring about legal reform. In addition to campaigning for the eight-hour working day through maximum hour legislation, the National Labor Union favored currency and banking reform, women's voting rights, and ultimately a national labor political party.

THE GREAT UPRISING OF 1877

The 1870s ushered in an era of intense and violent labor conflict that would continue into the 20th century. Throughout this period, the rhetoric of protecting the individual liberty to hire or work on terms of one's own choosing was used to justify the armed repression of unions, and the resulting story of labor history is "written in blood."[13] A massive depression in the mid-1870s caused severe unemployment and wage cuts, and union membership plummeted. A six-month coal strike in eastern Pennsylvania in 1875 involved open battles between strikers and company-paid police. The coal company hired an agent of the Pinkerton National Detective Agency—an organization that emerges repeatedly in employers' strikebreaking efforts in U.S. labor history—to infiltrate the miners. The strike ended when the miners agreed to a 20-percent wage *reduction*, and based on the Pinkerton agent's testimony—perhaps fabricated—10 miners were hanged for killing several mine bosses.[14]

But this was just the beginning. In response to a 10-percent wage cut (on top of wage cuts in earlier years of the depression), workers on one railroad and then another, and another, went on strike in July 1877. The strike quickly spread until railroad activity in large sections of the country was affected. Large crowds stopped trains, spiked switches, and took over depots and roundhouses. Two hundred federal troops were first sent to Martinsburg, West Virginia, and violence flared elsewhere. Nine people were killed in rioting in Baltimore; the state militia fired into a crowd in Pittsburgh, killing 20 and prompting a night of conflict, fire, and destruction that resulted in $5 million of railroad property damage.[15]

These events became known as the **Great Uprising of 1877** because this was much more than a railroad strike. More workers were involved than in any other labor conflict of the 1800s.[16] Many of these were not railroad workers—coal miners, ironworkers, and others significantly aided the railroad workers in many locations. Black longshoring workers in Texas and sewer workers in Kentucky struck for higher pay.[17] Chicago and St. Louis experienced general strikes in which thousands of workers shut down many businesses in the two cities. State militia and federal troops were used to forcefully end demonstrations and restore order in many locations. Yet despite its widespread intensity, the uprising ended nearly as quickly as it began, and railroad traffic resumed normal operations at the end of the month.

The Great Uprising of 1877 is probably more notable for what it represents than what it accomplished. The numerous strikes clearly reflected pent-up grievances of workers in many industries and locations struggling with the forces of industrialization and the conflict between labor and capital. The uprising also demonstrates the shared concerns of workers and is frequently used to define the beginning of the modern era in U.S. labor relations—one in which capital and labor are often sharply at odds. By some accounts, business fears of future labor insurrections led to more aggressive strategies to repress labor activity.[18] Alternatively, by showing that federal and state troops would protect business

Labor Relations Application The Infamous Pinkertons

Lurking in the shadows of many of the bitterest labor conflicts of the 19th century was the Pinkerton National Detective Agency. Founded in 1850 by Allan Pinkerton, the Pinkerton agency started off spying on dishonest railroad conductors and then gathering intelligence as spies during the Civil War. After the war Pinkerton detectives tracked some of the most notorious criminals of the era, including Jesse James and Butch Cassidy and the Sundance Kid. The company logo became an unblinking eye above the motto "We never sleep," which is the source of the expression "private eye."

In the sphere of labor relations, the Pinkerton agency provided guards and detectives. A railroad hired the agency in 1873 to infiltrate the secret association of its Irish coal miners—the alleged Molly Maguires. An agent successfully became a secretary of the local union and sent numerous labor activity reports to the company. Though this was never proved, some accused this spy of being an "agent provocateur"—that is, of initiating violence to get the Molly Maguires in trouble. Thereafter Pinkerton detectives were used extensively as labor spies, and charges of being agents provocateur more than once accompanied their discovery. One Pinkerton operative even infiltrated the legal defense team for the radical union leader Big Bill Haywood, who was accused of conspiring to murder a former governor of Idaho in retaliation for breaking a miners' strike in 1899. In the 1930s Pinkertons were still used as spies inside various labor unions—in fact at least 50 members of the United Auto Workers were actually Pinkerton agents.

In addition to infiltrating unions, the Pinkerton agency provided armed guards to companies. Pinkerton guards were involved in at least 70 strikes between 1877 and 1892, often accompanied by violence. By one account, the Pinkerton agency had 2,000 active agents and 30,000 in reserve—a total greater than the standing army of the United States at the time. The intense gun battles between Pinkertons and strikers, such as when 300 Pinkertons descended upon Homestead, Pennsylvania, in 1892, made the Pinkertons look more like a mercenary army than the protectors of corporate private property. By the end of the 19th century, 24 states had outlawed the importation of armed guards from other states.

In the 20th century strikebreaking became big business, and numerous agencies specialized in providing strikebreakers and armed guards. While not nearly as violent, union avoidance consulting still remains a thriving business in the 21st century. The Knights of Labor have long faded from U.S. history, but the Pinkerton Agency pioneered these "Knights of Capital."

References: Jeremy Brecher, *Strike!* (Boston: South End Press, 1972); J. Anthony Lukas, *Big Trouble: A Murder in a Small Western Town Sets Off a Struggle for the Soul of America* (New York: Simon and Schuster, 1997); Frank Morn, *"The Eye That Never Sleeps": A History of the Pinkerton National Detective Agency* (Bloomington: Indiana University Press, 1982); Stephen H. Norwood, *Strikebreaking and Intimidation: Mercenaries and Masculinity in Twentieth-Century America* (Chapel Hill: University of North Carolina Press, 2002); Robert Michael Smith, *From Blackjacks to Briefcases: A History of Commercialized Strikebreaking and Unionbusting in the United States* (Athens: Ohio University Press, 2003); Frederick Voss and James Barber, *We Never Sleep: The First Fifty Years of the Pinkertons* (Washington, DC: Smithsonian Institution Press, 1981).

property, the events of 1877 may have made big business "emboldened to confront labor rather than bargain with it."[19] In either case, the Great Uprising of 1877 laid the foundation for future labor–management conflict, not cooperation. More broadly, the Great Uprising of 1877 can be seen as a "social earthquake."[20] Some of the violent attacks on railroad property may have resulted not from work-related grievances but from frustration with the invasion of railroads into local communities, often against the wishes of local residents and small retail shop owners.[21] But whether rooted in work or community, individuals turned to collective action, protest, and sometimes violence when they felt otherwise powerless.

UPLIFT UNIONISM

One union that survived the depression of 1873–1878 was the Noble and Holy Order of the Knights of Labor. The **Knights of Labor** started as a union in the garment industry and emphasized secrecy to prevent employers from breaking it. Like many fraternal organizations of the time, the Knights of Labor initially had various rituals, passwords, and secret signs.[22] If a member wanted to know if someone else was a member, he would say, "I am

Violence during the Great Uprising of 1877: Workers Forcibly Stopping a B&O Train in Martinsburg, West Virginia, July 17, 1877

A Pittsburgh Train Yard after a Night of Destruction Prompted by the Killing of Workers by the State Militia, July 22, 1877

a worker," to which the correct response was "I too earn my bread with the sweat of my brow."[23] The top leader was called the Grand Master Workman. As the union expanded outside the garment industry, secrecy was dropped in 1881. For a brief time in the mid-1880s, the Knights of Labor was the most influential labor organization in the United States with 700,000 members in 1886.[24] Yet its decline was equally rapid, and 15 years later the organization had effectively faded away.

The Knights of Labor: Objectives and Strategies

A primary concern of the Knights of Labor was the moral worth, not just the material wealth, of a person.[25] So the Knights of Labor is traditionally considered the major U.S. example of **uplift unionism**, a philosophy in which a union "aspires chiefly to elevate the moral, intellectual, and social life of the worker."[26] Decent wages and working conditions were important because they served, in the words of one Grand Master, "the divine nature of man":

> [The Knights of Labor] must base its claims for labor upon higher ground than participation in the profits and emoluments, and a lessening of the hours and fatigues of labor. These are only physical effects and objects of a grosser nature, and, although imperative, are but the stepping-stone to a higher cause, of a nobler nature. The real and ultimate reason must be based upon the more exalted and divine nature of man, his high and noble capability for good. Excessive labor and small pay stints and blunts and degrades those God-like faculties, until the image of God, in which he was created and intended by his great Author to exhibit, are scarcely discernible.[27]

Shorter working hours were therefore needed so that workers would have greater time for education and moral betterment.

Organizationally the Knights of Labor consisted of numerous local assemblies—as many as 1,500 at one point—and membership was open to nearly everyone.[28] In fact the Knights of Labor wanted to unite all "producers," a group that included the equivalent of today's white-collar and professional workers as well as farmers, shopkeepers, and even employers.[29] The central conflict was not with employers; it was with those who controlled money and who were perceived as not "producing"—bankers, stockbrokers, and lawyers.[30] And consistent with the emphasis on morality, gamblers and liquor dealers were also excluded. But otherwise the Knights of Labor was broadly inclusive and emphasized the solidarity of all producers—including African Americans and women—as underscored by its motto, "An injury to one is a concern to all."[31]

To accomplish its goals, the Knights of Labor emphasized cooperation and education.[32] The ultimate goal was replacing capitalism with a system of producer cooperatives in which producers (not bankers and absentee owners) would own and control businesses. The bringing together of capital and labor into small cooperatives was believed to harmonize the interests of labor and capital (ending labor conflict) and avoid the problems of monopoly. Workers would regain a sense of control and autonomy, which industrialization and wage work were removing; and work would be restored to its noble purpose of serving personal and psychological needs and serving God. This latter goal rested on the then-common assumption that producing a tangible product (e.g., a barrel or a plow) was superior to contributing a less tangible service (e.g., management expertise or investment capital).[33] This view may seem simplistic today, but remember that industrialization was a new phenomenon and that corporations and the nature of employment as we know it today were just emerging and were causing great upheaval throughout society. As such, the Knights of Labor's reform agenda sought to replace capitalism with a different system rather than simply cushion capitalism's perceived negative effects on workers.[34] In fact, replacing the wage system with producer cooperatives was seen as a way to restore democracy because capitalism's inequalities and the wage system's degradation of workers were viewed as undermining the values and skills needed for a healthy, participative democracy.[35]

The top leadership of the Knights of Labor opposed the use of strikes and boycotts. These economic weapons might achieve higher wages and shorter working hours; but remember that in the philosophy of the Knights of Labor, these economic improvements were not important in their own right. Broader reform to serve the divine nature of humanity through the creation of producer cooperatives and through individual education and moral betterment could not be achieved through strikes and boycotts—at least not in the eyes of the national leadership. There was also a practical element to this emphasis on education over strikes and boycotts: The leaders remembered labor's defeats during the strikes of the 1870s (recall the Great Uprising of 1877).[36]

The Knights of Labor: Conflicts and Demise

The reality of strike activity, however, did not always match these theoretical ideals. In fact, the Knights of Labor's largest success was arguably the 1885 Southwest System rail strike, in which a startling victory was won over this very large railroad system controlled by robber baron Jay Gould.[37] This strike is popularly viewed as the first instance in which a U.S. union stood equal to a large, powerful corporation and as causing the Knights of Labor's dramatic growth in 1886.[38] Victory was short-lived, however. The leadership's lack of emphasis on collective bargaining let Gould settle with weak language—not even union recognition was achieved.[39] In fact, only a year later Gould successfully broke a violent strike with the help of Pinkerton spies.

Contributing to this defeat and the overall demise of the Knights of Labor was the most famous event associated with the Knights of Labor: the **Haymarket Tragedy.** A significant movement during the mid-1880s was the drive for an eight-hour workday. In 1884, May 1, 1886, was established by the forerunner of the American Federation of Labor as the effective date for the eight-hour day. (This is the modern origin of May Day—International Workers' Day—celebrated in many countries.) Numerous strikes occurred in 1886 to support this May 1 deadline, although consistent with the national leadership's emphasis on education rather than conflict, the Knights of Labor encouraged workers to write essays about the eight-hour day rather than strike.[40] In Chicago's Haymarket Square, a rally to protest police repression of May Day strikers ended with police firing into the departing protesters after a bomb was tossed into the police ranks. The bomb thrower was never identified, but the Haymarket Tragedy caused near hysteria that anarchists and radicals were starting an uprising. Depictions in the media were sensationalized. In "the most celebrated trial of the late 19th century," eight anarchist leaders were found guilty of murder for killing the police.[41] The evidence was fabricated, the judge was exceptionally biased, and all the jurors openly admitted to being prejudiced against the defendants. One juror was even a relative of one of the dead police officers. None of this prevented four of the eight defendants from being hanged.

The Knights of Labor organization was not directly involved in the Haymarket Tragedy, but it was the most visible labor organization at that time and was therefore greatly weakened by the public backlash against organized labor. The Knights of Labor was also undone by employers' antiunion activities, including the use of strikebreakers and labor spies. And the Knights of Labor suffered from conflicts with workers, trade assemblies, and independent trade unions that wanted more vigorous campaigns for improvements in bread-and-butter issues such as wages, hours of work, and working conditions, not moral betterment.[42]

PURE AND SIMPLE CRAFT UNIONISM

In response to the perceived failure of the Knights of Labor's leadership to address everyday working issues, representatives from 25 national unions created a new labor federation in December 1886 called the **American Federation of Labor** (AFL).[43] The first president of the AFL was Samuel Gompers, an official from the Cigar Makers' International Union, who would eventually be president with only a one-year interruption until his death nearly 40 years later in 1924. The AFL and Gompers are central figures in the development of U.S. labor relations (see Figure 3.2).

FIGURE 3.2
A Time Line of Labor History between 1875 and 1925

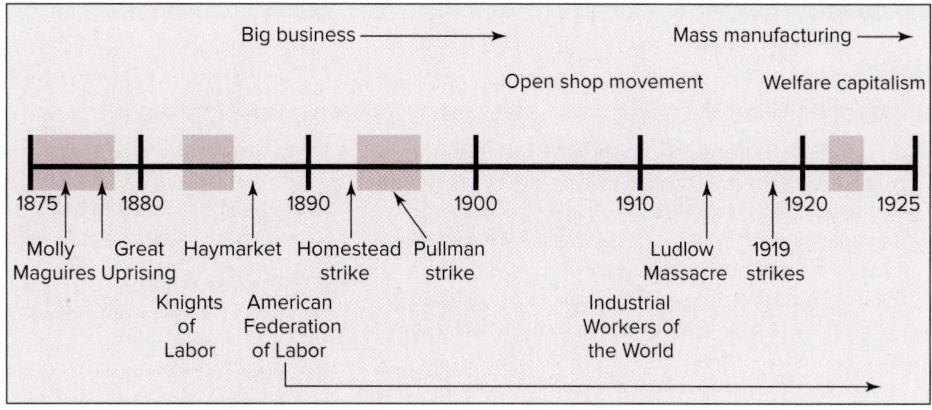

Note: Shading indicates economic depressions.

The AFL and Its Unions: Objectives and Strategies

It is important to understand that the AFL was a union *federation*, not a labor union per se. The member unions, not the AFL, pursued the primary labor relations functions of bargaining with employers, leading strikes, and resolving grievances. The AFL was a support organization for the independent unions.[44] The AFL sometimes coordinated bargaining and strikes when multiple unions were involved, and it provided financial assistance to striking unions. The AFL also resolved jurisdictional disputes when more than one union wanted to represent the same group of workers and, to a lesser extent, provided education and political lobbying. The AFL initiated organizing drives in occupations without a national union, with the goal of ultimately creating a new national union for that occupation.[45] In contrast with the Knights of Labor, each union that joined the AFL was explicitly granted the autonomy to control its own affairs.[46]

The AFL and its affiliated unions are the classic examples of a **business unionism** philosophy.[47] In contrast to the uplift unionism of the Knights of Labor, the business unionism of the AFL and its unions emphasizes immediate improvements in basic employment conditions—wages, hours, and working conditions. Business unionism accepts capitalism and the need for employers to make a profit, but seeks to win labor's fair share of the profits through collective bargaining backed up by the threat of striking. This is a pragmatic, business like approach to employee representation, or unionism "pure and simple"—not an idealistic approach based on morality and cooperatives (or at the other extreme, revolution). In the words of Gompers, "Economic betterment—today, tomorrow, in home and shop, was the foundation upon which trade unions have been built."[48] Business unionism continues to be the dominant philosophy of U.S. labor unions in the 21st century.

Beyond a business unionism philosophy, there are several additional central features of the AFL unions. Most AFL unions wholeheartedly endorsed a system of **craft unionism.** In this approach, unions were divided along craft lines—that is, by occupation or trade. Each union could focus on the unique concerns of workers in a single occupation and overcome this weakness of the Knights of Labor. Moreover, the craft unionism of the AFL was focused on *skilled* crafts such as printers, machinists, carpenters, cigar makers, and iron molders. Most AFL unions were openly hostile toward unskilled labor and represented only skilled workers. In fact, the Knights of Labor's inclusion of unskilled workers was a point of frustration among the trade unions that led to the formation of the AFL.[49] The structure of the AFL unions was further guided by the principle of **exclusive jurisdiction,** in which only one union should represent workers in a craft. For example, the single carpenters' union was entitled to represent carpenters; it could not represent other

Business Unionism

One of the earliest definitions of business unionism remains accurate today:

> It aims chiefly at more, here and now, for the organized workers of the craft or industry, in terms mainly of higher wages, shorter hours, and better working conditions, regardless for the most part of the welfare of the workers outside the particular organic group, and regardless in general of political and social considerations, except in so far as these bear directly upon its own economic ends. It . . . accepts as inevitable, if not as just, the existing capitalistic organization and the wage system, as well as existing property rights and the binding force of contract. It regards unionism mainly as a bargaining institution and seeks its ends chiefly through collective bargaining, supported by such methods as experience from time to time indicates to be effective in sustaining and increasing its bargaining power.

This describes the AFL craft unions in the first part of the 20th century, the CIO industrial unions three decades later, and today's private and public sector AFL–CIO unions. But why is this called "business unionism"?

> The truth is that the outlooks and ideals of this dominant type of unionism are those very largely of a business organization. Its successful leaders are essentially business men and its union are organized primarily to do business with employers—to bargain for the sale of the product it controls.

Reference: Robert Franklin Hoxie, *Trade Unionism in the United States* (New York: D. Appleton, 1917), pp. 45–46, 336.

occupations, and no other union could represent carpenters. An important function of the AFL was to resolve jurisdictional disputes; but as with other issues, the AFL lacked formal power to force rulings on the member unions.[50]

By the 1890s industrialization and the factory system were firmly in place. There were 160,000 miles of railroad tracks, coal provided power for a vast range of machines so that most major industries were mechanized, and the United States was truly becoming an industrial nation.[51] Workers were increasingly becoming subservient to machines, but skilled craftsmen in many industries—iron rollers, glassblowers, and coal miners, to name just a few—still had special knowledge of the production processes and therefore had some discretion or control over their work and their helpers.[52] In the words of the militant union leader Big Bill Haywood, "The manager's brains are under the workman's cap."[53] AFL unions and their members generally accepted this factory system (some sooner than others) but sought to maintain skilled worker control over the production process in addition to decent wages and hours of work.

As such, an important activity of the AFL unions was establishing and maintaining job standards through work rules. These rules frequently pertained to apprenticeship standards, tasks reserved for union members, undesirable or unskilled job duties that union members did not have to do (to prevent degradation of the craft), work allocation procedures, and other standards.[54] Before the 1900s these work rules were often established unilaterally by the unions and enforced by refusing to work on any other terms and by fining or expelling members who undermined these standards.[55] Wage rates might be negotiated with employers, but skilled workers believed that their skilled status as craftsmen entitled them to establish work standards. Control over decision making was seen as necessary to promote human dignity and to reinforce the mental and civic skills needed for active participation in a democratic society.[56]

The AFL and Its Unions: Conflicts with Employers

A critical struggle in the development of U.S. labor relations in the early 20th century therefore revolved around employers' efforts to weaken the AFL's desired level of worker control and establish supervisory supremacy in production decisions.[57] One of the most violent examples of this struggle for workplace control was the **Homestead strike** at the

HR Strategy Labor Negotiations, 1890s Style

You are in charge of a steel mill in the 1890s. A craft union represents less than one-quarter of the mill's employees; the rest are not represented by a union. The contract with this union is expiring. What do you do to prepare for negotiations with the union?

Now suppose this particular mill is the only operation in your company with a union. Your boss is vacationing out of the country and has left clear instructions that he doesn't want any union interference in his company. Your boss is one of the richest men in the world. Remember that in the 1890s no laws protected workers' rights to belong to unions. How do you approach negotiations?

In 1892 at the Homestead Works owned by Andrew Carnegie, Henry Clay Frick prepared for negotiations with the Amalgamated Association of Iron and Steel Workers by ordering the construction of a fence around the mill and running down to the river that bordered the mill. This fence was 11 feet high, made with two-inch-thick boards and topped with barbed wire. Every 25 feet was a three-inch hole at shoulder height. The workers called this "Fort Frick." A second component of Frick's negotiation preparations was to contract with the Pinkerton National Detective Agency for 300 armed Pinkertons. These guards were to secretly enter the mill via the river and secure the mill for the strikebreakers that Frick was presumably also arranging to bring in from other states. Then Frick's final offer to the union was for a 12–15 percent wage reduction. When this was refused, he closed the mill for the Fourth of July holiday and reopened it on a nonunion basis. The existing employees had to reapply for jobs.

References: Jeremy Brecher, *Strike!* (Boston: South End Press, 1972); William Serrin, *Homestead: The Glory and Tragedy of an American Steel Town* (New York: Vintage Books, 1992).

steel mill owned by Andrew Carnegie in Homestead, Pennsylvania. Of the 3,800 workers at the mill, the 800 most skilled belonged to the Amalgamated Association of Iron and Steel Workers, an AFL-affiliated craft union. The Amalgamated at Homestead was the last union in Carnegie's operations, and he was determined to wrest control of Homestead away from the skilled union members—and their 58 pages of work rules—when their contract expired in 1892.[58] When the union refused to accept 12–15 percent wage cuts, the mill was shut down. Management announced that the mill would reopen on July 6, 1892, as a nonunion operation. As the sun rose on July 6, hundreds of skilled and unskilled workers gathered on the mill property along the adjacent river armed with rifles, pistols, rocks, and fence posts to meet two barges containing 300 armed Pinkertons, who were supposed to secretly secure the mill property so that strikebreakers could be brought in. When the Pinkertons tried to come ashore, a gun battle broke out. No one knows who fired first, but the battle raged for hours. The Pinkertons eventually surrendered, but not before at least seven strikers and three Pinkertons were killed. On July 12, 4,000 soldiers of the Pennsylvania militia arrived in Homestead and secured the mill. Aided by new technology that reduced the skills needed for steelmaking, strikebreakers reopened the mill 7 days later.[59]

By October perhaps a thousand strikebreakers had been brought in—guarded by the state militia—and perhaps 100 strikers had returned to work. By the end of November the strike was officially over; only 400 of the 2,200 strikers who had reapplied for jobs were rehired.[60] In 1892 profits in Carnegie's steel operations were $4 million, and by the end of decade they would be $40 million; Carnegie sold these operations in 1901 for $480 million.[61] In the year after the strike, wages for skilled workers dropped significantly while the 12-hour workday continued. A union would not return to the Homestead mill until the 1930s—with the protection of a new labor law and the efforts of an industrial union to organize all workers, skilled and unskilled.

In a decade filled with violent clashes between strikers, strikebreakers, Pinkertons, and other armed agents, and of strikes broken by state militia or federal troops—from a streetcar strike in New Orleans to a miners' strike in Coeur d'Alene, Idaho—the second great labor history event of the 1890s was the **Pullman strike** in 1894. The Pullman Palace Car Company produced Pullman railroad cars in Pullman, Illinois. During the depression that started in 1893, Pullman cut wages by an average of 28 percent and laid off about one-quarter of the workers.[62] Management pay and stockholders' dividends were not reduced, nor was the rent charged to workers for company-owned housing.[63] After rent was deducted from his paycheck, one worker was reportedly left with a paycheck for 2 cents. Pullman workers joined an independent union led by Eugene V. Debs: the American Railway Union, which included both railroad employees and workers that made railroad cars (as at Pullman). Unlike the AFL craft unions with their principle of exclusive jurisdiction, the American Railway Union included multiple occupations—though as was common at the time, only white workers.

In May 1894 three grievance committee members at Pullman were discharged. When Pullman refused to arbitrate any disputed issues, workers struck and Pullman closed the plant. In solidarity, the railroad workers who belonged to the American Railway Union refused to handle Pullman cars on the railroads. The railroads fired anyone who honored this boycott, and the rest of each train crew often struck in support of these discharges. The Pullman dispute therefore quickly expanded into a national railroad strike (recall the "King Debs" drawing in Figure 2.1). The railroads started to put mail cars behind Pullman cars so when workers detached the Pullman cars, the mail would be disrupted. Aided by the U.S. attorney general, who was on the board of directors of one of the struck railroads, federal troops were placed on the trains in July 1894.[64] This drastically changed the tenor of the strike, and violence erupted. In various conflicts 13 people were killed, and more than 700 railroad cars were destroyed by angry strikers in Chicago. Debs was arrested for conspiracy to disrupt the mail and served 6 months in jail. With federal troops protecting the trains and the leader of the American Railway Union in jail, the strike died out.[65]

WORKERS OF THE WORLD UNITE!

The first part of the new century—the early 1900s—was marked by sharp contrasts. The richest 1 percent of households controlled 45 percent of total U.S. wealth—the highest concentration ever.[66] Almost unimaginable wealth was accumulated by industrialists like Carnegie, Rockefeller, Morgan, and Vanderbilt while millions of workers and their families, including many new immigrants, struggled with day-to-day survival. Whether in rural, company-owned towns or urban tenements, families lived in fear of unemployment, accidents, poor health, and making ends meet.[67] While railroad tycoon Jay Gould earned \$10,000,000 a year, the average unskilled worker earned \$10 a week, which meant his family could barely afford a run-down, two-room (not two-bedroom) apartment without running water.[68] Many children had to work to supplement family incomes. This period was an era of tremendous industrial growth, but also of relatively stagnant wages and dangerous working conditions.[69]

The early 20th century was the age of big business. The increased size and power of major corporations were graphically illustrated by the trusts—the companies that were able to monopolize and dominate their industries. By 1905 the Standard Oil Company refined nearly 25 million barrels of oil (85 percent of the market); U.S. Steel had more than 150,000 employees and 200 mills (60 percent of the steel industry); and International Harvester manufactured more than 500,000 agricultural harvesting machines (85 percent of the market).[70] The size of individual factories also continued to grow because the economical use of new mechanized production methods often required a large-scale operation—for example, steel mills were not cost-effective unless they produced at least 2,500 tons a day.[71] The rise of big business created important contrasts, especially between large corporations and individual workers, and between professional managers and unskilled laborers. Scientific management, or "Taylorism" after Frederick Winslow Taylor, decomposed skilled

Labor Relations Application Child Labor in Early 20th–Century America

A vivid illustration of why union leaders and social reformers fought for institutional checks and balances—through unions, laws, or otherwise—in the early 20th-century labor market is the problem of child labor. Many of the first textile mill workers in the 1830s were women and children. Compared to men, women and children were less productive on small New England farms, and therefore mill owners could attract them into the factories at a cheaper wage. By 1900 child labor had greatly expanded to the point that it was hard to ignore as a societal issue. It was estimated that nearly 2 million children aged 10–14 (20 percent of this age group) were gainfully employed in 1900. In many cases these were not safe, part-time after-school jobs, but rather were dangerous and dirty jobs in which children worked more hours than many adults today.

To spur change, several social reformers and philanthropists formed the National Child Labor Committee (NCLC) in 1904. For the NCLC, Lewis Hine took over 7,000 black-and-white photographs, often disguising himself as a fire inspector, insurance salesman, or photographer of machines rather than child workers. These photographs remain as powerful images of the abusive nature of child labor. Two of his photographs are reproduced here; the reference note points to collections of more photographs. Here were some of the worst industries for child labor:

- *The coal industry:* Breaker boys worked 9 or 10 hours per day hunched over fast-moving conveyors of coal, picking out rocks from the coal and breathing in thick coal dust. Others worked with their fathers half a mile underground, loading coal into cars.
- *Textile mills:* Girls spun cotton into yarn on large spinning frames for nine or more hours a day, perhaps six days a week. They received a break when boys were brought in several times a day to frantically replace all the full bobbins of yarn with empty ones. These boys were called doffers and either played or swept the factory in between doffing.
- *Glassmaking:* Boys worked on teams with skilled glassblowers, doing various unskilled aspects of glassmaking. The pace was quick (to keep up with the glassblowers, who were paid piece rates), and the furnaces were extremely hot. Because molten glass had to be kept at a constant temperature day and night, many

Breaker Boys at the Ewen Breaker, South Pittston, Pennsylvania (1911) Photograph by Lewis Hine, who wrote, "The dust was so intense at times as to obscure the view. This dust penetrated the utmost recesses of the boys' lungs. A kind of slave driver sometimes stands over the boys, prodding or kicking them into obedience."

U.S. National Archives

Young Textile Mill Workers, London, Tennessee (1910), Photograph by Lewis Hine, who wrote "Two of the tiny workers, a raveler and a looper in London Hosiery Mills."

Library of Congress [LC-DIG- nclc-02006]

glassmaking factories worked around the clock. Boys would often work the day shift one week and the night shift the next.

- *Agriculture and food processing:* From almost their birth, children would accompany their parents into the fields and food processing plants, and would start helping when they were old enough—perhaps at age 3 or 4. A study of a cranberry bog harvest found that half of the child pickers were less than 10 years old. Lewis Hine also photographed children harvesting cotton and sugar beets, shucking oysters and shrimp, and preparing vegetables for canning.
- *Messenger services:* In cities many boys worked day and night as messengers. The telephone network was not yet completely established, so messengers relayed many communications as well as parcels. But the messenger boys also worked at night, running errands for hotels, restaurants, and brothels.

References: Russell Freedman, *Kids at Work: Lewis Hine and the Crusade against Child Labor* (New York: Clarion Books, 1994)—good source of photographs; Hugh D. Hindman, *Child Labor: An American History* (Armonk, NY: M. E. Sharpe, 2002); John R. Kemp, *Lewis Hine: Photographs of Child Labor in the New South* (Jackson: University of Mississippi Press, 1986)—good source of photographs. Many Lewis Hine photographs are also available online through the U.S. National Archives at www.archives.gov/research/arc/ (enter "523064" in the search box).

jobs into basic repetitive tasks, creating sharp contrasts between professional, scientifically trained managers and unskilled occupations while also creating a contradiction between "scientific" job design and the assignment of workers based on racial and ethnic biases.[72] When Henry Ford added the assembly line to narrowly defined jobs in 1913, the mass manufacturing model was established for much of the rest of the century.

The labor movement was also rife with contrasts. In the Homestead strike skilled and unskilled workers stood together, but this was the exception rather than the norm. Most of the AFL-affiliated craft unions focused exclusively on skilled, white crafts*men* and excluded unskilled, minority, immigrant, and female workers.[73] Even the American

Railway Union, which embraced unskilled workers, discriminated against African American workers. There was also tension between the dominant craft union approach and a perceived need by other workers and union leaders for industrial unionism—that is, organizing workers of all occupations within an industry into a single union. Though affiliated with the AFL, the United Mine Workers (UMW) is an early example of an industrial union because it tried to unionize all employees in the mining industry, led in part by the colorful Mother Jones.[74] The UMW also stood out from other unions of the time in its acceptance of African American workers.[75]

Within the labor movement, divergent views of business unionism and pure and simple unionism were another sharp contrast in this period. During the Pullman strike, the Gompers-led AFL refused to support Eugene Debs's industrial union, the American Railway Union. Although this refusal may partly have reflected a pragmatic decision not to join a losing cause, it also shows a fundamental difference between the conservative business unionism philosophy and more militant alternatives.[76] In fact, as Gompers and other AFL leaders watched judges and the armed forces violently repress strikes and labor demonstrations that were publicly labeled as radical—such as the Great Uprising of 1877 and the eight-hour-day strikes of 1886—the conservatism of business unionism in seeking narrow economic gains for workers rather than more radical reforms to capitalism was reinforced.[77] In contrast, other labor leaders reacted to this repression by pursuing more radical, militant approaches. From 1905 to 1925, the visible radical and militant approach was that of the **Industrial Workers of the World** (IWW), often referred to by its nickname the "Wobblies." The perspective of the IWW was cleverly captured by one of its leaders: "I've never read Marx's *Capital,* but I have the marks of capital all over me."[78]

The IWW: Objectives and Strategies

The IWW is the major U.S. example of **revolutionary unionism,** a philosophy that emphasizes

> the complete harmony of interests of all wage workers as against the representatives of the employing class, and seeks to unite the former, skilled and unskilled together, into one homogeneous fighting organization. It repudiates, or tends to repudiate, the existing institutional order and especially individual ownership of production means, and the wage system.[79]

In terms of the intellectual schools of thought presented in Chapter 2, this philosophy is rooted in critical, Marxist, or radical industrial relations thought that believes in class-based employment relationship conflict. Consequently, revolutionary unionism tries to create working-class solidarity rather than solidarity by occupation or industry and ultimately seeks to overthrow capitalism. From this perspective, the labor movement is seen as an agent for revolution.

Founded in 1905 out of frustration with the discrimination and conservatism of the AFL, the IWW was inclusive and radical. Recall that the American Railway Union lost the Pullman strike when, among other things, the AFL and craft-based railroad unions refused to help. Events like this fostered the IWW's industrial union emphasis on working-class solidarity and inclusiveness. Its goal was to form "One Big Union" that embraced all workers—skilled and unskilled, young and old, native-born and immigrant, white and nonwhite, male and female—across all industries. The radical component of the IWW's philosophy can also be traced to events like the Pullman strike and miners' strikes, in which the IWW leaders felt that elected officials, judges, police, and the army helped employers break strikes. These IWW leaders turned to more radical viewpoints that emphasized the need for worker control of economic and political institutions.[80] And seeing elected officials and judges as effectively controlled by employers, the IWW

Labor Relations Application Mother Jones: The Most Dangerous Woman in America

One of the most colorful and determined individuals in the U.S. labor movement in the early 1900s was Mother Jones. Born as Mary Harris in 1837 in Ireland, by the time she was 35 years old she had experienced religious persecution in Ireland, the Irish potato famine, racial and ethnic hatred in Memphis after the Civil War, the death of her husband and children from yellow fever, and the great Chicago fire of 1871, which destroyed her belongings. In the 1890s—when she was nearly 60 years old—Mary Jones developed into Mother Jones—a grandmotherly figure dressed in long, black Victorian dresses who traveled the country raising hell on behalf of workers and their families, especially in the coal wars of Pennsylvania, West Virginia, and Colorado. From her experiences, she developed a sense of radicalism in which worker power, militancy, and ultimately control were needed to counter the overwhelming economic and political power of big business and secure decent lives for the working class as well as true democracy. One of her most well-known slogans was "Pray for the dead and fight like hell for the living."

Mother Jones often served as a union organizer for the United Mine Workers. Before the 1930s organizing usually meant leading a strike because companies would not recognize a union unless forced to. Mother Jones would therefore travel around coal country, rallying the rank-and-file miners with fiery speeches, leading public demonstrations to put pressure on the corporate enemies, and raising money to feed strikers' families. Her fighting spirit is revealed by her December 1902 description of a West Virginia coal strike:

> The wind blows cold this morning, but these cruel coal barons do not feel the winter blast; their babes, nay even their poodle dogs are warm and have a comfortable breakfast, while these slaves of the caves, who in the past have moved the commerce of the world, are out on the highways without clothes or shelter. Nearly 3,000 families have been thrown out of the corporation shacks to face the cold blasts of winter weather.

Her fiery independence was also demonstrated in her willingness to clash with national union leaders when she thought they were compromising with business owners too readily, and in her contempt for judges who tried to clamp down on her speeches. In fact the experiences of Mother Jones show the extent to which workers' civil liberties were violated to repress union activity. In West Virginia she was arrested in 1902 for violating a judge's order that prevented all demonstrations, even those on union property. In Colorado in 1914 a National Guard general deported her from mining country to Denver and arrested her upon her return—twice—though charges were never filed against her. In contrast, the mine owners' armed guards were rarely detained for killing strikers and their families.

Mine owners and other industrialists hated and feared Mother Jones, even in her 70s, for the power she had to inspire rank-and-file workers of nearly all skills and ethnic origins to fight for a better life. She is perhaps the most vivid personification of the "outside agitator" frequently attacked by management, even today. It should be obvious that outside agitation does not cause the conditions that spark worker discontent, but nevertheless Mother Jones "held great power over mine families . . . [her] speeches articulated the discontents of the coal towns; her body offered a model of physical courage; her spirit taught hope and perseverance." To those in power, she was the most dangerous woman in America between 1900 and 1920.

Reference: Elliot J. Gorn, *Mother Jones: The Most Dangerous Woman in America* (New York: Hill and Wang, 2001). Quotations are from pp. 98–99 and 183.

Mother Jones (1924)

Library of Congress [LC-DIG-npcc-12396]

Why "Wobblies"?

It's not immediately obvious how one goes from "Industrial Workers of the World" (IWW) to the nickname "Wobblies." There are at least four potential origins for this nickname:

- An immigrant worker in the early 1900s allegedly referred to the IWW, in broken English, as the "I-Wobble-U-Wobble-U" (or by some accounts "I-Wobble-Wobble"). This is the leading explanation.
- The nickname "Wobbly" might have come from "wobbly saw"—a popular saw in lumber camps where there were IWW members.
- IWW detractors allegedly started the "Wobbly" nickname because of the IWW's instability or as a way of accusing individual members of being drunks, and then the nickname was adopted by the IWW as a convenience.
- "Wobbly" may have been a code name for sabotage—a tactic of the IWW.

Reference: www.iww.org/history/icons/wobbly (accessed June 8, 2016).

leaders felt that reform could not be achieved through voting.[81] Instead direct worker action was emphasized:

> As defined by Wobblies, direct action included any step taken by workers at the point of production that improved wages, reduced hours, and bettered conditions. It encompassed conventional strikes, intermittent strikes, silent strikes, passive resistance, sabotage and the ultimate direct action measure: the general strike.[82]

The mission of the "One Big Union" was therefore to engage in a class struggle with capitalists.

The IWW's direct action philosophy is called syndicalism.[83] Unlike the Knights of Labor, the IWW did not overlook short-term improvements in working conditions; these short-term improvements were viewed as important victories for bettering workers and for advancing the larger struggle against the capitalists. Signed contracts, however, were viewed negatively by the IWW as legitimizing the capitalist system and restricting the IWW's ability to choose when to engage in direct action (rather than having to wait until a contract expired). The IWW also developed a rich tapestry of songs, poems, stories, skits, and visual images to convey its message and reinforce working-class solidarity.[84] In fact today's most well-known union song, "Solidarity Forever," was originally a Wobbly song.

The IWW: Conflicts and Demise

Consistent with the IWW's inclusiveness, its biggest victory was the Lawrence, Massachusetts, textile workers' strike in 1912.[85] After a wage reduction, the workers spontaneously walked out, and within three days 20,000 employees were on strike. Many of the strikers were Italian immigrants, but there were also significant numbers from Germany, Poland, Russia, and elsewhere—at least 25 nationalities in all.[86] It was an intense strike: Dynamite was planted to discredit the IWW, martial law was declared after a clash killed one worker, the strike leaders were arrested, and police brutality made national news. The strikers maintained their unity, however, and after two months the textile companies agreed to the strikers' demands. The IWW also fought on behalf of miners, loggers, and migratory agricultural workers in the West—sometimes with success, sometimes without.[87]

Unsurprisingly, employers and AFL unions were hostile toward the IWW and its radical agenda. World War I further heightened fears and led to greater repression of the IWW.[88] In fact, as part of an anticommunist red scare, Big Bill Haywood and 100 other Wobblies were found guilty of essentially opposing the war and sent to prison in 1918. An IWW leader was lynched in Montana. And in Bisbee, Arizona, labor radicalism met corporate

The Philosophy of the Industrial Workers of the World

The working class and the employing class have nothing in common. There can be no peace so long as hunger and want are found among the millions of working people and the few, who make up the employing class, have all the good things of life.

Between these two classes a struggle must go on until the workers of the world organize as a class, take possession of the earth and the machinery of production, and abolish the wage system . . . conditions can be changed and the interest of the working class upheld only by an organization formed in such a way that all its members in any one industry, or in all industries if necessary, cease work whenever a strike or lockout is on in any department thereof, thus making an injury to one an injury to all.

Instead of the conservative motto "A fair day's wage for a fair day's work," we must inscribe on our banner the revolutionary watchword "Abolition of the wage system."

It is the historic mission of the working class to do away with capitalism. The army of production must be organized, not only for the everyday struggle with capitalists, but also to carry on production when capitalism shall have been overthrown. By organizing industrially we are forming the structure of the new society within the shell of the old.

Source: Preamble to the IWW Constitution (1908).

vigilantism: The sheriff and 2,000 anti-IWW townspeople rounded up 1,200 striking copper miners in the middle of the night at gunpoint, put them on railroad cattle cars, and forcibly deported them to the New Mexico desert, where they were stranded without food or water in the July heat.[89] A railroad company provided transportation; the telegraph company agreed not to let any messages leave Bisbee. The IWW survived in a meaningful way for only a few more years.

Although the IWW exists today (and is actively organizing Starbucks' and Jimmy John's employees), its greatest activity occurred between 1905 and 1925. Even during this period, there were probably no more than 60,000 Wobblies at any one time; and though its revolutionary aims were not embraced by others, the IWW's inclusiveness and emphasis on social justice provided sparks (and sometimes tactics) for the industrial unions that would mushroom in the 1930s, and some activists today continue to advocate direct action by workers to challenge perceived corporate domination.[90] In the short run, however, the IWW's radicalism likely increased employer hostility toward labor unions.

STAYING UNION-FREE IN THE EARLY 1900s

Until the Great Depression of the 1930s, employer resistance to unions in the 20th century consisted mostly of the open shop movement and then the strategy of welfare capitalism. Craft unions wanted to control the standards of their crafts by (1) restricting entry to skilled workers to maintain high wage levels and (2) having workers rather than employers determine all aspects of work to maintain worker dignity. A central goal of the AFL craft unions was therefore the closed shop—a workplace closed to all except union members, with the union controlling who could become a member. Naturally employers strenuously opposed closed shops because they wanted to control hiring and the nature of work.[91] Beginning around 1903, employers launched a large-scale effort to achieve what they labeled the open shop. This label should not be taken literally—an open shop is not open to all workers, union and nonunion (or white and black). Rather, an open shop is a thoroughly nonunion

Solidarity Forever

The folk song "Solidarity Forever" is the U.S. labor movement's unofficial anthem. It is widely embraced today by many mainstream unions and is often sung at rallies, demonstrations, and picket lines. However, it was written by Wobbly songwriter Ralph Chaplin in 1915 to be "full of revolutionary fervor." You can hear the song by searching online for "solidarity forever mp3." If you want to sing along, the tune is that of the "Battle Hymn of the Republic."

Solidarity Forever

When the union's inspiration through the workers' blood shall run
There can be no power greater anywhere beneath the sun,
Yet what force on earth is weaker than the feeble strength of one?
But the Union makes us strong.

Chorus:

Solidarity forever!
Solidarity forever!
Solidarity forever!
For the Union makes us strong.

Is there aught we hold in common with the greedy parasite
Who would lash us into serfdom and would crush us with his might?
Is there anything left to us but to organize and fight?
For the Union makes us strong.

It is we who plowed the prairies; built the cities where they trade;
Dug the mines and built the workshops; endless miles of railroad laid;
Now we stand outcast and starving, 'midst the wonders we have made;
But the Union makes us strong.

All the world that's owned by idle drones is ours and ours alone.
We have laid the wide foundations, built it skyward stone by stone.
It is ours, not to slave in, but to master and to own
While the Union makes us strong.

They have taken untold billions that they never toiled to earn,
But without our brain and muscle not a single wheel can turn.
We can break their haughty power, gain our freedom when we learn
That the Union makes us strong.

In our hands is placed a power greater than their hoarded gold,
Greater than the might of armies magnified a thousand-fold.
We can bring to birth a new world in the ashes of the old
For the Union makes us strong.

Reference: The quote is from Joyce L. Kornbush (ed.), *Rebel Voices: An I.W.W. Anthology* (Ann Arbor: University of Michigan Press, 1964), p. 26.

operation of employees selected by the employer. The **open shop movement** was therefore a concerted drive by employers and their employers' associations in the early 1900s to create and maintain union-free workplaces.

The Open Shop Movement

To the public, the open shop movement portrayed an ideology of individual freedom. Unions were depicted as violating individual liberties by denying workers the ability to choose where to work and on what terms.[92] This was a very public campaign, as underscored by the advertisement from 1921 shown in Figure 3.3. In the advertisement, note the emphasis on *individual* liberties: "the right to work unmolested" (in other words, without a union), the "independence" of employees, "individual initiative," and the "free exercise . . . of their natural and constitutional rights." This rhetoric of individualism went so far that the open shop movement was renamed the American Plan in the 1920s.[93] Employers further used the rhetoric of individual liberty to argue that unions should not be allowed to interfere with management's control of its private property (its business).[94] As such, the advertisement in Figure 3.3 further equates the open shop with the "liberty and independence" of the employer that protects the employer's "natural and constitutional rights."

FIGURE 3.3
Open Shop Advertisement, Minneapolis (circa 1921)

Source: *The Iron Trade Review* (March 17, 1921)

Not heavily publicized, however, was that this drive for individual liberty was conducted by sophisticated local and national alliances of powerful employers and employers' associations.[95] In other words, the open shop movement consisted of well-orchestrated *collective* activity by business. In Minneapolis over 200 employers formed an organization in 1903 called the Citizens Alliance, which openly promoted the open shop and fought unions until the 1940s. In the name of *individual* liberty, the Citizens Alliance *collectively* created a trade school to educate skilled workers who were also schooled in the importance of individualism, blacklisted union supporters, operated a network of hundreds of labor spies, and recruited a private army when necessary. Dues payments to the Citizens Alliance were used to provide financial assistance to struck employers (just like a union strike fund); and if this was not enough, the business community threatened to boycott businesses that agreed to a union's terms (just like a union boycott). These activities and the recruitment of strikebreakers were facilitated by national employers' associations such as the National Association of Manufacturers (just as a union might get support from the AFL). Employers were also often successful in using court-ordered injunctions to break strikes (see Chapter 4). These are exactly the types of collective activities that were being publicly vilified as "un-American" when conducted by workers and their unions. And Minneapolis was not unique: There were hundreds of open shop organizations in major cities around the country in the first few decades of the 20th century.[96]

Some employers also exploited racial and ethnic tensions to foster open shops. Employers mixed nationalities or had them complete with one another in a divide-and-rule strategy that sought to prevent worker solidarity on class lines.[97] Many AFL craft unions were

Labor Relations Application Who Was the Most-Favored Strikebreaker?

Between 1890 and 1940 strikebreaking was a highly profitable business in U.S.—but not European—labor relations. Numerous strikebreaking agencies specialized in providing armed guards, labor spies, and replacement workers to struck firms—perhaps by the thousands on very short notice. One agency advertised that it could deliver 10,000 strikebreakers within 72 hours. These private armies often clashed violently with strikers and their supporters. Strikebreaking agencies managed the recruitment, training, compensation, feeding, housing, security, and work of the strikebreakers. In fact these agencies often assumed complete control over the operation of struck firms.

Which of these four groups do you think were the preferred strikebreakers?

- African Americans?
- Criminals?
- The unemployed?
- College students?

All of these were used in large numbers as strikebreakers, but college students were preferred. College students were instrumental in breaking these and other strikes in the early 20th century:

Minneapolis flour millers' strike (1903): University of Minnesota students.

New York subway strike (1905): Columbia students.

Pacific Gas and Electric Company strike (1913): Stanford students.

Boston police strike (1919): Harvard students.

New England telephone operators' strike (1919): MIT students.

Pennsylvania Railroad strike (1920): Princeton students.

San Francisco dockworkers' strike (1934): University of California–Berkeley students.

College students were especially attractive for several reasons. Unlike the other groups listed, college students were generally from the upper class and therefore had no sympathy for the working class. African Americans and the unemployed often developed sympathy for those on strike—especially if they were lured into being strikebreakers by not being told that the jobs were available because of a strike. College students were more skilled than the other groups, yet athletes and other young people had the brawn to endure not only physical work but also confrontations with strikers. Finally, unlike the other groups of strikebreakers, college students were viewed by the public as respectable and therefore helped the struck firm's public relations (consider the public's reaction to having college students versus criminals operate local transit systems).

From the perspective of the college students, strikebreaking was simply another adventurous extracurricular activity—like wild fraternity parties—and a chance to assert their masculinity. College presidents often encouraged strikebreaking to please wealthy trustees and donors. Some even created courses to help prepare students for strikebreaking, such as courses at MIT and Harvard in railroad engineering.

Reference: Stephen H. Norwood, *Strikebreaking and Intimidation: Mercenaries and Masculinity in Twentieth-Century America* (Chapel Hill: University of North Carolina Press, 2002).

discriminatory and openly hostile toward anyone except white men. The Pullman Company trained African American workers for skilled positions to keep the skilled labor force divided by racial tension and therefore nonunion. Pullman locations in which the labor movement was weaker saw fewer African American workers hired for skilled positions because the threat of unionization was not as strong. Worker solidarity across occupations was also weakened through racial and gender segregation—on Pullman cars, for example, conductors were always white and porters were always black; men cleaned the exterior of the railroad cars, women the interior. As another example of discrimination, to keep wages low, female clerical workers were fired when they got married.[98]

The open shop movement was sometimes characterized by open warfare. Professional strikebreaking companies provided a complete array of strikebreaking services: trained workers, armed guards, food and medical supplies, cots, and the like.[99] In other cases police and the National Guard repressed strikes, sometimes violently and illegally. During one strike the National Guard used military tribunals to prosecute more than 100 civilian strikers while denying them defense attorneys; other violations of strikers' civil liberties were common.[100] The Ludlow Massacre is often used to illustrate the extent to which employers would go to maintain an open shop. In 1913 workers struck the Rockefeller-owned coal mines in southern Colorado for union recognition and improved wages and working conditions. The strikers were forced out of their company-owned homes and moved into tent colonies, including one in Ludlow. Guerilla warfare broke out between strikers and the company's private army.[101] The stockholders were told that this strike was over the closed shop; and John D. Rockefeller, Jr., testified before a congressional hearing in April 1914 that he would stand by the principle of the open shop even if, as the question was posed to him, "it costs all your property and kills all your employees."[102] Two weeks later a gun battle broke out between the strikers and the Colorado militia, which was staffed essentially by company hirelings and guards. After the shooting killed perhaps 10 strikers, the militia overran the tent colony at Ludlow. The tents were soaked with kerosene and lit on fire. Two women and 11 children died hiding in a hole under a tent.[103] The Rockefeller-owned mine never did recognize the union. Four million workers were involved in strikes in 1919, including a general strike that paralyzed Seattle; huge coal mine, textile, and steel strikes; and a strike by Boston police.[104] In 1921 over 10,000 frustrated coal miners fought a weeklong armed battle at Blair Mountain, West Virginia, against deputies funded by nonunion mine owners determined to keep the United Mine Workers out of southern West Virginia. Federal troops caused the miners to give up the battle, and the mines remained nonunion until the 1930s.[105]

Welfare Capitalism

The negative publicity about this type of violence and the destructiveness of bitter strikes caused some companies to switch from aggressively suppressing unions to avoiding unions through less confrontational methods. Dating back to the late 1800s, some companies implemented a strategy of welfare work, which tried to create harmony between workers and their employers by creating a familylike company spirit and enhancing the welfare of workers.[106] Elements of welfare work included attractive company housing, recreational programs, libraries, landscaped factory grounds, profit sharing, and pension plans. The structure of work, however, was determined by scientific management and the push to decompose and standardize job tasks; workers were literally driven by supervisors in the foreman's empire. In the aftermath of the Ludlow Massacre and the labor shortages and unrest of World War I, welfare work evolved into the creation of the personnel management function, and the 1920s were thereby characterized by welfare capitalism.

Welfare capitalism sought to win worker loyalty and increase efficiency by improving supervisory practices, implementing orderly hiring and firing procedures, providing wage incentives, offering protective insurance benefits, creating a positive culture, improving the physical work environment and safety, and providing employee voice.[107] Depending on one's perspective, welfare capitalism represents either a sophisticated managerial strategy to control the workplace and prevent unionization, or the beginnings of today's strategic human resource management and high-performance workplaces.[108] Nevertheless, union avoidance by killing the labor movement with kindness was at least one important aspect of welfare capitalism.[109] Note further that employers lobbied against legislating the same types of benefits provided by welfare capitalism; employers wanted their employees to be dependent on, and therefore loyal and tied to, the company—not the government, a local community, or a union (a pattern that continues today).[110]

The most controversial aspect of welfare capitalism—then and now—was the attempt to provide employee voice or industrial democracy through employee representation plans or company unions. One of the first examples was the Rockefeller Plan, crafted to offset the negative publicity of the Ludlow Massacre, in which a committee of equal numbers of managers and elected employee representatives would meet to resolve labor issues.[111] These types of employee representation plans are often called company unions because they are similar to a union in that workers and managers meet to discuss work issues, but they are established and often run by the company. By the mid-1920s it was estimated that there were over 400 company unions covering more than 1 million workers.[112]

The debate over company unions—which still rages today (see Chapter 10)—is whether they provide legitimate employee voice or are management-dominated schemes that are manipulated to keep independent unions out. In other words, are company unions sham unions? Company unions could not strike and did not have the authority to force management to discuss specific issues. But they did provide an open channel of communication with management and a forum to present grievances; to prevent unionization, companies made concessions to the employee representatives at least sometimes. Unlike the AFL craft unions at the time, the Pullman Company's employee representation plans were integrated, and African American workers served as representatives equal to whites. Pullman also negotiated wage increases and other improvements with the employee representation plans several times in the 1920s.[113] However, these agreements coincided with periods of union activity when the threat of unionization was high. The company also discriminated against workers who did not support the employee representation plans. The struggle by the Brotherhood of Sleeping Car Porters, an independent union, to organize the Pullman porters was portrayed in no uncertain terms as a drive to break porters from the chains of the company-dominated representation plan. The Brotherhood of Sleeping Car Porters would eventually become the first African American union to sign a contract with a major corporation, but not until the great union upsurge in the New Deal of the 1930s.

Online Exploration Exercise: Explore some online labor history exhibits (e.g., see *www.library.arizona.edu/exhibits/bisbee/* or *www.depts.washington.edu/labhist/strike/*). To what extent did these events result from managerial choices? labor choices? the environment? How did they influence subsequent actions and events?

A NEW DEAL FOR WORKERS: LEGAL PROTECTION AND INDUSTRIAL UNIONS

On October 24, 1929, the stock market unexpectedly crashed. Consumer purchasing slowed and unemployment increased. Weak farm prices put farmers out of business; panics wiped out savings accounts, and banks closed. And then the economy plunged into the Great Depression. By 1933 the country's gross national product had declined by 29 percent, the steel industry was operating at 12 percent of capacity, the unemployment rate was nearly 25 percent with 15 million unemployed workers, and many others were working only part-time.[114] Many companies that had implemented welfare capitalism programs in the 1920s abandoned them and slashed wages and jobs.[115] Bread lines, evictions, and cardboard settlements of homeless families became common; thousands roamed the country looking for work. Today's unemployment insurance system had yet to be created, and the local poverty relief programs could not keep up with the incredible needs. Although economic activity partially rebounded in the mid-1930s, mass unemployment was a problem throughout the decade, and the Great Depression effectively lasted for the entire 1930s (see Figure 3.4). The widespread poverty is hard to describe in words, and at the time no one knew when it would end.

The severity of the Great Depression shook the intellectual foundations of the U.S. economy. The wisdom of relying on the invisible hand of free markets and the nation's elite—big business in particular—to promote widespread economic prosperity and security

FIGURE 3.4
A Time Line of Labor History between 1925 and 1960

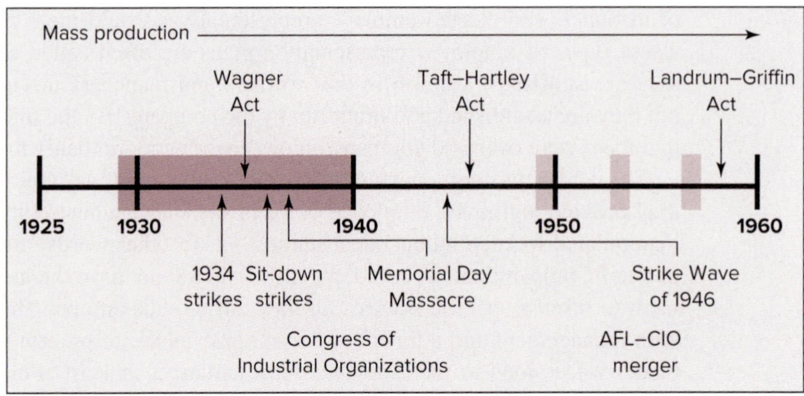

Note: Shading indicates economic depressions; light shading indicates recessions.

was discarded. Franklin Delano Roosevelt was elected president in 1932 and pledged "a new deal for the American people."[116] The New Deal program of the Roosevelt presidency would ultimately create an active government role in guaranteeing the welfare and security of the population, including federally mandated minimum wages and overtime premiums, unemployment insurance and Social Security systems, and through the Wagner Act in 1935, explicit protections for workers trying to form unions. With respect to the schools of thought from Chapter 2, government policy started following pluralist industrial relations thinking rather than mainstream economics in this period.

Striking for New Labor Legislation

As will be described in Chapter 4, New Deal legislation starting with the National Industrial Recovery Act (NIRA) in 1933 encouraged and emboldened workers to form unions. The AFL unions enjoyed a modest resurgence, and employers rushed to establish company unions to avoid independent unionization. In fact membership in company unions nearly equaled membership in AFL unions, with each group having from 2.5 to 3 million members.[117] But the NIRA was weak, and there were tremendous strikes in 1934 as workers again clashed with employers who refused to recognize their independent unions.

A successful strike for recognition at a Toledo auto parts plant resulted in an extended battle between strikers (joined by the unemployed) and the Ohio National Guard.[118] In Minneapolis 3,000 truck drivers and helpers struck after the trucking companies refused to bargain with Teamsters Local 574.[119] By infiltrating the union, the business leaders' Citizens Alliance lured strikers into an alley, where they were brutally beaten by police. After additional violence, Local 574 agreed to an election to see if workers wanted to unionize, but the employers refused. Martial law was declared, and the National Guard took over the city. Around the same time, all of San Francisco was paralyzed by a general strike.[120] San Francisco longshoremen struck for union recognition and an end to the shape-up system in which foremen selected workers by choosing them from a large crowd of hopefuls each morning. The strike spread up and down the Pacific coast. After police and the National Guard broke through the picket lines, 130,000 workers from many industries and occupations in San Francisco struck in support of the longshoremen. And this was not even the biggest strike of 1934—375,000 textile workers from Maine to Alabama struck to protest the firing of union supporters, the stretch-out (assigning more looms to each worker), and the failure of Roosevelt's New Deal to fulfill its promises of justice for workers.[121] Songs of protest such as "The Big Fat Boss and the Worker" and "Cotton Mill Colic" that were spread by traveling folk singers and radio broadcasts helped give the workers a voice and contributed to a shared sense of oppression and struggle across otherwise isolated mill towns.[122]

The Rise of Industrial Unionism

In 1935 Congress passed the Wagner Act, which encouraged unionization, enacted legal protections for workers, and outlawed company unions. The Wagner Act will be presented in detail in Chapter 4; the key point here is that the U.S. federal government became supportive of union organizing and bargaining. By 1941 union membership tripled to about 8.4 million, or 23 percent of workers.[123] This explosion in union membership was certainly connected to the new legal protections of the Wagner Act, but a second issue was also tremendously important: the rise of industrial unionism. Recall that the AFL emphasized craft unionism—organizing *skilled* workers into unions by craft or occupation. Craft unionism "reflected the industrial world of a half-century earlier: small shops, a simple technology, and the highly skilled workman."[124] In contrast, **industrial unionism** seeks to organize all the workers in a workplace or industry regardless of their occupations or skill levels.

The mismatch between craft unionism and the emerging modern workplace was vividly revealed in the 1919 steel strike. At the start of a coordinated drive to unionize steelworkers at the end of World War I, no fewer than 24 AFL unions claimed jurisdiction over various occupations. In the ensuing strike for union recognition, the steel companies used all the tactics of the open shop movement—strikebreakers, negative publicity campaigns associating unionism with radicalism, blacklisting, martial law, and state militia—so there were many reasons for the strike's complete failure. But attempting to organize the industry along craft lines with 24 different unions contributed to this failure: the individual unions insisted on following their own procedures, some fought over jurisdictional issues, organizers were uncoordinated, and each union was unwilling to contribute the financial resources needed to counter the steel industry.[125] The steel industry would not be unionized until the late 1930s—and then by an industrial union, not multiple craft unions.

Industrial unions emerged as a significant force in the mid-1930s, but the roots of industrial unionism are much older. The Knights of Labor and the Industrial Workers of the World were both industrial unions. In 1913 Mother Jones accurately saw into the future: "I know Industrial Unionism is coming, and you can't stop it."[126] Mother Jones had extensive experience with industrial unionism because even though it was part of the AFL, the United Mine Workers was an industrial union for the coal industry. By a special AFL exception, it represented all workers in the mines and around them, including skilled workers typically represented by other AFL craft unions, such as carpenters.[127] Several other unions within the AFL, such as the Amalgamated Clothing Workers, were also essentially industrial unions.[128]

The rise of industrialized, mass manufacturing industries created huge numbers of unskilled and semiskilled factory workers in autos, rubber and tires, farm and construction machinery, airplanes, electrical products, and elsewhere. The jurisdictional disputes between competing unions that had plagued the AFL since the 1890s intensified with the rise of these mass manufacturing industries.[129] The issue boiled over at the AFL's convention in 1935.[130] On one side were the old-line, conservative craft union leaders who looked down on the unskilled mass-production workers and who saw industrial unionism as a threat to their own power. One such leader was the other Big Bill in U.S. labor history: Big Bill Hutcheson, leader of the carpenters' union, who wanted jurisdiction over any worker who worked with wood regardless of industry. On the other side were the leaders of unions that were already organized along industrial lines, led by the president of the United Mine Workers, John L. Lewis. Lewis particularly wanted to aggressively organize the steel industry to strengthen his union's power in coal (because coal fed, and was often owned by, the steel industry); he felt that an industrial union approach was necessary (recall the 1919 strike). Personality conflicts between various leaders magnified the disagreements. At the 1935 convention Lewis was (again) unable to muster sufficient AFL support for launching organizing drives of mass-production workers by industrial unions. To underscore this conflict, Hutcheson called Lewis a bastard; the 225-pound Lewis responded by sending the equally large Hutcheson sprawling with a punch to the jaw.

Within a month, Lewis and the leaders of seven other unions formed the Committee for Industrial Organization (CIO) to pursue unionization of the mass manufacturing industries through industrial unionism. These unions were later suspended from the AFL. Mass-production workers were ripe for unionization—the work was physically difficult, the hours were long, and the supervision was arbitrary and abusive. Workers were looking for more equity, but also voice:

> When Armour's pork division grievance committee complained to the plant superintendent about a speed-up and the lack of a relief man, Superintendent Renfro responded, "You've been getting along for a good many years this way. What's the difference now?" Crawford Love, hog-kill steward, told him frankly, "The difference is this. I've been up there for eighteen years, and for eighteen years we've been breaking our hearts for the company, but now we've got a chance to say something about it."[131]

The CIO launched or supported organizing drives in the auto, steel, rubber, and radio industries and would become a very visible force in U.S. society.[132] The intense conflicts and ultimate successes of these drives are revealed by the events between 1936 and 1941 in autos and steel.

Sitting Down for Union Recognition

Despite the Wagner Act, the major automakers and steelmakers took a hard line against unionizing attempts. As in the 19th century, companies extensively used labor spies to infiltrate unions and thereby weaken or break them.[133] In fact, a government investigation found that one local union of General Motors workers was so thoroughly infiltrated that after the company fired all the workers who were members, only seven members were left. All were officers, and all were spies working for seven different agencies.[134] More generally, the Pinkertons alone infiltrated 93 separate unions.[135] While General Motors relied on espionage, Ford did not hesitate to supplement spying with brass knuckles. Ford's infamous Service Department of over several thousand ex-boxers, violent criminals, and thugs arbitrarily ruled the factories with intimidation and force. Union organizers in several cities were brutally beaten in broad daylight while police watched, and one was even tarred and feathered.[136]

The Visibility of the Rise of the CIO

Source: *Common Sense* (December 1937).

Against this backdrop, the watershed **General Motors sit-down strike** began in December 1936 when workers in Flint, Michigan, took over two Chevrolet plants by sitting down and refusing to work or leave the plant.[137] At the time, Flint was the heart of General Motors, the world's premiere corporation, and the most important issue was getting General Motors to recognize the United Auto Workers (UAW) as the employees' bargaining agent. Workers in Cleveland, Toledo, Detroit, and elsewhere followed suit and sat down in their factories, but the center of the strike was Flint. Strict discipline was maintained inside the plants by union leaders, and company property was not damaged; food was brought to the strikers by outside union members and the women's auxiliary. In early January 1937 police tried to recapture one plant with tear gas, but in the Battle of the Running Bulls, they were repulsed by fire hoses and strikers who threw two-pound car door hinges at them from the roof. The battle ended when women broke through the police lines and joined the picket line in front of the plant.[138] The governor then ordered the National Guard to Flint to preserve peace, and a stalemate ensued. General Motors refused to negotiate until its plants were evacuated, but the UAW figured that if the plants were evacuated, General Motors would have no incentive to bargain. Faced with a governor who refused to order the National Guard to forcibly evacuate the plants—likely with considerable bloodshed and loss of life—General Motors agreed to recognize the UAW on February 11, 1937, and the six-week strike ended. With the exception of Ford—whose Service Department's violence suppressed unionization until 1941—this victory at General Motors was followed by a strong wave of unionization throughout the auto industry.

The ramifications of the UAW's victory in the General Motors sit-down strike spread beyond the auto industry. In 1936 Lewis and the CIO created the Steel Workers Organizing Committee (SWOC) to unionize the steel industry.[139] The steel industry was full of

The Women's Emergency Brigade Outside a Chevrolet Plant in Flint, Michigan (1937) The sticks they are carrying were used to break the windows to release the tear gas affecting the sit-down strikers.

employee representation plans (company unions), so the companies and the SWOC vied for the workers' support.[140] In the aftermath of the UAW's sit-down strike and with the SWOC apparently winning more support than the company unions, the dominant steelmaker, U.S. Steel, announced in March 1937 that it had secretly negotiated an agreement with Lewis. A group of smaller steel manufacturers matched the terms of U.S. Steel's contract with the SWOC but refused to recognize the union. A government investigation later revealed that in preparation for a strike, one of these steel companies stockpiled 8 machine guns, 190 shotguns, 314 rifles, 453 revolvers, over 80,000 rounds of ammunition, and over 3,100 canisters of tear gas.[141] The expected recognition strike began in May 1937. Outside Republic Steel in Chicago, the police defied the courts by arresting peacefully picketing workers. A protest was thus called for Memorial Day. Marching to the steel mill, strikers and their families met a line of police that refused to let them proceed. Police fired into the crowd, killing 10 marchers. Seven of them were shot in the back. More than 50 were injured from gunfire or billy clubs. This event became known as the Memorial Day Massacre, but union recognition would not be achieved until 1941.[142] The SWOC would eventually become the United Steelworkers of America, and with the UAW would be among the most important industrial unions in the postwar period.

A New Federation to Rival the AFL

After the CIO organizing drives resulted in viable unions, it formally became the **Congress of Industrial Organizations** (CIO) in 1938. This new federation of industrial unions rivaled the AFL federation of craft unions. There were now roughly 35 industrial unions affiliated with the CIO, and their growth was spectacular. Conservative estimates reveal that by 1941 the CIO had 2.85 million members—an increase of 2 million members from 1936.[143] CIO industrial unions dominated the auto, steel, and rubber industries. The wave of CIO energy was not limited to the industrial centers of the Midwest. For example, CIO unions led organizing drives and strikes of Mexican American workers throughout the Southwest and West—such as pecan shellers in Texas, sugar beet harvesters in Colorado, copper miners in Arizona, and cannery workers in California.[144] As such, the CIO achieved the broadest base of support that the U.S. labor movement has ever known:

> The CIO had successfully organized the unskilled workers into industrial unions and broken through the narrow lines of craft unionism fostered by the AFL. It had welcomed, as the [AFL] had never done, immigrants, blacks, and women, without regard to race, sex, or nationality.[145]

On the other hand, by the end of the decade the CIO unions were becoming centralized and grassroots initiatives increasingly took a backseat to leadership control.[146] Accompanying this shift was a movement from community-based to workplace-based unionism. With the decreased emphasis on community and an increased portrayal of the workplace and unionism in masculine terms (recall Figure 3.4), women were relegated to marginal roles.[147] Most CIO unions "wanted women to join unions, organize auxiliaries, and even shape union culture, but they did not make much room for them on center stage"; and "by reinforcing the patriarchal family, the CIO did not encourage workers to challenge traditional gender relationships as much as ethnic and racial ones."[148] These issues have become significant concerns in the workplace of the 21st century.

It is also important not to overstate the differences between the two federations by the start of World War II. In their first years, the CIO unions relied heavily on aggressive workplace tactics—most visibly demonstrated by the sit-down strikes—and were significantly aided by communists, socialists, and other radicals. But unfavorable legal rulings—most visibly a 1939 Supreme Court decision that sit-down strikes are illegal—set the CIO unions on the path toward embracing the AFL's business unionism philosophy that emphasizes stable

Labor Relations Application A. Philip Randolph and the Brotherhood of Sleeping Car Porters

Before the rise of automobiles and airplanes, long-distance passenger travel used railroads. The most luxurious method of railroad travel was in a Pullman sleeping car. Passengers' needs were handled by porters, who combined the roles of host and servant. And all 10,000 Pullman porters were African American men. Being a Pullman porter was probably the best job a recently freed slave could obtain—it was a prestigious position that paid more than unskilled labor. But the job was full of indignities: the company exclusively hired African American workers to fit racist stereotypes that blacks were servile and that whites would find it more luxurious to be served by blacks; porters were subjected to bigotry from passengers and other railroad employees (e.g., conductors who were always white) in a segregated society.

Porters had to pay for their uniforms and even the rags used to shine the passengers' shoes. They could be ordered to make an extra trip without any advance notice; and a porter filling in for a sick coworker might not get paid for six hours of preparation work such as making beds. Until the 1920s all porters were referred to as "George"—after the company founder's name, George Pullman. To redress these inequities and indignities, porters turned to unionization. In the early 1920s Pullman created an employee representation plan to forestall unionizing activity. In frustration, some workers formed the Brotherhood of Sleeping Car Porters (BSCP) in 1925 and asked A. Philip Randolph to be its leader.

The BSCP fought battles on several fronts in the 1920s. Though the BSCP was a craft union, the AFL would not grant the BSCP status as a national union on par with other AFL unions until 1935. For its part, the company fired or reassigned union supporters and continued to use the representation plan to reduce support for the union (recall Figure 3.4). The representation plan supposedly "won" the termination of the "George" policy, although many porters credited union pressure. In the early 1930s the BSCP's membership of roughly 4,000 fell to 650 during the Depression, but the BSCP continued its struggle to become the recognized union for Pullman porters.

Under the tireless leadership of Randolph, the BSCP rebounded during the upsurge of union activity and legislative support in Roosevelt's New Deal. The BSCP finally won an election to represent the porters in 1935—as such, it was not only the CIO industrial unions that thrived in this period. Two years later the BSCP became the first African American union to sign a contract with a major U.S. corporation. Randolph went on to become an important civil rights leader, and in many respects the struggle of the BSCP laid the foundation for the postwar civil rights movement. The 1955 bus boycott in Montgomery, Alabama, after Rosa Parks was arrested, was organized by a Pullman porter. And A. Philip Randolph organized the 1963 March on Washington in which Martin Luther King delivered his famous "I have a dream" speech.

References: William H. Harris, *Keeping the Faith: A. Philip Randolph, Milton P. Webster, and the Brotherhood of Sleeping Car Porters, 1925–37* (Urbana: University of Illinois Press, 1991); Jack Santino, *Miles of Smiles, Years of Struggle: Stories of Black Pullman Porters* (Urbana: University of Illinois Press, 1989); Larry Tye, *Rising from the Rails: Pullman Porters and the Making of the Black Middle Class* (New York: Henry Holt, 2004).

workplace collective bargaining to improve wages and working conditions.[149] Moreover, the AFL had a larger membership and made gains during the 1930s as well.[150] Much of the CIO's success was in durable goods manufacturing, where large corporations dominated. The more decentralized AFL unions grew significantly in other sectors with smaller employers: trucking, construction, service industries, and retail trade. Industrial unionism, therefore, might be well suited to mass manufacturing, but other models might better fit other situations.

WARTIME AND POSTWAR LABOR RELATIONS

World War II was particularly important for the development of U.S. labor relations.[151] War production ended the mass unemployment of the 1930s. This new labor market power allowed unions to strengthen their weak spots—such as at Ford and the smaller steelmakers in 1941. At the same time government leaders wanted to keep union militancy under control, so strikes would not interfere with the production of airplanes, tanks, and other defense products. A National War Labor Board (NWLB) was created by President Roosevelt with a tripartite structure: It consisted of representatives of business, labor, and government. The NWLB's function was to resolve labor disputes to keep war production moving. The result was that organized labor essentially traded its right to strike in return for enhanced workplace security. This further institutionalized labor unions—union membership rose by 6 million workers to a union density of 36 percent—and also enhanced the power of union leaders at the expense of the rank and file, and ultimately created a bureaucratic form of unionism. In particular, rank-and-file militancy was channeled into bureaucratic grievance procedures (see Chapter 9). The NWLB also created fringe benefits such as holiday pay, shift differentials, and health insurance benefits to work around wage controls. All these features—bureaucratic, centralized unions, formal grievance procedures, and extensive benefits—remain central in U.S. labor relations today and can be traced to the wartime need for stable production. While there was a significant amount of wartime labor–management cooperation, threats to the traditional dominance of white men in the workplace brought challenges and conflict. Wartime production demands drew women into factory work in unprecedented numbers—think "Rosie the Riveter"—but unions did little to prevent their equally quick postwar purge; instead unionism as a male institution was reinforced.[152] Efforts to open up better jobs to African American workers led to hate strikes in Philadelphia, Detroit, and elsewhere as white workers refused to work with nonwhites, sometimes quietly supported by managers in order to weaken a union. Due to supportive unions, seniority systems, and grievance procedures, more progress was made integrating African American workers than women, but racial and ethnic challenges would continue.[153]

Cementing the Postwar Model of Labor Relations

The end of World War II brought on the **Great Strike Wave of 1945–46.** For the 12 months beginning in August 1945, 4,600 strikes occurred involving 4.9 million workers and resulted in nearly 120 million lost worker-days.[154] There were large yet relatively peaceful strikes in autos, steel, coal, rail, oil refining, longshoring, meatpacking, and electrical products. This level of strike activity surpassed any other year in U.S. history. Important causes included decreased employee earnings with the inevitable postwar production slowdown, rising prices with the lifting of wartime price controls, and a renewed drive by management to reassert its workplace control and cost discipline (which had waned during the war because costs could be passed through to government contracts).[155] This strike wave led to major changes in the Wagner Act through the passage of the Taft–Hartley Act in 1947 (see Chapter 4).

The strike with the most lasting significance during this wave was the UAW strike at General Motors.[156] Walter Reuther, the ambitious leader of the UAW, wanted to link workers' and consumers' interests and therefore demanded a 30-percent wage increase without an increase in auto prices. Reuther demanded that General Motors open its financial books when it claimed that it could not afford such an increase, and 200,000 General Motors, workers went on strike in November 1945. General Motors was adamant about retaining its right to manage both in the boardroom and on the shop floor. After 113 days Reuther declared victory, but corporate America really won: General Motors did not open its books and retained its right to manage. This established the postwar model of union representation: unions could negotiate for higher wages, better benefits, and favorable seniority provisions, but they would not be involved in production decisions. From this point forward, union contracts increased in length and detail while shop floor activism was curtailed by the workplace rule of law.[157] The workplace rule of law was increasingly enforced by college-educated foremen under pressure to speed up the pace of work; grievance resolution became more formal, and injury rates increased.[158]

The largely bureaucratic nature of U.S. unions was further cemented in the late 1940s and 1950s when opposition groups within the major CIO unions were driven out under

Labor Relations Application The Most Dangerous Man in Detroit

Born in 1907 to German immigrant parents, Walter Reuther moved to Detroit in 1927, lured by the possibility of working as a skilled die maker in the world's biggest and most celebrated auto factory: Ford's River Rouge plant. Reuther was simultaneously becoming enthusiastic about the socialist ideas taught to him earlier by his parents.

Intrigued by the Soviet five-year plan to industrialize, he left Ford in 1932 to work with his brother in a Soviet auto plant initially established by Ford. Before arriving in the Soviet Union, the brothers witnessed firsthand the rise of the antisocialist Nazi regime in Germany. By 1936 Reuther was back in Detroit and actively involved in the organizing efforts of the newly emerging United Auto Workers (UAW) union, often working closely with communist and socialist activists, who were the most active organizers in 1930s Detroit. He quickly became a member of the UAW executive board and in 1937 was beaten by Ford's Service Department goons when handing union literature to Ford workers. This highly publicized event, known as the Battle of the Overpass, elevated Reuther's visibility.

The UAW of the 1930s and 1940s was rife with intense political factions; Reuther distanced himself from the communists and socialists and consolidated his power. But an ambitious vision of labor's role in the economy and society remained important to him:

> The kind of labor movement we want is not committed to a nickel-in-the-pay-envelope philosophy. We are building a labor movement, not to patch up the world so men can starve less often and less frequently, but a labor movement that will remake the world so that the working people will get the benefit of their labor.

During World War II Reuther famously proposed a plan in which the corporations, organized labor, and the government would work together to produce 500 planes a day. At the end of the war, he demanded that General Motors (GM) raise wages 30 percent without increasing car prices in a bid to link workers with consumers. GM stood strong, however, and a 113-day strike failed.

In 1946 he was elected president of the UAW—a position he would hold for the rest of his life. Under his principled yet tightly controlling leadership, the UAW won great gains in living standards for autoworkers through collective bargaining. These gains, however, went in the opposite direction of Reuther's social vision: companies agreed to generous wages and benefits in return for retaining the right to manage. Detailed, formal contracts became the norm. With the UAW representing nearly the entire auto industry, Reuther was the most powerful man in Detroit in the 1950s.

UAW President Walter Reuther (2nd from right), Brotherhood of Sleeping Car Porters President A. Philip Randolph (3rd from right), Martin Luther King (left side), and other civil rights leaders holding hands leading the August 1963 March on Washington for Jobs and Freedom

Nationally, he was perhaps the most visible union leader of his generation. In the 1960s Reuther turned his social vision toward the civil rights movement. He was one of the lead marchers in the 1963 March on Washington and gave a speech just before Martin Luther King's "I have a dream" speech. To the end he was trying to broaden the mainstream labor movement's "nickel-in-the-pay-envelope" philosophy: Reuther died in a plane crash in 1970 en route to a UAW worker education center he was helping build in northern Michigan. Reuther's vision for broader social and economic equality and justice, however, could never be achieved solely at the bargaining table, no matter how much bargaining power the UAW wielded. It was during the turbulent times of the early 1900s, when Mother Jones was associated with the specter of class warfare, that a labor leader could be the most dangerous woman in America. By the 1950s unions had been contained to the workplace, and despite his tremendous efforts, Walter Reuther could only be the most dangerous man in Detroit.

References: Nelson Lichtenstein, *The Most Dangerous Man in Detroit: Walter Reuther and the Fate of American Labor* (New York: Basic Books, 1995); John Barnard, *American Vanguard: The United Autoworkers during the Reuther Years, 1935–1970* (Detroit: Wayne State University Press, 2004); The quote is from Melvyn Dubofsky and Foster Rhea Dulles, *Labor in America: A History*, 8th ed. (Wheeling, IL: Harlan Davidson, 2010), p. 339.

the guise of rooting out communists during the beginnings of the Cold War. Allegedly communist-controlled unions were expelled from the CIO.[159] This led to raiding attempts as CIO unions tried to win bargaining rights in units represented by the expelled unions;[160] this raiding activity was in addition to the ongoing raids between AFL and CIO unions. Such raids consumed precious resources for little gain, and in 1955 the AFL and CIO reconciled. A single, united federation was born: the American Federation of Labor–Congress of Industrial Organizations (AFL–CIO).[161]

Public attention to the labor movement in the 1950s largely focused on allegations of union corruption—as captured by the classic 1954 movie *On the Waterfront*, in which Marlon Brando portrays a boxer wrestling with his guilt over providing muscle for a corrupt union boss on the New Jersey docks. Fears of union corruption and the presence of mafia-infiltrated local unions led to the passage of a major federal law (the Landrum–Griffin Act) in 1959, which will be discussed in the next chapter. The 1960s witnessed the start of another upsurge in union membership—this time among teachers, police, and other employees of various local, state, and federal governments.[162] As in the private sector, public sector workers' attempts to unionize to fight low wages, onerous working conditions, and other indignities date back to the early 1800s. Government employers fought back with yellow dog contracts and restrictive legislation. In 1959 Wisconsin passed the first law protecting public sector collective bargaining; since that time the federal government and a number of other states followed. As a result, public sector union density exploded and today many of the occupations with the highest level of union representation are in the public sector. The development of firefighter unions illustrates the trajectory of public sector unionism (see the accompanying "Public Sector Labor Relations" box). In contrast to this rise in public sector unionism, postwar U.S. union density in the private sector peaked at around 35 percent in the mid-1950s (recall Figure 1.4).

A Turbulent End to the 20th Century

For private sector unions, the remaining decades of the 20th century would be years of turbulence and decline (see Figure 3.5). One source of labor movement turbulence was the postwar civil rights movement. The question of race and ethnicity in the U.S. labor movement is a thorny one.[163] There is no question that African American and Mexican American workers faced pervasive discrimination and were often relegated to the most menial, dangerous, and low-paying jobs. Throughout the historical development of U.S. labor relations, there are examples where unions contributed to this problem either passively or actively, and other examples where unions fought to break down discriminatory practices. The AFL craft unions are well known for their history

FIGURE 3.5
A Time Line of Labor History between 1960 and 2000

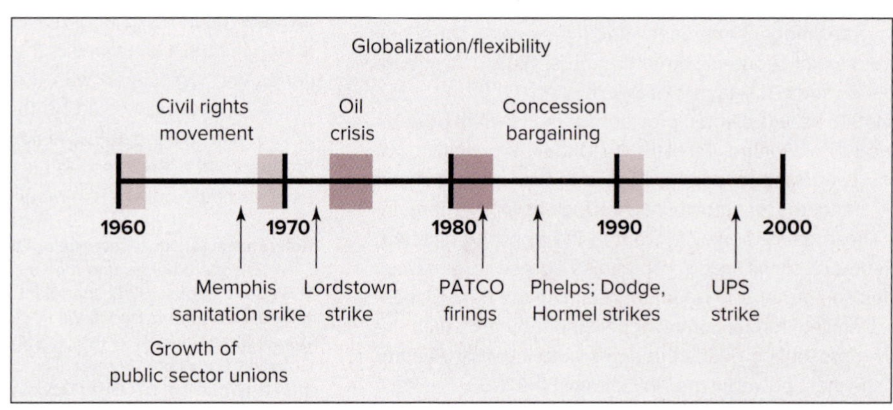

Note: Shading indicates economic recessions.

Labor Relations Application Public Sector Labor Relations: The Development of Firefighters' Unions

The development of public sector unions parallels that of private sector unions and reflects many of the same important themes, such as worker frustration and union success tied to the business cycle and public opinion. As an example, consider firefighters. Professional firefighters date back to the 1850s, when steam-powered pumps ended the need for numerous volunteers to pump water at a fire by hand. The first worker organizations among firefighters were mutual aid or benevolent societies in the late 1800s, in which workers would contribute money to a central fund to pay accident and death benefits to firefighters or their families.

The first firefighter union was established in Chicago in 1901, and it later affiliated with the AFL. During World War I labor shortages increased workers' leverage, and by 1918 one-quarter of the country's full-time firefighters were unionized. The unions started as locals and then in 1918 formed the International Association of Fire Fighters. Early issues that sparked workers to unionize included pay, working hours, and political favoritism. There were a variety of firefighter strikes during this period, but the most notorious public sector strike was by Boston police in 1919. The governor, Calvin Coolidge, who would become president of the United States, sent in the National Guard to end significant looting. As a result, public sector unionism was viewed negatively, and many jurisdictions outlawed public sector strikes, if not public sector unions entirely.

In Illinois the firefighter unions in some cities disbanded while others continued without legal protection. Firefighters, and other public sector employees, increasingly turned to political lobbying to win gains such as wage increases or safety improvements. For example, Illinois firefighters successfully lobbied for a state minimum wage law in 1937 and a state-mandated reduction in weekly work hours in 1941.

The private sector unionization wave during the New Deal of the 1930s spurred organizing among firefighters, but this was done without legal protection. Public sector unions therefore continued to depend on political power. Some states began passing laws to protect public sector unionization in the 1960s, but not Illinois. National public sector union membership grew significantly in this period. In Illinois—even without protective legislation—in the social turbulence of the late 1960s, firefighter frustration over wages and working conditions resulted in a number of strikes.

Without a regularized or legally sanctioned mechanism for settling disputes, conflicts continued. In one extreme case, firefighters in Normal, Illinois, went on strike for 56 days in 1978. The striking firefighters were sentenced to 42 days in jail for violating a restraining order, and the fire station was declared to be a work release center so that the firefighters spent half their time in jail and half their time on "work release" protecting the city against fires. After other strikes, including a 23-day strike in Chicago in 1980, Illinois passed a public sector collective bargaining law in 1985. As in the private sector, the development of public sector unionization followed a rocky path to stability. Today, over 60% of U.S. firefighters are unionized.

Reference: Michael G. Matejka, *Fiery Struggle: Illinois Fire FightersBuild a Union, 1901–1985*. (Chicago: Illinois Labor History Society, 2002).

of excluding African American workers, but even progressive CIO leaders like Walter Reuther had difficulties ending discriminatory practices that were embedded in rank-and-file workers and their local unions. Southern workplaces, in particular, remained largely segregated until the 1960s; at paper mills, for example, there were separate entrances, pay clocks, pay windows, bathrooms, water fountains, and cafeterias for blacks and whites.[164] From 1946 to 1953 the CIO aggressively tried to organize workers in the South, but this "Operation Dixie" failed partly because many Southern white workers refused to join together with African American workers.[165] Where unions did exist in the South, black workers were commonly segregated into Jim Crow locals with seniority ladders separate from white workers. As such, labor relations reflected larger societal patterns of discrimination.

During the civil rights movement in the 1950s and 1960s, the CIO's sit-down strikes of the 1930s inspired the sit-ins that desegregated Southern restaurants. While the AFL–CIO generally remained on the sidelines or helped the civil rights movement quietly, the Brotherhood of Sleeping Car Porters and the UAW contributed significant amounts of money and leadership. In fact, these two unions played instrumental roles in the 1963 March on Washington, famously remembered for Martin Luther King's "I have a dream" speech. The Civil Rights Act of 1964 outlawed discriminatory practices by both employers and unions, but issues of social and economic justice continue to be closely intertwined.[166] In Memphis, the 1968 killing of two African American sanitation workers by an unsafe garbage compactor unleashed years of pent-up frustration over racism and oppression, and over 1,000 black sanitation workers went on strike. For 2 months participants in the **Memphis sanitation strike** demanded not only improved wages and working conditions but also civil rights and respect—goals immortalized by their signs, which said simply, "I am a man." The strike was a major civil rights event that included peaceful marches and violent race riots. Martin Luther King was in Memphis supporting the strike in April 1968 when he was assassinated, and the city finally compromised with the strikers 2 weeks later. The workers won improved wages, promotions on the basis of seniority rather than racism, a nondiscrimination clause, and recognition for their union.[167]

Another source of postwar turbulence for the U.S. labor movement was the economy. The stability of the mass manufacturing system was undermined by the oil crisis of the 1970s followed by increased globalization and financialization (see Chapters 10 and 11). Intense competitive pressures resulted in a period of concession bargaining in the early 1980s. Under the threat of significant job loss, many unions agreed to wage freezes or cuts, benefit reductions, and looser work rules; the most visible examples were in the auto and steel industries.[168] More generally, the 1980s are believed to represent the return of a much more adversarial labor–management climate. In 1981 President Reagan fired the air traffic controllers during the illegal **PATCO strike** and hired replacement workers (see the "Ethics in Action" feature at the end of this chapter). To many observers the PATCO strike emboldened private sector employers to take a hard-line approach with their unions, though the true linkage may never be known.[169] With or without the PATCO strike as a model, a number of bitter strikes in the 1980s and 1990s involved management's use of permanent strike replacements: the Phelps-Dodge copper strike in Arizona (1983), the Hormel meatpacking strike in Minnesota (1985), the International Paper strike in Maine (1987), the Greyhound bus strike (1990), the Ravenswood aluminum strike in West Virginia (1990), the Bridgestone-Firestone tire strike in Illinois (1995), and the Detroit newspaper strike (1995), to name just a few.[170] Harkening back to the earlier era of the Pinkertons, the provision of antiunion consultants, armed guards, and surveillance forces continues to be big business.[171] Many of these more recent strikes ended in defeat for the strikers, though in 1997 the Teamsters mobilized rank-and-file militancy, built public support for the plight of part-time workers, and won a highly visible 15-day strike of 185,000 United Parcel Service workers.

Frustration with the direction of the labor movement even resulted in a rare contested election for the leadership of the AFL–CIO. In 1995 John Sweeney, president of the Service Employees International Union (SEIU), and a slate of insurgents defeated the longtime officials selected by outgoing AFL–CIO president, Lane Kirkland. Sweeney's subsequent efforts to shake up the AFL–CIO and its affiliate unions included devoting significant resources to union organizing and political mobilization—including a program called Union Summer, in which college students spend a summer working on organizing campaigns.

LABOR RELATIONS IN THE 21ST CENTURY

The challenging times of the late 20th century have continued for labor unions into the 21st century (see Figure 3.6). Globalization continues to undermine labor's bargaining power by putting domestic workers into competition with low-cost alternatives. Downward pressures on labor costs are now magnified by the rise of financialization in which corporations

FIGURE 3.6
A Time Line of Labor History in the 21st Century

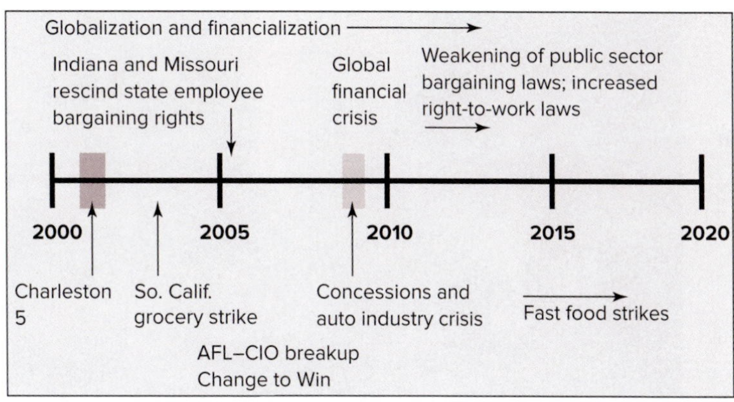

Note: Shading indicates economic recessions.

are increasingly driven by financial concerns such as boosting stock prices to satisfy Wall Street expectations and increase the value of executive stock options, and in which corporations and private equity firms seek profits through financial transactions rather than through the delivery of valuable goods and services. And private-sector union density has dropped to less than 10 percent.

Sharp increases in the costs of employee benefits are also a problem in many industries. For example, with the threat of Walmart moving into the southern California grocery industry, the unionized grocery chains demanded significant cuts in health insurance benefits. When negotiations broke down and Vons workers went on strike in October 2003, the other grocery chains locked out their employees, and the strike/lockout by 60,000 workers dragged on for 4 months before the union agreed to the industry's two-tiered wage and benefit system (subsequently ended in the next negotiating round in 2007). In 2007 Ford, General Motors, and Chrysler transferred their liability for retiree health care obligations to the UAW by establishing a $50 billion fund to be managed by the UAW. This was a risky move by the UAW, but it was seen as preventing the complete loss of benefits that might have occurred if the automakers attempted to shed these obligations in bankruptcy court. The UAW agreed to more concessions in 2009 when the automakers received federal bailout money and filed for bankruptcy; in return, the UAW's health fund now owns more than 15 percent of General Motors and more than 50 percent of Chrysler. In 2012, American Airlines and the maker of Twinkies filed for bankruptcy and sought significant wage and pension cuts from their unions. Even very high-paid employees are not immune to pressures for concessions in a weak economic environment, as illustrated by the 18-week National Football League (NFL) lockout and the 23-week National Basketball Association (NBA) lockout that occurred during 2011. Various companies and unions react differently to such tremendous pressures, and labor relations practices have become more divergent. Some labor–management relationships have become more adversarial, whereas others are trying to create stronger union–management partnerships (see Chapter 10).[172]

In the public sector, union density continues to hover around 35 percent (recall Figure 1.4). Public sector unionism, therefore, is one of the labor movement's strongest areas and cannot be ignored in contemporary labor relations.[173] But even here labor unions now face a challenging environment because public sector unions are seen by conservatives as a roadblock to reducing the size of government.[174] In 2005, newly elected Republican governors in Indiana and Missouri rescinded bargaining rights for state employees. In 2011, a wave of proposed bills in state legislatures sought to weaken or restrict public

On April 15, 2015, fast-food workers held rallies in over 200 U.S. cities for higher pay and union rights.

sector unions. One of the most dramatic of these was enacted in Wisconsin, but not until after the state experienced several weeks of intense worker and union protests. Wisconsin Governor Walker's Budget Repair Bill repealed collective-bargaining rights for some public sector employees, limited collective bargaining for other employees to wages, prohibited dues collection through paycheck deduction, and required annual votes of unionized workers to maintain certification. As another example of the turbulent labor relations environment in the public sector, a newly enacted law in Ohio that would also have limited public sector bargaining rights was overturned by voters. In 2015, the Nevada legislature debated proposed legislation that critics dubbed the "union armageddon" bill because of the extent to which it would have restricted public sector collective bargaining. With the election of Donald Trump in 2016, Republican control of the White House, Senate, and House of Representatives might also bring about legislative and other changes unfavorable to labor unions in the private and public sectors.

The economic and political environment continues to pressure the labor movement to change. Union mergers have washed away many historical distinctions between craft and industrial unions.[175] Today diverse occupations and industries are frequently represented in a single general union. The United Steelworkers union represents not only steelworkers but also employees across the entire manufacturing spectrum plus nurses, public school food service workers, and public sector clerical, technical, and professional employees. The Teamsters union literally represents occupations from A (airline pilots) to Z (zookeepers). As a result, general unionism has largely replaced craft unionism and industrial unionism.

Online Exploration Exercise: Search online for events in labor history that occurred in your city, state, or region. How are these events consistent with and/or different from the major themes of the time periods of labor history outlined in this chapter? For inspiration, see *www.chicagolabortrail.org/*.

Within the AFL–CIO, there have also been debates over how to reverse labor's declining influence, with some unions favoring more emphasis on organizing and less emphasis on political activity. In fact, divisions on this issue led seven large unions that favored organizing over political activity to break-away in 2005 and form a new labor federation, the Change to Win federation. As of 2016, however, only SEIU, the Teamsters, and the United Farm Workers remained in Change to Win. The AFL-CIO also created a community organization called Working America to assist nonunion workers in advocating for their rights through political mobilization and by increasing awareness of steps workers can take to be more empowered on their jobs (see *www.fixmyjob.com*). Whether the structural changes in the labor movement can overcome the effects of globalization, financialization, and other environmental factors is a major question for the future of U.S. labor relations.

Despite these challenges for the labor movement, millions of productive unionized workers go to work each day protected by unionized contracts negotiated without strikes, and there are pockets of vibrancy. SEIU has organized thousands of health care workers, including home care workers. Some unions have reached out to immigrant workers and incorporated their languages and cultural traditions.[176] In addition to the AFL-CIO's Working America, unions are also increasingly supporting nonunion workers through what has been called "alt-labor"—worker centers like the Restaurant Opportunities Center and other organizations that seek gains through education, protest, lobbying, lawsuits, and other means, especially in situations where formal union recognition is very difficult to achieve such as in the fast-food industry.[177] Perhaps the most visible tactic is the one-day strike/protest to create publicity and worker solidarity, such as the series of fast-food strikes in conjunction with the Fight for $15 starting in 2012. This initiative has resulted in employers increasing wages and lawmakers raising minimum wages.[178] There is also the potential for greater international labor solidarity. In one notable case where labor rights are inseparable from civil rights, police overzealously broke up a longshoring union's protest against the use of nonunion dockworkers in Charleston, South Carolina, in 2001 and arrested five protesters. This union is the state's most powerful black organization, and a nasty mix of racism and conservative political ambition caused the South Carolina attorney general to prosecute the "Charleston 5" for trumped-up rioting charges. Labor activists from around the globe came to the aid of the Charleston 5—such as when Spanish dockworkers put pressure on a Danish shipping company that was trying to avoid the union in Charleston—and the serious charges were dropped.[179]

In conclusion, the largest unions and watershed strikes in various eras often involve traditional blue-collar occupations—railroad workers in the 1870s, skilled craft steelworkers in the 1890s, coal miners in the early 1900s, and semiskilled auto assemblers in the 1930s—but the history of U.S. labor is not strictly a blue-collar affair. During the 20th century waitresses, actors, university clerical workers and professors, teachers, hotel and casino workers, journalists, athletes, agricultural workers, nurses, and airline pilots unionized.[180] Even doctors, university teaching assistants, and nude models have tried to form unions. The details may differ, but the fundamental reasons are universal: to seek greater equity and increased voice in the workplace through collective action with coworkers. Studying labor history reveals the various forces that may cause workers to seek unionization and the wide-ranging organizational and policy responses. And thus the historical record provides a rich foundation for understanding the development of the U.S. labor relations system and options for its future.

Key Terms

National Labor Union, *68*
Great Uprising of 1877, *68*
Knights of Labor, *69*
uplift unionism, *71*
Haymarket Tragedy, *72*
American Federation of Labor, *72*
business unionism, *73*
craft unionism, *73*
exclusive jurisdiction, *73*
Homestead strike, *74*
Pullman strike, *75*
Industrial Workers of the World, *79*
revolutionary unionism, *79*
open shop movement, *83*
welfare capitalism, *86*
industrial unionism, *89*
General Motors sit-down strike, *91*
Congress of Industrial Organizations, *92*
Great Strike Wave of 1945–46, *94*
Memphis sanitation strike, *98*
PATCO strike, *98*

Reflection Questions

1. *Nonunion Application.* The history of labor relations and the history of human resource management are inseparable. Nonunion managers can therefore learn a lot about what workers want and about the pros and cons of alternative human resource management strategies by understanding labor history. Reflect back upon the events and labor organizations presented in this chapter and identify some reactions of workers and of labor unions to employers' practices and strategies. Next, describe how these reactions inspired a new generation of human resource management strategies.
2. How are the lyrics of "Solidarity Forever" (p. 83) consistent with the IWW's beliefs? How is it ironic that today's mainstream unions have adopted this song as their own? What parts of the lyrics would today's mainstream unions agree with?
3. Look at the reasons listed by employers for being nonunion in the open shop handout in Figure 3.3. How would an AFL leader have responded to these reasons? Is the open shop movement consistent with today's human resource management approach?
4. Describe how the Knights of Labor, the American Federation of Labor, and the Industrial Workers of the World differed in their views of efficiency, equity, and voice. How about employers? What were their views of efficiency, equity, and voice during the open shop movement? Did these views change during the period of welfare capitalism?
5. The AFL, IWW, and CIO were all created out of frustration with the existing dominant form of unionism at the time. Explain. What does this imply about the future of U.S. unionism?
6. It's been written, "The attempt of persons to understand the forces remaking their world and, by organization, to control them, constitutes, indeed, the major motif of the social history of the late nineteenth century."[181] Describe how this statement applies to workers and their unions in different periods of labor history. How were employers more successful than employees in controlling these forces through creating and shaping their organizations?

Ethics in Action The PATCO Strike

Arguably the most significant U.S. labor relations event in the latter part of the 20th century was the failed strike by air traffic controllers belonging to the Professional Air Traffic Controllers Organization (PATCO) in 1981. Against a backdrop of long-term private sector union membership decline and robust unionism in the public sector, it is perhaps appropriate that this event occurred in the public sector: Air traffic controllers are U.S. federal government employees who work for the Federal Aviation Administration (FAA), a government agency. As we will discuss in Chapter 4, it is illegal for unions of federal government employees to strike.

Being an air traffic controller is stressful; a mistake can cause a plane crash. Controllers first formed a union in 1968—a common time for the formation of public sector unions. During the 1970s PATCO fought with the FAA over wages and working conditions, and several times engaged in coordinated sick-outs because striking was illegal. In June 1981 PATCO negotiators tentatively accepted a new contract that (if approved by Congress) would give substantial pay raises, increased severance pay, and an enhanced voice in operating and safety policy making. The membership rejected this agreement. President Reagan warned that strikers would be discharged because federal sector strikes are illegal; but on August 3, 1981, PATCO members went on strike. Military controllers, retirees, supervisors, and air traffic controllers who did not strike were put to work by the FAA, and after 10 days the system was functioning at about 70 percent of normal capacity. Four hours after the start of the strike, President Reagan gave the strikers 48 hours to return to work or be fired. Over 11,000 did not return and were fired. PATCO was decertified.

There are two competing views on why the PATCO membership struck. One view is that PATCO figured that a disruption of air traffic would force Congress to grant it the legal right to strike and to negotiate wages (which is also illegal in the federal sector), but the union leadership blundered by overestimating its power. As such, the workers foolishly turned down a generous contract. The alternative view is that the workers were striking out of frustration with autocratic, even paramilitary, FAA supervisors and managers. As such, the Reagan administration is also to blame for taking an exceptionally hard line during negotiations and the strike. In either case the firing of the striking air traffic controllers was a public and devastating defeat for organized labor. By many accounts (but not all), the failed PATCO strike established an antiunion climate in which it became acceptable for private sector employers to aggressively weaken or break unions during the 1980s and 1990s.

As a footnote, the new controllers voted to unionize in 1987 and are now represented by the National Air Traffic Controllers Association.

QUESTIONS

1. Was it ethically acceptable for the air traffic controllers to strike?
2. Was it ethically acceptable for President Reagan to fire the striking air traffic controllers?

Note: These questions do not ask whether the actions were legal or illegal—that issue is clear. The question is whether the actions were ethical.

References: Herbert R. Northrup, "The Rise and Demise of PATCO," *Industrial and Labor Relations Review* 37 (January 1984), pp. 167–84; Richard W. Hurd and Jill K. Kriesky, "Communications: 'The Rise and Demise of PATCO' Reconstructed," *Industrial and Labor Relations Review* 40 (October 1986), pp. 115–22.

End Notes

1. Nelson Lichtenstein et al., *Who Built America? Working People and the Nation's Economy, Politics, Culture, and Society,* Volume 2 (New York: Worth Publishing, 2000); James Wolfinger, *Running the Rails: Capital and Labor in the Philadelphia Transit Industry* (Ithaca, NY: Cornell University Press, 2016).
2. Melvyn Dubofsky and Foster Rhea Dulles, *Labor in America: A History,* 8th ed. (Wheeling, IL: Harlan Davidson, 2010).
3. Joseph G. Rayback, *A History of American Labor* (New York: Free Press, 1966).
4. Lichtenstein et al., *Who Built America?;* William Serrin, *Homestead: The Glory and Tragedy of an American Steel Town* (New York: Vintage Books, 1992).
5. Sidney Pollard, *The Genesis of Modern Management: A Study of the Industrial Revolution in Great Britain* (Cambridge, MA: Harvard University Press, 1965); E. P. Thompson, "Time, Work-Discipline, and Industrial Capitalism," *Past and Present* 38 (December 1967), pp. 56–97.
6. Philip S. Foner, *First Facts of American Labor* (New York: Holmes and Meier, 1984).
7. Rayback, *A History of American Labor.*
8. Dubofsky and Dulles, *Labor in America.*
9. Rayback, *A History of American Labor.*
10. Jonathan Grossman, *William Sylvis, Pioneer of American Labor* (New York: Columbia University Press, 1945).
11. Dubofsky and Dulles, *Labor in America.*
12. Dubofsky and Dulles, *Labor in America*; Grossman, *William Sylvis, Pioneer of American Labor*; Rayback, *A History of American Labor.*
13. Cedric de Leon, *The Origins of Right to Work: Antilabor Democracy in Nineteenth-Century Chicago* (Ithaca, NY: Cornell University Press, 2015); Paul A. Gilje, *Rioting in America* (Bloomington: Indiana University Press, 1996), p. 3. Wolfinger, *Running the Rails.*
14. Richard O. Boyer and Herbert M. Morais, *Labor's Untold Story* (Pittsburgh: United Electrical, Radio, and Machine Workers of America, 1955); Kevin Kenny, *Making Sense of the Molly Maguires* (New York: Oxford University Press, 1998).
15. Jeremy Brecher, *Strike!* (Boston: South End Press, 1972); Dubofsky and Dulles, *Labor in America*; Philip S. Foner, *The Great Uprising of 1877* (New York: Monad Press, 1977); Rayback, *A History of American Labor.*
16. Rayback, *A History of American Labor.*
17. Brecher, *Strike!*; Foner, *The Great Uprising of 1877.*
18. Dubofsky and Dulles, *Labor in America.*
19. Charles Perrow, *Organizing America: Wealth, Power, and the Origins of Corporate Capitalism* (Princeton, NJ: Princeton University Press, 2002), p. 179.
20. Jack Beatty, *Age of Betrayal: The Triumph of Money in America, 1865–1900* (New York: Knopf, 2007), p. 234.
21. David O. Stowell, *Streets, Railroads, and the Great Strike of 1877* (Chicago: University of Chicago Press, 1999).
22. Gregory S. Kealey and Bryan D. Palmer, *Dreaming of What Might Be: The Knights of Labor in Ontario, 1880–1900* (Cambridge: Cambridge University Press, 1982); Rayback, *A History of American Labor.*
23. Kealey and Palmer, *Dreaming of What Might Be,* p. 286.
24. Norman J. Ware, *The Labor Movement in the United States 1869–1895: A Study in Democracy* (New York: D. Appleton, 1929).
25. Philip Taft, *Organized Labor in American History* (New York: Harper and Row, 1964).
26. Robert Franklin Hoxie, *Trade Unionism in the United States* (New York: D. Appleton, 1917), p. 47.
27. Quoted in T. V. Powderly, *Thirty Years of Labor: 1859 to 1889* (Columbus, OH: Excelsior Publishing House, 1889), p. 163.
28. Ware, *The Labor Movement in the United States 1869–1895.*
29. Melton Alonza McLaurin, *The Knights of Labor in the South* (Westport, CT: Greenwood Press, 1978).
30. Hoyt N. Wheeler, *The Future of the American Labor Movement* (Cambridge: Cambridge University Press, 2002).
31. Kealey and Palmer, *Dreaming of What Might Be*; Ware, *The Labor Movement in the United States 1869–1895.*

32. McLaurin, *The Knights of Labor in the South;* Ware, *The Labor Movement in the United States 1869–1895.*
33. Ware, *The Labor Movement in the United States 1869–1895.*
34. Wheeler, *The Future of the American Labor Movement.*
35. Clayton Sinyai, *Schools of Democracy: A Political History of the American Labor Movement* (Ithaca, NY: Cornell University Press, 2006); Josiah Bartlett Lambert, *"If the Workers Took a Notion": The Right to Strike and American Political Development* (Ithaca, NY: Cornell University Press, 2005).
36. Ware, *The Labor Movement in the United States 1869–1895.*
37. Dubofsky and Dulles, *Labor in America*; Ware, *The Labor Movement in the United States 1869–1895.*
38. John R. Commons, *History of Labour in the United States,* Volume II (New York: Macmillan, 1918).
39. Ware, *The Labor Movement in the United States 1869–1895.*
40. Dubofsky and Dulles, *Labor in America.*
41. Paul Avrich, *The Haymarket Tragedy* (Princeton, NJ: Princeton University Press, 1984), p. 260.
42. Dubofsky and Dulles, *Labor in America*; Ware, *The Labor Movement in the United States 1869–1895.*
43. Dubofsky and Dulles, *Labor in America*; Philip Taft, *The A.F. of L. in the Time of Gompers* (New York: Harper and Brothers, 1957).
44. Dubofsky and Dulles, *Labor in America.*
45. Taft, *The A.F. of L. in the Time of Gompers.*
46. Dubofsky and Dulles, *Labor in America*; Taft, *The A.F. of L. in the Time of Gompers.*
47. Hoxie, *Trade Unionism in the United States.*
48. Samuel Gompers, *Seventy Years of Life and Labor* (New York: E.P. Dutton, 1925), p. 286.
49. Dubofsky and Dulles, *Labor in America.*
50. Taft, *The A.F. of L. in the Time of Gompers.*
51. Daniel Nelson, *Managers and Workers: Origins of the Twentieth Century Factory System in the United States, 1880–1920,* 2nd ed. (Madison: University of Wisconsin Press, 1994); Rayback, *A History of American Labor.*
52. David Montgomery, *Workers' Control in America: Studies in the History of Work, Technology, and Labor Struggles* (Cambridge: Cambridge University Press, 1979); Nelson, *Managers and Workers.*
53. Quoted in Montgomery, *Workers' Control in America,* p. 9.
54. Selig Perlman, *A Theory of the Labor Movement* (New York: Macmillan, 1928).
55. Montgomery, *Workers' Control in America.*
56. Sinyai, *Schools of Democracy.*
57. Montgomery, *Workers' Control in America*; Nelson, *Managers and Workers*; Christopher L. Tomlins, *The State and the Unions: Labor Relations, Law, and the Organized Labor Movement, 1880–1960* (Cambridge: Cambridge University Press, 1985).
58. Brecher, *Strike!*; Serrin, *Homestead.*
59. Brecher, *Strike!*; Serrin, *Homestead.*
60. Serrin, *Homestead.*
61. David Montgomery, *The Fall of the House of Labor* (Cambridge: Cambridge University Press, 1987); Serrin, *Homestead.*
62. Susan Eleanor Hirsch, *After the Strike: A Century of Labor Struggle at Pullman* (Urbana: University of Illinois Press, 2003).
63. Brecher, *Strike!*; Dubofsky and Dulles, *Labor in America.*
64. David Ray Papke, *The Pullman Case: The Clash of Labor and Capital in Industrial America* (Lawrence: University Press of Kansas, 1999).
65. Brecher, *Strike!*; Dubofsky and Dulles, *Labor in America*; Hirsch, *After the Strike.*
66. J. Bradford DeLong, "Robber Barons," in Anders Aslund and Tatyana Maleva (eds.), *Series of Lectures on Economics: Leading World Experts at the Carnegie Moscow Center* (Moscow: Carnegie Endowment for International Peace, 2002), pp. 179–208.
67. James R. Green, *The World of the Worker: Labor in Twentieth-Century America* (New York: Hill and Wang, 1980).

68. Matthew Josephson, *The Robber Barons: The Great American Capitalists, 1861–1901* (New York: Harcourt, Brace, and Company, 1934), p. 378; Lichtenstein et al., *Who Built America?*, p. 176.

69. Melvyn Dubofsky, *Industrialism and the American Worker, 1865–1920*, 2nd ed. (Arlington Heights, IL: Harlan Davidson, 1985); Rayback, *A History of American Labor.*

70. Eliot Jones, *The Trust Problem in the United States* (New York: Macmillan, 1923); Serrin, *Homestead.*

71. David Brody, *Workers in Industrial America: Essays on the Twentieth Century Struggle* (New York: Oxford University Press, 1980).

72. Robert Kanigel, *The One Best Way: Frederick Winslow Taylor and the Enigma of Efficiency* (New York, Penguin, 1997); Montgomery, *Workers' Control in America*; Nelson, *Managers and Workers*; Frederick Winslow Taylor, *The Principles of Scientific Management* (New York: Harper and Brothers, 1911); David Roediger and Elizabeth Esch, *The Production of Difference: Race and the Management of Labor in U.S. History* (New York: Oxford University Press, 2012).

73. Philip S. Foner, *Organized Labor and the Black Worker, 1619–1981* (New York: International Publishers, 1981); William H. Harris, *The Harder We Run: Black Workers since the Civil War* (New York: Oxford University Press, 1982); Taft, *The A.F. of L. in the Time of Gompers.*

74. Simon Cordery, *Mother Jones: Raising Cain and Consciousness* (Albuquerque: University of New Mexico Press, 2010); Elliot J. Gorn, *Mother Jones: The Most Dangerous Woman in America* (New York: Hill and Wang, 2001).

75. Foner, *Organized Labor and the Black Worker*; Harris, *The Harder We Run.*

76. Nick Salvatore, *Eugene V. Debs: Citizen and Socialist* (Urbana: University of Illinois Press, 1982).

77. Lambert, *If the Workers Took a Notion*.

78. J. Anthony Lukas, *Big Trouble: A Murder in a Small Western Town Sets Off a Struggle for the Soul of America* (New York: Simon and Schuster, 1997), p. 233.

79. Hoxie, *Trade Unionism in the United States,* p. 48.

80. Melvyn Dubofsky, *We Shall Be All: A History of the Industrial Workers of the World,* abridged ed. (Urbana: University of Illinois Press, 2000); Salvatore, *Eugene V. Debs.*

81. Dubofsky, *We Shall Be All*; Patrick Renshaw, *The Wobblies: The Story of Syndicalism in the United States* (Garden City, NY: Doubleday, 1967).

82. Dubofsky, *We Shall Be All,* p. 90.

83. Ralph Darlington, *Syndicalism and the Transition to Communism: An International Comparative Analysis* (Aldershot, Hampshire: Ashgate, 2008).

84. Joyce L. Kornbush (ed.), *Rebel Voices: An I.W.W. Anthology* (Ann Arbor: University of Michigan Press, 1964).

85. Dubofsky, *We Shall Be All*; Dubofsky and Dulles, *Labor in America*; Anne Huber Tripp, *The I.W.W. and the Paterson Silk Strike of 1913* (Urbana: University of Illinois Press, 1987).

86. Renshaw, *The Wobblies.*

87. Dubofsky, *We Shall Be All.*

88. Dubofsky, *We Shall Be All*; Renshaw, *The Wobblies.*

89. Dubofsky, *We Shall Be All*; Renshaw, *The Wobblies*; Jonathan D. Rosenblum, *Copper Crucible: How the Arizona Miners' Strike of 1983 Recast Labor–Management Relations in America* (Ithaca, NY: ILR Press, 1998).

90. Dubofsky and Dulles, *Labor in America*; Immanuel Ness, "Workers' Direct Action and Factory Control in the United States," in Immanuel Ness and Dario Azzellini (eds.), *Ours to Master and to Own: Workers' Control from the Commune to the Present* (Chicago: Haymarket Books, 2011), pp. 302–21; Immanuel Ness (ed.), *New Forms of Worker Organization: The Syndicalist and Autonomist Restoration of Class-Struggle Unionism* (Oakland: PM Press, 2014).

91. Montgomery, *Workers' Control in America.*

92. Hirsch, *After the Strike*; William Millikan, *A Union against Unions: The Minneapolis Citizens Alliance and Its Fight against Organized Labor, 1903–1947* (St. Paul: Minnesota Historical Society, 2001).

93. Irving Bernstein, *The Lean Years: A History of the American Worker, 1920–1933* (Boston: Houghton Mifflin, 1960); Dubofsky and Dulles, *Labor in America*; Taft, *Organized Labor in American History.*

94. Thomas Klug, "Employers' Strategies in the Detroit Labor Market, 1900–1929," in Nelson Lichtenstein and Stephen Meyer (eds.), *On the Line: Essays in the History of Auto Work* (Urbana: University of Illinois Press, 1989), pp. 42–72; Millikan, *A Union against Unions.*

95. Millikan, *A Union against Unions.*

96. Dubofsky and Dulles, *Labor in America.*
97. Roediger and Esch, *The Production of Difference*.
98. Hirsch, *After the Strike.*
99. Stephen H. Norwood, *Strikebreaking and Intimidation: Mercenaries and Masculinity in Twentieth-Century America* (Chapel Hill: University of North Carolina Press, 2002); Robert Michael Smith, *From Blackjacks to Briefcases: A History of Commercialized Strikebreaking and Unionbusting in the United States* (Athens: Ohio University Press, 2003).
100. Lambert, *If the Workers Took a Notion.*
101. Dubofsky and Dulles, *Labor in America*; Gorn, *Mother Jones.*
102. H.M. Gitelman, *Legacy of the Ludlow Massacre: A Chapter in American Industrial Relations* (Philadelphia: University of Pennsylvania Press, 1988), p. 15.
103. Dubofsky and Dulles, *Labor in America*; Gitelman, *Legacy of the Ludlow Massacre*; Thomas G. Andrews, *Killing for Coal: America's Deadliest Labor War* (Cambridge: Harvard University Press, 2008).
104. Lichtenstein et al., *Who Built America?*; Joseph E. Slater, *Public Workers: Government Employee Unions, the Law, and the State, 1900–1962* (Ithaca, NY: Cornell University Press, 2004).
105. Robert Shogan, *The Battle of Blair Mountain: The Story of America's Largest Labor Uprising* (Boulder, CO: Westview Press, 2004).
106. Sanford M. Jacoby, *Employing Bureaucracy: Managers, Unions, and the Transformation of Work in American Industry, 1900–1945* (New York: Columbia University Press, 1985); Nelson, *Managers and Workers.*
107. Bernstein, *The Lean Years*; Lizabeth Cohen, *Making a New Deal: Industrial Workers in Chicago, 1919–1939* (Cambridge: Cambridge University Press, 1990); Jacoby, *Employing Bureaucracy*; Sanford M. Jacoby, *Modern Manors: Welfare Capitalism since the New Deal* (Princeton: Princeton University Press, 1997); Frank Koller, *Spark: How Old-Fashioned Values Drive a Twenty-First-Century Corporation* (New York: PublicAffairs, 2010); Gerald Zahavi, *Workers, Managers and Welfare Capitalism: The Shoeworkers and Tanners of Endicott Johnson, 1890–1950* (Urbana: University of Illinois Press, 1988).
108. Bruce E. Kaufman, *Managing the Human Factor: The Early Years of Human Resource Management in American Industry* (Ithaca, NY: Cornell University Press, 2008); David Fairris, *Shopfloor Matters: Labor–Management Relations in Twentieth-Century American Manufacturing* (London: Routledge, 1997).
109. Dubofsky and Dulles, *Labor in America*; Bernstein, *The Lean Years*; Wolfinger, *Running the Rails.*
110. Cohen, *Making a New Deal*; Jennifer Klein, *For All These Rights: Business, Labor, and the Shaping of America's Public–Private Welfare State* (Princeton, NJ: Princeton University Press, 2003).
111. Gitelman, *Legacy of the Ludlow Massacre*; Bruce E. Kaufman, "The Case for the Company Union," *Labor History* 41 (August 2000), pp. 321–50; John D. Rockefeller, Jr., *The Personal Relation in Industry* (New York: Boni and Liveright, 1923).
112. Bernstein, *The Lean Years*; Dubofsky and Dulles, *Labor in America.*
113. Hirsch, *After the Strike.*
114. Irving Bernstein, *A Caring Society: The New Deal, the Worker, and the Great Depression* (Boston: Houghton Mifflin, 1985); Lichtenstein et al., *Who Built America?*; Cass R. Sunstein, *The Second Bill of Rights: FDR's Unfinished Revolution and Why We Need It More Than Ever* (New York: Basic Books, 2004).
115. Jacoby, *Modern Manors*; Chiaki Moriguchi, "Did American Welfare Capitalists Breach Their Implicit Contracts during the Great Depression? Preliminary Findings from Company-Level Data," *Industrial and Labor Relations Review* 59 (October 2005), pp. 51–81.
116. David M. Kennedy, *Freedom from Fear: The American People in Depression and War, 1929–1945* (New York: Oxford University Press, 1999), p. 98; Lichtenstein et al., *Who Built America?*, p. 393; Sunstein, *The Second Bill of Rights.*
117. Dubofsky and Dulles, *Labor in America.*
118. Irving Bernstein, *Turbulent Years: A History of the American Worker, 1933–1941* (Boston: Houghton Mifflin, 1970); Brecher, *Strike!*; Philip A. Korth and Margaret R. Beegle, *I Remember Like Today: The Auto-Lite Strike of 1934* (East Lansing: Michigan State University Press, 1988).
119. Bernstein, *Turbulent Years*; Philip Korth, *Minneapolis Teamsters Strike of 1934* (East Lansing: Michigan State University Press, 1995); Millikan, *A Union against Unions.*

120. Bernstein, *Turbulent Years*; Brecher, *Strike!*; Bruce Nelson, *Workers on the Waterfront: Seamen, Longshoremen, and Unionism in the 1930s* (Urbana: University of Illinois Press, 1988); David F. Selvin, *A Terrible Anger: The 1934 Waterfront and General Strikes in San Francisco* (Detroit: Wayne State University Press, 1996).
121. Bernstein, *Turbulent Years*; Brecher, *Strike!*; Janet Irons, *Testing the New Deal: The General Textile Strike of 1934 in the American South* (Urbana: University of Illinois Press, 2000); John A. Salmond, *The General Textile Strike of 1934: From Maine to Alabama* (Columbia: University of Missouri Press, 2002).
122. Vincent J. Roscigno and William F. Danaher, *The Voice of Southern Labor: Radio, Music, and Textile Strikes, 1929–1934* (Minneapolis: University of Minnesota Press, 2004).
123. Bernstein, *Turbulent Years.*
124. Bernstein, *Turbulent Years,* p. 353.
125. David Brody, *Steelworkers in America: The Nonunion Era* (Cambridge: Harvard University Press, 1960); David Brody, *Labor in Crisis: The Steel Strike of 1919* (Philadelphia: J. B. Lippincott, 1965).
126. Gorn, *Mother Jones,* p. 193.
127. Taft, *The A.F. of L. in the Time of Gompers.*
128. Steve Fraser, "Dress Rehearsal for the New Deal: Shop-Floor Insurgents, Political Elites, and Industrial Democracy in the Amalgamated Clothing Workers," in Michael H. Frisch and Daniel J. Walkowitz (eds.), *Working-Class America: Essays on Labor, Community, and American Society* (Urbana: University of Illinois Press, 1983), pp. 212–55.
129. Taft, *The A.F. of L. in the Time of Gompers*; Philip Taft, *The A.F. of L. from the Death of Gompers to the Merger* (New York: Harper and Brothers, 1959).
130. Bernstein, *Turbulent Years*; Dubofsky and Dulles, *Labor in America*; Taft, *The A.F. of L. from the Death of Gompers to the Merger.*
131. Cohen, *Making a New Deal,* p. 321.
132. Walter Galenson, *The CIO Challenge to the AFL: A History of the American Labor Movement, 1925–1941* (Cambridge: Harvard University Press, 1960).
133. Jerold S. Auerbach, *Labor and Liberty: The LaFollette Committee and the New Deal* (Indianapolis: Bobbs-Merrill, 1966).
134. Norwood, *Strikebreaking and Intimidation.*
135. Smith, *From Blackjacks to Briefcases.*
136. Norwood, *Strikebreaking and Intimidation.*
137. Bernstein, *Turbulent Years*; Brecher, *Strike!*; Sidney Fine, *Sit-down: The General Motors Strike of 1936–1937* (Ann Arbor: University of Michigan Press, 1969); John Barnard, *American Vanguard: The United Autoworkers during the Reuther Years, 1935–1970* (Detroit: Wayne State University Press, 2004).
138. Sol Dollinger and Genora Johnson Dollinger, *Not Automatic: Women and the Left in the Forging of the Auto Workers' Union* (New York: Monthly Review Press, 2000).
139. Paul F. Clark, Peter Gottlieb, and Donald Kennedy (eds.), *Forging a Union of Steel: Philip Murray, SWOC, and the United Steelworkers* (Ithaca, NY: ILR Press, 1987).
140. Bernstein, *Turbulent Years.*
141. From the La Follette Committee's investigation of Youngstown Sheet and Tube; see United States Senate, Subcommittee of the Committee on Education and Labor, *Violations of Free Speech and Rights of Labor,* Part 27 (Washington, DC: U.S. Government Printing Office, 1939), pp. 11393–4.
142. Michael Dennis, *The Memorial Day Massacre and the Movement for Industrial Democracy* (New York: Palgrave Macmillan, 2010).
143. Galenson, *The CIO Challenge to the AFL,* p. 585.
144. Zaragosa Vargas, *Labor Rights Are Civil Rights: Mexican American Workers in Twentieth Century America* (Princeton, NJ: Princeton University Press, 2005).
145. Dubofsky and Dulles, *Labor in America,* p. 282.
146. Cohen, *Making a New Deal*; Nelson Lichtenstein, *The Most Dangerous Man in Detroit: Walter Reuther and the Fate of American Labor* (New York: Basic Books, 1995).
147. Elizabeth Faue, *Community of Suffering and Struggle: Women, Men, and the Labor Movement in Minneapolis, 1915–1945* (Chapel Hill: University of North Carolina Press, 1991).
148. Cohen, *Making a New Deal,* p. 359.

149. Robert H. Zieger and Gilbert J. Gall, *American Workers, American Unions: The Twentieth Century,* 3rd ed. (Baltimore: Johns Hopkins Press, 2002); James Gray Pope, "Worker Lawmaking, Sit-Down Strikes, and the Shaping of American Industrial Relations, 1935–1958," *Law and History Review* 24 (Spring 2006), pp. 45–113; Bernstein, *Turbulent Years; NLRB v. Fansteel Metallurgical Corp.*, 306 U.S. 240 (1939).
150. Christopher L. Tomlins, "AFL Unions in the 1930s: Their Performance in Historical Perspective," *Journal of American History* 65 (March 1979), pp. 1021–42.
151. James B. Atleson, *Labor and the Wartime State: Labor Relations and Law during World War II* (Urbana: University of Illinois Press, 1998); Dubofsky and Dulles, *Labor in America*; Nelson Lichtenstein, *Labor's War at Home: The CIO in World War II* (Cambridge: Cambridge University Press, 1982); Taft, *Organized Labor in American History*; Zieger and Gall, *American Workers, American Unions.*
152. Ruth Milkman, "Rosie the Riveter Revisited: Management's Postwar Purge of Women Automobile Workers," in Nelson Lichtenstein and Stephen Meyer (eds.), *On the Line: Essays in the History of Auto Work* (Urbana: University of Illinois Press, 1989), pp. 129–52.
153. James Wolfinger, "World War II Hate Strikes," in Aaron Brenner, Benjamin Day, and Immanuel Ness (eds.), The Encyclopedia of Strikes in American History (Armonk, NY: M.E. Sharpe, 2009), pp. 126–37; Nelson Lichtenstein, *State of the Union: A Century of American Labor* (Princeton, NJ: Princeton University Press, 2013).
154. Taft, *Organized Labor in American History,* p. 567.
155. Zieger and Gall, *American Workers, American Unions.*
156. Lichtenstein, *Labor's War at Home*; Lichtenstein, *The Most Dangerous Man in Detroit*; Barnard, *American Vanguard.*
157. Victor G. Devinatz, "An Alternative Strategy: Lessons from the UAW Local 6 and the FE, 1946–52," in Cyrus Bina, Laurie Clements, and Chuck Davis (eds.), *Beyond Survival: Wage Labor in the Late Twentieth Century* (Armonk, NY: M.E. Sharpe, 1996), pp. 145–60; Kim Moody, *An Injury to All: The Decline of American Unionism* (London: Verso, 1988); Fairris, *Shopfloor Matters.*
158. David Fairris, "Institutional Change in Shopfloor Governance and the Trajectory of Postwar Injury Rates in U.S. Manufacturing, 1946–1970," *Industrial and Labor Relations Review* 51 (January 1998), pp. 187–203.
159. Moody, *An Injury to All*; Zieger and Gall, *American Workers, American Unions;* Taft, *Organized Labor in American History.*
160. Devinatz, "An Alternative Strategy."
161. Taft, *The A.F. of L. from the Death of Gompers to the Merger*; Taft, *Organized Labor in American History.*
162. Slater, *Public Workers.*
163. Foner, *Organized Labor and the Black Worker*; Rick Halpern, *Down on the Killing Floor: Black and White Workers in Chicago's Packinghouses, 1904–54* (Urbana: University of Illinois Press, 1997); Harris, *The Harder We Run;* Michael K. Honey, *Southern Labor and Black Civil Rights: Organizing Memphis Workers* (Urbana: University of Illinois Press, 1997); Timothy J. Minchin, *The Color of Work: The Struggle for Civil Rights in the Southern Paper Industry, 1945–1980* (Chapel Hill: University of North Carolina Press, 2001); Robert Rodgers Korstad, *Civil Rights Unionism: Tobacco Workers and the Struggle for Democracy in the Mid-Twentieth-Century South* (Chapel Hill: University of North Carolina Press, 2003); Vargas, *Labor Rights Are Civil Rights*; Robert H. Zieger, *For Jobs and Freedom: Race and Labor in America since 1865* (Lexington: The University Press of Kentucky, 2007).
164. Minchin, *The Color of Work.*
165. Barbara S. Griffith, *Operation Dixie and the Defeat of the CIO* (Philadelphia: Temple University Press, 1988).
166. Nancy MacLean, *Freedom Is Not Enough: The Opening of the American Workplace* (Cambridge: Harvard University Press, 2006).
167. Michael K. Honey, *Going Down Jericho Road: The Memphis Strike, Martin Luther King's Last Campaign* (New York: W.W. Norton, 2007).
168. John P. Hoerr, *And the Wolf Finally Came: The Decline of the American Steel Industry* (Pittsburgh: University of Pittsburgh, 1988); Harry C. Katz, *Shifting Gears: Changing Labor Relations in the U.S. Automobile Industry* (Cambridge: MIT Press, 1985).
169. Michael H. LeRoy, "The PATCO Strike: Myths and Realities," in Paula B. Voos (ed.), *Proceedings of the Forty-Ninth Annual Meeting* (Madison, WI: Industrial Relations Research Association, 1997), pp. 15–22.

170. Julius Getman, *The Betrayal of Local 14* (Ithaca, NY: ILR Press, 1998); Dave Hage and Paul Klauda, *No Retreat, No Surrender: Labor's War at Hormel* (New York: William Morrow, 1989); Tom Juravich and Kate Bronfenbrenner, *Ravenswood: The Steelworkers' Victory and the Revival of American Labor* (Ithaca, NY: Cornell University Press, 1999); Barbara Kingsolver, *Holding the Line: Women in the Great Arizona Mine Strike of 1983* (Ithaca, NY: ILR Press, 1989); Peter Rachleff, *Hard-Pressed in the Heartland: The Hormel Strike and the Future of the Labor Movement* (Boston: South End Press, 1993); Rosenblum, *Copper Crucible*; Bruce M. Meyer, *The Once and Future Union: The Rise and Fall of the United Rubber Workers, 1935–1995* (Akron, OH: University of Akron Press, 2002).
171. Norwood, *Strikebreaking and Intimidation*; Smith, *From Blackjacks to Briefcases.*
172. Harry C. Katz and Owen Darbishire, *Converging Divergences: Worldwide Changes in Employment Systems* (Ithaca, NY: ILR Press, 2000).
173. Slater, *Public Workers*. Robert Hebdon, Joseph E. Slater, and Marick F. Masters, "Public Sector Collective Bargaining: Tumultuous Times," in Howard R. Stanger, Paul F. Clark, and Ann C. Frost (eds.), *Collective Bargaining under Duress: Case Studies of Major North American Industries* (Champaign, IL: Labor and Employment Relations Association, 2013), pp. 255–95.
174. Lichtenstein, *State of the Union*; Richard B. Freeman and Eunice Han, "The War Against Public Sector Collective Bargaining in the US," *Journal of Industrial Relations* 54 (June 2012), pp. 386–408.
175. Gary Chaison, *Union Mergers in Hard Times: The View From Five Countries* (Ithaca, NY: ILR Press, 1996); Gary Chaison, *When Unions Merge* (Lexington, MA: Lexington Books, 1986).
176. Ruth Milkman (ed.), *Organizing Immigrants: The Challenge for Unions in Contemporary California* (Ithaca, NY: ILR Press, 2000); Immanuel Ness, *Immigrants, Unions, and the New U.S. Labor Market* (Philadelphia: Temple University Press, 2005).
177. Josh Eidelson, "Alt-Labor," *American Prospect* (January 29, 2013); Janice Fine, *Worker Centers: Organizing Communities at the Edge of the Dream* (Ithaca, NY: Cornell University Press, 2006); Janice Fine, "Alternative Labour Protection Movements in the United States: Reshaping Industrial Relations?" *International Labour Review* 154 (March 2015), pp. 15–26.
178. David Rolf, *The Fight for Fifteen: The Right Wage for a Working America* (New York: The New Press, 2016).
179. Suzan Erem and E. Paul Durrenberger, *On the Global Waterfront: The Fight to Free the Charleston 5* (New York: Monthly Review Press, 2008).
180. Paul F. Clark, John T. Delaney, and Ann C. Frost (eds.), *Collective Bargaining in the Private Sector* (Champaign, IL: Industrial Relations Research Association, 2002); Dorothy Sue Cobble, *Dishing It Out: Waitresses and Their Unions in the Twentieth Century* (Urbana: University of Illinois Press, 1991); Randy Shaw, *Beyond the Fields: Cesar Chavez, the UFW, and the Struggle for Justice in the 21st Century* (Berkeley: University of California Press, 2008); Leon Fink and Brian Greenberg, *Upheaval in the Quiet Zone: A History of Hospital Workers' Union, Local 1199* (Urbana: University of Illinois Press, 1989); Toni Gilpin et al., *On Strike for Respect: The Clerical and Technical Workers' Strike at Yale University, 1984–85* (Urbana: University of Illinois Press, 1995); John P. Hoerr, *We Can't Eat Prestige: The Women Who Organized Harvard* (Philadelphia: Temple University Press, 1997); George E. Hopkins, *Flying the Line: The First Half Century of the Air Line Pilots Association* (Washington, DC: The Air Line Pilots Association, 1982); Marjorie Murphy, *Blackboard Unions: The AFT and the NEA, 1900–1980* (Ithaca, NY: Cornell University Press, 1990); Fran Quigley, *If We Can Win Here: The New Front Lines of the Labor Movement* (Ithaca, NY: Cornell University Press, 2015).
181. Sigmund Diamond, *The Nation Transformed: The Creation of an Industrial Society* (New York: George Braziller, 1963), p. 18.

Chapter **Four**

Labor Law

Advance Organizer

It is impossible to understand contemporary U.S. labor relations without a careful examination of labor law. U.S. labor law grants rights to workers, unions, and companies, gives them responsibilities, and makes certain behaviors illegal. The major labor relations processes are therefore critically shaped by the specific provisions of labor law. A foundation for understanding these processes is studying labor law.

Learning Objectives

By the end of this chapter, you should be able to

1. **Understand** how a legal system can either promote or repress unionization.
2. **List** the major provisions of U.S. labor laws and their underlying logic and rationale, especially with respect to the Wagner Act, Taft–Hartley Act, and Landrum–Griffin Act.
3. **Understand** the role of the National Labor Relations Board and similar state agencies in U.S. labor relations.
4. **Compare** the similarities and differences between U.S. private and public sector law.
5. **Discuss** the criticisms of U.S. labor law and possible directions for reform.

Contents

U.S. labor relations have been closely intertwined with the U.S. legal system for over two centuries. Since the New Deal in the 1930s, U.S. labor laws have explicitly protected workers' union activity primarily by making it illegal for companies to prevent unionization through intimidation or manipulation. Before that time, few laws specifically targeted union activity, but business laws and judicial rulings on conspiracy and other issues were applied to workers' actions. It is difficult to imagine a labor relations system in which at least some aspects of the law are not important. Suppose we throw out all existing labor laws with the intent of letting labor and management do what they choose. Would you let workers take over a factory during a strike? Would you let supervisors threaten physical harm to employees who support a union? Would you allow violent or destructive picketing to the same extent as peaceful picketing? Most people would probably answer no to these questions, which inject legal rulings into labor relations. Labor relations are always critically shaped by the legal system, whether or not there are explicit labor laws.

Consequently, to understand labor relations it is imperative to consider the legal aspects. The major processes in today's U.S. labor relations system—organizing new unions, bargaining contracts, and resolving disputes and grievances—are not entirely legal in nature, but labor law has defined important aspects of these processes. Throughout this chapter, therefore, do not divorce these legal elements—whether court decisions or provisions in labor laws—from the underlying objectives. In addition to learning how labor law works, dig deeper and connect the how and the why. Understanding the objectives of labor law and their intellectual foundations makes the operation of specific legal provisions more readily comprehensible. In particular, the New Deal industrial relations system seeks to balance efficiency, equity, and voice in the U.S. employment relationship and is rooted in the industrial relations school of thought (recall Chapter 2). This perspective determined what form today's labor laws took, what provisions were written into them, and what language was used. These legal details will make more sense if you remember this objective of balancing efficiency, equity, and voice.

Another important strategy for understanding U.S. labor law is recognizing the theme of striking a balance between property rights and labor rights. To balance efficiency, equity, and voice, many legal rules and court decisions try to balance property rights and labor rights. You might not agree with the specific balance in a certain case, but in many areas of labor law it is instructive to consider the conflicting rights and how they are weighed against each other. Before the New Deal in the 1930s, legal doctrine generally favored property rights and individual liberty, consistent with the mainstream economics school of thought. As such, if there were conflicting rights, private property and individual liberty often won out over the interests or rights of labor. But today's laws seek a balance, consistent with the industrial relations school of thought.

This evolution in the legal doctrine pertaining to unions and union activity represents a shift from common law to statutory law, and within statutory law a shift from business law to labor law. Common law is a body of law based on customs, traditions of acceptable behavior, and judicial precedent, often stemming back to English legal principles from several centuries ago (see Table 4.1).[1] Important areas of common law include conspiracy, breach

TABLE 4.1
Some Important Legal Terms

Common Law Laws based on custom and judicial precedent, dating back several centuries into English jurisprudence. Examples include conspiracy, property rights, and employment-at-will. With statutory law, one of the two major categories of law.

Conspiracy: Common law doctrine making it a crime for two or more individuals to plot to deprive someone else of their rights or property.

Contract: A legally binding and enforceable agreement between two parties governed by common law.

Injunction: A court order requiring an individual or an organization to stop a proposed or current action on the belief that the action would cause irreparable harm or damage. A common example in the 1800s was a court order preventing picketing.

Due Process: Core standards of legal treatment, such as the right to a fair trial and to hear and present evidence.

Statutory Law Laws (statutes) passed by legislatures. With common law, one of the two major categories of law. Business, labor, and employment law are three examples. The implementation of statutory law is shaped by judicial interpretation of the written statutes; over time, the accumulation of judicial precedents creates a body of case law for a particular statute.

Business Law: Laws written to govern business activities. A major example of business law is antitrust law to prevent monopolies, especially the Sherman Antitrust Act (1890).

Labor Law: Laws written to govern the collective employment relationship (unions and union activity). Major examples include the Wagner Act (1935) and the Taft–Hartley Act (1947).

Employment Law: Laws written to establish minimum standards for the individual employment relationship. Major examples include the Civil Rights Act (1964) prohibiting discrimination, the Occupational Safety and Health Act (1970), and the Family and Medical Leave Act (1993).

of contract, property rights, and the employment-at-will doctrine. In contrast, statutory law consists of laws (statutes) enacted by legislatures, not judges. Three categories of statutory law are particularly relevant for labor relations: business law (laws applying to businesses, such as antitrust laws), labor law (laws written explicitly for unions and union activity), and employment law (laws pertaining to the individual rather than the collective employment relationship). Between 1800 and 1932, workers who tried to act collectively to influence their wages and working conditions were subjected to common-law principles, and starting in 1890, also to business laws. The year 1932 marks the birth of U.S. labor law; since then unions and union activity have been primarily governed by statutory laws written explicitly for labor relations activities (see Table 4.2). It is to these developments that we now turn.

TABLE 4.2
Labor Law Timeline

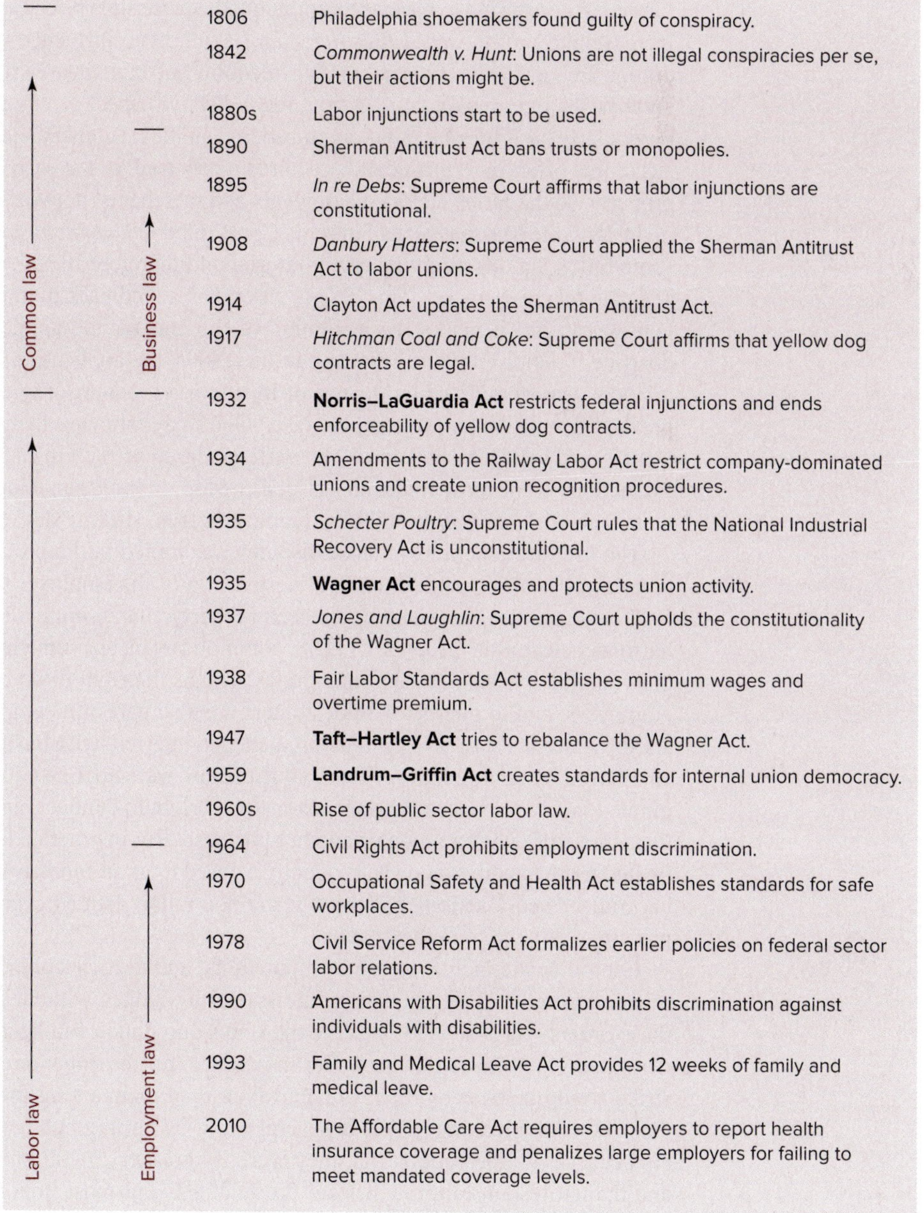

Common law (1806–1932); Business law (1890–1932); Labor law (1932–); Employment law (1964–)

1806	Philadelphia shoemakers found guilty of conspiracy.
1842	*Commonwealth v. Hunt*: Unions are not illegal conspiracies per se, but their actions might be.
1880s	Labor injunctions start to be used.
1890	Sherman Antitrust Act bans trusts or monopolies.
1895	*In re Debs*: Supreme Court affirms that labor injunctions are constitutional.
1908	*Danbury Hatters*: Supreme Court applied the Sherman Antitrust Act to labor unions.
1914	Clayton Act updates the Sherman Antitrust Act.
1917	*Hitchman Coal and Coke*: Supreme Court affirms that yellow dog contracts are legal.
1932	**Norris–LaGuardia Act** restricts federal injunctions and ends enforceability of yellow dog contracts.
1934	Amendments to the Railway Labor Act restrict company-dominated unions and create union recognition procedures.
1935	*Schecter Poultry*: Supreme Court rules that the National Industrial Recovery Act is unconstitutional.
1935	**Wagner Act** encourages and protects union activity.
1937	*Jones and Laughlin*: Supreme Court upholds the constitutionality of the Wagner Act.
1938	Fair Labor Standards Act establishes minimum wages and overtime premium.
1947	**Taft–Hartley Act** tries to rebalance the Wagner Act.
1959	**Landrum–Griffin Act** creates standards for internal union democracy.
1960s	Rise of public sector labor law.
1964	Civil Rights Act prohibits employment discrimination.
1970	Occupational Safety and Health Act establishes standards for safe workplaces.
1978	Civil Service Reform Act formalizes earlier policies on federal sector labor relations.
1990	Americans with Disabilities Act prohibits discrimination against individuals with disabilities.
1993	Family and Medical Leave Act provides 12 weeks of family and medical leave.
2010	The Affordable Care Act requires employers to report health insurance coverage and penalizes large employers for failing to meet mandated coverage levels.

THE COMMON LAW OF LABOR RELATIONS: CONSPIRACIES AND INJUNCTIONS

In the beginning there was no labor law. But there were (and are) common-law doctrines pertaining to conspiracy, property rights, and breach of contract. Throughout the 19th century and in the first three decades of the 20th century, workers who collectively tried to influence their wages and working conditions by forming unions, striking, and leading boycotts were subjected to these common-law doctrines. Chapter 3 noted that Philadelphia shoemakers formed the first permanent union in the United States in the 1790s. The Philadelphia shoemakers also have the dubious honor of marking the start of the **conspiracy doctrine** in labor relations: Their union was the first convicted of being an illegal conspiracy in 1806. By joining together and refusing to work unless their terms were met, the shoemakers were viewed as conspiring to harm the community because shoe prices and unemployment would increase and profits would fall. *Individual* attempts to influence wages and working conditions are consistent with individual freedom; but in mainstream economics thought that emphasizes free-market competition, the *collective* aspect of union activity was viewed as particularly harmful, and thus was considered an illegal conspiracy.[2] Note that conspiracy is a criminal offense, so prosecution required a jury trial. In the early 1800s jurors had to own property, so the juries included employers and merchants, not workers.[3]

In 1842 the Massachusetts Supreme Court ruled in *Commonwealth v. Hunt* that although some union actions might be conspiratorial and therefore illegal, labor unions are not per se unlawful conspiracies. This case is viewed as a landmark in granting unions some legal legitimacy, and it marks the beginning of the end for the application of the conspiracy doctrine to labor relations.[4] Starting in the 1880s, the application of common law to labor relations was dominated by the use of **injunctions**—court-ordered restraints on action to prevent harm or damage to someone else.[5] One study estimates that at least 4,300 injunctions were issued between 1880 and 1930, with increased activity in each decade of that period.[6] Injunctions were most frequently issued to stop or limit picketing during strikes, though there were also cases of prohibiting employees from striking or even from unionizing.

The use of injunctions in labor disputes was rooted in the property rights area of common law. If a strike caused physical destruction of the employer's factory, machines, railroad cars, and the like, the link between property and an injunction to prevent irreparable harm was clear. But "property" in U.S. common law means something significantly broader than tangible physical assets: Intangibles such as the right to do business, to hire and fire employees, and to interact with customers are also part of an employer's property rights.[7] As such, any strike or boycott that threatened to interfere with business could potentially be challenged by an injunction. Note that if the law were applied equally, judges should have granted injunctions equally when a company's right to conduct business was threatened by the actions of either a union or another business. But in practice labor seems to have been treated more harshly—judges frequently refused to grant injunctions to restrain potentially harmful business actions but often restrained union actions even though the same legal principles applied to both situations.[8]

Central to the increased use of injunctions, and to their controversy, is that temporary restraining orders and injunctions are issued by judges without full hearings. In theory, these orders' purpose is to preserve the status quo until a full hearing with witnesses, evidence, and the like can be held. But in practice, full hearings rarely occurred because the strike would be over by then. In fact, rather than maintaining the status quo, injunctions contributed to breaking strikes in several ways: by turning public opinion away from strikers because of a perception that they were lawbreakers; by draining the unions' financial and human resources through legal proceedings; and most importantly, by demoralizing

Court-Ordered Injunctions to Protect Employers' Property Rights and Liberty to Make Yellow Dog Contracts Were Common in the First Three Decades of the 20th Century

Source: *The Striker* from *Minneapolis Labor Review*, October 23, 1936.

strikers through fear and confusion.[9] These consequences might have been justified if each injunction was based on a careful evaluation of the specific evidence of potential harm to property rights presented in each instance. Indeed, there were undoubtedly cases where an injunction was warranted to protect private property from unlawful destruction. But in many other cases sweeping injunctions were quickly issued based on questionable evidence without a full hearing and in response to a standard, generic employer request that was nearly identical to employers' submissions in hundreds of other injunction cases. Consequently, organized labor felt that employers and judges were abusing the legal protection of employers' property rights by turning the injunction into a powerful antiunion legal weapon that broke strikes and unions in the late 1800s and early 1900s.

In the 1900s, labor injunctions were also applied to yellow dog contracts.[10] A **yellow dog contract** is a promise by a worker not to join or support a union; refusal to agree to such conditions meant either termination or not being hired. The courts viewed these contracts as legally enforceable, binding contracts because, in their view, employees signed them voluntarily and were not economically coerced into agreement because of a lack of other jobs. As such, a union's attempt to organize employees could result in an injunction because an outside third party should not be allowed to try to break up valid contracts. If a union ignores such an injunction, there can be significant penalties for contempt of court, so yellow dog contracts were an effective antiunion device. Some states passed laws outlawing yellow dog contracts, but they were ruled unconstitutional because they violated the liberty of employers and employees to freely make contracts incorporating whatever terms they desire.[11]

THE BUSINESS LAW OF LABOR RELATIONS: UNIONS AS CORPORATIONS

Recall from Chapter 3 that corporations increased in size during the 19th century, and toward the end of the 1800s some were huge monopolies or trusts that dominated entire industries. As a result, Congress passed the Sherman Antitrust Act in 1890 to outlaw monopolies and prevent their negative economic and social effects. Note that this is statutory law, not common law, and is premised on the mainstream economics promotion of competition. This law remains in effect today, and it has been the basis for lawsuits trying to break up Microsoft between 1997 and 2001 and for challenging Ticketmaster's monopoly in event ticketing. Violators can be punished by triple damages.

The particular concern for labor relations is whether the Sherman Antitrust Act applies to labor unions. However, the language of the act does not explicitly include or exclude labor unions.[12] *If* a union is viewed as a "combination . . . in restraint of trade or commerce" or represents an attempt "to monopolize any part of the trade or commerce," then this act applies to unions as well as corporations. This question went to the Supreme Court in the **Danbury Hatters case** (1908).[13] After a failed strike, the United Hatters of North America initiated a nationwide boycott of hats made by a Danbury, Connecticut, nonunion company in 1902.[14] In the *Danbury Hatters* case the Supreme Court ruled that the union boycott violated the Sherman Antitrust Act, and a later ruling held individual union members responsible for over $200,000 in damages.[15] In a different case, Samuel Gompers and the American Federation of Labor were found guilty of violating the act by placing a stove company on its "We Don't Patronize" list in its magazine;[16] here free speech was forced to take a back seat to antitrust law.[17] Given that the mainstream economics school of thought views labor unions as labor market monopolies, it is unsurprising that the Supreme Court applied the Sherman Antitrust Act to labor unions.

During this period Congress was debating a follow-up act to clarify some weaknesses of the Sherman Antitrust Act. Organized labor lobbied hard for this legislation to exempt unions from antitrust law.[18] The new law was the Clayton Act (1914), which Gompers hailed as a great victory for labor because it included this statement: "The labor of a human being is not a commodity or article of commerce." But contrary to labor's proclamations, the Clayton Act simply gave unions the legal right to exist; it did not unambiguously exempt them from antitrust laws.[19] Other aspects of the Clayton Act actually increased labor's burdens under antitrust laws because it became easier for employers to seek injunctions. And because the philosophy of the Supreme Court did not change, the act was narrowly interpreted to labor's disadvantage. For example, the Clayton Act allowed peaceful strikes and picketing, but the Supreme Court so narrowly construed this language that *any* picketing that involved even two people was *assumed* not to be peaceful and could therefore be prevented with an injunction.[20]

Between 1890 and 1932, therefore, business law was applied to union activities in ways unfavorable to organized labor (as were common-law injunctions and the coercive force of the police, militia, and army). Perhaps the most lasting development in this era, however, was the emergence of the legal view that unions are legitimate but need to be controlled by legal regulation to make sure they serve the public interest.[21] The 19th-century philosophy of Gompers and the AFL was that unions were voluntary associations of workers, not incorporated organizations. As such, freedoms to unionize, strike, and boycott were rooted in individual liberty, and the government should not interfere.[22] But the *Danbury Hatters* case revealed a risk—individual members were liable for damages—and the unwillingness of the courts to sanction all voluntary actions, such as nationwide boycotts. Meanwhile, the industrial relations school of thought developed its pluralist rather than individualist vision: Corporations and unions are both formal institutions that should serve the public interest and counterbalance each other (recall Chapter 2). In this business law era, adherents to this school successfully laid the foundation for transforming the legal treatment of unions (and corporations) from voluntary associations beyond the state's control to legally sanctioned organizations with corresponding rights and obligations in a pluralist society, including serving the public interest and living up to collective bargaining agreements. Republicans, too, wanted labor controlled, so both they and the industrial relations school promoted responsible unionism.[23] This institutionalized rather than voluntaristic vision of labor unions—legally sanctioned, tightly regulated, and party to enforceable union contracts—would become more firmly cemented in the labor laws of the 1930s and 1940s, and it still dominates U.S. labor relations today. As we will see, this transition to institutionalization benefited workers and unions by granting them legal protections, but in return workers and unions are constrained to operate within the parameters of the law and therefore must comply with restrictions on strikes, secondary boycotts, and other activities.

KEEPING COURTS OUT OF LABOR RELATIONS: THE NORRIS–LAGUARDIA ACT

Because of the potential for abuse, especially with so much power concentrated in a single judge's hands with no checks and balances, the labor injunction was despised not only by union leaders and members but also by sympathetic lawmakers and reformers. In fact, the AFL supported at least one anti-injunction proposal in Congress in every year between 1895 and 1914.[24] Events in the early 1920s brought anti-injunction legislation to the fore again. Narrow Supreme Court rulings deflated labor's faith in the Clayton Act. And in 1922 a judge issued "one of the most notorious injunctions in American legal history" during a strike by railroad shop workers.[25] Not only did this expansive injunction make striking illegal regardless of how peaceful it was, it restricted free speech by banning any type of "persuasion" to convince workers to strike and even made it illegal to "annoy any employees of said railroad companies."[26]

Between 1924 and 1931 anti-injunction legislation failed to get enough votes in Congress. But with the onset of the Great Depression in the early 1930s, the political composition of Congress changed, and in 1932 the **Norris–LaGuardia Act** was enacted.[27] The policy declaration for this act is presented in Table 4.3. Note carefully the intellectual foundations: organized corporations (essentially individual shareholders who have unionized by pooling their resources and hiring experts to look out for their best interests) are significantly more powerful than unorganized individual workers, and this imbalance in bargaining power forces workers to accept substandard wages and working conditions (recall the conditions of the labor problem from Chapter 2). As such, in the industrial relations school of thought, workers should be able to unionize to balance corporate power and thus obtain decent wages and working conditions. But how should this unionization be promoted? The last 20 words in Table 4.3 reveal the answer: The Norris–LaGuardia Act seeks to protect unionization efforts by limiting the "jurisdiction and authority of the courts of the United States." In other words, this act seeks to remove the courts from labor relations.

TABLE 4.3
The Norris–LaGuardia Act (1932)

Section 2. Whereas under prevailing economic conditions, developed with the aid of governmental authority for owners of property to organize in the corporate and other forms of organization, the individual unorganized worker is commonly helpless to exercise actual liberty of contract and to protect his freedom of labor, and thereby to obtain acceptable terms and conditions of employment, wherefore, though he should be free to decline to associate with his fellows, it is necessary that he have full freedom of association, self-organization, and designation of representatives of his own choosing, to negotiate the terms and conditions of employment, and that he shall be free from the interference, restraint, and coercion of the employers of labor, or their agents, in the designation of such representatives or in self-organization or in other concerted activities for the purpose of collective bargaining or other mutual aid or protection; therefore, the following definitions of and limitations upon the jurisdiction and authority of the courts of the United States are enacted.

More concretely, the Norris–LaGuardia Act forbids federal courts from issuing injunctions that interfere with strikes, payment of strike benefits, publicizing a dispute (as long as it is not fraudulent), peaceful picketing, and workers joining unions.[28] The conditions under which injunctions can be issued were also severely limited. As such, the popular name for this act is the federal anti-injunction act. The act further makes yellow dog contracts unenforceable and ends the criminal conspiracy doctrine of labor unions. Finally, by broadly defining permissible labor disputes, the act effectively exempts labor unions from the Sherman Antitrust Act. The Norris–LaGuardia Act therefore marks the end of the common law and business law eras in labor relations, and the start of the labor law era that governs labor relations today. But the Norris–LaGuardia Act simply tries to remove the courts from labor relations. The act does not give labor unions or workers any new rights or enforcement mechanisms. These are the next steps toward today's labor law.

PRELUDES TO A NATIONAL POLICY

Franklin Delano Roosevelt was elected president of the United States several months after the passage of the Norris–LaGuardia Act in 1932. The Great Depression had been wreaking economic havoc for 3 years, and 1933 was to be even worse.[29] Widespread unemployment, poverty, homelessness, and hunger shook the country's faith in the wisdom of laissez-faire government policies supporting free markets to promote economic prosperity and security. Roosevelt promised "a new deal for the American people," which meant creating an *active* government role in promoting and guaranteeing the welfare of the population.[30] The industrial relations school of thought, not mainstream economics or human resource management, underlies this New Deal philosophy (recall Chapter 2). Because of imperfect markets, conflicts of interest in the employment relationship between workers and owners, and the importance of employees as human beings, government regulation and labor unions are important for balancing power between employees and employers, which promotes economic stability and prosperity as well as fairness and democracy—efficiency, equity, and voice.[31]

Prelude 1: The National Industrial Recovery Act

But at the beginning of the Roosevelt presidency, the existing labor legislation was passive, not active: The Norris–LaGuardia Act simply tried to remove the courts from labor relations by clamping down on the rampant use of labor injunctions by judges hostile to unions. The Norris–LaGuardia Act did not actively protect or promote union activity, and it did little to combat employers' open shop tactics (described in Chapter 3): infiltrating unions with spies, using armed guards and professional strikebreaking agencies to break strikes, firing union activists, creating racial tension to divide workers, and using nonunion employee representation plans (company unions) to prevent the creation of independent labor unions. On the other hand, the most pressing issue in 1933 was not union busting, it was massive unemployment. As such, an early New Deal initiative was the National Industrial Recovery Act (NIRA) in 1933. The NIRA contained a public works program to create jobs and an ambitious framework for establishing industry codes of fair competition for preventing destructive competition and promoting economic recovery.[32]

Echoing the declaration of the Norris–LaGuardia Act, and over the opposition of business, Section 7(a) of the NIRA also specified that each industry code of fair competition must contain the following:

> Employees shall have the right to organize and bargain collectively through representatives of their own choosing, and shall be free from the interference, restraint, and coercion of the employers of labor, or their agents, in the designation of such representatives or in

> self-organization or in other concerted activities for the purpose of collective bargaining or other mutual aid or protection.

This language emboldened workers to focus their pent-up frustration on unionizing, but the lack of specific enforcement provisions could not prevent continued employer opposition.[33] A National Labor Board chaired by Senator Robert Wagner of New York was created to help settle labor disputes, but without specific enforcement powers it was ineffective.[34] Employers also established sham company unions in an attempt to minimally comply with the NIRA without recognizing independent labor unions.[35]

The ineffectiveness of the NIRA and the National Labor Board in achieving industrial peace was starkly demonstrated by the intense strikes of 1934 described in Chapter 3. And the broader failure of the NIRA to restructure power relations between workers and employers, improve wages and working conditions, and reduce unemployment was graphically illustrated by the 170,000 Southern textile workers who also went on strike in 1934.[36] In contrast to the New Deal's promise of justice for the working class and reduced unemployment, layoffs increased as the remaining textile mill hands were worked to exhaustion by the stretch-out (assigning more looms to each worker). And in spite of Section 7(a), thousands of union supporters were fired. Since the NIRA's textile industry code was written and administered by the owners of the mills, workers struck out of extreme frustration and a sense of powerlessness. Various institutions failed the workers, and the strike was a major defeat; but it highlighted the need for new legislation. Though it was never intended as a long-term solution, the NIRA was ruled unconstitutional by the Supreme Court in May 1935 because the authority granted by the NIRA to the U.S. president to approve the codes of fair competition was seen as excessive.[37]

Prelude 2: The Railway Labor Act

Even before the NIRA was struck down by the Supreme Court, Senator Wagner had been working to craft a stronger labor relations law with enough teeth to counter corporate resistance and thus improve U.S. capitalism by creating increased worker purchasing power, industrial peace, fairness, and industrial democracy through unionization.[38] Moreover, there were already the experiences of a major industry to draw on—the railroad industry. Recall from Chapter 3 that some of the most destructive strikes in labor history occurred in the railroad industry, including the Great Uprising of 1877 and the Pullman strike of 1894. Because railroads were the backbone of the entire economy, congressional efforts to achieve industrial peace specifically in this industry dated back to the Arbitration Act of 1888.[39] A series of attempts to improve the regulation of railroad labor relations before the 1920s was unsuccessful, so the railroad industry and its unions were asked by President Coolidge to jointly develop procedures for achieving labor peace. The result was a unique bill that was jointly crafted by labor and management, and enacted into law as the **Railway Labor Act** in 1926.[40] Airlines were added to the act in 1936, and both industries are still regulated by this act today.[41]

The primary purpose of the Railway Labor Act is to avoid strikes and other forms of labor–management conflict that disrupt interstate commerce and weaken the economy. Thus the act protects the rights of employees to form labor unions, provides government mediation of bargaining disputes, and establishes adjustment boards to resolve grievances. Consistent with American values, note the importance of individualism—unions specifically are not granted rights; rather, individual employees are granted the right to select a union to represent them. Moreover, these rights are procedural (such as the right to choose a bargaining representative or to engage in collective bargaining) rather than substantive (such as a specific wage rate), which is also consistent with individual free choice. As such, U.S. labor policy has important Republican origins.[42]

But how should individual choices about unionization be made effective? A major shortcoming of the initial Railway Labor Act was failing to provide a mechanism for

Labor Relations Application Senator Robert F. Wagner: Father of U.S. Labor Law

The development of U.S. labor law is a complex story with many events and actors; but if there is a single father of U.S. labor law, it would be Senator Robert F. Wagner. Wagner was born in Germany in 1877, the youngest of seven children, and emigrated to New York City with his family when he was 9 years old. As the youngest, Wagner was able to attend public school, college, and law school while being supported by the rest of his family.

Wagner was elected to the New York legislature in 1904 and was appointed chairman of the New York State Factory Investigating Commission in 1911 after the horrendous 1911 Triangle Shirtwaist factory fire killed over 100 seamstresses because of locked fire exits. Along with Frances Perkins, Wagner spent 4 years comprehensively touring factories across the state and saw firsthand the deplorable working and living conditions of many individuals. In response, Wagner sponsored numerous state laws to improve fire safety, establish safety standards for machinery, limit child labor, and control tenement home work. This would continue to be the foundation for his thinking throughout his political career: the need for government to place checks and balances on economic markets to protect the unlucky and promote prosperity for all.

As a state judge in the early 1920s, Wagner became the first judge to issue an injunction compelling an employer rather than a union to abide by the terms of a collective bargaining agreement it had agreed to. In 1926 he was elected to the U.S. Senate, where he immediately continued to champion workers' issues. Both before and after his colleague from the New York State Senate, Franklin Delano Roosevelt, was elected president in 1932, Wagner advocated using public spending to create jobs to increase workers' purchasing power, which would both improve their living standards and further boost the economy by giving them money to spend. As one of the most respected and influential senators of the time, Wagner was instrumental in shaping the National Industrial Recovery Act (NIRA), which contained a large public works component.

When strikes erupted after the NIRA's Section 7(a) guaranteed workers the right to organize, Wagner was appointed to head the National Labor Board. This appointment shifted Wagner's attention from public works projects to collective bargaining. As Wagner witnessed labor relations firsthand, he became convinced that the way to achieve economic prosperity and decent working and living standards was through equality of bargaining power between labor and management. Without this equality, companies were able to keep wages low—which, Wagner believed, not only maintained substandard living conditions and threatened democracy by leaving workers voiceless and powerless but also kept the economy depressed because of insufficient purchasing power. Wagner witnessed how company-dominated unions were powerless to raise wages and therefore were not a worthy substitute for independent labor unions.

Wagner continued to press for stronger labor relations legislation—in addition to strong public works programs, unemployment insurance, and a social security program that were being championed by Secretary of Labor Perkins—in order to achieve industrial peace and economic prosperity that "rests upon freedom, not restraint; upon equality, not subservience; upon cooperation, not dominance." In 1935 Wagner mustered sufficient support for the National Labor Relations Act (commonly and appropriately referred to as the Wagner Act), which continues today as the basis of U.S. labor law. Wagner continued to champion the government's role in improving economic and social issues, including public housing and fair employment practices, until he was forced to retire from the Senate in 1949 due to health problems. His last speech on the Senate floor was, unsurprisingly, in objection to the Taft–Hartley Act that substantially modified the Wagner Act in 1947. He died in his old Manhattan neighborhood in 1953, but his legacy of progressive labor policies remains.

Reference: J. Joseph Huthmacher, *Senator Robert F. Wagner and the Rise of Urban Liberalism* (New York: Atheneum, 1968); the quote is from p. 193.

determining when an employer would have to recognize a union as the employees' representative.[43] In fact, while nonunion employee representation plans sometimes served workers' needs in other industries, the railroad industry extensively manipulated company unions to keep independent labor unions out, both before and after the passage of the Railway Labor Act in 1926.[44] Consequently the act was strengthened in 1934 by restricting company-dominated unions and by establishing the National Mediation Board to conduct secret ballot elections to determine whether a union should represent employees. If a union wins support from a majority of workers, the union is certified as the exclusive representative of all the workers in that craft or class, and the company must bargain with that union. Senator Wagner's efforts at a national labor policy developed along similar lines.

Prelude 3: The Amalgamated Clothing Workers

As a third prelude to a national labor relations law, there was also the philosophy of some union leaders like Sidney Hillman, leader of the Amalgamated Clothing Workers (ACW) union. The garment industry was traditionally characterized by destructive competition—anyone could sew clothes as a subcontractor, and desperate workers undercut each other. Purchasing power was low, working and living conditions were lousy, and larger manufacturers were undercut. In the 1910s and 1920s the ACW brought stability and order to the garment industry through strong collective bargaining and an orderly grievance procedure. The militancy of small work groups was replaced by the discipline of "responsible" union leaders and union contracts. This was an early example of a union working cooperatively with employers and the government to create economic stability, increased purchasing power, and fair economic outcomes while also providing some form of employee voice. This experience proved to be a "dress rehearsal for the New Deal."[45]

SOLVING LABOR PROBLEMS: THE WAGNER ACT

When the NIRA was ruled unconstitutional in 1935, President Roosevelt finally endorsed Senator Wagner's efforts at creating stronger labor legislation, and one of the most radical pieces of U.S. legislation was passed relatively quickly.[46] The **Wagner Act,** or the National Labor Relations Act (NLRA), was signed into law by President Roosevelt on July 5, 1935. This act builds upon previous legislative attempts to promote and protect workers' abilities to unionize in the private sector if they so choose (see the accompanying box, "Senator Wagner Presents His Labor Relations Bill to Congress"). As amended in 1947 and 1959, the Wagner Act remains the centerpiece of today's U.S. labor law in the private sector. In other words, corporate and union leaders in the 21st century must thoroughly understand the objectives and provisions of the Wagner Act.

The Principles of the Wagner Act

The Wagner Act encourages collective bargaining in the private sector by protecting workers' rights to join and form labor unions. These objectives are rooted in the industrial relations principal beliefs:

- Labor is more than a commodity.
- Labor and management are not economic or legal equals (in other words, there is an imbalance of bargaining power).
- There is at least some conflict of interest between workers and employers that cannot be resolved by unitarist management policies, but this is pluralist employment relationship conflict, not class-based or societal conflict.
- Employee voice is important.[47]

From other intellectual perspectives, the Wagner Act is difficult to understand and is viewed as a harmful protection of monopoly labor (mainstream economics), unnecessary support of adversarial third parties (human resource management), or an imperfect attempt to empower labor that inadequately challenges capital's power (critical industrial relations).[48] But in the industrial relations school, unequal bargaining power is at the heart of

In Their Own Words Senator Wagner Presents His Labor Relations Bill to Congress (March 1935)

Mr. Chairman and members of the committee, the National Labor Relations bill does not present a single novel principle for the consideration of Congress. It is designed to further the equal balance of opportunity among all groups that we have always attempted to preserve despite the technological forces driving us toward excessive concentration of wealth and power.

. . .

I am not pleading for any special group. It is well recognized today that the failure to spread adequate purchasing power among the vast masses of the consuming public disrupts the continuity of business operations and causes everyone to suffer.

. . .

The government policy of fixing minimum wages and maximum hours is not a definitive solution. It is merely the foundation upon which can be built the mutual endeavors of a revived industry and a rehabilitated labor. This process of economic self-rule must fail unless every group is equally well represented. In order that the strong may not take advantage of the weak, every group must be equally strong. Not only is this common sense; but it is also in line with the philosophy of checks and balances that colors our political thinking. It is in accord with modern democratic concepts which reject the merger of all group interests into a totalitarian state.

. . .

Our alternatives are clear. If we allow Section 7(a) [of the NIRA] to languish, we shall be confronted by intermittent periods of peace at the price of economic liberty, dangerous industrial warfare, and dire depressions. On the other hand, if we clarify that law and bolster it by adequate enforcement agencies, we shall do much to round out the program for a balanced economic system founded upon fair dealing and common business sense.

Source: National Labor Relations Board, *Legislative History of the National Labor Relations Act 1935* (Washington, DC: U.S. Government Printing Office, 1949), pp. 1408–13.

the labor problem, and equalizing bargaining power through unionization is the solution (recall Chapter 2). One does not need to agree with the industrial relations school, but understanding its perspective is critical for understanding U.S. labor law and its goal of protecting union activity to balance efficiency, equity, and voice:

- Efficiency: Increasing the purchasing power of workers, reducing disruptive strike activity, and largely maintaining employer's property rights.[49]
- Equity: Achieving fair employment conditions and protections against exploitation.[50]
- Voice: Providing democracy in the workplace.[51]

In the later words of Senator Wagner, "The spirit and purpose of the law is to create a free and dignified workingman who has the economic strength to bargain collectively with a free and dignified employer in accordance with the methods of democracy."[52]

The full text of the Wagner Act can be found in Appendix A at the end of this book, and its central provisions are summarized in Table 4.4. The core of the Wagner Act, Section 7, echoes the NIRA's Section 7(a):

> Employees shall have the right to self-organization, to form, join, or assist labor organizations, to bargain collectively through representatives of their own choosing, and to engage in other concerted activities for the purpose of collective bargaining or other mutual aid or protection.

Note that this protects more than formal union activities like bargaining over a contract; spontaneous acts by small groups of nonunion employees can also be protected by Section 7 (see "Take the Section 7 Quiz"). The remainder of the Wagner Act essentially tries

TABLE 4.4
The Central Provisions of the Wagner Act (1935)

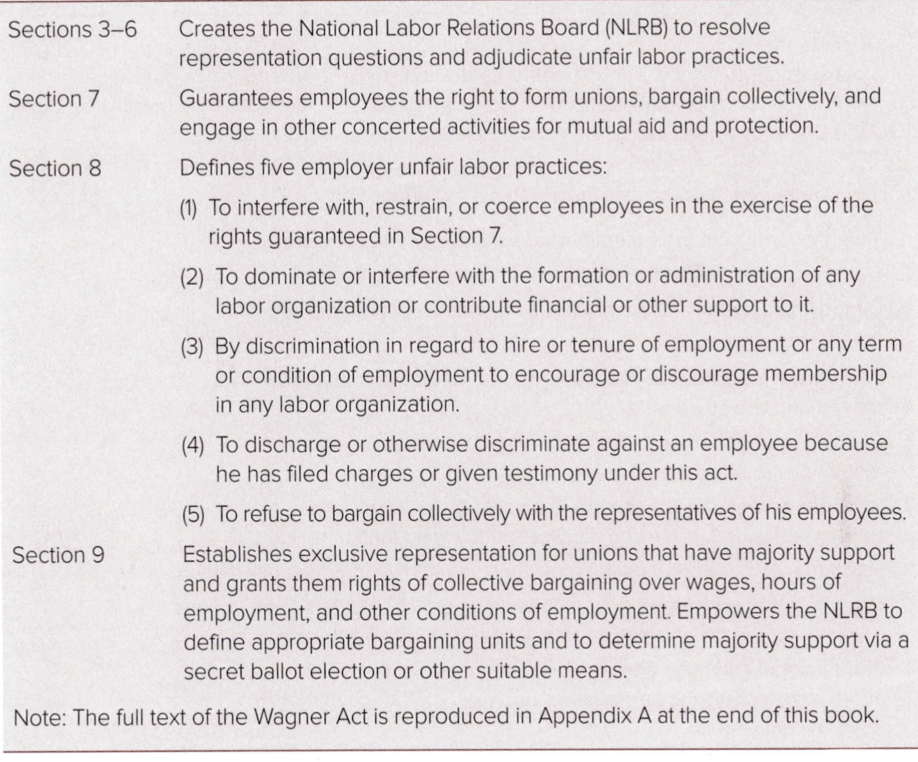

Sections 3–6	Creates the National Labor Relations Board (NLRB) to resolve representation questions and adjudicate unfair labor practices.
Section 7	Guarantees employees the right to form unions, bargain collectively, and engage in other concerted activities for mutual aid and protection.
Section 8	Defines five employer unfair labor practices: (1) To interfere with, restrain, or coerce employees in the exercise of the rights guaranteed in Section 7. (2) To dominate or interfere with the formation or administration of any labor organization or contribute financial or other support to it. (3) By discrimination in regard to hire or tenure of employment or any term or condition of employment to encourage or discourage membership in any labor organization. (4) To discharge or otherwise discriminate against an employee because he has filed charges or given testimony under this act. (5) To refuse to bargain collectively with the representatives of his employees.
Section 9	Establishes exclusive representation for unions that have majority support and grants them rights of collective bargaining over wages, hours of employment, and other conditions of employment. Empowers the NLRB to define appropriate bargaining units and to determine majority support via a secret ballot election or other suitable means.

Note: The full text of the Wagner Act is reproduced in Appendix A at the end of this book.

to make Section 7 a reality rather than hollow words. As such, the act builds from earlier legislative failures and shortcomings in three important ways:

- Granting a certified, majority-status union the right to be the exclusive representative of the relevant employees and specifying a certification procedure for establishing whether a majority of workers want union representation.
- Defining illegal employer actions that undermine Section 7.
- Creating an independent agency, the National Labor Relations Board (NLRB), to enforce the act.

Let's consider each of these in turn.

Exclusive Representation and Certifying Majority Status

First the Wagner Act explicitly establishes **exclusive representation** when a union has the support of a majority of a group of employees. In other words, with majority support a union is the *only* representative of that group of workers—there cannot be another union or a company union representing some employees in the group. Exclusive representation is unique to North America and stems from Senator Wagner's experience under the NIRA, which did not mandate exclusive representation.[53] Without exclusivity, companies established company unions even when a majority of employees wanted an independent union, and then manipulated the company unions to weaken the independent unions. Exclusive representation was established by the Wagner Act to prevent this problem. Note that any percentage of workers could have been specified for determining when a union becomes the exclusive representative. But using a simple majority as the decision rule is the most consistent with democracy and is therefore what the Wagner Act specifies.

Labor Relations Application Take the Section 7 Quiz

"Employees shall have the right to self-organization, to form, join, or assist labor organizations, to bargain collectively through representatives of their own choosing, and to engage in other concerted activities for the purpose of collective bargaining or other mutual aid or protection" (Wagner Act, Section 7).

Indicate whether each scenario is protected activity under Section 7. Protected or not?

1. Trying to form a union to negotiate wages and working conditions. ________
2. Going on strike and peacefully picketing for improved benefits. ________
3. Destroying company property while striking for improved benefits. ________
4. Discussing wages with coworkers. ________
5. Individually meeting with your supervisor to request improved lighting for you and two coworkers. ________
6. Circulating a flyer among coworkers to build support for a plan for employees to buy the company. ________
7. In a nonunion workplace, joining with several coworkers and refusing to work until the company provides a paid lunch break. ________
8. Insisting that a coworker be present when you think you will be disciplined. ________
9. Using the company e-mail system to send an e-mail message to coworkers pointing out the disadvantages of your employer's new vacation plan. ________
10. From a home computer after work, posting comments on Facebook about a coworker's job performance and asking other coworkers to add their comments. ________
11. Distributing obscene or malicious cartoons to protest a supervisor's actions. ________
12. Refusing to work under conditions that you and others reasonably believe pose a high risk of death or serious injury. ________

The answers are at the end of this chapter.

Establishing the principle of exclusive representation with majority support begs the question of how to determine majority support, and therefore union recognition, in practice. Recall from labor history that before 1935 the primary method for forcing employers to recognize unions was by striking. In fact, the major strikes in 1934 were over recognition, so this issue was fresh in Senator Wagner's mind. These strikes disrupted the economy as well as workers' lives, and the Wagner Act sought to help both by replacing these strikes with an orderly procedure. What's the natural method in a democratic society for determining what a majority of individuals prefer? A secret ballot vote. So the Wagner Act allows secret ballot elections to determine whether a majority of workers support a specific union. Technically the Wagner Act allows secret ballot elections or "any other suitable method," but elections are now the dominant method, and this will be the focus of Chapter 6 on union organizing. If a union is certified as the exclusive representative of a group of workers after a secret ballot election, the employer must bargain with that union over wages, hours, and other terms and conditions of employment (Chapter 7). However, the obligation to bargain with a union that represents a *minority* of workers has interestingly and perhaps inappropriately faded away (see "What About Nonmajority Unions?").[54]

Unfair Labor Practices

To make the organizing and bargaining processes effective, the second major element of the Wagner Act specifies illegal employer actions, which are called **unfair labor practices**

TABLE 4.5
Examples of Employer Unfair Labor Practices

Section 8(a)(1): Interference, Restraint, or Coercion That Undermines Section 7	Section 8(a)(3): Discrimination to Encourage or Discourage Union Membership
• Circulating an antiunion petition. • Surveillance of union activities beyond what's necessary for security of company property. • Threatening employees with job loss or demotion or physical harm if they support a union. • Promising benefits such as wage increases if employees reject a union. • Interrogating employees about their union sympathies. • Preventing employees from talking about a union or wearing union buttons when it doesn't interfere with their work duties or customers. • Note: All of the examples provided below for Sections 8(a)(2)–8(a)(5) also violate section 8(a)(1). *Section 8(a)(2): Domination of a Labor Organization (Company Union Ban)* • Initiating the formation of a union. • Providing financial support to a union. • Creating a nonunion employee representation plan. • Creating a labor–management committee that discusses wages and working conditions with some give-and-take with management, but in which managers retain decision-making power and control the committee's agenda, structure, and continued existence.	• Firing a union supporter or someone trying to form a union. • Transferring a union supporter to a less desirable job or promoting a union opponent to a better job. • Refusing to hire someone because of past union sympathies or membership. • Closing part of a business for antiunion reasons. *Section 8(a)(4): Discrimination for Filing Charges or Testifying under the NLRA* • Firing a worker who files an unfair labor practice charge. *Section 8(a)(5): Refusal to Bargain with a Certified Union* • Refusing to meet with a certified union. • Failing to bargain in good faith—that is, without a sincere attempt to reach agreement. • Never making counterproposals. • Changing wages, benefits, or other terms of employment without negotiating first. • Dealing directly with individual employees to circumvent the union. • Refusing to provide relevant information. • Refusing to bargain with a certified union as the exclusive representative of *all* bargaining unit employees.

(see Table 4.5). The first unfair labor practice [Section 8(a)(1)] prohibits employers from interfering, restraining, or coercing employees who are exercising their Section 7 rights. Refer to the "Take the Section 7 Quiz" box: for each example of protected activity, Section 8(a)(1) makes it illegal for employers to take adverse actions against employees who engage in activities protected by Section 7. This does not require employers to yield to employees' demands; for example, there is no legal obligation to provide the improved benefits, lighting, or lunch breaks demanded in entries 2, 5, and 7 of the quiz. Rather, the key point is that the employer cannot punish employees for making these demands. Such punishment would be considered interference, restraint, or coercion under Section 8(a)(1) and would therefore be illegal. So employees can "self-organize" by talking to their managers as a group, rather than as individuals, and be protected against reprisals even if they do not form a formal union.

Section 8(a)(1) is the "universal enforcer" because it covers all employer violations of employee rights.[55] As a result, this is the only unfair labor practice that is technically necessary to enforce the Wagner Act, but four other unfair labor practices were included to reinforce the illegality of four of the most problematic issues at the time.[56] Employers are explicitly reminded that they cannot fire or otherwise discriminate against employees who are trying to form a union [Section 8(a)(3)]. It is also reinforced that it is illegal for companies to dominate a labor organization [8(a)(2)]—this bans company unions, which Senator Wagner experienced as being sham unions that management manipulated to prevent workers from forming legitimate, independent unions.[57] Company unions were also perceived as weak and thus undermined Senator Wagner's objective of increasing employee bargaining power to prevent destructive competition, increase workers' purchasing power, and thus stimulate the economy.[58] This unfair labor practice received renewed attention in the 1990s because it potentially hinders corporate employee involvement initiatives (see Chapter 10). Finally, in the 1930s some employers would agree to bargain with a union that had majority support, but they would not recognize the union as the exclusive representative of all the employees (in other words, the employer would agree to apply the resulting contractual terms only to union members). To promote stable collective bargaining arrangements, Section 8(a)(5) reminds employers that when a union has majority support, the employer must recognize the union as the exclusive representative of *all* employees and bargain with it accordingly.[59] In short, it is an unfair labor practice for an employer to refuse to bargain with a certified majority union as the exclusive representative; this will be discussed in Chapter 7.

The National Labor Relations Board

How should secret ballot elections be conducted and allegations of unfair labor practices be resolved? The final component of the Wagner Act creates the **National Labor Relations Board** (NLRB),[60] which is an independent federal agency devoted to conducting representation elections and adjudicating unfair labor practices. The NLRB now has two parts—(1) a general counsel's office that conducts representation elections and investigates and prosecutes unfair labor practices and (2) a five-member board of presidential appointees (also called the National Labor Relations Board or the board for short) that hears and decides cases. If a group of workers or a union wants an employer to recognize and bargain with a union, they generally approach a regional office of the NLRB to manage the process and determine—usually through a secret ballot vote—whether the union has majority support. This process will be discussed in detail in Chapter 6.

If an individual believes an unfair labor practice has occurred, they can file charges with an NLRB regional office. If the regional office finds merit in the charge, a hearing will be held before an administrative law judge, during which evidence can be presented and witnesses examined and cross-examined. The administrative law judge issues a formal decision that can be appealed by the general counsel to the five-member board. Violators can be ordered to cease and desist from their illegal activities and, when relevant, to offer reinstatement with back pay to illegally discharged workers. The NLRB can seek enforcement of its rulings in federal court. Although the NLRB is criticized by some as weak—for example, punitive damages or fines are not allowed—this is a significantly stronger enforcement mechanism than appeared in previous labor laws. The NLRB currently receives over 20,000 unfair labor practice allegations and requests for nearly 3,000 representation elections each year.[61]

The First Years of the Wagner Act

The Wagner Act was immediately controversial.[62] Laissez-faire proponents attacked the act as greatly extending the federal government's reach into private affairs and therefore interfering with economic efficiency as well as individual and corporate liberty. In contrast, New Deal reformers felt that the overall structure of private property and economic exchange was maintained: The Wagner Act "did not dictate the terms and conditions of employment, but rather endorsed a process by which the parties could shape their own substantive contract terms."[63] As such, the act protects worker choice regarding unionization and provides an

Labor Relations Application What About Nonmajority Unions?

Since the 1940s U.S. labor relations have emphasized exclusive representation with majority support. But consider a situation in which some workers, but less than 50 percent, want a union to collectively bargain for them. Around the time of the Wagner Act in the mid-1930s, it was not uncommon for companies to bargain with a union in this situation, and the resulting contract would apply only to union members. In fact, the famous 1937 General Motors sit-down strike discussed in Chapter 3 resulted in a members-only agreement because the UAW did not have majority support. In this situation the union is called a minority union or a nonmajority union because it represents only a minority of the workers. It is clear from Section 7 of the Wagner Act that workers have the right to engage in this type of concerted activity; but is a company required to bargain with a nonmajority union when there is no majority union present?

Some legal scholars argue that a company must indeed bargain with a nonmajority union; failure to do so interferes with an employee's Section 7 rights and is therefore a Section 8(a)(1) unfair labor practice. Section 8(a)(5) was added late in the drafting of the Wagner Act and makes it explicit that a company must treat a union with majority support as the exclusive representative because there was significant employer resistance to exclusive representation (employers wanted to be able to continue to use company unions even when a majority of workers supported an independent union). But, some argue, Section 8(a)(5) was not intended to limit employers' bargaining obligation to cases of majority support.

Perhaps ironically, in the late 1930s and early 1940s unions were so successful in winning majority support that the use of nonmajority unionism faded away. And with it the legal doctrine that employers must bargain with nonmajority unions also faded from memory. As a result, without majority support a union today is considered a nonentity in the workplace, and U.S. labor relations have become in essence an all-or-nothing affair—a union is entitled to represent either all or none of the employees. But nonmajority unionism can provide representation to groups of workers who would otherwise be denied the opportunity, and it can also let unions demonstrate their effectiveness and generate majority support. Whether unions will revive their use of nonmajority unionism, and whether the NLRB and the courts will change to an interpretation of the NLRA that requires employers to bargain with nonmajority unions in the absence of a union with majority support, remain to be seen.

References: Charles J. Morris, *The Blue Eagle at Work: Reclaiming Democratic Rights in the American Workplace* (Ithaca, NY: Cornell University Press, 2005); Catherine Fisk and Xenia Tashlitsky, "Imagine a World Where Employers Are Required to Bargain with Minority Unions," *ABA Journal of Labor and Employment Law* 27 (Fall 2011), pp. 1–22.

affirmative obligation for employers to bargain with a majority union, but it does not require agreement or specific outcomes. Senator Wagner argued that his act increased rather than decreased individual freedom by granting workers the same opportunities to join together as were enjoyed by employers: Employers formed associations to discuss common problems and search for solutions, so why not employees?[64] Some business leaders hoped that unions could help stabilize their industries by preventing marginal employers from undercutting wage rates and labor standards and by increasing workers' purchasing power.[65]

Nevertheless, many employers openly flouted the new law.[66] Recall from Chapter 3 that the historic General Motors sit-down strike and Memorial Day Massacre occurred in 1937—*after* the passage of the Wagner Act. In fact nearly two-thirds of the tremendous number of strikes in 1937 were exactly what the act sought to prevent: union recognition strikes.[67] On the legal front, the new NLRB spent its first two years defending its existence.[68] Federal judges issued injunctions against the NLRB, and 2 months after the passage of the Wagner Act, conservative lawyers attached to the American Liberty League declared that the Wagner Act was unconstitutional.[69] The American Liberty League was bankrolled by major corporations; and in that period of misinformation and resistance, this pronouncement fueled legal attacks on the NLRB as well as continued opposition to unions and the new law. Not until the Supreme Court's 1937 ruling in

NLRB v. Jones and Laughlin Steel Corp., which declared the act constitutional, could the NLRB wholeheartedly attend to the business of enforcing the nation's new labor policy (see the "Digging Deeper" feature at the end of this chapter).[70]

Online Exploration Exercise: Whether or not graduate assistants should be protected by labor law in terms of trying to organize unions and bargain collectively continues to be a hotly contested issue. Explore the Coalition of Graduate Employee Unions website (*www.thecgeu.org*) to learn about the employment issues of concern for graduate students. In light of these issues, should graduate assistants be seen as workers who should be protected by labor law?

REBALANCING THE SYSTEM: THE TAFT–HARTLEY ACT

Although the Wagner Act grew out of the experience of earlier laws, it was a major increase in government intervention in economic and social affairs and continued to be controversial even after its constitutionality was affirmed: "Scarcely had the ink dried on the President's signature establishing the NLRA as part of our national policy when bills to repeal or amend the Act began pouring into the congressional mills."[71] In the decade after the Wagner Act, union membership nearly quadrupled from 4 million to more than 15 million, and many felt that unions were too strong, lacked a sense of public responsibility, were controlled by communists or corrupt union bosses, and should be bound by the same responsibilities and restrictions that employers faced under the Wagner Act.[72] Remember that the Wagner Act specified only employer unfair labor practices; unions were not restricted in any way. The pressures for reforming (or discarding) the Wagner Act boiled over with the Great Strike Wave of 1945–46 that followed the end of World War II. Recall from Chapter 3 that for the 12 months beginning in August 1945, 4,600 strikes occurred involving 4.9 million workers and resulting in nearly 120 million lost worker-days.[73] There were large strikes in autos, steel, coal, rail, oil refining, longshoring, meatpacking, and electrical products. This level of strike activity surpassed any other year in U.S. history and magnified the perceived need to bring unions under control.

The Principles of the Taft–Hartley Act

A popular framework for thinking about labor law is to consider a pendulum that can range from strong bargaining power for labor on one side to strong bargaining power for companies on the other side (recall Figure 2.3). If the pendulum is too far to one side, either labor or management will have too much power, which will be bad for society as a whole. For much of the 19th and early 20th centuries, the absence of specific laws pertaining to collective bargaining left labor relations subject to common-law and business-law rulings shaped by classical economic beliefs about the importance of free markets. The pendulum favored employers—injunctions were issued, strikes broken, union leaders jailed, and union supporters blacklisted. The Wagner Act in 1935 sought to move the pendulum to the middle of the power spectrum by restraining employers' abilities to repress unionization. However, by 1946 many believed that the Wagner Act had overcorrected the earlier problems: The pendulum swung through the middle and too far toward labor. Proposals for reform sought to fix the perceived excesses of the Wagner Act to move the pendulum to the middle of the spectrum.[74]

Labor issues are not always high on the national agenda, but labor relations issues in the 1930s and 1940s were a big deal. In fact, 17 bills to reform labor law were introduced

In Their Own Words Representative Hartley Reports His Labor Relations Bill to Congress (1947)

During the last few years, the effects of industrial strife have at times brought our country to the brink of general economic paralysis. Employees have suffered, employers have suffered—and above all, the public has suffered.

. . .

In 1945 approximately 38,000,000 man-days of labor were lost as a result of strikes. And that total was trebled in 1946, when there were 116,000,000 man-days lost and the number of strikes hit a new high of 4,985. The resulting loss in national wealth is staggering.

. . .

For the last 14 years, as a result of labor laws ill-conceived and disastrously executed, the American workingman has been deprived of his dignity as an individual. He has been cajoled, coerced, intimidated, and on many occasions beaten up, in the name of the splendid aims set forth in Section 1 of the National Labor Relations Act. His whole economic life has been subject to the complete domination and control of unregulated [labor union] monopolists. . . . He has been forced into labor organizations against his will. . . . He has been prohibited from expressing his own mind on public issues. He has been denied any voice in arranging the terms of his own employment. He has frequently against his will been called out on strikes. . . . In many cases his economic life has been ruled by Communists and other subversive influences.

. . .

The employer's plight has likewise not been happy. He has witnessed the productive efficiency in his plants sink to alarmingly low levels. He has been required to employ or reinstate individuals who have destroyed his property and assaulted other employees. . . . He has seen the loyalty of his supervisors undermined by the compulsory unionism imposed upon them by the National Labor Relations Board.

. . .

The bill attacks the problem in a comprehensive—not in a piecemeal—fashion. It is neither drastic, oppressive, nor punitive. . . . It does not take away any rights guaranteed by the existing National Labor Relations Act. It does, however, go to the root of the evils and provides a fair, workable, and long-overdue solution to the problem.

Source: National Labor Relations Board, *Legislative History of the National Labor Management Relations Act, 1947* (Washington, DC: U.S. Government Printing Office, 1948), pp. 294–96.

on the opening day of Congress in 1947—the first Congress controlled by Republicans since 1930.[75] The proposal that was ultimately enacted in 1947 was the **Taft–Hartley Act,** also known as the Labor Management Relations Act. The Taft–Hartley Act significantly amends the Wagner Act. These acts are still the basis of U.S. labor law and together are often referred to as the National Labor Relations Act (NLRA). Whereas the opening of the Wagner Act emphasizes inequalities between labor and management and therefore the need to promote collective bargaining, the Taft–Hartley Act, in contrast, declares,

> Industrial strife . . . can be avoided or substantially minimized if employers, employees, and labor organizations each recognize under law one another's legitimate rights in their relations with each other, and above all recognize under law that neither party has any right in its relations with any other to engage in acts or practices which jeopardize the public health, safety, or interest. It is the purpose and policy of this Act . . . to prescribe the legitimate rights of both employees and employers . . . , to provide orderly and peaceful procedures for preventing the interference by either with the legitimate rights of the other, to protect the rights of individual employees in their relations with labor organizations . . . , and to protect the rights of the public in connection with labor disputes affecting commerce.

TABLE 4.6
The Central Changes of the Taft–Hartley Act (1947)

Section 2	Excludes supervisors and independent contractors.
Sections 3–6	Expands and restructures the National Labor Relations Board (NLRB).
Section 7	Guarantees employees the right to refrain from forming unions, bargaining collectively, and engaging in other concerted activities.
Section 8(a)	Modifies the third employer unfair labor practice to outlaw the closed shop.
Section 8(b)	Defines six union unfair labor practices: (1) To restrain or coerce employees in the exercise of the rights guaranteed in Section 7. (2) To cause an employer to discriminate against employees except for failure to pay required union dues. (3) To refuse to bargain collectively with the employer. (4) To engage in secondary boycotts and certain forms of strikes and picketing. (5) To require excessive or discriminatory membership fees. (6) To force an employer to pay for services not performed (featherbedding). [(7) was added in 1959: To picket an employer to demand recognition except in limited circumstances.]
Section 8(c)	Grants employers the right to express views and opinions except for threats and promises (employer free speech).
Section 8(d)	Defines the bargaining obligation as meeting in good faith with respect to wages, hours, and other terms and conditions of employment, but as not requiring agreement.
Section 9	Specifies secret ballot elections for determining questions of majority support for both certification and decertification cases.
Section 14(b)	Allows states to pass right-to-work laws.
Sections 201–204	Create the Federal Mediation and Conciliation Service to provide voluntary mediation.
Sections 206–210	Empower the U.S. president to petition a court to suspend a strike that is deemed a national emergency strike.

Note: The full text of the Taft–Hartley Act is reproduced in Appendix A at the end of this book.

To accomplish these objectives, the Taft–Hartley Act amends and adds to the Wagner Act in diverse and far-reaching ways; the full text is in Appendix A, and the major provisions are summarized in Table 4.6. These changes can be usefully divided into three categories:

- Restrictions on union actions.
- Enhanced rights of individuals and employers.
- New dispute resolution procedures.[76]

Taft–Hartley Restrictions on Unions

Union actions are restricted in the Taft–Hartley Act primarily by the addition of six union unfair labor practices (a seventh was added in 1959 to restrict picketing for union recognition). The Wagner Act's employer unfair labor practices remain and appear in Section 8(a); Section 8(b) was created for the union unfair labor practices. The first three parallel the employer unfair labor practices: to restrain or coerce employees in the exercise of the rights guaranteed in Section 7 [8(b)(1)], to cause or attempt to cause an employer to discriminate against employees except for failing to pay any required union dues [8(b)(2)], and to refuse to bargain collectively with the employer [8(b)(3)].

Of the remaining three unfair labor practices, only 8(b)(4) is significant. This unfair labor practice prohibits unions from engaging in secondary boycotts and other forms of strikes and picketing that involve "innocent" employers. The term secondary boycott comes from the fact that a secondary rather than a primary employer is targeted—that is, a company that does not directly employ the workers who are involved in the dispute. For example, consider a strike against the maker of potato chips that is sold in a local grocery store. A secondary boycott would occur if the union picketed the grocery store to tell consumers not to shop at the store. This is illegal because the grocery store is a secondary employer; the workers on strike work for the potato chip maker, not the grocery store. In contrast, it would be legal for the union members to "picket the product" outside the grocery store and tell consumers not to buy the specific brand of chips because of a labor dispute: This action specifically targets the primary employer and is therefore acceptable.

Union actions are also restricted by a change that outlaws closed shop agreements. A **closed shop** agreement is a provision negotiated into a collective bargaining agreement that requires the employer to hire only union members. In other words, the workplace is closed to all except union members. Employers viewed this as especially pernicious because the employers cannot hire whomever they choose; rather, they must hire union members. In contrast, a **union shop** allows anyone to be hired; but to remain employed, workers must join the union within a certain amount of time (commonly 30 days). An **agency shop** is similar; but rather than joining the union, workers must pay dues. Both are allowed by the Taft–Hartley Act, though later Supreme Court rulings rendered union shops enforceable only as agency shops in which workers can be forced to pay only the fraction of union dues that is germane to bargaining and administering union contracts, called an "agency fee" or "fair-share fee" (see Chapter 9); union shop clauses cannot compel workers to formally join unions.[77]

Section 14(b) of the Taft–Hartley Act allows states to pass **right-to-work laws** that prohibit union or agency shop agreements.[78] As of 2016, there are 26 right-to-work states, which is what states with right-to-work laws are called (see Figure 4.1). At a political level, right-to-work laws are arguably the most controversial topic in labor relations today. Most right-to-work laws are decades old, but starting in 2012 there was a push by conservative groups to enact new right-to-work laws, which included surprising successes in Michigan (2013) and Wisconsin (2015). The effects of right-to-work laws have long been debated, with proponents claiming that right-to-work laws improve employment growth and other

FIGURE 4.1
Right-to-Work States (unshaded) with Dates of Enactment

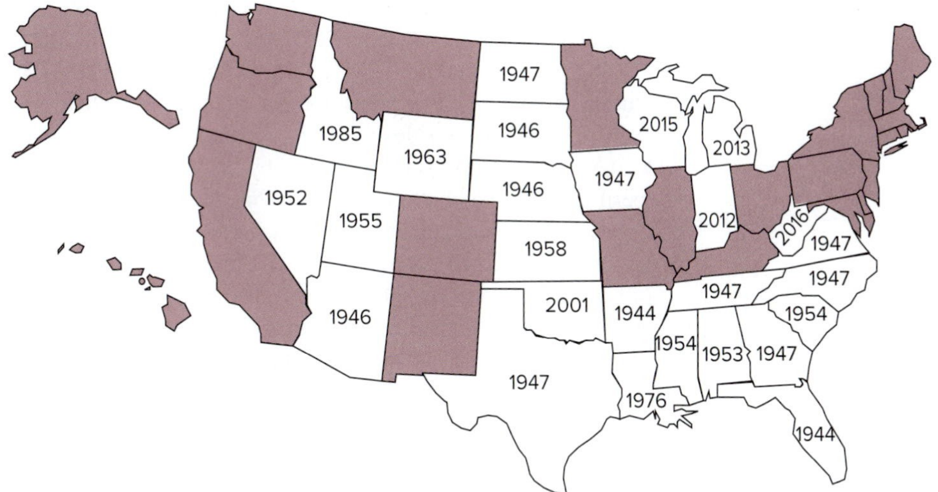

economic outcomes while detractors counter that it is impossible to isolate the effects of right-to-work laws from many other differences between right-to-work and non-right-to-work states. On balance, the empirical evidence is mixed.[79] More important than these economic angles are the principles that underlie arguments pro and con. Repeating 19th century arguments emphasizing the individual freedom to contract, right-to-work advocates label union and agency shops as "compulsory unionism" that violates individual freedoms by depriving workers of their right to freely choose whether or not to become a union member and pay union dues.[80] In contrast, unions argue that it is unfair to allow free riders to benefit from union representation without sharing the costs by paying their fair share and that majority rule is a basic feature of democratic institutions and any dues paying requirements are subject to majority approval. Most controversially, unions and their supporters see the arguments for right-to-work laws as a smokescreen for the true conservative agenda: strengthening its political and legislative power by weakening the labor movement as a key political opponent. Indeed, support for and against right-to-work laws commonly falls along party lines, with Republicans in favor of these laws and Democrats opposed.

Enhancing the Rights of Individuals and Employers

The second major category of the Taft–Hartley Act provisions enhances the rights of individuals and employers. These provisions again reflect the view that unions were too strong and the resulting perceived need to bolster the rights of other parties in the employment relationship. Section 7 is expanded from the Wagner Act to give individuals the right to refrain from concerted activity, and Section 9 is revised to add a decertification procedure by which individuals can oust their bargaining agent if they no longer desire union representation. Employers are granted rights by the employer's free speech provision [Section 8(c)]. This provision lets employers express views about unionization as long as these expressions do not contain threats or promises. This is an important aspect of union organizing campaigns and will therefore be discussed in Chapter 6. Additionally, to serve employers' demands for unquestioned loyalty among supervisors, supervisors were excluded from protection of the act. Supervisors can try to unionize, but it's not an unfair labor practice to fire them in response. Another right granted to employers is the ability to file unfair labor practice charges against unions.[81]

New Dispute Resolution Procedures

Finally, the Taft–Hartley Act addressed various dispute resolution mechanisms. The NLRB had been sharply attacked by business since its creation; the Taft–Hartley Act restructured the NLRB to separate the investigation/prosecution and judicial aspects of the agency (unlike all other federal agencies) and also prevented it from undertaking economic analyses—changes that significantly weakened the agency and forced it to become singularly legal rather than pragmatic.[82] The board was also expanded to five members. To facilitate resolution of bargaining disputes, the act created the Federal Mediation and Conciliation Service (FMCS) to provide voluntary mediation to labor and management negotiators. Also, the U.S. president was authorized by the act to petition the courts to stop strikes that "imperil the national health or safety." This national emergency strike provision is unsurprising when one remembers that this act was passed in the aftermath of the tremendous strike wave in 1945–46, though its provisions are used infrequently.

In sum, if unions were too powerful, the various amendments to the Wagner Act that were implemented by the Taft–Hartley Act in 1947 can be viewed as restoring a needed balance among individuals, unions, and employers. On the other hand, organized labor saw the Taft–Hartley Act as an opportunistic effort by business and conservative politicians to roll back labor's protections and therefore labeled it the "Slave Labor Act." This label might be more accurate for the more draconian original proposal in the House of Representatives than the final law that was passed, but it clearly underscores labor's strong opposition.[83]

In this view, restrictions on secondary boycotts undermined union solidarity and prevented the strong from aiding the weak; the employer's free speech provision legitimized employer interference in what should be a worker-only issue (whether to join a union); not protecting supervisor unions relegated the labor movement to representing only blue-collar workers; and the act generally made unions even more dependent on government control.[84] Union leaders also felt victimized by the Taft–Hartley requirement that union leaders sign an affidavit swearing that they are not communists (this provision is no longer in effect). Many unions had already purged communists from their organizations, but the Taft–Hartley Act publicly equated unionism with communism. Business leaders did not have to sign such affidavits, only union leaders.[85] Advocates of the industrial relations school of thought opposed the Taft–Hartley Act amendments as injecting too much government regulation into labor relations (such as with broad and vague union unfair labor practices).[86] President Truman vetoed the Taft–Hartley Act, but his veto was easily overridden by an alliance of Republicans and conservative Southern Democrats. As such, the Taft–Hartley Act remains at the heart of U.S. labor law—and by some accounts, organized labor's weakness—in the 21st century.

FIGHTING UNION CORRUPTION: THE LANDRUM–GRIFFIN ACT

In 1956 a New York journalist appeared on national television with dark glasses and bandaged hands and generated widespread public outrage about labor movement corruption. After publishing a newspaper column about organized crime in the New York garment and trucking industries, this journalist had been blinded in an acid attack linked to New York gangster Johnny Dio.[87] A congressional investigating committee was formed in response; and through the McClellan committee hearings in 1957–1959, the American public learned about the links among Teamsters leader Jimmy Hoffa, Johnny Dio, and other organized crime figures and their use of sweetheart contracts (in return for kickbacks, union officials would ignore an employer's contract violations such as substandard wages, though they would still collect union dues), personal loans from union health and welfare funds, and violence to keep resistant employers and employees in line.[88] In fact, the committee eventually published 58 volumes of hearings and reports—34 about the Teamsters and the rest about four other unions.[89] The McClellan committee concluded that rank-and-file union members lacked a voice and often the right to vote in internal union affairs, national union leaders abused their power over locals and union finances, and violence was used to keep members in line. This represented just 5 out of 200 or so national unions, so it is important not to overstate the extent of union corruption; nevertheless there were (and continue to be) unfortunate examples of mafia-infiltrated unions and corrupt union leaders.[90]

Congress responded by debating various bills to address concerns with union democracy, financial transparency, and some revisions to the National Labor Relations Act (NLRA). As a result, the **Landrum–Griffin Act** was passed in 1959.[91] As emphasized by its opening declaration, this act focuses on internal union affairs:

> In order to accomplish the objective of a free flow of commerce it is essential that labor organizations, employers, and their officials adhere to the highest standards of responsibility and ethical conduct in administering the affairs of their organizations, particularly as they affect labor–management relations. The Congress further finds, from recent investigations in the labor and management fields, that there have been a number of instances of breach of trust, corruption, disregard of the rights of individual employees, and other failures to observe high standards of responsibility and ethical conduct which require further and supplementary legislation that will afford necessary protection of the rights and interests of employees and the public generally as they relate to the activities of labor organizations, employers, labor relations consultants, and their officers and representatives.

In Their Own Words Representative Landrum Introduces a Labor–Management Reform Bill (1959)

Mr. Chairman, together with the gentleman from Michigan [Representative Griffin], I have today introduced a nonpartisan bill, dealing with the tremendously vital issue of labor–management reform legislation. We did so only after the most thorough consideration, and in light of what we feel to be absolutely necessary in this field, if free and democratic processes in the industrial relations of our great Nation are to survive.

. . .

I would call to the Members' attention that the interim report of the McClellan committee found that there has been a significant lack of democratic processes in certain unions, that one-man dictatorships have thrived—in some instances for 20 to 30 years—and that through intimidation and fear, the rank-and-file union member has been deprived of a voice in his own union affairs.

. . .

One of the basic underlying principles of both the Wagner Act of 1935 and the Taft–Hartley Act of 1947 has been the rights of employees—under the first to be free from employer domination, under the second to be free from union domination. That further legislation, however, dealing with union democracy is needed in 1959 cannot be challenged. As one union official put it in his testimony, "We believe that the control of the union by its membership is the best way to insure its democracy and keep the officers in line—I believe that the best demonstration of democracy in action, is where the people directly handle their own union business." This [our] bill seeks to accomplish, by insuring effective membership control . . . . Under the bill we propose, all unions of whatever size would be required to report pertinent financial data, informing the membership of possible conflicts of interest, and other shady deals . . .

. . .

In conclusion, Mr. Chairman, let me say that the bill the gentleman from Michigan and I have introduced is not an antiunion bill, it is not a union busting bill, it is not an anticollective bargaining bill. It would not impinge in any way upon the lawful and legitimate purposes and activities of American labor unions. It is a bill which would restore the control of union affairs to union members.

Source: National Labor Relations Board, *Legislative History of the National Labor Relations Act 1959,* Vol. II (Washington, DC: U.S. Government Printing Office, 1959), pp. 1517–19.

To achieve union democracy, the Landrum–Griffin Act creates a bill of rights for union members that guarantees all union members equal rights of participation in internal union affairs, including voting and expressing views (see Table 4.7). Democratic standards for the election of union officers are also established.

Increased democracy should reduce union corruption, but the Landrum–Griffin Act tries to prevent union corruption and labor racketeering in three additional ways. First, unions and their officers are required to disclose financial records by filing reports with the U.S. Department of Labor; these reports can be viewed at *www.dol.gov/olms/*. In fact, the formal name of the Landrum–Griffin Act is the Labor–Management Reporting and Disclosure Act. This reporting is intended to increase the transparency of union governance to prevent abuse—foreshadowing the attempts to increase the transparency of corporate governance 40 years later in the wake of the Enron scandal. Second, the act restricts the use of union trusteeships. National unions can take over the operation of a local union and replace the elected officers with an appointed trustee; the act tries to ensure that this power is used for legitimate purposes (cleaning up a corrupt local) rather than illegitimate ones (removing local leaders that are political opponents of the national leadership or installing a corrupt leader who is beholden to the national leadership). Third, the Landrum–Griffin Act establishes the fiduciary responsibility of union leaders.

TABLE 4.7
The Central Provisions of the Landrum–Griffin Act (1959)

Title I: Bill of Rights of Members of Labor Organizations

- Equal rights for all union members to nominate candidates for office, vote in union elections, attend meetings, and participate in deliberations.
- Freedom of speech and assembly for union members.
- Dues amounts must be approved by a majority vote.
- Safeguards against improper discipline or expulsion of union members.
- All union members are entitled to receive a copy of the collective bargaining agreement.

Title II: Reporting by Labor Organizations and Employers

- Unions must adopt a constitution and bylaws and file them with the Department of Labor.
- Unions must report the following information to the Department of Labor:
  - Names and titles of officers as well as their salaries and any loans made to them.
  - Initiation fees and dues.
  - Procedures for auditing financial records, approving contracts, and the like.
  - Financial assets, liabilities, receipts, and expenditures.
- Union members are entitled to look at union records to verify this information.
- Officers and employees of unions must report financial interests, transactions, or loans between them and any business whose employees are represented by the union.
- Employers must report payments or loans to union officials.
- Employers must report any contracts with labor relations consultants.

Title III: Trusteeships

- Unions must report and justify trusteeships to the Department of Labor.
- Standards for trusteeships are outlined.

Title IV: Union Elections

- All national unions must elect officers through democratic procedures at least every five years.
- All local unions must elect officers through a secret ballot vote at least every three years.
- Neither union funds nor employer donations can be used to finance a campaign for union office.
- Mailing lists of union members must be made equally available to all candidates for office.

Title V: Safeguards for Labor Organizations

- Union officers have a fiduciary duty to the union and its members.
- Significant loans to officers and employees of the union are prohibited.
- Convicted criminals of certain offenses (e.g., bribery, extortion, embezzlement, murder) are prohibited from holding positions of authority in labor unions within five years of ending their prison sentence.

Title VI: Miscellaneous Provisions

- Picketing to extort an employer is illegal.

Title VII: NLRA Amendments

- Permanently replaced strikers are allowed to vote only in NLRB elections that occur within 12 months of the start of the strike.
- Some loopholes with respect to Section 8(b)(4)'s ban on secondary boycotts are closed.
- A seventh union unfair labor practice [(8(b)(7)] is added restricting picketing for union recognition.
- Hot cargo agreements are banned.
- Prehire agreements in the construction industry are allowed.

Note: The full text of the act is available online at www.law.cornell.edu/uscode/text/29/chapter-11.

Although the overwhelming purpose of the Landrum–Griffin Act is to increase internal union democracy and prevent union corruption, it also amended the National Labor Relations Act in a few minor ways. The rights of permanently replaced strikers to participate in NLRB elections were confined to the first 12 months of a strike; the Section 8(b)(4) restrictions on secondary boycotts were revised; a seventh union unfair labor practice [Section 8(b)(7)] was added to restrict picketing for union recognition; and hot cargo agreements were outlawed [Section 8(e)]. In labor relations, hot cargo consists of goods that are made by nonunion workers or by a company that is being struck; a hot cargo agreement is a union contract clause giving members the right to refuse to handle hot cargo. The Landrum–Griffin Act also created special exceptions in various areas for the construction industry because of its short-term nature of employment.

Regulating Unions' Political Contributions

A concern related to the Landrum-Griffin Act's focus on the internal operation of labor unions is the use of union funds for political purposes. Indeed, the annual financial reports that unions must file under the Landrum-Griffin Act now include a separate entry for reporting political expenditures. Of particular worry to some is that unions force workers to pay dues and then use those funds to support political candidates and other causes that the workers might not support. Indeed, labor unions are active participants in the political arena, as are many corporations and business groups, but there is a complex set of statutes and case law that governs the financial aspects of their political participation.[92]

The Taft-Hartley Act prohibits unions from making donations directly to candidates for federal office, but subsequent federal campaign finance laws allow unions to use their funds to disseminate political information to their members and to establish separate political action committees (PACs), which can directly support candidates. These campaign finance laws prohibit the use of dues money to support union-sponsored PACs; rather, union members need to be solicited for voluntary contributions to a union-sponsored PAC. Corporations and unions, however, found ways around these restrictions by funding "electioneering communications" that did not explicitly say to vote for or against a specific candidate, but essentially achieved this message through its content. A campaign finance law in 2002 therefore tried to limit this practice, but in 2010 the Supreme Court ruled that these restrictions violate the free speech protections of the First Amendment.[93] So while corporations and unions are still prohibited from contributing directly to candidates (this needs to be done through a PAC), a wide range of other political expenditures, financed by union dues, are permitted.

However, if a unionized worker objects to the spending of union funds on political activities, the worker is free to resign his or her membership in the union and therefore not pay dues. In non-right-to-work states, it is likely that nonmembers might still have to pay some fraction of regular dues, but because of important judicial rulings, these nonmembers can object to, and not have to pay for, political activities and other activities not germane to collective bargaining.[94] Consequently, there are ways for individuals to avoid having their money spent on political activities. The use of dues money in the political arena, however, remains a highly charged political issue, and in recent years a number of federal and state "paycheck protection" acts have been proposed. These proposals would convert these judicial protections into statutory protections and in some cases deepen these rulings, for example, by requiring union members to grant approval explicitly for political expenditures.[95]

EXTENSIONS TO GOVERNMENT EMPLOYEES: PUBLIC SECTOR LABOR LAW

The next major developments in U.S. labor law occurred in the public sector—government employees at the federal, state, and local levels. By 1959 the legislative framework for private sector labor law was nearly completely established, but it was just on the verge of erupting in the public sector. The National Labor Relations Act (NLRA) applies to private sector employers and workers nationwide. In contrast, public sector labor law has 51 separate jurisdictions—the U.S. federal government for federal employees and the 50 states for state and local government workers. Thus there can be significant differences in public sector labor law across jurisdictions.

Public sector unionization dates back to the 19th century: There was a strike in 1836 in the federal shipyards, a national teachers' union was established in 1857, postal workers formed unions as early as 1863, and firefighters and police began organizing around the turn of the century.[96] However, in the wake of a 1919 strike by Boston police that resulted in looting and violence, public sentiment became, in the words of Calvin Coolidge, who was governor of Massachusetts at the time, "there is no right to strike against the public safety by anybody, anywhere, any time."[97] As such, early laws and legal rulings treated attempts to bargain with governments as interfering with the responsibility of *elected* government officials to establish public policies and protect the public interest. In the 1950s, this aversion to public sector unions started weakening in the face of worsening public sector employment conditions and a new legal respect for the freedom of association.[98] The first public sector law giving government employees the right to engage in collective bargaining was passed by Wisconsin in 1959; the federal government and a number of other states followed in the 1960s. Since then public sector union membership has increased from less than 1 million in 1960 to over 7 million today—that is, from a union density of 10 percent to 35 percent (recall Figure 1.4).

Federal Sector Bargaining Rights

In the federal sector President Kennedy established limited bargaining rights, exclusive representation, and unfair labor practices for federal employees with Executive Order 10988 in 1962.[99] Subsequent presidents revised this initial structure, and the resulting bargaining system was codified into law by Congress in 1978 through the **Civil Service Reform Act.**[100] This act protects most federal sector workers, though supervisors, the military, security agencies (like the FBI), the Post Office, and several other agencies are excluded. Postal employees are covered under the NLRA (but cannot legally strike), and it is illegal for military personnel to unionize. The major elements of the labor relations system for federal workers set forth in the Civil Service Reform Act parallel the NLRA framework: exclusive representation with majority support, certification elections, employer and union unfair labor practices, and an agency (the Federal Labor Relations Authority) that administers elections and unfair labor practice charges (see Table 4.8). However, there are some important differences between

TABLE 4.8
The Civil Service Reform Act and The NLRA: Similar . . . But Different

	Comparison with the NLRA	
Major Features of the Civil Service Reform Act	**Similar**	**Different**
Grants employees the right to form unions and engage in collective bargaining.	✓	
Applies to many federal government employees.		X
Exclusive representation with majority support is a key principle.	✓	
A union with the support of 10 percent but less than 50 percent of the bargaining unit has consultation rights.		X
Unfair labor practices are specified.	✓	
An agency conducts elections to determine majority support and adjudicates unfair labor practice charges.	✓	
Negotiable issues exclude wages and benefits; bargaining is generally limited to policies and procedures.		X
Explicitly grants management rights (the right to determine mission and budgets, to hire, assign, direct employees, and other managerial functions) to managers.		X
Strikes are prohibited.		X

Note: The full text of the Civil Service Reform Act is available online at www.law.cornell.edu/uscode/text/5/part-III/subpart-F/chapter-71.

the two systems. In particular, strikes are prohibited, wages and benefits are excluded from bargaining, and unions with minority but not majority support have consultation rights so that a federal agency must consult with the union before changing working conditions (see Chapter 13). As long as one remembers that this is an oversimplification, labor law for federal employees can be summarized as "the NLRA without the right to strike."

State and Local Government Bargaining Rights

Labor relations for state and municipal workers are governed by the laws and courts of each state. First note that the courts have decided that preventing public sector workers from unionizing violates freedom of assembly and speech (this differs from the private sector because in the public sector the employer is a government), but there is no constitutional right of bargaining.[101] Thus questions of public sector labor law focus on bargaining. With this in mind, start by considering four categories of state public sector bargaining laws: comprehensive laws, narrow laws, no laws, and prohibitive laws. Comprehensive laws broadly grant nearly all government occupations—teachers, firefighters, police, state employees, and the like—the right to collectively bargain, whereas narrow laws apply to one or several occupations only. For example, Hawaii, Iowa, and New York have comprehensive laws; Wyoming's narrow law covers only firefighters; and Indiana's covers only teachers. States with no laws are silent on whether public sector bargaining is legal, whereas prohibitive laws ban it. All told, 29 states have comprehensive laws, 14 have narrow laws or executive orders, 3 have no laws, and laws in 3 states prohibit bargaining (see Table 4.9).[102] In states with no laws, bargaining still occurs; this underscores the important distinction between unprotected and illegal union activity.[103]

Unsurprisingly, the bargaining laws (where present) vary tremendously from state to state in operational details. The sentiment of "there is no right to strike against the public safety by anybody, anywhere, any time" is still widespread, so most public sector bargaining laws prohibit strikes for all public sector employees. Some states even harshly penalize strikers; for example, New York's Taylor law imposes a "two for one" penalty for each day someone is on strike—their lost pay for the day plus a fine equal to their day's pay. In contrast, some states allow strikes by nonessential workers—teachers, bus drivers, state workers, college professors—while banning strikes by essential workers—firefighters, police, prison guards. Public sector bargaining laws also differ in the types of dispute resolution procedures used as substitutes for strikes (see Chapter 8). There are additional operational differences in the scope of bargaining, the legality of the agency shop, and the wording of unfair labor practices. But the laws are generally based on exclusive representation with majority rule, certification elections, unfair labor practices, and administration via a specialized agency.[104] As long as one remembers that this is an oversimplification, labor law for state and municipal employees—where it exists—can be summarized as "the NLRA *usually* without the right to strike."

Online Exploration Exercise: Find a state bargaining law online. Is this a comprehensive law? How is it similar to the NLRA framework? How is it different?

Ongoing Controversies Over Public Sector Unionization

In recent years, the issue of public sector bargaining laws has resurfaced as a highly charged political issue. As noted above, opposition to public sector unionization in earlier decades was based on a belief that unionization undermined governmental authority and therefore democracy. But now, opponents of big government see public

TABLE 4.9
Five Types of State Public Sector Bargaining Laws

Comprehensive	Narrow	No Law	Prohibitive	Broad but Shallow
(bargaining rights for nearly all occupations)	(no bargaining rights for some occupations)	(bargaining neither protected nor banned)	(bargaining is prohibited)	(comprehensive coverage with limited rights)
(29 states)	(14 states)	(3 states)	(3 states)	(1 state)
Alaska*	Alabama	Louisiana*	North Carolina	Wisconsin
Arkansas	Arizona	Mississippi	South Carolina	
California*	Colorado*	West Virginia	Virginia	
Connecticut	Georgia			
Delaware	Idaho			
Florida	Indiana			
Hawaii*	Kentucky			
Illinois*	Missouri			
Iowa	Nevada			
Kansas	North Dakota			
Maine	Oklahoma			
Maryland	Tennessee			
Massachusetts	Texas			
Michigan	Wyoming			
Minnesota*				
Montana*				
Nebraska				
New Hampshire				
New Jersey*				
New Mexico				
New York				
Ohio*				
Oregon*				
Pennsylvania*				
Rhode Island				
South Dakota				
Utah				
Vermont*				
Washington				

Note: *denotes the right to strike for teachers and/or state workers (by law or court ruling).

sector unions as "too powerful because they sustain a strong and intrusive state, not because they subvert it."[105] In states with public sector bargaining laws, therefore, Republican lawmakers have increasingly tried to limit or abolish bargaining rights. For example, newly elected Republican governors in Indiana and Missouri removed bargaining rights for state workers in 2005. Since that time, there have been hundreds of proposals introduced in numerous states. These proposals are commonly rationalized by saying that public sector unions are too strong and therefore state and local governments can no longer afford to pay the wages and benefits negotiated by public sector unions. For example, the Wisconsin bill that passed in 2011 repealing collective bargaining rights for some public sector employees and limiting collective bargaining for other employees was titled the Budget Repair Bill. This leads to a fifth category of public sector bargaining laws in Table 4.9: broad coverage but shallow rights. In Wisconsin, public sector unions are limited to only bargaining over base wages, and wage increases greater than the rate of inflation are prohibited unless approved by a public referendum. Though it did not pass, in 2015, the Nevada considered legislation that critics dubbed the "union armageddon" bill because of the extent to which it would have restricted public sector bargaining.

Labor unions and their supporters argue that the real motivation behind these attempts to roll back public sector unionization policies is to weaken the political power of unions because they traditionally support Democratic rather than Republican lawmakers and oppose significant reductions in government services. For example, Wisconsin's Budget Repair Bill also prohibited dues collection through paycheck deduction and required annual votes of unionized workers to maintain certification. These sharply divided perspectives and the passionate nature of these debates were very visibly highlighted by the events in Wisconsin in 2011–12, including Democratic lawmakers hiding in Illinois to prevent a vote on the bill, weeks of intense worker and union protests around the state capitol, legal challenges after the bill was enacted, and the collection of over 1 million signatures to trigger a special election to recall Governor Walker.[106] In 2016, all eyes were on a Supreme Court case (*Friedrichs v. California Teachers Association*) that would have prohibited agency fee arrangements and thus made the entire public sector a "right-to-work" sector; Justice Antonin Scalia's sudden death, however, left the Court split so a lower court ruling affirming public sector agency fees was left intact, at least for the time being. As long as the political environment remains polarized and partisan, legislative and judicial conflicts over public sector unionization will likely continue.

LABOR LAW IN PRACTICE: NLRB DECISIONS AND REFORM

The statutes that comprise U.S. labor law are quite static. In the private sector, in particular, most of today's laws governing labor–management relations were written in 1935 and 1947. The Landrum–Griffin Act made some minor modifications, but the major focus of that act was internal union affairs rather than interactions between labor and management. In 1974, the NLRA was amended to include private sector hospitals and to provide stringent notice requirements before hospital unions could strike.[107] Except for changes in state-level right-to-work laws, these are the only changes since 1947 worth mentioning here. However, a second important component of labor law is much more dynamic and voluminous: the accumulated body of case law developed through National Labor Relations Board (NLRB) and court decisions and precedents. The same is generally true on a smaller scale for public sector labor law, albeit with greater variation. In practice, both the stable statutes and the dynamic case law are criticized by various advocates, so reforming the NLRA is a perennial debate in labor relations.

NLRB Decisions and Precedents

The NLRA contains numerous general standards—interference, restraint, domination, discrimination, good faith—but in practice, what do these standards mean? The NLRB must apply the facts of specific cases to these general legal principles to determine if violations have occurred (you can try this with the "Labor Law Discussion" cases at the end of the chapter). When the NLRB hears a case, it issues a written decision that may serve as a precedent for future cases; a sample decision is presented in Appendix C at the end of this book. Between 1935 and 2016, the NLRB issued 364 volumes of decisions. It is difficult to keep up with these rulings, but labor relations professionals need to be generally aware of this body of case law. Moreover, some NLRB and court precedents are so important that they have become part of everyday labor relations jargon: *Beck* rights (from the 1988 Supreme Court decision *Communication Workers of America v. Beck* described in Chapter 9), the *Mackay* doctrine (Chapter 8), *Weingarten* rights (Chapter 9), the *Borg–Warner* doctrine (Chapter 7), the *Excelsior* list (Chapter 6), and the *Wright Line* test, to name a few.

The ***Wright Line* test** illustrates the importance of precedents for guiding legal decision making, and it pertains to the heart of U.S. labor law: the dividing line between legitimate employee discipline and discharge on the one hand, and unlawful retaliation for union activity on the other (an 8(a)(3) unfair labor practice). Under the *Wright Line* test established by a 1980 NLRB decision, the NLRB general counsel (the prosecution) must first show that (1) the disciplined or discharged employee was engaged in protected activity, (2) the employer was aware of the activity, and (3) the activity was a substantial or motivating reason for the employer's action.[108] If the general counsel establishes these facts, the burden of proof shifts to the employer to prove that it would have taken the same action even if the employee had not engaged in protected activity. Human resource managers therefore must be able to document that employee discipline and termination are applied consistently and for valid job-related reasons, and that the reasons for discipline are not a pretext for discriminating against organizing activity. This shows how labor law matters for the everyday practice of labor relations, even in nonunion situations.

A major theme in many areas that the NLRB has to adjudicate is balancing property rights with labor rights. The *Wright Line* test tries to balance employers' rights and needs to discipline and discharge poor performers with employees' rights to engage in protected activity under the NLRA. Preventing employees from wearing pro-union buttons and other insignia interferes with protected activity and therefore violates Section 8(a)(1)—unless the employer can demonstrate a legitimate business need. Employers can use surveillance equipment to monitor employees to maintain security, but aggressive surveillance that might be used to retaliate against union supporters is viewed by the NLRB as going beyond the need to protect property rights and violates labor rights. Sticky issues in labor law pertaining to union organizing, bargaining, and strikes will be presented in subsequent chapters; these issues also often involve difficulties in balancing property rights with labor rights.

NLRB case law—the dynamic, interpretive aspect of labor law—enables the law to accommodate new situations that were not present in 1935 and 1947 and to therefore balance property rights and labor rights in a changing environment. For example, are a company's restrictions on employee use of its e-mail system a legitimate use of property rights, or do they violate labor rights by interfering with concerted activity such as discussing working conditions? Such questions are addressed by NLRB decisions. However, the NLRB framework for adjudicating U.S. labor law has critics. The board's five members who decide cases are political appointees. While allegations that the NLRB is overly politicized are generally overstated, few deny that there are political influences on major NLRB rulings or major rule-making changes, which opens up the NRLB to criticism from the party not in power.[109] Other labor supporters argue that the NLRB lacks sufficient remedial powers—in particular, the lack of punitive damages means that employers find it cost-effective to commit unfair labor practices.[110] If this is true, the penalties for labor law violators need to be strengthened. Unions are also critical of how employers can manipulate NLRB hearings and judicial appeals to create legal delays that frustrate union organizing and bargaining.

Debating the Need for Labor Law Reform

Beyond the operation of the NLRB, there are a number of ongoing labor law controversies. As more employees are asked to exercise independent judgment or delegate minor tasks to coworkers, who exactly is a supervisor under the NLRA has become a contentious legal issue, especially as employers have increasingly tried to exclude nurses and others from coverage under the act.[111] In fact, it is estimated that 20 to 25 percent of private sector workers lack the protections of the NLRA because they are supervisors or independent contractors or because they work for businesses that are too small to be covered or in excluded industries such as agriculture. Moreover, approximately one-third of public sector workers (excluding the military) are not covered by a bargaining law.[112] The increased importance of undocumented immigrant workers for the U.S. economy highlights another controversial area: Undocumented workers are protected under the NLRA, but the 2002 *Hoffman Plastic* Supreme Court decision denies back pay awards to undocumented workers when their NLRA rights are violated.[113] The NLRA protects the right to strike, but the Supreme Court lets employers use permanent strike replacements.[114] One can also argue that judges have rewritten the NLRA through legal rulings that significantly weaken the original law.[115] So there continue to be calls to reform substantive aspects of the NLRA.[116] Union proponents favor expanding NLRA coverage to supervisors, streamlining the certification election process to determine majority support, and banning the use of permanent strike replacements.

These issues will be addressed in subsequent chapters, and although Congress has debated various reform proposals, none have passed. A recent example is the Employee Free Choice Act that would certify unions based on signed authorization cards rather than an election (see Chapter 6), authorize the use of first contract arbitration, and mandate stiffer penalties for violators. The Employee Free Choice Act was passed by the U.S. House of Representatives in 2007, but a lack of Senate support and the threat of a veto by President Bush killed it. After the election of President Obama, this bill was promptly reintroduced in Congress in 2009 and received a lot of media attention, but it was not voted on. It is unlikely to be acted on during the Trump administration.

Others criticize the NLRA framework for reducing labor unions to economic agents. Rather than seeing freedom of association and the right to strike as fundamental civil liberties that support democracy, workers are legally protected only when they pursue narrow economic interests such as higher wages.[117] Taking this a step further, critical scholars advocate more sweeping changes that would shift U.S. labor law away from seeing unions as limited workplace advocates of workers (as in the industrial relations school) toward broader visions of unions as key institutions of the working class across workplaces and throughout the political and economic aspects of society (as in the critical industrial relations school).[118] Such changes require weakening the dominance of employers' property rights, increasing union participation in corporate governance, and removing barriers to broad-based working-class solidarity like the prohibition on secondary boycotts. In a different vein, advocates of using joint (nonunion) labor–management committees for improving workplace issues lobby for a loosening of the Section 8(a)(2) ban on company-dominated unions; this too has been considered by Congress but has not been enacted (see Chapter 10).[119]

An alternative view is that the NRLA assumptions—especially a sharp divide between managers and workers in stable, mass manufacturing industries—no longer match the 21st-century world of work based on knowledge workers in a global system of flexible production.[120] The industrial relations school of thought implies that new institutions should be created to place checks and balances on free markets; promote efficiency, equity, and voice; and balance property rights with labor rights.[121] From a business perspective, typically rooted in mainstream economic or human resource management thought (recall Chapter 2), institutional checks are largely unnecessary, and the NLRA is seen as interfering with the achievement of economic prosperity through free markets and individual action. From these perspectives, the NLRA should be weakened or even repealed.[122] A number of recent congressional proposals have therefore sought to reduce funding for the NLRB, block NLRB appointees, limit proposed NLRB election rules, and limit the NLRB's enforcement powers. These various perspectives on labor law reform are important for thinking about future directions for U.S. labor relations, and they will be revisited in Chapter 13. But first, the next few chapters discuss the major processes of the current U.S. labor relations system—union organizing, bargaining, and grievance resolution. Understanding the development of the NLRA out of the industrial relations school of thought is a vital foundation for understanding these processes.

POSTSCRIPT: THE RISE OF EMPLOYMENT LAW

In U.S. legal and business circles it is common to distinguish between labor law, which focuses on workers' *collective* actions, and **employment law,** which pertains to *individual* employment rights. In the absence of explicit laws, the U.S. employment relationship is governed by the employment-at-will doctrine, which means employees can be hired under any conditions and fired at any time for *any* reason. Under the employment-at-will doctrine, outstanding job performers can be fired because their supervisors dislike them, because of their gender or their race, or for any other arbitrary reason—and in return, employees are free to quit at any time.

The earliest attempts to temper the at-will doctrine occurred in the area of safety and health as various states enacted laws specifying minimum safety standards around 1900, though these laws were generally ineffective.[123] Many states also passed workers' compensation laws between 1910 and 1920, and they are now universal. Because of these workers' compensation policies, employees do not have to sue their employers in court to collect damages if they are injured on the job; rather, employees are now guaranteed a set schedule of benefits.[124] This tempers the at-will doctrine by requiring workers' compensation insurance and by prohibiting an employee from being fired in retaliation for filing a valid workers' compensation claim. Workers' compensation laws were probably passed much earlier than other employment laws because *employers* benefit substantially: They are shielded from litigation expenses and the possibility of large damage awards.

During the Great Depression adherents to the industrial relations school of thought believed that both unionization and government regulation of the employment relationship were necessary for balancing efficiency, equity, and voice. Unions can help equalize bargaining power between employers and unionized employees, while laws can ensure minimum standards for all employees.[125] Consequently, the New Deal period not only saw the passage of the Wagner Act promoting unionization but also advanced employment law through the passage of the Social Security Act (1935) and the Fair Labor Standards Act (FLSA, 1938). The Social Security Act established what has grown into OASDHI: old age, survivors, disability, and health insurance, which provides federal monetary assistance and health care coverage to retirees, the disabled, and their dependents. This legislation also

Nonunion Application Frances Perkins: Mother of the New Deal

If Senator Wagner is the father of U.S. labor law (recall the box from earlier in the chapter), then Frances Perkins should be considered the mother of the New Deal. Born in 1880 from descendants of early New England families, Perkins was concerned with the plight of the poor from an early age. After graduating from Mount Holyoke, she volunteered in Chicago at the famous Hull House, a charitable community center for poor immigrant workers. From there, Perkins moved to Philadelphia where she worked to shut down agencies that lured women to Philadelphia with the promise of factory jobs and instead forced them into sexual slavery as prostitutes. She also interviewed many factory girls who were paid less than men, relegated to the worst jobs, and discriminated against within labor unions.

A few years later, Perkins ran the New York City office of the National Consumer League fighting dangerous working conditions, excessive working hours for women, and child labor. She witnessed the tragic Triangle Shirtwaist fire firsthand in 1911, and she became an influential figure, along with Wagner, in the subsequent investigations and reform movements. In 1919, at the age of 38, Perkins was appointed to the New York Industrial Commission, a state agency overseeing factory safety and regulation. This was a major appointment at a time when women did not yet have the right to vote and the leadership ranks of government, business, and labor were dominated by men. When he was elected governor of New York in 1928, Franklin Delano Roosevelt promoted Perkins to chair this commission. With the onset of the Great Depression, Perkins advocated for investigations into the problems of unemployment and urged the creation of unemployment insurance systems which did not yet exist in the United States.

When Roosevelt was elected U.S. president in 1932, he appointed Perkins as secretary of the Department of Labor. The challenges she faced were enormous—nearly a quarter of the U.S. workforce was unemployed, the idea of federal legislation regulating work was widely seen as unconstitutional, the Department of Labor she inherited was disorganized if not corrupt, and a woman had never before held a presidential cabinet post. The challenges further increased with the outbreak of bitter strikes in the mid-1930s. But she worked tirelessly—so tirelessly that her chauffeur was run ragged and quit.

Perkins was a champion of workers rather than of the labor unions of her day. Her concern with providing a voice for the workers led her to help bring about Section 7(a) of the National Industrial Recovery Act (NIRA), but it was Wagner (who by then was a U.S. senator) who initially championed the National Labor Relations Act. Indeed, Perkins's greater interest in the NIRA was a public works component to provide work for the unemployed, and her monumental accomplishments, which were yet to come, were aimed at benefitting all workers and their families. In particular, Perkins was the driving force behind the passage of the Social Security Act and the Fair Labor Standards Act, all while enduring sharp personal attacks by opponents of these initiatives and by those uncomfortable with a woman in a position of power and influence. By overcoming these attacks, broad segments of the labor force would be protected by minimum wages, overtime premiums, child labor restrictions, unemployment insurance, and old-age insurance (Social Security) for the first time in U.S. history.

Perkins served as Secretary of Labor for 12 years, a period that included much of the Great Depression and World War II. During the war, she promoted the contributions of female factory workers and ensured that Roosevelt and Winston Churchill would support the continuation of the International Labor Organization as an international agency advocating for workers. Perhaps the only major goal that she was unable to achieve was an issue that remains highly contested today—universal health insurance to further enhance the security of workers and their families.

Owing to Frances Perkins's intellectual abilities, determination, passion, and untiring efforts, she was perhaps the one individual most responsible for the lasting legacies of the New Deal for the American worker. More generally, this New Deal period was, in her own words, a "turning point in our national life—a turning from careless neglect of human values and toward an order . . . of mutual and practical benevolence within a free competitive industrial economy."

Reference: Kirstin Downey, *The Woman Behind the New Deal: The Life and Legacy of Frances Perkins, FDR's Secretary of Labor and His Moral Conscience* (New York: Doubleday, 2009). Quote is from p. 337.

established a system of state unemployment insurance benefits programs administered under the Federal Unemployment Tax Act. The FLSA created a federal national minimum wage, a mandatory overtime premium for covered workers for hours worked in excess of a weekly standard (now 40 hours), and restrictions on child labor.

As noted earlier, private sector labor law was largely enacted before 1960. By that time employment law consisted of various forms of social insurance (workers' compensation, unemployment insurance, Social Security) and protective employment standards (minimum wages, maximum hours, and child labor restrictions). Between the 1960s and the present, private sector labor law has received little attention by lawmakers while employment law has exploded.[126] Consistent with the civil rights movement of the 1960s, many new employment laws target discriminatory employment practices. The Equal Pay Act of 1963 prohibits discriminating between men and women in determining compensation for equal jobs. Title VII of the Civil Rights Act of 1964 prohibits employment discrimination by both employers and unions on the basis of race, color, religion, sex, or national origin. The Age Discrimination in Employment Act (1967) extends Title VII's protections to age discrimination against employees over the age of 40, and the Americans with Disabilities Act (1990) adds disabled individuals to the list of protected classes. The Civil Rights Act of 1991 strengthens these nondiscriminatory laws by adding the possibility of compensatory and punitive damages, not just back pay.

Other employment laws passed since the 1960s mandate employment conditions beyond the wage, hours, and child labor provisions specified by the FLSA. The Occupational Safety and Health Act (1970) obligates employers to provide safe workplaces and empowers the Occupational Safety and Health Administration (OSHA) to determine specific safety standards. The Employee Retirement Income Security Act (ERISA, 1974) establishes basic requirements for employer-sponsored pension plans and other benefits to protect employees against abuse and loss of benefits; some of these requirements and protections were strengthened in 2006 in the Pension Protection Act. The Worker Adjustment and Retraining Act (WARN, 1989) requires employers to provide advance notice of mass layoffs, and the Family and Medical Leave Act (FMLA, 1993) guarantees employees 12 weeks of unpaid leave to care for themselves, their parents, or their children. The Affordable Care Act (often called "Obamacare", 2010) requires employers to report health insurance coverage and penalizes large employers for failing to meet mandated coverage levels. Finally, state courts have developed a patchwork of limited exceptions to the employment-at-will doctrine, such as when a dismissal violates a public policy or when an employee handbook constitutes a valid employment contract.

The rise of employment law is a significant feature of the modern U.S. employment relationship and is important for labor relations. On a practical level, these laws directly affect labor relations by providing standards that both employers and unions must fulfill, such as nondiscrimination or family leave. Moreover, research shows that unions facilitate the fulfillment of the promises of employment law, such as the receipt of unemployment insurance benefits.[127] On a broader level, the sufficiency of employment law protections against the potential abuses of the employment-at-will doctrine provides a basis for evaluating the need for labor unions in the 21st-century employment relationship. In other words, does employment law give nonunion workers sufficient levels of equity and voice? By some accounts, employment law has made unions obsolete by providing basic protections, and the rise of employment law may therefore underlie the long-term decline in union density.[128] Other observers think the exceptions to the employment-at-will doctrine are still quite limited. Age discrimination, for example, is permissible toward workers under the age of 40, and many other areas are untouched by employment law—workers have been fired for living with someone without being married, smoking, drinking, motorcycling, and other legal activities outside work.[129] Workers can even be fired for saying, "Blacks have rights too," to a coworker.[130] In contrast to the standard of just cause discipline and discharge prevalent in union contracts (Chapter 9), the current nonunion exceptions to the employment-at-will doctrine do not amount to broad protections against unfair dismissal for nonunion workers. Whether this narrowness of employment law is evaluated as sufficient for the 21st-century employment relationship (as in the mainstream economics and human resource management schools of thought) or not (as in the industrial relations and critical industrial relations schools of thought) has important ramifications for the future role of labor unions.

Key Terms

conspiracy doctrine, *114*
injunctions, *114*
yellow dog contract, *115*
Danbury Hatters case, *116*
Norris–LaGuardia Act, *117*
Railway Labor Act, *119*
Wagner Act, *121*
exclusive representation, *123*
unfair labor practices, *124*
National Labor Relations Board, *126*
NLRB v. Jones and Laughlin Steel Corp., 128
Taft–Hartley Act, *129*
closed shop, *131*
union shop, *131*
agency shop, *131*
right-to-work law, *131*
Landrum–Griffin Act, *133*
Civil Service Reform Act, *137*
Wright Line test, *141*
employment law, *143*

Reflection Questions

1. A Kenyan proverb states, "When elephants fight, it is the grass that suffers." How is U.S. labor law premised on this belief? Describe specific provisions in U.S. labor law that are intended to address this concern.
2. Outline the arguments in support of the Taft–Hartley Act. Outline the opposing arguments.
3. In U.S. politics, the Democratic party has generally been more supportive of labor unions than the Republican party. Explain why it makes sense that the Wagner Act was sponsored by a Democrat, the Taft–Hartley Act by two Republicans, and the Landrum–Griffin Act by one of each.
4. One of the main tasks of the NLRB is applying the facts of a certain case to the general principles of the NLRA to determine if an unfair labor practice has been committed. To gain a greater understanding of this process, answer the questions in the "Labor Law Discussion" cases that follow.
5. In both the private and public sectors, a sharp increase in union membership coincides with the passage of protective legislation. A longstanding debate is whether increased demand for unionization causes new legislation or vice versa.[131] Explain how causality can work in both directions. In which direction is labor law more important? Which direction do you think is more realistic?
6. Draw pictures to represent the NLRA's employer and union unfair labor practices.
7. Reconsider the examples of protected and unprotected concerted activity in "Take the Section 7 Quiz." Explain how each ruling tries to balance property rights and labor rights.

Labor Law Discussion Case 1: Let's Do Lunch—Insubordination or Protected Activity?

BACKGROUND

Bird Engineering manufactures go-carts and minibikes in Nebraska and annually purchases and sells goods and services valued in excess of $50,000 using sources outside Nebraska. The plant includes a lunchroom and a break room that have vending machines, but no cafeteria. The vending machines contain chips, cookies, peanuts, sometimes rolls, soup, hot chocolate, and coffee. No employees are represented by a labor union.

Production is cyclic with peak production in November, so night shifts and temporary employees are generally added to various production departments beginning in August. Because of thefts of employee and company property, unauthorized use of company property, suspicion of drinking during lunch breaks, and employees returning tardy from lunch breaks, management implemented a closed campus rule for night shift employees. Under this new policy, night shift employees were prohibited from leaving the plant during the night shift lunch break. This is legal by Nebraska state law.

The welding department added a night shift a week after the closed campus rule was instituted, and the welding department was not aware of this rule. After management learned that the welding department was violating the closed campus rule, five night shift employees of the welding department were called to the supervisor's office, informed of the closed campus rule, and told by their supervisor that they would be terminated if they left the plant building during their lunch break. The five employees protested that the policy was illegal and asked to be granted permission to leave for lunch because they did not bring any lunch with them to work that day. Their request was denied.

The five employees decided to protest the closed campus rule by following their past practice of leaving the premises for lunch. Termination slips were issued to them when they returned from their lunch outing 30 minutes later.

That same evening, at about 10:30 p.m. (the normal lunch break time for the night shift), a sixth employee, Christina Hodgeman, was preparing to go to her van and eat her lunch when her supervisor informed her that if she left the building she would be fired. Hodgeman normally ate her lunch in her van in the parking lot and had been told when she was hired a month ago that employees were permitted to go to the parking lot but should clock out. She had been absent the previous three days because of the flu and asked permission to go to her van to get her lunch and medication. This request was denied. Feeling that she needed her medication, Hodgeman responded, "Well, if there's no other alternative, then write me out a termination slip." The supervisor obliged.

NATIONAL LABOR RELATIONS ACT EXCERPT

RIGHTS OF EMPLOYEES. SECTION 7.
Employees shall have the right to self-organization, to form, join, or assist labor organizations, to bargain collectively through representatives of their own choosing, or to engage in other concerted activities for the purpose of collective bargaining or other mutual aid or protection, and shall also have the right to refrain from any or all of such activities except to the extent that such right may be affected by an agreement requiring membership in a labor organization as a condition of employment as authorized in Section 8(a)(3).

UNFAIR LABOR PRACTICES. SECTION 8.

(a) It shall be an unfair labor practice for an employer

(1). to interfere with, restrain, or coerce employees in the exercise of the rights guaranteed in Section 7.

QUESTIONS

1. Are the six employees covered by the NLRA? Does it matter that they are not represented by a labor union?
2. Consider the five employees who left together. Assuming that the employees are covered by the NLRA, did Bird Engineering violate Section 8(a)(1) by firing the five employees? In other words, were they discharged for activities that are protected by Section 7? (*Hint:* If the employees were on strike, it is protected activity. If their action was insubordination, it is not protected.)
3. Consider the sixth employee who went to her van to get her medicine. Assuming that the employees are covered by the NLRA, did Bird Engineering violate Section 8(a)(1) by firing her?
4. If Bird Engineering violated the NLRA, what is the appropriate remedy?

Labor Law Discussion Case 2: Fired for Poor Driving, or Talking with a Union Organizer?

BACKGROUND

La Gloria Gas and Oil Company operates a Texas refinery that employs 14 truck drivers that are not represented by a union. The drivers deliver oil products to various industrial clients, sometimes several hours away. Linda Taylor, a former state trooper, works part-time for La Gloria monitoring the drivers' driving patterns by secretly following them. Every 2 weeks to 6 months she submits written reports to the company listing various infractions she observes: following too closely, speeding, failing to stop at railroad tracks, missing a mud flap, and the like. No driver had been disciplined or discharged for the violations reported by Taylor.

One of the drivers, Jose Garcia, questioned his supervisor, Chris Mueller, about why the drivers didn't receive any benefits and was told in response, "You work for La Gloria, so you got what you want, but there's no benefits." Around the same time, Garcia received some union literature. He then contacted a union organizer and talked with some other drivers about unionizing. He met with the organizer at the union hall a couple of times. With two other drivers, he also met with the organizer at a local restaurant. All of these events occurred in a span of about 6 weeks.

The day after the meeting at the restaurant, supervisor Mueller approached another worker who was at that meeting and asked, "What's the rumor that I am hearing?" The worker explained that the drivers had met with a union organizer because they were upset at the lack of benefits. He did not name the other workers at the meeting. The next day a similar exchange occurred with another worker who was at the restaurant. Both workers indicated that Mueller was agitated and upset and remarked that the refinery would probably get rid of the trucks if the drivers unionized, which would also put him out of a job. Mueller was even more upset when Garcia's name came up.

Two days later Taylor monitored Garcia's driving and called in a report to Mueller the next day. Taylor indicated that Garcia intermittently exceeded the speed limit, ran a red light, and left his turn signal on for a long time. Mueller then fired Garcia for these traffic violations and for two prior incidents of insubordination. Garcia denies that he ran a red light or exceeded the speed limit. Garcia denies being disciplined for the prior incidents of insubordination. The written memos in his personnel file are questionable—they contain little factual documentation and could have been made after the fact.

DISCUSSION

Section 8(a)(3) of the NLRA makes it an unfair labor practice for an employer "to encourage or discourage membership in any labor organization" "by discrimination in regard to hire or tenure of employment or any term or condition of employment." The scenario in this case is a classic 8(a)(3) unfair labor practice question. The employer claims to have valid, job-related reasons for disciplining or firing an employee while the employee feels that these reasons are an excuse to justify firing a union supporter. The question for the NLRB is whether the employer's claims are legitimate or are instead simply a pretext for firing the employee because of his union activity. It is important for management and union practitioners to understand how the NLRB analyzes and decides these cases.

When an alleged 8(a)(3) violation hinges on the employer's motivation (such as valid job performance issues versus retribution for union activity), the NLRB applies the framework established by *Wright Line,* 251 NLRB 1083 (1980) [approved by the Supreme Court in *NLRB v. Transportation Management Corp.,* 462 U.S. 403 (1983)]. In this framework the general counsel (the prosecution) must first show that (1) the employee was engaged in protected activity, (2) the employer was aware of the activity, and (3) the activity was a substantial or motivating reason for the employer's action. If the general counsel establishes these facts, the burden shifts to the employer to prove that it would have taken the same action even if the employee had not engaged in protected activity.

QUESTIONS

1. How would you argue the first three requirements on behalf of the discharged employee? (1) Garcia was engaged in protected activity, (2) the employer was aware of the activity, and (3) the activity was a substantial or motivating reason for Garcia's discharge.
2. Assuming that the first three requirements are established, how would you argue on behalf of the employer that Garcia would have been discharged even if he had not engaged in his protected activity?
3. If you were a member of the NLRB, how would you rule? What is the remedy?

Labor Law Discussion Case 3: Is Body Language Protected Activity?

BACKGROUND

The Health Care and Retirement Corporation (HCR) owns and operates over 100 nursing homes in 27 states. Corporate headquarters are in Toledo, Ohio. One of the nursing homes is located in rural Ohio and is called Heartland. Heartland is a 100-bed facility with about 65 people employed in the nursing department (10 staff nurses [8 licensed practical nurses, 2 registered nurses] and 55 nurse aides). No employees at Heartland are represented by a union.

The nurse aides have the most contact with the residents of Heartland—bathing, dressing, feeding, emptying bed pans, and so on. The nurses are responsible for making sure that the needs of the residents are fulfilled—checking on the health status of the residents, administering medicine, communicating with physicians. Nurses also perform the duties of nurse aides when an insufficient number of nurse aides show up for work.

While night shift nurses have little to do with assigning aides' duties, the day shift nurses are responsible for telling the aides what residents they are responsible for. The nature of the aides' work makes them fairly interchangeable. Also, assignments are often done by following old patterns or letting the aides decide coverage among themselves. Nurses are responsible for trying to find replacement aides when an aide does not show up for work, but they have no authority to order an aide to come in. Nurses have no authority to authorize overtime. Disciplining and performance appraisals of the aides are conducted by the director of nursing, not a staff nurse (although nurses can make comments about an aide's performance in an "employee counseling form"). At night and on weekends, the staff nurses are the most senior personnel at the facility. The director of nursing (or an assistant) is on call and is normally contacted when nonroutine matters arise.

Barbara Young was hired in July to be the new administrator at Heartland. She was quite inexperienced, however, and was overworked. In December Ms. Young switched the Heartland's pharmacy from a local pharmacy (whose owner had close ties with the community) to a chain pharmacy located 40 miles away. This drastically increased the paperwork duties of the nurses (although it is perhaps the case that this increase occurred because Heartland and the local pharmacy were not completing the forms required by state regulations). The community was offended by this action, and Heartland experienced a drop in new admissions (some of this community discontent was fueled by the nurses).

The director of nursing position was vacant between December and February of the next year. The facility was understaffed, especially among nurse aides, and little was being done to hire new personnel. In January three staff nurses asked to meet with Young. They wished to discuss several actions by Young that the nurses thought were detrimental to the residents and affected the work of the nurses and aides. Young replied that, due to her busy schedule, they should set up an appointment for later in the week.

Instead the three nurses traveled to corporate headquarters in Toledo the next day, where they met with a vice president and with Bob Custer, HCR's director of human resources. In this meeting the three nurses expressed four primary problems:

1. There were insufficient aides employed at Heartland (and substandard wages and recruiting perpetuated this ongoing problem).
2. Little discipline was taken with regard to aides' absenteeism, which placed more burden on the aides who showed up for work.
3. The pharmacy switch.
4. Communications problems between Young and Heartland's nurses.

The nurses were told that an investigation of their complaints would be launched and that they would not be harassed for speaking out.

A week later Custer met with Heartland's department heads (Young was not present). The department heads liked Young, knew the nurses had complained about Young, and assumed that Custer would fire her. The department heads supported Young in their meeting with Custer and also talked about the unprofessional behavior of the three nurses. Custer subsequently asked each person at the meeting for the names of the people he or she thought responsible for the tension at Heartland. Two of the three nurses appeared on every response; the third was on many.

Custer also met with Young. During their discussion Young remarked to Custer about the three nurses' lack of cooperation with management. Young also mentioned that some employees had, among other things, started a rumor about an affair between Custer and Young. A few days later Custer met with the facility's aides. The complaints about Heartland were greatest among aides who worked the same shift as the three nurses. Custer took this as further evidence that the three nurses were the root of the problem.

During February the three nurses received a variety of disciplinary notices. The circumstances surrounding their disciplinary notices for missing an "in-service" (internal training session) were typical of the situations for which they were disciplined: Only six nurses attended, but the three were the only absent nurses to receive warnings. Additionally Heartland's policy is to give two weeks' notice before any mandatory in-service; in this instance only a few days' notice was given. As a second example, a state audit found many minor mistakes by all the nurses in their unit, but only the three were disciplined.

In March HR Director Custer met with Heartland's nurses to announce that

- The pay for aides would be increased to hire more aides.
- Young would not be fired.
- The pharmacy situation would not be changed back.

Custer perceived the demeanor and tone of the meeting to be resistance to change and emphatic refusal to get on board and make Heartland a good facility. Custer believed the three nurses were responsible for this attitude among the nurses and concluded that they should be fired. The demeanor of the meeting, Custer admitted, was conveyed to him by the three nurses crossing their arms and rolling their eyes as Custer talked. Custer therefore concluded that the three nurses were unwilling to change their mode of operation and attitude to improve the facility. Thus Custer decided they should leave. When they refused to resign, they were fired.

QUESTIONS

1. Are the nurses covered by the NLRA? Remember that the NLRA excludes supervisors from protection under the act using the following definition:

   2(11) The term "supervisor" means any individual having authority, in the interest of the employer, to hire, transfer, suspend, lay off, recall, promote, discharge, assign, reward, or discipline other employees, or responsibly to direct them, or to adjust their grievances, or effectively to recommend such action, if in connection with the foregoing the exercise of such authority is not of a merely routine or clerical nature, but requires the use of independent judgment.
2. Create a list of possible reasons that the three nurses were fired. Determine whether each reason is protected by Section 7.
3. If you were a member of the NLRB, would you rule that HCR violated Section 8(a)(1) of the NLRB by discharging the three nurses (assuming that they are covered by the NLRA)? Why or why not?

Digging Deeper The Constitutionality of the Wagner Act

The Wagner Act radically increased congressional regulation of what had been private affairs, and hence it was controversial. A conservative group of lawyers declared the act unconstitutional, and despite their lack of jurisdiction, this declaration summed up the opinions of many. In fact, some believe that certain lawmakers voted for the act under the assumption that it would be struck down by the Supreme Court as unconstitutional. There were two major reasons why many believed Congress was exceeding its powers granted by the U.S. Constitution.[132]

First, remember that Congress can regulate only specific things such as war, immigration, banking, and interstate and foreign commerce. Where's the power to regulate labor relations? Congress based its power to govern labor unions and collective bargaining on its constitutional authority to regulate interstate commerce, but this justification was not widely accepted in 1935. Railroads were clearly part of interstate commerce, but the Wagner Act applied to manufacturing, coal mining, retail stores, and other businesses that operated in fixed locations. Many argued that a strike at a single manufacturing facility disrupted *production* but not interstate *commerce*. Earlier Supreme Court decisions rejected a connection between labor relations and interstate commerce, except for railroads.

Second, the Constitution's fifth amendment guarantees that no one will "be deprived of life, liberty, or property, without due process of law." It was widely argued that regulating labor relations deprived companies and individuals of their liberty and property rights without due process—employers cannot establish company unions or fire workers because of union status, for example, and unionized employees have to work at the terms negotiated by the union, not themselves. In fact, numerous Supreme Court rulings in the first three decades of the 20th century struck down various employment laws on this basis of violating the liberty to contract.

With so much opposition to the Wagner Act and the NLRB, it wasn't hard to find a test case for the courts to decide these legal questions. In 1936 the NLRB ruled that steel manufacturer Jones and Laughlin was guilty of violating the act by firing employees for trying to form a union. Jones and Laughlin fought the case by arguing that they did not affect interstate commerce and thus were not covered by the act. A federal appeals court agreed. However, the Supreme Court agreed to hear the case. By a slim 5–4 vote, the Supreme Court upheld the constitutionality of the Wagner Act in its 1937 *NLRB v. Jones and Laughlin Steel Corp.* decision by ruling that manufacturing strikes affected interstate commerce and that employers were not denied due process of law. In the shadow of Roosevelt's court-packing plan and the sit-down strikes—two serious crises—the Court indicated that in an advanced, integrated economy, strikes in one establishment affect businesses in other states. With respect to due process, the Court followed an earlier Railway Labor Act ruling and stated that the act did not interfere with employers' normal ability to hire and fire employees; rather, the target of the act is protecting free employee choice of bargaining representatives.

This landmark decision not only upheld the constitutionality of the Wagner Act, thus giving legitimacy to the U.S. system of labor relations, but also provided the legal foundation for additional government laws pertaining to employment such as minimum wage and civil rights legislation.

Answers to "Take the Section 7 Quiz"

1. Protected: This is the classic form of concerted activity that the Wagner Act seeks to protect—employees joining together to increase their bargaining power to improve their employment conditions.
2. Protected: Striking or threatening to strike is the primary way for employees to succeed in improving their employment conditions as envisioned by the Wagner Act.
3. Unprotected: Although strikes are central to the Wagner Act framework, the Section 7 rights are not unlimited, and they do not protect outrageous or illegal behavior such as destroying company property, vandalism, or violence.
4. Protected: The Wagner Act empowers employees to work together to improve their employment conditions.
5. Protected: Even though the meeting was attended by an individual, not a group, that individual was acting on behalf of others and therefore is concerted activity.
6. Unprotected: This one is tricky. Circulating a flyer is concerted activity, but building support for employee ownership is an issue for the workers as owners, not employees. The act promotes the improvement of working conditions; ownership issues are beyond the scope and therefore beyond the protection of the act.
7. Protected: This is a strike and is therefore protected. Being represented by a union is not necessary. Nonunion employees are entitled to engage in collective actions to improve their working conditions.
8. Unprotected: Neither union nor nonunion workers have the right to insist on a coworker's presence, but union workers do have the right to union representation when discipline is likely (this is a form of mutual aid or protection that will be discussed in Chapter 9).
9. Protected: The content of this message would be considered mutual aid and thus protected by the act. But what about the sending of this e-mail message using the company's e-mail system? Typically, workers do not have a statutory right to use an employer's equipment for Section 7 activity. However, because e-mail is such "a natural gathering place" for employees to discuss terms and conditions of employment, the NLRB allows employees to use company e-mail systems for non-business purposes, including Section 7 activity, during non-work time.
10. Protected: Social media activity during nonwork hours using personal equipment is generally protected if it pertains to terms and conditions of employment, is concerted, and is not defamatory or otherwise destructive. In this situation, commenting on a coworker's job performance can be considered related to terms and conditions of employment because of the implications for working conditions and staffing levels, and because the worker was soliciting other coworkers' feedback, it is concerted activity. This would be unprotected, however, if the comments were so harsh as to be considered bullying.
11. Unprotected: Actions that are malicious, defamatory, or insubordinate lose protection. Spontaneous outbursts of profanity can be protected if they result from the "heat of the moment" and frustration over working conditions.
12. Protected: Consistent with the spirit of the Wagner Act, employees have the right to protect themselves from harm. But if the workers do not have a genuine belief that the situation is dangerous, then a refusal to work is insubordination, which is not protected by the act. Also, there needs to be a concerted element, and an individual worker acting alone might not be protected.

Additional Reading: Calvin William Sharpe, "'By Any Means Necessary'—Unprotected Conduct and Decisional Discretion under the National Labor Relations Act," *Berkeley Journal of Employment and Labor Law* 20 (1999), pp. 203–53; Kenneth T. Lopatka, *NLRA Rights in the Nonunion Workplace* (Arlington, VA: BNA Books, 2010).

End Notes

1. Norman F. Cantor, *Imagining the Law: Common Law and the Foundations of the American Legal System* (New York: HarperCollins, 1997); Mary Ann Glendon, Paolo G. Carozza, and Colin B. Picker, *Comparative Legal Traditions in a Nutshell,* 3rd ed. (St. Paul, MN: Thomson West, 2008).
2. Charles O. Gregory and Harold A. Katz, *Labor and the Law,* 3rd ed. (New York: Norton, 1979); Benjamin J. Taylor and Fred Witney, *Labor Relations Law,* 5th ed. (Englewood Cliffs, NJ: Prentice Hall, 1987).
3. Taylor and Witney, *Labor Relations Law.*
4. Gregory and Katz, *Labor and the Law*; Taylor and Witney, *Labor Relations Law.*
5. Felix Frankfurter and Nathan Greene, *The Labor Injunction* (New York: Macmillan, 1930); Gregory and Katz, *Labor and the Law*; Taylor and Witney, *Labor Relations Law.*
6. William E. Forbath, *Law and the Shaping of the American Labor Movement* (Cambridge, MA: Harvard University Press, 1991).
7. Taylor and Witney, *Labor Relations Law.*
8. William E. Forbath, "The New Deal Constitution in Exile," *Duke Law Journal* 51 (October 2001), pp. 165–222.
9. Frankfurter and Greene, *The Labor Injunction*; Taylor and Witney, *Labor Relations Law*; Edwin E. Witte, *The Government in Labor Disputes* (New York: McGraw-Hill, 1932).
10. Gregory and Katz, *Labor and the Law*; Joel Seidman, *The Yellow-Dog Contract* (Baltimore: Johns Hopkins University Press, 1932); Taylor and Witney, *Labor Relations Law*; Witte, *The Government in Labor Disputes.*
11. For example, *Adair v. U.S.,* 208 U.S. 161 (1908); *Coppage v. State of Kansas,* 236 U.S. 1 (1915).
12. Taylor and Witney, *Labor Relations Law.*
13. *Loewe v. Lawlor,* 208 U.S. 274 (1908).
14. Daniel R. Ernst, *Lawyers against Labor: From Individual Rights to Corporate Liberalism* (Urbana: University of Illinois Press, 1995).
15. *Lawlor v. Loewe,* 235 U.S. 522 (1915).
16. *Gompers v. Bucks Stove and Range Company,* 221 U.S. 418 (1911).
17. Taylor and Witney, *Labor Relations Law.*
18. Ernst, *Lawyers against Labor.*
19. Taylor and Witney, *Labor Relations Law.*
20. *American Steel Foundries v. Tri-City Central Trades Council,* 257 U.S. 184, 206–7 (1921).
21. Ernst, *Lawyers against Labor*; Ruth O'Brien, *Workers' Paradox: The Republican Origins of New Deal Labor Policy, 1886–1935* (Chapel Hill: University of North Carolina Press, 1998).
22. Clayton Sinyai, *Schools of Democracy: A Political History of the American Labor Movement* (Ithaca, NY: Cornell University Press, 2006).
23. O'Brien, *Workers' Paradox*; Christopher L. Tomlins, *The State and the Unions: Labor Relations, Law, and the Organized Labor Movement, 1880–1960* (Cambridge: Cambridge University Press, 1985).
24. Witte, *The Government in Labor Disputes.*
25. Melvyn Dubofsky, *The State and Labor in Modern America* (Chapel Hill: University of North Carolina Press, 1994), p. 95; Colin J. Davis, *Power at Odds: The 1922 National Railroad Shopmen's Strike* (Urbana: University of Illinois Press, 1997).
26. Frankfurter and Greene, *The Labor Injunction,* p. 254.
27. Dubofsky, *The State and Labor in Modern America*; Forbath, *Law and the Shaping of the American Labor Movement.*
28. Gregory and Katz, *Labor and the Law*; Taylor and Witney, *Labor Relations Law.*
29. David M. Kennedy, *Freedom from Fear: The American People in Depression and War, 1929–1945* (New York: Oxford University Press, 1999); Nelson Lichtenstein et al., *Who Built America? Working People and the Nation's Economy, Politics, Culture, and Society,* Volume 2 (New York: Worth Publishing, 2000).
30. Cass R. Sunstein, *The Second Bill of Rights: FDR's Unfinished Revolution and Why We Need It More Than Ever* (New York: Basic Books, 2004).
31. John W. Budd, *Employment with a Human Face: Balancing Efficiency, Equity, and Voice* (Ithaca, NY: Cornell University Press, 2004); Thomas A. Kochan, Harry C. Katz, and Robert B. McKersie, *The Transformation of American Industrial Relations* (New York: Basic Books, 1986).

32. Ellis W. Hawley, *New Deal and the Problem of Monopoly: A Study in Economic Ambivalence* (Princeton, NJ: Princeton University Press, 1966); Colin Gordon, *New Deals: Business, Labor, and Politics in America, 1920–1935* (New York: Cambridge University Press, 1994).
33. Irving Bernstein, *Turbulent Years: A History of the American Worker, 1933–1941* (Boston: Houghton Mifflin, 1970); Dubofsky, *The State and Labor in Modern America*; Janet Irons, *Testing the New Deal: The General Textile Strike of 1934 in the American South* (Urbana: University of Illinois Press, 2000); Stanley Vittoz, *New Deal Labor Policy and the American Industrial Economy* (Chapel Hill: University of North Carolina Press, 1987).
34. Dubofsky, *The State and Labor in Modern America*; James A. Gross, *The Making of the National Labor Relations Board: A Study in Economics, Politics, and the Law* (Albany: State University of New York Press, 1974); Taylor and Witney, *Labor Relations Law.*
35. Bruce E. Kaufman, "Accomplishments and Shortcomings of Nonunion Employee Representation in the Pre–Wagner Act Years: A Reassessment," in Bruce E. Kaufman and Daphne Gottlieb Taras (eds.), *Nonunion Employee Representation: History, Contemporary Practice, and Policy* (Armonk, NY: M. E. Sharpe, 2000), pp. 21–60; Daniel Nelson, "The AFL and the Challenge of Company Unionism, 1915–1937," in Bruce E. Kaufman and Daphne Gottlieb Taras (eds.), *Nonunion Employee Representation: History, Contemporary Practice, and Policy* (Armonk, NY: M. E. Sharpe, 2000), pp. 61–75; O'Brien, *Workers' Paradox.*
36. Irons, *Testing the New Deal.*
37. *Schecter Poultry Corp. v. United States,* 295 U.S. 495 (1935); Bernstein, *Turbulent Years.*
38. Irving Bernstein, *The New Deal Collective Bargaining Policy* (Berkeley: University of California Press, 1950); Bernstein, *Turbulent Years*; O'Brien, *Workers' Paradox*; Vittoz, *New Deal Labor Policy and the American Industrial Economy.*
39. Gerald G. Eggert, *Railroad Labor Disputes: The Beginnings of Federal Strike Policy* (Ann Arbor, University of Michigan Press, 1967).
40. Charles M. Rehmus, "Evolution of Legislation Affecting Collective Bargaining in the Railroad and Airline Industries," in Charles M. Rehmus (ed.), *The Railway Labor Act at Fifty: Collective Bargaining in the Railroad and Airline Industries* (Washington, DC: National Mediation Board, 1976), pp. 1–22.
41. Douglas L. Leslie (ed.), *The Railway Labor Act* (Washington, DC: Bureau of National Affairs, 1995).
42. O'Brien, *Workers' Paradox.*
43. Dana E. Eischen, "Representation Disputes and Their Resolution in the Railroad and Airline Industries," in Charles M. Rehmus (ed.), *The Railway Labor Act at Fifty: Collective Bargaining in the Railroad and Airline Industries* (Washington, DC: National Mediation Board, 1976), pp. 23–70.
44. Nelson, "The AFL and the Challenge of Company Unionism."
45. Steve Fraser, "Dress Rehearsal for the New Deal: Shop-Floor Insurgents, Political Elites, and Industrial Democracy in the Amalgamated Clothing Workers," in Michael H. Frisch and Daniel J. Walkowitz (eds.), *Working-Class America: Essays on Labor, Community, and American Society* (Urbana: University of Illinois Press, 1983), pp. 212–55.
46. Bernstein, *The New Deal Collective Bargaining Policy*; Dubofsky, *The State and Labor in Modern America.*
47. Budd, *Employment with a Human Face.*
48. Dan C. Heldman, James T. Bennett, and Manuel H. Johnson, *Deregulating Labor Relations* (Dallas: Fisher Institute, 1981); Karl E. Klare, "Judicial Deradicalization of the Wagner Act and the Origins of Modern Legal Consciousness, 1937–1941," *Minnesota Law Review* 62 (March 1978), pp. 265–339; David Montgomery, *Workers' Control in America: Studies in the History of Work, Technology, and Labor Struggles* (Cambridge: Cambridge University Press, 1979); Morgan O. Reynolds, *Power and Privilege: Labor Unions in America* (New York: Universe Books, 1984); Katherine V.W. Stone, "The Post-War Paradigm in American Labor Law," *Yale Law Journal* 90 (June 1981), pp. 1509–80; Tomlins, *The State and the Unions*; Leo Troy, *Beyond Unions and Collective Bargaining* (Armonk, NY: M. E. Sharpe, 1999).
49. Bruce E. Kaufman, "Why the Wagner Act? Reestablishing Contact with Its Original Purpose," in David Lewin, Bruce E. Kaufman, and Donna Sockell (eds.), *Advances in Industrial and Labor Relations,* Volume 7 (Greenwich, CT: JAI Press, 1996), pp. 15–68; Kochan, Katz, and McKersie, *The Transformation of American Industrial Relations.*
50. Bernstein, *The New Deal Collective Bargaining Policy*; William E. Forbath, "Caste, Class, and Equal Citizenship," *Michigan Law Review* 98 (October 1999), pp. 1–91.

51. Craig Becker, "Democracy in the Workplace: Union Representation Elections and Federal Labor Law," *Minnesota Law Review* 77 (February 1993), pp. 495–603.
52. Leon H. Keyserling, "Why the Wagner Act?" in Louis G. Silverberg (ed.), *The Wagner Act: After Ten Years* (Washington, DC: Bureau of National Affairs, 1945), pp. 5–33 at 31.
53. Gross, *The Making of the National Labor Relations Board*; O'Brien, *Workers' Paradox.*
54. Charles J. Morris, *The Blue Eagle at Work: Reclaiming Democratic Rights in the American Workplace* (Ithaca, NY: Cornell University Press, 2005); Catherine Fisk and Xenia Tashlitsky, "Imagine a World Where Employers Are Required to Bargain with Minority Unions," *ABA Journal of Labor and Employment Law* 27 (Fall 2011), pp. 1–22.
55. Morris, *The Blue Eagle at Work*, p. 101.
56. Morris, *The Blue Eagle at Work*.
57. Michael H. Leroy, "What Do NLRB Cases Reveal About Non-Union Employee Representation Groups? A Typology from Post-*Electromation* Cases," in Paul J. Gollan et al. (eds.), *Voice and Involvement at Work: Experience with Nonunion Representation* (London: Routledge, 2014), pp. 366–93; Bruce E. Kaufman, "Experience with Company Unions and their Treatment under the Wagner Act: A Four Frames of Reference Analysis," *Industrial Relations* 55 (January 2016), pp. 3–39.
58. Bruce E. Kaufman, "The Case for the Company Union," *Labor History* 41 (August 2000), pp. 321–50; Kaufman, "Experience with Company Unions and their Treatment under the Wagner Act."
59. Morris, *The Blue Eagle at Work*.
60. Gross, *The Making of the National Labor Relations Board*; National Labor Relations Board, *NLRB: The First 50 Years* (Washington, DC: 1985).
61. National Labor Relations Board, Graphs and Data, available at www.nlrb.gov/news-outreach/graphs-data.
62. Bernstein, *Turbulent Years*; Dubofsky, *The State and Labor in Modern America*; Gross, *The Making of the National Labor Relations Board*.
63. Kochan, Katz, and McKersie, *The Transformation of American Industrial Relations*, p. 24.
64. National Labor Relations Board, *Legislative History of the National Labor Relations Act 1935* (Washington, DC: U.S. Government Printing Office, 1949), pp. 512–16.
65. Gordon, *New Deals*.
66. Jerold S. Auerbach, *Labor and Liberty: The LaFollette Committee and the New Deal* (Indianapolis: Bobbs-Merrill, 1966); Dubofsky, *The State and Labor in Modern America.*
67. James B. Atleson, *Labor and the Wartime State: Labor Relations and Law during World War II* (Urbana: University of Illinois Press, 1998).
68. Gross, *The Making of the National Labor Relations Board*; Taylor and Witney, *Labor Relations Law.*
69. Bernstein, *Turbulent Years*; Gross, *The Making of the National Labor Relations Board*; National Lawyers Committee of the American Liberty League, *Report on the Constitutionality of the National Labor Relations Act* (September 5, 1935).
70. *NLRB v. Jones and Laughlin Steel Corporation,* 301 U.S. 1 (1937).
71. Harry A. Millis and Emily Clark Brown, *From the Wagner Act to Taft–Hartley: A Study of National Labor Policy and Labor Relations* (Chicago: University of Chicago Press, 1950), p. 332.
72. Millis and Brown, *From the Wagner Act to Taft–Hartley.*
73. Philip Taft, *Organized Labor in American History* (New York: Harper and Row, 1964), p. 567.
74. Fred A. Hartley, *Our New National Labor Policy: The Taft–Hartley Act and the Next Steps* (New York: Funk and Wagnalls, 1948).
75. Millis and Brown, *From the Wagner Act to Taft–Hartley.*
76. Taylor and Witney, *Labor Relations Law.*
77. *NLRB v. General Motors,* 373 U.S. 734 (1963); *Communication Workers of America v. Beck,* 487 U.S. 735 (1988).
78. Raymond Hogler, "The Historical Misconception of Right to Work Laws in the United States: Senator Robert Wagner, Legal Policy, and the Decline of American Unions," *Hofstra Labor and Employment Law Journal* 23 (Fall 2005), pp. 101–52.
79. Benjamin Collins, "Right to Work Laws: Legislative Background and Empirical Research," Congressional Research Service, 2012; Gordon Lafer, "Working Hard to Make Indiana Look Bad: The Tortured, Uphill Case for 'Right-to-Work,'" Economic Policy Institute Briefing Paper #333, 2012.

80. Cedric de Leon, *The Origins of Right to Work: Antilabor Democracy in Nineteenth-Century Chicago* (Ithaca, NY: Cornell University Press, 2015).
81. Taylor and Witney, *Labor Relations Law.*
82. James A. Gross, *The Reshaping of the National Labor Relations Board: National Labor Policy in Transition 1937–1947* (Albany: State University of New York Press, 1981); James A. Gross, *Broken Promise: The Subversion of U.S. Labor Relations Policy, 1947–1994* (Philadelphia: Temple University Press, 1995); Tomlins, *The State and the Unions.*
83. Joseph G. Rayback, *A History of American Labor* (New York: Free Press, 1966); Tomlins, *The State and the Unions;* Dubofsky, *The State and Labor in Modern America*; Taft, *Organized Labor in American History.*
84. Nelson Lichtenstein, *State of the Union: A Century of American Labor* (Princeton, NJ: Princeton University Press, 2013); Tomlins, *The State and the Unions.*
85. Lichtenstein, *State of the Union*; Sinyai, *Schools of Democracy.*
86. Dubofsky, *The State and Labor in Modern America*; Millis and Brown, *From the Wagner Act to Taft–Hartley.*
87. Thaddeus Russell, *Out of the Jungle: Jimmy Hoffa and the Remaking of the American Working Class* (New York: Knopf, 2001).
88. R. Alton Lee, *Eisenhower and Landrum–Griffin: A Study in Labor–Management Politics* (Lexington: University Press of Kentucky, 1990); Russell, *Out of the Jungle*; Taft, *Organized Labor in American History.*
89. Janice R. Bellace and Alan D. Berkowitz, *The Landrum–Griffin Act: Twenty Years of Federal Protection of Union Members' Rights* (Philadelphia: Industrial Research Unit, University of Pennsylvania, 1979).
90. James B. Jacobs, *Mobsters, Unions, and Feds: The Mafia and the American Labor Movement* (New York: New York University Press, 2006).
91. Bellace and Berkowitz, *The Landrum–Griffin Act*; Lee, *Eisenhower and Landrum–Griffin*; Taylor and Witney, *Labor Relations Law.*
92. Marick F. Masters, Raymond Gibney, and Thomas J. Zagenczyk, "Worker Pay Protection: Implications for Labor's Political Spending and Voice," *Industrial Relations* 48 (October 2009), pp. 557–77.
93. *Citizens United v. Federal Election Commission*, 558 U.S. 50 (2010).
94. *Machinists v. Street*, 367 U.S. 740 (1961); *Abood v. District Board of Education*, 431 U.S. 209 (1977); *Communication Workers of America v. Beck*, 487 U.S. 735 (1988).
95. Masters, Gibney, and Zagenczyk, "Worker Pay Protection."
96. Joseph E. Slater, *Public Workers: Government Employee Unions, the Law, and the State, 1900–1962* (Ithaca, NY: Cornell University Press, 2004); Richard C. Kearney and Patrice M. Mareschal, *Labor Relations in the Public Sector,* 5th ed. (Boca Raton: CRC Press, 2014).
97. Francis Russell, *A City in Terror: 1919, The Boston Police Strike* (New York: Viking, 1975), p. 191; Sterling D. Spero, *Government as Employer* (New York: Remsen Press, 1948).
98. Kearney and Mareschal, *Labor Relations in the Public Sector*; B.V.H. Schneider, "Public Sector Labor Legislation—An Evolutionary Analysis," in Benjamin Aaron, Joyce M. Najita, and James L. Stern (eds.), *Public Sector Bargaining,* 2nd ed. (Washington, DC: Bureau of National Affairs, 1988), pp. 189–228.
99. Schneider, "Public Sector Labor Legislation."
100. Kearney and Mareschal, *Labor Relations in the Public Sector*; Taylor and Witney, *Labor Relations Law.*
101. Kearney and Mareschal, *Labor Relations in the Public Sector*; Taylor and Witney, *Labor Relations Law.*
102. Milla Sanes and John Schmitt, "Regulation of Public Sector Collective Bargaining in the States," Center for Economic and Policy Research, 2014.
103. Schneider, "Public Sector Labor Legislation."
104. Janet McEneaney and Robert P. Hebdon, "Public Sector Labor Law and Experience in New York State," in Joyce M. Najita, and James L. Stern (eds.), *Collective Bargaining in the Public Sector: The Experience of Eight States* (Armonk, NY: M. E. Sharpe, 2001), pp. 161–94; Kearney, *Labor Relations in the Public Sector.*
105. Lichtenstein, *State of the Union*, p. 282.

106. Michael D. Yates (ed.), *Wisconsin Uprising: Labor Fights Back* (New York: Monthly Review Press, 2012); Robert Hebdon, Joseph E. Slater, and Marick F. Masters, "Public Sector Collective Bargaining: Tumultuous Times," in Howard R. Stanger, Paul F. Clark, and Ann C. Frost (eds.), *Collective Bargaining under Duress: Case Studies of Major North American Industries* (Champaign, IL: Labor and Employment Relations Association, 2013), pp. 255–95.
107. Taylor and Witney, *Labor Relations Law.*
108. 251 NLRB 1083 (1980) [approved by the Supreme Court in *NLRB v. Transportation Management Corp.,* 462 U.S. 403 (1983)].
109. Ronald Turner, "Ideological Voting on the National Labor Relations Board," *University of Pennsylvania Journal of Labor and Employment Law* 8 (Spring 2006), pp. 707–64; Samuel Estreicher "Depoliticizing the National Labor Relations Board: Administrative Steps," *Emory Law Journal* 64 (2015), pp. 1611–20.
110. Morris M. Kleiner and David Weil, "Evaluating the Effectiveness of National Labor Relations Act Remedies: Analysis and Comparison with Other Workplace Penalty Policies," in Cynthia L. Estlund and Michael L. Wachter (eds.), *Research Handbook on the Economics of Labor and Employment Law* (Northampton, MA: Edward Elgar, 2012), pp. 209–47
111. Marley S. Weiss, "*Kentucky River* at the Intersection of Professional and Supervisory Status: Fertile Delta or Bermuda Triangle," in Laura J. Cooper and Catherine L. Fisk (eds.), *Labor Law Stories* (New York: Foundation Press, 2005), pp. 353–98; Steven E. Abraham, Adrienne E. Eaton, and Paula B. Voos, "Supreme Court Supervisory Status Decisions: The Impact on the Organizing of Nurses," in Richard N. Block et al. (eds.), *Justice on the Job: Perspectives on the Erosion of Collective Bargaining in the United States* (Kalamazoo, MI: Upjohn, 2006), pp. 163–89.
112. General Accounting Office, *Collective Bargaining Rights: Information on the Number of Workers with and without Bargaining Rights*, GAO-02-835 (Washington, DC: United States General Accounting Office, 2002).
113. *Hoffman Plastic Compounds, Inc. v. NLRB*, 535 U.S. 137 (2002); Catherine L. Fisk and Michael J. Wishnie, "The Story of *Hoffman Plastic Compounds, Inc. v. NLRB:* Labor Rights without Remedies for Undocumented Immigrants," in Laura J. Cooper and Catherine L. Fisk (eds.), *Labor Law Stories* (New York: Foundation Press, 2005), pp. 399–438.
114. Julius G. Getman and Thomas C. Kohler, "The Story of *NLRB v. Mackay Radio and Telegraph Co.*: The High Cost of Solidarity," in Laura J. Cooper and Catherine L. Fisk (eds.), *Labor Law Stories* (New York: Foundation Press, 2005), pp. 13–53.
115. Ellen Dannin, *Taking Back the Workers' Law: How to Fight the Assault on Labor Rights* (Ithaca, NY: Cornell University Press, 2006).
116. Stephen F. Befort and John W. Budd, *Invisible Hands, Invisible Objectives: Bringing Workplace Law and Public Policy into Focus* (Stanford, CA: Stanford University Press, 2009); Charles B. Craver, *Can Unions Survive? The Rejuvenation of the American Labor Movement* (New York: New York University Press, 1993); Sheldon Friedman, Richard W. Hurd, Rudolph A. Oswald, and Ronald L. Seeber (eds.), *Restoring the Promise of American Labor Law* (Ithaca, NY: ILR Press, 1994); William B. Gould, *Agenda for Reform: The Future of Employment Relationships and the Law* (Cambridge: MIT Press, 1993).
117. Josiah Bartlett Lambert, *"If the Workers Took a Notion": The Right to Strike and American Political Development* (Ithaca, NY: Cornell University Press, 2005).
118. George Feldman, "Unions, Solidarity, and Class: The Limits of Liberal Labor Law," *Berkeley Journal of Employment and Labor Law* 15 (1994), pp. 187–272; Karl E. Klare, "Workplace Democracy and Market Reconstruction: An Agenda for Legal Reform," *Catholic University Law Review* 38 (Fall 1988), pp. 1–68; Katherine Van Wezel Stone, "Labor and the Corporate Structure: Changing Conceptions and Emerging Possibilities," *University of Chicago Law Review* 55 (Winter 1988), pp. 73–173.
119. Michael H. LeRoy, "Employee Participation in the New Millennium: Redefining a Labor Organization under Section 8(a)(2) of the NLRA," *Southern California Law Review* 72 (September 1999), pp. 1651–723; Edward E. Potter and Judith A. Youngman, *Keeping America Competitive: Employment Policy for the Twenty-First Century* (Lakewood, CO: Glenbridge Publishing, 1995).
120. Charles C. Heckscher, *The New Unionism: Employee Involvement in the Changing Corporation* (New York: Basic Books, 1988); Katherine V. W. Stone, *From Widgets to Digits: Employment Regulation for the Changing Workplace* (Cambridge: Cambridge University Press, 2004).
121. Budd, *Employment with a Human Face*; Befort and Budd, *Invisible Hands, Invisible Objectives*.
122. Morgan Reynolds, "A New Paradigm: Deregulating Labor Relations," *Journal of Labor Research* 17 (Winter 1996), pp. 121–28; Richard Epstein, "The Deserved Demise of EFCA (and Why the NLRA Should Share its Fate)," in Cynthia L. Estlund and Michael L. Wachter (eds.), *Research Handbook on the Economics of Labor and Employment Law* (Northampton, MA: Edward Elgar, 2012), pp. 177–208.

123. John F. Burton, Jr., and James R. Chelius, "Workplace Safety and Health Regulations: Rationale and Results," in Bruce E. Kaufman (ed.), *Government Regulation of the Employment Relationship* (Madison, WI: Industrial Relations Research Association, 1997), pp. 253–93.
124. Dawn D. Bennett-Alexander and Laura P. Hartman, *Employment Law for Business,* 8th ed. (Boston: McGraw-Hill/Irwin, 2015).
125. Bruce E. Kaufman, "Labor Markets and Employment Regulation: The View of the 'Old' Institutionalists," in Bruce E. Kaufman (ed.), *Government Regulation of the Employment Relationship* (Madison, WI: Industrial Relations Research Association, 1997), pp. 11–55.
126. Bennett-Alexander and Hartman, *Employment Law for Business*; Befort and Budd, *Invisible Hands, Invisible Objectives*.
127. John W. Budd and Brian P. McCall, "The Effect of Unions on the Receipt of Unemployment Insurance Benefits," *Industrial and Labor Relations Review* 50 (April 1997), pp. 478–92; David Weil, "Implementing Employment Regulation: Insights on the Determinants of Regulatory Performance," in Bruce E. Kaufman (ed.), *Government Regulation of the Employment Relationship* (Madison, WI: Industrial Relations Research Association, 1997), pp. 429–74.
128. James T. Bennett and Jason E. Taylor, "Labor Unions: Victims of Their Political Success?" *Journal of Labor Research* 22 (Spring 2001), pp. 261–73.
129. Lewis Maltby, *Can They Do That? Retaking Our Fundamental Rights in the Workplace* (New York: Portfolio, 2009).
130. *Bigelow v. Bullard*, 901 P.2d 630 (Nev. 1995).
131. Gregory M. Saltzman, "Bargaining Laws as a Cause and Consequence of the Growth of Teacher Unions," *Industrial and Labor Relations Review* 38 (April 1985), pp. 335–51.
132. Richard C. Cortner, *The Jones & Laughlin Case* (New York, Knopf, 1970); Gross, *The Making of the National Labor Relations Board*; Taylor and Witney, *Labor Relations Law.*

Chapter **Five**

Labor and Management: Strategies, Structures, and Constraints

Advance Organizer

The previous two chapters described the historical development and legal framework of the U.S. labor relations system. This chapter examines the strategies and organizational structures used by labor unions and employers to achieve efficiency, equity, and voice. The extent to which these strategies and structures succeed depends on the constraints of the employment environment.

Learning Objectives

By the end of this chapter, you should be able to

1. **Compare** the traditional U.S. union strategies (especially business unionism, job control unionism, and the servicing model) and their alternatives (especially social unionism, employee empowerment unionism, and the organizing model).
2. **Understand** the organizational structure of unions and the labor movement in the United States.
3. **Discuss** the range of possible management strategies toward labor unions and how they relate to human resource strategies and business strategies.
4. **Analyze** how the labor relations environment, including ethics, influences and constrains labor relations outcomes.

Contents

The heart of labor relations is conflict between the goals of employees and employers. This can be an intimidating image, but it should not be. It does not mean that labor and management are consumed in an all-out war and continually attack each other. In fact, the striking feature of most workplaces is the amount of daily cooperation, not conflict or competition.[1] But what sets the study and practice of labor relations apart from other approaches, such as human resource management, is the acceptance of conflict in the employment relationship. As described in Chapter 2, labor relations scholars and practitioners who adhere to the pluralist industrial relations school of thought believe that there is an inherent conflict of interest in the employment relationship. Although employees and employers have shared interests, conflict is also natural and to be expected, not pathological and to be suppressed. Labor law therefore seeks to design systems and policies to manage this conflict to create productive workplaces that balance efficiency with equity and voice (Chapter 4).

Within this legal framework, labor unions and employers design strategies and build organizational structures to pursue their objectives. This chapter describes these strategies and organizational structures, concluding with a discussion of the major aspects of the environment that also constrain and affect labor and management's abilities to achieve their goals.

LABOR UNION STRATEGIES

U.S. labor history reveals a variety of alternative union strategies—from the political emphasis of the National Labor Union to the business unionism of the AFL to the revolutionary approach of the IWW (Chapter 3). Since the 1950s, however, U.S. labor unions have primarily followed just one of these—a business unionism philosophy. Within this approach, the dominant collection of strategies are summarized in the left side of Table 5.1: within a business unionism philosophy, the use of a servicing model to pursue job control unionism through industrial unions. In this mode, equity is achieved through generous

TABLE 5.1
Traditional Union Strategies (left-side column) and 21st-Century Alternatives (right-side column)

Business Unionism		*Social Unionism*
Strong workplace unions.	↔	Strong community networks.
Collective bargaining is key.	↔	Workplace, social, and political action.
Acceptance of capitalist institutions.	↔	Critical of status quo.
Equity through workplace union protection.	↔	Equity through social justice.
Voice through workplace union representation.	↔	Voice through political and social movement.
Servicing Model		*Organizing Model*
Pay dues in return for protection through collective bargaining and grievance procedures.	↔	Mobilize workers for empowerment and action.
Workers consume union services.	↔	Workers participate in union and workplace activities including organizing.
Job Control Unionism		*Employee Empowerment Unionism*
Focus on specific job rights.	↔	Focus on creating procedures for empowerment.
Seniority and job classification are important.	↔	Skills are important.
Equity through standardization and equal treatment.	↔	Equity through fair processes.
Voice through union representatives.	↔	Voice through empowerment.
Industrial Unionism		*Craft or Occupational Unionism*
Represent all workers at a single workplace.	↔	Represent workers in a single occupation in different workplaces.
Bargaining power from controlling entire workplace.	↔	Responsiveness to a homogeneous occupation.

wage and benefit packages, seniority-based layoff and promotion procedures, restrictions on discipline and discharge for just cause only, and due process protections in the grievance procedure. Voice is achieved through representation at the bargaining table and in the grievance procedure. Collective bargaining is institutionalized, and the union contract becomes the "workplace rule of law."[2] This section begins by explaining these elements of the traditional U.S. union strategy. Attention then turns to pressures for change, and the arguments calling for unions to embrace one or more of the strategic approaches presented in the right side of Table 5.1 as better ways to achieve equity and voice in the 21st century.

The Traditional Collection of U.S. Union Strategies

U.S. labor unions have traditionally embraced a **business unionism** philosophy.[3] In this approach, the key to achieving equity and voice is collective bargaining in the workplace, through which unions win wage gains, benefits, grievance procedures, and protective work rules. This philosophy accepts the legitimacy of capitalism and the need for employers to make a profit. Labor's goal is to secure a fair share of these profits through collective bargaining. John L. Lewis, longtime president of the United Mine Workers and leader of the industrial union movement in the 1930s, clearly described the U.S. business unionism outlook:

> Trade unionism is a phenomenon of capitalism quite similar to the corporation. One is essentially a pooling of labor for the purpose of common action in production and sales. The other is a pooling of capital for exactly the same purpose. The economic aims of both are identical—gain.[4]

In other words, this is a businesslike approach to employee representation, or unionism "pure and simple."[5]

An abusive variant of business unionism can be called "hold-up unionism" or "jungle unionism."[6] If unrestrained competition, especially in periods of high unemployment, leads to individual needs for survival, a jungle unionism strategy is to take whatever you need or can by whatever means necessary—like the law of the jungle. Among the most egregious examples are the tactics of Jimmy Hoffa's Teamsters in the 1930s and 1940s, in which strikes and boycotts were readily supplemented with bombings, brawls, flying squadrons, and other means of violence and coercion to organize drivers and warehouse workers in the highly competitive Detroit transportation, retail, and wholesale industries.[7] It is important, however, not to generalize the pattern of a handful of corrupt unions to the many that are not.

To carry out their business unionism philosophy, U.S. labor unions traditionally have represented workers by using a **servicing model.**[8] Here a union is like an insurance company: Workers pay dues, and in return they are protected against bad times—arbitrary supervisors, the vagaries of markets, workplace accidents, and the like. In this conceptualization, workers do not participate in a union; rather, they consume union services, especially collectively bargained contracts and representation in the grievance procedure. Workers are serviced by union officials: Problems are solved *for* the workers, not *by* the workers. This is a passive form of employee representation; the only active participants are union officials.

How to specifically represent or "service" workers is shaped by the business environment. Through much of the 20th century, the dominant method of work organization was scientific management, in which jobs were divided into specialized tasks. A typical example is assembly-line production in which each worker repeats just a few operations on each item as it passes by on the assembly line, although narrow job classifications can be found in many occupations and industries—grocery store checkout clerks, financial services data entry clerks, and hotel room cleaners, for example. In addition to creating detailed job classifications, employers have traditionally been adamant about maintaining their managerial prerogatives—discipline, production, scheduling, marketing, pricing, investment, and other managerial functions.[9]

In this environment, unions have sought to protect their members from volatile managers and markets by negotiating detailed, legalistic union contracts that tie employee rights to narrowly defined jobs while removing labor from business decision making.[10] This is called **job control unionism** because a central element is replacing arbitrary management control with union-negotiated seniority systems for allocating jobs and determining pay and benefits. Equity and voice are pursued through predictable wage increases, generous benefits, seniority-based layoff and promotion systems, limitations on discipline and discharge for just cause only, and grievance procedures. Since World War II, then, U.S. labor relations have been characterized by a sharp break between collective bargaining over wages and rights linked to jobs on one hand, and managerial authority over business functions on the other.

Another dimension to union strategy is whether unions represent workers along craft/occupational or industrial lines. **Craft unionism,** or occupational unionism, involves a single union representing only workers in a single occupation or craft, such as separate unions for electricians, carpenters, and painters. This was common before the rise of the modern factory (recall the AFL unions described in Chapter 3), and it remains prevalent today in the construction industry. Occupational unionism might also be well suited to the workforce of the future if workers are increasingly mobile and identify more with an occupation than with a specific company.[11] In contrast, **industrial unionism** focuses on an industry rather than a craft. Industrial unions seek to represent workers of all occupations within an industry. For example, an industrial union at an appliance factory represents janitors, assembly-line workers, and skilled workers such as electricians; an industrial union at a hotel represents employees who work at the front desk, in the bar, restaurant, and kitchen, on the loading dock, in the back office, in the laundry room, and in the rooms as cleaners.

Alternative Union Strategies for the 21st Century

The traditional union strategies are under great pressure to change in the 21st century. These pressures come from changes in the external business environment (or political environment for public sector unions) and also from critics within the labor movement itself. On the business side, management has been fighting the rigidities of job control unionism since the 1980s because of the greater needs for flexibility and quality that have arisen with increased foreign and nonunion competition (see Chapter 10). At the same time, a desire to revitalize a weakened labor movement has caused some labor movement supporters to criticize the conservatism of the longstanding business unionism philosophy along with the union member apathy that is created by the passivity of the servicing model. The labor movement has therefore been debating and experimenting with alternatives to its traditional strategies (see the right side of Table 5.1).

Unfortunately these debates often confuse different dimensions of union strategies. The traditional collection of union strategies combines a workplace focus with passive rank-and-file participation. Alternative strategies can change only one, or both, of these dimensions. To understand these debates more clearly, then, it is important to distinguish between what can be called the scope and the soul of employee representation (see Table 5.2). The *scope* of representation describes the breadth of the representation activities—in particular, whether union activity is concentrated in the workplace or in the broader political and social arenas. A business unionism focus on collective bargaining is a workplace scope of representation; an alternative approach embracing community and social activism represents a broader social scope. The *soul* of representation captures how the representation is pursued or delivered, especially regarding the extent of rank-and-file participation.

TABLE 5.2
The Soul and Scope of Employee Representation

		Scope of Representation	
		Workplace (Business Unionism)	Social Arena (Social Unionism)
Soul of Representation	Union Officials (Passive Servicing Model)	Job control unionism, Traditional craft unionism	European social partnerships
	Union Members (Active Organizing Model)	Employee empowerment unionism	Social movement unionism

The rank and file are passive in the servicing model; alternative strategies seek to instead actively engage the rank and file in union activities.

Consider first the two rows in Table 5.2. In contrast to the common servicing model, some argue that unions should embrace an **organizing model.**[12] This approach views unions as institutions of active worker participation, empowerment, and mobilization. Organizing drives to unionize nonunion workers are not led solely by full-time union staff members, but rely heavily on internal organizers: workers themselves who talk about forming a union with their coworkers and thereby create more internal organizers. Once unionized, problems are not solved for workers as in the servicing model; rather, workers play an active part in resolving their own problems. Workers do not consume equity and voice; they participate in their attainment and continually serve as internal organizers to create vibrant unions. This is an active form of representation, and the soul of the representation process consists of the rank-and-file union members. In other words, in the servicing model, a union is like a vending machine—you put in your money, push a button (make a phone call), and get a desired service in return—whereas in the organizing model, a union is like a health and fitness club—you get a tour, see how it works, and what you get out of it depends on how much of a personal investment you make. As another important contrast, the servicing model sees the relationship between a worker and his or her union as a narrow economic exchange that develops only weak ties between leaders and union members; the organizing model sees this as a social exchange with the potential for developing strong social ties not only between leaders and members but also among members.[13]

While staying within the workplace focus of the business unionism philosophy (column 1 of Table 5.2), labor and management have experimented with different ways of moving away from the servicing model toward an organizing model (i.e., from row 1 to row 2 in Table 5.2). Some of these alternatives to job control unionism can be loosely grouped together as **employee empowerment unionism** (see Table 5.1).[14] Rather than establishing standardized outcomes, such as tying wages to jobs or layoffs to seniority as are typical in job control unionism, employee empowerment unionism establishes the framework of procedures in which workers are then empowered to determine their own outcomes. Consider union strategies in professional sports. These unions focus less on negotiating specific outcomes and instead have established the parameters within which individual players negotiate their own salaries.[15] These parameters include minimum standards and provisions for resolving disputes. A similar model is used for actors and might also be appropriate for college professors, doctors, and other occupations.

Professional athletes and actors are perhaps unique examples because the individual employees negotiate their own salaries; but as companies move toward teamwork and various mechanisms for employee involvement and decision making, examples of employee empowerment unionism are increasing. Skill-based pay is one example: labor and management negotiate the parameters of the system, and workers are responsible for upgrading their skills and reaping rewards for doing so. Union involvement in establishing standards for a team to select new members or a team leader is another example in which the union's role is not negotiating outcomes, but negotiating processes for empowering individual employees. Finally, the clerical workers at Harvard University bargained for a problem-solving system that replaces a traditional grievance procedure with a framework that empowers employees to resolve their own workplace problems.[16]

Now consider the columns in Table 5.2. The workplace scope of representation common in U.S. labor relations contrasts with the **social unionism** philosophy that is frequently observed in Europe. Adherents to a social unionism philosophy see labor unions as more than workplace mechanisms for winning economic gains; rather, unions are viewed as integral participants in a community's and country's civic and political activities (see Table 5.1). In other words, the scope of representation is the broader social and political arena. Labor's influence comes less from strong bargaining power in the workplace and more from social and political power. The pursuit of equity and voice is not limited to negotiating favorable contract language governing the rules of the workplace, but extends to broader concerns of social justice throughout society.

Like business unionism, however, the soul of social unionism can be union leaders with passive rank-and-file participation—consistent with a servicing model of representation (row 1 in Table 5.2)—or active union member participation—consistent with an organizing model of representation (row 2 in Table 5.2). European social partnership arrangements in which the top union and business leaders negotiate agreements with the government on broad social and economic issues are examples of social unionism with passive rank-and-file participation (see Chapter 12). Union lobbying for minimum wage increases, civil rights legislation, or other broad reforms without grassroots participation are other examples in which the rank and file are largely passive. An historical example from Chapter 3 is the National Labor Union and its emphasis on the political arena.

In contrast, social *movement* unionism embraces labor unions as part of a broader social movement of community, social, and political activist groups that relies on active grassroots participation and mobilization. In this way, social movement unionism could also be called "whole-worker organizing" because it seeks to integrate rather than separate out work issues from the rest of a person's life and thereby "seeks to engage 'whole workers' in the betterment of their lives."[17] Social movement unionism in the United States is often advocated as a basis for revitalizing the labor movement because rank-and-file activism can provide the means to increase organizing, especially among traditionally overlooked groups such as immigrant workers, and to resist management demands for concessions. The sociopolitical activism of social movement unionism is also frequently rooted in a belief that the employment relationship is characterized by deep sociopolitical class conflict rather than economic conflicts that can be mediated by workplace-focused institutions (recall the contrast between the critical and pluralist industrial relations schools in Chapter 2). In other words, "if class struggle is not restricted to the workplace, then neither should unions be."[18] An historical example from Chapter 3 is the IWW and its emphasis on drastic social change.

THE STRUCTURE OF THE U.S. LABOR MOVEMENT

The primary focus of this chapter is the strategies used by labor unions and employers to achieve efficiency, equity, and voice, but students and practitioners of labor relations should also understand the structure of the U.S. labor movement. According to the U.S. Department of Labor, in 2015 there were 14,795,000 union members in the private and public sectors combined. An additional 1.6 million workers were covered by union contracts but were not union members, which brings the total number of U.S. workers covered

TABLE 5.3
U.S. Union Membership and Coverage Statistics, 2015

	Union Members		Workers Covered by a Union Contract	
	Number	**Percentage**	**Number**	**Percentage**
Total	14,795,000	11.1	16,441,000	12.3
Full-time workers	13,340,000	12.2	14,768,000	13.5
Part-time workers	1,431,000	5.9	1,646,000	6.7
White				
Men	6,222,000	11.2	6,875,000	12.4
Women	5,079,000	10.2	5,752,000	11.6
African American				
Men	1,097,000	14.5	1,174,000	15.5
Women	1,149,000	12.8	1,253,000	13.9
Hispanic or Latino ethnicity				
Men	1,211,000	9.6	1,346,000	10.6
Women	892,000	9.2	1,019,000	10.5

Source: U.S. Department of Labor.

by unions to 16,441,000, or 12.3 percent of all employed workers. As shown in Table 5.3, union density is significantly higher in full-time than in part-time jobs and is slightly higher among men than women. Moreover, relative to whites, union density is higher among African American workers but lower among workers of Hispanic or Latino ethnicity. These figures also imply that 47 percent of union members are women, 24 percent are members of minority groups, and 49 percent are in the public sector.

Table 5.4 illustrates the range of union coverage rates across different occupations, industries, and states. Union density is quite low for sales and managerial positions but is between 15 and 20 percent for blue-collar manual occupations and nearly 40 percent for teachers, police, and firefighters. A similar pattern is evident across industries, with service-related industries having low union coverage, whereas union coverage rates in manufacturing, construction, transportation, and utilities are above average. Finally, there are significant regional differences in union membership. Southern and southwestern states generally have the lowest union densities, while northern industrial states have the highest. These differences in union densities can have important effects on bargaining power and labor relations outcomes.

Local Union Structures

Most union members have the greatest contact with their local union. A local union may represent many workers from a single workplace (an industrial local), workers in a single occupation from several workplaces (a craft local), or multiple occupations in multiple workplaces in multiple industries (an amalgamated local). Craft and amalgamated locals are likely to have an elected business agent to administer the contracts that have been negotiated with the various employers. Most worksites also have one or more elected or appointed shop stewards. These individuals are the primary point of contact for most unionized employees, and the stewards' most important responsibility is processing grievances that have been filed within their work groups. Local unions are governed by a president and executive committee who are democratically elected. There may also be a negotiation committee and a grievance committee. Some local unions may be active in local politics and in trying to organize new members. Individual

TABLE 5.4
Union Contract Coverage by Industry, Occupation, and State, 2015

Occupation			Percentage
Farming, fishing, and forestry			2.5
Management, business, and financial			5.4
Sales and office occupations			7.5
Service occupations			11.7
Production, transportation, and material moving			15.1
Installation, maintenance, and repair			15.7
Construction and extraction			18.3
Professional and educational			18.9
Industry			
Private wage and salary workers			7.4
Agriculture and related industries			1.7
Financial activities			2.8
Professional and business services			3.3
Leisure and hospitality			3.6
Other services			3.9
Wholesale and retail trade			5.1
Mining			6.5
Education and health services			9.9
Information			9.9
Manufacturing			10.0
Construction			14.0
Transportation and utilities			20.3
Government workers			39.0
Federal			32.3
State			33.6
Local			45.0
States			
Lowest Five		**Highest Five**	
South Carolina	2.9	New York	26.0
North Carolina	4.1	Alaska	21.7
Georgia	5.1	Hawaii	21.7
Utah	5.2	Washington	18.0
Texas	5.6	Connecticut	17.4

Source: U.S. Department of Labor.

workers can participate in the local union in formal (e.g., being an officer) or informal ways (e.g., talking with new members), and unions can foster greater participation by creating positive attitudes and a supportive local union culture that result in high levels of union commitment.[19]

The local leadership positions, including the shop stewards, can be either full-time or part-time depending on the size and complexity of the local union. In some cases this local union may be an independent organization and not part of a national union; for example, the Kaiser Permanente Nurse Anesthetists Association or the Southwest Airlines Pilots' Association. But nearly all local unions are part of a **national union**.

National Union Structures

There are approximately 100 national unions in the United States. The largest are the National Education Association (NEA) with over 3 million members and the Teamsters, United Food and Commercial Workers (UFCW), Service Employees International Union (SEIU), and American Federation of State, County, and Municipal Employees (AFSCME), each with over 1 million members. The NEA has over 14,000 locals, and the UFCW has over 1,000 locals. Some national unions are called "internationals" because they also have locals in Canada; for example, the UFCW's full name is the United Food and Commercial Workers International Union.

While local unions are the focal point of most rank-and-file members' contact with the union, the greatest power and authority generally lie with the national unions. National unions charter the local unions and often have final approval authority over local actions. Although the labor movement has such diverse structures that generalizations do not apply universally, most national unions are responsible for organizing new members, providing research and training, lobbying legislators, providing strike benefits, and supervising the collective bargaining process. When bargaining with larger companies, the national union may directly handle collective bargaining. With smaller companies, a local union's negotiating committee may take the lead, but often with the support and advice of a national union staff member.

The national unions are structured to support these activities. National unions generally have a number of departments, divisions, and regions. Departments consist of specialized staff in important functional areas. Common departments include organizing, collective bargaining, research, education or training, and government affairs. Divisions or conferences focus on important industries or occupations within a national union and provide the opportunity for coordination and networking within these areas. For example, the International Brotherhood of Boilermakers has divisions for construction, railroad, shipbuilding, and appliances. It is also common for national unions to have regional or district offices to serve the local unions. The basic nature of a typical national union is summarized in Figure 5.1.

As with the local unions, national unions are governed through traditional democratic methods. National union officers are periodically elected either directly by the membership or indirectly through elected delegates. Each national union has a constitution that spells out the union's bylaws and procedures. Overall policy directions and changes to the constitution are made through periodic conventions attended by delegates elected by the union's membership. Although unions have increased their use of formal human resources, financial, and strategic planning processes, improving the management and strategic planning skills of union leaders is needed.[20]

Historically it was easy to distinguish between national craft unions representing workers in a single craft, such as the United Brotherhood of Carpenters or the International Brotherhood of Electrical Workers, and national industrial unions representing all workers in a single industry, such as the United Steelworkers of America (USW) or the United Auto Workers (UAW). But unions have diversified and merged over the years, so there is now less of a distinction.[21] In fact, today many U.S. unions represent workers from diverse occupations and industries. For example, as the result of multiple mergers, the USW's full name is now the United Steel, Paper and Forestry, Rubber, Manufacturing, Energy, Allied Industrial and Service Workers International Union. The USW represents not only workers in numerous metal and manufacturing industries but also nurses, pharmacists, home health aides, librarians, zookeepers, bus drivers, police officers, university clerical workers, and many others. Many U.S. unions today would therefore be better described as **general unions** rather than as true industrial or craft unions.

FIGURE 5.1
The Structure of the U.S. Labor Movement

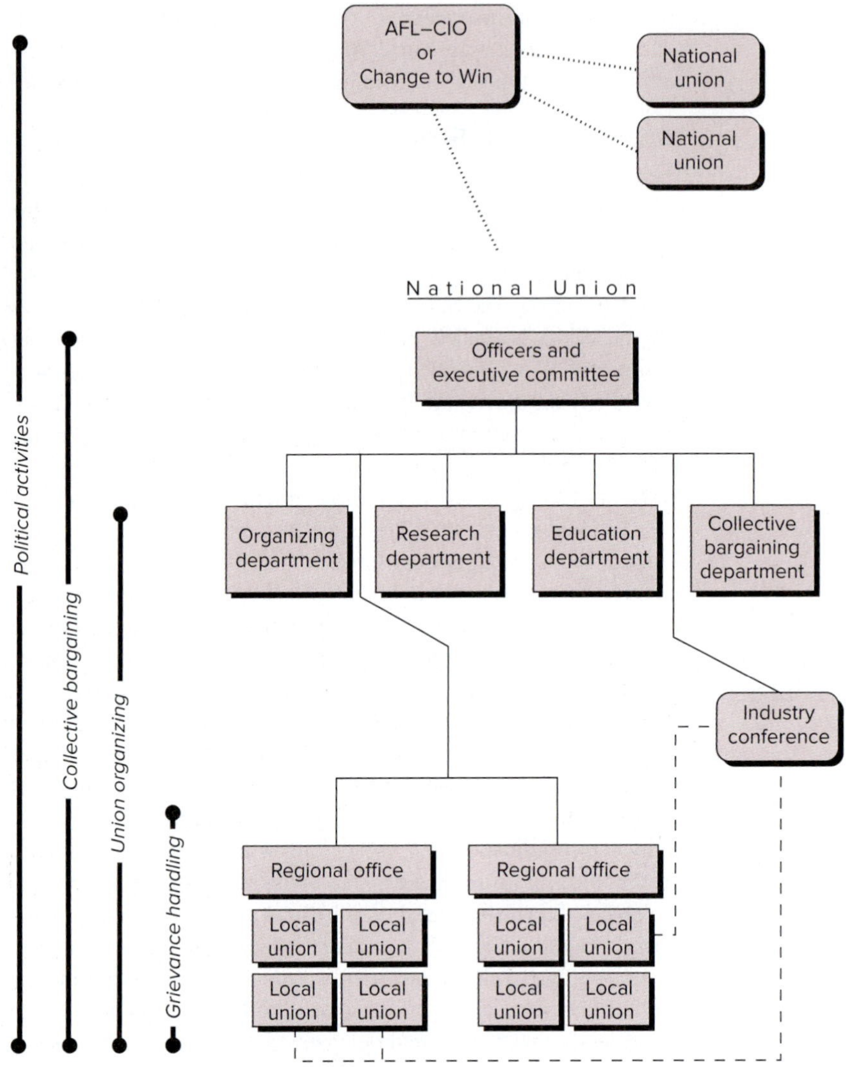

The Pros and Cons of General Unions

One persistent question for the U.S. labor movement is whether the increased strength that the national unions gain by increasing their membership and financial base through mergers and diverse organizing activity outweighs the potential problems with being responsive to the increasingly disparate needs and situations of individual workers. One critic has gone so far as to characterize opportunistic mergers and organizing activity as "nickel-and-dime business unionism" that lacks a coherent strategy for representing diverse workers.[22] Also, mergers do not always go smoothly. The Union of Needletrades, Industrial and Textile Employees merged with the Hotel Employees and Restaurant Employees International Union in 2004 to form the cleverly named UNITE HERE. But culture clashes and leadership conflicts erupted into an internal war, and in 2009, nearly 25 percent of the membership left to affiliate with SEIU.

A related question relates to union competition for members, or **rival unionism.** Merger activity reduces interunion competition, as when one of the Teamsters' fiercest rivals, the Brewery Workers, joined the Teamsters. But diverse organizing activity among general unions increases competition among unions, as when the Steelworkers compete with both service employees' and nurses' unions to organize nursing home employees. The question for the labor movement is whether this competition is a waste of precious resources or whether it causes better representation. The former is a popular view, but as a counterexample, it appears that many truck drivers and warehouse workers significantly benefited from competition between the Teamsters and rival unions in the 1930s–1950s as the threat of losing members to rivals caused union leaders to bargain more aggressively and win greater gains.[23] Perhaps the benefits of competition that cause corporations to innovate and strive for better goods and services also apply to labor unions.[24]

National and International Union Federations

Another important component of the structure of each country's labor movement is one or more national labor federations. A labor federation is an association of labor unions that provides support and leadership to the labor movement. To better understand the place of labor federations in the overall power structure, it is instructive to compare the levels of the labor movement to the levels of government in the United States. Local unions are like state governments—they have their own elected officials and can pursue their own policies and conduct their own activities within the parameters set by a superior authority. For state governments the superior authority is the U.S. federal government, and for local unions it is their parent national union. Thus, national unions are like the federal government in that they have the ultimate authority. A labor federation is like the United Nations—it provides overall leadership and important services, but membership is voluntary. Like the United Nations, a labor federation cannot force its members to comply with its decisions.

Between 1955 and 2005 there was one major national labor federation in the United States: the American Federation of Labor–Congress of Industrial Organizations (**AFL–CIO**). The AFL–CIO consists of 56 national unions that represent 12.5 million workers. A fraction of the union dues collected by each member union is forwarded to the AFL–CIO to fund its operations. Figure 5.2 shows the organizational structure of the AFL–CIO. As with the national unions, there are specialized departments, called programmatic departments, as well as divisions for specific industries or occupations, called trade and industrial departments. Specialized departments include civil and human rights, international affairs, organizing, and several pertaining to the AFL–CIO's political function: legislative, political, and public policy. Trade and industrial departments include building and construction trades, food and allied services, maritime trades, and professional employees. The AFL–CIO also has affiliated state federations and local labor councils that provide opportunities for the labor movement to cooperate at the state and local levels. Figure 5.2 also emphasizes the AFL–CIO's relationship with a number of other groups. The AFL–CIO plays an important leadership role in the direction and coordination of the U.S. labor movement, but most of the organizing, negotiating, and grievance handling is done by local and national unions, not the AFL–CIO. The AFL–CIO is a support organization, analogous to the National Association of Manufacturers or the Chamber of Commerce on the employer side. As such, its main functions are political lobbying, research, education, and overall coordination and direction.

In 2005, disagreements among AFL–CIO affiliated unions over how much to target resources toward organizing instead of political activity led seven organizing-focused unions to break-away from the AFL–CIO and form a new labor federation called Change to Win.[25] As of 2016, however, only three unions remained in Change to Win and the AFL–CIO clearly remains as the leading U.S. labor federation.

Labor federations and individual unions also have international links and alliances with labor movements from around the globe. For example, the AFL–CIO is a member of the International Trade Union Confederation (ITUC)—a federation of national union federations. Similarly, individual unions participate in international organizations for their

FIGURE 5.2 AFL–CIO Organization Chart

Source: AFL–CIO.

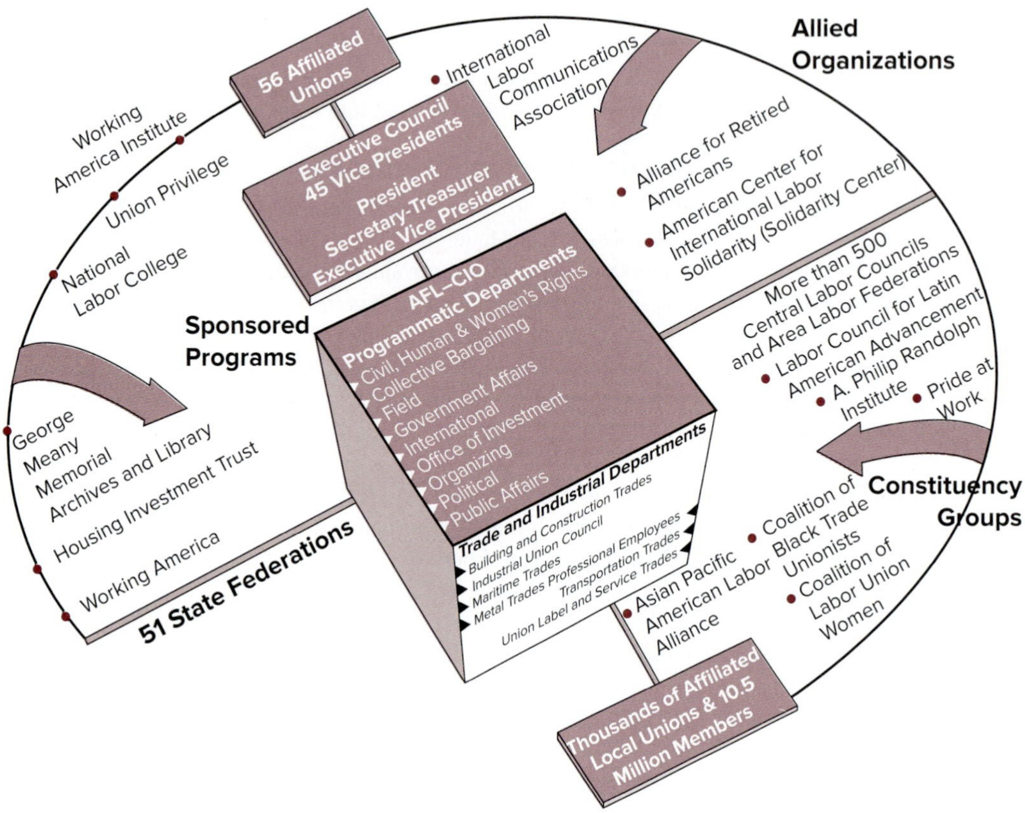

industries. For example, the UAW belongs to the International Metalworkers' Federation. These global union federations provide the same type of communication, coordination, research, and education functions as the AFL–CIO, but at a global level.

Union Democracy

Because providing voice is a primary role of labor unions, it is imperative that unions be democratic. Democracy in unions is also championed because of the belief that democratic unions more effectively represent their members.[26] **Union democracy** can be analyzed along three dimensions: procedural, behavioral, and substantive.[27] Procedurally, U.S. law (the Landrum–Griffin Act) mandates basic democratic procedures within unions, including free speech and election provisions. Behaviorally, unions appear to be more democratically vibrant at the local than the national level. Although participation rates of rank-and-file members at local union meetings are low, attendance rises for voting on contracts and strikes. Many national leaders are regularly reelected; there is greater leader turnover at the local level.

Even if officer turnover is low, however, the presence of opposition can keep leadership responsive to its membership. This is the substantive dimension, and between 70 and 80 percent of union members report being at least somewhat satisfied with their ability to influence local union leaders, bargaining agendas, and the selection of national leaders.[28]

While there is room for improvement, the generally positive record on the substantive dimension is adequate if one accepts the servicing model of unionism (recall Table 5.1).

Advocates for the organizing model, however, point to the dismal record along the behavioral dimension of democracy as a major obstacle to creating a vibrant labor movement, especially because of entrenched union bureaucracies and socially conservative union leaders.[29] Managerial pressures for employee involvement in workplace decision making can also undermine union democracy by eroding employee commitment to their union and lowering participation in union affairs.[30] In extreme cases union leaders can be corrupt and unions can be infiltrated by the mafia (as portrayed in the HBO series *The Sopranos*).[31] National unions can use trusteeships to clean up local abuses, and in the worst instances corrupt officials can be prosecuted under the federal Racketeer Influenced and Corrupt Organizations Act (RICO), as was the case for the national leadership of the Teamsters.

Last, note that outside of critical circles, it is unusual to raise questions about "corporate democracy." And yet, union democracy is a well-recognized concept. This contrast highlights significant differences in the organizational nature of labor organizations and corporations. Conceptually, labor unions are bottom-up organizations that ideally serve the interests of the rank-and-file members. Leaders at all levels of labor organizations are therefore elected, and members are entitled to vote, express opinions, and the like. In contrast, corporations are top-down organizations designed to serve the interests of their owners. Employees are not entitled to elect their leaders; rather, leaders are appointed by those in higher levels in the organizational structure and have formal authority over those at lower levels. These differences are important for understanding the distinct goals, strategies, and decision-making processes of labor unions and corporations. At the same time, other aspects of labor and corporate organizations can be similar, especially in terms of hierarchical structures, formalized procedures, specialized functions, and other elements of large-scale bureaucracies.[32]

Online Exploration Exercise: Find descriptions of the structure of national unions on various union sites (on many sites there is a link for "About Union Name"). How similar are the structures? Can you find differences in structures that are related to differences in the environment? One source of links to union sites is *www.aflcio.org/About/AFL-CIO-Unions*.

MANAGEMENT STRATEGIES

A dominant—perhaps even *the* dominant factor—in contemporary labor relations, and in the world economy more generally, is the corporation. In fact, many union strategies are developed in reaction to managerial strategies, and whether unions are good or bad for the bottom line depends on how managers act toward employees and unions.[33] So managerial choices are important. To think about managerial strategies in labor relations, consider two possible management attitudes toward labor unions: acceptance and avoidance. Theoretically there is a third possibility: union encouragement, but there is little doubt that except in rare situations, U.S. corporations prefer to be nonunion.[34] To the extent that management works toward remaining nonunion, or becoming nonunion if already unionized, this is **union avoidance.** To the extent that management accepts, perhaps begrudgingly, the presence of a union or a drive to establish a union, this is union acceptance. How these attitudes translate into labor relations strategies depends on the organization's approach to human resources more generally, which is in turn rooted in its business strategy.

Business Strategies

It is common to divide business strategies into two general types: cost leadership strategies (emphasizing low cost) and differentiation strategies (emphasizing product quality and features).[35] A cost leadership business strategy is likely pursued through a human resources strategy that seeks to minimize labor costs (see Table 5.5). Efficiency stems from low costs and high output, so labor is driven and treated as a commodity or machine. Equity and voice are seen in market-based terms, and efficiency is paramount. A stereotypical example is a traditional mass production assembly line where supervisors push employees to work harder and threaten them with discipline or discharge if they fail to produce. Such approaches are consistent with the well-known Theory X of management, in which workers are assumed to dislike work and must therefore be commanded and controlled through threats of punishment.[36] The result is a "low road" human resources approach that is largely autocratic.

In contrast, a differentiation business strategy is likely pursued through a "high road" human resources strategy that develops, rewards, and perhaps even empowers employees to create a loyal and productive workforce (see Table 5.5). Equity and voice are important components of this strategy because fair treatment and protective benefits (equity) and individual voice mechanisms such as open-door policies can foster loyalty, satisfaction, and therefore productivity. In contrast to the traditional Theory X, this human resources strategy is consistent with Theory Y, in which managers motivate employees by establishing conditions of commitment and responsibility.[37] More extensive approaches might even employ a strategic business partner HR strategy in which employees are seen as a source of competitive advantage; employees are thus empowered in high-performance workplaces.[38] In management theory this approach is similar to Theory Z, which features participative decision making.[39] The overall approach is paternalistic, or, in the high-performance model, strategic.

TABLE 5.5
Human Resources Patterns and Labor Relations Strategies

	Human Resources and Industrial Relations Patterns	
	Autocratic	**Paternalistic/Strategic**
Business Strategy	Cost leadership	Differentiation
Human Resources Strategy	Minimize labor costs	Develop, reward, and empower employees
Supervision	Drive	Inspire
Management's View of		
Efficiency	Low cost and high output	Loyal, productive, and empowered workforce
Equity	Market outcomes are fair	Fair treatment; protective benefits
Voice	If you don't like it, quit	Open-door policies; formal employee involvement programs
Employees as	Commodities or machines	Assets
Labor Relations Strategy		
If Union Acceptance	Adversarial	Participatory
If Union Avoidance	Suppression	Substitution

Nonunion Application The Corporation

A corporation is an organization that is allowed by law to function essentially as a person with specific rights (such as the ability to purchase property) and duties (such as abiding by the law). Investors purchase shares of the corporation, and these shareholders therefore collectively own the corporation (these shares might also be called "stocks," and these shareholders might therefore be called "stockholders"). These shares might be publicly traded on a stock market (a publicly traded company) or not (a privately owned company). Note that the shareholders own, but do not manage, the corporation. Investors purchase shares with the expectation that the executives and managers will work hard on their behalf, make a profit, and increase the values of the shares.

Corporations have come to dominate the economic landscape only in the last 200 years. In the 1600s pepper and other spices from southeastern Asia were in great demand in Europe. But spice voyages were very risky—one storm, an encounter with pirates, an outbreak of scurvy, or some other hazardous event could wipe out the entire investment. To avoid the potential for a huge loss in a single voyage, merchants bid for "shares" of a voyage. Moreover, as spice voyages, mines, and utilities became bigger and more complex, their expense could no longer be financed by a sole merchant or by a small number of partners. Thus the now-common practice of purchasing shares in a corporation was born. Early corporations, however, were viewed with suspicion. Before this time, even the largest businesses were partnerships in which the owners knew each other personally and were all actively involved in running the business. The separation of ownership and management inherent in a corporation was a significant break from what people were familiar with. Many feared that when shareholders did not personally know the managers, the managers would be able to take advantage of the shareholders. In fact corruption was common at times, and corporations were banned in England from 1720 until 1825.

By pooling resources, corporations can be efficient economic organizations; and with the rise of railroads in the 1800s, corporations became widespread. Individual investors, however, still faced a significant risk—*personal* liability for a company's debts regardless of the amounts of their initial investments. In the late 1800s England and the United States enacted limited liability laws so that individual investors can lose only the amounts of their initial investments (not their houses, cars, personal savings, and the like). Through various court rulings, the legal nature of a corporation also developed into that of a person "with its own identity, separate from the flesh-and-blood people who were its owners and managers and empowered, like a real person, to conduct business in its own name, acquire assets, employ workers, pay taxes, and to go to court to assert its rights and defend its actions."

As a result, corporations have taken on a life of their own. And it is largely a single-minded life. So that managers cannot take advantage of shareholders, corporations are legally bound to make money for the shareholders. Managers must act in the interests of shareholders—not in the interests of workers, consumers, or the environment except to the extent that these interests are aligned with increased profits. Supporters emphasize the incredible economic efficiencies that can result. But detractors caution against placing too much faith in corporate self-interest: A corporation is in business to make money, not to promote other things that real humans value such as democracy, empathy, relationships, justice, and dignity—especially when, unlike a real person who can be put in jail, it is hard to punish corporations for their transgressions.

So what's the bottom line? For a corporation, it is returning profits to shareholders. This undeniably creates great economic wealth, but it also provides incentives for resisting unions, polluting the environment, and avoiding taxes. For a society, the bottom line should be more than just profits. Corporations are not real people—they are created through the legal system and given certain privileges (recall limited liability, for example) in return for serving the public interest. It is therefore legitimate for a labor relations system—as well as national and global economic systems—to ensure that corporations continue to serve the public interest.

References: Joel Bakan, *The Corporation: The Pathological Pursuit of Profit and Power* (New York: Free Press, 2004); the quote is from p. 16; Howard Gospel and Andew Pendleton (eds.), *Corporate Governance and Labour Management: An International Comparison* (Oxford: Oxford University Press, 2005); Thom Hartmann, *Unequal Protection: The Rise of Corporate Dominance and the Theft of Human Rights* (New York: Rodale, 2002); Marjorie Kelly, *The Divine Right of Capital: Dethroning the Corporate Aristocracy* (San Francisco: Berrett-Koehler, 2001); Penny Le Couteur and Jay Burreson, *Napoleon's Buttons: How 17 Molecules Changed History* (New York: Jeremy P. Tarcher/Putnam, 2003).

Labor Relations Strategies

The autocratic and paternalistic/strategic patterns help reveal the importance of managerial attitudes toward unions (see the last two rows of Table 5.5). First consider the autocratic approach. A union acceptance strategy in this type of organization would likely consist of adversarial negotiations in which labor and management negotiators challenge and threaten each other during negotiations. Strikes and grievance activity would also be expected to be higher than average as management fights to keep labor costs down and unions react to this aggressiveness. But management does not seek to oust the union. In contrast, a union avoidance strategy in an autocratic organization is **union suppression** (see Table 5.6).[40] Some might call this union busting. Union suppression tactics include harassment, demotion, or firing of union supporters. Recall from Chapter 4 that this behavior is illegal in the United States, but studies suggest that it is nevertheless common.[41] Another set of union suppression tactics involves either proactively or reactively shifting work from locations that are unionized (or are threatening to unionize): plant closings, outsourcing, bankruptcies, and double-breasting (the opening of nonunion operations in the same market, a popular strategy in construction). Recent examples include the outsourcing of jobs to low-wage countries in the private sector and the privatization of services in the public sector. Decisions to not make new investments in unionized facilities in favor of targeting new investment toward nonunion locations are also part of a union suppression strategy.[42] Finally, an aggressive union suppression strategy in a unionized workplace might include tactics to decertify (kick out) the union, engage in surface bargaining (going through the motions without intending to reach agreement), and use permanent strike replacements to take the jobs of union supporters. These tactics will be covered in greater detail in later chapters, and, as we will discuss, many are of questionable legality.

In an autocratic organization, a union avoidance strategy is union suppression; in a paternalistic/strategic organization, a union avoidance strategy is **union substitution.**[43] In short, management adopts policies and practices to keep unions out by making them unnecessary (see Table 5.6). Central features of this strategy include paying above-market wages and benefits (often comparable to unionized compensation packages), providing employment security, giving employees opportunities for training and development, and instituting informal grievance procedures or at least complaint mechanisms. Authoritarian supervision is replaced with more respectful, coaching methods of supervision, and attitude surveys are used to monitor employee satisfaction. Employees are made to feel like they are part of the organization, and have voice, with information sharing and participatory mechanisms such as quality circles. Through these equity and

TABLE 5.6
Union Avoidance Tactics

Union Suppression	Union Substitution
Firing or harassing union supporters	Above-market pay and benefits
Screening out pro-union applicants	Opportunities for training and development
Plant closings/bankruptcy	Respectful supervision
Subcontracting/outsourcing	Complaint or grievance procedures
Investing in nonunion sites	Employment security
Surface bargaining	Attitude surveys
Using permanent strike replacements	Information sharing
Facilitating decertification	Consultation/participation mechanisms

voice mechanisms, employers hope to create not only loyal and productive workers but also workers who feel they do not need a union. This is essentially the goal of welfare capitalism and modern human resource management and reflects a unitarist view of the employment relationship (Chapter 2).[44] In fact, one of the first health insurance plans stemmed from an attempt by DuPont to expand its employee insurance benefits and thwart an organizing drive.[45] Union substitution tactics are generally legal when pursued as a consistent human resource management strategy; but, for example, if compensation is manipulated in response to a specific union organizing drive, this might be illegal interference under Section 8(a)(1) of the National Labor Relations Act. Moreover, voice mechanisms that are viewed as company-dominated unions violate Section 8(a)(2); this important controversy will be discussed in Chapter 10.

Last, a union acceptance attitude in a paternalistic/strategic organization results in a participatory labor relations strategy in which the union is enlisted as a partner to help the business create high-performance work systems. In this system, employee involvement programs, work teams, and other practices are jointly established by representatives of management and the workers rather than unilaterally imposed by management. This has the potential for being more effective than in a nonunion situation because a union has the potential to better articulate true employee concerns, and individuals will speak more freely when employees are not afraid of management reprisal.[46]

Labor Relations Strategies in Practice

The history of human resources and industrial relations in the U.S. automobile industry provides good examples of these different labor relations strategies. Henry Ford implemented a form of paternalistic welfare capitalism with his $5-a-day plan in 1914.[47] This is consistent with a union avoidance strategy in the paternalistic pattern of Table 5.5. After a recession in the early 1920s, however, Ford adopted a more antagonistic strategy and aggressively fought any attempts at unionization by its workers for the next 20 years. Ford became famous for its so-called Service Department—essentially an internal police force composed of criminals and informers—which used spying, intimidation, and violence to suppress union activity.[48]

In the postwar period the United Auto Workers (UAW) became entrenched at Ford, and resistance to unions became prohibitively expensive. Ford then adopted a union acceptance strategy that accepted, but sought to contain, the presence of the UAW (recall the discussion of job control unionism from earlier in this chapter). More recently, however, competitive price and quality issues have caused Ford to adopt a participative strategy in which union members and leaders are empowered with greater input into production and business decisions.[49] Similarly, in the 1970s General Motors tried a union avoidance strategy (its "Southern strategy") of opening new, nonunion plants in the southern United States. The UAW was successful in pressuring General Motors to end this policy because of its corporatewide leverage.[50] Today General Motors has more of a union acceptance strategy, although it is generally believed to lag behind Ford in employee involvement. Finally, a popular example of a unionized high-performance work system was the (now-defunct) team-based production system used to make Saturn cars in which unionized employee teams had extensive decision-making authority over production decisions.[51]

The auto and other manufacturing industries, however, are no longer the pacesetters for the rest of American business. Rather, some argue that Walmart is creating the template for 21st-century capitalism in the United States and around the world.[52] In particular, Walmart is obsessive about continually and aggressively reducing costs to "squeeze more out of every penny."[53] Walmart's business model is therefore highly centralized to take advantage of standardized policies, scale economies, and data mining.[54] Walmart's human resource strategies fit with this business strategy—policies are centralized and standardized, store managers' labor costs are carefully policed by Walmart's headquarters, worker behavior is tightly proscribed, and wages and benefits are low.[55] Walmart is also aggressively antiunion. If a manager suspects any union activity, a rapid response team is dispatched from headquarters to squelch this threat; antiunion videos are shown, supervisors meet with employees one-on-one, employees are closely watched, and union supporters are reportedly fired.[56] When butchers in one store voted for a union, Walmart ceased employing butchers by switching to selling prepackaged meats in all its stores. When employees at a store in Quebec voted to unionize, Walmart closed the store. These are classic examples of a union suppression strategy and are consistent with a 21st-century business model that emphasizes low costs.

THE LABOR RELATIONS ENVIRONMENT

Labor leaders and corporate managers struggle with the development of strategies and organizational structures because their goals can be difficult to achieve. Labor and management must contend not only with each other's sometimes conflicting strategies but also with the pressures, constraints, and opportunities of the **labor relations environment.** This section highlights four important dimensions of this environment: legal, economic, sociopolitical, and ethical.

The Legal Environment

The legal system in every country establishes the framework for labor–management interactions. The clearest component of the legal environment is the set of laws explicitly pertaining to labor relations. As discussed in Chapter 4, the National Labor Relations Act (NLRA) establishes the processes for forming new unions and for bargaining union contracts in the U.S. private sector. The legal environment is not confined to labor law, however. Some U.S. employment standards are established by the Fair Labor Standards Act (minimum wages and overtime payments), the Civil Rights Act (nondiscrimination), the Occupational Health and Safety Act (workplace safety), and the Family and Medical Leave Act (unpaid leave), to name just a few major laws. Tax laws, bankruptcy codes, and deregulation can also affect labor relations.[57] Common law—law based on tradition and precedent rather than created by statutes enacted by lawmakers—is also important. For example, common-law doctrine on property rights affects union organizing by forbidding union organizers from the employer's premises. Perhaps most significantly, the U.S. employment relationship is governed by the employment-at-will doctrine (see Chapter 1). In the absence of legislative (especially antidiscrimination laws) or contractual restrictions (most widely associated with union contracts), employees can generally be discharged or quit at any time for any reason. This at-will relationship is established by the legal environment.

The Economic Environment

The economic environment includes the labor market, the market for the employer's products or services, markets for other factors of production, financial markets, and the state of the overall economy. Within the framework established by common and statutory laws, the economic environment critically determines workers' employment options. If the labor market is tight—that is, if unemployment is low and jobs are easy to find—a frustrated employee might quit and find a better job elsewhere. Or because a tight labor market makes it hard for employers to find new employees, a frustrated employee might use his or her leverage to win favorable gains from an employer. In a weak labor market with high levels of unemployment, employees might be reluctant to form a union for fear of being fired and unable to find a new job. Similarly, employees might be less willing to strike when the labor market is weak, and collective bargaining settlements are therefore expected to favor employers. Reducing complex jobs to simple, repetitive tasks ("deskilling"), perhaps using emerging technologies, can be a way for an organization to enhance its bargaining power by shifting demand away from expensive employees with specific knowledge to easy-to-replace, less-skilled employees.[58]

It is not just the labor market that is important. Labor demand—the strength of an employer's need for employees—is a derived demand; it is derived from employers' competitive positions in markets for their goods and services.[59] Labor demand for airline pilots stems from their role in satisfying customers' demands for flights. As routes, types of aircraft, and passengers' needs change, the demand for pilots changes accordingly. Employers that do not deliver competitive products and services will face declining market shares and therefore declining labor demand. The product market is therefore a particularly important part of the labor relations environment.[60] And across diverse industries, increased competitive pressures from globalization, increased nonunion competition, technology, and deregulation have placed significant pressures on labor relations in the United States and around the globe.[61] The 2016 strike involving nearly 40,000 workers in Verizon's landline and wired Internet business stemmed from changes in the competitive landscape due to continued consumer shifts to cell phone and wireless products. Whether a global supply or value chain is producer-driven (as in autos) or buyer-driven (as in clothing) can also significantly affect labor relations.[62]

Lastly, financial markets are increasingly being recognized as another important dimension of the labor relations environment. In a trend that has been labeled "financialization," corporations are increasingly focused on financial concerns such as boosting stock prices to satisfy Wall Street expectations and increase the value of executive stock options (Chapter 11). Financialization also includes an increased pursuit of profits through financial transactions rather than through the delivery of valuable goods and services.[63] Financialization affects the labor relations environment by shaping corporate goals that in turn shape strategies toward employee issues generally, and labor unions specifically, including decisions on how corporations allocate resources: for example, by using corporate cash reserves to repurchase its stock rather than invest in new equipment.[64]

Several major elements of the U.S. economic environment are summarized in Figure 5.3. The recessions, indicated by the shaded regions, and the unemployment rate portray the cyclic nature of the U.S. economy as the economy strengthens and weakens. The sharp increase in

FIGURE 5.3
The U.S. Macroeconomic Record, 1960–2015

Sources: Lawrence Mishel, Josh Bivens, Elise Gould, and Heidi Shierholz, *The State of Working America,* 12th ed. (Ithaca, NY: Cornell University Press, 2012) and various government sources.

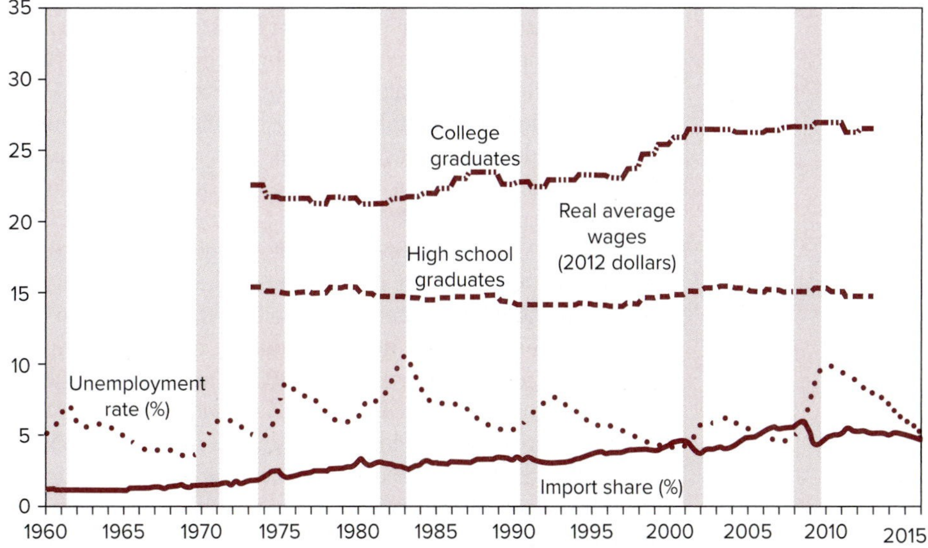

Shaded regions denote recessions.

unemployment in the early 1980s, for example, accompanied an intense period of **concession bargaining** in which many unions agreed to wage, benefit, and work rule concessions (or givebacks) to try to save jobs—a scenario repeated more than once in the first two decades of the 21st century as the major auto companies, airlines, and newspapers teetered on the edge of survival.[65] Increased globalization is represented by the import share trend (imports as a fraction of gross domestic product), which quadrupled between 1960 and 2000. Globalization represents a major shift in the environment and is the focus of Chapter 11. Finally, the average real wages for high school graduates and college graduates show that real wages for high school graduates have been stagnant since the 1970s and that the earnings gap between less educated and more educated workers has increased significantly.

Online Exploration Exercise: Identify a local company or some other business organization that is of interest. Search online to find information on the economic environment for that company. Try to find labor market information as well as company-level, industry-level, and economy-wide information regarding consumer demand, ability to pay, and other factors. Are there trends in other dimensions of the labor relations environment that are relevant for this company?

The Sociopolitical Environment

The sociopolitical environment captures factors stemming from the social and political arenas that influence labor and management. The social part of the labor relations environment can favor labor or management depending on the extent of social support for each group. In other words, employment outcomes can be influenced by public attitudes toward labor unions. The fast-food strikes in 2016 were aimed at publicizing the plight of fast-food workers to shift public opinion in their favor and create pressure for the industry to increase wages.[66] In a comparative context, the relative success of labor unions in Canada versus the United States can be partially explained by greater social acceptance of collective action, and therefore lack of acceptability of antiunion management behavior.[67] It is also commonly believed that the firing of the public sector air traffic controllers by President Ronald Reagan during the (illegal) PATCO strike in 1981 created a climate in which it was acceptable for private sector employers to actively fight unions and resist their legal strikes (see Chapter 4).[68] The British government's role in defeating the 1984–1985 National Union of Mineworkers strike is viewed similarly (see Chapter 12).[69]

Business and labor can also lobby political leaders for favorable treatment. In Minneapolis the hotel employees' union successfully pressured the city to include provisions for employer neutrality in any organizing campaigns at a hotel that was being developed with public assistance.[70] In this case the political environment affected the labor relations environment by making it easier for unions to organize new workplaces. Unions that represent workers at public utilities such as phone companies can lobby for rate increases (so the employer can afford higher wages) and mandated service improvements (which might require hiring additional employees). In fact, some employee groups rely on political lobbying rather than collective bargaining to improve wages and working conditions. As an example, the International Union of Gaming Employees does not pursue collective bargaining but tries to protect the interests of casino dealers by filing lawsuits to alleviate problems of secondhand smoke and by lobbying for better safety standards to prevent repetitive motion injuries.[71] Because of their shunning of collective bargaining, such groups are often referred to as associations rather than unions. Associations can grow into "full-fledged" unions that engage in collective bargaining.[72] For example, the National Educational Association started as a lobbying association on behalf of teachers but now also bargains for them.

Labor Relations Application The Government's Role in Labor Relations

The government (or in academic discussions, "the state") has several roles in labor relations. The role that receives the most attention was covered in Chapter 4: the *regulative* role. Labor law regulates individuals, unions, and companies in the context of union organizing, collective bargaining, and other collective activities, while employment law regulates the individual employment relationship. The regulative role provides the legal context of the bargaining environment. But there are four other roles a government can assume: an employer role, a facilitative role, a structural role, and a constitutive role.

The government as *employer* is the subject of public sector labor relations. The federal and state governments make the rules for their own behavior because they are both the regulator of public sector labor laws and the employer of public sector employees. In this situation, the government has a vested interest in making laws that favor its role as employer, especially with respect to employees that provide essential services.

In the *facilitative* role, the government facilitates the nature of labor relations by establishing social norms or attitudes and by providing various services. The PATCO and NUM strikes in the 1980s are often credited with establishing antiunion climates in the United States and Great Britain. This contributes to the political and social dimensions of the labor relations environment. Moreover, by providing training, statistics, and mediation, the government can facilitate the practice of labor relations.

The *structural* role of government consists of economic policies that help shape or structure the economic environment for labor relations. This includes fiscal policy, monetary policy, international trade agreements, and social safety nets (such as unemployment insurance, Social Security, workers' compensation, and welfare).

In the *constitutive* role, the government establishes how economic and social relationships, including the employment relationship, are established or constituted. A government that establishes a capitalist, marketbased economy emphasizes the importance of property rights; labor rights are often of secondary importance. For example, managers have a fiduciary obligation to serve the shareholders, but no corresponding obligation to employees.

In sum, the constitutive dimension establishes the broadest parameters for labor relations (such as a capitalistic society), and within this overall system, the regulative role creates the legal framework for labor relations, the structural role partially determines the economic climate, and the facilitative role contributes toward the attitudinal climate and the capabilities of the parties. In U.S. labor relations, the regulative role is generally the focal point, but these other roles of government are intertwined and should not be overlooked.

Nonunion Application: *Read this box again while replacing each occurrence of "labor relations" with "human resource management" and note how the different roles of government also influence the environment for managing human resources.*

Reference: John Goddard, *Industrial Relations, the Economy, and Society,* 4th ed. (Concord, Ontario: Captus Press, 2011).

The Ethical Environment

Suppose a major employer in your community closes a local facility, lays off the workers, and opens a new plant in another country to take advantage of lower labor costs. How do you feel? Is this acceptable because it improves economic efficiency, which will benefit consumers through lower prices? Or because business owners have a right to use their private property as they choose? Alternatively, is this plant closing troubling because it treats workers simply as factors of production? Or because it doesn't seem fair as some benefit at the expense of others? Or because it doesn't seem like the right thing to do? Or because it doesn't respect relationships and communities that have been established?

Each of these responses represents a different ethical standard for whether the action is right or wrong. Business ethics studies moral standards as they apply to the business context and is therefore important for understanding and evaluating labor relations behaviors, policies, and outcomes. While ethics studies right and wrong, you should not narrowly view ethics as simply restricting behavior. Rather, think of business ethics as an important motivating force for and potential constraint on behavior.[73] An ethical framework that emphasizes efficiency produces very different behaviors than one in which individuals are expected to treat others with dignity. Comparing ethical theories is a valuable way of considering different perspectives on labor relations that illuminates why individuals, employers, unions, or elected officials make specific choices.

Table 5.7 summarizes six key ethical theories (for additional details, see the "Digging Deeper" feature at the end of this chapter). The first two provide an ethical foundation for the neoliberal market ideology. Utilitarianism defines ethical actions as those that maximize aggregate welfare ("utility") so aggregate economic prosperity is highlighted, irrespective of how it is achieved. Libertarianism sees actions that infringe on others' freedoms as unethical and therefore emphasizes property rights and freedom from governmental (or labor union) interference. In contrast, Kantian ethical theory (in which individuals have a duty to respect human dignity) and Rawlsian justice ethics (in which there is an ethical concern for the least well-off) both highlight a concern with how workers are treated. These two ethical theories imply that work should not be experienced in a way that undermines human dignity and citizenship. Finally, the ethics of virtue and of care highlight the ethical value of our individual actions and our special relationships with others.

Again, the external environment establishes the parameters for decision makers, but specific actions within these parameters result from choices made by individual employees, managers, union leaders, and shareholders. One important influence on

TABLE 5.7 Six Ethical Frameworks

Ethics of . . .	Influential Thinkers	Focal Point	Tools	Immoral Acts
Utility	Jeremy Bentham John Stuart Mill	Greatest good for the greatest number	Cost–benefit analysis	Inefficient or welfare-reducing behavior
Liberty	John Locke	Freedom as the negative right to be left alone	Property rights	Forcing individuals to use themselves or their property against their will (including taxation for redistribution)
Duty	Immanuel Kant	Respect for human dignity	Categorical imperative	Treating others in ways you would not want to be treated; treating people only as means, not also as ends
Fairness	John Rawls	Justice through liberty, equal opportunity, and concern for the least well-off	Veil of ignorance; difference principle	Placing efficiency above liberty, equal opportunity, and concern for the least well-off
Virtue	Aristotle	Moral character to achieve happiness (flourishing)	Specific virtues (such as friendliness and truthfulness)	Actions contrary to virtues (vices) that prevent flourishing
Care	Carol Gilligan	Nurturing personal relationships	Caring for people	Failing to develop special relationships; relationships based on exploitation, disrespect, or injustice

these choices is ethics.[74] In fact, the widespread codes of ethics developed by corporations, labor unions, and professional associations for their employees and members underscore the belief that ethical foundations shape behavior. As a concrete example of managerial choice, consider Johnsonville Sausage's response to a 2015 fire that destroyed one of its Wisconsin meat processing plants. While a new plant was built, rather than laying off its 120 workers, the company continued to pay full wages and benefits in return for volunteering in the community. The environment gave the company options, but an ethical consideration—in this case an emphasis on the special relationships with the workers and local community—determined the final course of action. This decision isn't typical, however; business decisions made with a sole focus on efficiency and profit maximization represent another underlying ethical framework—the ethics of utility.

As such, ethics is not just philosophy; it provides an additional framework for a better understanding of labor relations (see Table 5.8).[75] Arguments against labor unions on the grounds that they impair efficiency or intrude on property rights reflect utilitarian and libertarian ethical beliefs. Arguments for labor unions because they provide equity and voice that respect human dignity, fairness, and the importance of community reflect the ethics of duty, justice, virtue, and care. In fact, the campaign to form a union of Harvard University clerical and technical workers in the 1980s was inspired largely by the ethics of care's emphasis on developing interpersonal relationships (see Chapter 6). The continuing managerial drive for greater flexibility in deploying labor and the continued resistance by workers and unions reflect in part a clash between utilitarian concerns with efficiency and Kantian concerns with the quality of human life. The sometimes violent protests over globalization stem from the utilitarian emphasis on free trade to increase efficiency clashing with the other ethical frameworks that emphasize human rights and fairness. To understand behavior and outcomes—and in making your own decisions—pay attention not only to the legal, economic, and sociopolitical environment but also to ethics. This is equally true for both labor and management, and in unionized and nonunion situations.

TABLE 5.8
Examples of Ethical Foundations in Labor Relations

The Ethics of . . .	Labor Relations Examples
Utility	A management desire to be "union-free" based on a cost–benefit analysis. Provision of equity and voice only because they increase productivity.
Liberty	Employer participation in the union organizing process because of the rights of private property and free speech.
Duty	Employees are entitled to voice because they are rational human beings who should not be treated only as a means to some other end.
Fairness	Unions negotiating compressed wage structures that narrow the gap between unskilled and skilled workers in the name of fairness.
Virtue	"Might does not make right." Rather, establish productive workplaces or engage in collective bargaining based on excellence and integrity.
Care	Recent union initiatives to organize workers by developing special relationships with the workers, especially in female-dominated occupations.

Key Terms

business unionism, *161*
servicing model, *161*
job control unionism, *162*
craft unionism, *162*
industrial unionism, *162*
organizing model, *163*
employee empowerment unionism, *163*
social unionism, *164*
national union, *167*
general union, *167*
rival unionism, *168*
AFL–CIO, *169*
union democracy, *170*
union avoidance, *171*
union suppression, *174*
union substitution, *174*
labor relations environment, *176*
concession bargaining, *178*

Reflection Questions

1. Of the union strategies in Table 5.1, which ones do you think are best for the 21st-century world of work? Are some strategies always better, or does this depend on the environment?
2. Describe the pros and cons of union mergers for (a) two unions that represent workers in the same industry and (b) two unions that represent workers in different industries. Should U.S. law encourage, discourage, or remain neutral on union mergers?
3. There is longstanding debate over "American exceptionalism"—the extent to which the low levels of support for unionization and a socialist movement make the United States unique among industrialized democratic countries. There might also be a management side: American management has been exceptionally antiunion compared to managers in other countries.[76] Why do you think this is?
4. It is almost universally accepted that labor unions, but not companies, must be democratic. Why is there this dichotomy? What does this dichotomy imply about the organizational structures and sources of power for labor unions and for corporations?
5. Employees might respond to workplace injustice in one of five ways: quitting, individual voice (such as complaining), collective voice (including forming a union), resistance (including work withdrawal such as absenteeism, reduced work effort, and work avoidance, or perhaps even sabotage), and silence. How might union strategies, managerial strategies, and the external environment shape which response an individual worker chooses? What else might affect whether workplace injustice causes an individual to support a labor union over the other options for dealing with injustice?

HR Strategy Achieving Quality

A contemporary challenge for business, managers, and employees is achieving exceptional levels of quality in the production and delivery of goods and services. To serve this goal, quality guru W. Edwards Deming articulated 14 points for management:

1. Create constancy of purpose toward improvement of product and service, with the aim to become competitive and to stay in business, and to provide jobs.
2. Adopt the new philosophy: We are in a new economic age. Western management must awaken to the challenge, must learn their responsibilities, and take on leadership for change.
3. Cease dependence on inspection to achieve quality. Eliminate the need for inspection on a mass basis by building quality into the product in the first place.
4. End the practice of awarding business on the basis of price tag. Instead, minimize total cost. Move toward a single supplier for any one item, on a long-term relationship of loyalty and trust.
5. Improve constantly and forever the system of production and service to improve quality and productivity, and thus constantly decrease costs.
6. Institute training on the job.
7. Institute leadership. The aim of supervision should be to help people and machines and gadgets to do a better job. Supervision of management is in need of overhaul as well as supervision of production workers.
8. Drive out fear, so that everyone may work effectively for the company.
9. Break down barriers between departments. People in research, design, sales, and production must work as a team to foresee problems of production and in use that may be encountered with the product or service.
10. Eliminate slogans, exhortations, and targets for the workforce asking for zero defects and new levels of productivity. Such exhortations only create adversarial relationships, as the bulk of the causes of low quality and low productivity belong to the system and thus lie beyond the power of the workforce.
11. a. Eliminate work standards (quotas) on the factory floor. Substitute leadership.
    b. Eliminate management by objective. Eliminate management by numbers, numerical goals. Substitute leadership.
12. a. Remove barriers that rob the hourly worker of his right to pride of workmanship. The responsibility of supervisors must be changed from sheer numbers to quality.
    b. Remove barriers that rob people in management and in engineering of their right to pride of workmanship. This means (among other things) abolishment of the annual merit rating and of management by objective.
13. Institute a vigorous program of education and self-improvement.
14. Put everybody in the company to work to accomplish the transformation. The transformation is everybody's job.

QUESTIONS

1. Do you agree with these principles?
2. How can unions help pursue these 14 principles?
3. How might unions hinder these 14 principles?
4. What factors determine whether a union helps or hinders achievement of these 14 principles?

Reference: W. Edwards Deming, *Out of the Crisis* (Cambridge, MA: MIT Press, 1986), pp. 23–24.

Digging Deeper Business Ethics

Ethical theories describe what should be of fundamental importance in society, and these standards provide a way of evaluating specific labor relations practices and outcomes. Of course, there are differing views of which ethical standards are best, but these theories provide a basis for debating these standards. An understanding of business ethics can also help managers and labor union officials make decisions. Business and labor leaders face numerous complex issues with conflicting obligations, trade-offs between costs and benefits, clashes between principles and outcomes, and winners and losers. Studying business ethics can help you become "more comfortable facing moral complexity" and can provide "a renewed sense of purpose and vision" for business and labor leaders struggling with this complexity.[77] This is especially important in the context of human resources and industrial relations because of the direct impact on workers' lives, and it is also particularly important in the workplace of the 21st century with the potential for electronic monitoring, genetic testing, and other emerging issues.[78] Studying business ethics will not provide easy answers to these difficult issues, but it will help you more fully identify and evaluate the consequences of alternative courses of action. This section outlines six major ethical theories that are particularly relevant to business ethics and labor relations, and concludes with an ethical analysis template to help tackle thorny ethical problems.

THE ETHICS OF UTILITY

The ethics of utility—utilitarianism—focuses on maximizing net social welfare ("utility"). As such, the key to utilitarianism is creating the "greatest good for the greatest number." Utilitarianism is a consequentialist moral theory: Actions are judged simply by their consequences. Actions are morally good if they maximize aggregate welfare in which the greatest benefits are produced with the lowest costs compared to alternative actions.[79] In fact, the utilitarian calculation of totaling costs and benefits is the same cost–benefit analysis used in the economic analysis of policy or business decisions. Cost–benefit analysis operationalizes utilitarianism.[80] This is graphically illustrated by the Ford Motor Company's calculation in the 1960s that moving the gas tank in its new small car, the Pinto, would cost $137 million in manufacturing expenses but would save only $49 million in preventing the expected 180 deaths, 180 serious burn injuries, and 2,100 burned cars.[81] Because the costs outweighed the benefits, Ford did not modify the design of its notorious exploding Pinto. In the ethics of utility, this was morally acceptable. If the negative aspects of unions described in Chapter 2 outweigh the socially beneficial contributions, then in utilitarian terms, labor unions are socially harmful and should not be allowed.

Economic efficiency also provides a strong link between utilitarianism, economics, and business. Standard economic theory indicates that "the greatest good for the greatest number" is achieved through competitive markets, profit-maximizing behavior, and efficiency. Consequently, "the enterprise of business harbors a fundamentally utilitarian conception of the good society."[82] Union avoidance strategies to maximize profits, as well as human resource management strategies to provide equity because it improves the bottom line, reflect a utilitarian belief system: "managerial opposition to unions is pragmatic, and motivated by competitive pressures . . . they evaluate unionism as a net cost in the cost–benefit ratio of the performance of the company, and that is why they oppose unionization."[83] These decisions are not independent of ethics—they are the ethics of utility.

The logic of utilitarian business thinking is powerful: Individuals pursuing their self-interests in competitive markets will maximize efficiency, and therefore welfare. Moreover, employee compensation packages will equal the value that employees contribute. More productive workers will earn a higher wage, and less productive workers will earn less. Because of a popular belief that hard work should be rewarded accordingly, this theoretical prediction has evolved into a value statement that "factors of production *ought to be paid* the value of their marginal product," which has been called "marginal productivity justice."[84] This is a utilitarian ethical philosophy; but outside of economics, business, and conservative political thought, the *normative* value of this logic is not well accepted. In fact, if there are market imperfections and other inequalities within society, laissez-faire utilitarianism degenerates into ethical egoism, in which ethical behavior is the unabashed pursuit of individual self-interest irrespective of the greater good. Moral philosophers reject the legitimacy of ethical egoism because it relies on the unsupportable assumption that our own interests are more important than everyone else's.[85] Another criticism of utilitarianism is that the ends justify the means.[86] Rights and virtues are irrelevant, distributive justice and minimum living standards are not a concern, and communities and relationships are important only so far as they increase aggregate welfare. Only the consequences matter.

THE ETHICS OF LIBERTY

The ethics of liberty, or libertarianism, emphasizes individual freedom. In this ethical system restrictions on anyone's behavior are justified only if they are needed to prevent harm to others. Unless your actions harm others, you should be free to do as you please. Strong property rights are therefore central to the libertarian philosophy, and the role of government is to protect individuals and their property. Taxes and other forms of redistribution from the wealthy to the poor that are not purely voluntary are seen as coercive takings of private property that violate the primary right of liberty. As long as the distribution of wealth in society is the result of fair acquisition and exchange (such as the lack of coercion and fraud), then it is just, even if it is extremely unequal.[87]

Like utilitarianism, the ethics of liberty strongly advocates free markets. While utilitarianism supports free markets because they are viewed as the best way to achieve efficiency and to maximize utility, libertarianism supports free markets because of the primacy of liberty. Individuals should have the right to interact with others in free markets. Chapter 4 showed that this primacy of property rights and the freedom to pursue unregulated economic relationships dominated U.S. labor law before the 1930s. Moreover, continuing struggles with workers' rights versus property rights in U.S. labor law, such as whether union organizers can be banned from private premises, partly reflect this libertarian view of the sanctity of property rights.

Libertarianism can be criticized for its narrow conception of liberty. In simple terms, are people who are starving truly free? Why should the freedom from harm to private property always trump other freedoms such as the freedom from hunger?[88] Fraud, slavery, theft, and other actions also challenge the justice of existing patterns of property rights and resources, which undermines the libertarian premise that free marketplace transactions are just. Recall further that the industrial relations school believes that labor and management have unequal bargaining power and asymmetric information (Chapter 2). If this is true, the extent to which unregulated marketplace transactions are free—and therefore just—is questionable.

THE ETHICS OF DUTY

Traditionally the most important contrast to the ethics of utility is the ethics of duty because, rather than judging actions based on their consequences, judgments are based on the action itself. Most literally, people have a duty to act in certain ways—for example not to lie, even if it does not produce the best outcome. The most important advocate of the ethics of duty is the 18th-century German philosopher Immanuel Kant. Kantian moral philosophy is based on three equivalent formulations of the categorical imperative:

1. Act only on that maxim by which you can at the same time will that it should become a universal law (formula of universal law).
2. Act in such a way that you always treat humanity, whether in your own person or in the person of any other, never simply as a means, but always at the same time as an end (formula of the end itself).
3. So act as if you were through your maxims a law-making member of a kingdom of ends (formula of the kingdom of ends).[89]

These principles are based on the view that human beings are rational and therefore capable of self-determination and self-governance.[90] Everyone is therefore entitled to dignity and respect. Using people simply to increase your own wealth, for example, treats them only as a means and violates the intrinsic value and sanctity of human life (formula of the end itself). Because everyone has equal intrinsic value, universal application of standards of behavior is critical (formula of the universal law). Note that this means you must be willing to be treated as you treat others—similar to the Golden Rule. And everyone's intrinsic value must be respected in social interactions (formula of the kingdom of ends). Full respect for human dignity and a moral kingdom of ends also requires concern for the welfare of others.

The moral principles embodied in the categorical imperative specify our duties: We have a duty to act so that our actions are universal and never treat individuals as only a means, even at the expense of aggregate welfare. In labor relations, this implies that workers are entitled to equity and voice. To refuse to hire people because of their race, gender, or union sympathies, for example, violates the first formulation of the categorical imperative if we are not willing to be discriminated against in the same manner. Discrimination also violates the formula of the end itself because discriminatory treatment for arbitrary reasons violates the equal sanctity of all human life.[91]

It can be argued that Kantian moral philosophy also gives managers a moral obligation to stockholders to pursue profits to increase shareholder wealth: A manager who ignores profitability violates an implied promise between managers and shareholders and thus violates the categorical imperative. But this is not the same as *maximizing* shareholder wealth at the expense of all other concerns.[92] Therefore, an employment relationship guided by the Kantian ethics of duty should provide efficiency *and* equity *and* voice.

Kant's emphasis on universal, unwavering rules can be criticized for understating the importance of virtues, or what it means to be a good person in everyday life.[93] Universal rules are also challenged by situations such as protecting an innocent person by telling a lie. Proponents of property rights and liberty object to the Kantian implication of concern for others rather than a focus on individual liberties. Kantian moral philosophy also ignores the development of relationships.

THE ETHICS OF FAIRNESS

The most important example of the ethics of fairness, or justice, is John Rawls's theory of distributive justice, which adds a concern with the distribution of outcomes to the Kantian standards of equality and freedom. Rawlsian justice is based on individuals determining societal standards and outcomes from behind a "veil of ignorance" in which they do not yet know their own characteristics (such as race, gender, social status, and abilities). In simple terms, think of this as dividing a cake without knowing which piece you'll receive. The principles that Rawls believes rational, self-interested, and equal individuals will agree to are these:

1. Each person is to have an equal right to the most extensive total system of equal basic liberties compatible with a similar system of liberty for all (liberty principle).
2. Social and economic inequalities are to be arranged so that they are both
   a. to the greatest benefit of the least advantaged (difference principle) and
   b. attached to offices and positions open to all under conditions of fair equality of opportunity (principle of equal opportunity).[94]

The first principle, the liberty principle, is the highest priority and includes the right to vote, freedom of speech, freedom from oppression, private property rights, and freedom from arbitrary arrest and seizure. Principle 2a, the difference principle, allows inequalities in outcomes, but these inequalities must also benefit the least well-off members of society. Principle 2b emphasizes equality of opportunity—differential outcomes are allowed, but these should reflect legitimate differences in ability and effort, not arbitrary or discriminatory factors. In short, Rawlsian fairness combines political liberty with equal opportunity and distributive justice. Efficiency is important, but it does not trump political liberties, equal opportunity, and concern for the least well-off. The importance of this Rawlsian ethics of fairness for labor relations is to highlight the importance of social justice.

THE ETHICS OF VIRTUE

The previous four ethical theories strike some people as cold and unfeeling—there is an emphasis on outcomes or duties or rights or difference principles, but where is human goodness or moral character? In contrast, the ethics of virtue focuses on the type of person each individual ought to be. This framework can be traced back to Aristotle over 2,000 years ago in ancient Greece. In this tradition, virtues are the characteristics that make a person a good human being and are necessary to live a good life as part of, and in service to, a social community. Moral behavior flows from virtues—not by the application of rules but from the virtuous moral character of individuals. A contemporary Aristotelian ethical framework is described in Table 5.9. Note the importance of using virtues to serve not only your own interests but greater social purposes as well.

As applied to business ethics, virtue ethics sees corporations as human communities with a vital sense of purpose that contribute to, and have responsibilities

TABLE 5.9 An Aristotelian Ethical Framework

Community: People are not primarily individualists but are members of organized social groups with extensive shared and communal interests. Human meaning and identification stem from being part of communities.

Excellence: Individual qualities of moral character—virtues—necessary for living the good life. Requires serving social purposes, not just individual needs. Important contemporary virtues include

Honesty	Fairness	Trust
Friendliness	Honor	Loyalty
Compassion	Charisma	Justice

Membership: Roles for each individual (in personal life, business, and society) provide the context for using virtues. These roles might conflict, but context-specific virtues should not override greater social purposes.

Integrity: Unity of character and moral courage. Requires harnessing all the virtues to create a whole person.

Judgment: With virtues instead of universal rules, and with conflicting roles, individuals need good judgment to develop integrity and make good (ethical) decisions. Generally requires consideration of all options, interests, and consequences.

Holism: Concern for the whole. Virtues should be the driving force for all behavior. All virtues should be harnessed to create integrity and good judgment. Integrity and good judgment should be directed toward the greater social purposes of the relevant communities.

Reference: Robert C. Solomon, *Ethics and Excellence: Cooperation and Integrity in Business* (New York: Oxford University Press, 1992).

in, the larger social community.[95] Corporations are collections of mutually dependent individuals, not isolated competitors, and individual excellence and virtues contribute to the success of the individual and the community. As a member of the global community, corporate excellence is defined by service to the broader community, not by a singular focus on making money. Service in the form of quality goods and services will result in profits if done well, but a blind focus on profits should not be the sole driving force; profit is "a means of encouraging and rewarding hard work and investment, building a better business, and serving society better," not "an end in itself."[96] As applied to labor relations, actions that undermine a holistic sense of community are unethical. Moreover, if the adjectives for an employer or a union are vices, such as greedy, selfish, dishonest, or corrupt, then the employer or the union is acting unethically.[97] In the ethics of virtue, labor relations should instead be characterized by cooperation, integrity, honesty, fairness, and tolerance.

THE ETHICS OF CARE

The ethics of care highlights the importance of special interpersonal relationships, such as with parents, children, neighbors, coworkers, or friends. Caring in this sense refers not to simply caring *about* something, but caring *FOR* someone—nurturing their well-being.[98] This ethical framework was initially developed in the 1980s using feminist theories, especially the claim that the feminine voice consists of "defining the self and proclaiming its worth on the ability to care for and protect others."[99] Thus moral judgments are not based on rules or principles; rather, the ethics of care relies on the deeper context of each particular situation, especially the implications for relationships. This framework is similar to a specialized version of virtue ethics with a focus on virtues that are important to personal relationships, such as sympathy, compassion, fidelity, love, and friendship.[100] Moreover, within the ethics of care it is acceptable—and maybe even encouraged—to treat people you have relationships with differently. But in developing and nurturing these special relationships, one must guard against positive nurturing becoming discriminatory favoritism, especially in the workplace.[101]

Although the ethics of care is rooted in feminist theory, it is certainly not relevant only to women. As applied to labor relations, the ethics of care focuses our attention on the relationships between employers and employees and between companies and the local communities. Deceiving employees is unethical because this demonstrates a lack of care.[102] Because this ethical framework legitimizes special treatment, corporate decisions such as whether to invest in an existing unionized plant or open a new nonunion plant in another location should pay particular attention to the existing relationships with the current workers and the local community.

In sum, the use of business ethics in labor relations is important in providing a basis for evaluating behavior and outcomes as well as understanding actions. Many participants and observers, both probusiness and prolabor, in the U.S. labor relations system feel that it needs fixing. In other words, the labor relations system is not fulfilling some basic standards. But what are those standards? The six ethical frameworks provide the basic standards against which both the labor relations system and the participants' behavior should be understood and evaluated. Similarly, when you confront difficult decisions—as a manager, employee, or union leader—these six ethical theories provide a framework for analyzing your options and the associated positive and negative consequences. Table 5.10 provides a template that incorporates the six ethical theories into a process for analyzing morally complex problems. This template can be applied to ethical questions in later chapters and to real-world situations you confront.

TABLE 5.10 An Ethical Analysis Template

For a proposed action . . .

1. *Identify the benefits.* Be as specific as possible about people or groups of people whose material, financial, or personal well-being will be improved.
2. *Identify the harms.* Be as specific as possible about people or groups of people whose material, financial, or personal well-being will be worsened.
3. *Identify rights.* Be as specific as possible about people or groups of people whose rights will be exercised or strengthened.
4. *Identify rights violations.* Be as specific as possible about people or groups of people whose rights will be violated or weakened.
5. *Identify the impact to the person making the decision.*
6. *State the moral problem.* Use the format "Is it right that (insert decision maker and action) given that (insert harms and rights violations)?" For example, is it right that company XYZ hires workers to replace strikers given that the strikers will potentially lose their jobs, the union may be broken, and the local residents may be divided by violence?
7. *Consider the ethics of utility.* Total the overall costs and benefits. Is net welfare improved or worsened? Does the proposed action increase or decrease efficiency?
8. *Consider the ethics of liberty.* Does the action violate individual liberty? If some rights are exercised and some are harmed, can they be prioritized? Does liberty take precedence over outcomes?
9. *Consider the ethics of duty.* Does the action respect human dignity? Does it treat people only as a means? Should the action be universal? Would you accept being treated in this way?
10. *Consider the ethics of fairness.* Is distributive justice respected? Do the least well-off benefit from this action? Would you choose this course of action from behind a veil of ignorance knowing that you might either benefit or be harmed by the action after the veil is lifted?
11. *Consider the ethics of virtue.* Is this action consistent with individual excellence and virtues in service of a larger social purpose? Could you be proud of this action?
12. *Consider the ethics of care.* How does the action affect special relationships? Does it nurture relationships?
13. *Identify several alternatives.* Be simultaneously creative and realistic.
14. *Support your decision.* What are the three most important ethical principles that support your decision as morally right?

Reference: Adapted from LaRue Tone Hosmer, "Standard Format for the Case Analysis of Moral Problems," *Teaching Business Ethics* 4 (May 2000), pp. 169–80.

End Notes

1. John Godard, *Industrial Relations, the Economy, and Society,* 4th ed. (Concord, Ontario: Captus Press, 2011); Robert C. Solomon, *Ethics and Excellence: Cooperation and Integrity in Business* (New York: Oxford University Press, 1992); Cynthia Estlund, *Working Together: How Workplace Bonds Strengthen a Diverse Democracy* (Oxford: Oxford University Press, 2003).
2. David Brody, *Workers in Industrial America* (New York: Oxford University Press, 1980), p. 217; Victor G. Devinatz, "An Alternative Strategy: Lessons from the UAW Local 6 and the FE, 1946–52," in Cyrus Bina, Laurie Clements, and Chuck Davis (eds.), *Beyond Survival: Wage Labor in the Late Twentieth Century* (Armonk, NY: M. E. Sharpe, 1996), pp. 145–60.
3. Robert Franklin Hoxie, *Trade Unionism in the United States* (New York: D. Appleton, 1917).
4. Sidney Lens, *The Crisis of American Labor* (New York: Sagamore Press, 1959), p. 81.
5. David Brody, "Labor's Crisis in Historical Perspective," in George Strauss, Daniel G. Gallagher, and Jack Fiorito (eds.), *The State of the Unions* (Madison, WI: Industrial Relations Research Association, 1991), pp. 277–311.
6. Hoxie, *Trade Unionism in the United States*; Thaddeus Russell, *Out of the Jungle: Jimmy Hoffa and the Remaking of the American Working Class* (New York: Knopf, 2001).
7. Russell, *Out of the Jungle.*
8. Jack Fiorito and Paul Jarley, "Trade Union Morphology," in Paul Blyton et al. (eds.), *Sage Handbook of Industrial Relations* (London: Sage, 2008), pp. 189–208.
9. Howell John Harris, *The Right to Manage: Industrial Relations Policies of American Business in the 1940s* (Madison: University of Wisconsin Press, 1982).
10. Harry C. Katz, *Shifting Gears: Changing Labor Relations in the U.S. Automobile Industry* (Cambridge, MA: MIT Press, 1985); Thomas A. Kochan, Harry C. Katz, and Robert B. McKersie, *The Transformation of American Industrial Relations* (New York: Basic Books, 1986).
11. Dorothy Sue Cobble, "Lost Ways of Unionism: Historical Perspectives on Reinventing the Labor Movement," in Lowell Turner, Harry C. Katz, and Richard W. Hurd (eds.), *Rekindling the Movement: Labor's Quest for Relevance in the Twenty-First Century* (Ithaca, NY: ILR Press, 2001), pp. 82–96; Katherine V. W. Stone, *From Widgets to Digits: Employment Regulations for the Changing Workplace* (Cambridge, England: Cambridge University Press, 2004).
12. Andy Banks and Jack Metzgar, "Participating in Management: Union Organizing on a New Terrain," *Labor Research Review* 14 (Fall 1989), pp. 1–55; Bill Fletcher, Jr., and Richard W. Hurd, "Beyond the Organizing Model: The Transformation Process in Local Unions," in Kate Bronfenbrenner et al. (eds.), *Organizing to Win: New Research on Union Strategies* (Ithaca, NY: ILR Press, 1998), pp. 37–53; Fiorito and Jarley, "Trade Union Morphology."
13. Ed Snape and Tom Redman, "Exchange or Covenant? The Nature of the Member–Union Relationship," *Industrial Relations* 43 (October 2004), pp. 855–73; Paul Jarley, "Unions as Social Capital: Renewal through a Return to the Logic of Mutual Aid?" *Labor Studies Journal* 29 (January 2005), pp. 1–26.
14. John W. Budd, *Employment with a Human Face: Balancing Efficiency, Equity, and Voice* (Ithaca, NY: Cornell University Press, 2004).
15. Roger I. Abrams, *The Money Pitch: Baseball Free Agency and Salary Arbitration* (Philadelphia: Temple University Press, 2000); Kenneth M. Jennings, *Swings and Misses: Moribund Labor Relations in Professional Baseball* (Westport, CT: Praeger, 1997).
16. John Hoerr, *We Can't Eat Prestige: The Women Who Organized Harvard* (Philadelphia: Temple University Press, 1997).
17. Jane McAlevey with Bob Ostertag, *Raising Expectations (and Raising Hell): My Decade Fighting for the Labor Movement* (London: Verso, 2012), p. 14; Lowell Turner and Richard W. Hurd, "Building Social Movement Unionism: The Transformation of the American Labor Movement," in Lowell Turner, Harry C. Katz, and Richard W. Hurd (eds.), *Rekindling the Movement: Labor's Quest for Relevance in the Twenty-First Century* (Ithaca, NY: ILR Press, 2001), pp. 9–26; Paul Johnston, "Organize for What? The Resurgence of Labor as a Citizen Movement," in Turner, Katz, and Hurd, *Rekindling the Movement: Labor's Quest for Relevance in the Twenty-First Century,* pp. 27–58.
18. Bill Fletcher, Jr., and Fernando Gapasin, *Solidarity Divided: The Crisis in Organized Labor and a New Path toward Social Justice* (Berkeley: University of California Press, 2008), p. 174; Rick Fantasia and Kim Voss, *Hard Work: Remaking the American Labor Movement* (Berkeley: University of California Press, 2004); McAlevey, *Raising Expectations (and Raising Hell).*
19. Paul F. Clark, *Building More Effective Unions*, 2nd ed. (Ithaca, NY: Cornell University Press, 2009).

20. David Weil, *Turning the Tide: Strategic Planning for Labor Unions* (Lexington, MA: Lexington Books, 1994); Paul F. Clark and Lois S. Gray, "Changing Administrative Practices in American Unions: A Research Note," *Industrial Relations* 44 (October 2005), pp. 654–58; Barbara L. Rau, "The Diffusion of HR Practices in Unions," *Human Resource Management Review* 22 (March 2012), pp. 27–42.
21. Fiorito and Jarley, "Trade Union Morphology"; Gary Chaison, *Union Mergers in Hard Times: The View From Five Countries* (Ithaca, NY: ILR Press, 1996).
22. Kim Moody, *An Injury to All: The Decline of American Unionism* (London: Verso, 1988), p. 205.
23. Russell, *Out of the Jungle*.
24. Kye D. Pawlenko, "Reevaluating Inter-Union Competition: A Proposal to Resurrect Rival Unionism," *University of Pennsylvania Journal of Labor and Employment Law* 8 (Spring 2006), pp. 651–706.
25. Fletcher and Gapasin, *Solidarity Divided*; Gary Chaison, "The AFL–CIO Split: Does It Really Matter?" *Journal of Labor Research* 28 (May 2007), pp. 301–11; Rachel Aleks, "Estimating the Effect of 'Change to Win' on Union Organizing," *Industrial and Labor Relations Review* 68 (May 2015), pp. 584–605.
26. George Strauss, "Union Democracy," in George Strauss, Daniel G. Gallagher, and Jack Fiorito (eds.), *The State of the Unions* (Madison, WI: Industrial Relations Research Association, 1991), pp. 201–36; Robert Bruno, *Reforming the Chicago Teamsters: The Story of Local 705* (DeKalb: Northern Illinois Press, 2003).
27. Fiorito and Jarley, "Trade Union Morphology"; Strauss, "Union Democracy."
28. Richard B. Freeman and Joel Rogers, *What Workers Want* (Ithaca, NY: ILR Press, 1999); Daniel G. Gallagher and George Strauss, "Union Membership Attitudes and Participation," in George Strauss, Daniel G. Gallagher, and Jack Fiorito (eds.), *The State of the Unions* (Madison, WI: Industrial Relations Research Association, 1991), pp. 139–74; Robert Bruno, "Consenting to Be Governed: Union Transformation and Teamster Democracy," in David Lewin and Bruce Kaufman (eds.), *Advances in Industrial and Labor Relations*, Volume 11 (Amsterdam: Elsevier Science, 2002), pp. 95–122.
29. Ray M. Tillman and Michael S. Cummings (eds.), *The Transformation of U.S. Unions: Voices, Visions, and Strategies from the Grassroots* (Boulder, CO: Lynne Rienner Publishers, 1999); Nelson Lichtenstein, *State of the Union: A Century of American Labor* (Princeton, NJ: Princeton University Press, 2013); Fantasia and Voss, *Hard Work;* McAlevey, *Raising Expectations (and Raising Hell)*.
30. Ann C. Frost, "Union Involvement in Workplace Decision Making: Implications for Union Democracy," *Journal of Labor Research* 21 (Spring 2000), pp. 265–86.
31. James B. Jacobs, *Mobsters, Unions, and Feds: The Mafia and the American Labor Movement* (New York: New York University Press, 2006); Bruno, *Reforming the Chicago Teamsters*.
32. John Child, Ray Loveridge, and Malcolm Warner, "Towards an Organizational Study of Trade Unions," *Sociology* 7 (January 1973), pp. 71–91; Fiorito and Jarley, "Trade Union Morphology."
33. Dionne Pohler and Andrew Luchak, "Are Unions Good or Bad for Organizations? The Moderating Role of Management's Response," *British Journal of Industrial Relations* 53 (September 2015), pp. 423–459; Joel Cutcher-Gershenfeld, Dan Brooks, and Martin Mulloy, *Inside the Ford-UAW Transformation: Pivotal Events in Valuing Work and Delivering Results* (Cambridge: MIT Press, 2015).
34. Sanford M. Jacoby, *Modern Manors: Welfare Capitalism since the New Deal* (Princeton, NJ: Princeton University Press, 1997); Freeman and Rogers, *What Workers Want;* Kochan, Katz, and McKersie, *The Transformation of American Industrial Relations*.
35. Michael E. Porter, *Competitive Strategy* (New York: Free Press, 1980).
36. Douglas McGregor, *The Human Side of Enterprise* (New York: McGraw-Hill, 1960).
37. McGregor, *The Human Side of Enterprise*.
38. Eileen Appelbaum and Rosemary Batt, *The New American Workplace: Transforming Work Systems in the United States* (Ithaca, NY: ILR Press, 1994).
39. William G. Ouchi, *Theory Z: How American Business Can Meet the Japanese Challenge* (Reading, MA: Addison-Wesley, 1981).
40. Thomas A. Kochan and Harry C. Katz, *Collective Bargaining and Industrial Relations: From Theory to Policy and Practice*, 2nd ed. (Homewood, IL: Irwin, 1988).
41. John Schmitt and Ben Zipperer, *Dropping the Ax: Illegal Firings during Union Election Campaigns, 1951–2007* (Washington, DC: Center for Economic and Policy Research, 2009); Kate Bronfenbrenner and Tom Juravich, "It Takes More Than House Calls: Organizing to Win with a Comprehensive Union Building Strategy," in Kate Bronfenbrenner et al. (eds.), *Organizing to Win: New Research on Union Strategies* (Ithaca, NY: ILR Press, 1998), pp. 19–36; John Logan, "The Union Avoidance Industry in the United States," *British Journal of Industrial Relations* 44 (December 2006), pp. 651–75.

42. Kochan, Katz, and McKersie, *The Transformation of American Industrial Relations.*
43. Kochan and Katz, *Collective Bargaining and Industrial Relations*.
44. Jacoby, *Modern Manors*; Karen Legge, *Human Resource Management: Rhetorics and Realities* (Basingstoke, UK: Macmillan Press, 1995); Jennifer Klein, *For All These Rights: Business, Labor, and the Shaping of America's Public–Private Welfare State* (Princeton, NJ: Princeton University Press, 2003).
45. Klein, *For All These Rights*.
46. Barry Bluestone and Irving Bluestone, *Negotiating the Future: A Labor Perspective on American Business* (New York: Basic Books, 1992); Adrienne E. Eaton and Paula B. Voos, "Productivity-Enhancing Innovations in Work Organization, Compensation, and Employee Participation in the Union versus the Nonunion Sectors," in David Lewin and Donna Sockell (eds.), *Advances in Industrial and Labor Relations*, Volume 6 (Greenwich, CT: JAI Press, 1994), pp. 63–109.
47. Stephen Meyer, *The Five Dollar Day: Labor Management and Social Control in the Ford Motor Company, 1908–1921* (Albany: State University of New York Press, 1981).
48. Meyer, *The Five Dollar Day*; Nelson Lichtenstein, *The Most Dangerous Man in Detroit: Walter Reuther and the Fate of American Labor* (New York: Basic Books, 1995); Stephen H. Norwood, *Strikebreaking and Intimidation: Mercenaries and Masculinity in Twentieth-Century America* (Chapel Hill: University of North Carolina Press, 2002).
49. Bluestone and Bluestone, *Negotiating the Future;* Cutcher-Gershenfeld, Brooks, and Mulloy, *Inside the Ford-UAW Transformation.*
50. Kochan, Katz, and McKersie, *The Transformation of American Industrial Relations.*
51. Saul A. Rubinstein and Thomas A. Kochan, *Learning from Saturn: Possibilities for Corporate Governance and Employee Relations* (Ithaca, NY: ILR Press, 2001).
52. Nelson Lichtenstein (ed.), *Wal-Mart: The Face of Twenty-First Century Capitalism* (New York: The New Press, 2006).
53. Ellen Israel Rosen, "How to Squeeze More out of a Penny," in Nelson Lichtenstein (ed.), *Wal-Mart: The Face of Twenty-First Century Capitalism* (New York: The New Press, 2006), pp. 243–59.
54. James Hoopes, "Growth through Knowledge: Wal-Mart, High Technology, and the Ever Less Visible Hand of the Manager," in Nelson Lichtenstein (ed.), *Wal-Mart: The Face of Twenty-First Century Capitalism* (New York: The New Press, 2006), pp. 83–104; Charles Fishman, *The Wal-Mart Effect: How the World's Most Powerful Company Really Works—and How It's Transforming the American Economy* (New York: Penguin Press, 2006).
55. Rosen, "How to Squeeze More out of a Penny"; Barbara Ehrenreich, *Nickel and Dimed: On (Not) Getting By in America* (New York: Henry Holt, 2001).
56. Steven Greenhouse, "At a Small Shop in Colorado, Wal-Mart Beats a Union Once More," *The New York Times*, February 26, 2005.
57. Michael H. Belzer, *Sweatshops on Wheels: Winners and Losers in Trucking Deregulation* (New York: Oxford University Press, 2000); Howard R. Stanger, "Hard Times and Hard Bargaining in the Newspaper Industry" in Howard R. Stanger, Ann C. Frost, and Paul F. Clark (eds.), *Collective Bargaining Under Duress: Case Studies of Major North American Industries* (Champaign, IL: Labor and Employment Relations Association, 2013), pp. 201–53.
58. Harry Braverman, *Labor and Monopoly Capital: The Degradation of Work in the Twentieth Century* (New York: Monthly Review Press, 1974); David Montgomery, *Workers' Control in America: Studies in the History of Work, Technology, and Labor Struggles* (Cambridge, England: Cambridge University Press, 1979).
59. Alfred Marshall, *Principles of Economics,* 8th ed. (New York: Macmillan, 1920).
60. William Brown, "The Influence of Product Markets on Industrial Relations," in Paul Blyton et al. (eds.), *Sage Handbook of Industrial Relations* (London: Sage, 2008), pp. 113–28.
61. Howard R. Stanger, Paul F. Clark, and Ann C. Frost (eds.), *Collective Bargaining under Duress: Case Studies of Major North American Industries* (Champaign, IL: Labor and Employment Relations Association, 2013).
62. Mark S. Anner, *Solidarity Transformed: Labor Responses to Globalization and Crisis in Latin America* (Ithaca, NY: Cornell University Press, 2011).
63. Natascha van der Zwan, "Making Sense of Financialization," *Socio-Economic Review* 12 (January 2014), pp. 99–129; Gerald F. Davis, *Managed by the Markets: How Finance Reshaped America* (New York: Oxford University Press, 2009).

64. William Lazonick, *Sustainable Prosperity in the New Economy? Business Organization and High-Tech Employment in the United States* (Kalamazoo, MI: Upjohn Institute, 2009); Eileen Appelbaum and Rosemary Batt, *Private Equity at Work: When Wall Street Manages Main Street* (New York: Russell Sage Foundation, 2014); Christian E. Weller (ed.), *Inequality, Uncertainty, and Opportunity: The Varied and Growing Role of Finance in Labor Relations* (Champaign, IL: Labor and Employment Relations Association, 2015).
65. Paula B. Voos (ed.), *Contemporary Collective Bargaining in the Private Sector* (Madison, WI: Industrial Relations Research Association, 1994); Stanger, Clark, and Frost, *Collective Bargaining under Duress.*
66. David Rolf, *The Fight for Fifteen: The Right Wage for a Working America* (New York: The New Press, 2016).
67. Daphne Gottlieb Taras, "Collective Bargaining Regulation in Canada and the United States: Divergent Cultures, Divergent Outcomes," in Bruce E. Kaufman (ed.), *Government Regulation of the Employment Relationship* (Madison, WI: Industrial Relations Research Association, 1997), pp. 295–341.
68. Steve Babson, *The Unfinished Struggle: Turning Points in American Labor, 1877–Present* (Lanham, MD: Rowman and Littlefield, 1999); Lichtenstein, *State of the Union.*
69. Brian Towers, *The Representation Gap: Change and Reform in the British and American Workplace* (Oxford: Oxford University Press, 1997).
70. John W. Budd and Paul K. Heinz, "Union Representation Elections and Labor Law Reform: Lessons from the Minneapolis Hilton," *Labor Studies Journal* 20 (Winter 1996), pp. 3–20.
71. C. Jeffrey Waddoups and Vincent H. Eade, "Hotels and Casinos: Collective Bargaining during a Decade of Expansion," in Paul F. Clark, John T. Delaney, and Ann C. Frost (eds.), *Collective Bargaining in the Private Sector* (Champaign, IL: Industrial Relations Research Association, 2002), pp. 137–77.
72. Casey Ichniowski and Jeffrey S. Zax, "Today's Associations, Tomorrow's Unions," *Industrial and Labor Relations Review* 43 (January 1990), pp. 191–208.
73. Robert C. Solomon, *Ethics and Excellence: Cooperation and Integrity in Business* (New York: Oxford University Press, 1992); John W. Budd and James G. Scoville, "Moral Philosophy, Business Ethics, and the Employment Relationship," in John W. Budd and James G. Scoville (eds.), *The Ethics of Human Resources and Industrial Relations* (Champaign, IL: Labor and Employment Relations Association, 2005), pp. 1–21.
74. Manuel G. Velasquez, *Business Ethics: Concepts and Cases,* 7th ed. (Upper Saddle River, NJ: Pearson, 2012).
75. Budd and Scoville, "Moral Philosophy, Business Ethics, and the Employment Relationship"; John T. Delaney, "Ethical Challenges in Labor Relations," in John W. Budd and James G. Scoville (eds.), *The Ethics of Human Resources and Industrial Relations* (Champaign, IL: Labor and Employment Relations Association, 2005), pp. 203–28.
76. Sanford M. Jacoby, "American Exceptionalism Revisited: The Importance of Management," in Sanford M. Jacoby (ed.), *Masters to Managers: Historical and Comparative Perspectives on American Employers* (New York: Columbia University Press, 1991), pp. 173–200.
77. Solomon, *Ethics and Excellence,* pp. 4–5.
78. Paul Schumann, "A Moral Principles Framework for Human Resource Management Ethics," *Human Resource Management Review* 11 (Spring/Summer 2001), pp. 93–111; Richard S. Rosenberg, "The Technological Assault on Ethics in the Modern Workplace," in John W. Budd and James G. Scoville (eds.), *The Ethics of Human Resources and Industrial Relations* (Champaign, IL: Labor and Employment Relations Association, 2005), pp. 141–71.
79. Velasquez, *Business Ethics*; Tom L. Beauchamp and Norman E. Bowie (eds.), *Ethical Theory and Business,* 8th ed. (Upper Saddle River, NJ: Prentice Hall, 2009); Daniel M. Hausman and Michael S. McPherson, *Economic Analysis and Moral Philosophy* (Cambridge, England: Cambridge University Press, 1996).
80. Hausman and McPherson, *Economic Analysis and Moral Philosophy.*
81. Velasquez, *Business Ethics.*
82. Beauchamp and Bowie, *Ethical Theory and Business,* p. 22.
83. Leo Troy, *Beyond Unions and Collective Bargaining* (Armonk, NY: M.E. Sharpe, 1999), p. 54.
84. Peter D. McClelland, *The American Search for Justice* (Cambridge, MA: Basil Blackwell, 1990), pp. 19 and 59 (emphasis in original).
85. James Rachels and Stuart Rachels, *The Elements of Moral Philosophy,* 8th ed. (Boston: McGraw-Hill, 2015).

86. Beauchamp and Bowie, *Ethical Theory and Business;* Norman E. Bowie, *Business Ethics: A Kantian Perspective* (Malden, MA: Blackwell, 1999); Hausman and McPherson, *Economic Analysis and Moral Philosophy;* Solomon, *Ethics and Excellence;* Velasquez, *Business Ethics.*

87. Robert Nozick, *Anarchy, State, and Utopia* (New York: Basic Books, 1974).

88. Jack Donnelly, *Universal Human Rights in Theory and Practice*, 2nd ed. (Ithaca, NY: Cornell University Press, 2003); Alan Gerwith, *The Community of Rights* (Chicago: University of Chicago Press, 1996).

89. Immanuel Kant, *Groundwork of the Metaphysics of Morals* (1785), pp. 17/402, 66–67/429, 80/436.

90. Bowie, *Business Ethics;* Roger J. Sullivan, *Immanuel Kant's Moral Theory* (Cambridge, England: Cambridge University Press, 1989).

91. Norman E. Bowie and Ronald F. Duska, *Business Ethics,* 2nd ed. (Englewood Cliffs, NJ: Prentice Hall, 1990).

92. Bowie, *Business Ethics.*

93. Solomon, *Ethics and Excellence.*

94. John Rawls, *A Theory of Justice* (Cambridge, MA: Harvard University Press, 1971), pp. 83 and 250.

95. Solomon, *Ethics and Excellence.*

96. Solomon, *Ethics and Excellence,* p. 47.

97. Schumann, "A Moral Principles Framework for Human Resource Management Ethics."

98. Nel Noddings, *Caring: A Feminine Approach to Ethics and Moral Education,* 2nd ed. (Berkeley: University of California Press, 2003); Velasquez, *Business Ethics.*

99. Carol Gilligan, *In a Different Voice: Psychological Theory and Women's Development* (Cambridge, MA: Harvard University Press, 1982), p. 79.

100. Beauchamp and Bowie, *Ethical Theory and Business.*

101. Velasquez, *Business Ethics.*

102. Schumann, "A Moral Principles Framework for Human Resource Management Ethics."

Chapter Six

Union Organizing

Advance Organizer

In the U.S. labor relations system, if a group of employees wants their employer to bargain with them collectively rather than individually, they typically need to form a union and formally demonstrate that a majority of the employees support this union. This chapter discusses the behavioral, strategic, and legal aspects of this union organizing process.

Learning Objectives

By the end of this chapter, you should be able to

1. **Discuss** the basic procedural steps and legal standards for how new unions are formed in the United States. This is called the organizing process.
2. **Explain** why individuals vote for or against a union in a representation election.
3. **Understand** the tactics used by employers to weaken individual support for unions and why these tactics are controversial.
4. **Understand** the traditional tactics used by unions to strengthen individual support for unions and the pressures for developing new strategies.
5. **Compare** the pros and cons of the existing certification election process and options for reform.

Contents

The previous chapter described the organizational structure of U.S. unions—which are typically large, bureaucratic organizations with many members and locations (like many corporations). In contrast, to start this chapter, let's return to the fundamental conception of a labor union described in Chapter 1: A group of workers who join together to influence the nature of their employment. Suppose some employees want to get a vacation policy changed. The individuals can "self-organize" by meeting with each other and then collectively approach management to ask that the policy be changed. As long as these activities do not interfere with their work, we saw in Chapter 5 that U.S. labor law protects the members of this group from reprisals so they cannot be fired, demoted, or disciplined. But they can be ignored; management has no legal obligation to deal with this group. To force the employer to bargain with them, the employees must *organize* themselves into a union. So if the group's request to change the vacation policy is ignored, the individuals have four options: (1) They can look for work elsewhere, (2) they can endure the existing vacation policy, (3) they can be disruptive and possibly cause the employer to reconsider (while running the risk of being disciplined for their disruptive activities), or (4) they can try to form a labor union. If they successfully form a legally recognized union, the employer will have a legal obligation to bargain with them.

You can probably think of numerous ways in which a union can be formed. A few employees could initiate a strike and then round up support (as in the 1930s sit-down strikes); union supporters could get workers to sign cards or a petition and present the results to management along with a threat to strike if management ignores their request; or the employees could have a secret ballot election in which the union and employer must abide by the decision of the majority. Since the passage of the National Labor Relations Act (NLRA) in 1935, U.S. public policy has favored the last option. Most U.S. unions are organized (formed) through secret ballot elections administered by the National Labor Relations Board (NLRB). The first major U.S. labor relations process—the organizing process—is therefore principally shaped by the NLRA and the procedural and legal aspects of NLRB elections. These **representation elections** answer questions of whom the employees want to represent them. The most significant type of representation election is a certification election—an election to determine whether a union will be certified as the bargaining agent of the employees. Both the U.S. union organizing process and this chapter are largely about certification elections—how employees can get an election held, what determines how individuals vote, what constitutes acceptable or objectionable election conduct by both labor and management, how union and employer strategies affect employee voting behavior, and why the election process is heavily criticized by labor unions.

THE ORGANIZING TIME LINE

A union organizing drive—that is, a campaign to organize nonunion workers into a union that is recognized by the employer as representing the employees—typically follows a common sequence of steps (see Figure 6.1).

Initiating an Organizing Drive

The first step is initiation. In theory, there are three possible initiators of an organizing drive: one or more employees, a union, or an employer. The last possibility might seem odd, but as an example, in the 1960s and 1970s some agricultural companies signed contracts with the Teamsters rather than risk having their employees choose the more militant United Farm Workers. Note that this interferes with employee free choice, and therefore employer-initiated organizing drives are illegal [Section 8(a)(1) unfair labor practices under the NLRA]. Thus our concern is with employee- or union-initiated campaigns.

An employee-initiated organizing drive is perhaps the classic scenario. Low pay, excessive overtime, harsh supervision, lack of respect and voice, or numerous other factors cause dissatisfied employees to talk with each other about forming a union to increase their collective strength. These employees might try to form a union on their own or, more frequently, contact a union organizer who works for an existing union in their area, industry, or occupation. In either case this is an employee-initiated campaign.

Alternatively, unions may initiate organizing campaigns by advertising, distributing information, and trying to contact employees to show the benefits of unionization. There are two types of union-initiated campaigns: strategic and opportunistic. Strategic campaigns are those in which organizing a particular workplace will enhance a union's ability to effectively represent existing employees. For example, the United Auto Workers (UAW) frequently tries to organize the nonunion U.S. manufacturing plants of the Japanese auto companies such as Honda to maintain its bargaining power in that industry. On the other hand, opportunistic campaigns attempt to increase a union's membership by organizing dissatisfied workers who are "ripe" for unionization but who do not have a strategic fit with the existing membership, such as when the United Steelworkers of America tries to organize nursing home workers.

FIGURE 6.1
The Union Organizing Process

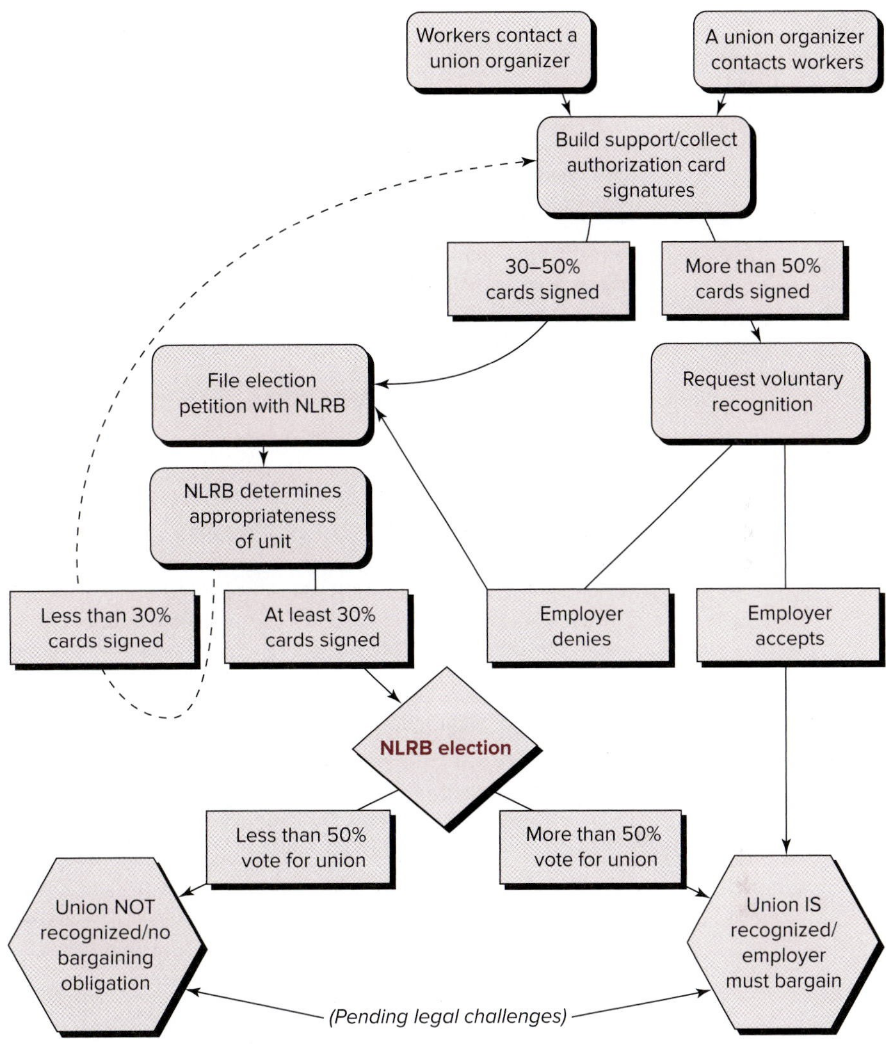

Building and Documenting Support

In any case, once an organizing drive has been initiated, the next step in the union organizing time line is building support (see Figure 6.1). This generally involves meeting interested employees outside the workplace and distributing information. Organizing also involves raising expectations—what someone should expect from their job, their employer, a potential union, and ultimately, themselves and their co-workers.[1] If an organizing drive is to continue, sooner or later employees must concretely express support for having a union represent them. The most important method in U.S. labor relations for showing this support is to sign an **authorization card.** An authorization card is a preprinted form containing something like "I authorize [union name] to represent me for the purposes of collective bargaining" which employees fill out and sign (see Figure 6.2). Collecting signed authorization cards is a crucial part of the union organizing process because the cards demonstrate the interest in unionization to three important parties: union organizers, the employer, and if necessary, the NLRB. Some union organizers will not continue to devote their time and resources to a campaign if they cannot collect a certain number of signatures in a certain time period.

FIGURE 6.2
A Union Flyer with Authorization Card for University of California (UC) Professional Employees

Source: University Professional & Technical Employees, CWA 9119.

UC staff professionals are central to the University's research, medical, and educational missions, but often our work is not given the recognition it deserves. We need an effective organization to give us a voice in determining our future at the University. The ability to negotiate a union contract will guarantee that our voices will be heard.

We need to have a say in how our compensation system works. Increasing workloads, uncertain job security, and rising health care costs can no longer remain unchallenged. Thousands of other UC employees have already won the right to collectively negotiate with the University over the issues important to them. Now it's our turn to get the recognition we deserve.

UP
TE

UNIVERSITY PROFESSIONAL & TECHNICAL EMPLOYEES, CWA 9119

Take a step for *real* change by filling out the card below. It will be given to the California Public Employment Relations Board with a petition for a secret ballot election to give UC staff professionals an opportunity to vote for UPTE-CWA representation.

Professionals eligible to sign a card: Administrative Analysts, Student Affairs Officers, Programmer Analysts, Administrative Specialists, Accountants, Program Reps, Analysts, Computer Network Technicians, Statisticians, Library Asst. V., Senior & Principal Writers & Editors, Learning Skills Counselors, and other job titles.

Questions? Please call (510) 704-UPTE.

UPTE is the union for UC professional and technical employees at the campuses, medical centers, and national labs. UPTE is a democratic, member-run union. Since 1990 UPTE-CWA has won union elections benefiting more than 11,000 UC technical, research, and health care professionals. With UPTE-CWA as their representative these employees have made many gains on the job including better wages, more layoff protections, and enhanced career development.

Now it's our turn to have a voice at the bargaining table. Imagine the power of thousands of UC staff professionals joining together to work for solutions that benefit all employees.

PLEASE MAIL THIS CARD TO UPTE, PO Box 4443, BERKELEY, CA 94704. DO NOT FAX.

Campus ________

Authorization Card

Yes! I want UPTE-CWA Local 9119 to be my union for the purpose of negotiating wages, hours, and working conditions with the University of California.

Please print legibly

Name ______________________________ Home Phone ( ) __________
LAST FIRST MIDDLE INITIAL

Home Address ______________________________

City/State/Zip ______________________________

Job Title/Classification ______________ Department ______________

Work Mailing Address ______________ Work Phone ( ) __________

Actual Work Location ______________ E-mail ______________
BUILDING and ROOM

Date ______________ Signature ______________

More importantly, authorization cards show the employer that employees want union representation. Recognizing a union that lacks majority support violates the NLRA.[2] But if a union gathers signed cards from more than 50 percent of the employees, it can ask the employer to recognize the union as the bargaining agent of the employees. If the employer is agreeable, a neutral party can examine the cards and determine if truly more than 50 percent of the employees signed cards. If so, the employer can recognize the union and is then obligated to bargain with the union. This is called voluntary recognition, and when this occurs, the union organizing process is over (see the right-hand side of Figure 6.1). Recognition based on authorization cards is called **card check recognition** or a majority sign-up procedure.

Unions are aggressively pushing for card check recognition procedures, both through legislative action (such as the Employee Free Choice Act discussed at the end of this chapter) that would require employers to accept card check recognition and through agreements with specific companies to voluntarily accept card check recognition. But unless the Employee Free Choice Act or similar legislation is enacted, card check recognition will probably continue to be the exception rather than the norm because employers typically refuse to recognize unions voluntarily.

Alternatives to Voluntary Recognition

What happens after an employer declines a request for voluntary recognition? First consider the pre-NLRA era before 1935. In this era employees had only one option: Step up the pressure on the company to force it to change its stance. As a result employees would launch a **recognition strike**—a strike to try to compel the employer to recognize their union. Recall from Chapter 3 that the Ludlow Massacre, the 1934 general strikes in San Francisco and Minneapolis, the General Motors sit-down strike, the Memorial Day Massacre, and the Memphis sanitation strike were all recognition strikes. And recall further how costly these strikes were—in loss of human life, human suffering, lost profits, and economic disruption. A major goal of the NLRA is to replace these costly recognition strikes with an orderly alternative. What is the natural, orderly mechanism in a democratic society for determining the wishes of the majority? An election.

The 1935 passage of the NLRA therefore created a certification procedure in which employees can petition the NLRB for an election to determine if a union has the support of a majority of the employees. Although there are restrictions on recognitional picketing, the NLRA does not ban recognition strikes per se but rather tries to make them obsolete by giving employees a safer alternative that does not involve lost wages and the risk of being replaced by new employees during a strike. Most recognition questions today are settled through NLRB representation elections rather than through strikes.

Contemporary examples reinforce the NLRA's logic. For example, graduate student teaching assistants at Yale University have been trying to form a union since the early 1990s. A major complicating factor, however, has been whether in the eyes of the law these individuals are employees or students. Except for 2000–2004 and again starting in August 2016, the NLRB has ruled that graduate assistants at private universities are students, not employees, and are therefore not covered under the NLRA.[3] Absent access to the NLRB certification election process, the only way for the graduate assistants to force Yale to recognize their union is through economic pressure tactics. In fact, at the end of the 1995 fall semester, the Graduate Employees and Students Organization (GESO) led a grade strike—the graduate assistants refused to hand in grades for the classes they were teaching—to try to force the university to recognize the GESO as their union. The strike failed, and the conflict between the graduate assistants and the university continues to fester. Yale graduate assistants struck again for a week in 2005 to try to win recognition for their union. This time they were joined by Columbia University teaching assistants also striking for recognition. Whether in the form of sit-down strikes, grade strikes, or traditional strikes, U.S. labor law tries to prevent this type of disruptive activity by allowing secret ballot elections to decide questions of representation among workers covered by the NLRA.

NLRB REPRESENTATION ELECTIONS

Types of Elections

The several types of NLRB representation elections correspond to different questions of representation, but all have the same goal: To determine the wishes of the majority of employees. The most frequent type is the **certification election,** which is used in a nonunion location to ascertain if a majority of employees want to become unionized—that is, to designate a specific union as their bargaining agent. If so, the NLRB uses the election results to *certify* this union as the bargaining agent. Most certification elections have just one union on the ballot (so the choice is between a specific union and no union), but some have multiple unions vying for representation rights. In these cases runoff elections between the top vote getters might be needed to determine the wishes of the majority.

The opposite of a certification election is a **decertification election.** This type of election is used to determine whether a majority of unionized employees no longer wish to be represented by their union. If so, this union is decertified and loses the right to represent and bargain for these employees. A small number of decertification elections decertify the existing union and certify a new union; this is a raid election in which employees can choose between their existing union, a challenging (raiding) union, and no union. Most decertification elections result in a workplace going from union to nonunion. The NLRB conducts over 1,700 representation elections each year; approximately 85 percent are certification elections (see Table 6.1).[4] Unions win roughly two-thirds of certification elections and lose about 60 percent of decertification elections. This chapter largely focuses on certification elections. Most of the issues discussed are similar for decertification elections.

TABLE 6.1
Some Notable NLRB Representation Elections

First	December 1935: Fort Wayne (Indiana) knitting mill employees.
Longest	112 days: maritime seamen on 20 ships (1965).
Most remote	Island of Tinian (Northern Marianas): Micronesian Telecommunications Co. employees (1984).
Most complex	Bituminous coal industry: 2,200 staffers providing ballots to 311,000 eligible workers at 2,000 mines in 31 states in 22 hours (1945).
Largest	Steel industry: 686,000 workers (1945).
Largest in a single plant	Ford's River Rouge Plant (Dearborn, Michigan): 78,000 eligible workers (1941).
Smallest	Two employees: Various instances, including one election for two grave diggers.
Most recent	Today (unless you are reading this on a weekend).

Source: National Labor Relations Board, *NLRB: The First 50 Years* (Washington, DC: 1985).

Getting the NLRB to Conduct an Election

To request that the NLRB conduct a certification election, a group of employees or a union must file a petition form with the NLRB (you can see a blank 502 (RC) form at *www.nlrb.gov/resources/forms*). This petition must be supported by a demonstration of sufficient interest among the employees for such an election. "Sufficient interest" is defined by the NLRB as 30 percent. This is perhaps the most important use of signed authorization cards—the typical way to demonstrate sufficient interest is to provide signed authorization cards from at least 30 percent of the employees. Many unions wait until they have cards from more than 50 percent, but 30 percent is the legal minimum. Authorization cards are presumed valid for one year. Thirty percent is also the threshold for demonstrating that there is sufficient interest for holding a decertification election, though this would be demonstrated through signatures on an employee petition or other means, not by authorization cards.

In addition to verifying sufficient interest, the NLRB must deal with several other details before scheduling a representation election. First, unless there are unusual circumstances, the NLRB will not allow more than one election in a 12-month period. Second, elections will not be authorized within 12 months of any union certification.[5] Third, a decertification election cannot be held when there is a valid collective bargaining agreement in place (up to a limit of three years); this is called the contract bar doctrine.

Finally, the NLRB must handle the most contentious aspect of the petition—defining the occupations and geographical locations included in a certification election. A union will be certified as the exclusive bargaining representative for employees when a majority of them support the union, but to what set of employees does this refer? For example, in a grocery store, does this mean just full-time cashiers, all cashiers, all hourly employees, all employees including managers, or some other group? For a grocery chain with multiple stores in a single city, is the unit limited to a single store or does it include multiple locations?

Determining the Appropriate Bargaining Unit

When a petition for a certification election is filed with the NLRB, a definition of the relevant jobs and locations is proposed by the party filing the petition, such as this:

> All full-time and regular part-time licensed dealers employed by the Employer at its Connecticut Casino, including poker dealers, table game dealers, and dual rate dealers; but excluding all other employees, office clerical employees, and guards, professional employees and supervisors as defined in the Act.[6]

If the employer objects to this definition, the NLRB must make a determination. Section 9(b) of the NLRA states that the NLRB "shall decide in each case whether, in order to assure to employees the fullest freedom in exercising the rights guaranteed by this Act, the unit appropriate for the purposes of collective bargaining shall be the employer unit, craft unit, plant unit, or subdivision thereof." (National Labor Relations Board, H.R. 3094. 112th: Workforce Democracy and Fairness Act.) Thus the group of occupations and locations relevant to the certification election is referred to as the **appropriate bargaining unit;** employees in these occupations can vote in the election and will be represented by the union if the union wins the election.

But how should the appropriate unit be determined? Security guards cannot be in the same unit with other employees. Individuals who are not defined as employees by the NLRA, such as supervisors and managers, are excluded from NLRB-defined bargaining units. In some cases this can be a critical issue and can even end an organizing drive if enough employees are excluded. College professors can be seen as managerial because of their control over curricula, courses, and admissions; registered nurses can be seen as supervisors because they direct the work of less skilled health care workers (more about this soon); and graduate students are often ruled to be students rather than employees.[7]

Once the supervisory, managerial, and other exclusions are resolved, the NLRB's determination of the appropriate bargaining unit is generally based on grouping together the jobs that share a community of interest. In manufacturing it is common to include all production and maintenance employees in a single facility; this is called an industrial unit because it follows the industrial unionism model. Drivers, clerical employees, and workers at other locations of the same employer may or may not be included based on specific circumstances, such as whether there are common human resource policies or significant similarities and interactions between employee groups.[8] In contrast, under the Railway Labor Act, bargaining units are narrow in occupation but broad in geography and include all an employer's locations.[9] But under the NLRA there is great diversity: Some units span many occupations and diverse locations, whereas under other circumstances the NLRB might rule that a single occupation in one location is appropriate (a craft rather than industrial unit). In some cases a bargaining unit consists of only two employees. The NLRB's determination of the appropriate bargaining unit can be contentious because the union and the employer each want the unit defined to maximize their own chance of winning the election. In fact, unions fare significantly better in smaller rather than larger elections, and in elections with more homogeneous rather than heterogeneous skill and racial groups.[10]

Ultimately determining the appropriate bargaining unit, including who is a supervisor or a managerial employee and which employees share a community of interest, must be done case by case because the details can vary from one workplace to another. The hearing for one case involving college professors took 19 days and resulted in a 112-page decision.[11] The resulting delays in some of these cases can weaken or end an organizing drive. In fact, once the appropriate bargaining unit is determined, the petition for a certification election might no longer be supported by signed authorization cards from at least 30 percent of the relevant employees. For example, in the Harvard University case discussed in the accompanying "Labor Relations Application," when the NLRB expanded the bargaining unit in 1984 to include all Harvard University clerical and technical workers, not just those in the medical area, the size of the bargaining unit tripled from 1,200 to 3,600 employees. The union had been collecting cards only in the medical area, so with this expansion it no longer had 30 percent. In such a situation the union must return to the start of the time line in Figure 6.1—building support and collecting signed authorization cards. In the Harvard University case the union spent nearly four additional years collecting enough cards to demonstrate sufficient interest for a certification election based on the new unit.[12] But not all unions are successful in this endeavor; and because of changed unit definitions, antiunion campaigns, delays litigating unfair labor practice allegations, and other events that erode support for unionization, fewer than 70 percent of all petition filings result in elections.[13]

The Supervisor Controversy

The exclusion of supervisors from NLRB-determined bargaining units and from the protections of the NLRA against reprisal for union activity has become particularly important as the skill requirements for many jobs have increased: If everyone who occasionally directs another worker to do something is deemed to be a supervisor, countless workers will find themselves outside the NLRA protections. Unions also fear that companies are intentionally giving employees just enough responsibility to make them legally seen as supervisors with the express intent of removing them from the NLRA protections and thus making it harder for employees to unionize.

Each time this issue is brought before the NLRB, it must determine who is and is not a supervisor by applying the statutory definition contained in the NLRA:

> 2(11) The term "supervisor" means any individual having authority, in the interest of the employer, to hire, transfer, suspend, lay off, recall, promote, discharge, assign, reward, or discipline other employees, or responsibly to direct them, or to adjust their grievances, or effectively to recommend such action, if in connection with the foregoing the exercise of such authority is not of a merely routine or clerical nature, but requires the use of independent judgment.

Labor Relations Application The Appropriate Bargaining Unit for Harvard University Clerical and Technical Workers

Harvard University's medical area consists of its medical, dental, and public health schools and is located about three miles from the main Harvard campus. The medical area employs approximately 1,200 clerical and technical workers. These employees are similar to the 2,400 clerical and technical workers throughout the rest of the university in typing manuscripts, handling correspondence, and performing technical duties, though in the medical area the work is more medically oriented and perhaps includes more health hazards. There are relatively more technical workers than clerical workers in the medical area compared to the rest of Harvard. Of the Harvard clerical and technical employees in the medical area that transfer between jobs, approximately 80 percent stay within the medical area. Human resource policies are established centrally for all of Harvard; the medical area is the only campus unit to have its own human resources office. This office is responsible for hiring new employees but must comply with the centrally established job classification and wage system.

In the early 1970s a handful of women employed in Harvard University's medical area started a group to bring attention to discriminatory treatment against female workers. Out of frustration with Harvard's unresponsiveness, this movement grew into a campaign to unionize, and in 1975 a petition was filed with the NLRB to conduct an election for clerical and technical employees in the medical area.

QUESTIONS

1. As the human resources director for Harvard University, do you object to the definition of the bargaining unit? In other words, would you rather have an election for all clerical and technical workers at Harvard, not just those in the medical area? What are the risks and benefits?
2. As the NLRB, how would you decide on the appropriate bargaining unit if Harvard objected?

References: *Harvard College*, 229 NLRB No. 97 (1977); *Harvard College*, 269 NLRB No. 151 (1984).

The key legal difficulties are how to interpret these functions (e.g., what do "assign," "responsibly direct," and "independent judgment" mean?) and how to weight them (e.g., what if only 10 percent of a worker's tasks are supervisory?).[14] After much anticipation by unions and employers, in 2006 the Bush-appointed NLRB issued its *Kentucky River* decisions that created new definitions for assign, responsibly direct, and independent judgment.[15] These new definitions have been criticized by labor and its supporters for making it easier to exclude supervisory and professional employees from NLRB-defined bargaining units and from the NLRA's protections.[16] Remember that being excluded from NLRA protection does not mean it is illegal to form a union. But by splitting workers deemed to be supervisors or professionals from other employees, unions can be weakened, and without NLRA protection for the excluded employees, they can be fired for trying to organize. Increased supervisory exclusions from the NLRA are therefore seen by the labor movement as another example of the continued erosion of employee rights to form labor unions. Consequently, the labor movement supported the proposed Re-Empowerment of Skilled and Professional Employees and Construction Tradesworkers Act (the RESPECT Act), which would remove "assign" and "responsibly" directly from the definition of supervisor and would require the other supervisory functions to be a majority of an individual's job in order for him or her to be considered a supervisor. On the other hand, the Obama-appointed board was criticized by business groups for its narrow application of the *Kentucky River* rules in issuing decisions that reject employers' claim that certain workers are supervisors.[17] These controversies over who is a supervisor are likely to continue.

Scheduling the Election

Once all the details are ironed out—sufficient interest, timeliness, and unit definition—the NLRB will schedule an election. Elections are supervised and monitored by NLRB officials and usually take place at the employees' worksite—aboard ships and in factories, warehouses, offices, restaurants, movie studios, sports stadiums, and train yards. In special circumstances mail ballots are allowed. Each eligible worker can vote using a secret ballot. Voter turnout is often quite high—around 80 percent on average.[18] Half of all elections are held within 33 days of a petition being filed, and over 95 percent are held within 56 days.[19] Challenges to a unit definition can drastically lengthen the election timetable, and a few elections might not occur until a year or more after a petition is filed. In this period between filing the petition and conducting the election, the most intense campaigning by both unions and employers takes place—all with the intent of shaping how each individual worker votes in the election.

In 2015, the NLRB implemented new elections rules to streamline the process and reduce delays. This includes postponing hearings on some issues until after an election. For example, if a union wins or loses by a wide margin, then a small number of disputed ballots are irrelevant. Rather than delaying the election by having a hearing to resolve these disputes ahead of time, a hearing will be held after the election only if it's necessary to determine the outcome. Due to the shortened timeframe for conducting an election, SHRM and other business groups have labeled this the "ambush election" rule.[20]

Online Exploration Exercise: Search for sites and/or videos that support and criticize the election rules implemented by the NLRB in 2015 (hint: in addition to "NLRB election rule," another search term to try is "ambush election"). What are the main criticisms? Are they valid? Develop an argument to support "ambush election" as an accurate label. Develop a counter argument to reject "ambush election" as an accurate label.

INDIVIDUAL VOTING DECISIONS

In the most common scenario, an individual worker voting in a representation election receives a preprinted ballot asking, "Do you wish to be represented for the purpose of collective bargaining by [union name]?" and is instructed to mark the appropriate box—yes or no. An important question in labor relations is what influences individual workers to vote yes to form a union or no to remain nonunion. Research on U.S. workers typically reveals that demographic factors such as age and gender are *not* important predictors of how people vote in representation elections.[21] Rather, the voting decision is believed to be much more practical and is based on the perceived costs and benefits of unionization as well as on individual attitudes toward unions. As such, two starting points for the voting decision are typically identified: frustration and personal utility maximization.[22] In the frustration models, only dissatisfied workers or those frustrated by perceived workplace injustice will consider unionizing. In broad terms, frustration models can be thought of as psychological models because they are rooted in discrepancies between desired and actual employment conditions. In contrast, utility maximization models are economic models: Rational workers will consider unionization if it increases their well-being and the benefits outweigh the costs; job dissatisfaction is not required. Most studies support the importance of frustration/dissatisfaction rather than utility maximization.[23]

Job dissatisfaction and utility maximization are only the starting points, however. In order for these features to translate into a vote for unionization, three additional items are important: (1) A worker needs to feel that the union will be effective in improving things in the specific workplace, (2) a worker usually must not have negative views about unions in general, and (3) the social environment of the workplace must be favorable to unionization (see Figure 6.3). The first item is called **union instrumentality:** the degree to which an individual thinks a union will be instrumental (successful) in improving the workplace.[24] Unsurprisingly, workers who do not think a union will make a positive difference in their workplace are unlikely to vote for a union even if they are dissatisfied with their wages, working conditions, or other aspects of their jobs. Workers' fears that a union will bring conflict to the workplace can be viewed as an important negative dimension of union instrumentality.[25] In fact, union instrumentality is believed by some to be the most consistent predictor of union support.[26] Workers' beliefs that their unions lack instrumentality also increase the likelihood that they will vote against union representation in decertification elections.[27]

The second item often identified as important for determining whether frustrated or dissatisfied workers will vote for a union is attitudes toward unions in general.[28] Whereas union instrumentality is a belief about a specific union in your specific workplace, this second dimension pertains to broader images of unions. On the negative side, these general attitudes might include views of unions as autocratic, discriminatory, corrupt, outdated, bureaucratic, or conflictual. Negative stereotypes of unions are prominent in American culture, so unions need to work hard to overcome these antiunion attitudes in organizing drives.[29] In contrast, general positive attitudes can include beliefs that unions improve working conditions, help ensure that workers are treated fairly, and lobby for needed protective labor legislation. Positive attitudes might stem from previous experience in unionized workplaces or from having a parent or a spouse who is a union member.[30]

The third item that affects whether job dissatisfaction translates into a pro-union vote pertains to social aspects of the workplace. At one level this involves what has been labeled social pressure. Social pressure measures the extent to which an individual thinks his or her coworkers support the union—especially respected coworkers.[31] More generally, social aspects of the workplace capture the basic fact that unionization is ultimately a social or collective rather than individual activity.[32] Workplace-level employee solidarity and social identification are important factors in determining whether workers will try to correct perceived workplace injustices individually or collectively.[33] In other words, if workplace solidarity is low and workers have more of an individual rather than collective social identity, job dissatisfaction is not likely to translate into pro-union support. Interestingly, sometimes low-wage immigrant workers are more likely to unionize than low-wage native workers because of the greater collective social identity of immigrant workers that results when they self-select or are forced into living together and working in concentrated occupational niches such as New York City's West African grocery delivery workers or Pakistani "black-car" drivers.[34]

Finally, note that the description of individual decisions about whether to unionize captured by Figure 6.3 is largely North American. In the United States and Canada, the decision to join

FIGURE 6.3
The Individual Voting Decision in NLRB Representation Elections

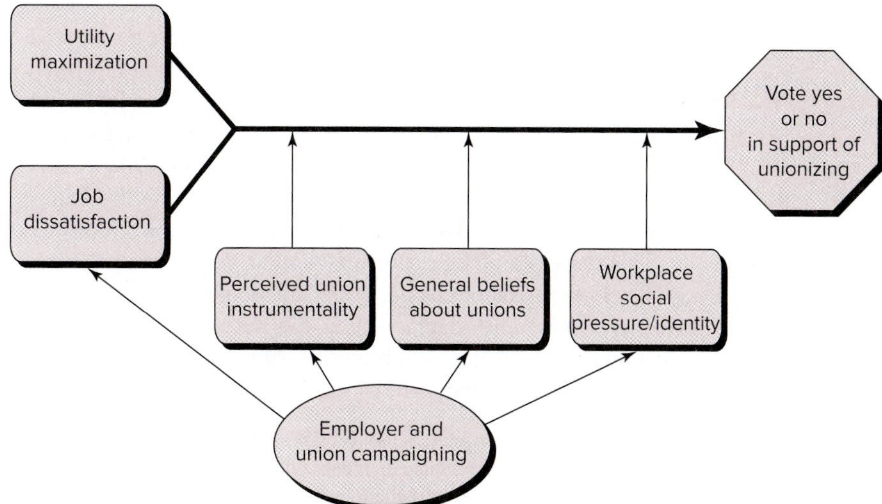

a union is closely linked to collective representation in the workplace. In continental Europe, in contrast, collective bargaining often occurs at the industry level and does not depend on whether a majority of workers in a workplace support a specific union (see Chapter 12). As such, an alternative explanation for why workers join unions focuses on political and ideological beliefs. But this applies more to European workers than North American workers; in some European countries, workers might also join unions for the pragmatic reason of getting access to unemployment insurance benefits.[35] In the United States, however, whether to vote for and join a union is tightly linked to whether one wants collective bargaining in their workplace. Consequently, each NLRB representation election is an important contest for unions and companies, and campaigning by both sides to affect whether individuals vote for or against union representation is a significant component of the U.S. union organizing process.

NLRB ELECTION STANDARDS

In the days and weeks leading up to NLRB representation elections, employers and unions typically conduct intense campaigns to bolster support for their sides. Unions try to create a social climate in the workplace that supports collective rather than individual action while highlighting reasons why employees should be dissatisfied with their jobs, how the union will be effective in improving their jobs (union instrumentality), and that unions in general are a positive societal force. On the other hand, employers try to make employees feel satisfied with their jobs, question the effectiveness of and need for unions in improving the workplace, negatively portray unions as dues-hungry or corrupt, and emphasize the value of individual rather than collective action. In short, employer and union campaigns try to affect the key determinants of how individuals vote in representation elections (see Figure 6.3). Various campaign tactics will be discussed in the next two sections; but first ask yourself whether there should be any limits or restrictions on employer and union campaigning. Remember that NLRB representation elections are not about employers or unions. Rather, the NLRA authorizes these elections to determine whether the *workers* want union representation.

The key legal standard for NLRB representation elections is therefore employee free choice. Campaigning by employers and unions is permitted by the NLRA's employer's free speech provision [Section 8(c)]:

> The expressing of any views, argument, or opinion, or the dissemination thereof, whether in written, printed, graphic, or visual form, shall not constitute or be evidence of an unfair labor practice under any of the provisions of this Act, if such expression contains no threat of reprisal or force or promise of benefit.

But this right is not unlimited—threats and promises are not allowed. Why? Because threats and promises can interfere with employee free choice. Union supporters might not vote for a union if they are afraid they will be fired if the union wins; employees who do not favor unionization might not vote against a union if union organizers have threatened them with physical violence. So to promote the key standard of employee free choice, the NLRB has established boundaries for employer and union campaigning: Campaign tactics that hamper, restrict, or interfere with *employee* free choice in deciding whether to have union representation are prohibited.[36]

This principle of free choice is similar to the typical standard for political elections: Well-informed voters are important for democracy, but buying votes through bribes or violence undermines democracy and is not allowed. Consequently, the NLRB evaluates election conduct using its **laboratory conditions doctrine,** also known as the *General Shoe* doctrine (after the name of the NLRB decision that created this doctrine):

> In election proceedings, it is the [NLRB's] function to provide a laboratory in which an experiment may be conducted, under conditions as nearly ideal as possible, to determine the uninhibited desires of the employees. It is our duty to establish those conditions; it is

> also our duty to determine whether they have been fulfilled. When, in the rare extreme case, the standard drops too low, because of our fault or that of others, the requisite laboratory conditions are not present and the experiment must be conducted over again.[37]

When the NLRB feels that election campaigning or other conduct causes employees to vote differently from their true preferences, the election results will be thrown out and a new election conducted (consider this yourself with "Labor Law Discussion Case 4" at the end of this chapter). The clearest violations of laboratory conditions are the NLRA's employer and union unfair labor practices: interfering with or coercing employees [Sections 8(a)(1) and 8(b)(1)], establishing a company-dominated sham union [8(a)(2)], and discriminating against employees on the basis of union support [8(a)(3)]. The classic example is firing union activists, which can affect the outcome of an election in several ways. Pro-union votes are kept from the election. Individuals who are key in spreading information about the union and creating a workplace climate supportive of collective action are removed. And other employees may be afraid to support the union for fear of being fired next. Firing (or otherwise discriminating against) union activists because of their union support therefore interferes with employee free choice and is illegal. Threatening to close a work site if a union wins an election or promising wage increases if the union loses amounts to buying votes and interferes with free choice. These actions are therefore prohibited. Improving wages, benefits, and working conditions before an election in order to defeat a union is also illegal interference.

But the laboratory conditions standard goes beyond unfair labor practices.[38] In other words, election conduct need not rise to the severity of a clear unfair labor practice in order to violate laboratory standards and therefore trigger a new election. For example, employer or union campaign tactics that inflame racial prejudices are not necessarily unfair labor practices, but they can create a tense environment in which employee free choice is affected. Lies and other distortions or misrepresentations of facts are also not unfair labor practices but can undermine free choice. Even though the NLRB has largely abandoned the view that lies and misrepresentations by themselves distort laboratory conditions—its logic is that workers can see through such propaganda—in extreme cases where the "pervasiveness of misrepresentation or the artfulness of deception during an election campaign renders employees so unable to separate truth from untruth that their free and fair choice is affected," a new election will be held.[39] Finally, the actions of a third party—that is, individuals not under the direction of the employer or the union, such as individual employees, the mayor or chief of police, or business and labor union leaders from other companies and unions—cannot be unfair labor practices but nevertheless can negatively impact laboratory conditions (see "Labor Law Discussion Case 5").

EMPLOYER CAMPAIGNING

Employer campaign tactics try to influence the four key determinants of individual voting decisions: job dissatisfaction, union instrumentality, general union attitudes, and collective social identity (recall Figure 6.3). At a minimum these tactics usually include providing pro-company and antiunion information and opinions to the employees. This is generally legal. Some companies are more aggressive and supplement this information with the manipulation of wages, benefits, working conditions, and job assignments as well as with threats, promises, rumors, layoffs, and firings. Antiunion committees might be formed, supervisors might be reassigned, and parties might be thrown. Many of these more aggressive activities can distort laboratory conditions and are therefore prohibited. These efforts might be led by full-time antiunion consultants. Two helpful acronyms to remember are FOE and TIPS. Providing workers with facts, opinions, and personal experiences ("FOE") pertaining to unions is generally legal, but it is illegal for managers to threaten, intimidate, make a promise to, or spy on workers ("**TIPS**").

Communicating with Employees

Information and opinions are shared with employees using a variety of methods. Supervisors might meet with employees individually or in small groups. Letters or e-mail messages might be sent to workers. The letters in Figure 6.4 are representative of common employer messages: The first letter tries to weaken workers' perceptions of union instrumentality, and the second portrays unions more generally in negative terms. Strikes and paying dues

FIGURE 6.4
Management Campaign Letters to Employees

Source: Adapted from actual letters from a company's website, modified to preserve anonymity.

Dear Employee of ABC:

With the election expected to be soon, many employees continue to ask:

EXACTLY WHAT CAN THE UNION GUARANTEE ME IF THEY GET ELECTED?

Not much. Here are the facts.

FACT: If the union wins the election, it wins only the right to bargain with ABC as your exclusive negotiating agent.

FACT: While the union and ABC both would be required by law to bargain "in good faith," the law would not require ABC to agree with the union on any union proposal or promise made to you during the campaign (your supervisor has proof).

FACT: If the union made demands to which ABC could not or would not agree, the union would ultimately have two choices:

1. DROP THEIR DEMAND, OR
2. STRIKE

FACT: Bargaining for a first contract is often a lengthy and complex process with uncertain results … and while bargaining goes on, your wages and benefits are **FROZEN** until changed, if at all, by a contract.

FACT: If and when a contract is finally agreed to, you may wind up with more, the same, or less than you now have.

I hope this is helpful. We've heard that the union organizers are promising employees "big" pay raises, "free" day care, etc. Sadly, as other employees have found out, there is often a **big** difference between what unions promise and what they actually deliver. It's just one more reason to vote "**NO**" union.

Sincerely,

W. Leiserson
Senior Vice President, Human Resources

Dear Employee:

"Member Decline Threatens U.S. Unions"

That's the headline of a recent news story about the current state of union membership. As you can see, union officials are worried; and they should be. Despite their recent efforts, union membership as a percentage of the total U.S. workforce continues to drop—from a high of 35% in 1955 to just 12% last year.

And just how do these union officials intend to solve this problem? At their recent convention in Las Vegas, they decided:

1. to spend more of their members' money on political campaigns, and
2. to raise the dues payments that union members now pay!

In fact, the same union that is chasing you here at ABC has already announced their plan **to increase members' dues each year for the next three years**! (See your supervisor for proof).

Ask yourself:

- **Do I want to pay money to help unions bail themselves out?**
- **Would I want my money spent on political campaigns?**
- **If unions have so much to offer employees, why aren't there more "takers"?**

If you have questions, please feel free to see your supervisor or any other member of management.

Sincerely,

W. Leiserson

Senior Vice President, Human Resources

are also frequent themes. Another important employer tactic for sharing information and opinions is the **captive audience meeting**—a group meeting held in the workplace during working hours in which employees are forced to listen to management's antiunion and pro-company presentations (captive audience speeches). Such meetings are legal as long as they are not within 24 hours of the election and steer clear of "TIPS."[40] Captive audience meetings are hotly debated—employers justify them on the basis of property and free speech rights; unions criticize them as giving employers an unfair advantage in communicating with, and perhaps pressuring, the employees.

These forms of communication are acceptable if they consist of "FOE" (Facts-Opinions-Experiences), but are unacceptable if managers are overly aggressive and deploy "TIPS" (Threaten-Intimidate-Promise-Spy). Sometimes, however, there is a fine line between predictions or opinions on one hand and threats on the other.[41] Suppose an employer tells employees that if a union increases labor costs too much, the plant will have to close. Is this an opinion, a prediction, or a threat? Or suppose an employer tells employees that similar facilities have closed after being organized by this same union. Is this a factual statement or an implied threat? It depends. Predictions based on objective facts that some events will likely occur because of forces beyond the employer's control (like competitive forces) are acceptable; statements that convey the impression that these events are inevitable or at the discretion of the employer are prohibited threats. An acceptable conversation between a supervisor and an employee also becomes objectionable if it turns into an interrogation about the employee's views of unionization. A visit to an employee's home by a management official is grounds for invalidating an election—because the employer controls an employee's job, visiting him or her at home is viewed as intimidating and coercive.[42]

Employer Restrictions on Employees and Union Organizers

Another employer campaign tactic is to use no solicitation rules. The employer can use its private property rights to prohibit outside organizations from entering the workplace and interacting with workers. As long as these rules are equally enforced for all types of outside organizations, union organizers can be denied access to employees in the workplace, except in extreme circumstances when unions have no other access to employees (such as in remote mining camps).[43] Union organizers can even be banned from shopping mall parking lots.[44] Note carefully that this applies to outside union organizers, not the employer's employees.[45]

Employees can discuss unionization in the workplace, but such conversations can be restricted to nonwork hours, and if they interfere with production or customers, to nonwork locations such as an employee cafeteria.[46] As such, some unions, especially in the construction industry, have tried a tactic called salting in which paid union organizers try to get hired as regular employees (and therefore "salt" or enrich the workplace) for the purpose of organizing the workers.[47] In a controversial ruling, the Supreme Court decided that salts are employees under the NLRA and therefore protected against discrimination in hiring and firing.[48] But to be protected, a salt must also have a genuine interest in working for the employer.[49]

Restrictions on both employees and nonemployee union organizers must be equally enforced. Consider an organization that allows its employees to sell Girl Scout cookies in working areas but restricts employee discussions of unions to nonwork areas, or allows Boy Scouts into the workplace to sell holiday wreaths but prohibits union organizers from the premises. Isolated charitable acts will be overlooked.[50] But if employees are allowed to repeatedly sell Girl Scout cookies to other workers during work time, such activities are likely not disruptive. To then restrict discussions of unionization by claiming that they are disruptive is disingenuous and amounts to discriminating against union activity.[51] For the same reason, discriminatory enforcement of no solicitation rules is objectionable interference with employee rights to organize unions.[52]

Currently the sharpest debates are over employee use of company e-mail systems. It is well established in labor law that employees do not have a statutory right to use their employer's traditional office equipment for union organizing or other Section 7 rights, whether it be bulletin boards, telephones, or copiers. Until 2014, employer e-mail systems were treated the same way such that employees did not have a right to use employer e-mail systems for Section 7 activity.[53] But in a controversial 2014 decision, the Obama-appointed NLRB ruled that because e-mail is such "a natural gathering place" for employees to discuss terms and conditions of employment, employees who already have access to a company e-mail system are allowed to use it for non-business purposes, including Section 7 activity, during non-work time.[54] Unlike other types of business equipment, the NLRB noted, employee use of e-mail is unlikely to prevent others from using it and is unlikely to add additional usage costs. If an employer wants to limit employee use of e-mail for union organizing or other Section 7 activity, it needs to show concrete costs (such as large e-mail attachments interfering with the e-mail system's operation) or that special circumstances make it necessary to restrict its employees' rights in order to maintain production or discipline. Relatedly, an employer can monitor e-mail messages on its own e-mail system, but cannot do this in a discriminatory fashion, such as increasing its monitoring during an organizing drive or monitoring union supporters more intensely than others. Note that in all of these situations, the NLRB is trying to find a balance between workers' rights and employers' property rights.

Union Avoidance Consultants

The use of outside union avoidance consultants and lawyers is a prominent component of employers' campaigns.[55] Consultants can help managers take advantage of tactics such as captive audience meetings and train supervisors in union avoidance methods. Unions, however, view union avoidance consultants as another element of a deck stacked in favor of employers who can hold captive audience meetings, ban union organizers from the workplace, and hire expensive consultants to lead sophisticated communications and public relations campaigns. Moreover, at least some union avoidance consultants aggressively seek to break unions by resorting to almost any means necessary—a less publicly visible descendant of the aggressive strikebreaking agencies like the Pinkertons in the 19th century (described in Chapter 3). This is labor relations at its worst: lies, threats, promises, manipulation, harassment, espionage, abuse, and firings.[56] In one extreme case in South Carolina in 1999, a 17-year employee with no record of violence challenged his plant manager to let the employees talk with a union organizer. The following day the employer notified the local sheriff that this employee was threatening workers, so the sheriff's deputies surrounded him at gunpoint on his way to work and forcibly took him to the local hospital. Based on what the employer told the sheriff, the employee was involuntarily committed to a mental hospital. He was held for two weeks against his will and forcibly injected with antipsychotic drugs until a lawyer could obtain his release.[57]

With the help of attorneys and consultants, another employer tactic is delay.[58] By challenging the proposed bargaining unit definition in an election petition, an employer can slow down the election time line and delay the election date for a couple of months or more. The 1975 unit determination case for Harvard University clerical and technical workers was stretched out by the university's lawyers to include more than 20 days of hearings; and in a similar case at Yale University, the university's lawyers submitted a witness list of over 300 individuals.[59] Research shows that election delays reduce the likelihood of union certification.[60] Why is delay a significant tactic in the employer's favor? The employer gains more time to campaign against the union; employee turnover may result in the loss of union supporters; perceptions of union instrumentality might be weakened as the union appears helpless to counter the employer's legal maneuverings; and critical union momentum is lost. As noted earlier, new NLRB election rules implemented in 2015 seek to reduce election delays.

Ethics in Action A Union Avoidance Consultant Tells All

Marty Levitt spent more than 20 years as a union avoidance consultant, aggressively directing campaigns to prevent unions from winning representation elections. Then he had a change of heart and publicly revealed his past activities, offering a glimpse into the big business of labor relations consulting. Here are some of his revelations:

> There are many forms of union busting. Some labor consultants and attorneys take on unions that already represent a workforce, squeezing negotiators at the bargaining table, forcing workers out on strike, harassing union officers. My career took another path. I refined the specialty . . . called "counterorganizing drives," battling nonunion employees as they struggled to win union representation. The enemy was the collective spirit. I got hold of that spirit while it was still a seedling; I poisoned it, choked it, bludgeoned it if I had to, anything to be sure that it would never blossom into a united workforce, the dreaded foe of any corporate tyrant.
>
> For my campaigns I identified two key targets: the rank-and-file workers and their immediate supervisors. The supervisors served as my front line. I took them hostage on the first day and sent them to antiunion boot camp. I knew that people who didn't feel threatened wouldn't fight. So through hours of seminars, rallies, and one-on-one encounters, I taught the supervisors to despise and fear the union. I persuaded them that a union organizing drive was a personal attack on them, a referendum on their leadership skills, and an attempt to humiliate them. I was friendly, even jovial at times, but always unforgiving as I compelled each supervisor to feel he was somehow to blame for the union push and consequently obliged to defeat it.
>
> . . .
>
> Although I took on the supervisors face-to-face, my war on union activists was covert. To stop a union proponent—a "pusher," in the antiunion lexicon—the buster will go anywhere, not just to the lunchroom, but into the bedroom if necessary. The buster is not only a terrorist; he is also a spy. My team and I routinely pried into workers' police records, personnel files, credit histories, medical records, and family lives in search of a weakness that we could use to discredit union activists.
>
> Once in a while, a worker is impeccable. So some consultants resort to lies. To fell the sturdiest union supporters in the 1970s, I frequently launched rumors that the targeted worker was gay or was cheating on his wife. . . . If even the nasty stories failed to muzzle an effective union proponent, the busters might get the worker fired.
>
> . . .
>
> Not only were working people crushed by the cruelty of the union busters, but the companies themselves were raped, as consultants and attorneys conspired to wring as much as they could out of their clients. The executives paid whatever they were asked, the consultants having convinced them that a union organizing effort amounted to the worst crisis of their business lives. In the end I understood that a union busting campaign left a company financially devastated and hopelessly divided and almost invariably created an even more intolerable work environment than before. . . .

QUESTIONS

1. Show how the type of union busting described here is unethical in all six ethical theories presented in Chapter 5.
2. Given that this type of union busting is unethical in all six perspectives, why do some managers hire such consultants? Why do some people become union busting consultants? Is it simply because some people are unethical, or are there more complex reasons?

Source: Martin Jay Levitt and Terry Conrow, *Confessions of a Union Buster,* pp. 2–4.

The Controversies over Employer Campaign Tactics

Employer campaigning during NLRB representation elections is a controversial topic in U.S. labor relations. Some argue that union representation is a question solely for workers, and employers should not be granted rights as formal participants in the process—free speech should be allowed, but not the right to object to the definition of the unit, to use special campaign tactics like captive audience speeches, and to challenge the results.[61] The usual counterarguments are that the employers' property rights give them the right to participate in the process, that unions are too powerful without a fair counterweight of employer campaigning, and that employers need to speak for the antiunion employees and deliver their message.

More pragmatically, there is also significant debate over the practical questions of the prevalence and significance of employer campaigning. Some campaign tactics are hard to observe or measure (such as informal supervisor conversations with employees), and most are undertaken quietly (especially the illegal ones). Using NLRB data on illegal discharge unfair labor practices, it has been estimated that workers were illegally fired in 25 percent of representation election campaigns during the 2000s and that there is nearly a 2 percent chance that any pro-union worker involved in an organizing drive will be illegally fired. If union activists represent 10 percent of pro-union workers, this means that there is a 20 percent chance that union activists will be fired.[62] Moreover, employees perceive the chances of retribution for organizing activity to be high: In one survey 41 percent of non-union respondents agreed that "it is likely I will lose my job if I try to form a union," and 79 percent of all respondents said it is "very" or "somewhat" likely that "nonunion workers will get fired if they try to organize a union."[63]

More generally, research seems to reveal a pattern of broad-based employer campaigning during NLRB representation elections.[64] This research often relies on the reports of union organizers, so it might overstate (if organizers or their inside sources intentionally or unintentionally inflate the amount of employer resistance) or understate (if organizers do not observe all the campaigning) the true level of employer campaigning. With this in mind, Table 6.2 presents some typical statistics. Note that a large fraction of employers reportedly use outside consultants, one-on-one meetings between workers and supervisors, and multiple captive audience meetings.

But do these tactics matter? This is the most debated question. Relative to their peers in other industrialized countries, American managers appear to be exceptionally hostile toward unions and have significantly stronger traditions of using union avoidance tactics.[65] Various studies find that employer antiunion campaign tactics reduce the likelihood that employees will vote for unions in NLRB representation elections and that unions are less likely to win these elections.[66] In contrast, a famous study in the 1970s found that most workers already had their minds made up before employer campaigning began and therefore that employer tactics do not matter.[67] On the other hand, a reanalysis of this study's data revealed that because many elections are decided by thin margins, captive audience meetings as well as objectionable threats and actions toward union supporters can affect enough votes to shift the outcome of the election.[68] Yet another study found that employer unfair labor practices did not reduce the probability of unions winning an election, but they did reduce overall union success rates by decreasing the likelihood that a petition filing would result in an election being held.[69] And the debate continues.

TABLE 6.2
The Frequency of Employer Campaign Tactics

Tactic	Frequency
One-on-one meetings with supervisors	77%
Used outside consultant	75%
More than five captive audience meetings	53%
Threatened cuts in wages or benefits	47%
Assisted an antiunion committee	30%
Discharged workers not reinstated	29%
Distributed pay stubs with dues deducted	23%
Gave wage increase	18%

Reference: Kate Bronfenbrenner, "No Holds Barred—The Intensification of Employer Opposition to Organizing," *EPI Briefing Paper No. 235* (Washington, DC: Economic Policy Institute, 2009).

Labor Relations Application The Case against Employer Campaigning

"The major counterargument [to proposals to limit employer campaigning] made by employers—especially the majority who do not engage in this most egregious breaking of labor law tradition—is that they are denied what should be their equal right to campaign for the allegiance of employee voters. This is said to be the equivalent of a political election that allows the Democratic party, but not the Republicans, to campaign effectively for voter support in political elections.

The fallacy in that analogy and argument is that it mistakenly assumes that an affirmative vote for the union . . . means that the union is now *governing* employers (or even employees). All that a successful employee verdict does is give the union the mandate to *represent* employees in negotiations with the employer under labor law. Under employment law, we would never dream of suggesting that the employer should have an affirmative right and opportunity to campaign against the employee's decision about whether to hire a law firm (and if so, which one) when challenging employer policies regarding occupational safety or sexual harassment, for example."

. . .

"The more apt political analog of the role of the employer in a representation election is the role of a foreign government in an American election. Canada, for example, has a significant interest in which party is elected to govern the United States; selection of one party rather than the other may make life considerably easier or more difficult for the Canadian government in negotiations over defense, trade, natural resources, energy, foreign investment, and so on. Yet no one would argue that Canadian government agencies should therefore have a right to participate in an American election campaign in order to try to persuade United States citizens to vote for a party that would be favorable to Canadian interests. After all, it is the job of the United States government to advance the interests of its own citizens when those interests conflict with the interests of Canadians; Canadians have their own government to defend their interests irrespective of the electoral verdict in the United States."

. . .

"The law should not restrain the employer's freedom to say what it will about collective bargaining—censorship in the representation campaign has the same offensive flavor that it has in politics or in the arts—but there is no principle of fairness that requires that the representation process be structured to facilitate employer opposition to unionization."

Sources: Paul C. Weiler, "A Principled Reshaping of Labor Law for the Twenty-First Century," *University of Pennsylvania Journal of Labor and Employment Law* 3 (Winter 2001), p. 190; Paul Weiler, "Promises to Keep: Securing Workers' Rights to Self-Organization under the NLRA," *Harvard Law Review* 96 (June 1983), pp. 1814–15.

In sum, by many accounts employers devote a lot of time and money to campaigning against unions in NLRB representation elections. Some campaign tactics are legal (recall "FOE"), though still criticized by labor supporters; other tactics are illegal (recall "TIPS"), and union busting can be "a very dirty business."[70] Given the resources spent on campaigning, managers must perceive them as effective in reducing the likelihood that a union organizing drive will be successful. Moreover, the evidence points toward the presence of significant incentives to avoid unions at all costs. One-third of nonunion managers believe that their careers will be harmed if their employees unionize.[71] And they are probably right: In one study, managers in establishments without any union organizing activity had a 21 percent chance of being promoted and a 2 percent chance of being fired; in similar establishments that experienced an organizing drive, not a single manager was promoted and 15 percent were fired.[72]

UNION CAMPAIGNING

Like employers, unions can campaign to influence the four key determinants of individual voting decisions in NLRB representation elections (recall Figure 6.3). An example of a union campaign flyer is shown in Figure 6.5—note the emphasis on the implicit messages regarding

FIGURE 6.5
A Union Campaign Flyer

Source: Reprinted by permission of GESO.

Got fully subsidized dependent health care?

In 1998, due in great part to GESO organizing, Yale agreed to subsidize half of the cost of dependent health care. Like the rest of the employees on campus working over 20 hours per week, graduate students should be provided with a *full* subsidy, along with affordable child care and reasonable parental leave.

>>Contact an organizer. Show your support for these benefits so graduate students with families can worry about completing their degrees, not what will happen if their spouses or children become sick or injured.

Organizing toward a written and binding contract.

For more information: www.geso.org or 203/624-5161

job dissatisfaction (all other employees have a *full* subsidy for dependent health care) and union instrumentality (if we unionize, we can also win a full subsidy). But beyond some of these basic similarities between employer and union campaigning, there are significant differences. Labor law tries to balance the rights of employers and unions during the organizing process, but because of employers' power over their property and employees, the tactics available to each side differ. From a behavioral and strategic rather than legal perspective, U.S. unions have not traditionally devoted extensive resources to campaign tactics (though some unions are trying to change this practice).[73] Yet in many ways, unions need to make more important decisions than employers. In fact, the organizing process is perhaps the primary area of labor relations in which unions are the proactive rather than the reactive party. Unions, not employers, need to figure out what type of representation philosophy fits best with various types of workers—factory workers, office employees, professionals, women, recent immigrants, and the like—and what type of campaign tactics support these philosophies.

Communicating with Employees

From a legal standpoint, the laboratory conditions doctrine applies to union as well as employer actions. If union threats or harassment distort employee free choice, the election results can be invalidated and a new election held. NLRB rulings, however, have traditionally been less likely to conclude that union promises undermine laboratory conditions.[74] Rather, the NLRB typically holds the perspective that

> Employees are generally able to understand that a union cannot obtain benefits automatically by winning an election but must seek to achieve them through collective bargaining. Union promises . . . are easily recognized by employees to be dependent on contingencies beyond the union's control and do not carry with them the same degree of finality as if uttered by an employer who has it within his power to implement promises of benefits.[75]

In fact, unions have little to offer employees except promises that they will try to win gains for the employees.[76] One of the vexing problems for unions, however, is how to get this message to employees.

Recall from the previous section that employers can force employees to attend captive audience meetings and listen to captive audience speeches. At the same time, property rights can be used to enforce no solicitation rules banning union organizers from the workplace and the surrounding private property such as parking lots. So how can union organizers contact employees? In lieu of workplace access, once a representation election is scheduled, an NLRB rule requires employers to give the union a list of names, addresses, and available personal email addresses and phone numbers of the employees eligible to vote in the election. This is called an ***Excelsior* list** (named after the 1966 *Excelsior Underwear* decision) and must be provided within two days of the NLRB scheduling an election.[77] Unions can then contact employees or visit them at home.[78] Unlike employers, unions are allowed home visits:

> There is a substantial difference between the employment of the technique of individual interviews by employers on the one hand and by unions on the other. Unlike employers, unions often do not have the opportunity to address employees in assembled or informal groups, and never have the position of control over tenure of employment and working conditions which imparts the coercive effect to systematic individual interviews conducted by employers. Thus, not only do unions have more need to seek out individual employees to present their views, but, more important, [unions] lack the relationship with the employees to interfere with their choice of representatives thereby.[79]

Some employees might view home visits as invasions of privacy, but with no workplace access, unions have little choice. Some unions also use websites and Facebook pages to provide campaign information, but they have to figure out how to direct employees to these sites.

Strategies to Create Worker Activism

Union campaigning has traditionally focused on distribution of flyers and letters through mailings and handbilling (the classic picture of a union organizer standing outside the factory gate handing out flyers).[80] Even if we update this to include e-mail mailings, individual workers are passive recipients of information; there is no personal contact, and they are not actively involved in building their union. Unions are increasingly supplementing these traditional tactics with new methods for developing personal relationships with workers—such as house calls and small group meetings—and for getting workers actively involved in the campaign, such as rallies and using workers as volunteer organizers (see Table 6.3). In fact, research has shown that these tactics are often more important than employer campaigning in influencing the outcome of NLRB representation elections, especially when used as a comprehensive union-building strategy.[81] Until these new campaign tactics become more widespread, however, the conventional wisdom will likely continue to be true: More often than not, employer campaigning is more comprehensive, sophisticated, and aggressive (and expensive) than union campaigning.

Union organizing tactics are closely related to the type of message unions want to deliver. Passive campaign tactics like mailings and handbilling are consistent with the servicing model of union representation. Recall from the previous chapter that in this model workers consume union services, especially collectively bargained contracts and

TABLE 6.3
The Frequency of Union Campaign Tactics

The traditional union campaign tactics are mailings and handbilling. Tactics to create more personal contact with individual employees and to get them actively involved are starting to be used:

Tactic	Frequency
Made house calls	58%
Used solidarity days (supporters wear buttons, etc.)	56%
Held union rallies	41%
Made house calls to at least half the unit	39%
Held 10 or more small group meetings	39%
Used coalitions with community groups	30%
Surveyed at least 70% one-on-one	21%
Used 10 or more rank-and-file volunteers	17%

Reference: Kate Bronfenbrenner and Tom Juravich, "It Takes More Than House Calls: Organizing to Win with a Comprehensive Union Building Strategy," in Kate Bronfenbrenner et al. (eds.), *Organizing to Win: New Research on Union Strategies* (Ithaca, NY: ILR Press, 1998), pp. 19–36.

representation in the grievance procedure. Problems are solved *for* the workers, not *by* the workers. And who is the source of these problems? Management. The employer is therefore portrayed in campaign literature as the enemy. The union is a source of protection, and unionism becomes "us versus them" adversarialism (see Figure 6.6).

In contrast, the organizing model views unions as vehicles for worker participation and empowerment.[82] Problems are not solved *for* workers—workers are directly involved in solving their own problems. Workers do not consume equity and voice—they participate in their attainment. Traditional passive union campaign tactics cannot be used to organize a new union based on active rank-and-file participation. A different type of unionism requires a different type of campaigning. To be successful, these campaigns use the types of tactics listed

FIGURE 6.6
A Union Campaign Flyer

Sometimes Things Are Not What They Seem!

Beware of Management's Tricks.

Management often tries to convince you that they are on your side. They say your interests are the same and that we are all just one big, happy family.

Management uses mandatory meetings on company time to trick you into believing that it's in your best interest to believe that a union is not needed here.

They tell you that management will take care of you. The truth is that they are in business to make money. If making money means paying you less and providing fewer benefits that is what they will do.

The company makes money because of your hard work. You need a union to protect your rights.

The only guarantee of keeping good wages and increasing your benefits is a union contract—not management's promises.
Don't get the wool pulled over your eyes.

Let's Get It In Writing – A Union Contract!

in Table 6.3—extensive one-on-one personal contact, active rank-and-file volunteers, and rallies to build collective identity. Much of the focus of labor advocates today is on developing these active campaign tactics to increase organizing success and build stronger labor unions.[83]

These tactics that emphasize grassroots involvement rather than reliance on outside, full-time, paid union organizers reflect Saul Alinsky's "iron rule of organizing": "Never do for others what they can do for themselves."[84] In such a campaign, existing workers take the lead in talking with their coworkers about the possibility of unionizing. To put this in perspective, consider how differently you might react if you were approached by a full-time union organizer whom you had never met or by a coworker whom you've known and respected for several years. Note also that existing employees have greater access to their coworkers than do outside union organizers because of the no solicitation rules and ability to use company e-mail systems discussed earlier in this chapter. Beyond the benefits that flow from volunteer rank-and-file organizers being better able to connect with their coworkers, the extensive use of such volunteers can build a much stronger local union organization. Following the iron rule of organizing creates new leaders by increasing personal responsibility, confidence, communication skills, and self-respect; creates a sense of vibrancy and life through participation; and roots the local union more strongly into the local community.[85]

Many advocates believe that such tactics are necessary when employers seem to have the upper hand. As such, these new tactics can be aggressive and militant. A combination of public rank-and-file activism and alliances with community groups and worker centers has been effective in overcoming the language barriers and fears of immigrant and other marginalized workers by tapping into their strong social networks and by creating campaigns that are more responsive to the particular concerns of these workers.[86] Perhaps the most heralded successes in this regard are the Justice for Janitors campaigns (see the accompanying "Labor Relations Application" box). The Fight for $15 movement in the fast-food industry in the 2010s has embraced similar tactics of public activism to try to organize and empower low-paid workers.

But these tactics that emphasize rank-and-file involvement do not have to be aggressively militant. Clerical and technical workers at Harvard University were successfully organized by a grassroots campaign that focused on developing personal relationships.[87] This campaign explicitly rejected the traditional passive campaign tactics and the traditional "us versus them" adversarial mind-set. A prominent campaign theme was "It's not anti-Harvard to be pro-union." The workers were seeking empowerment, not protection. This philosophy is perhaps a good approach for organizing female workers, and it's no coincidence that the clerical and technical workers at Harvard and the lead organizers were overwhelmingly female.[88] In fact, this organizing style is rooted in the ethics of care (Chapter 5), which is rooted in feminist thought. This emphasis on empowerment, involvement, and by extension independent judgment can also be a good model for professional employees who are looking for additional workplace voice but do not view their employers as enemies. Professional workers typically do not want outside third parties to "service" them and to create an adversarial, inflexible workplace.[89] In organizing campaigns, professionals therefore "respond best to a democratic structure that allows them to take control of their own organization and use it to gain influence and respect and to enhance their professionalism."[90] Again, unions are the proactive party in the organizing process and need to determine the best types of representation for different workplaces—and then develop comprehensive organizing campaigns to support them.

Online Exploration Exercise: Search for sites that are focused on organizing new workers (hint: one possible search term is "workers united"), or try to find some relevant Twitter feeds (example: @UnionizeTmobile). What types of issues are emphasized in the different campaigns? What tactics are used? What are the pros and cons of using online sites for organizing?

Labor Relations Application Organizing Immigrant Workers: Justice for Janitors and Beyond

Organizing immigrant and other marginalized workers is a major challenge for the U.S. labor movement in the 21st century. In many large cities, a majority of the jobs that have traditionally been keys to union strength—manual jobs with few educational requirements—are held by recent immigrants. In fact, first- and second-generation immigrants were an important part of the rise of the CIO industrial unions. Particular issues for organizing immigrant workers include language barriers, high turnover, employer power, employers' attempts to manipulate ethnic conflict, and among undocumented immigrants, the fear of deportation even though the NLRA does not exclude undocumented workers from its protections. Do not assume, however, that immigrant workers are not receptive to unionism; rather, many have had positive experiences with unions or other efforts at challenging institutionalized authority in their home countries.

One of the most celebrated success stories of organizing immigrant workers is the Justice for Janitors campaigns created by the Service Employees International Union (SEIU) to organize janitors at large commercial properties. Organizing commercial janitors involves a number of special challenges beyond the fact that many are immigrant workers. Building owners contract with cleaning services to provide janitorial services rather than directly hiring their own janitors. Consequently, building owners can switch contractors if one becomes unionized, and it is difficult to pressure the primary employer because it is not the building owner. Picketing a building, for example, can be an illegal secondary boycott. Furthermore, because cleaning service contractors have janitors at numerous properties around a city, organizing cannot focus on a single building—the appropriate bargaining unit as defined by the NLRB is all the janitors working for a single contractor at all its properties.

For these reasons, traditional union campaign tactics are not successful in organizing commercial janitors. In the mid-1980s the SEIU launched a more militant strategy. Because the building owners hold the true power but are shielded from NLRB elections because janitorial services are contracted out, the SEIU focuses on bringing public pressure to the owners and forcing them to support unionization without an election. To a large degree, this strategy depends critically on extensive rank-and-file involvement in organizing. To generate sufficient publicity and galvanize community support, the Justice for Janitors campaigns rely on extensive, if not daily, public demonstrations that would not be possible without high levels of worker involvement. To end these "in your face" tactics, building owners pressure the contractors to recognize the SEIU and negotiate union contracts. For example, in Los Angeles the number of unionized janitors grew from fewer than 2,000 to over 20,000 as a result of a Justice for Janitors campaign.

The Justice for Janitors campaigns have been successful in winning contracts without NLRB elections by mobilizing the janitors to help themselves. By creating high levels of participation, these campaigns can harness the strong social networks within immigrant communities and develop strong alliances with other community groups such as churches and immigrant rights groups. The importance of these groups is illustrated by the number of worker centers that help immigrant and other marginalized workers with many social justice issues like discrimination and wage theft in addition to union organizing. Borrowing the public activism tactics of the Justice for Janitors campaigns, the Centro de Trabajadores Unidos en la Lucha (the Center of Workers United in Struggle) in Minneapolis pressured Target Corporation into its 2014 adoption of a Responsible Contractor Policy for the cleaning contracts for Target retail stores which will assure janitors the right to organize. Finally, extensive rank-and-file participation forces unions to be more responsive to the particular interests and concerns of various groups of workers. These techniques are therefore being championed by the labor movement as good not just for organizing immigrant and marginalized workers, but for organizing all workers.

References: Ruth Milkman (ed.), *Organizing Immigrants: The Challenge for Unions in Contemporary California* (Ithaca, NY: ILR Press, 2000); Jane Williams, "Restructuring Labor's Identity: The Justice for Janitors Campaign in Washington, D.C.," in Ray M. Tillman and Michael S. Cummings (eds.), *The Transformation of U.S. Unions: Voices, Visions, and Strategies from the Grassroots* (Boulder, CO: Lynne Rienner Publishers, 1999), pp. 203–18; Ruth Milkman and Ed Ott (eds.), *New Labor in New York: Precarious Worker Organizing and the Future of Unionism* (Ithaca, NY: Cornell University Press, 2014); Janice Fine, "Alternative Labour Protection Movements in the United States: Reshaping Industrial Relations?" *International Labour Review* 154 (March 2015), pp. 15–26.

THE CERTIFICATION ELECTION PROCESS: HELP OR HINDRANCE?

The union certification process established by the NLRA in 1935 was initially a great victory for workers wanting union representation. Firing union supporters was made illegal, and rather than having to strike for recognition, workers could petition the NLRB for a democratic determination of whether a majority of workers favored unionizing. In the first few years after 1935, the NLRB used a variety of methods to determine majority status: authorization cards, petitions, union membership applications, employee affidavits of membership, strike participation, and employee testimony.[91] The Taft–Hartley Act amendments in 1947, however, explicitly stated that if "a question of representation exists, [the NLRB] shall direct an election by secret ballot" [Section 9(c)]. Later the Supreme Court ruled that an employer can request a secret ballot election, even if majority status as indicated by signed authorization cards is not in doubt.[92] Early NLRB decisions also excluded employers from participating in the certification process, but the Supreme Court and Section 8(c) of the Taft–Hartley Act explicitly authorize (noncoercive) employer participation in the process.[93] The certification process has therefore changed from a quick procedure with minimal employer involvement to a formal and often lengthy election procedure with extensive employer participation, including not only campaigning but also legal challenges to proposed bargaining units and election results.

Criticisms of the NLRA Certification Process

While the certification process has undergone this transformation, private sector union density has fallen from 35 percent in the 1950s to less than 10 percent today. Labor unions and their supporters frequently argue that employer resistance, including campaigning during representation elections, is primarily responsible for this extended decline in U.S. union density.[94] To illustrate the difficulty of this process, one study of over 22,000 petitions for certification elections filed with the NLRB found that only 8,100 resulted in union election victories, and only 4,600 resulted in signed contracts within a year of victory.[95] In other words, unions need to file five petitions to successfully gain one new bargaining unit with a signed contract. Three aspects of the NLRA certification process are criticized most frequently: unequal access to employees, the lack of penalties for violators of the NLRA, and the length of the election process.

First let's consider the criticism of unequal access. Employers can meet with employees informally, conduct captive audience meetings, and enforce no solicitation rules against union organizers while unions merely get a list of employee contact information after the election date is set. Some think this unequal access to employees gives employers an unfair advantage. Possibilities for reform include banning employer captive audience meetings, giving unions the right to hold captive audience meetings, requiring a certain number of campaign debates, or allowing unions to send e-mail messages using the company's system.[96] In fact, for a few years in the 1950s, the NLRB granted unions a right of reply—if an employer used a captive audience speech, it also had to give the union an equal opportunity to address the employees.[97] Other possibilities are to make *Excelsior* lists available at any time, or after a union collects 30 percent signed authorization cards.[98] Others advocate greater union access to employees at work more generally.[99] In particular, rather than placing the burden on the union to show that no other channels of communication exist, the burden could be on the employer to show that greater physical or electronic access for union organizers interferes with the business (the current standard for attempts to restrict employees from discussing unionization).

A second criticism of the NLRA certification process is the lack of penalties for violators. When a company violates Section 8(a)(3) by illegally discharging a union supporter,

Labor Relations Application The Women's Movement Meets the Labor Movement at Harvard

During the women's movement in the early 1970s, a handful of women employed in Harvard University's medical area started a group to bring attention to discriminatory treatment against female workers. Out of this grew a full-fledged push to unionize clerical and technical workers. Medical workers voted against unionizing in a 1977 election, and the union again lost a narrow vote in 1983 after Harvard posted armed guards outside the polling place. When a third petition was filed in 1983, the NLRB expanded the unit to include all clerical and technical employees throughout Harvard.

By the time the NLRB issued its unit determination ruling in 1984, the United Auto Workers (UAW) was leading the organizing drive and using its traditional organizing tactics, especially passive handbilling that emphasizes the need for strong union protection against harsh working conditions and employers concerned more with profits than people. But the clerical and technical workers were predominantly women fighting against the paternalism of Harvard. They had no interest in replacing this with the paternalism of the UAW. And the Harvard employees were not anti-Harvard—they wanted more respect in a nonadversarial workplace. The grassroots organizers (former Harvard employees) therefore emphasized building one-on-one relationships rather than getting signatures on authorization cards.

In 1985 the grassroots organizers split from the UAW and formed an independent organization: the Harvard Union of Clerical and Technical Workers (HUCTW). In 1986 the HUCTW gave up on letters, flyers, and other paper forms of communication—largely because they couldn't afford it but also because they wanted to create an active campaign. "No longer could a pro-union worker become an activist merely by handing out pieces of paper. Now she or he had to talk to people." The slogan "It's not anti-Harvard to be pro-union" became a central theme of the campaign. The union also emphasized broad issues such as voice and self-representation rather than specific issues like better wages:

> We believe in self-representation. We are building our union for this reason, and not out of anger or negativity. Responsible, self-respecting adults should represent themselves in important matters affecting their lives. We have until now allowed Harvard to decide everything to do with our work lives. Now we are ready to participate as equals in making those decisions.

The central campaign tactic became one-on-one organizing: "The objective of one-on-one organizing was to establish a personal relationship with each worker and to introduce him or her to other workers through union activities, so that in the end a very large number of workers were 'connected' to one another in a complex web of relationships." Feminist thought emphasizing the importance of relationships rather than power was thus incorporated into the labor movement.

To get an election, the HUCTW eventually had to collect signed authorization cards and filed an election petition in 1988 supported by cards from 60 percent of the workers. Harvard actively campaigned against the union for the two months leading up to the election. While remaining largely autonomous, the HUCTW was now affiliated with the American Federation of State, County, and Municipal Workers, and Harvard tried to paint a picture of a large, strike-prone, dues-hungry union that would bring conflict and rigidity into the workplace. But with the strong one-on-one relationships that had been developed, many workers were inoculated against this standard antiunion rhetoric.

In May 1988 the HUCTW won the NLRB representation election in a close vote; and after Harvard dropped its opposition to the union, a number of workers voluntarily joined the union, and membership jumped to 75 percent. Several years later the person who led Harvard's campaign *against* the HUCTW offered the following assessment:

> [The HUCTW] knew us better than we did. We didn't know our employees in this huge decentralized place. They organized employees that we didn't know existed. . . . If they had stayed with the UAW, they would have put out a flyer, and we would have put out a flyer, and we would have beaten them. [The HUCTW] understood intuitively what the people were hungering for and nurtured it. . . . They want to be in relationships rather than putting up their dukes.

The HUCTW remains a vibrant union at Harvard today (see *www.huctw.org*).

Reference: John P. Hoerr, *We Can't Eat Prestige: The Women Who Organized Harvard* (Philadelphia: Temple University Press, 1997). The quotes are from pp. 155, 183, 197, and 211.

the worst penalty the company faces is minor: offering reinstatement with full back pay to the employee. And the company can reduce the back pay award by the amount the employee has earned elsewhere since discharge. Many see this as an inadequate deterrent to violating the NLRA and propose reforming the NLRA to allow compensatory and punitive damage awards (as is the case under antidiscrimination laws such as the Civil Rights Act) rather than allowing only back pay awards.[100] With respect to elections, if the NLRB finds that laboratory conditions have been corrupted by employer, union, or third-party actions, the typical remedy is to throw out the election results and conduct a new election. In some instances this happens several times. In rare cases in which the NLRB believes that the union had majority support but extreme employer misconduct has eroded this support and has also been so pernicious as to make an election pointless, the NLRB can issue a ***Gissel* bargaining order** instead of trying to restore laboratory conditions and conducting a new election.[101] A *Gissel* bargaining order requires the employer to recognize and bargain with the union even though the usual election results are lacking. As such, there are three ways in which a union can win recognition: voluntary recognition, an NLRB representation election, and a bargaining order. But bargaining orders are issued only rarely and only for the most extreme cases in which multiple, severe unfair labor practices have been committed.

A third criticism of the NLRB certification process is its length. Typically elections are not held until two months after the filing of the election petition, and employers' legal maneuverings can lengthen this period. Many believe that the worst violations occur during this period, when the campaigning on both sides is the most intense.[102]

NLRB elections are supposed to be the democratic method for settling representation questions. But it's questionable whether NLRB elections fulfill the standards for democratic elections.[103] Democratic elections should be free of intimidation, but many workers are fired for trying to form unions. Freedom of speech is essential for democratic elections, but employers can limit free speech in the workplace. Democratic elections also require reasonably balanced financial resources and access to voters, but employers typically have much greater resources and access to employees.

For labor supporters, therefore, the NLRB certification process has some major weaknesses. If these weaknesses are in fact responsible for the decline in U.S. union density, then reform is warranted. But there are other possible explanations for this decline. Structural, or compositional, changes are partly responsible: declining employment in traditionally unionized industries such as manufacturing combined with faster employment growth in Southern states, increased numbers of women in the labor force, and increases in education and skill levels.[104] This structural explanation, however, begs important questions about why certain industries, occupations, regions, or workers are more or less receptive to unionization. Another possible explanation is that the demand for unions by nonunion employees has declined—perhaps because of increased employment laws, improved human resource management practices, or unresponsive unions that have failed to stay in touch with the contemporary workforce.[105] There is no single, universally accepted explanation of why union density has declined, but the true answer is critically important for determining whether reforms to the NLRB certification process are needed.

Organizing Outside the NLRB Certification Process

Without waiting for this academic debate to be settled, or for labor law to be reformed, more and more unions are explicitly trying to organize new workers outside the NLRB certification process. In fact, the AFL–CIO claims that in recent years, more workers have been organized outside NLRB elections than through such elections.[106] For example, the

Justice for Janitors campaigns use public demonstrations to pressure commercial property owners and cleaning service contractors into recognizing unions without going through the NLRB election process. Unions are also trying to organize outside the NLRB by negotiating neutrality and card check agreements with employers in which employers agree to remain neutral in organizing drives and to recognize the union based on signed authorization cards.[107] For example, thousands of AT&T wireless employees have unionized using this card check recognition process, including network technicians, retail sales associates, and call center workers.

The Hotel Employees and Restaurant Employees union (now UNITE-HERE) has also occasionally succeeded in pressuring local governments to include these types of provisions in lease agreements when new hotels are constructed with public funds. In one case the union staffed a table in the employee cafeteria to talk with interested workers and after 32 days had sufficient cards to be recognized through a card check recognition procedure.[108] Compare this to the months (sometimes years) of hostility and warfare in standard NLRB elections. Finally, workers outside the scope of the NLRA (or other legislation) of course must also organize outside the NLRB. Notable examples are graduate assistants at private universities and agricultural workers. In California, for example, before a state law in the mid-1970s established a recognition election process, Cesar Chavez and the United Farm Workers were forced to rely on national boycotts of grapes and lettuce as well as public demonstrations (such as a 340-mile protest march from Delano to Sacramento) to win recognition for fieldworkers. At the same time, most companies resist card check agreements, and some labor activists have criticized campaigns for card check agreements that are high-level affairs pursued by national union staff disconnected from rank-and-file workers because organizing ultimately needs to be worker-focused.[109] So while organizing outside the NLRB election process has become an important issue in labor relations, it is not without its own challenges.

In a different vein, one can argue that the NLRA obligates employers to bargain with unions on a members-only basis when a union represents less than a majority of employees.[110] Therefore, another strategy for unions is to concentrate on building organizations within workplaces and signing up union members rather than on winning elections. The benefits that accrue to a small number of union members through members-only bargaining and representation can then build support among skeptical workers and perhaps ultimately create majority support and full-fledged exclusive representative status. This has the potential to drastically reshape the union organizing process, but conventional wisdom that emphasizes an all-or-nothing approach to winning majority support through NLRB elections is deeply ingrained in U.S. labor relations. Only time will tell whether members-only organizing and bargaining take hold legally and practically.

Is the Employee Free Choice Act the Answer?

To remedy the perceived deficiencies in the NLRB certification election process, in recent years the labor movement has aggressively lobbied for the enactment of the Employee Free Choice Act. As introduced in Congress in March 2009, the Employee Free Choice Act would amend the NLRA in four significant ways. First, the act would provide for card check recognition by specifying, "If the [NLRB] finds that a majority of the employees in a unit appropriate for bargaining has signed valid authorizations designating the individual or labor organization specified in the petition as their bargaining representative and that no other individual or labor organization is currently certified or recognized as the exclusive representative of any of the employees in the unit, the [NLRB] shall not direct an election but shall certify the individual or labor organization as the representative." Second, if labor and management are unable to reach agreement on a first contract after a new union is certified, an arbitration panel would impose a two-year contract upon the parties. Third, penalties for violating the NLRA during an organizing drive or first contract campaign would be strengthened by providing for treble damages (three times an individual's back pay award) for unlawful discrimination [8(a)(3) unfair labor practices] and civil penalties up to $20,000 [8(a)(1) and (3) unfair labor practices]. Fourth, the NLRB would be required to seek injunctive relief in the courts when employers commit 8(a)(1) and (3) unfair labor practices during organizing drives and first contract campaigns.

The card check recognition part of the Employee Free Choice Act has received the most publicity. Supporters argue that a card check recognition procedure is needed because employers have hijacked the election process through sophisticated and sometimes illegal campaigning, manufactured legal delays, and other tactics that have been discussed in this chapter. Card check recognition is seen as a way to avoid many of these problems because these tactics are particularly severe in the weeks that lead up to an election. Card check recognition is common in Canada, and research shows that management opposition under card check regimes is significantly less effective in thwarting unionization efforts than in traditional election regimes.[111]

Critics of the proposed Employee Free Choice Act, on the other hand, characterize it as antidemocratic by depriving workers of the secret ballot vote. There is a risk that workers will sign cards simply to stop pro-union workers from pestering or threatening them, though survey evidence does not support this contention.[112] By removing the election process, the Employee Free Choice Act is also portrayed as undermining informed employee decision making by reducing employer campaigning opportunities. But if employers were truly concerned with an informed electorate, they would not go to the lengths currently witnessed in denying unions access to employees to share their views. When he was Walmart CEO, Lee Scott was candid about his opposition to the act's intention of making organizing unions easier: "We like driving the car and we aren't going to give the steering wheel to anybody but us."[113]

Although it has not received as much public attention, the proposal for first contract arbitration is also important. Successfully obtaining union recognition does not guarantee that a union contract will be achieved. Conventional wisdom is that 25 to 30 percent of newly unionized bargaining units fail to overcome managerial resistance and secure a first contract, but at least one estimate puts this figure as high as 45 percent.[114] Critics argue that such a process would allow outsiders to impose terms and conditions of employment, but this is exactly the intent—the risk of arbitration is intended to provide an incentive to bargain rather than seeking ways to avoid negotiating a contract. In the words of a government-appointed commission that studied this issue, "once a majority of workers has voted [to unionize] the debate about whether a bargaining relationship is to be established should be over. At this point, the parties' energies and the public's resources should turn to creating an effective ongoing relationship that is suited to the needs of their workplace."[115] Evidence from Canada indicates that mandated first contract arbitration encourages voluntary settlements.[116] In the United States, arbitration is a well-established method for resolving bargaining disputes in the public sector and typically results in contracts that reflect compromise positions, not provisions that are out of line with competitors (see Chapter 8).

The labor movement campaigned hard for Barack Obama during the presidential election of 2008 and hoped to be rewarded by President Obama's support for the act. However, after the drawn-out debates over health care reform, political support for the Employee Free

Choice Act waned, and it was not voted on. If the Employee Free Choice Act is introduced again, one possible change that might make it slightly less controversial would be to add safeguards against the possibility of undue influence of union coercion in card signing campaigns, such as requiring signed cards to be accompanied by an individual's payment of the first month of union dues, setting the card check threshold at 55, 60, or even 70 percent of a defined unit of employees, and allowing the NLRB to require a secret ballot election if there are concerns about misinformation, misunderstandings, or union coercion.[117] Another safeguard would be to allow employees to secretly withdraw their support during a cooling-off period before final certification was granted.[118] An alternative is to provide for instant or snap elections in which a certification election must be held within a certain period, such as five days. Evidence from Canada suggests that this can be effective when paired with the expedited processing of unfair labor practice allegations.[119] Yet another option is to allow employees to cast confidential votes online or via telephone anytime after a union demonstrates sufficient interest to the NLRB, and once the union achieves majority support, or some other threshold, these votes could be used to demand recognition from the employer.[120]

Though unlikely during the Trump administration, passage of the Employee Free Choice Act would represent the most significant revision to the NLRA in 70 years, and it would likely make it easier for workers to successfully form unions and bargain collectively with their employers. But there would still be outstanding issues, such as unequal access to employees during organizing drives, the ability of unions to craft representational strategies that give workers what they want, and at a more fundamental level, the difficulty of getting an election held at all. Noting that the NLRA was enacted during a period of worker activism (recall the strikes of 1934), one could argue that with today's less activist workforce, "the law is like a cage built for a lion that instead confines a lamb" such that the steps for workers to get an election held are too onerous.[121] This is reflected in union attempts to organize outside the NLRB and the extreme rarity of workers themselves rather than a union filing an election petition. This leads to a more significant reform possibility: requiring that NLRB elections be conducted automatically on an annual basis in all workplaces to see if workers want to be unionized or continue to be unionized, just like political elections are regularly held to determine political representation.[122]

However, while there are various reform possibilities, the reality is that significant legal reform is unlikely in the foreseeable future. In 2014, for example, intense business lobby objections caused the NLRB to abandon its attempt to require employers to display a poster that informs employees of their existing rights and provides examples of illegal campaign tactics (see *www.nlrb.gov/poster*). This requirement would not have changed the election procedure; it only would have required displaying a poster similar to posters that are already required for minimum wages and other employee rights. That even this modest proposal generated significant controversy and legal challenge strongly suggests that the passage of the Employee Free Choice Act or other legislation that significantly changes the NLRA is unlikely.

In conclusion, this chapter has focused on the private sector union organizing process in the United States as governed by the NLRA and NLRB. This practice of using secret ballot elections to determine majority support and to bestow exclusive representation rights to a union is not representative of how unions are formed outside North America (see Chapter 12), but the process in the U.S. railway and airline industries under the Railway Labor Act and National Mediation Board is quite similar. Moreover, for occupations covered by a public sector bargaining law, the organizing process in the U.S. public sector also

Labor Relations Application Public Sector Labor Relations: Union Organizing

Recall from Chapter 4 that federal government employees are covered by the Civil Service Reform Act while state and local government employees fall within the jurisdiction of each state, which may or may not have a law pertaining to a specific occupation. Thus the organizing process for public sector employees varies from jurisdiction to jurisdiction.

In states without laws, or for occupations outside the coverage of narrow laws, workers can still form unions, but there is no established legal machinery for granting recognition to these unions. This is analogous to the pre-1935 situation in the private sector. These workers therefore must resort to economic and political pressure tactics to win recognition. Workers can try to pressure local school boards and other government officials through demonstrations and lobbying, but the most powerful weapon is the recognition strike. In fact, Martin Luther King Jr. was assassinated while visiting Memphis to support sanitation workers who were striking for recognition. Firefighters, teachers, college professors, and many other occupations in numerous states have won recognition for their unions through recognition strikes or threats of such strikes. Graduate student teaching assistants are also exempted from many state bargaining laws, but students at the University of Massachusetts–Amherst and the University of Illinois used strikes, sit-ins, and class boycotts to pressure these universities into agreeing to elections that were won by unions.

For federal, state, and local government employees covered by bargaining laws, the union certification process typically closely parallels the NLRA system described in this chapter. In the federal sector, individuals who wish to be represented by a union must file a petition with the Federal Labor Relations Authority (FLRA). The FLRA clarifies any unit definition questions, and if the petition is supported by 30 percent signed authorization cards, an election will be called (subject to the usual bars such as a contract already being in place). State laws are similar, with state agencies handling the representation process. Like the NLRB, many jurisdictions use a "community of interest" standard to define appropriate bargaining units. Public sector bargaining units are often small—in one study, half of all (nonfederal) public sector elections were for bargaining units of fewer than 15 employees. Some states also allow card check recognition if only one union is present and if management does not object. Some states extensively use mail ballots.

Perhaps the most striking difference between private and public sector representation elections is the win rate. In the private sector, unions typically win about two-thirds of elections; in the public sector the win rate is 85 percent. The margin of victory is also significantly higher in the public sector: In elections won by unions, over 80 percent of employees, on average, voted for the union. It is widely believed that public sector employers do not aggressively campaign against unions during organizing drives. Perhaps this explains the stark differences in win rates between private and public sector elections.

State-level initiatives to weaken laws pertaining to public sector unionization over the past 10 years have focused more on restricting the scope of bargaining and limiting the ability of unions to collect dues than on the certification process. But in 2011, Oklahoma and New Hampshire repealed their card check election provisions while Wisconsin enacted an annual recertification requirement requiring an established union to win an election every year to maintain its status as the authorized bargaining agent of the employees.

References: Kate Bronfenbrenner and Tom Juravich, *Union Organizing in the Public Sector: An Analysis of State and Local Elections* (Ithaca, NY: ILR Press, 1995); Richard C. Kearney and Patrice M. Mareschal, *Labor Relations in the Public Sector,* 5th ed. (Boca Raton: CRC Press, 2014).

closely follows the NLRA philosophy and machinery (see the accompanying "Public Sector Labor Relations" box). And in both the U.S. private and covered public sectors the certification of a majority union as the exclusive representative of employees obligates their employer to bargain with the union. After all, from a functional perspective this is why employees organize—to compel their employer to bargain with them collectively rather than individually. Bargaining is therefore the second major process of labor relations, and it is the topic of the next chapter.

Key Terms

representation election, *196*
authorization card, *197*
card check recognition, *199*
recognition strike, *199*
certification election, *200*
decertification election, *200*
appropriate bargaining unit, *201*
union instrumentality, *204*
TIPS, *207*
laboratory conditions doctrine, *206*
captive audience meeting, *209*
Excelsior list, *215*
Gissel bargaining order, *221*

Reflection Questions

1. Outline the pros and cons of the NLRA's election-based union recognition process. Why do labor unions seem to criticize this process more than businesses? Describe some alternative means for deciding questions of representation. What do you think would be best for the workplaces and workforce of the 21st century? Refer back to the "Labor Relations Application: The Case against Employer Campaigning" box on p. 213—should employers be excluded from the representation process?
2. In a concise paragraph, paraphrase what you have learned about union strategies in organizing drives to describe these strategies to a new union organizer.
3. Bob Ulrich, CEO of nonunion retailer Target, justifies his company's antiunion philosophy by saying that Target "simply doesn't believe that third-party representation would add anything for our customers, our employees, or our shareholders. We just do not believe it's productive and adds value."[123] Critique this stance.
4. Should employees be allowed to use company e-mail systems to discuss common work-related concerns pertaining to their wages, benefits, and other terms and conditions of employment? How about to discuss unionizing? If not, what types of restrictions should companies be allowed to place on the use of their e-mail systems?
5. The "HR Strategy" box that follows contains four scenarios of union organizing drives that end with different decision points for management. Follow the instructions at the beginning of the box to analyze these scenarios. Remember that the tone adopted by management will likely influence future relationships with the employees, and, if it is successful, the union.
6. *Nonunion Application.* Prepare an outline to record a brief video using a phone or other device that could be used to explain to managers the usefulness of "TIPS" not only as a guideline for avoiding inappropriate actions during a union organizing drive but also as a guideline for good managerial practice in situations that have nothing to do with unionization.

HR Strategy Responding to a Union Organizing Drive

For each of the four scenarios here, you are the HR manager and you need to

1. Outline your various alternatives in responding to the union organizing drive.
2. Develop and support a specific recommended course of action to present to upper management.

ACME AUTO PARTS

Acme Auto Parts is a small nonunion manufacturer of auto parts located in a small town in the South. The work is repetitive and routine. There are no particular skill or educational requirements for the production employees. Acme sells nearly all its parts to the Big Three automakers (Ford, General Motors, and Chrysler) according to the specifications they provide. The highly unionized Big Three have largely outsourced the manufacturing of parts. Many of their traditional parts suppliers have closed their unionized operations in Michigan and opened nonunion plants in the South and in Mexico. The Big Three, however, continue to face competitive cost pressures from the Japanese car companies and therefore are continually trying to wring cost concessions from their suppliers.

The parts workers at various companies that are still represented by the United Auto Workers (UAW) face demands for concessions during every contract negotiation. The UAW is therefore trying to organize the nonunion parts factories. You have seen UAW organizers in town trying to contact Acme workers for the past few weeks. This morning you overheard two workers talking about the UAW.

THE ZINNIA

The Zinnia is a 300-room hotel in the central business district of a major Midwestern metropolitan area. This is a full-service hotel—a hotel providing a wide variety of services including food and beverage facilities and meeting rooms—that caters to individual business travelers, convention attendees, and local businesspeople who need meeting space. The Zinnia emphasizes outstanding service and amenities and is owned by a prominent local real estate magnate, Ms. Lucy Baldercash, who closely monitors the management and financial performance of her diversified properties.

Many of this city's major hotels are unionized, and the Zinnia's wage rates are equal to the local union wage scale. You feel that while the Zinnia's employee benefit package is modest compared to what the union has been able to extract from your unionized competitors, it is competitive with other low-skilled occupations in the area—and is particularly generous for the undocumented immigrants that you have quietly hired to fill the dishwashing and room cleaning positions. You also feel that your unionized competitors are saddled with myriad work rules that restrict flexibility.

The local union organizes aggressively and isn't afraid to have public marches and demonstrations in support of its goal of social justice. But you thought your workers were content, and you were astonished to learn this morning that Zinnia workers have been quietly signing authorization cards. You received notice from the NLRB that a petition was filed by the local hotel union requesting an election covering back-of-the-house workers (kitchen, laundry, and room cleaning employees—not front-of-the-house employees like bellhops, bartenders, and waitresses) and that this petition was supported by signed authorization cards from 40 percent of the workers.

SCHOOL DISTRICT 273

School District 273 is a medium-sized public school district in a Northeastern state with a comprehensive bargaining law that includes teachers. The bargaining law allows strikes (except for police, firefighters, and prison guards) and also allows unions to be recognized through a card check recognition procedure if the employer does not object. Otherwise a representation election will be conducted when a petition is supported by 30 percent signed authorization cards. No employees in District 273 are represented by a union, though teachers in many neighboring districts are.

District 273 receives 75 percent of its funding from the state based on a statewide per-student funding formula; the remainder comes from local property taxes and fees. To balance the state budget, school funding was reduced by 10 percent. School budgets are also being squeezed by rising health care costs. And teachers are frustrated by the state's emphasis on standardized test scores; they feel they are losing control over educational standards and curriculum. A grassroots unionization effort started among some teachers at the district's high school near the beginning of the school year. It is now the middle of the school year, and the leaders of this grassroots effort—which they are now calling the District 273 Teacher's Association—claim to have signed authorization cards from 70 percent of the teachers, including large numbers at all the district's schools. They have asked the school board to voluntarily recognize their union and schedule bargaining sessions to hear their concerns and negotiate a contract that preserves teachers' input into the educational process.

WOODVILLE HEALTHCARE

Woodville HealthCare is a for-profit health care provider formed through the merger of several networks of physicians. It operates 50 managed care clinics and employs 400 doctors in the West. The merger has resulted in a major restructuring of operations. Several clinics have been closed, and a number of new operating guidelines have been implemented. Doctors are now required to see more patients; specialty medical procedures and non-generic prescriptions must be approved by the medical authorization department; and expensive procedures can negatively affect a doctor's salary.

Some doctors contacted a national doctors' union that is affiliated with one of the largest U.S. unions, and an organizing drive was launched. After a petition was filed with the NLRB, Woodville filed objections and argued that the doctors were supervisors and therefore excluded from the NLRA. The NLRB eventually ruled that 100 of the doctors had supervisory responsibilities, but that 300 were nonmanagerial doctors. Woodville then spent $300,000 (plus staff time) on an anti-union campaign leading up to last week's election for the 300 nonmanagerial doctors. The election results were 142 voting in favor of the union, 128 against.

This is a slim seven-vote margin, and you have until tomorrow to decide whether to appeal the results of the election by filing objections with the NLRB. Several days before the election, the union's website reported salary figures for Woodville's top executives that were grossly inflated. You have also investigated several allegations of inappropriate union campaigning on the day of the election but have uncovered only weak evidence. Your attorney predicts that there is a 20 percent chance an appeal would succeed.

Labor Law Discussion Case 4 Does a Meeting with a Supervisor Interfere with Employee Free Choice?

BACKGROUND

The International Association of Bridge, Structural, and Ornamental Iron Workers was conducting an organizing drive at a plant of the NVF Company. The election unit was determined to be all production and maintenance employees including truck drivers, shipping and receiving clerks, and all other plant clerical employees employed by NVF Company at its Hartwell, Georgia, facility, but excluding all office clerical employees, professional employees, guards, and supervisors as defined in the NLRA. An election to determine union certification was scheduled for August 16.

During the months of July and August leading up to the election, Matt Rust, general manager of the Hartwell plant, called employees into his office in groups of five or six. The purpose of the meetings was to discuss the upcoming NLRB election. Rust's remarks were not coercive, but he did express NVF's reasons for wanting the employees to vote against union representation. He solicited the employees to vote against the union. Approximately 95 percent of the employees eligible to vote participated in this type of meeting with Rust.

The employees were familiar with the general manager's office from prior experiences. For example, employees previously visited that office to obtain loans or discuss grievances. There was no other suitable location to hold such meetings.

The results of the election held on August 16 were as follows:

International Association of Bridge, Structural, and
Ornamental Iron Workers . . . . 64 votes
No union . . . . 95 votes

Shortly after the election of August 16, the union filed timely objections with the NLRB.

POTENTIALLY RELEVANT PRECEDENT

In *General Shoe Corp.* (1948) the company president brought into his office 25 groups of 20–25 employees on the day before a certification election. Each group was read the same intemperate antiunion address. The employer had also instructed foremen to propagandize employees in their homes. The NLRB invalidated the results of the election because one could not assume that the results "represented the employees' own true wishes." This decision was not, however, based on the finding of an unfair labor practice.

QUESTIONS

1. Should the election be ruled invalid? On what basis? If so, what is the appropriate remedy?
2. Do the size of the groups (five or six) and the percentage of voters involved (95%) matter?

Labor Law Discussion Case 5 Does Community Activity Interfere with Laboratory Conditions?

BACKGROUND

The International Hod Carriers' Building and Common Laborers' Union of America was conducting an organizing drive of production employees at the Monarch Rubber Company. An election to determine the preference of a majority of the workers for collective representation was scheduled for Friday, July 19.

On Thursday, July 18, the local newspaper, the *Times Record,* ran the following full-page advertisement:

> *The Times Record* Thursday July 18 A10
> Proudly serving Roane County since 1932
>
> Dear Monarch Rubber Employee,
>
> On the eve of the union election, one should fully consider the advantages and disadvantages of having a Union.
>
> The advantages and benefits to be obtained *without* a Union are clear: full employment, improved working conditions, increased earnings, and a larger future plant, to name but a few.
>
> The disadvantages of voting *for* a Union are: intermittent unemployment, AND, by union domination—
>
> a complete LOSS OF YOUR JOB!
>
> WE URGE ALL MONARCH RUBBER EMPLOYEES TO VOTE TO KEEP THEIR JOBS!
>
> VOTE <u>AGAINST</u> THE UNION.
>
> Sponsored by: A Group of Business People

The results of the election held on Friday, July 19, were as follows:

International Hod Carriers' Building and Common Laborers' Union of America	54 votes
No union	58 votes

There were 121 eligible voters. Seven ballots were challenged by the union. On July 24, the union filed timely objections with the National Labor Relations Board.

Upon investigation, it was found that on July 10, Samuel Quail, publisher of the *Times Record,* met with Kristin Day, vice president of Monarch Rubber. Quail showed Day the text of the newspaper ad. Day pointed out various items in the ad that did not pertain to the situation at Monarch Rubber. Furthermore, Quail informed Day of his intention to approach the Chamber of Commerce about sponsoring the ad. Day did not respond to this remark.

On July 15, Quail met with the treasurer of the Roane County Chamber of Commerce. Despite Quail's exhortation, the organization would not sponsor or pay for the newspaper advertisement. Consequently, Quail inserted the advertisement in Thursday's (July 18) edition of the *Times Record* free of charge and without a sponsor.

Upon seeing the advertisement in the paper, Day contacted Quail and disavowed any and all responsibility for the ad.

QUESTIONS

1. Should the election be ruled invalid? If so, what is the appropriate remedy?
2. Does Monarch Rubber have any responsibility for the ad? Does it matter?

End Notes

1. Jane McAlevey with Bob Ostertag, *Raising Expectations (and Raising Hell): My Decade Fighting for the Labor Movement* (London: Verso, 2012).
2. *International Ladies' Garment Workers (Bernhard-Altmann Texas Corp.) v. NLRB*, 366 U.S. 731 (1961).
3. Robert A. Epstein, "Breaking Down the Ivory Tower Sweatshops: Graduate Student Assistants and Their Elusive Search for Employee Status on the Private University Campus," *St. John's Journal of Legal Commentary* 20 (Fall 2005), pp. 157–98; *Columbia University*, 364 NLRB No. 90 (2016).
4. National Labor Relations Board, Statistical Tables, available at www.nlrb.gov/news-outreach/graphs-data.
5. Douglas E. Ray, Calvin William Sharpe, and Robert N. Strassfield, *Understanding Labor Law* (New York: Mathew Bender, 1999).
6. National Labor Relations Board, Regional Director, Region 34, "Decision and Direction of Election, Foxwoods Resort Casino," Case No. 34-RC-02230 (October 24, 2007).
7. *Point Park University v. NLRB* (D.C. Cir., 2006); *NLRB v. Yeshiva University*, 444 U.S. 672 (1980); Marley S. Weiss, "*Kentucky River* at the Intersection of Professional and Supervisory Status: Fertile Delta or Bermuda Triangle," in Laura J. Cooper and Catherine L. Fisk (eds.), *Labor Law Stories* (New York: Foundation Press, 2005), pp. 353–98; *Brown University*, 342 NLRB No. 42 (2004).
8. Ray, Sharpe, and Strassfield, *Understanding Labor Law*.
9. Douglas L. Leslie (ed.), *The Railway Labor Act* (Washington, DC: Bureau of National Affairs, 1995).
10. Rebecca S. Demsetz, "Voting Behavior in Union Representation Elections: The Influence of Skill Homogeneity and Skill Group Size," *Industrial and Labor Relations Review* 47 (October 1993), pp. 99–113; Henry S. Farber, "Union Success in Representation Elections: Why Does Unit Size Matter?" *Industrial and Labor Relations Review* 54 (January 2001), pp. 329–48; John-Paul Ferguson, "The Eyes of the Needles: A Sequential Model of Union Organizing Drives, 1999–2004," *Industrial and Labor Relations Review* 62 (October 2008), pp. 3–21; John-Paul Ferguson, "Racial Diversity and Union Organizing in the United States, 1999–2008," *Industrial and Labor Relations Review* 69 (January 2016), pp. 53–83.
11. *Point Park University v. NLRB* (D.C. Cir., 2006).
12. John P. Hoerr, *We Can't Eat Prestige: The Women Who Organized Harvard* (Philadelphia: Temple University Press, 1997).
13. Ferguson, "The Eyes of the Needles."
14. Brett Huckell, "Who's the Boss? Supervisors, Professionals, Independent Judgment, and the NLRA: A Post-*Oakwood Healthcare* Review," *Labor Law Journal* 59 (Fall 2008), pp. 236–64.
15. *Oakwood Healthcare, Inc.*, 348 NLRB No. 37 (2006); *Golden Crest Healthcare Center*, 348 NLRB No. 39 (2006); *Croft Metals, Inc.*, 348 NLRB No. 38 (2006); Weiss, "*Kentucky River* at the Intersection of Professional and Supervisory Status."
16. Steven E. Abraham, Adrienne E. Eaton, and Paula B. Voos, "Supreme Court Supervisory Status Decisions: The Impact on the Organizing of Nurses," in Richard N. Block et al. (eds.), *Justice on the Job: Perspectives on the Erosion of Collective Bargaining in the United States* (Kalamazoo, MI: Upjohn, 2006), pp. 163–89; Anne Marie Lofaso, "The Vanishing Employee: Putting the Autonomous Dignified Union Worker Back to Work," *Florida International Law Review* 5 (Spring 2010), pp. 495–549.
17. "Narrowing the Definition of a 'Supervisor' under the National Labor Relations Act," *Hunton & Williams LLP* (January 12, 2016).
18. Henry Farber, "Union Organizing Decisions in a Deteriorating Environment: The Composition of Representation Elections and the Decline in Turnout," *Industrial and Labor Relations Review* 68 (October 2015), pp. 1126–56.
19. National Labor Relations Board, Statistical Tables, available at www.nlrb.gov/news-outreach/graphs-data.
20. Jeffrey M. Hirsch, "NLRB Elections: Ambush or Anticlimax?" *Emory Law Journal* 64 (2015), pp. 1647–68.
21. Julian Barling, Clive Fullagar, and E. Kevin Kelloway, *The Union and Its Members: A Psychological Approach* (New York: Oxford University Press, 1992); Jack Fiorito and Angela Young, "Union Voting Intentions: Human Resource Policies, Organizational Characteristics, and Attitudes," in Kate Bronfenbrenner et al. (eds.), *Organizing to Win: New Research on Union Strategies* (Ithaca, NY: ILR Press, 1998), pp. 232–46; John Godard, "Union Formation," in Paul Blyton et al. (eds.), *Sage Handbook of Industrial Relations* (London: Sage, 2008), pp. 377–405.

22. Hoyt N. Wheeler and John A. McClendon, "The Individual Decision to Unionize," in George Strauss, Daniel G. Gallagher, and Jack Fiorito (eds.), *The State of the Unions* (Madison, WI: Industrial Relations Research Association, 1991), pp. 47–83.
23. Barling, Fullagar, and Kelloway, *The Union and its Members*; Richard B. Freeman and Joel Rogers, *What Workers Want* (Ithaca, NY: ILR Press, 1999); John Godard, "Uncertainty and the Correlates of Union Voting Propensity: An Organizing Perspective," *Industrial Relations* 50 (July 2011), pp. 472–96; Godard, "Union Formation"; Steven L. Premack and John E. Hunter, "Individual Unionization Decisions," *Psychological Bulletin* 103 (1988), pp. 223–34; Paul F. Clark, *Building More Effective Unions*, 2nd ed. (Ithaca, NY: Cornell University Press, 2009).
24. Barling, Fullagar, and Kelloway, *The Union and its Members*; Satish P. Deshpande and Jack Fiorito, "Specific and General Beliefs in Union Voting Models," *Academy of Management Journal* 32 (December 1989), pp. 883–97; Godard, "Union Formation."
25. Larry Cohen and Richard W. Hurd, "Fear, Conflict, and Union Organizing," in Kate Bronfenbrenner et al. (eds.), *Organizing to Win: New Research on Union Strategies* (Ithaca, NY: ILR Press, 1998), pp. 181–96.
26. Jack Fiorito, Daniel G. Gallagher, and Charles R. Greer, "Determinants of Unionism: A Review of the Literature," in Kenneth M. Rowland and Gerald R. Ferris (eds.), *Research in Personnel and Human Resource Management, Volume 4* (Greenwich, CT: JAI Press, 1986), pp. 269–306.
27. Barling, Fullagar, and Kelloway, *The Union and its Members*; Barry A. Friedman, Steven E. Abraham, and Randall K. Thomas, "Factors Related to Employees' Desire to Join and Leave Unions," *Industrial Relations* 45 (January 2006), pp. 102–10.
28. Deshpande and Fiorito, "Specific and General Beliefs in Union Voting Models"; Godard, "Union Formation"; Wheeler and McClendon, "The Individual Decision to Unionize"; Heejoon Park, Patrick P. McHugh, and Matthew M. Bodah, "Revisiting General and Specific Union Beliefs: The Union-Voting Intentions of Professionals," *Industrial Relations* 45 (April 2006), pp. 270–89; Seymour Martin Lipset and Noah M. Meltz, with Rafael Gomez and Ivan Katchanovski, *The Paradox of American Unionism: Why Americans Like Unions More Than Canadians Do but Join Much Less* (Ithaca, NY: Cornell University Press, 2004); Clark, *Building More Effective Unions*.
29. Lawrence Richards, *Union-Free America: Workers and Antiunion Culture* (Urbana: University of Illinois Press, 2008).
30. Alex Bryson and Rafael Gomez, "Buying into Union Membership," in Howard Gospel and Stephen Woods (eds.), *Representing Workers: Trade Union Recognition and Membership in Britain* (London: Routledge, 2003), pp. 72–91; Julian Barling, E. Kevin Kelloway, and Eric H. Bremermann, "Preemployment Predictors of Union Attitudes: The Role of Family Socialization and Work Beliefs," *Journal of Applied Psychology* 76 (October 1991), pp. 725–31.
31. Jeanette A. Davy and Frank Shipper, "Voter Behavior in Union Certification Elections: A Longitudinal Study," *Academy of Management Journal* 36 (February 1993), pp. 187–99.
32. John Kelly, *Rethinking Industrial Relations: Mobilization, Collectivism and Long Waves* (London: Routledge, 1998); Christina Cregan, Timothy Bartram, and Pauline Stanton, "Union Organizing as a Mobilizing Strategy: The Impact of Social Identity and Transformational Leadership on the Collectivism of Union Members," *British Journal of Industrial Relations* 47 (December 2009), pp. 701–22; Hoyt N. Wheeler, *Industrial Conflict: An Integrative Theory* (Columbia: University of South Carolina Press, 1985).
33. Randy Hodson, *Dignity at Work* (Cambridge, England: Cambridge University Press, 2001); Kelly, *Rethinking Industrial Relations*.
34. Immanuel Ness, *Immigrants, Unions, and the New U.S. Labor Market* (Philadelphia: Temple University Press, 2005).
35. Wheeler and McClendon, "The Individual Decision to Unionize"; Claus Schnabel, "Union Membership and Density: Some (Not So) Stylized Facts and Challenges," *European Journal of Industrial Relations* 19 (September 2013), pp. 255–72.
36. National Labor Relations Board, *Outline of Law and Procedure in Representation Cases* (Washington, DC: U.S. Government Printing Office, 2005); Ray, Sharpe, and Strassfield, *Understanding Labor Law*; Benjamin J. Taylor and Fred Witney, *Labor Relations Law*, 7th ed. (Englewood Cliffs, NJ: Prentice Hall, 1996).
37. *General Shoe Corp.*, 77 NLRB 124, 127 (1948).
38. Taylor and Witney, *Labor Relations Law*.
39. *Dayton Hudson Dept. Store v. NLRB*, 987 F.2d 359, 365 (6th Cir. 1993), on remand 314 NLRB No. 129 (1994), affd. 79 F.3d 546 (1996).
40. *Peerless Plywood Co.*, 107 NLRB 427 (1954).

41. National Labor Relations Board, *Outline of Law and Procedure in Representation Cases*; Taylor and Witney, *Labor Relations Law.*
42. *Plant City Welding and Tank Co.,* 119 NLRB 131 (1957).
43. *NLRB v. Babcock & Wilcox Co.,* 351 U.S. 105 (1956).
44. *Lechmere, Inc. v. NLRB,* 112 U.S. 841 (1992); Cynthia L. Estlund, "Labor, Property, and Sovereignty after *Lechmere,*" *Stanford Law Review* 46 (January 1994), pp. 305–59.
45. Ray, Sharpe, and Strassfield, *Understanding Labor Law.*
46. *Republic Aviation v. NLRB,* 324 U.S. 793 (1945).
47. Cory R. Fine, "Union Salting: Reactions and Rulings since *Town and Country,*" *Journal of Labor Research* 23 (Summer 2002), pp. 475–85; James L. Fox, "'Salting' the Construction Industry," *William Mitchell Law Review* 24 (1998), pp. 681–712.
48. *NLRB v. Town and Country Electric,* 516 U.S. 85 (1995).
49. *Toering Electric Company*, 351 NLRB No. 18 (2007).
50. *Hammary Mfg. Corp.,* 265 NLRB 57 (1982).
51. *New York Telephone Company,* 304 NLRB No. 33 (1991).
52. *NLRB v. Stowe Spinning Co.,* 336 U.S. 226 (1949); *Price Chopper,* 325 NLRB 186 (1997).
53. Christine O'Brien, "Employees on Guard: Employer Policies Restrict NLRA-Protected Concerted Activities on E-mail," *Oregon Law Review* 88 (2009), pp. 195–253.
54. *Purple Communications, Inc.*, 361 NLRB No. 126 (2014) at p. 1.
55. John J. Lawler, *Unionization and Deunionization: Strategy, Tactics, and Outcomes* (Columbia: University of South Carolina Press, 1990); John Logan, "The Union Avoidance Industry in the United States," *British Journal of Industrial Relations* 44 (December 2006), pp. 651–75.
56. Martin Jay Levitt and Terry Conrow, *Confessions of a Union Buster* (New York: Crown Publishers, 1993).
57. http://abcnews.go.com/onair/2020/2020_000128_unions_feature.html (accessed August 14, 2003).
58. Lawler, *Unionization and Deunionization*; Levitt and Conrow, *Confessions of a Union Buster*; Paul Weiler, "Promises to Keep: Securing Workers' Rights to Self-Organization under the NLRA," *Harvard Law Review* 96 (June 1983), pp. 1769–827.
59. Toni Gilpin, Gary Isaac, Dan Letwin, and Jack McKivigan, *On Strike for Respect: The Clerical and Technical Workers' Strike at Yale University, 1984–85* (Urbana: University of Illinois Press, 1995); Hoerr, *We Can't Eat Prestige*.
60. Chris Riddell, "The Causal Effect of Election Delay on Union Win Rates: Instrumental Variable Estimates from Two Natural Experiments," *Industrial Relations* 49 (July 2010), pp. 371–86.
61. Paul C. Weiler, "A Principled Reshaping of Labor Law for the Twenty-First Century," *University of Pennsylvania Journal of Labor and Employment Law* 3 (Winter 2001), pp. 177–206; Weiler, "Promises to Keep."
62. John Schmitt and Ben Zipperer, "Dropping the Ax: Illegal Firings during Union Election Campaigns, 1951–2007" (Washington, DC: Center for Economic and Policy Research, 2009).
63. Richard B. Freeman and Joel Rogers, "Who Speaks for Us? Employee Representation in a Nonunion Labor Market," in Bruce E. Kaufman and Morris M. Kleiner (eds.), *Employee Representation: Alternatives and Future Directions* (Madison, WI: Industrial Relations Research Association, 1993), pp. 13–80 at p. 31.
64. Kate Bronfenbrenner, "The Role of Union Strategies in NLRB Certification Elections," *Industrial and Labor Relations Review* 50 (January 1997), pp. 195–212; Kate Bronfenbrenner, "No Holds Barred—The Intensification of Employer Opposition to Organizing," *EPI Briefing Paper No. 235* (Washington, DC: Economic Policy Institute, 2009); Richard B. Freeman and Morris M. Kleiner, "Employer Behavior in the Face of Union Organizing Drives," *Industrial and Labor Relations Review* 43 (April 1990), pp. 351–65; Lawler, *Unionization and Deunionization*.
65. Sanford M. Jacoby, "American Exceptionalism Revisited: The Importance of Management," in Sanford M. Jacoby (ed.), *Masters to Managers: Historical and Comparative Perspectives on American Employers* (New York: Columbia University Press, 1991), pp. 173–200; Daphne Gottlieb Taras, "Collective Bargaining Regulation in Canada and the United States: Divergent Cultures, Divergent Outcomes," in Bruce E. Kaufman (ed.), *Government Regulation of the Employment Relationship* (Madison, WI: Industrial Relations Research Association, 1997), pp. 295–341; Rick Fantasia and Kim Voss, *Hard Work: Remaking the American Labor Movement* (Berkeley: University of California Press, 2004).

66. Bronfenbrenner, "The Role of Union Strategies in NLRB Certification Elections"; Bronfenbrenner "No Holds Barred"; Freeman and Kleiner, "Employer Behavior in the Face of Union Organizing Drives"; Lawler, *Unionization and Deunionization*.
67. Julius G. Getman, Stephen B. Goldberg, and Jeanne B. Herman, *Union Representation Elections: Law and Reality* (New York: Russell Sage, 1976).
68. William T. Dickens, "The Effect of Company Campaigns on Certification Elections: *Law and Reality* Once Again," *Industrial and Labor Relations Review* 36 (July 1983), pp. 560–75.
69. Ferguson, "The Eyes of the Needles."
70. Levitt and Conrow, *Confessions of a Union Buster,* p. xi.
71. Freeman and Rogers, *What Workers Want*.
72. Freeman and Kleiner, "Employer Behavior in the Face of Union Organizing Drives."
73. Jack Fiorito and Paul Jarley, "Union Organizing and Union Revitalization in the United States," *Proceedings of the Sixtieth Annual Meeting* (Champaign, IL: Labor and Employment Relations Association, 2008), pp. 92–100; Richard W. Hurd, "Contesting the Dinosaur Image: The Labor Movement's Search for a Future," *Labor Studies Journal* 22 (Winter 1998), pp. 5–30.
74. Taylor and Witney, *Labor Relations Law.*
75. *Smith Co.,* 192 NLRB 1098, 1101 (1971).
76. Ray, Sharpe, and Strassfield, *Understanding Labor Law*.
77. *Excelsior Underwear,* 156 NLRB 1236 (1966).
78. Leonard Bierman, "Toward a New Model for Union Organizing: The Home Visits Doctrine and Beyond," *Boston College Law Review* 27 (December 1985), pp. 1–35.
79. *Plant City Welding and Tank Co.,* 119 NLRB 131, pp. 133–34 (1957).
80. Richard B. Peterson, Thomas W. Lee, and Barbara Finnegan, "Strategies and Tactics in Union Organizing Campaigns," *Industrial Relations* 31 (Spring 1992), pp. 370–81.
81. Bronfenbrenner, "The Role of Union Strategies in NLRB Certification Elections"; Kate Bronfenbrenner and Tom Juravich, "It Takes More Than House Calls: Organizing to Win with a Comprehensive Union Building Strategy," in Kate Bronfenbrenner et al. (eds.), *Organizing to Win: New Research on Union Strategies* (Ithaca, NY: ILR Press, 1998), pp. 19–36.
82. Andy Banks and Jack Metzgar, "Participating in Management: Union Organizing on a New Terrain," *Labor Research Review* 14 (Fall 1989), pp. 1–55; Bill Fletcher, Jr., and Richard W. Hurd, "Beyond the Organizing Model: The Transformation Process in Local Unions," in Kate Bronfenbrenner et al. (eds.), *Organizing to Win: New Research on Union Strategies* (Ithaca, NY: ILR Press, 1998), pp. 37–53.
83. Gregor Gall (ed.), *The Future of Union Organising: Building for Tomorrow* (Basingstoke, UK: Palgrave Macmillan, 2009); Gregor Gall (ed.), *Union Revitalisation in Advanced Economies: Assessing the Contribution of Union Organising* (Basingstoke, UK: Palgrave Macmillan, 2009); Bill Barry, *From First Contact to First Contract: A Union Organizer's Handbook* (Annapolis: Union Communication Services, 2012); McAlevey, *Raising Expectations (and Raising Hell).*
84. Saul D. Alinsky, *Rules for Radicals: A Practical Primer for Realistic Radicals* (New York: Random House, 1971).
85. Bruce Nissen and Seth Rosen, "Community-Based Organizing: Transforming Union Organizing Programs from the Bottom Up," in Bruce Nissen (ed.), *Which Direction for Organized Labor? Essays on Organizing, Outreach, and Internal Transformations* (Detroit: Wayne State University Press, 1999), pp. 59–73; Barry, *From First Contact to First Contract.* McAlevey, *Raising Expectations (and Raising Hell).*
86. Ness, *Immigrants, Unions, and the New U.S. Labor Market*; Ruth Milkman and Ed Ott (eds.), *New Labor in New York: Precarious Worker Organizing and the Future of Unionism* (Ithaca, NY: Cornell University Press, 2014); Janice Fine, "Alternative Labour Protection Movements in the United States: Reshaping Industrial Relations?" *International Labour Review* 154 (March 2015), pp. 15–26.
87. Hoerr, *We Can't Eat Prestige.*
88. Marion Crain, "Gender and Union Organizing," *Industrial and Labor Relations Review* 47 (January 1994), pp. 227–48; Kris Rondeau and Gladys McKenzie, "Women's Ways of Organizing," *Labor Research Review* 18 (1991), pp. 45–59.
89. Cohen and Hurd, "Fear, Conflict, and Union Organizing"; Victor G. Devinatz, "The Fears of Resource Standardization and the Creation of an Adversarial Workplace Climate: The Struggle to Organize a Faculty Union at Illinois State University," in David Lewin and Bruce Kaufman (eds.), *Advances in Industrial and Labor Relations, Volume 11* (Amsterdam: Elsevier, 2002), pp. 145–79.

90. Cohen and Hurd, "Fear, Conflict, and Union Organizing," p. 195.
91. Craig Becker, "Democracy in the Workplace: Union Representation Elections and Federal Labor Law," *Minnesota Law Review* 77 (February 1993), pp. 495–603.
92. *Linden Lumber Division, Summer & Co. v. NLRB,* 419 U.S. 301 (1974).
93. *NLRB v. Virginia Electric and Power Company,* 314 U.S. 469 (1941).
94. Gary N. Chaison and Joseph B. Rose, "The Macrodeterminants of Union Growth and Decline," in George Strauss, Daniel G. Gallagher and Jack Fiorito (eds.), *The State of the Unions* (Madison, WI: Industrial Relations Research Association, 1991), pp. 3–46; Phil Comstock and Maier B. Fox, "Employer Tactics and Labor Law Reform," in Sheldon Friedman et al. (eds.), *Restoring the Promise of American Labor Law* (Ithaca, NY: ILR Press, 1994), pp. 90–109; Richard B. Freeman, "Why Are Unions Faring So Poorly in NLRB Representation Elections?" in Thomas A. Kochan (ed.), *Challenges and Choices Facing American Labor* (Cambridge, MA: MIT Press, 1985), pp. 45–64; Michael Goldfield, *The Decline of Organized Labor in the United States* (Chicago: University of Chicago Press, 1987); James A. Gross, *Broken Promise: The Subversion of U.S. Labor Relations Policy, 1947–1994* (Philadelphia: Temple University Press, 1995); Weiler, "Promises to Keep."
95. Ferguson, "The Eyes of the Needles."
96. Bierman, "Toward a New Model for Union Organizing"; Charles B. Craver, *Can Unions Survive? The Rejuvenation of the American Labor Movement* (New York: New York University Press, 1993); Samuel Estreicher, "Labor Law Reform in a World of Competitive Product Markets," *Chicago-Kent Law Review* 69 (1993), pp. 3–46; Jeffrey M. Hirsch, "The Silicon Bullet: Will the Internet Kill the NLRA?" *George Washington Law Review* 76 (February 2008), pp. 262–304.
97. *Bonwit Teller, Inc.,* 96 NLRB 608 (1951).
98. Craver, *Can Unions Survive?*; Estreicher, "Labor Law Reform in a World of Competitive Product Markets"; Randall J. White, "Union Representation Election Reform: Equal Access and the *Excelsior* Rule," *Indiana Law Journal* 67 (Winter 1991), pp. 129–67.
99. Estlund, "Labor, Property, and Sovereignty after *Lechmere*"; Karl E. Klare, "Workplace Democracy and Market Reconstruction: An Agenda for Legal Reform," *Catholic University Law Review* 38 (Fall 1988), pp. 1–68; Sarah Korn, "Property Rights and Job Security: Workplace Solicitation by Nonemployee Union Organizers," *Yale Law Journal* 94 (December 1984), pp. 374–93.
100. Craver, *Can Unions Survive?*; William B. Gould, *Agenda for Reform: The Future of Employment Relationships and the Law* (Cambridge, MA: MIT Press, 1993); Morris M. Kleiner and David Weil, "Evaluating the Effectiveness of National Labor Relations Act Remedies: Analysis and Comparison with Other Workplace Penalty Policies," in Cynthia L. Estlund and Michael L. Wachter (eds.), *Research Handbook on the Economics of Labor and Employment Law* (Northampton, MA: Edward Elgar, 2012), pp. 209–47.
101. *NLRB v. Gissel Packing Company,* 395 U.S. 575 (1969); Laura J. Cooper and Dennis R. Nolan, "The Story of *NLRB v. Gissel Packing*: The Practical Limits of Paternalism," in Laura J. Cooper and Catherine L. Fisk (eds.), *Labor Law Stories* (New York: Foundation Press, 2005), pp. 191–239.
102. Commission on the Future of Worker–Management Relations, *Report and Recommendations* (Washington, DC: U.S. Departments of Labor and Commerce, 1994); Gould, *Agenda for Reform*; Weiler, "Promises to Keep."
103. David L. Cingranelli, "International Election Standards and NLRB Representation Elections," in Richard N. Block et al. (eds.), *Justice on the Job: Perspectives on the Erosion of Collective Bargaining in the United States* (Kalamazoo, MI: Upjohn, 2006), pp. 41–56.
104. Chaison and Rose, "The Macrodeterminants of Union Growth and Decline."
105. James T. Bennett and Jason E. Taylor, "Labor Unions: Victims of Their Political Success?" *Journal of Labor Research* 22 (Spring 2001), pp. 261–73; Henry S. Farber and Alan B. Krueger, "Union Membership in the United States: The Decline Continues," in Bruce E. Kaufman and Morris M. Kleiner (eds.), *Employee Representation: Alternatives and Future Directions* (Madison, WI: Industrial Relations Research Association, 1993), pp. 105–34; Leo Troy, *Beyond Unions and Collective Bargaining* (Armonk, NY: M. E. Sharpe, 1999); McAlevey, *Raising Expectations (and Raising Hell).*
106. James Brudney, "Neutrality Agreements and Card Check Recognition: Prospects for Changing Paradigms," *Iowa Law Review* 90 (March 2005), pp. 819–86.
107. Paul F. Clark, John T. Delaney, and Ann C. Frost (eds.), *Collective Bargaining in the Private Sector* (Champaign, IL: Industrial Relations Research Association, 2002); Adrienne E. Eaton and Jill Kriesky, "Dancing with the Smoke Monster: Employer Motivations for Negotiating Neutrality and Card Check Agreements," in Richard N. Block et al. (eds.), *Justice on the Job: Perspectives on the Erosion of Collective Bargaining in the United States* (Kalamazoo, MI: Upjohn, 2006), pp. 139–60; Julius G. Getman, *Restoring the Power of Unions: It Takes a Movement* (New Haven, CT: Yale University Press, 2010).

108. John W. Budd and Paul K. Heinz, “Union Representation Elections and Labor Law Reform: Lessons from the Minneapolis Hilton,” *Labor Studies Journal* 20 (Winter 1996), pp. 3–20.
109. Jane McAlevey, “The Crisis of New Labor and Alinsky’s Legacy: Revisiting the Role of the Organic Grassroots Leaders in Building Powerful Organizations and Movements,” *Politics & Society* 43 (September 2015), pp. 415–41.
110. Charles J. Morris, *The Blue Eagle at Work: Reclaiming Democratic Rights in the American Workplace* (Ithaca, NY: Cornell University Press, 2005); Catherine Fisk and Xenia Tashlitsky, “Imagine a World Where Employers Are Required to Bargain with Minority Unions,” *ABA Journal of Labor and Employment Law* 27 (Fall 2011), pp. 1–22.
111. Godard, “Union Formation”; Chris Riddell, “Union Certification Success under Voting versus Card-Check Procedures: Evidence from British Columbia, 1978–1998,” *Industrial and Labor Relations Review* 57 (July 2004), pp. 493–517; Terry Thomason, “The Effect of Accelerated Certification Procedures on Union Organizing Success in Ontario,” *Industrial and Labor Relations Review* 47 (January 1994), pp. 207–26.
112. Adrienne E. Eaton and Jill Kriesky, “NLRB Elections versus Card Check Campaigns: Results of a Worker Survey,” *Industrial and Labor Relations Review* 62 (January 2009), pp. 157–72.
113. Kimberly Morrison, “Wal-Mart Focuses On Improving Assets, Products,” *The Morning News* (Springdale, Arkansas), October 28, 2008.
114. Bronfenbrenner and Juravich, “It Takes More Than House Calls”; Commission on the Future of Worker–Management Relations, *Fact Finding Report* (Washington, DC: U.S. Departments of Labor and Commerce, 1994); Ferguson, “The Eyes of the Needles.”
115. Commission on the Future of Worker–Management Relations, *Report and Recommendation*, p. 21.
116. Susan J. T. Johnson, “First Contract Arbitration: Effects on Bargaining and Work Stoppages,” *Industrial and Labor Relations Review* 63 (July 2010), pp. 585–605; Chris Riddell, “Labor Law and Reaching a First Collective Agreement: Evidence From a Quasi-Experimental Set of Reforms in Ontario,” *Industrial Relations* 52 (July 2013), pp. 702–36; Bradley R. Weinberg, “A Quantitative Assessment of the Effect of First Contract Arbitration on Bargaining Relationships,” *Industrial Relations* 55 (July 2015), pp. 449–77.
117. Stephen F. Befort and John W. Budd, *Invisible Hands, Invisible Objectives: Bringing Workplace Law and Public Policy into Focus* (Stanford, CA: Stanford University Press, 2009).
118. Brishen Rogers, “‘Acting Like A Union’: Protecting Workers’ Free Choice By Promoting Workers’ Collective Action,” *Harvard Law Review Forum* (2010), pp. 38–54.
119. Michele Campolieti, Chris Riddell, and Sara Slinn, “Certification Delay under Elections and Card-Check Procedures: Empirical Evidence from Canada,” *Industrial and Labor Relations Review* 61 (October 2007), pp. 32–58.
120. Benjamin I. Sachs, “Enabling Employee Choice: A Structural Approach to the Rules of Union Organizing,” *Harvard Law Review* 123 (January 2010), pp. 655–728.
121. Michael M. Oswalt, “Automatic Elections,” *UC Irvine Law Review* 4 (May 2014), pp. 801–56.
122. Oswalt, “Automatic Elections.”
123. Chris Serres, “Teflon Target,” *Star Tribune*, May 22, 2005, pp. D1, D4.

Chapter **Seven**

Bargaining

Advance Organizer

Once a union is organized by a group of employees and recognized by an employer through the process outlined in the previous chapter, the next goal of the employees is for the union to negotiate a contract with the employer. Most contracts are then renegotiated every two to three years. This chapter discusses the behavioral, strategic, and legal aspects of collectively bargaining contracts in U.S. labor relations.

Learning Objectives

By the end of this chapter, you should be able to

1. **Sketch** the steps of the bargaining.
2. **Define** the different types of bargaining structures.
3. **Discuss** the determinants and importance of bargaining power.
4. **Explain** the legal parameters of the U.S. bargaining process.
5. **Outline** the four subprocesses of bargaining (distributive bargaining, integrative bargaining, attitudinal structuring, and intraorganizational bargaining), their purposes, and their tactics.
6. **Understand** the pressures for changing from traditional to integrative bargaining, and why this is difficult.

Contents

One of the main goals of the U.S. labor relations system is to allow employees to *negotiate* their terms and conditions of employment with their employer as a group, instead of individually taking or leaving whatever their employer offers unilaterally. As a result, "the union at work is the union negotiating a contract."[1] Through the process of collective bargaining, employers and unions negotiate terms and conditions of employment, and put these terms into written contracts, also called collective bargaining agreements. In the United States these contracts are legally binding and typically last one to five years, with a three-year duration being the most common. U.S. union contracts usually include the following subjects:

- *Compensation:* wages, benefits, vacations and holidays, shift premiums, profit sharing.
- *Personnel policies and procedures:* layoff, promotion, and transfer policies, overtime and vacation rules.
- *Employee rights and responsibilities:* seniority rights, job standards, workplace rules.
- *Employer rights and responsibilities:* management rights, just cause discipline and discharge, subcontracting, safety standards.

- *Union rights and responsibilities:* recognition as bargaining agent, bulletin board, union security, dues checkoff, shop stewards, no strike clauses.
- *Dispute resolution and ongoing decision making:* grievance procedures, committees, consultation, renegotiation procedures.

Compensation items might also be referred to as economic issues, and the other areas are called administrative or language issues.

But how are these contracts actually negotiated? You can probably imagine the scene: a cluttered conference table littered with paper, laptops, water bottles, and coffee cups flanked by a management team lined up on one side, with their union/employee counterparts on the other. Everyone is tired from a marathon negotiating session. No one wants a strike or a lockout, but at least some on each side think they can get a better deal. So discussions continue—sometimes in measured tones, sometimes with great animation and emotion, sometimes across the table, and sometimes in private management-only and union-only caucuses. Options are explored, trade-offs considered, and proposals refused and countered at the right time, all while trying to discern the other side's strategies and motivations. Bargaining can be exhilarating and exhausting, intimidating yet intriguing. But much more is involved than meets the eye: months of preparation, a bargaining environment that determines relative bargaining power, legal standards that bind the parties, alternative negotiating strategies to choose from, and constituencies not present at the table who will be the ultimate judges of the negotiation's outcomes.

This chapter follows the negotiating process from preparation to agreement, and for each step of the process explores the major concepts that negotiators should understand about labor–management bargaining. To complement this analytical approach (or what some might call the "science of bargaining") the Zinnia bargaining simulation described in Appendix D provides the opportunity to experience the dynamism of bargaining firsthand—that is, to practice the "art of bargaining." You will then be ready to do what all labor negotiators do: prepare-explore-agree-implement.

PREPARING TO BARGAIN

A time line of the negotiation process is shown in Figure 7.1. Note that the longest portion of the time line is the preparation stage, which usually begins at least several months before bargaining begins, or even 18 months before the start of a particularly large, complex, or pattern-setting negotiation.[2] First, a team must be assembled. For the employer team, managerial roles typically determine bargaining team responsibilities, whereas union bargaining committees are usually elected by the rank and file. Also, a national union staff representative might assist or lead the negotiations for the union. The next step in preparing for negotiations is collecting information. Managers might collect external benchmarking data on labor costs and other items and should also review the organization's financial performance and strategic plans. The union negotiating committee will likely survey the rank and file to identify their top priorities, such as wage increases, benefits improvements, additional vacation days, or new contractual language governing specific policies such as layoffs or promotions. Union negotiators might also consult with their national union regarding compensation and benefits trends, recent settlements, and strategic advice. Both sides should also conduct thorough reviews of how the expiring collective bargaining agreement has performed, and sections of the contract that have created problems should be noted. For example, if contract language on the assignment of overtime has generated numerous grievances, the negotiating teams might want to consider negotiating a revised procedure for assigning overtime.

FIGURE 7.1
The Bargaining Time Line

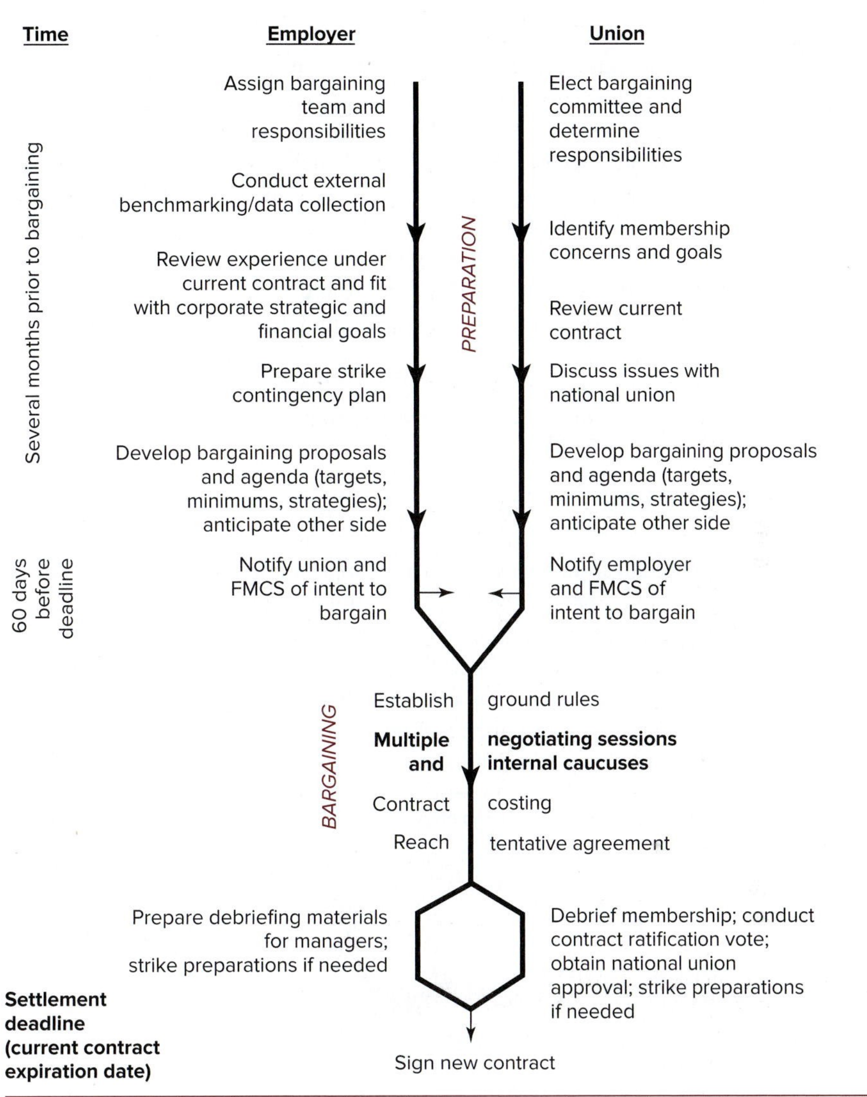

These pieces of information form the basis for each side to determine five essential things:

1. Their interests (what they are really concerned about).
2. Options for achieving their interests.
3. External benchmarks of fairness.
4. The other side's interests.
5. Their best alternative to a negotiated agreement (BATNA) (described later in this chapter).[3]

From these, both bargaining teams develop targets, priorities, and strategies. For example, a company's negotiators might want to negotiate a wage freeze, increased health care co-pays, more flexible language on job transfers, and a host of other changes, but it should also prioritize these desired changes by considering the importance of each one for its operational and strategic objectives. Similarly, the rank and file likely want improvements on many fronts, but the union negotiating team will need to use responses to a bargaining survey and other information to determine which changes are the most important and the most feasible. Extensive checklists for both employer and union negotiators are available to help guide preparation activities.[4] Creating a strike contingency plan is another important aspect of bargaining preparations (see Chapter 8). Sixty days before the existing contract expires, or 90 days in the health care industry, the parties provide official notification to each other and to the Federal Mediation and Conciliation Service that they intend to negotiate a new contract (you can see monthly lists of these F-7 filings at *www.fmcs.gov/resources/documents-and-data/*). The bargaining teams then establish a schedule of bargaining sessions and set ground rules. If the parties desire, a joint training session might also be completed at this time. And then it is time to bargain.

Before we turn to the bargaining table, however, two important topics set the stage for understanding what happens there. First, the bargaining structure describes the organizational nature of the negotiations—that is, what workplaces the negotiations cover. Second, the bargaining environment determines the relative bargaining power of the two parties.

BARGAINING STRUCTURE

Recall from Chapter 6 that an appropriate bargaining unit is defined during the representation process. This unit is the minimal unit for collective bargaining. Once certified, however, multiple units can be combined into a single larger bargaining unit for the purposes of negotiating a contract if the parties agree. The resulting organizational structure for the collective bargaining process is called the **bargaining structure.** Graphical representations of four major examples of the bargaining structure are presented in Figure 7.2. Bargaining

FIGURE 7.2
Four Types of Bargaining Structures

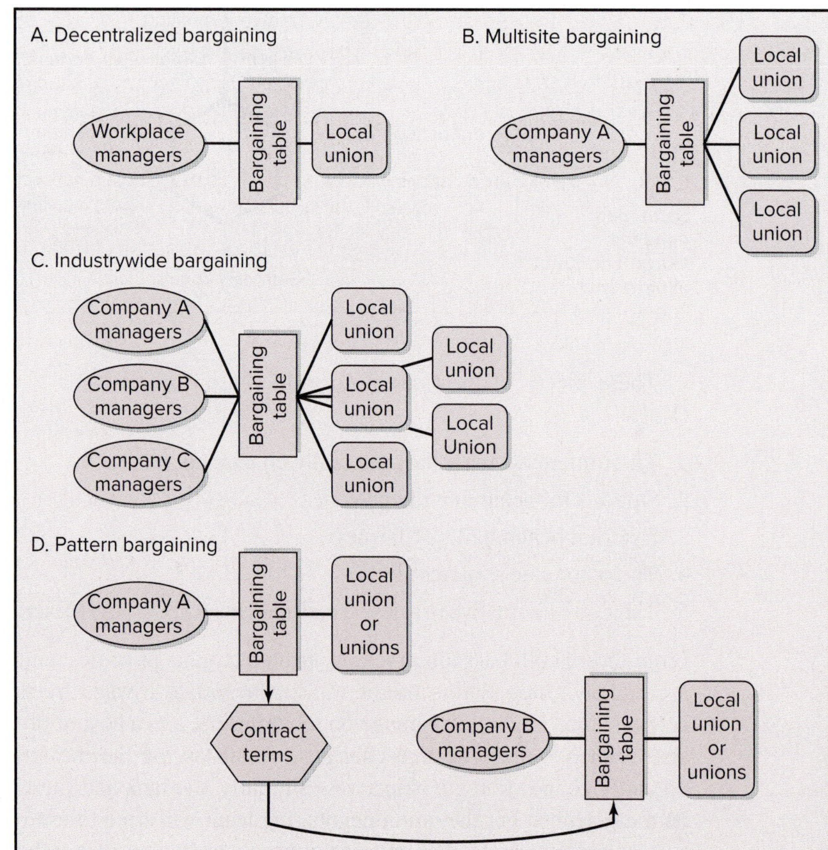

structures range from decentralized to centralized. A very decentralized bargaining structure involves a limited group of employees in a single workplace—for example, meat cutters in a single grocery store or school bus drivers in a single school district. At the other end of the range, a very centralized bargaining structure involves numerous occupations, locations, and companies, such as the industrywide bargaining that occurred between the basic steel manufacturers and the United Steelworkers union between the 1950s and 1980s.[5]

The conventional wisdom is that in many situations, employers prefer decentralized bargaining structures to have local unions compete against one another for jobs (this is called "whipsawing") and to tailor contracts to local situations. Unions are generally believed to prefer more centralized structures because they can consolidate their power and prevent whipsawing by negotiating uniform contracts (this is called "taking wages out of competition"). Compared to many other countries, the bargaining structure in the United States is typically decentralized. Before competitive pressures intensified in the 1970s, less than 15 percent of union contracts in manufacturing covered more than one employer, and the most common bargaining structure consisted of multiple sites within a single company but was less than completely firmwide.[6] Since then the bargaining structure in the United States (and in many other countries) has become more decentralized.[7] Industrywide arrangements such as in basic steel have broken apart into company-by-company negotiations, and in previously firm-centered negotiations, plant-level variation has become more important. The leading explanations for this trend appear to be that employers have been able to use their greater bargaining leverage to force more decentralization and also that both firms and workers like the flexibility and opportunities for employee involvement in decision making allowed by decentralized bargaining structures (see Chapter 12).

Another type of bargaining structure is **pattern bargaining.** For example, the United Auto Workers (UAW) explicitly selects Ford, General Motors, or Chrysler as the target company for its auto industry contract negotiations every three years. The union bargains exclusively with that target company until an agreement is reached. That target settlement is then used by the union as the pattern for subsequent negotiations in the auto industry and other manufacturing industries.[8] Note that this sequential bargaining process is an informal way of achieving a more centralized bargaining structure—unions negotiate with one company at a time, but the contracts that follow the pattern end up being similar (though not identical). Before the 1980s, pattern bargaining was a prominent feature of collective bargaining in many industries. Consistent with the broad trend toward decentralization, pattern bargaining appears to have weakened since 1980, but it has not disappeared.[9] Pattern bargaining can help unions take wages out of competition, but there are also intraorganizational bargaining reasons: Within the UAW, for example, internal union political pressures stemming from rank-and-file comparisons of different contracts cause negotiators to pattern contracts after each other, even across different industries.[10]

When determining the desired bargaining structure, labor and management negotiators face a trade-off between power and responsiveness. Compared to a centralized bargaining structure, decentralized bargaining can be more responsive to local needs because the issues are often more homogeneous and the negotiators are close to their constituents. But decentralized bargaining can also reduce labor's bargaining power. If a union is negotiating only for meat cutters in a single grocery store, the union likely has little strike leverage because management can weather the strike simply by replacing the small number of meat cutters and by continuing to earn profits at other grocery stores owned by the same company. Compare this weak strike leverage to the more common grocery store bargaining structures in which the United Food and Commercial Workers negotiates a single contract for all grocery stores in a metropolitan area or for all stores in a single chain. In the former case it is more difficult to hire replacement workers because of the number of positions that need to be filled; in the latter scenario, a company for which all locations are shut down by a strike loses all sources of revenue. However, as negotiations become more centralized, the number of issues increases, labor and management negotiators become further removed from their constituents, and it is more difficult to tailor local solutions for specific problems. The current trend is toward greater decentralization, in the United States and elsewhere, to be more flexible and responsive to local needs of both workers and companies; but this is not without its costs and critics because decentralization reduces labor's bargaining power.

BARGAINING POWER AND THE BARGAINING ENVIRONMENT

Bargaining does not take place in a vacuum. The negotiators know that they are situated in a complex environment that provides opportunities and constraints. Consequently, what happens at the bargaining table reflects differences in relative **bargaining power** between labor and management. In fact, a critical reason that U.S. labor law protects workers' efforts at forming unions and engaging in collective bargaining is to better balance bargaining power between a company and its employees. But what is bargaining power? A popular conceptualization is "the ability to secure another's agreement on one's own terms."[11] This ability depends on the relative costs of agreeing and disagreeing. If management calculates that it is more costly to disagree with a union's proposed contract terms and endure a strike than it is to agree to the proposal, then management will accept the proposal. Unions face the same calculation. Thus the side that can impose greater disagreement costs on the other will be in a more powerful position.

Strikes are the most important way for unions to impose disagreement costs on employers, so relative bargaining power is closely related to a union's strike leverage. A union with strong strike leverage can impose significant costs on management through a strike, and labor in this situation has strong bargaining power relative to the employer. The contract terms that result from this negotiation are expected to favor the employees. The reverse is true if a union has weak strike leverage.

Analyzing relative bargaining power—or strike leverage—consists of identifying the important elements of the **bargaining environment.** The bargaining environment is the diverse set of external influences on labor and management as they sit at a bargaining table negotiating a contract. Chapter 5 described how legal, economic, and sociopolitical pressures shape the ability of employers and unions to achieve their labor relations goals. Considering the bargaining environment is a specific application of this more general inquiry—namely to the question of achieving bargaining goals via a combination of employers' ability to pay (or alternatively, to withstand strikes) and unions' ability to mount successful strikes. Table 7.1 provides some examples from the grocery industry. The concepts derived from these examples are easily extended to other industries or occupations (go ahead, try it!).

The dimensions of the bargaining environment apply equally well to the private and public sectors (see Table 7.2 for a public sector example). Laws specify what public sector employers and unions can and cannot do. The labor market determines how easily striking workers can be replaced or find comparable jobs elsewhere. Labor-saving technology, such as single-operator garbage trucks that hydraulically lift garbage cans, puts the same pressure on public sector collective bargaining as in the private sector.[12] But there are at least two key differences between the public and private sectors. First, although some services can be privatized or outsourced, essential services must still be provided. Public sector management does not have the option of moving to a different location in search of lower labor costs. This places an important constraint on the business strategies available to public sector managers. Second, public services are not bought and sold in economic

TABLE 7.1
The Bargaining Environment: Examples from the Grocery Industry

Dimension	Examples
1. Legal	• Grocery stores can legally hire replacement workers during strikes.
	• Grocery store wages are anchored by the level of the minimum wage.
	• Unions cannot block the introduction of new technologies like scanners.
2. Economic	• Grocery store employees can be easily replaced in a loose labor market (high unemployment), and it may be difficult for workers to find work elsewhere.
	• Increased grocery store competition with restaurants and discount retailers reduces the grocery industry's ability to pass costs to consumers, and gives customers alternatives during a strike.
	• Technological change reduces demand for skilled meat cutters and makes it easier for grocery stores to find replacement workers.
3. Sociopolitical	• Unions can lobby against zoning permits for discount retailers that bring increased product market competition.
	• The community might support a strike if it sympathizes with the plight of part-time grocery workers.

TABLE 7.2
The Bargaining Environment: Examples for Public School Teachers

Dimension	Examples
1. Legal	• Depending on state law, the school district might not have a legal obligation to collectively bargain, and teachers might not have the right to strike.
	• Some key working and operational conditions might be set by state law, such as tenure protections, the number of instructional days per year, and student testing requirements.
2. Economic	• State-mandated teacher certification might shelter teachers from labor market competition while also making it harder for teachers to leave their state to find teaching jobs.
	• Traditional school districts might face competition from private schools, online schools, and charter schools (note: this is also a sociopolitical issue because lawmakers determine the types of approved and funded alternative schools).
3. Socio-political	• Unions can work with parents and other community members to lobby for increased taxpayer funding.
	• Taxpayers may revolt if taxes are too high.
	• Teachers unions are under attack from conservative groups for protecting poor teachers and opposing pay-for-performance.
	• School board members are elected.

markets; instead the levels of services are ultimately determined by voters, taxpayers, and elected officials in the political arena. This heightens the importance of the sociopolitical dimension of the bargaining environment.

In fact, these differences lead some to argue that public sector collective bargaining should be prohibited because public sector unions are too powerful.[13] In the private sector, if one brand of car is too expensive, consumers can purchase competing brands. Consumers are not dependent on a single manufacturer, and the threat of lost business restrains labor's demands. In the public sector, when there is only one service provider—one police department, for example—residents depend on this sole source of services. It is argued that this dependence makes labor—the police officers, for example—too powerful economically and politically and therefore distorts both the provision of public services and the democratic process. Magnifying these concerns, unions can also strengthen their bargaining power by convincing the public that there is a need for mutually beneficial services such as additional police officers.[14]

The evidence, however, does not support the contention that public sector unions have unlimited bargaining power.[15] Overpaid workers can be replaced by others willing to work for less. Some occupations face private sector competition or the threat of being replaced by technology. Many laws forbid public employees from striking. And in the absence of the market mechanism that disciplines managers and employees in the private sector against excessive labor costs, public sector managers and employees are disciplined by government budget restraints. The public's limited tolerance for paying for government services is reflected in taxpayer revolts, ballot initiatives to limit or reduce taxes, and the prominence of tax cuts as a major campaign issue in local, state, and federal elections. These pressures make their way back to the bargaining table in the public sector, just as market pressures do for the private sector bargaining table.

AT THE BARGAINING TABLE

Once at the bargaining table, negotiators need to use their communication, relationship-building, and problem-solving skills to reach an agreement that both sides find acceptable. Most labor negotiations involve the renegotiation of an expiring contract, and this contract anchors the negotiations. For starters, the side that wants to change the contract traditionally makes the opening proposals that mark the beginning of bargaining. When the company is healthy, unions present initial demands for improved wages, benefits, and work rules; when the company is struggling or the economy is weak, employers open with demands for concessions in wages, benefits, and work rules. From there, proposals are considered and counterproposals are made until an agreement is reached. It is common for negotiators to start with the easier items first and to leave difficult economic issues such as compensation for later. But negotiators should be cautious of prematurely locking themselves into resolutions of the easy issues because they might provide useful options for trade-offs when negotiations are in the final, difficult hours.[16]

Labor Negotiations as Theater

The dramatic structure of labor negotiations closely parallels a theatrical play.[17] The negotiators are actors and have roles, especially the lead negotiators with the leading parts. The audience for the actors' performances are other negotiators and the negotiators' constituents, especially upper management for management negotiators, union members for the union negotiators. These performances take place on a visible stage at the bargaining table. The audience has certain expectations of how the performance should proceed—that is, the constituents demand that their interests be strongly represented. As such, the lead negotiators need to put on a show. Table pounding and other aggressive tactics demonstrate the strength of the negotiators not to each other but to their constituents: "Getting members to be happy about the results is largely a matter of good theater—of enhancing confidence in the bargainer and using tensions to good effect."[18] This theater takes place on the front stage of negotiations (the bargaining table) for the other members of the bargaining committee to see.

But there is also a backstage: Experienced lead negotiators often meet with each other in private with no other bargaining team members present. In these meetings the negotiators can step out of their public roles, share information, and explore wide-ranging options. In contrast with the conflictual bargaining of the front stage, backstage interactions can have a problem-solving flavor. "While conflict is expressed in public, understanding is built up in private."[19] This front-stage, backstage dichotomy is driven by the social structure of labor negotiations: Negotiators have to demonstrate their leadership by satisfying the expectations of their constituents, being a strong advocate, and also producing an agreement.

The dramatic structure of labor negotiations makes negotiations more complex than they appear. Negotiators have to decipher whether the other negotiators are putting on a show or trying to communicate a legitimate point. And novice labor relations practitioners need to make sure they do not get swept up in the performance or get emotionally involved. Table pounding, yelling, and even personal attacks are likely a performance for the audience. Participants need to know their roles, understand the nature of the entire performance, and wait for their opportunities out of the spotlight backstage. Moreover, this dramatic structure applies equally well to the grievance procedure. Novices should be prepared for public performances during meetings and hearings to resolve grievances and should not take the process personally. In the words of one union rep, "I have had arbitration cases where I will bring in 25 guys and put the show on, and they don't remember I lost the case. They remember I worked over management."[20]

Negotiating Tools

Throughout the negotiations the participants use various negotiating tools. One essential tool is **contract costing,** which is used to evaluate proposals by estimating their monetary costs. A lump-sum bonus is perhaps the easiest proposal to cost—simply multiply the amount of the bonus by the number of employees who will receive it. But most proposals are more complex, and their costs might depend on employee seniority, future staffing levels, and other complicating factors.[21] Contract costing therefore often requires making projections of complex issues (such as how many employees will choose early retirement or use parental leave, how much health insurance premiums will rise over the next three years, or what the economic value is of loosening a restrictive work rule), and negotiators might disagree over these projections. Table 7.3 provides an example of costing a vacation-related proposal.

Another common tool for negotiators is a bargaining book.[22] Each side uses three-ring binders to create a complete record of the negotiation, including their agenda, proposals, supporting documents, proposals and materials received from the other side, and the minutes of each bargaining session. Each contract section can have its own entry where proposals, counterproposals, and agreements are tracked. It can also be useful for the bargaining book to include a summary sheet that shows the status of each section (pending, agreed, or withdrawn) at the end of each bargaining session. Negotiators might also receive assistance from neutral mediators (see Chapter 8).

Bargaining in Good Faith

Labor law is also present at the bargaining table. The National Labor Relations Act (NLRA) requires negotiators to bargain "in good faith" [Section 8(d)]. The dividing line between good faith and illegal bad faith bargaining, however, is not always clear (see this yourself with the "Labor Law Discussion" case at the end of this chapter). Consider four major examples of bad faith bargaining: making unilateral changes, direct dealing, refusing to provide information, and surface bargaining. A **unilateral change** occurs when an employer changes wages, benefits, or other terms and conditions of employment without first bargaining with the union. This includes both during contract negotiations and when

TABLE 7.3
Contract Costing Example

Contract Change: All workers with at least five years of seniority will receive an extra week of paid vacation annually.

Formula for Costing this Contract Change

200 workers × 5 days × 8 hours × $20.00 per hour × 1.5 per hour = $240,000 per year
(1) (2) (3) (4) (5)

Explanation for Each Numbered Element of this Formula

1. Number of workers affected: There are currently 200 employees with at least five years of seniority, so assume 200.
2. Each worker gets five extra days of vacation per year with this contract change.
3. The standard working day is eight hours.
4. Need to replace each vacationing worker with another employee: Assume that the average hourly wage for all employees in the bargaining unit is $20 per hour.
5. Overtime premium: When existing employees work extra to take the places of vacationing employees, they are working overtime and receive time and a half.

Note that this is just an estimate, and some complicating factors are ignored:

1. Turnover reduces the number of affected workers. But workers with four years of seniority this year will be eligible next year, workers with three will be eligible in two years, and so on.
2. Some workers might not take all their extra vacation days.
3. Some workers might not need to be replaced for an entire eight hours.
4. Because the extra vacation is for workers with more seniority, they might need to be replaced with workers with higher seniority. in which case the hourly wage for the replacements would be higher than the overall average of $20 per hour.
5. If there are extra workers or business is slow, the extra hours might not be overtime.

Also, if extra vacation increases morale and reduces turnover, the costs of this change can be offset by lower turnover costs (including the costs of recruitment, training, and lost productivity).

a contract is in force. An employer can make unilateral changes in mandatory bargaining items only after it has fulfilled its bargaining obligation by bargaining to an impasse. Unfortunately, "impasse" is another aspect of labor law that is fairly ambiguous and often requires NLRB interpretation of the specific facts of a case:

> Whether a bargaining impasse exists is a matter of judgment. The bargaining history, the good faith of the parties in negotiations, the length of the negotiations, the importance of the issue or issues as to which there is disagreement, the contemporaneous understanding of the parties as to the state of negotiations are all relevant factors.[23]

Once an impasse has been reached, however, the employer can legally implement the terms of its final offer to the union.[24]

The second example of bad faith bargaining is **direct dealing,** which occurs when an employer illegally tries to circumvent and undermine a union by interacting directly with the employees with respect to bargaining issues. For example, an employer cannot survey employees to gauge their support for specific bargaining proposals or striking—these are issues for employees to convey through their union at the bargaining table, and an employer survey erodes the union's bargaining power.[25] However, this does not prohibit all forms of communications with employees. Noncoercive communication from the employer to the employees that simply informs the employees about the status of negotiations is acceptable;

but if it undermines the union (such as by questioning the union's effectiveness), then it is illegal direct dealing and violates the employer's obligation to bargain in good faith with the union.[26]

A third example of bad faith bargaining is refusing to provide information in certain situations. Upon request, an employer has an obligation to provide information to the union that is necessary for representing the workers effectively. Examples of legitimate requests that the employer must comply with include wage information for employees, job evaluation data, standards for merit raises, the results of a local wage survey, and health and safety statistics.[27] Perhaps the most contentious information requests pertain to union requests for corporate financial data. Such information is not deemed necessary for collective bargaining, so unions are not entitled to receive it. But if an employer states that it cannot afford one of the union's bargaining proposals, the information becomes relevant and the employer is obligated to provide it.[28] There is a fine line here: If an employer says that it *cannot* pay, it must back this up by providing financial data; if an employer says that it *will not* pay because of a competitive disadvantage, there is no obligation to provide any financial information.[29] Unions must also comply with employer requests for information if it is relevant, although this situation arises less frequently than union requests.[30]

The fourth and most important example of bad faith bargaining is **surface bargaining,** which occurs when an employer or a union goes through the motions of bargaining but does not sincerely try to reach an agreement. Good faith bargaining requires that the parties must make "a serious attempt to resolve differences and reach a common ground."[31] Surface bargaining is a multifaceted concept, and in each case the NLRB looks at the specific facts and the totality of conduct, including delaying tactics, unreasonable bargaining demands, failure to designate an agent with sufficient bargaining authority, withdrawal of already agreed-upon provisions, making "take it or leave it" offers, refusing to make counterproposals, and arbitrary scheduling of meetings.[32] A difficulty with surface bargaining is distinguishing it from "hard bargaining." Proposals for wage cuts or other concessions that are justified by competitive concerns are hard bargaining, not illegal surface bargaining. A company can use its bargaining power to achieve a favorable settlement (hard bargaining) but not to undermine the sincere pursuit of an agreement (surface bargaining).

Online Exploration Exercise: Go to the NLRB site (*www.nlrb.gov*), navigate to the "Board Decisions" page within the "Cases and Decisions" section. Use the search box to find decisions containing the text "surface bargaining." What types of negotiator behaviors were ruled to be surface bargaining? What behaviors were acceptable as fulfilling the good faith bargaining standard?

Mandatory Bargaining Items

Labor law also affects what is discussed at the bargaining table. Specifically the NLRA requires good faith bargaining over "wages, hours, and other terms and conditions of employment" [Section 8(d)]. Based on this, many years ago the U.S. Supreme Court empowered the National Labor Relations Board (NLRB) to classify bargaining issues into three categories of bargaining items: mandatory, permissive, and illegal; this is called the *Borg-Warner* doctrine after the name of the Court's decision.[33] **Mandatory bargaining items** are wages, hours, and terms and conditions of employment; employers and unions have an obligation to bargain over these. At the other end of the spectrum, illegal bargaining items are those that would violate the law—such as closed shop provisions, policies that involve racial discrimination, or payment of wages below the legal minimum. Employers and unions are prohibited from bargaining over such items. The

TABLE 7.4
Examples of Mandatory and Permissive Bargaining Items

Mandatory	Permissive
Wage reductions/increases	Union representation on the board of directors
Bonus plans	Drug and alcohol screening for applicants
Health insurance payments	Benefits for retirees
Pension contributions	Interest arbitration
Work schedules and vacations	Bargaining unit expansion
Seniority provisions	Contract ratification procedures
Just cause discipline provisions	Plant closings
Grievance arbitration	
Food prices in the company cafeteria	
Lie detector and drug tests	
Subcontracting	
Effects of plant closings	

middle category—**permissive bargaining items**—includes everything not in the other two. Employers and unions can bargain over permissive items if they choose; but because they are outside the boundaries of the NLRA, the NLRB cannot order bargaining on these issues, and employees are not protected if they go on strike over these issues.

When there are disputes between negotiators about whether something is a mandatory bargaining item—for example, prices in the company cafeteria—the NLRB issues a ruling indicating whether the specific issue is included in their interpretation of "wages, hours, and other terms and conditions of employment." Some prominent examples of mandatory and permissive bargaining items are listed in Table 7.4. As one example, consider "effects bargaining." A managerial or business decision, such as whether to close a plant, is not a mandatory bargaining item, but the effects of that decision on workers, such as the layoff order or severance pay, are mandatory items.[34] As such, companies do not need to bargain over the decision to shut down facilities, but they must bargain with unions over layoff procedures, severance packages, and other effects of these closings.

BARGAINING SUBPROCESSES AND STRATEGIES

Seeing labor negotiations as theater, considering the tools negotiators use, and appreciating the importance of the legal standard of good faith bargaining over wages, hours, and other terms and conditions of employment are important for understanding labor negotiations. But what types of bargaining occur during labor negotiations, and what strategies do negotiators use? In a classic work, Richard Walton and Robert McKersie decomposed the overall labor negotiations process into four types of bargaining: distributive bargaining, integrative bargaining, attitudinal structuring, and intraorganizational bargaining (see Table 7.5).[35] In Walton and McKersie's terminology, these are the four subprocesses of negotiations—the four types of bargaining that take place in collective bargaining to negotiate a union contract. The first two subprocesses—distributive and integrative bargaining—are the major alternatives for negotiating terms and conditions of employment: adversarial bargaining over conflicts of interest, and collaborative problem solving for issues of mutual gain. Attitudinal structuring is the element of a negotiation that shapes the attitudes of labor

TABLE 7.5
The Four Subprocesses of Labor Negotiations

Subprocess	Focus	Where the Subprocess Occurs
Distributive bargaining	Resolving conflicts of interest; often adversarial.	At the bargaining table between labor and management negotiators.
Integrative bargaining	Solving joint problems (that do not involve conflicts of interest) by creating solutions for mutual gains; often collaborative.	At the bargaining table and in brainstorming sessions between labor and management negotiators and their committees.
Attitudinal structuring	Managing attitudes and the overall labor–management relationship; often trust-building.	At the bargaining table between labor and management negotiators, but spilling over to others.
Intraorganizational bargaining	Achieving consensus within each group; often complex.	Away from the bargaining table within each organization.

Reference: Richard E. Walton and Robert B. McKersie, *A Behavioral Theory of Labor Negotiations* (New York: McGraw-Hill, 1965).

and management toward each other. An attempt to increase the amount of trust between a company and a union is an example of an activity that falls within this subprocess. And intraorganizational bargaining captures the conflict resolution strategies used to reach a consensus *within* the union and *within* the employer's management ranks.

Collective bargaining in both the private and public sectors is a mixture of all four subprocesses for three reasons:

1. Mainstream industrial relations views employment relationship conflict as a **mixed motive**—a mixture of conflicts of interests and shared opportunities for mutual gain—so both distributive and integrative bargaining are important.
2. The employer–employee–union relationship is a long-term, ongoing affair, so attitudinal structuring is significant.
3. Both employers and unions have constituencies with diverse interests, so intraorganizational bargaining is present.

Distributive Bargaining

Think of some bargaining situations in everyday life. What scenarios come to mind? Buying a car? Haggling with your roommate over who's going to wash the dishes? Trying to get your boss to give you a day off next week? One way to approach these bargaining situations is by assuming that there is a strict conflict of interest: You want a lower price for the car and the salesperson wants a higher price, you want your roommate to wash the dishes and your roommate wants you to, you want a day off next week and your boss wants you to work. In labor relations, the simplest example is bargaining over wages—employees want to receive higher wages, and employers want to keep labor costs down. These types of bargaining scenarios are typically viewed as dividing a fixed pie—the more dishes your roommate washes, the fewer you are stuck with, or paying out an extra $10,000 in wages reduces profits by $10,000. **Distributive bargaining** is the familiar type of negotiation used to resolve these conflicts of interests—in other words, to *distribute* the shares of the fixed pie.[36] In distributive bargaining, the more one side receives, the less the other side receives, so this type of bargaining is also referred to as zero-sum bargaining. This can be an unfortunate label because there is value in reaching agreement so it is not the case that there are zero benefits; a better descriptor might be "constant-sum bargaining."

Distributive bargaining is the classic vision of collective bargaining: union and management negotiators pounding the table demanding more (the union) or less (the employer) and both trying to drive the hardest bargain possible. Wages, benefits, working conditions, and work rules are all viewed as conflictual issues—improvements benefit the workers and harm the company's bottom line (and vice versa). But if both sides are trying so hard to win, why bargain at all? Because the parties are interdependent.[37] Employers need workers to produce goods and services, and workers need to work to earn a living—but not at any cost. Parties will pursue and enter a negotiated agreement when the terms of this agreement are better than their alternatives. For workers, their alternatives include going on strike and looking for work elsewhere; for employers, the alternatives are taking a strike, trying to hire new employees, outsourcing, and moving. The best alternative to a negotiated agreement (BATNA) therefore determines what terms are minimally acceptable to either side.[38] It is important to be realistic when assessing your BATNA. Indeed, at least one mediator prefers the term "most likely alternative to a negotiated agreement" (MLATNA) to prevent the parties from being anchored by unachievable alternatives.

The expectation that a negotiated settlement will be better than a party's BATNA (or MLANTA) provides an incentive to bargain. The costs of a strike and hiring new employees give employers an incentive to bargain; the costs of unemployment and the uncertainties of trying to find a new job give employees an incentive to bargain. In distributive bargaining, each side's BATNA can be thought of as their threat point or resistance point—they will resist accepting terms less favorable than their BATNA and will threaten to quit the negotiations and walk away if they cannot obtain terms at least equal to their BATNA. It is common to graphically represent this situation as shown in Figure 7.3.[39] In the top half of Figure 7.3, the union's resistance point is a 2 percent wage increase while the employer's resistance point is a 5 percent wage increase. There is thus a positive settlement or bargaining range, and each side should be satisfied with any wage increase between 2 and 5 percent. In the bottom half of Figure 7.3, however, a settlement is not expected: The maximum the employer is willing to offer is 2 percent, and the minimum the union is willing to accept is 5 percent. If each side's BATNA is realistic, these parties are better off with their alternatives than with negotiating a settlement.

The top half of Figure 7.3 captures the traditional distributive bargaining scenario. Remember that the resistance points are the minimally acceptable terms. The parties also have a desired or target settlement. In distributive bargaining, each party's target is often the other side's resistance point.[40] In other words, each side wants to win as much as

FIGURE 7.3
Distributive Bargaining and the Settlement Range

Positive Settlement Range: Settlement Should Result

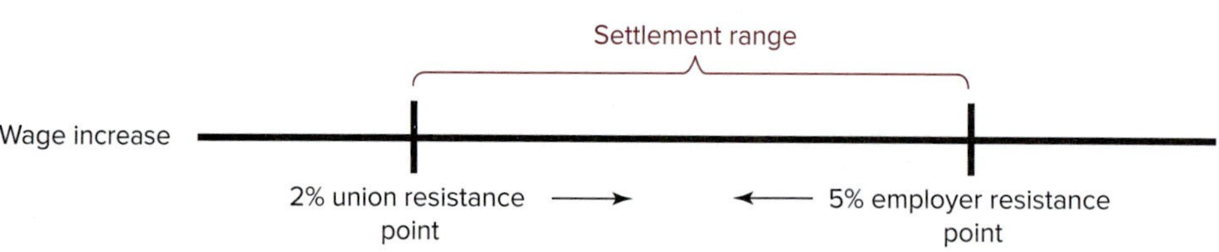

Negative Settlement Range: Settlement Is Difficult

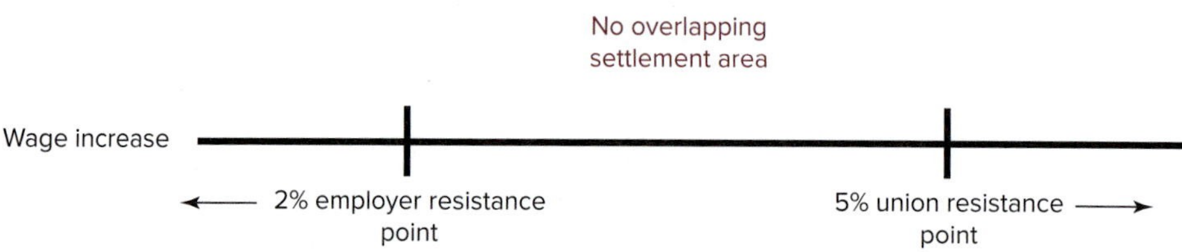

possible without driving the other side to walk away. Consequently, the major distributive bargaining strategies and tactics are rooted in power: trying to strengthen the image of your own resistance point while seeking out and weakening the other side's impression of their own resistance point.[41] Such tactics include carefully controlling and selectively presenting the information shared with the other side (typically only the chief negotiator gets to speak at the bargaining table), reacting emotionally to statements made by the other side (or not reacting at all), "educating" the other side about the implications of their proposals, and staking out strong positions. To make it look like they are making concessions, each side's opening positions might be excessively high or low while also including extra demands that only they know are unimportant, but this can increase the chance of escalation and misunderstanding.

Pressure tactics might also include increasing the other side's costs of not making an agreement, such as through union rallies that disrupt production and bring negative publicity to the employer. The careful sequencing of offers, counteroffers, and concessions lies at the heart of the distributive bargaining process, and these tactics are designed to quicken the pace and generosity of the other side's concessions while reducing the need to make your own concessions. Hardball tactics such as lies, bluffs, threats, and intimidation are also sometimes used to achieve these ends, but they may do more harm than good. At American Airlines, days after approving over $1 billion in concessions, the rank and file learned that the airline had concealed special pension protections for 48 top executives. The resulting anger led to the CEO's resignation, and the airline barely avoided bankruptcy by renegotiating the concession agreements to be more favorable to the employees. Hiding these executive perks during negotiations proved to be a costly bargaining tactic. Whether these hardball tactics are ethical is also subject to debate (see the "Ethics in Action" box at the end of the chapter).

With or without hardball tactics, each side's maneuvers are designed to win the most for their side, and distributive bargaining is therefore typically adversarial. Conflicts of interests over wages, benefits, working conditions, and work rules are a central component of collective bargaining in U.S. labor relations. But remember that labor and management have vital areas of common interest. Both want productive work systems and financially healthy organizations so employers can continue to provide quality jobs and returns on shareholders' investments. Finding the best solutions to these problems that involve mutual gain rather than conflicts of interest is pursued through a different type of bargaining: integrative bargaining.

Integrative Bargaining

Integrative bargaining seeks to unify (integrate) the common interests of the parties to a negotiation so that all can become better off.[42] Rather than trying to split a fixed pie as in distributive bargaining, integrative bargaining seeks to expand the size of the pie. Solving a production bottleneck by reconfiguring work flow, reallocating a benefits package that holds costs steady but increases employee satisfaction, and implementing a training program that improves productivity and wage rates are three examples in which both employees and employers benefit. Such integrative outcomes, however, are unlikely to result from the adversarial tactics and limited sharing of information in distributive bargaining. Rather, integrative bargaining is joint problem solving that relies heavily on trust and full communication (see Table 7.6). Integrative bargaining is also referred to as win–win bargaining (because both sides win by expanding the pie), mutual gains bargaining (because of the focus on creating mutual gains rather than resolving zero-sum conflicts), or interest-based bargaining (because of the focus on interests).

A key principle of integrative bargaining is focusing on interests rather than positions.[43] Negotiators in distributive bargaining are focused on positions: "I'll pay you $20,000 for

TABLE 7.6
Distributive and Integrative Bargaining

Distributive Bargaining		Integrative Bargaining
Conflict of interest	*Conflict*	Common interest
Distributing a fixed pie	*Imagery*	Integrating interests to increase the size of the pie
Positions	*Focus*	Interests
Of minor importance, gets weakened	*Trust*	Critical, is strengthened
Tightly controlled	*Information*	Free flowing
Chief spokesperson/lead negotiator only	*Participation*	All members of negotiating teams
Manipulating perceptions of positions, increasing costs of delay	*Tactics*	Brainstorming, using objective criteria
Table for pounding	*Important Prop*	Flip chart for brainstorming
Winning gains for your side through bargaining power	*Benefits*	Creating joint gain and stronger relationships
Too aggressive? Harmful to the relationship? How to innovate?	*Risks*	Selling out? Giving up too much?
Stress	*Difficulties for negotiators*	Giving up control, selling results to constituents, time-consuming
How to prevent adversarial tactics from damaging the relationship?	*Question marks*	How to distribute the increased gains?
Adversarial bargaining, hard bargaining, traditional bargaining	*Other labels*	Win–win bargaining, mutual gains bargaining, interest-based bargaining
Positional bargaining	*In sum*	Joint problem solving

this new car and not a nickel more" or "We demand a 5 percent wage increase." Such positions reinforce an adversarial bargaining climate as each side gets locked into defending its position. But this overlooks and obscures the more fundamental interests of each party that underlie its positions. Your interest is not getting a car for \$20,000—it is obtaining safe, reliable, and affordable transportation; the union's interest is not getting a 5 percent raise—it is ensuring that the workers are rewarded for their contributions to the company and can live comfortably. There might be several ways of satisfying these basic interests: Perhaps you could lease a car instead of buying one, or perhaps the union and company can provide rewards and security through a profit-sharing plan and a no-layoff guarantee. But these options will not be discovered when adversarial negotiators are focused on defending their positions.

After an issue is identified, the key second step in the integrative bargaining process is trying to understand each side's fundamental interests (see Figure 7.4). Some recommend capping the number of interests for an issue at nine so the process does not become too time-consuming.[44] Once the true interests are uncovered, the next step is generating options for satisfying these interests using basic problem-solving strategies such as brainstorming. Note that in contrast to the tight control of information in distributive bargaining,

FIGURE 7.4
The Integrative Bargaining Steps

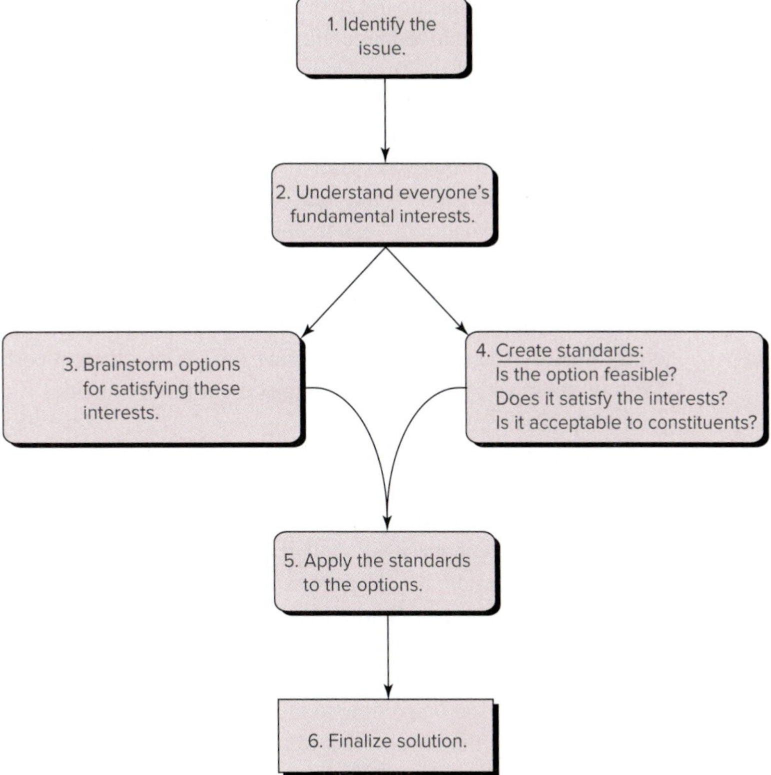

the brainstorming approach of integrative bargaining requires high levels of trust and extensive sharing of information.[45] All members of each side's bargaining committee—not just the lead negotiators—are expected to participate and contribute ideas because during the brainstorming phase, the parties should be trying to generate multiple options rather than worrying about which is the best one.[46] After numerous options for solving a particular problem have been identified, the negotiators must select one. The literature on integrative bargaining emphasizes using objective criteria that are established in advance to select the best solution.[47] These might be external standards of performance or fairness for a particular issue; others recommend using the consistent standards of feasibility, satisfaction of interests, and acceptability.[48] Armed with multiple options and a set of agreed-upon standards, the negotiators then determine the best solution by applying the standards to the options.

Distributive versus Integrative Bargaining in Labor Relations

One of the leading issues for labor–management relationships is what type of bargaining to use. Many academics and consultants advocate replacing distributive with integrative bargaining in labor negotiations to create more cooperative partnerships and healthy workplaces and organizations in a competitive environment.[49] But achieving this change in practice is exceptionally difficult.[50] The trouble stems partly from the overly simplistic illusion of a forced choice between distributive *or* integrative bargaining. If the employment relationship is characterized by mixed motive conflict, a mixture of distributive and integrative bargaining is appropriate for collective bargaining. Dividing the fruits of integrative bargaining is a task for distributive bargaining, so successful integrative bargaining ultimately creates a distributive bargaining situation later.

Although it is simplistic to say that collective bargaining should use integrative bargaining instead of distributive bargaining, it is reasonable to question whether labor negotiations use integrative bargaining enough. It is common for people generally to *assume* that a negotiating situation involves a conflict of interest—this is a mythical fixed-pie bias.[51] As a result, labor negotiators default to distributive bargaining tactics and miss opportunities for mutual gains through integrative bargaining. Instead, labor negotiators should start with integrative bargaining and then, if desired, turn to distributive bargaining when the mutual gains are exhausted.[52] Sometimes this is called modified integrative bargaining. It is even possible to negotiate wages and other economic items in an integrative fashion using a process developed by the Federal Mediation and Conciliation Service in 2015 called the Affinity Method of Collaborative Economic Bargaining. In this approach, negotiators jointly identify the issues before making proposals, create a costing methodology, brainstorm options, and jointly build an agreement that both sides find acceptable using open communication.

But moving away from distributive bargaining, whether in part or in full, is difficult. Negotiators need to overcome not only the mythical fixed-pie bias but also their old habits and strategies. Joint labor–management training in preparation for integrative bargaining is therefore often emphasized. And if collective bargaining is going to mix distributive and integrative tactics, it is important that distributive bargaining over some issues does not poison the relationship and prevent the successful pursuit of integrative bargaining on other issues.

Finally, seeing labor negotiations as theater reveals the difficulty of switching from traditional adversarial bargaining to more integrative approaches.[53] Traditional distributive bargaining fulfills the social roles that negotiators must play: "The traditional process is stable because the public rituals that are so common to it—displays of opposition, representation, and control—help negotiators achieve their personal and strategic goals and to manage the many political pressures that they face."[54] This is not to say the traditional system is perfect—front-stage conflict can get out of hand, signals might be misread, and many participants are left out. But it highlights the difficulties with changing to integrative bargaining. How can negotiators fulfill their social roles on a front stage of integrative bargaining when the audience—corporate executives and union members alike—demands a distributive bargaining performance and may see integrative bargaining as selling out?

Attitudinal Structuring

Integrative bargaining produces joint material gains and distributive bargaining divides these gains, but activities that occur during negotiations also shape the participants' attitudes toward each other. This aspect of a negotiation is Walton and McKersie's third subprocess: **attitudinal structuring.**[55] In other words, distributive and integrative bargaining produce a written contract, whereas attitudinal structuring creates a social contract that reflects the attitudinal quality of the relationship between labor and management.[56] Distributive and integrative bargaining are negotiation subprocesses for managing transactions; attitudinal structuring is a negotiation subprocess for managing relationships.[57]

Negotiators need to remember that attitudinal structuring will occur during negotiations even if the negotiators are not actively trying to manage the relationship. For example, the use of distributive bargaining tactics that focus on aggressive bargaining positions, restrict information sharing, and involve threats and other demonstrations of power can inadvertently create uncooperative and adversarial attitudes that will not only affect the tenor of the negotiations but also shape the continued attitudinal nature of the overall labor–management relationship. In this way, aggressive distributive bargaining tactics can undermine efforts at integrative bargaining and attempt to build lasting labor–management partnerships. It is therefore important for negotiators to judge "how hard to push one's temporary bargaining advantage or power if doing so might produce a negative reaction from a party to an ongoing relationship like a marriage, a work group, a strategic business partnership, or a labor–management relationship."[58] At the same time, the close personal interaction between labor and management negotiators that occurs during the bargaining process provides the opportunity for the parties to build trust and respect and therefore move toward a more cooperative and less conflict-laden relationship. Trust-building activities might include identifying common problems and mutual successes, sharing information, participating in off-site retreats and joint training sessions, and establishing formal participatory mechanisms such as problem-solving committees.[59] This important issue of changing the nature of labor–management relationships will be revisited in Chapter 10.

Intraorganizational Bargaining

If an unmarried person is buying a used car from another unmarried person, the negotiators need concern themselves with only the distributive and integrative bargaining subprocesses. However, if they anticipate repeated interactions, attitudinal structuring will also be important in shaping the ongoing attitudinal nature of their relationship. If one of them is married, that negotiator will also encounter *intra*organizational bargaining as the negotiator and his or her spouse try to reach consensus on the terms for buying or selling the car. **Intraorganizational bargaining** is the subprocess of the bargaining process that takes place within an organization—within the union and within the ranks of management.[60] The need for intraorganizational bargaining results from the presence of diverse interests within the constituency of a negotiator.

A diversity of interests is typically most visible on the union side. Employees with varying demographic characteristics may have different priorities: Older employees might be particularly interested in retirement benefits, younger workers in vacation, female and minority employees in equal opportunity policies, and workers with children in health insurance benefits. Some occupations might be in competition for wage increases, especially in bargaining units that contain both skilled and unskilled jobs. This is common in manufacturing bargaining units that include production as well as skilled maintenance workers. Lastly, in addition to different priorities for contract negotiations, employees might disagree about appropriate bargaining tactics, with some supporting a more adversarial and distributive approach and others a more conciliatory or integrative approach.

Union leaders and rank-and-file workers also have different priorities. Local union leaders might be more concerned with institutional issues such as union security, the number of union stewards, and access to employees at work; rank-and-file workers might be more concerned with bread-and-butter employment issues—compensation, benefits, and working conditions. That most U.S. unionized workers belong to diverse national or international unions further complicates intraorganizational bargaining. National union leaders need to balance the good of a specific bargaining unit and the greater good of all the union's members. Intense conflicts can arise, however, when a local union wants to accept concessions such as wage cuts or work rule changes to save their jobs, and a national union objects to prevent a downward spiral throughout an industry—or vice versa. In one extreme example that can be viewed in the documentary movie *Final Offer*, tensions between autoworkers in Canada and their U.S. parent union became so intense during the 1984 auto negotiations that the Canadian locals broke away from the UAW and formed their own union. Another example is described in the accompanying "Labor Relations Application" on the Hormel strike.

Intraorganizational bargaining is more visible on the union side of the bargaining process because unions are political institutions: bargaining agendas are created with rank-and-file input, leaders are elected, and contracts are approved by ratification votes (see the "Labor Relations Application: The Ross–Dunlop Debate").[61] But intraorganizational bargaining

Labor Relations Application Intraorganizational Bargaining at Hormel

On a Friday in April 1983 the large meatpacking company Wilson Foods filed for bankruptcy. Before the bankruptcy code was changed in 1984, employers used bankruptcy to void their collective bargaining agreements, and when Wilson's employees returned to work on Monday, their hourly wages had been slashed from $10.69 to $6.50. Wilson was losing money because of nonunion competition, the recession of the early 1980s, and a decade of neglect as its parent company cashed out its profits without reinvesting. Other major meatpacking companies demanded concessions from their workers, and by the end of 1983 much of the industry was paying between $6.00 and $8.25. Many of these workers were represented by the United Food and Commercial Workers (UFCW).

The national UFCW leadership agreed to the concessions with the hopes of stabilizing employment and then gradually bargaining wages back up over time. But UFCW Local P-9, representing 1,500 workers at Hormel's flagship plant in Austin, Minnesota—maker of Spam and other products—wasn't inclined to go along with this plan. Hormel's plants were modern and the company was profitable. P-9 members felt that they were working harder than before and saw no reason to grant wage and benefit concessions to a profitable company. In 1984, six other UFCW locals at Hormel agreed to a concessions package that reduced wages. Against the wishes of the national UFCW leadership, Local P-9 refused to negotiate, so Hormel implemented the "me too" provision in its contract that allowed it to follow the industry wage pattern and cut wages at the Austin plant from $10.69 to $8.25 in October 1984. Local P-9 insisted that the "me too" clause applied only to wage *increases*, but an arbitrator disagreed.

Local P-9's contract with Hormel expired in August 1985, and after a summer of unproductive bargaining sessions, it went on strike. The national UFCW unenthusiastically sanctioned the strike so strikers could receive strike benefits. By some accounts this strike stemmed partly from a failure of intraorganizational bargaining—the P-9 negotiating committee was unable or unwilling to prioritize and trim its long list of demands even though Hormel had greater bargaining leverage.

In December, federal mediators drafted a proposal that would essentially match the other Hormel plants. Hormel agreed to accept this proposal if P-9 members would. The national UFCW thought it was the best that could be achieved and recommended ratification. The leaders of Local P-9 thought everyone was selling them out. Neither the national UFCW leaders nor the Local P-9 leaders trusted the other side to reveal the true results of a vote, so they both conducted ratification votes. In both votes the proposal was rejected, though large numbers voted to accept the mediator's proposal.

By mid-February 1986 the Hormel plant in Austin was operating at almost full capacity with P-9 members who had crossed the picket lines and with newly hired replacement workers. With no contract in place and with replacement workers outnumbering P-9 members, the UFCW faced a serious threat of being decertified. The national UFCW leadership therefore began publicly criticizing the Local P-9 leadership. In March it withdrew authorization for the strike, and two months later it placed Local P-9 in trusteeship and removed the local leaders. Local P-9 in return sued the UFCW—its parent union—for $13 million for allegedly undermining its strike. This suit was dismissed, and the UFCW ended the strike. A contract was finally negotiated in August 1986.

The Hormel strike was one of the most bitter of the last part of the 20th century, and it reveals several layers of intraorganizational conflict. The failure of Local P-9 to manage intraorganizational bargaining by narrowing its demands likely contributed to the strike. Within Local P-9 a majority clearly supported the strike, but a dissident group fought for a settlement, and significant numbers crossed the picket lines. Local P-9 also differed in its views from the six other Hormel locals and especially with the national UFCW leadership. The Local P-9 leaders strongly believed that they were just in resisting concessions from a profitable corporation, and they received zealous support from many labor activists around the country. The national UFCW leadership in contrast felt that it was more prudent to preserve unionized employment in the meatpacking industry and to wait for a more favorable environment to fight for improvements. It is hard to adequately describe the level of distrust and conflict between the Local P-9 leaders and the national UFCW leadership. Intraorganizational conflict does not typically create such a bitter and costly strike, but it is a central feature of the U.S. collective bargaining process.

References: Dave Hage and Paul Klauda, *No Retreat, No Surrender: Labor's War at Hormel* (New York: William Morrow, 1989); Peter Rachleff, *Hard-Pressed in the Heartland: The Hormel Strike and the Future of the Labor Movement* (Boston: South End Press, 1993).

also occurs within the ranks of management.[62] In the bargaining process, top management is particularly concerned with the bottom-line financial impact; human resource professionals worry about the principles that are affected or established; supervisors are interested in how work gets done; and the negotiators want an agreement. During multiunit negotiations, managers from different geographical regions or business units may have different needs and constraints and therefore divergent bargaining goals.[63] As in the union case, these sometimes conflicting priorities need to be addressed before and during negotiations.

Intraorganizational bargaining occurs in varying ways; it might include both distributive and integrative bargaining tactics. Elected union bargaining committees often use surveys of rank-and-file desires to establish bargaining agendas before negotiations begin. Management negotiating teams typically research problem areas in the current contract and get feedback or direction from various levels of managers. While negotiations are under way, the teams periodically provide bargaining updates to their constituents to manage their expectations and help prepare them to accept a specific outcome. The bargaining teams frequently caucus during negotiations, and some of these committee-only meetings might involve heated discussions of bargaining priorities and strategies. Emotional outbursts, table pounding, and other distributive bargaining tactics might be used to persuade your own team members of the benefits of a certain position. Once the negotiators reach a tentative agreement, the bargaining teams need to sell this agreement to their constituents. As an experienced management negotiator once told me, coming out of negotiations, everyone needs a victory speech. This is another significant instance of intraorganizational bargaining in the collective bargaining process.

Online Exploration Exercise: Using the search term "bargaining update," find sites, videos, and other social media tools being used by unions to keep their members informed about negotiations (such as *www.geworkersunited.org*). What types of issues are emphasized on these sites? What issues seem common across different unions? What issues are specific to certain occupations? Do the sites suggest a more adversarial or cooperative bargaining relationship? Why is it hard to find similar sites on the management side?

REACHING AGREEMENT

Negotiations are almost always settled at the last minute. Settling earlier risks leaving the audience dissatisfied and suspicious that the negotiators have not fought for their interests as strenuously as possible. Even if it requires going right up to the bargaining deadline, successful negotiations conclude with a tentative agreement. An agreement is only tentative at this stage because union negotiators, and maybe the management side as well, must obtain formal approval before the settlement becomes official. On the union side, the approval process typically involves a contract ratification vote by the rank and file, though some union constitutions provide for approval by an elected executive committee. Some unions might also require the approval of the national union headquarters. Before a ratification vote, unions will usually have a membership meeting in which the terms of the agreement are presented to the rank and file and intraorganizational bargaining occurs as the leaders try to convince the members that the agreement is a good one. Union members then have the final say by voting to accept or reject the agreement.

On the employer side, management negotiators typically have the authority to agree to a final settlement, and intraorganizational bargaining takes place before the final agreement. However, if the union is told in advance, it is legal for management negotiators to agree to a tentative settlement subject to upper management approval.[64] In this case management

Labor Relations Application The Ross–Dunlop Debate

One of the most famous academic debates in U.S. industrial relations was launched by an exchange between Professors John T. Dunlop and Arthur M. Ross that occurred in the 1940s: Are labor unions economic or political organizations? The economic approach models unions as trying to maximize some type of utility function, just as corporations are assumed to maximize profits and individuals are assumed to maximize their utility. Dunlop argued that unions act to maximize their wage bill—the aggregate income earned by their members. In contrast, the political approach models unions as composed of individuals with diverse preferences and leaders with goals of their own that do not translate into a single well-defined union objective. Ross argued that the major challenge of union leaders and negotiators is to reconcile these diverse and often conflicting preferences into concrete bargaining objectives and that this reconciliation is a political process based on the relative political power of various groups within the union.

In the economic approach, bargaining outcomes are a function of the external environment that determines union bargaining power—the unemployment rate, corporate profitability, whether technology can be easily substituted for expensive labor, and the like. In contrast, in the political approach, "orbits of coercive comparisons" (as Ross labeled them) are an important determinant of bargaining outcomes:

> Comparisons are important to the worker. They establish the dividing line between a square deal and a raw deal. . . . Comparisons are crucially important within the union world . . . they measure whether one union has done as well as others. They show whether the negotiating committee has done a sufficiently skillful job of bargaining. They demonstrate to the union member whether he is getting his money's worth for his dues. A favorable contract ("the best contract in the industry") becomes an argument for reelection of officers, a basis for solidification and extension of membership, and an occasion for advancement within the union hierarchy.

So are unions economic or political institutions? Does bargaining reflect the external environment or internal union political struggles? Dunlop and Ross agreed that the answer is "both." Dunlop thought the economic aspects are more important, and Ross believed that the political aspects are unwisely overlooked; but neither argued for an exclusively economic or political approach to understanding labor union behavior. With respect to the bargaining process, the political aspects—that is, intraorganizational bargaining—must not be ignored.

References: John T. Dunlop, *Wage Determination under Trade Unions* (New York: Macmillan, 1944); Arthur M. Ross, *Trade Union Wage Policy* (Berkeley: University of California Press, 1948); the quote is from p. 51; Bruce E. Kaufman, "Models of Union Wage Determination: What Have We Learned since Dunlop and Ross?" *Industrial Relations* 41 (January 2002), pp. 110–58.

negotiators may have to sell the agreement to their bosses just as the union negotiators must sell it to the rank and file. In collective bargaining, "it takes three agreements to achieve one agreement—that is, an agreement within each party as well as one across the table."[65] If the contract is not ratified or approved, the negotiators might return to the bargaining table to negotiate a revised contract, or a strike or lockout might occur (Chapter 8). Once a contract settlement is approved, it is signed by the employer and the union and it is binding on both parties for the length specified in the contract (often three years).

Bargaining in the Public Sector

The process of collective bargaining in the public sector is similar to that in the private sector—the need for thorough preparation is equally great, the environment determines bargaining power, bargaining structures range from very decentralized (such as a small, specialized unit in a local school district) to centralized (such as state-level units), and negotiations involve dynamic mixtures of distributive bargaining, integrative bargaining, attitudinal structuring, and intraorganizational bargaining. But public sector bargaining includes additional complexities.

The diversity of legal jurisdictions governing public sector labor relations results in varying legal standards for bargaining across these jurisdictions. Some states, for example,

Nonunion Application Principles and Tools for Any Negotiator

The four subprocesses of labor negotiations are not just relevant to labor negotiations—rather, they might be present in *any* negotiation. Nonunion HR managers, for example, negotiate with people they are trying to recruit into the organization, with vendors for training or other products, and with higher-level executives for resources. These can involve varying levels of distributive bargaining, integrative bargaining, attitudinal structuring, and intraorganizational bargaining, including the different tactics involved for negotiating and managing relationships. Many of the other ideas presented in this chapter, such as the importance of preparation, diagnosing bargaining power and the bargaining environment, avoiding the fixed-pie bias, and depersonalizing others' front stage performances, are also equally relevant to negotiations outside of labor relations. Prepare-explore-agree-implement are the key steps in any successful negotiation. Understanding the important subprocesses, concepts, tactics, and lessons of labor negotiations will therefore make you a better negotiator in any situation.

have sunshine laws that require public sector negotiations to take place in the public (i.e., out in the sunshine).[66] Also, while the mandatory/permissive distinction for bargaining items is common in the public sector, some public sector jurisdictions place greater restrictions on the allowable bargaining subjects.[67] For federal government employees, the parties are prohibited from negotiating wages and benefits because these items are established through civil service rules. Consequently, mandatory bargaining items include policies and procedures rather than wages and benefits. At the state and local levels, some states allow a broad scope of bargaining, and a few provide for a narrow scope of bargaining.[68] At the narrow end, New Jersey allows bargaining only over mandatory items (there are no permissive items) and does not allow effects bargaining; at the extreme narrow end, Wisconsin restricts bargaining to wage increases less than the rate of inflation. At the broad end, Illinois and Pennsylvania are similar to the NLRA in requiring bargaining over wages, hours, and other terms and conditions of employment.

Other bargaining differences in the private and public sectors are caused by structural rather than legal differences. The management structures of public sector agencies are not as hierarchical as in the private sector, and often elected officials and professional managers share or compete for decision-making authority.[69] Special interest groups, voters, and taxpayers might also try to sway public decisions. Collective bargaining in the public sector is therefore sometimes characterized by **multilateral bargaining**—negotiations between more than two parties. Consider negotiations in a school district for a contract covering teachers. Important groups in these negotiations can include the teachers' union, the school superintendent, an elected school board, a parents' organization like the PTA, taxpayers' groups, and a state board of education. Even if only the first two are sitting at the bargaining table, the other groups can be vocal in trying to influence negotiations.

Multilateral bargaining also raises the possibility of an end run. Unions can appeal for support directly to these other groups, who in turn can pressure the management officials at the bargaining table. For example, suppose the police union helped campaign for the city mayor during the last election. During negotiations for a new contract for police officers, the union can ask the mayor for support in the hope that the mayor will pressure the city's negotiating team to settle on terms favorable to the police officers. As such, the union makes an end run around the city's negotiators. As another form of an end run, unions can also improve the results of their bargaining by lobbying. By selling the public on the need for services such as additional firefighters or smaller class sizes, unions can increase the size of public sector budgets and thereby increase both compensation and employment.[70] Or in the opposite direction, some police unions have been able to roll back unfavorable local policies such as mandatory name tags by lobbying the legislature to enact laws outlawing such policies.[71]

THE CONTEMPORARY BARGAINING PROCESS: CONTINUITY AND CHANGE

In both the private and public sectors, collective bargaining has traditionally been adversarial yet professional. But with the more challenging competitive environment that started in the late 1970s and continues today, collective bargaining has become increasingly divergent. A number of employers have tried to tackle labor cost issues through a forcing strategy: aggressive distributive bargaining tactics to force weakened labor unions to grant significant wage, benefit, and work rule concessions.[72] In fact, concession bargaining has been a prominent feature of the labor relations landscape in many industries since the 1980s. The most aggressive forcing strategies have often involved strikes and the use of replacement workers to take the place of striking workers (Chapter 8).[73] Unsurprisingly, many of these situations also witnessed an escalation in conflict that risked violence, continued distrust, and unanticipated costs to the employer.[74]

In contrast, other bargainers have tried to develop a more cooperative relationship through attitudinal structuring. Attempts to change the bargaining relationship between an employer and union from adversarial to integrative highlight important issues of change management and leadership for both corporate and labor leaders. Negotiators often express frustration with both the personal costs (stressful, marathon negotiating sessions that include threats, bluffs, and perhaps personal attacks) and the organizational costs (limited participation except by chief negotiators and last-minute settlements narrowly averting work stoppages) of adversarial bargaining sessions. Moreover, traditional bargaining sessions often reflect and contribute to an overall adversarial climate that pervades the entire labor–management relationship. Such a stereotypical, traditional relationship might include a culture of conflict, defensiveness, and entrenchment. There is little trust between the parties, and communication is limited to formal negotiating sessions every three years in which all the problems of the last three years are aired. Thus attempts to move away from an adversarial bargaining relationship are often intimately related to broader desires to change the entire labor relations climate.

But such changes often run into sharp opposition. Resistance to many types of organizational changes often stems from inertia, self-interest, peer pressure, misunderstanding, and other reasons; these same elements underlie resistance to changing a bargaining relationship from adversarial to more integrative (see Table 7.7). Strong traditions of adversarial bargaining (inertia) combined with suspicions about the other side's motive for change (self-interest) and leadership fears of appearing weak or of "selling out" (misunderstanding and peer pressure) are particularly important when labor and management negotiators try to change the tenor of the bargaining relationship. Other union leaders believe that it is their responsibility to serve as a counterweight to management, not to concern themselves with managerial interests through integrative bargaining.

Joint training programs to overcome resistance are therefore important.[75] Such programs can help address misperceptions of integrative bargaining, can involve negotiators from both sides to reduce the impression that a change is serving one side's hidden agenda, and can develop the participants' skills so they are comfortable with the process. Survey evidence shows that more than half of management and union negotiators have used

TABLE 7.7
Resistance to Changing Bargaining Relationships from Adversarial to Integrative

Reference: Column 1 is adapted from Thomas S. Bateman and Scott A. Snell, *Management: Competing in the New Era,* 5th ed. (Boston: McGraw-Hill/Irwin, 2002).

Resistance to Change Factors	Application to Labor Negotiations
General Reasons for Resistance to Change	
Inertia	
Difficult to try something new.	Strong tradition of adversarial negotiations in labor relations.
Timing	
Not a good time to try something new.	Difficult to change style or form in the middle of negotiations.
Surprise	
Sudden and unexpected occurrences can cause a negative reaction.	Management or labor might unilaterally develop a new approach and propose it to the other side without warning.
Peer pressure	
Group norms might sharpen resistance to change.	Strong antiunion or antimanagement group sentiment can reinforce suspicions about the other side's motives for change.
Change-Specific Reasons for Resistance to Change	
Self-interest	
A specific change might harm a certain person or group.	The more powerful side might see a different bargaining style as weakening its position.
Misunderstanding	
Incomplete or false information about a proposed change might cause resistance.	Some view integrative bargaining methods as giving up power and selling out.
Different assessments	
Different people might value elements of a change differently.	Management emphasis on efficiency; labor emphasis on equity and voice.

integrative bargaining principles, but negotiators differ in how they rate traditional and integrative approaches—management negotiators rate the integrative approach higher than the traditional approach, but union negotiators prefer traditional bargaining.[76]

This chapter has mostly focused on what might be called "institutional bargaining"—bargaining between unions and corporations or public sector organizations. This institutional bargaining is focused on the formal, periodic negotiation of a collective bargaining agreement. However, there is an important second level of negotiations—daily contests between workers and managers over working conditions, performance expectations, and the like. This has been called "fractional bargaining," but a more intuitive label is perhaps "employee bargaining."[77] Employee bargaining might take place through the grievance procedure (Chapter 9), but it might also occur informally between individual workers and supervisors, and it is also an important element of quality circles, work teams, and other initiatives to involve workers in workplace decision making (Chapter 10). Many of the concepts presented in this chapter are equally instructive for employee bargaining: distributive versus integrative bargaining strategies, the importance of BATNA and the environment, and the need for careful preparation as the foundation for negotiating success.

Bargaining between unions and employers is one of the important processes of U.S. labor relations. For individual labor relations professionals, bargaining is a dynamic and fascinating yet stressful activity that requires strong communication and problem-solving skills. Institutionally, collective bargaining serves efficiency, equity, and voice: Efficiency is served by having employers' interests represented at the bargaining table, equity can be achieved by harnessing employees' collective strength to better balance employers' power and produce fair outcomes, and voice is fulfilled by having the terms and conditions of employment negotiated rather than unilaterally imposed by someone else. In U.S. collective bargaining, the end result is almost always a written union contract. The content and the resolution of disputes that arise under the terms of these contracts are the subjects of Chapter 9. But first, the next chapter discusses what happens if bargaining fails.

Key Terms

bargaining structure, *240*
pattern bargaining, *241*
bargaining power, *242*
bargaining environment, *242*
contract costing, *245*
unilateral change, *245*
direct dealing, *246*
surface bargaining, *247*
mandatory bargaining item, *247*
permissive bargaining item, *248*
mixed motive, *249*
distributive bargaining, *249*
integrative bargaining, *251*
attitudinal structuring, *254*
intraorganizational bargaining, *255*
multilateral bargaining, *259*

Reflection Questions

1. In a concise paragraph, paraphrase what you have learned about bargaining strategies to inform a friend about the options for negotiating his or her starting salary and other items for a new job.
2. Distributive bargaining is sometimes referred to as "win–lose bargaining." Where does this label come from? How can it be misleading? Also, some people casually characterize any negotiated settlement as "a win–win." Why is this accurate in layperson's terms but inaccurate in light of how negotiation experts use the term *win–win*?
3. Choose one of the scenarios from the "HR Strategy: Responding to a Union Organizing Drive" box at the end of Chapter 6, and assume that the union wins recognition. As an HR manager, how would you prepare for negotiations? What type of information would be important for you? What type of bargaining priorities and strategies would you develop? How would your answers change if you were a union representative?
4. Why is it difficult for labor negotiators to switch from traditional to integrative bargaining? What recommendations would you make for negotiators trying to make this switch? Why is it more difficult for union negotiators to make this change compared to company negotiators?
5. Use the three fictitious newspaper articles that follow this question to analyze the bargaining environment for contract negotiations between copper producer Phelps Dodge and Morenci Miners Local 616. Create a traditional outline or a mind map (a radial outline) for one of the years. Use the major dimensions of the bargaining environment as your major categories. Note that the newspaper articles are based on fact but have been embellished for educational use.

Three Fictitious Newspaper Articles to Accompany Reflection Question 5

From the *Copper Era* (Clifton, Arizona):

PD, Miners Set to Bargain ... Again

Copper Prices Up; Local Union Confident

MORENCI, AZ; November 14, 1954. The rhetoric is heating up again in Clifton and Morenci as Mine-Mill Local 616 prepares to negotiate a new collective bargaining agreement with Phelps Dodge. The Morenci Miners Local 616 represents 2,000 open-pit mine laborers and mill and smelter production workers. The major issues this year appear to be medical coverage and the length of the agreement. Collective bargaining agreements between Morenci Miners Local 616 and Phelps Dodge have been one-year agreements since the first contract was signed after a 107-day strike in 1946. This year, the International Union of Mine, Mill, and Smelter Workers has been pushing for three year contracts for its 100,000 members nationally. The local union enters negotiations confidently. "The miners know how important the union is," says longtime Local 616 president David Velasquez.

The copper industry continues to benefit from several economic trends and forces. Automobiles and housing construction are two primary consumers of copper and the postwar boom in both industries continues to push copper prices higher. Pending legislation to create a federally funded interstate highway network would probably continue strong automobile demand, experts contend. Adding to demand in recent years was the Korean conflict. Phelps Dodge, the third largest domestic copper producer, has consequently realized an average return on its investment of close to 20 percent while the other copper producers' returns have been between 8 and 16 percent.

Nationally, aggregate union ranks continue to swell with more and more members each year, but the Mine-Mill negotiations are set against a backdrop of union rivalry and competition. While the 1952 deaths of AFL leader William Green and CIO leader Phillip Murray have reduced the fiery nature of the public feud between the two federations, and a no-raid agreement is rumored to be close to finalizing, there is still a long history of bitter divisions between the craft and industrial unions at Phelps Dodge. Morenci Miners Local 616 is one of 13 unions at the Morenci mine and the primarily Mexican-American miners local continues to be ostracized from the predominately white craft unions.

Adding to the inter-union conflict is the Mine-Mill's national leadership's Communist party sympathies. Mine-Mill and several other unions were expelled from the CIO in 1950 and the Steelworkers and Auto Workers unions have been trying to raid Mine-Mill locals ever since. A section of the Taft–Hartley Act has been used to deny Mine-Mill the protections of the National Labor Relations Board and the recently passed Communist Control Act opens up the national Mine-Mill leadership to criminal prosecution.

A planned union rally in Clifton was cut short by the arrival of the first television set in Clifton. Ironically, the first program broadcast was the trial of three leaders of the Farm Equipment Workers Union for alleged Communist activities. These trials are part of the ongoing investigations spearheaded by Senator Joseph McCarthy (R–WI). The mood could only have been more somber if the McClellan Committee hearings investigating union corruption had also been broadcast, but the Ed Sullivan Show followed the McCarthy hearing. Phelps Dodge continues to ban television sets in the company town of Morenci.

Continued

From the *Arizona Tribune* (Phoenix, Arizona):

USW-led Coalition to Bargain in Copper

Industrywide Strike Feared with New Bargaining Structure

SALT LAKE CITY, UT; March 16, 1967. Twenty-six unions have been meeting this week to hammer out plans for negotiating as a coalition against the copper industry when the major union contracts expire this summer. The coalition has been named the "Non-Ferrous Industry Conference" (NIC) and is being led by the United Steelworkers of America (USW), with significant assistance from the AFL–CIO's Industrial Union Department (IUD). Tomorrow the coalition members will vote on the NIC's bargaining goals, a 38-page booklet some have dubbed "Heaven in '67."

The coalition's main goal, however, is no secret: industrywide uniformity in collective bargaining agreements covering the Big Four copper companies' mining, manufacturing, and refining operations in the United States and Canada covering over 60,000 workers at 73 locations. A USW spokesperson said the two primary objectives are companywide master agreements and simultaneous expiration dates across the industry. This outcome would be a drastic departure from traditional copper bargaining. For example, in previous negotiations at Phelps Dodge, the second largest domestic copper producer with 15,000 employees nationally, management has agreed to similar contracts for its four Arizona mining properties, including milling and smelting operations, but separate negotiations have always been the rule for its refinery and fabrication operations located throughout the United States.

The 26 unions participating in the NIC are quite diverse and observers of the labor movement are watching with keen interest to see if the alliance holds. The diversity stems from copper's history of decentralized bargaining and representation. The USW primarily represents unskilled mine employees and mill and smelter production employees. The Operating Engineers represent power shovel operators, the Teamsters and various railroad craft unions represent workers who haul mined ore to mills, and numerous craft unions represent mill and smelter maintenance workers. The Auto Workers and other industrial unions represent myriad workers in copper refining and fabrication.

To explain the existing union solidarity in the NIC, experts point to 12 years of a united AFL–CIO and perhaps more importantly, to the recently finalized USW merger plans with the Mine, Mill, and Smelter Workers, or Mine-Mill. Mine-Mill has been plagued by Communist influences for two decades. The USW has been trying to raid Mine-Mill locals around the country for 15 years, but very rarely with success. Last year, a Supreme Court ruling reversed convictions against Mine-Mill leaders for allegedly lying on anticommunist oaths and in January, 40,000 Mine-Mill workers agreed to join the million-member USW. A majority of workers in copper now belong to the USW and it comes as no surprise that the USW is leading the NIC. According to conference participants, Joseph Molony, a USW vice president, is likely to be named chief negotiator for the NIC. Some of the other 25 unions, however, are nervous that USW attention will be diverted once steel negotiations begin. Steel contracts expire next summer.

The Johnson administration has publicly declined comment; insiders say that Defense Secretary Robert McNamara and Treasury Secretary Henry Fowler will be kept apprised of developments at the bargaining table when talks begin next month. Armed conflict in Vietnam continues to increase and labor experts are certain that any strike would be on an industrywide basis. "The IUD appears determined to bring stability to copper bargaining via industrywide bargaining–a stance likely to require an industrywide strike," says Jim Scoville, assistant professor of economics at Harvard University. Such a strike, sources say, could have negative implications for the war effort and for the country's balance of payments. The Taft–Hartley Act gives the president powers to force an 80-day cooling-off period for national emergency strikes, but no one knows whether Johnson would invoke these powers if there was an industrywide strike.

Coincidentally, governors from five western states have been meeting in Phoenix this week to discuss matters of mutual concern. The governors unanimously endorsed a statement calling for productive negotiations between the unions and the copper industry. The Arizona governor is particularly apprehensive due to copper's importance to the state economy. Roughly 60 percent of U.S. copper comes from Arizona and 10 percent of earnings in Arizona comes from copper employment.

Copper prices have been rising for most of the decade, but industry analysts caution that new deposits of copper have recently been discovered in Africa and South America. Currently, imports amount to 5 percent of U.S. consumption. The Big Four copper companies targeted by the NIC account for nearly 90 percent of all U.S. copper mining, smelting, and refining. The Big Four are all engaged primarily in the nonferrous metals industry with little diversification. Phelps Dodge, in particular, is known for being self-financing and rarely borrows capital on the open market. An IUD spokesperson estimates that military-related U.S. copper consumption will amount to 600 million pounds in 1967, or enough to build more than 15 million cars. Sources at the Pentagon say that the government is considering a 10 percent "set aside" of all U.S. copper production for defense purposes. Several professors call this proposal "previously unheard of."

Continued

From the *New York Journal* (New York, New York):

Phelps Dodge, Copper Unions Open Talks

1982 Losses, Kennecott Settlement Seen as Complicating Factors

NEW YORK, NY; May 4, 1983. Negotiations over new collective bargaining agreements between copper producer Phelps Dodge and 13 unions began today in Phoenix. Phelps Dodge lost $74 million in 1982 as the worst recession since the 1930s shut down automobile factories and new construction—copper's biggest customers. Industry analysts disagree about whether copper prices will rebound any time soon. While negotiators refused comment, Phelps Dodge is reportedly seeking $2 per hour wage cuts, an end to cost-of-living adjustments (COLA), and benefits reductions. Industry leader and SOHIO subsidiary Kennecott, however, surprised the industry last month by agreeing to a new contract containing only minor benefits concessions. The Kennecott settlement, which preserves wage rates and the COLA clause, "dropped a bombshell on the industry" says George Hildebrand, a labor relations expert at Cornell University.

The 13 unions have joined forces as the "Unity Council" and are jointly negotiating contracts covering 2000 workers at Phelps Dodge's remote Arizona properties in Morenci, Ajo, Douglas, and Bisbee. Union contracts for Phelps Dodge's Tyrone, New Mexico mine, mill, and smelter complex expire next year. The Unity Council dates back to 1967 when the unions' attempt to impose industrywide contracts failed. Since that time, the copper unions have followed a practice known as pattern bargaining in which the first settlement in each bargaining round sets the pattern for subsequent negotiations. Consequently, settlements every three years at Phelps Dodge have followed the pattern set at Kennecott or Anaconda, but only after a strike each time. In the last bargaining round, Phelps Dodge withstood a 90-day strike before conceding to the unions' demands. Pattern bargaining and COLAs yielded an annual wage increase of roughly 15 percent in the 1970s, according to Phelps Dodge.

In spite of these successes in the 1970s, observers argue that these are tough times for organized labor. President Reagan is widely believed to be unsympathetic, if not openly hostile, toward labor unions as illustrated by his appointments to the National Labor Relations Board and the firing of the air traffic controllers in 1981. Unions represent a smaller fraction of the workforce than at any other time since World War II and "employers are trying to bust unions like never before" says an AFL–CIO spokesperson. Organized labor has also criticized the Reagan administration's inflation-fighting tight monetary policy and the increased taxation of unemployment insurance benefits.

Labor is also fearful of a Supreme Court decision in *Belknap* v. *Hale*, which is expected some time this summer. A Kentucky court of appeals ruled that an employer who told new employees who were replacing striking workers that they were "permanent" could not discharge the replacements to make room for returning strikers without committing a breach of contract. Labor worries that the Supreme Court will affirm this ruling. Management has had the right to replace striking workers during a labor dispute since the 1938 *Mackay* ruling.

The copper industry has its own worries. Copper imports now account for over 20 percent of domestic consumption—and much of the imported copper is from state-owned mines in places like Chile and Zambia. Even after last month's modest copper price increase to 70¢ per pound, Phelps Dodge loses 10¢ on every pound of copper it produces. In addition to Phelps Dodge's $74 million loss for 1982, Anaconda lost $332 million, Kennecott $189 million, and ASARCO $38 million. According to industry insiders, however, Phelps Dodge is very close to introducing a new solvent extraction-electrowinning process which drastically reduces production costs, eliminates the need for smelting, and makes it cost-effective to extract copper from low-grade ore previously considered waste. Phelps Dodge's Douglas smelter employs 300 people and is the nation's largest polluter of sulfur dioxide.

The Unity Council is being led by the Steelworkers union (USW) a majority of Arizona miners. The Unity Council is following the broader industry goals established by the Nonferrous Industry Committee led by USW vice-president Frank McKee. McKee, 62, has publicly denounced the concession bargaining that has occurred in other industries, notably autos. His name is commonly mentioned as a possible successor to USW president Lloyd McBride who is seriously ill. George Seltzer, professor of industrial relations at the University of Minnesota, describes McKee as "a hard-line, bread-and-butter unionist."

The growing metropolis of Phoenix with its growing base of emerging companies is an odd setting for a classic Western standoff. But from Wall Street to Main Street Morenci, Arizona, where miners were laid off for six months last year and only two-thirds have returned to work, many eyes are focused on the negotiating table at a Phoenix hotel. Unlike many in the United States, the aging Morenci Miners, as they are known locally, have a strong understanding of history, but so, too, does Phelps Dodge.

Ethics in Action Is Bluffing Ethical?

A classic *Harvard Business Review* article argued that business is like a poker game. Because bluffing is a well-known part of both poker and business that everyone does to win, bluffing is ethically acceptable. This theme has been taken up in discussions over labor negotiations often with the same conclusions: Bluffing is part of the game and is therefore harmless because (a) everyone does it and (b) you need to protect yourself against the bluffing of others.

But not everyone agrees; critics emphasize the true nature of bluffing. Don't confuse bluffing with asking for a generous settlement. Opening a negotiation by asking for a 10 percent wage increase and then making compromises is not bluffing—this is readjusting your expectations after seeing the other side's resistance. Bluffing involves intentional deception. An employer claims it has replacement workers already lined up to continue production if the regular employees strike, but it doesn't. A union claims that the employees will strike if the employer insists on any health insurance co-pays, though it knows they won't. These types of deceptions are what bluffing is about.

QUESTIONS

1. With this precise definition of bluffing, do you think bluffing is widespread in labor negotiations?
2. Is bluffing ethical? Does it matter if it is widespread in labor negotiations?

References: Albert Z. Carr, "Is Business Bluffing Ethical?" *Harvard Business Review* 46 (January–February 1968), pp. 143–53; Chris Provis, "Ethics, Deception, and Labor Negotiation," *Journal of Business Ethics* 28 (November 2000), pp. 145–58.

Labor Law Discussion Case 6: Does the Duty to Bargain Preclude Unilateral Wage Increases?

BACKGROUND

Winn-Dixie Stores, Inc., operates a multistate chain of retail food stores. Its volume of business is such that it is engaged in interstate commerce. The United Food and Commercial Workers is the authorized bargaining agent for all employees (with the standard exceptions) engaged in the receiving, shipping, and processing of all food products at the Winn-Dixie warehouse in Jacksonville, Florida.

The previous collective bargaining agreement expired in February, and the two parties were continuing to negotiate a new agreement. On April 8 the company submitted a wage proposal to the union that would increase wages for employees in the bargaining unit by 56 to 81 cents per hour. The offer was rejected by the union. In letters dated April 17 and April 25, the union requested dates for the purpose of collective bargaining.

The company responded to the union in a letter dated May 3. The letter contained two proposals. First, the company suggested arranging a meeting to be held in early June. Second, the company proposed that the wage proposal dated April 8 "be put into effect immediately without prejudice to further bargaining on the subject." The union responded on May 6 by rejecting the wage proposal and emphasized its desire to bargain not only for "wage increases, but increases in pensions, vacations, hospitalization, and other fringe benefits as well as terms and conditions of employment."

The parties met for the purpose of collective bargaining on June 24. Each side discussed the current agreement section by section. Each side, for the most part, simply restated its previously announced bargaining positions. Additionally, the company again expressed its wish to implement the wage proposal of April 8. The company stated that such an increase was necessary to keep its wages competitive in the local labor market because Winn-Dixie warehouse employees had not received a wage increase in over 18 months. The company also stated that it did *not* intend to have the implementation of this wage increase foreclose further bargaining on the subject of wages. Again the union would not agree to this wage proposal. The union preferred to first reach agreement on premium pay, holidays, vacations, the pension plan, and arbitration.

Similar negotiating sessions occurred on July 1 and July 2. At the second of these two meetings the company informed the union that as of July 7, it was implementing the proposed wage increase. The company further proposed that the union and the company post joint notice of this increase, stating that it was an interim increase and further bargaining was still taking place. The union replied that it would not agree and that if the company implemented the increase, the union would file an unfair labor practice charge.

The company implemented the wage increase plan on July 7.

THE UNION'S POSITION

The unilateral change for wages of employees represented by the union violates Sections 8(a)(5) and 8(a)(1) of the National Labor Relations Act.

THE COMPANY'S POSITION

A unilateral change in wages or working conditions by an employer during negotiations, in the absence of an impasse, does not per se establish a failure of the duty to bargain. In fact, the union was given ample notice of the proposed changes, and there was adequate time for the union to make counterproposals.

QUESTIONS

1. You are an administrative law judge who has to decide this case. With which party do you agree? Why?
2. Does it matter that the parties were not at an impasse?

Digging Deeper Marshall's Conditions and Bargaining Power

A key determinant of labor's bargaining power is the strength of the employer's demand for labor. Specifically, labor's bargaining power is greater when labor demand is less responsive to wage changes (so a wage increase will not reduce employment much)—that is, when labor demand is less elastic in economics terminology. Marshall's conditions state that labor demand is less elastic when (1) labor is essential or difficult to replace, (2) demand for the resulting product or service is inelastic (less responsive to price changes), (3) labor accounts for a small fraction of the entire production cost, and (4) supply of the other factors of production is inelastic.[78] Considering these four conditions is a longstanding way to think about labor's bargaining power, as can be illustrated by considering the grocery industry.

The importance of the labor market for relative bargaining power is captured in the first dimension of Marshall's conditions. When the labor market is tight (low unemployment), it is more difficult to hire new employees, so labor's bargaining power will be higher. On the other hand, if grocery clerks, for example, do not need special skills, they are easily replaced by new hires and will have less bargaining power. Strike leverage that comes from perishable products is also a form of labor being difficult to replace because perishable products imply the need for immediate replacement of employees. On the other hand, weakened strike leverage because of a large inventory of nonperishable goods is a form of labor being easy to replace. For example, think of a warehouse-format grocery store that is already stocked with huge quantities of boxed and canned goods. In this case it might not take much labor to operate during a strike. Lastly, if it is easy to substitute machines for labor, such as by replacing grocery checkout clerks with self-service checkout stations, then labor is more easily replaced and its bargaining power is lower.

Industry ability to pay, market concentration, and the nature of product market competition are captured by Marshall's second condition. With greater demand for take-out food, grocery stores face increased competition from restaurants. This competition makes product demand for grocery stores more dependent on price and quality, which in turn reduces labor's bargaining power in grocery stores. For example, a wage increase for grocery employees cannot be passed along to consumers because they have significant alternatives. In many industries, though not in grocery stores, increased globalization reduces labor's bargaining power by making product demand more elastic through increased imports and by making the supply of other factors more elastic through increased capital mobility. Increased competitive pressure, whether from globalization, domestic nonunion competitors, or deregulation, is perhaps the single most important change in the bargaining environment in the postwar period.

With respect to Marshall's third condition, grocery store employees are a large fraction of total costs; thus even a small wage increase can translate into a large increase in total costs, so labor's power is lower. There is a tension between this condition and the first one, however: A union will generally have greater bargaining power if it represents all employees because it can be harder to replace the entire workforce during a strike.

Marshall's fourth condition reveals that labor demand is also related to the availability of other factors of production. If the cost of self-service checkout stands declines, labor's bargaining power also declines. The macroeconomic environment can also affect bargaining power through Marshall's conditions. When the economy is booming, consumers have more disposable income, which might make the demand for groceries less responsive to price changes (less elastic) and thus increase labor's bargaining power.

In addition to labor demand factors, the economic environment also affects labor supply and therefore bargaining power. While labor demand captures an employer's demand for labor, labor supply captures the willingness of individuals to offer their services as workers. When the economy is booming, it is likely to be easier for workers and their spouses to find another job during a strike. This additional income can change the workers' labor supply decisions and strengthen labor's bargaining position. The extent of union strike benefits, the amount of workers' savings, and whether striking workers are eligible for unemployment insurance can also factor into labor's bargaining power.

Reference: Alfred Marshall, *Principles of Economics,* 8th ed. (New York: Macmillan, 1920); George J. Borjas, *Labor Economics,* 6th ed. (Boston: McGraw-Hill/Irwin, 2012).

End Notes

1. Arthur M. Ross, *Trade Union Wage Policy* (Berkeley: University of California Press, 1948), p. 11.
2. Robert M. Cassel, *Negotiating a Labor Contract: A Management Handbook*, 4th ed. (Washington, DC: Bureau of National Affairs, 2010).
3. Roger Fisher and Danny Ertel, *Getting Ready to Negotiate: The Getting to YES Workbook* (New York: Penguin Books, 1995).
4. Maurice B. Better, *Contract Bargaining Handbook for Local Union Leaders* (Washington, DC: Bureau of National Affairs, 1993); Cassel, *Negotiating a Labor Contract.*
5. John P. Hoerr, *And the Wolf Finally Came: The Decline of the American Steel Industry* (Pittsburgh: University of Pittsburgh, 1988); Garth L. Mangum and R. Scott McNabb, *The Rise, Fall, and Replacement of Industrywide Bargaining in the Basic Steel Industry* (Armonk, NY: M. E. Sharpe, 1997).
6. Wallace E. Hendricks and Lawrence M. Kahn, "The Determinants of Bargaining Structure in U.S. Manufacturing Industries," *Industrial and Labor Relations Review* 35 (January 1982), pp. 181–95.
7. Harry C. Katz, "The Decentralization of Collective Bargaining: A Literature Review and Comparative Analysis," *Industrial and Labor Relations Review* 47 (October 1993), pp. 3–22; Robert J. Flanagan, "The Changing Structure of Collective Bargaining," in Paul Blyton et al. (eds.), *Sage Handbook of Industrial Relations* (London: Sage, 2008), pp. 406–19.
8. John W. Budd, "The Determinants and Extent of UAW Pattern Bargaining," *Industrial and Labor Relations Review* 45 (April 1992), pp. 523–39; Christopher L. Erickson, "A Re-Interpretation of Pattern Bargaining," *Industrial and Labor Relations Review* 49 (July 1996), pp. 615–34.
9. Budd, "The Determinants and Extent of UAW Pattern Bargaining"; John W. Budd, "Institutional and Market Determinants of Wage Spillovers: Evidence from UAW Pattern Bargaining," *Industrial Relations* 36 (January 1997), pp. 97–116.
10. John W. Budd, "The Internal Union Political Imperative for UAW Pattern Bargaining," *Journal of Labor Research* 16 (Winter 1995), pp. 43–55.
11. Neil W. Chamberlain and James W. Kuhn, *Collective Bargaining*, 2nd ed. (New York: McGraw-Hill, 1965), p. 170; Terry L. Leap and David W. Grigsby, "A Conceptualization of Collective Bargaining Power," *Industrial and Labor Relations Review* 39 (January 1986), pp. 202–13.
12. David Lewin, "Technological Change in the Public Sector: The Case of Sanitation Service," in Daniel B. Cornfield (ed.), *Workers, Managers, and Technological Change* (New York: Plenum, 1987), pp. 281–309.
13. Harry Wellington and Ralph K. Winter, Jr., *The Unions and the Cities* (Washington, DC: Brookings Institution, 1971).
14. Victor G. Devinatz, "The Real Difference between the Old Unionism and the New Unionism: A New Strategy for U.S. Public Sector Unions," *Journal of Collective Negotiations in the Public Sector* 28 (1999), pp. 29–39; Joseph E. Slater, *Public Workers: Government Employee Unions, the Law, and the State, 1900–1962* (Ithaca, NY: Cornell University Press, 2004).
15. Jeffrey H. Keefe, "A Reconsideration and Empirical Evaluation of Wellington's and Winter's, *The Union and the Cities*," *Comparative Labor Law and Policy Journal* 34 (Winter 2013), pp. 251–75.
16. Max H. Bazerman and Margaret A. Neale, *Negotiating Rationally* (New York: Free Press, 1992).
17. Raymond A. Friedman, *Front Stage, Backstage: The Dramatic Structure of Labor Negotiations* (Cambridge, MA: MIT Press, 1994).
18. Friedman, *Front Stage, Backstage*, p. 87.
19. Friedman, *Front Stage, Backstage*, p. 111.
20. Friedman, *Front Stage, Backstage*, p. 87.
21. Michael H. Granoff, Jay E. Grenig, and Moira J. Kelly, *How to Cost Your Labor Contract*, 2nd ed. (Washington, DC: Bureau of National Affairs, 2011).
22. Better, *Contract Bargaining Handbook for Local Union Leaders*; Cassel, *Negotiating a Labor Contract.*
23. *Taft Broadcasting*, 163 NLRB 475, 478 (1967).
24. *NLRB v. Katz*, 369 U.S. 736 (1962).
25. *Harris-Teeter Super Markets*, 310 NLRB 216 (1993).
26. *United Technologies Corp.*, 274 NLRB 1069 (1985), enfd. 789 F.2d 121 (2d Cir. 1986).
27. Linda G. Kahn, *Primer of Labor Relations*, 25th ed. (Washington, DC: Bureau of National Affairs, 1994).
28. *NLRB v. Truitt Mfg. Co.*, 351 U.S. 149 (1956); Kenneth G. Dau-Schmidt, "The Story of *NLRB v. Truitt Manufacturing Co.* and *NLRB v. Insurance Agents' International Union:* The Duty to Bargain in Good Faith," in Laura J. Cooper and Catherine L. Fisk (eds.), *Labor Law Stories* (New York: Foundation Press, 2005), pp. 107–48.

29. *Lakeland Bus Lines,* 335 NLRB No. 29 (2001).
30. Bruce S. Feldacker, *Labor Guide to Labor Law,* 4th ed. (Upper Saddle River, NJ: Prentice Hall, 2000).
31. *NLRB v. Insurance Agent's International Union,* 361 U.S. 477, 487 (1960).
32. *Atlanta Hilton and Tower,* 271 NLRB 1600 (1984).
33. *NLRB v. Wooster Division of Borg-Warner Corporation,* 356 U.S. 342 (1958).
34. *Fibreboard Paper Products Corporation v. NLRB,* 379 U.S. 203 (1964).
35. Richard E. Walton and Robert B. McKersie, *A Behavioral Theory of Labor Negotiations* (New York: McGraw-Hill, 1965).
36. Walton and McKersie, *A Behavioral Theory of Labor Negotiations.*
37. Roy J. Lewicki, David M. Saunders, and Bruce Barry, *Negotiation,* 5th ed. (Boston: McGraw-Hill/Irwin, 2006).
38. Roger Fisher, William Ury, and Bruce Patton, *Getting to YES: Negotiating Agreement Without Giving In,* 2nd ed. (New York: Penguin Books, 1991).
39. Howard Raiffa, *The Art and Science of Negotiation* (Cambridge, MA: Harvard University Press, 1982); and Walton and McKersie, *A Behavioral Theory of Labor Negotiations.*
40. Walton and McKersie, *A Behavioral Theory of Labor Negotiations.*
41. Lewicki, Saunders, and Barry, *Negotiation*; Walton and McKersie, *A Behavioral Theory of Labor Negotiations.*
42. Walton and McKersie, *A Behavioral Theory of Labor Negotiations*; Joel Cutcher-Gershenfeld, "Interest-Based Bargaining," in William K. Roche, Paul Teague, and Alexander J.S. Colvin, eds., *The Oxford Handbook of Conflict Management in Organizations* (Oxford: Oxford University Press, 2014), pp. 150–67.
43. Fisher, Ury, and Patton, *Getting to YES.*
44. Carolyn Brommer, George Buckingham, and Steven Loeffler, "Cooperative Bargaining Styles at FMCS: A Movement toward Choices," *Pepperdine Dispute Resolution Law Journal* 2 (2002), pp. 465–90.
45. Walton and McKersie, *A Behavioral Theory of Labor Negotiations.*
46. Better, *Contract Bargaining Handbook for Local Union Leaders.*
47. Fisher, Ury, and Patton, *Getting to YES;* Lewicki, Saunders, and Barry, *Negotiation.*
48. Brommer, Buckingham, and Loeffler, "Cooperative Bargaining Styles at FMCS."
49. Edward Cohen-Rosenthal and Cynthia E. Burton, *Mutual Gains: A Guide to Union–Management Cooperation,* 2nd ed. (Ithaca, NY: ILR Press, 1993); David S. Weiss, *Beyond the Walls of Conflict: Mutual Gains Negotiating for Unions and Management* (Chicago: Irwin, 1996).
50. Friedman, *Front Stage, Backstage.*
51. Margaret A. Neale and Max H. Bazerman, *Cognition and Rationality in Negotiation* (New York: Free Press, 1991).
52. Weiss, *Beyond the Walls of Conflict.*
53. Friedman, *Front Stage, Backstage.*
54. Friedman, *Front Stage, Backstage,* p. 115.
55. Walton and McKersie, *A Behavioral Theory of Labor Negotiations.*
56. Robert B. McKersie and Richard E. Walton, "From the Behavioral Theory to the Future of Negotiations," in Thomas A. Kochan and David B. Lipsky (eds.), *Negotiations and Change: From the Workplace to Society* (Ithaca, NY: ILR Press, 2003), pp. 301–14; Richard E. Walton, Joel E. Cutcher-Gershenfeld, and Robert B. McKersie, *Strategic Negotiations: A Theory of Change in Labor–Management Relations* (Boston: Harvard Business School Press, 1994).
57. Leonard Greenhalgh and Roy J. Lewicki, "New Directions in Teaching Negotiations: From Walton and McKersie to the New Millennium," in Thomas A. Kochan and David B. Lipsky (eds.), *Negotiations and Change: From the Workplace to Society* (Ithaca, NY: ILR Press, 2003), pp. 20–34.
58. Thomas A. Kochan and David B. Lipsky, "Conceptual Foundations: Walton and McKersie's Subprocesses," in Thomas A. Kochan and David B. Lipsky (eds.), *Negotiations and Change: From the Workplace to Society* (Ithaca, NY: ILR Press, 2003), pp. 15–19.
59. Walton and McKersie, *A Behavioral Theory of Labor Negotiations*; Walton, Cutcher-Gershenfeld, and McKersie, *Strategic Negotiations.*
60. Walton and McKersie, *A Behavioral Theory of Labor Negotiations.*

61. Ross, *Trade Union Wage Policy.*
62. Friedman, *Front Stage, Backstage*; Walton and McKersie, *A Behavioral Theory of Labor Negotiations.*
63. Robert B. McKersie et al., "Bargaining Theory Meets Interest-Based Negotiations: A Case Study," *Industrial Relations* 47 (January 2008), pp. 66–96.
64. *Mid-Wilshire Health Care Center,* 337 NLRB No. 7 (2001).
65. John T. Dunlop, *Dispute Resolution: Negotiation and Consensus Building* (Dover, MA: Auburn House Publishing, 1984), p. 10.
66. Richard C. Kearney and Patrice M. Mareschal, *Labor Relations in the Public Sector,* 5th ed. (Boca Raton, FL: CRC Press, 2014).
67. B.V.H. Schneider, "Public Sector Labor Legislation—An Evolutionary Analysis," in Benjamin Aaron, Joyce M. Najita, and James L. Stern (eds.), *Public Sector Bargaining,* 2nd ed. (Washington, DC: Bureau of National Affairs, 1988), pp. 189–228; Robert Hebdon, Joseph E. Slater, and Marick F. Masters, "Public Sector Collective Bargaining: Tumultuous Times," in Howard R. Stanger, Paul F. Clark, and Ann C. Frost (eds.), *Collective Bargaining under Duress: Case Studies of Major North American Industries* (Champaign, IL: Labor and Employment Relations Association, 2013), pp. 255–95.
68. Joyce M. Najita and James L. Stern (eds.), *Collective Bargaining in the Public Sector: The Experience of Eight States* (Armonk, NY: M. E. Sharpe, 2001).
69. Milton Derber, "Management Organization for Collective Bargaining in the Public Sector," in Benjamin Aaron, Joyce M. Najita, and James L. Stern (eds.), *Public Sector Bargaining,* 2nd ed. (Washington, DC: Bureau of National Affairs, 1988), pp. 90–123; Hervey A. Juris and Peter Feuille, *Police Unionism: Power and Impact in Public Sector Bargaining* (Lexington, MA: Lexington Books, 1973); Thomas A. Kochan, "A Theory of Multilateral Bargaining in City Governments," *Industrial and Labor Relations Review* 27 (July 1974), pp. 525–42.
70. Devinatz, "The Real Difference between the Old Unionism and the New Unionism"; Jeffrey Zax and Casey Ichniowski, "The Effects of Public Sector Unionism on Pay, Employment, Department Budgets, and Municipal Expenditures," in Richard B. Freeman and Casey Ichniowski (eds.), *When Public Sector Workers Unionize* (Chicago: University of Chicago Press, 1988), pp. 323–63.
71. Juris and Feuille, *Unionism.*
72. Walton, Cutcher-Gershenfeld, and McKersie, *Strategic Negotiations.*
73. Julius G. Getman, *The Betrayal of Local 14* (Ithaca, NY: ILR Press, 1998); Dave Hage and Paul Klauda, *No Retreat, No Surrender: Labor's War at Hormel* (New York: William Morrow, 1989); Jonathan D. Rosenblum, *Copper Crucible: How the Arizona Miners' Strike of 1983 Recast Labor–Management Relations in America* (Ithaca, NY: ILR Press, 1995); Walton, Cutcher-Gershenfeld, and McKersie, *Strategic Negotiations*.
74. Walton, Cutcher-Gershenfeld, and McKersie, *Strategic Negotiations.*
75. Joel Cutcher-Gershenfeld, "Bargaining over How to Bargain in Labor–Management Negotiations," *Negotiation Journal* 10 (October 1994), pp. 323–35.
76. Joel Cutcher-Gershenfeld and Thomas Kochan, "Taking Stock: Collective Bargaining at the Turn of the Century," *Industrial and Labor Relations Review* 58 (October 2004), pp. 3–26; Joel Cutcher-Gershenfeld et al., "Collective Bargaining in the Twenty-First Century: A Negotiations Institution at Risk," *Negotiation Journal* 23 (July 2007), pp. 249–65.
77. James W. Kuhn, *Bargaining and Grievance Settlements* (New York: Columbia University Press, 1962).
78. Alfred Marshall, *Principles of Economics,* 8th ed. (New York: Macmillan, 1920); George J. Borjas, *Labor Economics,* 5th ed. (Boston: McGraw-Hill/Irwin, 2010); Flanagan, "The Changing Structure of Collective Bargaining."

Chapter Eight

Impasses, Strikes, and Dispute Resolution

Advance Organizer

The goal of the bargaining process described in the previous chapter is for labor and management negotiators to reach an agreement on the terms and conditions of employment, usually in the form of a written union contract. Sometimes, however, negotiations are unsuccessful and impasses are reached. This chapter outlines what happens when impasses occur and the alternative methods for their resolution.

Learning Objectives

By the end of this chapter, you should be able to

1. **Explore** options for resolving bargaining disputes and impasses.
2. **Understand** different types of strikes and lockouts, their roles in labor relations, and their legal restrictions in the private and public sectors.
3. **Discuss** the controversies surrounding the use of strike replacements.
4. **Identify** other types of pressure tactics beyond strikes and lockouts and why they are being used more frequently than in the past.
5. **Compare** the major third-party dispute resolution mechanisms (mediation, arbitration, and fact-finding) and their strengths and weaknesses.

Contents

The previous chapter discussed the bargaining process, especially as it pertains to negotiating a union contract that specifies wages, benefits, and other terms and conditions of employment. In this process, negotiators do not have to reach an agreement. The National Labor Relations Act (NLRA) specifically states that the good faith bargaining obligation "does not compel either party to agree to a proposal or require the making of a concession" [Section 8(d)]. Public sector bargaining laws in many states use the same language. A bargaining impasse can therefore occur when labor and management negotiators fail to agree on a mutually acceptable set of terms and conditions of employment.

Bargaining impasses are rare. Of the thousands of intent to bargain notices filed annually with the Federal Mediation and Conciliation Service, only around 1 percent result in strikes.[1] Nevertheless, bargaining disputes or impasses and methods for their resolution are central topics in labor relations for several reasons. First, the possibility of a bargaining dispute underlies all labor negotiations because the threat of strikes, lockouts, and other pressure tactics—also known as economic weapons—can be used to try to force the other side to make additional concessions at the bargaining table. Second, bargaining in good faith to an impasse fulfills each side's legal bargaining obligation. This is significant because the employer is then free to implement the terms of its final offer (such as new wage rates or benefit packages) even over the objection of the union. Third, even though infrequent, major strikes can have devastating consequences for workers, employers, and the public and are therefore important to understand. Companies can lose customers and profits and see their stock prices decline; public sector agencies can lose the support of taxpayers and voters; workers can lose income and face severe emotional and financial strain, including struggling to pay for food and rent; communities might be divided and suffer economic losses; and the public can be deprived of important goods, services, and sources of transportation.

Fourth, some dispute resolution methods can be used before an impasse is reached (especially mediation), and others are designed to prevent an impasse from occurring (especially arbitration); thus their significance is greater than a low dispute rate might otherwise indicate. And finally, the method used to resolve bargaining disputes is a defining feature of different labor relations systems or laws. In the public sector, for example, striking is often illegal and a bargaining impasse typically triggers a mandatory dispute resolution mechanism, especially mediation, arbitration, or fact-finding. Students of labor relations should therefore understand the alternative methods of dispute resolution, along with their advantages and disadvantages.

There are two broad categories of disputes in labor relations: interest disputes and rights disputes. As the name suggests, **interest disputes** pertain to conflicts of interest—higher wages (the employees' interest) versus lower labor costs (the employer's interest), seniority-based layoffs versus merit-based layoffs, broad union input into managerial issues versus strict management rights to conduct business without interference. These conflicts of interest are the focus of contract negotiations. Compromises on these conflicts result in specific contractual terms—a wage and benefits package and language governing layoffs and management rights, for example. In contrast, rights disputes are disagreements over whether someone's rights have been violated. In labor relations, these rights are specified in the union contract. Rights disputes are therefore grievances—conflicts over the application and interpretation of a contract. The resolution of rights disputes is the focus of Chapter 9. The current chapter focuses on interest disputes—conflicts that occur during the negotiation of *new* contract terms, not over the interpretation of *existing* terms.

In learning about interest disputes, it is important to remember the concepts presented in the previous chapter on bargaining. The dimensions of the bargaining environment influence the alternatives to a negotiated agreement, and thereby determine each side's best alternative to a negotiated agreement (BATNA). A strong labor market, for example, enhances workers' BATNA because it is easy to find comparable jobs elsewhere; laws that allow the use of replacement workers during strikes can enhance employers' BATNA by making it easier to operate during a strike. Each side's BATNA, in turn, determines whether there is a positive settlement range, and therefore whether a settlement is likely to result without a bargaining dispute (recall Figure 7.3). But even with a positive settlement range, a bargaining dispute might occur because of negative attitudes that are generated by hard bargaining tactics (recall the attitudinal structuring bargaining subprocess), differing preferences within a union or an employer's management team (recall the intraorganizational bargaining subprocess), or other factors that will be described in this chapter.

STRIKES AND LOCKOUTS

A strike occurs when employees refuse to work until an employer changes its position on one or more issues. The *Oxford English Dictionary* traces this usage of the word *strike* to British sailors in 1768 who struck (lowered) their ships' sails to halt shipping until their

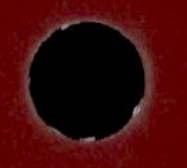

Labor Relations Application Children Workers, Children Strikers

Strikes to protest and force improvements in substandard wages, hours, and working conditions have occurred throughout history. It is therefore no surprise that in situations with significant numbers of child workers, children have attempted to improve their jobs by striking. Some notable strikes by children in the United States include these:

- *Patterson Cotton Mill strike* (New Jersey, 1828): Children struck for three weeks to change their lunch hour back to noon and to reduce daily working hours from 13½ to 9 hours. The strikers won the former but not the latter.
- *Lowell Textile Mill strike* (Massachusetts, 1836): Two thousand women and girls, including some as young as 10 or 11 years old, struck when a rent increase at the company-owned boardinghouses amounted to a 12 percent reduction in pay. After a month the strike was broken by evicting the workers from the boardinghouses.
- *Newsies strike* (New York City, 1899): At the turn of the century, newspapers in major cities were often sold by newspaper boys (newsies) between the ages of 8 and 15 hawking papers on street corners after school. The newsies bought the papers wholesale from the newspaper companies and kept whatever they took in from customers; unsold papers could not be returned. In 1899 two of the leading New York City publishers, William Randolph Hearst and Joseph Pulitzer, increased the wholesale price to the newsies while keeping the retail price unchanged. When the publishers refused to rescind this increase, newsies boycotted their papers. Striking newsies attacked other newsies who ignored the boycott, and in spite of their leaders being bought off by the publishers, the strike ended with a victory—the papers did not rescind the price increase but agreed to a policy of refunding newsies for their unsold papers each day.
- *Garment workers' strike* (New York City and Philadelphia, 1909–1910): In late November 1909, 20,000 girls and young, unmarried women struck almost 500 sewing factories in New York City for better wages, reduced hours, no fees for supplies, improvements in safety, and union recognition. Hundreds of strikers were beaten on the picket lines and then arrested. The sewing companies tried moving production to Philadelphia, but five days before Christmas, garment workers in Philadelphia also struck. By late January and early February, most of the workers had won wage improvements, a shorter workweek (52 hours), no supply fees, and an arbitration board to resolve grievances. However, the strike failed to win improvements in safety standards. A year later, a fire at one of the factories where workers demanded safety improvements—the Triangle Shirtwaist Company—killed 146 workers when oil-soaked rags caught on fire and the workers were trapped by locked fire exits.

Reference: Susan Campbell Bartoletti, *Kids on Strike!* (Boston: Houghton Mifflin, 1999).

Children on strike attempting to reduce their workweek from 60 to 55 hours in Philadelphia textile mills (circa 1900). After 2½ months, the strikers ran out of money and returned to work without the reduced workweek.

demands for a higher wage were met.[2] But by whatever name, strikes have occurred for thousands of years, including during construction of the pyramids in ancient Egypt.[3] In the United States, strikes have occurred across the full spectrum of industries and occupations, and even children around the turn of the century in 1900 struck for better pay and hours in various industries.[4] A strike is fundamentally an expression of protest and dissatisfaction, but it is also frequently intended to enhance labor's bargaining power by pressuring an employer: By withholding their labor, strikers seek to increase the employer's cost of disagreement by depriving the employer of profits (private sector) or the ability to satisfy the demands of taxpayers and voters (public sector). If such actions are costly enough, the employer will accept the employees' demands to avoid a threatened strike or settle an ongoing strike.

Types of Strikes

There are a variety of reasons why employees might strike, so there are a number of different types of strikes. Employees might strike to win better wages, benefits, and work rules; this is called an **economic strike.** Such strikes stem from bargaining impasses over mandatory bargaining items when union contracts are being negotiated. Economic strikes are the most frequent type of strikes in U.S. labor relations. Closely related to an economic strike is a **lockout**—an employer-initiated rather than worker-initiated work stoppage during a bargaining impasse. In an economic strike, workers refuse to work until their terms are met; in a lockout, an employer tells the workers not to return until they agree to the employer's terms.

A strike to protest an employer's unfair labor practice is an **unfair labor practice strike.** If employees are striking to force an employer to recognize and bargain with their union, it is called a recognition strike. Striking to support other workers who are on strike (e.g., by not crossing their picket line) is a sympathy strike. Most union contracts contain a no-strike clause prohibiting work stoppages over grievances during the life of the contract, and such strikes are therefore called wildcat strikes. Grievance arbitration is typically used instead of wildcat strikes (Chapter 9). If a union strikes to force an employer to assign certain work to its members, this is a jurisdictional strike.

The Legal Treatment of Strikes

It is important to differentiate between types of strikes because the U.S. legal system treats them differently (see Table 8.1). Economic strikes and unfair labor practice strikes are protected by Section 7 of the NLRA. As such, workers cannot be disciplined or discharged for participating in these types of strikes—to do so would be a Section 8(a)(1) unfair labor practice. As we will detail later in the chapter, however, this does not prevent economic strikers from being replaced. Remember that to be an economic strike, the dispute must be over mandatory bargaining items; permissive items are outside the boundaries of the NLRA, so strikes over these issues are not protected, and workers can be fired for participating in such a strike. Strikes over grievances are considered protected activity under the NLRA, but no-strike clauses in union contracts frequently forfeit this protection. As such, employees who participate in wildcat strikes can often be disciplined. Jurisdictional strikes are prohibited by the NLRA, so unions can be ordered to cease and desist from such strikes. These various limitations on the right to strike, including the legality of permanent strike replacements, reveal that U.S. public policy sees striking as an economic activity to pursue things like higher wages rather than a civil liberty rooted in freedom of association.[5]

The taxonomy of strikes presented in Table 8.1 also applies to public sector strikes, but all types of strikes are more likely to be illegal when conducted by government employees. Prohibiting public sector strikes is rooted in several traditional beliefs: that striking against the government is an unacceptable threat to the supreme authority of the government, that public sector employee bargaining power is too high because there are no market-based checks on their demands, and that government services are too critical to be interrupted. The commonly cited watershed event in creating widespread opposition to public sector strikes is the Boston police strike in 1919, which resulted in looting and violence after police officers walked off the job when their union leaders were suspended by the police commissioner. In the midst of this lawlessness, the Massachusetts Governor (later U.S. President) Calvin Coolidge expressed what would become the common sentiment toward

TABLE 8.1 Types of Strikes

Category	Definition	Private Sector Strikers Protected by the NLRA?
Economic strikes	Strikes over wages, benefits, and work rules (mandatory bargaining items) during contract negotiations. This is the classic form of strike in contemporary U.S. labor relations.	*Yes.* Workers cannot be disciplined or discharged. But workers can be replaced with both permanent and temporary strike replacements.
Unfair labor practice strikes	Strikes in protest against an employer's unfair labor practice(s).	*Yes.* Workers cannot be disciplined, discharged, or permanently replaced. But the NLRB must find that an unfair labor practice was committed.
Recognition strikes	Strikes to force an employer to recognize and bargain with a union. Occurred frequently in labor history, but the NLRA encourages the use of representation elections instead.	*Yes, but can picket for only 30 days.* Workers are protected, but can be permanently replaced. Picketing for recognition is essentially limited to 30 days. After 30 days, workers can strike but not picket.
Sympathy strikes	Strikes in support of other workers on strike.	*Maybe.* A no-strike clause in a contract might be a waiver of protection if the clause clearly includes sympathy strikes. In this case workers are not protected and can be disciplined or discharged. Otherwise sympathy strikes are protected, but strikers can be replaced.
Wildcat strikes	Strikes over grievances while a contract is still in force (not during contract negotiations).	*Occasionally.* A no-strike clause in a contract usually waives protection, so workers can be disciplined or discharged. Otherwise grievance strikes are protected, but strikers can be replaced.
Jurisdictional strikes	Strikes over the assignment of work to bargaining unit employees.	*No.* Jurisdictional strikes are prohibited by the NLRA.
Noneconomic strikes	Strikes over permissive bargaining items during contract negotiations.	*No.* The NLRA protects workers' efforts to improve only their wages, hours, and other terms and conditions of employment.
General or political strikes	Mass protests against government policies. Rare in the United States, but more common in Europe.	*No.* The NLRA protects workers' efforts to improve their terms and conditions of employment by bargaining with their employer.

Note: The same taxonomy (columns 1 and 2) applies to public sector strikes, but strikes by government employees are more tightly regulated than in the private sector and are more likely to be unprotected or even illegal (column 3).

public sector strikes: "There is no right to strike against the public safety by anybody, anywhere, any time."[6]

As such, strikes by federal government workers are prohibited and only 25 percent of states grant state and local public employees even a limited right to strike.[7] For example, in Hawaii only teachers, college faculty, and blue-collar state and local workers can strike; only economic strikes are allowed, and only after mediation, fact-finding, and a 60-day cooling-off period. Other types of strikes are illegal, and all other employees are considered essential and must use arbitration instead of striking.[8] On the other hand, a number of states not only prohibit all strikes but also specify penalties for violators.[9] New York's Taylor law, for example, imposes a "two for one" strike penalty—for each day workers are on strike, they lose their pay for the day plus a fine equal to their day's pay.[10] In both the private and public sectors, however, illegal strikes occur. For example, New York City transit workers struck for 60 hours in December 2005 and shut down the subway and bus system; strikers forfeited six days of pay under the Taylor law's two for one penalty, and a judge also fined the union $2.5 million for conducting an illegal strike.[11]

National Emergency Strikes

There is also a concern in private sector labor law with strikes that seriously harm the public interest. Because of the vital importance of railroads for the early 20th century economy, the Railway Labor Act empowers the president of the United States to create a presidential emergency board if a strike would "threaten substantially to interrupt interstate commerce to a degree such as to deprive any section of the country of essential transportation service" (Section 10).[12] A presidential emergency board has 30 days to investigate the dispute and issue a report, which typically contains nonbinding recommendations for a settlement. After the report is issued, a strike can occur after a 30-day cooling-off period. For the private sector more generally, the 1947 Taft–Hartley Act amendments to the NLRA created provisions for settling national emergency strikes following the Great Strike Wave of 1945–1946.[13] When the president believes that a strike or threatened strike "will imperil the national health or safety," she or he can appoint a board of inquiry to investigate and report on the disputed issues (Section 206). Upon receipt of this report, the president can seek a court-ordered injunction halting the strike or threatened strike for up to 80 days. Additional changes to the NLRA in 1974 provided for boards of inquiry in the health care industry if a strike would "substantially interrupt the delivery of health care in the locality concerned" (Section 213).

Unsurprisingly, these national emergency strike procedures are rarely used.[14] Research on the effects of strikes and lockouts affirms the rarity of strikes that should be considered emergencies. Work stoppages clearly have negative effects: Productivity declines, profits are lost, stock prices fall, and workers lose income and suffer from stress, but these effects are generally confined to the specific employer and workers involved in the strike.[15]

Lockouts

A lockout is similar to an economic strike in that it is a work stoppage that results from a bargaining dispute, but a lockout is initiated by the employer rather than the employees. It is useful to distinguish between defensive and offensive lockouts.[16] A defensive lockout occurs when an employer locks out employees to prevent losses from an expected strike. If an employer handles perishable goods and expects a strike but the union will not reveal the timing of its strike plans, the employer can lock out the employees to prevent losses stemming from the spoilage of its perishable products. This is a defensive action to protect the employer from significant economic losses.

In contrast, an offensive lockout occurs when an employer takes the initiative to pressure the union for a more favorable settlement. A common reason for taking this initiative is to control the timing of the work stoppage. For example, if professional athletes strike just before the playoffs, they will already have been paid for much of the season while the owners would lose significant revenue during this time of peak fan interest. To avoid this situation, the owners in the professional sports leagues have instead locked out their players when negotiations have reached an impasse, including both the NBA and NFL in 2011. While these professional sports lockouts are the most visible, lockouts have recently occurred in multiple industries, including sugar processing, tire manufacturing, hospitals, and the performing arts. The annual number of lockouts is still small, but the recent increase seems to suggest increased employer militancy in pursuing their bargaining goals.

Both defensive and offensive lockouts are legal (assuming an absence of illegal actions like surface bargaining) as long as they protect or support employers' bargaining positions. Lockouts are not legal if they are overly aggressive and appear to be an attempt to destroy the union.

Picketing

A key aspect of a strike or lockout is a picket line: Strikers or locked-out workers, their leaders, and their supporters march outside the struck employer's location(s) to publicize their dispute, convince the public not to patronize the business and workers not to cross the picket line, create solidarity among the strikers, and otherwise build support for their cause. In economic and unfair labor practice strikes, picketing is legal but with some legal limitations. Picket line misconduct such as violence or vandalism is not protected by the NLRA and can therefore result in discipline and loss of recall rights at the end of the strike, as well as potential criminal prosecution. Moreover, mass picketing that blocks entrances to an employer's property is also illegal.[17] Recall from Chapter 4 that injunctions were used in the early 20th century to severely restrain picketing. While not as extreme, injunctions by state courts are still used to restrain picketing, and it is not unusual for an injunction to limit the number of picketers at each entrance to an employer's property.

Picketing raises several other important issues. First, what about employees who want to work instead of strike and therefore cross their own union's picket line? This can be a very emotionally charged issue, but legally employees are allowed to do this. Unions have the right to discipline union members who cross a picket line, but union members also have the right to resign from the union and thus avoid discipline.[18] Discipline can consist of being expelled from the union and being assessed reasonable fines. Second, picketing gives rise to sympathy strikes—the refusal to cross another union's picket line. Sympathy strikes are protected by the NLRA, but sympathy strikers can be replaced. Moreover, a no-strike clause in a union contract might waive this protection.[19] Third, picketing to pressure an employer to recognize a union is explicitly limited by the NLRA to 30 days [Section 8(b)(7)(C)]. Recognition strikes are legal, but after 30 days such strikes typically cannot also include picketing (though there are some exceptions).[20] U.S. labor law seeks to discourage recognition strikes by making the certification election process available to employees (Chapter 6), but recognition strikes are nevertheless allowed. Finally, as we will discuss later in this chapter, the legality of picketing becomes complex when more than one employer is involved.

The Decline in Strike Activity

The largest U.S. work stoppages for each year between 2005 and 2015 are listed in Table 8.2. Note the variety of industries, issues, and dispute lengths. But while major work stoppages such as these still occur, U.S. strike activity in the 21st century is at an all-time low. The number of major strikes and lockouts (those involving at least 1,000 workers) exceeded 400 per year in the early 1950s, ranged between 250 and 425 in the early 1970s, and then plummeted to less than 20 today (see Figure 8.1). Public sector strikes account for perhaps 15 percent of these major strikes (and of those, 40 percent are illegal public sector strikes).[21] Relative to the total economy, the number of working days lost because of strikes is minuscule: In 2015 the days lost due to strikes involving at least 1,000 workers amounted to less than 1/100th of 1 percent of total working days. Even in the 1950s this figure was only 1/5th of 1 percent of total working days.[22] Some complicated data issues make it difficult to know exactly what fraction of all negotiations result in strikes, but the strike rate in large bargaining units (more than 1,000 workers) has declined from 15 percent in the 1970s to perhaps 5 percent in the 2000s.[23] Strike rates for all negotiations are even lower—perhaps even less than 1 percent in recent years.[24]

This sharp decline in U.S. strike activity since 1980 begs the question of why strikes occur. A simple view starts with the important interaction between bargaining power and strikes. Recall from the previous chapter that the threat of a strike is a major determinant of bargaining power. If the economy is strong, employees are not worried about losing their jobs, and replacement employees are difficult to find, the threat of a strike might be more

TABLE 8.2 Each Year's Largest Work Stoppage since 2010

2015
Around 6,600 oil refinery workers represented by the United Steelworkers in California, Indiana, Kentucky, Louisiana, Ohio, and Texas, Washington struck Shell Oil for over a month. This was part of national contract negotiations covering 30,000 workers at Shell, Exxon Mobil, Chevron, and other oil companies. Major issues: Safety issues and ensuring that maintenance work is done by union workers.

2014
A 131-day strike by 1,700 workers at FairPoint Communications didn't end until 2015. These workers were represented by the Communications Workers of America and the International Brotherhood of Electrical Workers, and they worked in what used to be Verizon's landline business in northern New England before being purchased by FairPoint. Major issues: Outsourcing, health care, and pensions.

2013
A four-week strike by 8,000 public school bus drivers belonging to the Amalgamated Transit Union in New York City affected 100,000 students. The strike resulted from the city's bidding out bus routes to private companies without wage, benefit, and seniority protections. Major issue: job protections.

2012
More than 26,000 Chicago public school teachers struck for a week. In addition to wage and benefits issues, educational issues like standardized testing were also in dispute. Four years later, the teachers struck for one day to pressure the state to provide more funding for education. Major issues: wage increases, re-hiring laid-off teachers, educational issues.

2011
In response to demands for numerous concessions and a perceived lack of progress at the bargaining table, 45,000 workers represented by the Communications Workers of America and the International Brotherhood of Electrical Workers struck telecommunications giant Verizon for two weeks and then returned to work without a new contract when Verizon signaled a willingness to negotiate. Major issue: benefits.

2010
A Chicago-area construction strike between the Mid-America Regional Bargaining Association and the Laborers International Union and International Union of Operating Engineers involved 15,000 workers and lasted three weeks. Major issue: wage increases to offset increased health care costs.

Source: Bureau of Labor Statistics Work Stoppages Program (www.bls.gov/wsp) and various news reports.

viable than in a weak economy with significant anxiety about job loss and with many available replacements. A company that has a significant inventory of finished products (such as automobiles) is probably less threatened by a strike than a company with little inventory. In fact, important bargaining tactics for both labor and management focus on strengthening or weakening the strike threat—such as building union solidarity to maximize the effect of a strike on an employer's bottom line, or on the part of management, arranging for replacement workers or moving production to other locations to minimize a strike's disruptions.

We might therefore be tempted to speculate that strike activity has declined since 1980 because labor's bargaining power has declined. But this confuses the *threat* of strikes with the *occurrence* of strikes. Bargaining power depends on the strength of the strike threat. If labor's bargaining power is high because employers face greater strike losses, employers should be more likely to give into labor's demands before strikes occur. As such, the threat of a strike is higher and wages will be higher, but the actual occurrence of strikes is not higher than when labor's bargaining power is lower.[25] In short, bargaining power and the threat of a strike should affect the extent to which bargaining outcomes favor labor or management, but not the occurrence of strikes.

More generally, because strikes are costly for all involved, they seem irrational on a strict cost–benefit basis: In standard economic thought, rational negotiators should be able to figure out the poststrike settlement and agree to it without a strike, and everyone would be better off.[26] Yet strikes are not completely irrational because in practice strike activity is not random, but instead is correlated with a number of factors (e.g., the unemployment rate, bargaining unit size, contract duration, and in the public sector, strike penalties).[27]

FIGURE 8.1
U.S. Major Strikes (1,000 workers or more), 1950–2015

Source: Bureau of Labor Statistics.

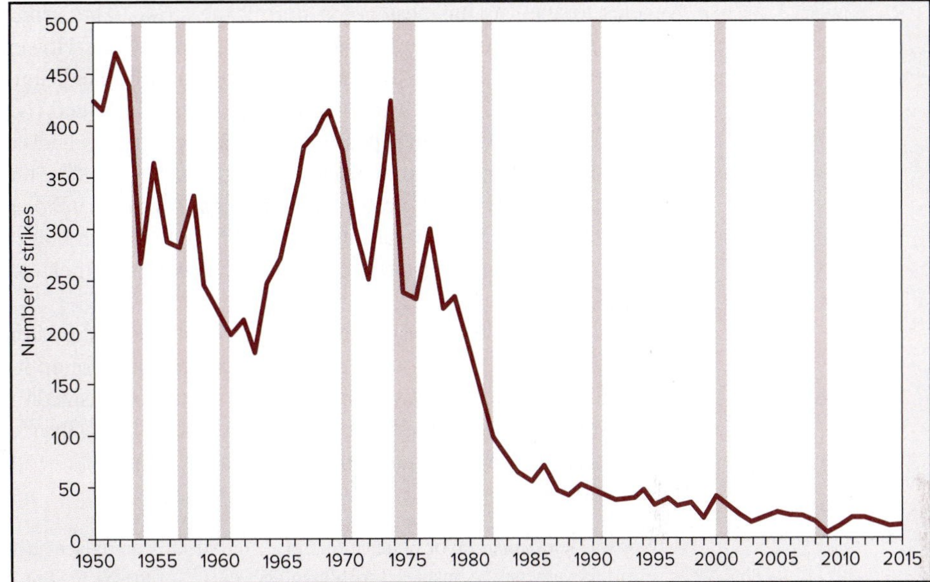

Note: Includes lockouts. Shaded regions denote recessions.

The economics approach to explaining why strikes occur typically focuses on problems of information (so, e.g., rational negotiators cannot figure out the poststrike settlement ahead of time). Other approaches broaden the narrow dollars-and-cents focus of *economic* rationality and examine other explanations for strikes such as the pursuit of workplace voice.[28] These various approaches to explaining why strikes occur are discussed in the "Digging Deeper" feature at the end of this chapter.

So what explains the decline in strike activity? Before the 1980s research often found that strike activity tracked the business cycle (more strikes during booms, fewer during recessions).[29] But as shown in Figure 8.1, strike activity declined consistently through the 1980s, 1990s, and 2000s irrespective of the business cycle. Alternatively, many academic theories of strikes hinge on the lack of full information possessed by negotiators and their constituents. Another explanation, therefore, is that the availability of information has increased—for example, through a decline in inflation uncertainty.[30] Lastly, there is a possible sociopolitical explanation: The steep decline in U.S. strike activity may result from the increased acceptability of using strike replacements that started in the 1980s.[31] Thus workers stopped striking in order to not lose their jobs.

Online Exploration Exercise: Use labor news sites such as *www.labourstart.org* or *www.labornet.org*, or other sources such as Facebook or Twitter, to find out about current strikes in the United States and in other countries. What are the main issues? How similar are the main issues across different strikes? Across countries?

STRIKE REPLACEMENTS

The *Mackay* Doctrine

Less than three months after the NLRA was signed into law in 1935, a number of telegraph operators for the Mackay Radio and Telegraph Company went on strike in San Francisco. The company brought in operators from its branches in New York, Chicago, and Los

Angeles to keep its business going during the strike. The strike did not go well for the strikers, and after four days they offered to return to work. However, five of the operators who were brought in from the other cities apparently liked San Francisco so much that they wanted to stay. There were now five fewer openings, and five striking operators were not allowed to return to their positions. These five strikers had been particularly active in the union and the strike—they were not, for example, the five employees with the lowest seniority or the lowest job performance ratings. An unfair labor practice charge was filed with the National Labor Relations Board (NLRB) alleging that the company violated the NLRA by discriminating against these five strikers for their active participation in the union and the strike.

In one of its earliest decisions pertaining to the NLRA, the Supreme Court in 1938 ruled against the Mackay Radio and Telegraph Company and found it guilty of discriminating against the five union activists. However, the Court emphasized that the key illegal act was singling out union activists. In an almost incidental remark, the Court indicated that absent such discrimination, it is legal to have employees do the work of striking individuals during an economic strike:

> Nor was it an unfair labor practice to replace the striking employees with others in an effort to carry on the business. Although Section 13 [of the NLRA] provides, "Nothing in this Act shall be construed so as to interfere with or impede or diminish in any way the right to strike," it does not follow that an employer, guilty of no act denounced by the statute, has lost the right to protect and continue his business by supplying places left vacant by strikers. And he is not bound to discharge those hired to fill the places of strikers, upon the election of the latter to resume their employment, in order to create places for them.[32]

Employees used or hired to do the work of individuals on strike are called strike replacements. But note carefully that the Supreme Court did more than just allow employers to hire strike replacements: In the last sentence of this passage the Court wrote that employers do not have to fire the replacements at the end of a strike in order to provide jobs to strikers who want to return to work. In other words, employers can hire **permanent strike replacements**—replacement workers who continue in their positions after the strike ends—as well as temporary strike replacements who are discharged at the end of the strike. This is known as the *Mackay* doctrine after the famous 1938 decision just quoted: ***NLRB v. Mackay Radio and Telegraph Co.*** Most other industrialized countries, however, do not allow permanent strike replacements.

Strikers who have been permanently replaced are not necessarily entitled to immediate reinstatement to their jobs after they end their strike. However, these employees cannot be fired in the literal sense—to do so would violate the NLRA's ban on discharging workers for engaging in protected activity [Sections 8(a)(1) and 8(a)(3)]. Rather, at the conclusion of a strike, returning strikers are placed on a priority recall list, and as jobs become available, employers must first offer jobs to the former strikers before hiring any new employees.[33] As a practical matter, the status of temporary or permanent replacements is determined by what the employer tells the replacement workers when they are hired.[34] If disputes arise later, the employer must prove that the replacements were told they were permanent; otherwise they will be considered temporary and must be terminated when strikers make an unconditional offer to return to work.

Replacement Workers in Unfair Labor Practice Strikes

Numerous other complications can arise when strike replacements are used, and the NLRB and the courts must then determine the legality of these scenarios (try this yourself with the "Labor Law Discussion" case at the end of this chapter). Of particular note is the question of whether employers can use permanent strike replacements during an unfair labor practice strike. The *Mackay* doctrine clearly establishes the legality of using permanent strike replacements in economic strikes, but other court decisions have determined that employers cannot use permanent replacements during an unfair labor practice strike (otherwise employers could benefit from their own illegal actions).[35] Unfair labor practice strikers are therefore entitled to immediate reinstatement. As a result, striking workers commonly claim that they are engaged in an unfair labor practice strike, but it is up to the NLRB to make that determination. This determination can be complicated; in short, if an unfair labor practice has "anything to do with" causing a strike or if it appears that the employer's unlawful conduct played a part in the employees' decision to strike, then the strike is an unfair labor practice strike.[36] Also, an employer's unfair labor practice during an economic strike can convert it to an unfair labor practice strike.

Replacement Workers in Lockouts

Whether a work stoppage is a strike or a lockout is also important for determining the legal use of replacement workers. Recall that a lockout is legal as long as it is not overly aggressive and is not an attempt to destroy the union. As such, employers can use *temporary* replacements during lockouts because this has been interpreted as legitimate support of the employer's bargaining position.[37] But to maintain a balance of power between employees and employers, hiring *permanent* replacements is not allowed.[38] This would be too destructive of employee rights: An employer could lock out employees against their wishes, hire permanent replacements, and decertify the union. These outcomes are also possible with a strike, but note the critical difference—in a strike employees choose to stop working, whereas in a lockout the employees are forced out.

Efforts to Ban Permanent Strike Replacements

The legal rulings that establish the doctrine surrounding the use of replacement workers in both strikes and lockouts largely date back to the 1960s and before. In fact, the *Mackay* decision was handed down in 1938 and was not controversial at that time.[39] The issue was a quiet one until the 1980s, but since then it has sparked one of the most intense debates in U.S. labor relations. What ignited this debate was the 1981 firing of the striking air traffic controllers by President Reagan during the illegal PATCO strike (Chapter 3). Labor supporters have frequently argued that this event set the tenor for labor relations in the 1980s and made it acceptable to replace workers during strikes, though the true linkage may never be known.[40] Two years later copper producer Phelps Dodge showed that permanent strike replacements could be used to effectively break a strike and decertify a union in a legal private sector strike.[41]

Although permanently replaced strikers have the right to priority recall when jobs become available, the NLRA specifies that they are eligible to vote in a decertification election only within 12 months of the start of the strike. A decertification election at Phelps Dodge occurred 15 months after the strike began, and unsurprisingly the unions were decertified because all the voters were either strike replacements or employees that crossed the picket lines. Permanent strike replacements were subsequently used in bitter strikes at Hormel (1985), International Paper (1987—see the accompanying "Ethics in Action" box), Greyhound (1990), Bridgestone–Firestone (1995), the *Detroit News* (1995), Northwest Airlines (2005), and elsewhere.[42] These high-profile examples underlie the belief in the labor movement that the use of strike replacements exploded in the 1980s, but the extent to which this truly represents an increase is unknown.[43]

Based on the results of these high-profile strikes, banning the use of permanent strike replacements was the labor movement's top legislative priority between 1985 and 1995. Labor argues that workers are essentially fired for striking, so other workers are afraid to strike. This destruction of the right to strike is asserted to disrupt the balance of the U.S.

Ethics in Action Strike Replacements or Scabs?

In 1987–1988 workers represented by the United Paperworkers International Union at the Jay, Maine, Lock Haven, Pennsylvania, and DePere, Wisconsin, plants of the International Paper Company struck for 17 months when the company demanded significant concessions. At the time, International Paper was earning record profits and refused to share its financial records with the union to justify the need for concessions. When the strikers were permanently replaced after a few weeks, the strike became very bitter and divided the union, families, and communities. Consider some perspectives of the participants in their own words:

A Mill Manager on the Company's Decision to Use Permanent Strike Replacements

We had enjoyed a stable workforce, with whom the company had a constructive relationship. We did not provoke the strike, nor did we have any interest or intent in replacing that workforce when the dispute began. However, the union left us with no choice. By striking, the union put the company in the position of either accepting conditions which would have clearly made the mill uncompetitive within the industry . . . or shutting down the mill, eliminating jobs not only there but in other parts of the company and in the community dependent on our producing and fulfilling our orders. The only alternative allowing us to continue to fulfill our commitments to our other employees, customers, communities, and shareholders was to hire permanent replacement workers.

The President of the United Paperworkers International Union on the Company's Demands

They were asking for stuff that we've had for 25 years in our contract [including the Christmas Day holiday]. And it was at a time when the profits with the company were setting records. And at the same time now, they gave the executives an average of a 38 percent increase in salary. It boggles your mind.

A Millworker/Former Union Steward/Onetime Temporary Supervisor on Striking

If we had accepted this contract or not voted to strike and worked without one, they could have squeezed 1,200 workers [at another plant] until they relented to the contract which was offered them. [*Note:* Three months earlier, Mobile, Alabama, workers continued working without a contract, and International Paper locked them out and hired temporary replacements.] Then . . . they could have squeezed us, and they could have done that to every plant . . . so we in essence would have been cutting our own throat anyway. This company was out to squeeze the worker, and they were going to do it systematically throughout the United States. I have no doubt in my mind. I sat on both sides and could see it coming.

A Replacement Worker on Taking the Job of a Striker

No. It wasn't really a hard decision. You had no choice, especially when you're in the construction business working like I was, $5.70 an hour. It doesn't take much to convince you—when somebody tells you you can make $16.00 an hour, and you've been trying to get into a paper mill. So if you have any family at all, then you'd be a fool not to go for it.

A Local Supporter of the Union on the Replacement Workers

In my book there is no redeeming a scab under any circumstances whatsoever. That means never, ever. . . . Scabs epitomize self-interest and would likely run their mothers over if it meant an extra buck or two. Scabs are scumbags.

A Striker on the Impact of the Strike and of Using Replacement Workers on the Community

It has put brother against brother, friend against friend, neighbor against neighbor. It will take many generations before the hurt and anger will heal.

QUESTIONS

1. Is it ethical for a company to use permanent strike replacements? How about temporary strike replacements?
2. Is it ethical for individuals to cross picket lines and become temporary or permanent strike replacements?
3. Is it ethical for unions and their supporters to attack strike replacements as "scabs" and try to prevent them from crossing picket lines?

References: Julius Getman, *The Betrayal of Local 14* (Ithaca, NY: ILR Press, 1998), pp. 32, 40, 71, 196, and 213; U.S. Congress, *Hearings on H.R. 5, The Striker Replacement Bill,* Hearings before the Subcommittee on Labor–Management Relations of the Committee on Education and Labor, House of Representatives, March 6 and 13, 1991 (Washington, DC: U.S. Government Printing Office, 1991), p. 244.

labor relations system and give employers vastly greater power. And using permanent replacements allows employers to rid themselves of their unions by forcing a strike through hard bargaining, hiring permanent strike replacements, and engineering a decertification election.[44] For labor, the use of permanent strike replacements is not about keeping a business operating during a strike—this could be accomplished with temporary replacements; it is about busting unions through intensified confrontation. The fact that some companies use professional "security" companies (some would say "strikebreaking" companies) that provide armed guards in combat fatigues or riot gear to intimidate strikers and protect replacement workers reinforces the suspicions of labor.[45]

On the other hand, business argues that the current system is balanced and that banning permanent strike replacements would favor unions. Without the threat of being permanently replaced, unions might strike more frequently for increased demands that would reduce competitiveness and destroy jobs. To business, the use of permanent strike replacements is not about busting unions—it is about maintaining competitiveness.

The labor movement would still like permanent strike replacements banned, but its inability to pass this legislation in the 1990s and the continued decline in union density has caused the labor movement to shift its legislative focus to reforming the certification process through the Employee Free Choice Act (Chapter 6). In what might prove to be a victory for labor, a 2016 NLRB decision ruled that permanent strike replacements will not be allowed if their use is motivated by an independent unlawful purpose, such as retaliation for striking.[46] In the public sector, only Minnesota bans the use of permanent strike replacements. Overall, then, the United States continues to be unusual among industrialized, democratic countries in the extent to which it allows permanent strike replacements.

OTHER PRESSURE TACTICS

Labor's primary economic weapon is the strike, but this is not the only tactic to pressure an employer. Boycotts, work slowdowns, and corporate campaigns also increase labor's bargaining power by imposing costs on employers, and therefore help win more favorable settlements for employees. Though the legality of such tactics is mixed, they have become more important and more frequent since the 1980s. The reason for this trend is straightforward: As the use of strike replacements (perceived or real) has increased, labor unions have turned to tactics in which employees do not risk losing their jobs by being permanently replaced in a strike. Additionally, boycotts and corporate campaigns can increase the pressure on a struck employer, especially when a strike is being neutralized by the use of replacement workers. In short, unions believe that employers have escalated economic warfare through the use of strike replacements, and unions have responded by searching for alternatives to strikes and also by further escalating conflicts with other pressure tactics. In the public sector, these other pressure tactics occur more frequently when strikes are prohibited.[47]

Boycotts

One pressure tactic that has a long history in labor relations is the boycott, which is a campaign to encourage a company's customers to stop doing business with it. As just one example, striking workers at Delta Pride's catfish processing plant in Mississippi were able to counter longstanding racial prejudice and economic disadvantage when a 1990's boycott of Delta Pride catfish was supported by consumers in St. Louis, Memphis, and elsewhere.[48] To understand the legality of boycotts, it is necessary to distinguish between primary and secondary employers. In the context of a bargaining dispute, a primary employer is the company for whom the workers involved in the bargaining dispute work; a secondary employer is an organization that does not employ the workers who are involved in the dispute but has some business ties to the primary employer. This distinction is important because in the U.S. private sector, a boycott is generally legal if it narrowly targets the primary employer, but Section 8(b)(4) of the NLRA prohibits **secondary boycotts** that target secondary employers. Consider the employees of a hotel who are demanding wage and benefit improvements from the hotel's management. The hotel is the primary employer, and the hotel's employees can legally launch a consumer boycott campaign by asking travelers to stay at a different hotel. But encouraging consumers to not patronize (in other words, to boycott) a local flower shop because it supplies flowers to the hotel is illegal because the flower shop is a secondary or neutral employer.

While this example might seem straightforward, note that the legal doctrine on boycotts can be quite complex.[49] What if the union just publicizes the fact that the flower shop does business with the hotel without explicitly asking consumers to boycott it? Or could the union boycott the flower shop if it is owned by the same corporate parent as the hotel? Or if the hotel's flower arrangements were done by hotel employees until the bargaining dispute, at which time the work was contracted out to the flower shop? The answers to these three scenarios are probably, probably not, and probably; but more importantly, in all such cases the NLRB tries to balance the rights of employees and employers.

Boycotts are frequently supported by picketing, and the legality of such conduct can be especially complex in the construction industry when employees of numerous companies are working at the same construction site. Suppose electricians are on strike against an electrical contractor, and they picket an entire construction site where they work alongside other construction trades that work for other contractors. This is called common situs picketing because it involves multiple employers at a common location or site. Common situs picketing that targets an entire worksite is illegal because it includes secondary or neutral employers.[50] It is now common for construction sites to include separate gates for different contractors so picketers are limited to the gate of their employer. But there can still be significant complications if the primary gate is too far removed from the public's eye, if there are mixed-use gates, or if there is a roving employer (such as a construction equipment repair company that is called to different job sites throughout the workday).[51] How the message is conveyed can also be controversial—as illustrated by the accompanying "Labor Relations Application" box describing the use of giant inflatable rats. In such cases the law seeks to balance the employees' right to publicize their dispute with the secondary or neutral employers' right to conduct business.

Work Slowdowns

A second pressure tactic is the work slowdown. Slowdowns try to pressure employers by imposing costs through lowered productivity, but without employees leaving their jobs and going on strike (and thereby facing the risk of being permanently replaced). Slowdowns can take various forms. Perhaps the most creative is a **work-to-rule campaign** in which employees do their work by exactly following the employer's rules. For example, if there is a safety rule that all machines must be inspected before use, a worker can spend 15 minutes at the start of each shift thoroughly checking every nut and bolt on the machine. And perhaps the machine will need to be inspected again after being turned off for lunch. Postal workers can check numerous zip codes, grocery clerks can do frequent price checks, and utility workers can scrupulously check for gas leaks. More generally workers can frequently ask supervisors questions to make sure they understand their tasks. When overtime is voluntary, workers can refuse to work overtime. The legal status of such actions is unsettled. On one hand, if workers are simply following management's rules, it's hard to argue that it is not acceptable.[52] On the other hand, if a work-to-rule campaign is interpreted as a withholding of work that has been

Labor Relations Application Without the NLRB's Muscle, Tony Soprano Loses to a Giant Inflatable Rat

During season four of the hit TV drama *The Sopranos*, mob figures Carmine Lupertazzi and Tony Soprano battle each other for the profits of a housing scam. After Tony has Carmine's new restaurant ransacked in the "Eloise" episode, Carmine tells his underboss, "I haven't wanted to do this, but it's gotta be . . . call the union." Cut to Tony's construction site and, consistent with popular media stereotypes, a corrupt union business agent drives up with a giant inflatable rat in the back of his pickup—complete with pink beady eyes, two big teeth, and claws poised to strike—and announces that because of the use of nonunion laborers, the job site is shut down until further notice.

This is an example of art imitating life—giant inflatable rats ranging from 10 to 30 feet tall have become a common sight at labor disputes. During a musicians' strike at Radio City Music Hall in New York City in 2005, striking workers were accompanied by a giant inflatable rat; management responded by putting a ferocious-looking inflatable cougar on top of the Radio City marquee. The use of inflatable rats has been especially common at construction sites to protest the use of nonunion labor. In this Sopranos episode, if the labor union had set up a picket line to stop electricians and other contractors' workers from working at the job site, this would have clearly been an illegal boycott under the NLRA's prohibition on secondary boycotts. But sometimes there aren't any pickets—just a giant inflatable rat.

Unions argue that this is free speech, but companies argue that this is illegal secondary picketing. In the absence of formal pickets, the NLRB has ruled that secondary "signal picketing" is illegal. Signal picketing is an action that effectively sends the same signal or message as picketing. So a debate has emerged: Are giant inflatable rats illegal signal pickets? Before 2011, the NLRB ruled that because employees know that the rat is a sign of labor protest, especially against "rat contractors" and their low wages and dangerous working conditions, displaying the inflatable rat is an illegal signal picket. A more recent decision, however, ruled that displaying an inflatable rat is a legal form of free speech as long as it is not accompanied by confrontational pickets or messages to interfere with the secondary employer's business. Rather than trying to outlast his mob rival with his job site shut down, Tony Soprano could have used the muscle of the NLRB.

Reference: Marion Crain and John Inazu, "Re-Assembling Labor," *University of Illinois Law Review* 2015 (2015), pp. 1791–846.

traditionally provided (literally slowing down work), then perhaps it is insubordination and is not protected by the NLRA.[53] The NLRB has yet to issue definitive rulings.

Another method for engaging in work slowdowns is the use of partial, quickie, or intermittent strikes.[54] A refusal to work overtime is a partial strike, a very short strike (such as one day or even one hour) is a quickie strike, and a series of repeated quickie strikes amounts to an intermittent strike. The goal of these job actions is to disrupt an employer's operations; but because these strikes are a surprise and very short, it is difficult for the employer to hire strike replacements. Such strikes, however, are often ruled to be

TABLE 8.3
Public Sector Work Slowdowns

Blue flu	Mass absenteeism among police officers, named after blue uniforms.
Heal-in	Doctors refusing to release patients.
Red flu or red rash	Same as the blue flu, but for firefighters.
Human error day	Intentional day of mistakes by clerical workers.
Chalk dust fever	Same as the blue flu, but for teachers.
Budgetitis	Mass absenteeism among public sector workers in protest over budget issues.

insubordination rather than legitimate protected activity, so employees can be disciplined and discharged for engaging in these types of strikes. In the public sector where strikes are often illegal, workers sometimes resort to quickie strikes by conducting coordinated days of mass absenteeism—for example, a number of police officers can catch the "blue flu" and all call in sick on the same day (see Table 8.3).[55] Work slowdowns are often part of a broader campaign of workplace tactics—sometimes called an inside game strategy—that includes visible demonstrations of worker solidarity such as wearing armbands and holding rallies in the parking lot before work.[56]

Corporate Campaigns

Another economic pressure tactic is the **corporate campaign** that seeks to bolster inside tactics with external pressure, typically directed at corporate headquarters by outsiders such as other members of the business and financial community, consumers, politicians, and government regulators. The union's strategy is to create negative publicity that causes these outsiders to pressure or withdraw support for the targeted company. It is common to trace the beginnings of corporate campaigns to the union campaign directed against the textile company J. P. Stevens in the late 1970s.[57] After years of being thwarted by union-busting techniques, the textile workers' union shifted its focus from the workplace to the corporate boardroom. Remember that it is common for a company's board of directors to include outside directors who are also executives of other companies. The J. P. Stevens board included the chairman of the cosmetics company Avon. When J. P. Stevens's aggressive antiunion conduct toward its female workers was publicized to women who used Avon products, Avon's chairman resigned from the J. P. Stevens board. The chairman of J. P. Stevens resigned from the board of a major bank when unions threatened to withdraw their pension funds from this bank. This type of high-level pressure is credited with causing J. P. Stevens to finally settle with the textile workers' union.

Since then the labor movement has continued to use corporate campaigns to increase its power. In addition to pressuring corporate directors and financial linkages with major banks, some corporate campaigns have expanded to include regulatory agencies, politicians, and activist organizations or causes. Such efforts can bring the labor movement into unexpected alliances. Labor activists are currently working with college students on the "Campaign to Stop Killer Coke" stemming from the killing of union supporters at Coca-Cola bottling plants in South America (see *www.killercoke.org*). Corporate campaigns also find labor unions working closely with environmental groups. Although there can be conflicts if workers see environmentalists as reducing jobs through environmental protections, they have also teamed up to push for sustainable jobs and a sustainable natural environment.[58] During labor disputes these two groups have a common interest in bringing a company's environmental violations to the attention of federal and state regulators. Corporate campaigns might also include consumer boycotts as part of their comprehensive strategies.

Labor Relations Application The Corporate Campaign against Ravenswood Aluminum

In October 1990 the Ravenswood Aluminum in Ravenswood, West Virginia, declared an impasse in its contract negotiations with the United Steelworkers and locked out 1,700 workers. Before the contract had even expired, several buses of replacement workers were in the company parking lot, and the replacement workers entered the plant almost immediately after the start of the lockout. The company also brought in guards with military-style clothing, riot shields, and video cameras.

Several union offers of significant concessions were summarily rejected without discussion by the company. The union filed unfair labor practice charges accusing the company of engaging in bad faith bargaining and in unilaterally implementing its final offer without reaching an impasse. But unfair labor practice cases take a while to be investigated and litigated by the NLRB; the Steelworkers wanted faster results. Consequently, the national Steelworkers leadership decided to launch a corporate campaign.

One tactic of the corporate campaign was to target consumers. Union members followed trucks from the Ravenswood plant to their destinations to determine what companies were using the finished aluminum products. These companies were then contacted by the union, and Anheuser-Busch, Miller Brewing, and Stroh's agreed to not use aluminum from Ravenswood in their cans rather than risk the negative publicity of being tied to Ravenswood.

The second tactic was targeting the owners and creditors of Ravenswood Aluminum. A Steelworkers team traced the company's complex ownership structure. The offices of major investors in New York and Connecticut were then picketed. A significant piece of the ownership puzzle was Marc Rich, America's most wanted white-collar criminal who had earlier fled to Switzerland to avoid being convicted of fraud, tax evasion, and trading with the enemy (by violating the U.S. embargo of Iranian oil). The Steelworkers worked with European labor unions to further uncover Rich's secret activities. Demonstrations were held outside his Swiss offices, and the unionists met with a major source of his financing in the Netherlands, NMB Postbank. This negative publicity started to scuttle Rich's deals with corporations and governments that were unaware of his shady dealings.

Lastly, when Ravenswood denied government safety inspectors access to the aluminum plant, the Steelworkers lobbied national politicians to investigate. This led to a wall-to-wall OSHA inspection and a citation for over 200 health and safety violations and a $600,000 fine. Environmental investigations—more negative publicity for the company—were then launched, and the company was sued for violating the Clean Water Act.

After more than a year of this intense corporate campaign the CEO of Ravenswood Aluminum was ousted and negotiations began again in April 1992. Because of the corporate campaign, "This time the whole world was watching . . . the U.S. Congress, the international and national news media, and financial investors worldwide. This was no longer a simple negotiation between a local union and a West Virginia employer." At the end of June 1992 the workers ratified a new contract containing wage, pension, and safety improvements and returned to work victorious.

Reference: Tom Juravich and Kate Bronfenbrenner, *Ravenswood: The Steelworkers' Victory and the Revival of American Labor* (Ithaca, NY: Cornell University Press, 1999); the quote is from p. 185.

Both the success and legality of corporate campaigns are debatable.[59] The campaigns against J. P. Stevens and Ravenswood Aluminum (see the accompanying "Labor Relations Application") are visible success stories; campaigns against Phelps Dodge, Hormel, and International Paper are visible failures.[60] At least one labor activist has criticized corporate campaigns for being disconnected from rank-and-file workers.[61] But many labor supporters see corporate campaigns as important tools for pressuring corporations who seem to hold all the power in a global economy, and in the process of conducting such campaigns, for building stronger, more vibrant labor organizations with greater rank-and-file participation and stronger links with other community groups.[62] Critics—who are also proponents of free markets—see corporate campaigns as manipulating the media and regulatory agencies to benefit unionized workers at the expense of consumers and nonunion workers, and as ineffective in stemming organized labor's decline.[63] Because corporate campaigns are outside the workplace, the legality of these campaigns is determined outside labor law. In particular, companies have tried to challenge corporate campaigns by charging unions with blackmail, extortion, and other illegal interference in business relations, primarily under the same law used to prosecute the mafia (the Racketeer Influenced and Corrupt Organization Act or RICO).[64] Free speech rights, however, have largely prevailed.[65]

THIRD-PARTY DISPUTE RESOLUTION

One way to settle a bargaining impasse is to let the parties resort to economic weapons—strikes, lockouts, corporate campaigns, boycotts, strike replacements, and the like. Escalating the costs of disagreement will bring the parties to a settlement, or the relationship will disintegrate as in the case of strikes that lead to decertification. In either case the dispute is resolved. But economic weapons can be very costly dispute resolution mechanisms, and the public interest might be better served by more proactive methods of resolving impasses. Third-party dispute resolution mechanisms use a neutral third party to settle bargaining impasses with the goal of avoiding costly strikes. In the private sector, a strong sense of property rights and the freedom to enter economic contracts of one's own choosing means that the use of third-party dispute resolution mechanisms is usually voluntary—they are rarely forced on labor and management. In the public sector, however, the primacy of serving the public interest means that third-party dispute resolution mechanisms are often compulsory—labor and management must use them before or instead of striking.

The three primary third-party dispute resolution mechanisms are mediation, arbitration, and fact-finding. In mediation, the neutral third party is a mediator who tries to facilitate an agreement but lacks the power to force an agreement. In arbitration, the neutral third party is an arbitrator who forces an agreement on both parties by issuing a ruling that specifies the settlement terms. In fact-finding, the neutral third party is a fact finder who investigates the dispute and makes nonbinding recommendations for a settlement. Hybrid mechanisms can also be created, such as "med–arb," in which the mediator becomes the arbitrator if mediation fails. These dispute resolution mechanisms differ in the amount of control the third party has over the dispute resolution process and the outcome (see Table 8.4).[66] A mediator has a high level of control over the negotiating process but not the outcome; an arbitrator has the opposite—a high level of control over the outcome but no involvement in the negotiating process. A fact finder lacks control over both the process and the outcome.

Although mediators and arbitrators both serve vital functions as third-party neutrals in labor relations, their career paths and skills are typically different. Mediators can be either independent practitioners or full-time employees of mediation agencies at the federal level (the Federal Mediation and Conciliation Service and the National Mediation Board) or the state level (such as the Pennsylvania Bureau of Mediation). In contrast, arbitrators usually either are full-time, self-employed arbitrators or are lawyers or university professors (typically in law or industrial relations) who arbitrate on a part-time basis.[67] Mediators and arbitrators rarely begin their careers in these positions; rather, individuals almost always develop expertise in labor relations in other ways before becoming mediators or arbitrators later in their careers. Significant experience in negotiating contracts as either a management or a labor negotiator

TABLE 8.4
Options for Third-Party Dispute Resolution

		Degree of Third-Party Control over the Negotiating Process	
		Low	**High**
Degree of Third-Party Control over the Outcome	Low	Fact-finding	Mediation
	High	Arbitration	Med–arb

seems particularly important for a career in mediation, whereas arbitrators tend to start their labor relations careers as lawyers or professors. Methods for obtaining work also differ: For each particular dispute, mediators are often assigned by the relevant mediation agency; arbitrators are usually picked by the labor and management negotiators. As will become apparent in the following sections, mediators need to be well-trained in conflict resolution and communication strategies; arbitrators tend to need analytical skills. Neither will succeed, however, if they are not impartial and do not have a deep understanding of labor relations.

MEDIATION

Mediation is a dispute resolution process in which a neutral third party—the mediator—helps negotiators avoid or resolve an impasse by reaching an agreement. Note that unlike striking or going to arbitration, the use of mediation does not need to wait until an impasse occurs. By definition mediators lack the authority to force a resolution by imposing a settlement on the negotiators; rather, mediation is essentially "assisted negotiation."[68] In practice mediation involves a series of meetings with the mediator—some joint meetings with the union and management negotiating teams together, and some individual meetings with only the union or management negotiators. Through these meetings, the mediation process typically evolves through several stages.[69] The first is setting the stage, in which the mediator collects information and establishes ground rules. One of the most important keys to success for mediators needs to be achieved during this stage: establishing a rapport so that the parties trust the mediator.[70] In the second stage, problem solving, the mediator works on clarifying the disputed issues and on developing alternative solutions. The focus of the mediator in the third stage, achieving a workable agreement, is encouraging the negotiators to reach a settlement.

A wide range of tactics can be used by mediators in these stages to help solve a bargaining impasse (see Table 8.5).[71] Depending on the types of tactics emphasized, individual

TABLE 8.5
Mediator Tactics in Labor Negotiations and in Nonunion Settings

To facilitate agreement and solve a bargaining impasse, mediators can try to . . .

. . . increase the level of objectivity among the negotiators by decreasing hostility, promoting cooperation, and focusing the negotiators away from personal conflicts and toward the bargaining issues.

. . . improve each negotiator's understanding of the other side's positions by accurately communicating information between the two sides.

. . . remove structural roadblocks in the negotiation process by changing the format of negotiations. Mediator tactics in this vein include revising agendas, chairing negotiating sessions, and forming subcommittees for specific issues.

. . . help shape new compromise proposals and make suggestions for mutual concessions.

. . . increase the perceived costs of disagreeing by highlighting the uncertainty of strikes or arbitration decisions.

. . . allow negotiators to save face. In particular, negotiators can make concessions under the guise of mediator pressure so as not to appear weak to their constituents and the other negotiators.

Nonunion Application: Having meditation skills can be useful for HR professionals who might be called upon to resolve disagreements within the workplace. Take a look at each of these tactics for labor mediators and consider how each might be useful for HR professionals in nonunion situations.

mediators can be classified as orchestrators or dealmakers.[72] Orchestrators focus on trying to facilitate productive negotiations; this is the traditional view of mediation that targets improved dialogue between negotiators. In contrast, dealmakers see negotiations as over when they enter and are therefore not very concerned with facilitating renewed negotiations. Dealmakers focus their attention on the bargaining issues and trying to pressure the negotiators to make concessions. Orchestrators think that if they can improve the climate and structure of negotiations, the parties will be able to resolve their differences on the issues. Dealmakers are more direct in their attempts to shape the final outcome—not the process—by getting the negotiators to change their positions and strike a deal. Dealmakers are more likely to produce agreements, but they are also more likely to be perceived as antagonistic or biased, which can reduce negotiators' acceptance of mediators.[73]

Depending on the sector, mediation can be voluntary or mandatory. Under the NLRA mediation is voluntary. Employers and unions are required to notify the Federal Mediation and Conciliation Service (FMCS) that they will be renegotiating a contract. This advance notice lets the FMCS offer the assistance of a mediator, but either party can refuse this offer. The Railway Labor Act, however, makes mediation mandatory for negotiators in the railway and airline industries. Railroads and airlines are prohibited from changing the existing terms and conditions of employment, and unions are forbidden from striking, until the National Mediation Board releases the parties from mediation. In difficult disputes the parties may be kept in mediation longer than they would like; but the objective of the mediator, and of the Railway Labor Act, is to resolve disputes without strikes and other forms of conflict. The National Mediation Board is also obligated to offer arbitration to the parties as a method for resolving their dispute, but either party can reject this offer. If the parties are released from mediation and one party rejects arbitration, a strike can legally occur after a 30-day cooling-off period.

A diverse pattern of voluntary and mandatory mediation is also present in public sector labor law across different states. A majority of state laws provide for some type of mediation, and some states have mediation agencies similar to the FMCS.[74] Public sector mediation is typically the first step in a multistep dispute resolution process. In states that allow public sector workers to strike, mediation is commonly required before strikes can legally occur (similar to the Railway Labor Act). Mediation is also frequently used before arbitration or fact-finding. In only a handful of states is mediation the final dispute resolution step.[75] In California, for example, if mediation fails to resolve a bargaining impasse for state employees, the terms and conditions of employment revert to those specified by the state's civil service laws.[76]

Online Exploration Exercise: Browse the Federal Mediation and Conciliation Service website (*www.fmcs.gov*) and YouTube channel. What types of activities does this agency pursue in order to promote dispute resolution? Does your state have comparable agency for public sector collective bargaining (see *www.alra.org/member_agencies.html*)? If so, how does it compare to the FMCS? If not, should your state have a comparable public sector agency? Why or why not?

INTEREST ARBITRATION

Arbitration resolves disputes by a neutral third-party arbitrator (or panel of arbitrators) issuing a settlement that is binding on the employer, union, and employees. A hearing is held, evidence is presented by each side, and an arbitrator issues a decision. This section focuses on **interest arbitration**—arbitration to resolve interest disputes that results in new contractual terms governing wages and terms and conditions of employment; grievance arbitration to settle rights disputes is also important in U.S. labor relations and will be described in the next chapter. Unlike mediation and fact-finding, interest arbitration *imposes* a settlement on the parties to the dispute. As such, once invoked arbitration has a 100 percent settlement rate. But a common objective in labor relations is to have parties peacefully settle their own differences.[77] The typical standard for arbitration, therefore, is the extent to which the threat of arbitration encourages negotiated rather than arbitrated settlements.

The two primary forms of interest arbitration are conventional arbitration and final offer arbitration. In conventional arbitration, the arbitrator is not constrained in deciding the settlement terms. The employer likely argues for a certain wage increase, the union tries to justify a higher wage increase, and the arbitrator can choose any wage increase seen as warranted. The uncertainty of what the arbitrator will choose and the loss of control by the negotiators over the settlement terms motivate negotiators to reach their own negotiated agreement without resorting to arbitration.[78] It has traditionally been believed that such a system suffers from the **chilling effect.**[79] In particular, if arbitrators simply split the difference between the positions of labor and management, each side might hold back from making compromises during negotiations. Suppose you are the management negotiator, and the union is demanding a 10 percent wage increase and you have offered 2 percent. If you make a concession to 4 percent and the union doesn't budge and you end up in arbitration, the wage increase will be 7 percent if the arbitrator splits the difference. If you had stayed at 2 percent, the arbitrator's award would have been less (6 percent). If negotiators follow this logic and refrain from making concessions during negotiations, the bargaining process is "chilled" by the possibility of conventional arbitration. Because many believe that arbitration should encourage negotiated settlements, the chilling effect is a significant concern in labor relations.

To try to lessen this potential chilling effect of conventional arbitration, final offer arbitration was created such that the arbitrator must choose between the union's final offer and the employer's final offer.[80] Final offer arbitration has two variations: (1) total package final offer arbitration, in which the arbitrator must select one party's final offer on all the disputed contract terms (e.g., wages, health insurance, holidays, and so on); and (2) issue-by-issue final offer arbitration, in which the arbitrator can choose either party's final offer on an issue-by-issue basis. The underlying logic of final offer arbitration is that because the arbitrator cannot choose a compromise value, it is riskier for a negotiator to present an extreme offer because this will increase the chances that the arbitrator chooses the other side's final offer.

However, if both sides present extreme offers, final offer arbitration is not necessarily any riskier than conventional arbitration, so both types of arbitration might induce a chilling effect. Additionally, if arbitrators weigh the reasonableness of each party's offer, then negotiators have an incentive to present moderate rather than extreme demands to the arbitrator in both types of arbitration (see the accompanying "Labor Relations Application" on arbitrator decision making).[81] As a result, the traditional thought on extreme offers undermining the value of conventional arbitration is overly simplistic. In fact, although dispute rates are higher under arbitration than strike regimes, empirical research does neither unequivocally support the superiority of either final offer or conventional arbitration in encouraging negotiated settlements nor find a pattern of extreme offers in either type of arbitration.[82]

Arbitration might also have a **narcotic effect**—that is, negotiators might become addicted to or overdependent on arbitration. For example, during difficult economic times if union negotiators settle for minimal gains for the employees, they risk accusations of being ineffective or of selling out. As such, the negotiators can instead take a tough bargaining stance and force arbitration. When the arbitrator awards minimal gains (as the economic environment warrants), the union negotiators can blame the arbitrator and deflect concerns about their own bargaining ability.[83] Similar incentives might be present among management negotiators. The narcotic effect posits that when negotiators see how they can "pass the buck" to the arbitrator, they will develop an overdependence on arbitration to settle their negotiations. In practice, the evidence in support of a narcotic effect is mixed.[84]

As with mediation, interest arbitration is voluntary in the private sector and often mandatory in the public sector. The most visible use of private sector interest arbitration is the final offer arbitration system used in major league baseball to determine player salaries. However, this arrangement is limited to a single issue (salary) and is not used to resolve bargaining disputes between the players' union and team owners. In 2009, when General Motors and Chrysler accepted government bailout money to stay in business, one of the conditions was a provision requiring interest arbitration instead of a strike if there was an impasse when negotiating the next round of collective bargaining agreements.[85] But settlements were reached without needing to use arbitration and this provision wasn't retained. Moving beyond these rare exceptions, private sector negotiators strongly prefer to remain in control of determining their settlements, and private sector interest arbitration is largely a nonevent.[86]

Most interest arbitration occurs in the public sector. In fact, more than 20 states have some form of *compulsory* arbitration statute for at least some public sector employees, especially essential occupations such as police officers and firefighters.[87] However, the specific details vary across states.[88] In Hawaii, for example, police and fire disputes are resolved by mandatory conventional arbitration. New Jersey allows the two parties to select the type of arbitration. If the two parties cannot agree, the statute mandates that final offer arbitration be used with economic issues treated as a package and noneconomic issues chosen issue-by-issue. Michigan police and firefighter bargaining units are covered by a compulsory arbitration method in which economic issues are settled via issue-by-issue final offer arbitration and noneconomic issues are settled via conventional arbitration. As a different example, Iowa uses a tri-offer arbitration system: The arbitrator in a dispute can choose from three offers on an issue-by-issue basis—the union's final offer, the employer's final offer, and a fact finder's recommendation. In the federal sector, bargaining disputes over terms and conditions of employment for postal employees that persist for 180 days are settled through interest arbitration using a panel of arbitrators. Empirical research generally supports the primary goal of these various forms of compulsory interest arbitration dispute resolution systems: preventing strikes.[89]

Some states use a hybrid mediation–arbitration procedure, often called "med–arb."[90] Although many states that use arbitration also use mediation as a first step, note carefully that med–arb is a special case in which the same neutral individual serves as both the mediator and the arbitrator. In other words, once the mediation process is exhausted, the mediator changes hats and becomes the arbitrator. The main advantage of med–arb over other third-party dispute resolution mechanisms is that the mediator–arbitrator develops detailed knowledge of the situation during the mediation phase that can result in a better arbitration award if arbitration becomes necessary.[91] The threat of arbitration might also give the mediator–arbitrator more leverage during the mediation phase—in other words, med–arb can be thought of as "mediation with a club."[92] On the other hand, negotiators may not be completely forthcoming during the mediation phase for fear that the revealed information could be used against them during the arbitration phase.[93] Also, few individuals are effective at both mediation and arbitration because different skills are needed for each.[94] As with other methods of dispute resolution, med–arb has advantages and disadvantages; but med–arb underscores the numerous possible systems of third-party dispute resolution.

Labor Relations Application How Do Arbitrators Make Decisions?

An arbitrator in an interest dispute is presented with arguments from both the union and employer regarding what wage increases and other terms and conditions of employment the arbitrator should award. How do arbitrators decide the terms of the award? The traditional wisdom in labor relations is that arbitrators split the difference between the final offers of labor and management. If the union requests two new paid holidays and the employer demands no new holidays, an arbitrator who splits the difference will award one additional paid holiday. An important debate is whether the traditional wisdom is accurate—do arbitrators really just split the difference?

First note that while mediators typically work full-time for a mediation agency, arbitrators are often independent and are frequently selected by the labor and management negotiators on a case-by-case basis. An arbitrator who develops a reputation as biased in favor of either labor or management will not be selected. Consequently, there is a powerful incentive for arbitrators to split the difference: to appear fair or impartial and therefore to continue one's career as an arbitrator. Moreover, while splitting the difference is easiest under conventional arbitration, similar behavior is also possible under final offer arbitration. In issue-by-issue final offer arbitration, for example, arbitrators can choose the union's offer on half the issues and the employer's offer on the other half. In total package final offer arbitration, the arbitrator can choose the union's final offer in one round and the employer's final offer in the next round (this is sometimes called a "flip-flop effect").

Now think about what's observed in practice. In states with final offer arbitration, it is common to find average union win rates (a union win is when the union's final offer is selected) close to 50 percent. So arbitrators split the difference. Or do they? Arbitrators have more information about a dispute than the final offers of the parties. Arbitrators know the strength or weakness of the economic environment, the terms of other settlements with the same employer, and the terms of settlements in comparable bargaining units elsewhere. As such it is likely that arbitrators have an independent view of a fair settlement. If arbitrators weigh the reasonableness of the final offers when making a decision, then union and management negotiators will position their offers around their estimate of the arbitrator's fair award belief. This behavior will yield union and management win rates close to 50 percent and will yield awards that appear to split the difference. But in this scenario the final offers do not determine the award via splitting the difference—just the opposite: The expected award determines the final offers submitted by each side.

Consequently, one cannot determine whether arbitrators split the difference simply by observing win rates close to 50 percent or by observing arbitrator awards that are close to the middle of the final offers. Such observations might reflect splitting the difference, or they might reflect the negotiators' views of the arbitrator's fair award belief. More sophisticated analyses of arbitrator behavior suggest that arbitrators do not simply split the difference. In an experiment in which arbitrators were presented with hypothetical scenarios, the awards depended both on the parties' final offers and on the facts of each scenario. Moreover, the facts were of much greater importance than the final offers.

In sum, labor relations needs to update its conventional wisdom. Arbitrator awards are influenced by the final offers of the negotiators, but arbitrator decision making is more complex than naïve splitting the difference. Arbitrators are also influenced by their own perceptions of a fair award based on the facts of the situation. This is consistent with provisions in some state laws that specify that arbitrators should base their awards on multiple criteria. For example, Oregon law (Section 243.746) states that arbitrators must base their findings on (1) the interest and welfare of the public, (2) the financial ability of the public sector employer to meet the costs of the proposed contract, (3) the ability of the employer to attract and retain qualified personnel at the wage and benefit levels provided, (4) the overall compensation presently received by the employees, (5) a comparison of the overall compensation of other employees performing similar services in comparable communities, (6) the cost of living, (7) the stipulations of the parties, and (8) other factors that are traditionally taken into consideration in determining wages, hours, and other terms and conditions of employment.

References: Orley Ashenfelter and David E. Bloom, "Models of Arbitrator Behavior: Theory and Evidence," *American Economic Review* 74 (March 1984), pp. 111–24; Max Bazerman and Henry S. Farber, "Arbitrator Decision Making: When Are Final Offers Important?" *Industrial and Labor Relations Review* 39 (October 1985), pp. 76–89; Henry S. Farber, "Splitting the Difference in Interest Arbitration," *Industrial and Labor Relations Review* 35 (October 1981), pp. 70–77; Richard A. Lester, *Labor Arbitration in State and Local Government* (Princeton, NJ: Princeton University Industrial Relations Section, 1984).

FACT-FINDING

Fact-finding is a third-party dispute resolution method in which a neutral third party—a fact finder—investigates a bargaining impasse and issues nonbinding recommendations for a settlement. Fact-finding is essentially nonbinding arbitration. Typically hearings allow each side to make its case, and then the fact finder issues a report containing specific terms of a settlement; but unlike in arbitration, these terms are not binding on the parties. Even without a binding award, however, the fact-finding report helps resolve the bargaining dispute in at least three ways.[95] First, by establishing a set of unbiased settlement terms, the fact-finding report can help the negotiators reevaluate their positions and find an acceptable compromise settlement. Second, as with the narcotic effect in arbitration, a fact-finding report can let union or management negotiators save face by making concessions under the guise of following the report rather than appearing weak. Third, making the fact-finding report public can use the glare of publicity to push the parties to a settlement—typically along the lines of the fact finder's recommendations because they are publicly viewed as neutral and fair.

But what happens if these avenues fail to produce a settlement? The public pressure that underlies the rationale of fact-finding frequently does not exist. As a last resort, a legislative body might need to intervene and legislate an end to the dispute. The fact-finding report is useful as a basis for the substance of this action, but enacting legislation is an inefficient way to end bargaining disputes. Moreover, absent legislative action, important questions arise about what happens next. If management can make unilateral changes after an unresolved impasse, what incentive does the employer have to bargain? Or if the status quo must be maintained and it is a concessionary environment, what incentive does the union have to bargain?

Nevertheless, fact-finding is firmly entrenched as an important component of U.S. labor relations. The emergency strike procedures in both the Railway Labor Act and the NLRA described earlier in this chapter are essentially fact-finding procedures. In the railroad industry in particular, Congress has occasionally legislated settlements based on the report of a presidential emergency board when this report fails to generate sufficient pressure for the parties to settle voluntarily.[96] In the public sector, fact-finding is specified as the final dispute resolution step in many state bargaining laws.[97] The statutory language governing Florida's use of fact-finding is presented as an example in the accompanying "Labor Relations Application"; note the explicit reliance on legislative action to end unresolved disputes, though this is not present in all state policies.

The widespread incorporation of fact-finding in state laws is perhaps a political compromise between unions' demands for binding arbitration and public sector employers' demands for only mediation as the final step for resolving interest disputes.[98] But it is reasonable to question whether this compromise effectively serves the labor relations process. Unlike arbitration, fact-finding does not guarantee a resolution, and unlike mediation, it does not assist the negotiators. In fact, fact-finding appears to actually increase labor conflict relative to public sector jurisdictions that settle disputes with strikes or arbitration.[99] In terms of Table 8.4, fact-finding has the worst of both worlds—low control over both the outcome and the negotiating process. As such, fact-finding is often evaluated negatively.[100]

WHAT'S BEST?

Bargaining impasses—threatened or real—are a central topic in labor relations. From a practical standpoint, preparing for any type of bargaining impasse, but especially a strike through the creation of a strike contingency plan, is complex and contains significant

Labor Relations Application Florida's Fact–Finding System

Florida's public sector bargaining law is an example of a system that uses fact-finding as the final dispute resolution step. Here is an excerpt from the Florida statute:
447.403 Resolution of impasses.—

. . .

3. The fact finder shall hold hearings in order to define the area or areas of dispute, to determine facts relating to the dispute, and to render a decision on any and all unresolved contract issues. . . . Within 15 calendar days after the close of the final hearing, the fact finder shall transmit his or her recommended decision to the [Florida Public Employees Relations Commission] and to the representatives of both parties. . . .
4. If the public employer or the employee organization does not accept, in whole or in part, the recommended decision of the fact finder:

a. The chief executive officer of the governmental entity involved shall, within 10 days after rejection of a recommendation of the fact finder, submit to the legislative body of the governmental entity involved a copy of the findings of fact and recommended decision of the fact finder, together with the chief executive officer's recommendations for settling the disputed impasse issues. . .;

b. The employee organization shall submit its recommendations for settling the disputed impasse issues to such legislative body and to the chief executive officer;

c. The legislative body or a duly authorized committee thereof shall forthwith conduct a public hearing at which the parties shall be required to explain their positions with respect to the rejected recommendations of the fact finder;

d. Thereafter, the legislative body shall take such action as it deems to be in the public interest, including the interest of the public employees involved, to resolve all disputed impasse issues; and

e. Following the resolution of the disputed impasse issues by the legislative body, the parties shall reduce to writing an agreement which includes those issues agreed to by the parties and those disputed impasse issues resolved by the legislative body's action taken pursuant to paragraph (d). The agreement shall be signed by the chief executive officer and the bargaining agent and shall be submitted to the public employer and to the public employees who are members of the bargaining unit for ratification. If such agreement is not ratified by all parties . . . the legislative body's action taken pursuant to the provisions of paragraph (d) shall take effect as of the date of such legislative body's action for the remainder of the first fiscal year which was the subject of negotiations. . . .

Note: Florida law refers to fact finders as "special magistrates." The excerpt here has been changed by replacing "special magistrate" with the more commonly used "fact finder" to avoid confusion.

challenges for labor relations professionals on both the management and union sides. From a policy perspective, there are a number of ways to resolve bargaining impasses—allowing the parties to use their economic weapons, providing mediation, requiring binding arbitration, publicizing a fact finder's recommendations, and various hybrid combinations of these alternatives. This naturally begs the question of what the best method is for resolving interest disputes. But there is no simple answer to this question. No method is best along all dimensions; rather, each of the alternatives involves trade-offs. Like other aspects of labor relations, dispute resolution systems need to strike a balance between these trade-offs.

Strikes and lockouts can be particularly inefficient and costly to employers, employees, and the public. But private sector unions and employers are almost always adamantly opposed to giving up the right to strike or to lock out employees. Employers insist on retaining control over the terms of the settlement (rather than handing control over to an arbitrator), while unions insist that striking is a fundamental right that underlies the ability of employees to achieve equity and voice. Whether the use of strike replacements destroys this right is an important question for the future of U.S. labor relations and again is a question of balancing the rights and interests of employers and employees.

HR Strategy Strike Contingency Plans

Undertaking a strike is a daunting task for both labor and management, and therefore it requires careful planning. Here are some major elements of developing a strike contingency plan.

EMPLOYER

- Appoint a strike coordinator.
- Notify customers and suppliers of the possible strike.
- Prepare a security plan to protect the premises.
- Develop either a shutdown plan or a plan for operating during the strike.
- If planning to operate during the strike, assess how many employees will cross the picket line, how to use supervisors and managers, and the availability of strike replacements.
- If using replacements, determine training needs, HR policies, and housing, food, recreational, and security needs.
- Determine the eligibility of strikers for health insurance and other benefits.
- Create a plan for communicating with the strikers.
- Create a public relations plan.
- Debrief participants on legal issues.

UNION

- Choose a strike committee to lead the strike.
- Establish a strike headquarters.
- Create a picket subcommittee to prepare picket signs and assign picket duty.
- Communicate with the national union regarding strike benefits and other forms of support.
- Establish support committees to reach out to other groups (other unions, food shelves, and local banks and stores for lines of credit for strikers).
- Develop activities to maintain solidarity and morale among the strikers.
- Determine a strategy for handling strike replacements and union members who cross the picket line.
- Evaluate corporate campaign options.
- Create a plan for communicating with the union members.
- Create a public relations plan.
- Debrief participants on legal issues.

QUESTIONS

For each of the scenarios in "HR Strategy: Responding to a Union Organizing Drive" at the end of Chapter 6, assume that the union won recognition and is now bargaining a contract.

1. As an HR manager developing a strike contingency plan, what particular concerns should you have in each scenario?
2. As a local union leader developing a strike contingency plan, what particular concerns should you have in each scenario?
3. For public sector negotiations in which strikes are illegal and bargaining impasses are instead resolved through arbitration, mediation, or fact-finding, which elements of the strike contingency plans presented in this box are unnecessary? Which elements should still be completed?

References: Maurice B. Better, *Contract Bargaining Handbook for Local Union Leaders* (Washington, DC: Bureau of National Affairs, 1993); Robert M. Cassel, *Negotiating a Labor Contract: A Management Handbook,* 4th ed. (Washington, DC: Bureau of National Affairs, 2010).

With respect to third-party dispute resolution, the process and outcome dimensions of Table 8.4 capture the trade-offs among different methods.[101] Fact-finding lacks significant control over both the negotiating process and the outcome. If public sentiment is absent (as it commonly is), fact-finding puts little pressure on the parties to resolve their dispute. Mediation lacks this same pressure but at least helps the parties improve the negotiating process. Therefore, if the primary goal of the dispute resolution system is putting pressure on negotiators to settle and guaranteeing a settlement, arbitration is best. However, if the goal of the dispute resolution system is assisting negotiators in resolving their own disputes—and thereby fostering healthy collective bargaining relationships—mediation is best. In practice, therefore, many labor relations systems combine various dispute resolution methods—especially (usually voluntary) mediation with economic weapons in the private sector and (sometimes mandatory) mediation with fact-finding in the public sector. And as the labor relations environment changes, the search for the "best" dispute resolution procedure continues.

Key Terms

Reflection Questions

1. Not all forms of strikes are protected by the NLRA. What types are protected? Unprotected? Does this make sense, or should all types of strikes be treated equally?
2. In a concise paragraph, paraphrase what you have learned about strike replacements to explain to your parents or spouse why this is such a controversial issue in labor relations. Should the NLRA be revised to prohibit the use of temporary or permanent strike replacements?
3. List the pros and cons of interest arbitration. Why do you think the usage of interest arbitration in the private sector is so low?
4. A state legislature is writing a public sector bargaining law and asks you to design the law's impasse procedures (strike, arbitration, mediation, fact-finding, or some combination). Outline a detailed plan. Do you allow workers to strike? Do you require any types of third-party dispute resolution procedures? How would you sell this plan to the various interested parties?

Labor Law Discussion Case 7: Replacing Strikers by Inverse Seniority: Saving Costs or Coercing Employees?

BACKGROUND

Child Care Services Inc. (CCSI) operates 12 child care centers. A local of the American Federation of State, County, and Municipal Employees (AFSCME) has represented the employees at CCSI for over 15 years with the most recent collective bargaining agreement covering 80 nonprofessional employees (four teachers were covered by a separate contract). In anticipation of the June 30 expiration date, CCSI (represented by attorney Donald Barrister and executive director Susan Gruber) and AFSCME (represented by AFSCME staff rep Elaine Mendez and five bargaining unit members) bargained between April and June. However, the parties were unable to reach agreement.

In a final attempt to craft a settlement, the two parties met on June 27. At this bargaining session, the union presented a proposal consisting of a $1,500 annual wage increase, employer-paid health insurance, shift assignments, and a few other items. CCSI countered with a final offer of no wage increase and sharing of health care costs. Barrister also said that if there was a strike, the child care centers would be operated by permanent replacements and strikers would be replaced by inverse seniority. In other words, employees with the most seniority would be replaced first.

Later that evening, the union held a membership meeting and the negotiating committee briefed the membership on the day's events. Many employees were upset at CCSI's plans to replace employees by inverse seniority, especially because the negotiating committee would be the first to be replaced: The employees on the committee were 1st, 2nd, 5th, 9th, and 19th on the seniority list. By a large margin, those present voted to reject the company's final offer and to go on strike.

On July 1, 54 employees went on strike while 26 did not. Over the next few months, 34 replacements were hired. During the strike there was no mention of unfair labor practice allegations or the inverse seniority replacement plan. The picket signs read, "On Strike for Fair Wages and Health Insurance." On July 25 Mendez met with Barrister and told him that the strike was over and made an unconditional offer to return to work. In January CCSI began offering reinstatement to the strikers by seniority.

QUESTIONS

1. Recall that the *Mackay* doctrine grants employers the right to hire replacement workers during an economic strike. CCSI indicated that it would replace striking employees by inverse seniority. Does this plan violate Section 8(a)(1) of the NLRA or is it allowable under the *Mackay* doctrine?
2. Assuming that the replacement plan violated the NLRA and was therefore an unfair labor practice, was the strike then an unfair labor practice strike?
3. Were the strikers entitled to be reinstated as of July 25? Does it matter whether or not the strike was an unfair labor practice strike?
4. During the administrative law judge hearings for this case, Gruber testified that the reason for replacing employees by inverse seniority was that it would save $40,000 because more senior employees are more expensive. However, it was unclear whether this explanation was offered to the union at the June 27 bargaining session or whether it was an afterthought used in defense during the hearings. Therefore, the NLRB remanded the case back to the administrative law judge for further factual investigation. Why is it important whether the cost-savings rationale was offered to the union on June 27?

Digging Deeper Why Do Strikes Occur? A Multidisciplinary Research Question

In the textbook economics model, individuals are rational and possess perfect information. In this framework it is difficult to explain why strikes occur. If labor and management negotiators have perfect information, they both know the terms of the contract settlement that will occur after a strike. The rational thing to do, therefore, is to agree to those terms without a strike and save everyone the expense of a strike.[102] But strikes obviously do occur. Why? Many explanations for strikes focus on the two assumptions embedded in the textbook economics model: perfect information and pure economic rationality.

LESS THAN PERFECT INFORMATION

Because rationality is at the heart of economics, most economic models of strikes focus instead on problems with the perfect information assumption. One of the first theories posited that strikes were mistakes that stemmed from imperfect information.[103] If union and management negotiators differ in their forecasts of inflation, for example, even rational negotiators will not be able to agree in advance on the poststrike settlement and a strike might occur.[104] Along similar lines, uncertainty about the other side's power and future economic trends can cause miscalculation or a divergence between labor and management negotiators and thus strikes.[105] This is another information-related model because uncertainty stems from a lack of perfect information. Lastly, private or asymmetric information explanations have been developed.[106] Suppose a firm has better information about its profitability than the union. The union wants high-profit firms to pay high wages and will allow low-profit firms to pay lower wages. With private information about profitability, all firms will claim to be low-profit. Consequently, the union can use a strike to screen true profitability by giving the firm two choices: a high wage with no strike or a lower wage after a strike. High-profit firms will take the former, and low-profit firms will choose the latter.

Two other economic models of strikes are also ultimately rooted in information issues. In the joint costs model, if the combined costs of a strike to labor and management are high, negotiators will work hard to avoid a strike.[107] On the other hand, if the joint costs of a strike are less than the expense of negotiating, strikes will occur. But how can the costs of a strike ever be less than those of negotiating? Because of information issues that make it costly (in time and frustration) to negotiate contracts that deal with every possible future contingency that might arise. The last economic model is rooted in information issues between union leaders and the rank and file.[108] In this model, rational union and management negotiators agree on the optimal settlement that avoids a strike, but rank-and-file workers have unrealistically high expectations. In the absence of convincing information, it sometimes takes a strike to lessen the workers' expectation of a high settlement.

BEYOND PURE ECONOMIC RATIONALITY

Outside of economics there is often less attachment to assuming that individuals are always fully rational in a narrow, dollars-and-cents, self-interested manner. Models of strike activity in other disciplines therefore embrace a broader conception of rational behavior and incorporate sociological and psychological influences such as social identities and emotions.

Mobilization theory posits that workers will mobilize for collective action (as in a strike) if there are leaders present when workers (1) suffer from perceived injustice, (2) blame management rather than themselves for their problems, and (3) feel a sense of collective rather than individual identity in the workplace.[109] In this thinking, strikes are not simply calculated attempts to increase wages; they are also expressions of discontent through the exercise of collective voice.[110] As such, strikes will depend not only on the costs and benefits of striking but also on the social relations and climate of the workplace. Organizational stability or institutional turmoil within the workplace, unions, and the labor movement can also affect strike activity.[111]

Conservative business and political groups occasionally blame strikes on troublemaking agitators—often branded as communists—who manufacture strikes by manipulating workers. While mobilization theory reveals the importance of leaders in collective action such as strikes, and while the personalities of labor and management negotiators can be important, it is inaccurate to blame strikes solely on manipulative leaders.[112] Legitimate worker dissatisfaction or injustice is needed to cause strikes.

A second model category that broadens the pure economic rationality assumption is behavioral models rooted in psychology. Work in this vein focuses on perception, motivation, and frustration.[113] If workers perceive situations differently from managers, are motivated to seek different goals than managers, and are frustrated in pursuit of these goals, strikes can result. Because of the powerful emotion of frustration, aggression can overwhelm pure economic calculations and result in strikes.[114]

A final explanation for strikes is that they are used occasionally as practice to make sure employers continue to appreciate the strike threat and therefore concede to union demands in negotiations without an actual strike:

> Weapons grow rusty if unused, and a union which never strikes may lose the ability to organize a formidable strike, so that its threats become less effective. The most able trade union leadership will embark on strikes occasionally, not so much to secure greater gains upon that occasion. . . . but in order to keep their weapon burnished for future use, and to keep employers thoroughly conscious of the union's power.[115]

In sum, strikes involve complex interactions of human behavior and the surrounding environment, often in stressful and challenging situations. There are a variety of possible explanations for why strikes occur, and few researchers probably believe that a single theory underlies all strikes. Rather, strikes likely stem from a combination of economic, social, organizational, political, and psychological factors. Explaining strikes continues to be a challenging, multidisciplinary research problem.[116]

End Notes

1. Federal Mediation and Conciliation Service, *Annual Report* (Washington, DC: U.S. Government Printing Office, various years).
2. Marcus Rediker, *Between the Devil and the Deep Blue Sea: Merchant Seaman, Pirates, and the Anglo-American Maritime World, 1700–1750* (Cambridge, England: Cambridge University Press, 1987).
3. J.J. Janssen, "Background Information on the Strikes of Year 29 of Ramesses III," *Oriens Antiquus* 18 (1979), pp. 301–8.
4. Aaron Brenner, Benjamin Day, and Immanuel Ness (eds.), *The Encyclopedia of Strikes in American History* (Armonk, NY: M.E. Sharpe, 2009).
5. Josiah Bartlett Lambert, *"If the Workers Took a Notion": The Right to Strike and American Political Development* (Ithaca, NY: Cornell University Press, 2005).
6. Francis Russell, *A City in Terror: 1919, The Boston Police Strike* (New York: Viking, 1975), p. 191; Joseph Slater, "Labor and the Boston Police Strike of 1919," in Aaron Brenner, Benjamin Day, and Immanuel Ness (eds.), *The Encyclopedia of Strikes in American History* (Armonk, NY: M.E. Sharpe, 2009), pp. 241–51; Sterling D. Spero, *Government as Employer* (New York: Remsen Press, 1948).
7. John Lund and Cheryl L. Maranto, "Public Sector Labor Law: An Update," in Dale Belman, Morley Gunderson, and Douglas Hyatt (eds.), *Public Sector Employment in a Time of Transition* (Madison, WI: Industrial Relations Research Association, 1996), pp. 21–57.
8. Joyce M. Najita, William J. Anzenberger, and Helene S. Tanimoto, "Essential Employee Strikes and Compulsory Arbitration Procedures: The Hawaii Public Sector Collective Bargaining Experience," in Joyce M. Najita and James L. Stern (eds.), *Collective Bargaining in the Public Sector: The Experience of Eight States* (Armonk, NY: M. E. Sharpe, 2001), pp. 222–56.
9. Lund and Maranto, "Public Sector Labor Law."
10. Janet McEneaney and Robert P. Hebdon, "Public Sector Labor Law and Experience in New York State," in Joyce M. Najita and James L. Stern (eds.), *Collective Bargaining in the Public Sector: The Experience of Eight States* (Armonk, NY: M. E. Sharpe, 2001), pp. 161–94.
11. Michael Hirsch, "Three Strikes Against the New York City Transit System," in Aaron Brenner, Benjamin Day, and Immanuel Ness (eds.), *The Encyclopedia of Strikes in American History* (Armonk, NY: M.E. Sharpe, 2009), pp. 277–86.
12. Donald E. Cullen, "Emergency Boards under the Railway Labor Act," in Charles M. Rehmus (ed.), *The Railway Labor Act at Fifty: Collective Bargaining in the Railroad and Airline Industries* (Washington, DC: National Mediation Board, 1976), pp. 151–86; Douglas L. Leslie (ed.), *The Railway Labor Act* (Washington, DC: Bureau of National Affairs, 1995); Charles M. Rehmus, "Emergency Strikes Revisited," *Industrial and Labor Relations Review* 43 (January 1990), pp. 175–90.
13. Donald E. Cullen, *National Emergency Strikes* (Ithaca, NY: New York State School of Industrial and Labor Relations, 1968); Harry A. Millis and Emily Clark Brown, *From the Wagner Act to Taft–Hartley: A Study of National Labor Policy and Labor Relations* (Chicago: University of Chicago Press, 1950); Rehmus, "Emergency Strikes Revisited."
14. Cullen, *National Emergency Strikes;* Rehmus, "Emergency Strikes Revisited."
15. Brian E. Becker and Craig A. Olson, "The Impact of Strikes on Shareholder Equity," *Industrial and Labor Relations Review* 39 (April), pp. 425–38; Bruce E. Kaufman, "Research on Strike Models and Outcomes in the 1980s: Accomplishments and Shortcomings," in David Lewin, Olivia S. Mitchell, and Peter D. Sherer (eds.), *Research Frontiers in Industrial Relations and Human Resources* (Madison, WI: Industrial Relations Research Association, 1992), pp. 77–129; Charles R. Stoner and Raj Arora, "An Investigation of the Relationship between Selected Variables and the Psychological Health of Strike Participants," *Journal of Occupational Psychology* 60 (March 1987), pp. 61–71.
16. Douglas E. Ray, Calvin William Sharpe, and Robert N. Strassfield, *Understanding Labor Law* (New York: Mathew Bender, 1999); Benjamin J. Taylor and Fred Witney, *Labor Relations Law,* 7th ed. (Englewood Cliffs, NJ: Prentice Hall, 1996).
17. Ahmed A. White, "Workers Disarmed: The Campaign against Mass Picketing and the Dilemma of Liberal Labor Rights," *Harvard Civil Rights-Civil Liberties Law Review* 49 (Winter 2014), pp. 59–124.
18. Bruce S. Feldacker, *Labor Guide to Labor Law,* 4th ed. (Upper Saddle River, NJ: Prentice Hall, 2000).
19. Taylor and Witney, *Labor Relations Law.*
20. *Local 707 Motor Freight Drivers (Claremont Polychemical Corp.),* 196 NLRB 613 (1972).
21. Robert Hebdon, "Public Sector Dispute Resolution in Transition," in Dale Belman, Morley Gunderson, and Douglas Hyatt (eds.), *Public Sector Employment in a Time of Transition* (Madison, WI: Industrial Relations Research Association, 1996), pp. 85–125.

22. "Major Work Stoppages in 2015," Bureau of Labor Statistics, U.S. Department of Labor (February 10, 2016).
23. Sheena McConnell, "Cyclical Fluctuations in Strike Activity," *Industrial and Labor Relations Review* 44 (October 1990), pp. 130–43; Michael H. Cimini and John K. Steinmeyer, "What Can You Tell Me about Collective Bargaining Expirations and Work Stoppages?" *Compensation and Working Conditions Online,* May 28, 2003, accessed June 23, 2003, at www.bls.gov/opub/cwc/cb20030522ar01p1.htm.
24. Federal Mediation and Conciliation Service, *Annual Report.*
25. Kaufman, "Research on Strike Models and Outcomes in the 1980s."
26. Alison L. Booth, *The Economics of the Trade Union* (Cambridge, England: Cambridge University Press, 1995); John R. Hicks, *The Theory of Wages* (London: Macmillan, 1932); Barry T. Hirsch and John T. Addison, *The Economic Analysis of Unions* (Boston: Allen and Unwin, 1986).
27. Kaufman, "Research on Strike Models and Outcomes in the 1980s"; McConnell, "Cyclical Fluctuations in Strike Activity"; Craig A. Olson, "Strikes, Strike Penalties, and Arbitration in Six States," *Industrial and Labor Relations Review* 39 (July 1986), pp. 539–51.
28. John Godard, "Strikes as Collective Voice: A Behavioral Analysis of Strike Activity," *Industrial and Labor Relations Review* 46 (October 1992), pp. 161–75.
29. Kaufman, "Research on Strike Models and Outcomes in the 1980s"; McConnell, "Cyclical Fluctuations in Strike Activity"; Albert Rees, "Industrial Conflict and Business Fluctuations," *Journal of Political Economy* 60 (October 1952), pp. 371–82.
30. Cynthia L. Gramm, Wallace E. Hendricks, and Lawrence M. Kahn, "Inflation Uncertainty and Strike Activity," *Industrial Relations* 27 (Winter 1988), pp. 114–29.
31. Jonathan D. Rosenblum, *Copper Crucible: How the Arizona Miners' Strike of 1983 Recast Labor–Management Relations in America,* 2nd ed. (Ithaca, NY: ILR Press, 1998); Robert H. Zieger and Gilbert J. Gall, *American Workers, American Unions: The Twentieth Century,* 3rd ed. (Baltimore: Johns Hopkins Press, 2002).
32. *NLRB v. Mackay Radio and Telegraph Co.,* 304 U.S. 333, 345–46 (1938); Julius G. Getman and Thomas C. Kohler, "The Story of *NLRB v. Mackay Radio and Telegraph Co.:* The High Cost of Solidarity," in Laura J. Cooper and Catherine L. Fisk (eds.), *Labor Law Stories* (New York: Foundation Press, 2005), pp. 13–53; Lambert, "*If the Workers Took a Notion*"; John Logan, "Permanent Replacements and the End of Labor's 'Only True Weapon,'" *International Labor and Working-Class History* 74 (Fall 2008), pp. 171–92.
33. *NLRB v. Fleetwood Trailer Co.,* 389 U.S. 375 (1967).
34. Ray, Sharpe, and Strassfield, *Understanding Labor Law.*
35. *Mastro Plastics Corp. v. NLRB,* 350 U.S. 270 (1956).
36. *NLRB v. Cast Optics Corp.,* 458 F.2d 398 (3d Cir. 1972), cert. denied 409 U.S. 850 (1972); *Larand Leisurelies,* 213 NLRB 197 (1974), enfd. 523 F.2d 814 (6th Cir. 1975).
37. *NLRB v. Brown,* 380 U.S. 278 (1965); *Harter Equipment,* 280 NLRB 597 (1986).
38. *Harter Equipment,* 293 NLRB 647 (1989).
39. Samuel Estreicher, "Collective Bargaining or 'Collective Begging'?: Reflections on Antistrikebreaker Legislation," *Michigan Law Review* 93 (December 1994), pp. 577–608.
40. Michael H. LeRoy, "The PATCO Strike: Myths and Realities," in Paula B. Voos (ed.), *Proceedings of the Forty-Ninth Annual Meeting* (Madison, WI: Industrial Relations Research Association, 1997), pp. 15–22; Logan, "Permanent Replacements and the End of Labor's 'Only True Weapon.'"
41. Barbara Kingsolver, *Holding the Line: Women in the Great Arizona Mine Strike of 1983* (Ithaca, NY: ILR Press, 1989); Rosenblum, *Copper Crucible.*
42. Julius Getman, *The Betrayal of Local 14* (Ithaca, NY: ILR Press, 1998); Dave Hage and Paul Klauda, *No Retreat, No Surrender: Labor's War at Hormel* (New York: William Morrow, 1989); Peter Rachleff, *Hard-Pressed in the Heartland: The Hormel Strike and the Future of the Labor Movement* (Boston: South End Press, 1993); Logan, "Permanent Replacements and the End of Labor's 'Only True Weapon.'"
43. Peter C. Cramton and Joseph S. Tracy, "The Use of Replacement Workers in Union Contract Negotiations: The U.S. Experience, 1980–1989," *Journal of Labor Economics* 16 (October 1998), pp. 667–701; Craig A. Olson, "The Use of Strike Replacements in Labor Disputes: Evidence from the 1880s to the 1980s" (unpublished paper, University of Wisconsin–Madison, 1991); John F. Schnell and Cynthia L. Gramm, "The Empirical Relations between Employers' Striker Replacement Strategies and Strike Duration," *Industrial and Labor Relations Review* 47 (January 1994), pp. 189–206.
44. Rick Fantasia and Kim Voss, *Hard Work: Remaking the American Labor Movement* (Berkeley: University of California Press, 2004).

45. Stephen H. Norwood, *Strikebreaking and Intimidation: Mercenaries and Masculinity in Twentieth-Century America* (Chapel Hill: University of North Carolina Press, 2002); Robert Michael Smith, *From Blackjacks to Briefcases: A History of Commercialized Strikebreaking and Unionbusting in the United States* (Athens: Ohio University Press, 2003); Logan, "Permanent Replacements and the End of Labor's 'Only True Weapon.'"
46. *American Baptist Homes of the West d/b/a Piedmont Gardens*, 364 NLRB No. 13 (2016).
47. Robert Hebdon and Robert Stern, "Do Public Sector Strike Bans Really Prevent Conflict?" *Industrial Relations* 42 (July 2003), pp. 493–512.
48. Philip M. Dine, *State of the Unions: How Labor Can Strengthen the Middle Class, Improve Our Economy, and Regain Political Influence* (New York: McGraw-Hill, 2008).
49. Ray, Sharpe, and Strassfield, *Understanding Labor Law;* Taylor and Witney, *Labor Relations Law.*
50. *NLRB v. Denver Building Trades Council,* 341 U.S. 675 (1951).
51. Feldacker, *Labor Guide to Labor Law.*
52. *Central Illinois Public Service Company,* 326 NLRB No. 80 (1998).
53. *Caterpillar, Inc.,* 322 NLRB No. 115 (1996).
54. Michael H. LeRoy, "Creating Order Out of CHAOS and Other Partial and Intermittent Strikes," *Northwestern University Law Review* 95 (Fall 2000), pp. 221–70.
55. Richard C. Kearney and Patrice M. Mareschal, *Labor Relations in the Public Sector,* 5th ed. (Boca Raton: CRC Press, 2014).
56. Dan La Botz, *A Troublemaker's Handbook: How to Fight Back Where You Work—And Win!* (Detroit: Labor Notes, 1991).
57. Hage and Klauda, *No Retreat, No Surrender;* Tom Juravich and Kate Bronfenbrenner, *Ravenswood: The Steelworkers' Victory and the Revival of American Labor* (Ithaca, NY: Cornell University Press, 1999); LaBotz, *A Troublemaker's Handbook.*
58. Laura Paskus, "In Search of Solidarity," *High Country News* 36 (May 24, 2004).
59. Paul Jarley and Cheryl L. Maranto, "Union Corporate Campaigns: An Assessment," *Industrial and Labor Relations Review* 43 (July 1990), pp. 505–24; Charles R. Perry, "Corporate Campaigns in Context," *Journal of Labor Research* 17 (Summer 1996), pp. 329–43.
60. Hage and Klauda, *No Retreat, No Surrender;* Getman, *The Betrayal of Local 14;* Juravich and Bronfenbrenner, *Ravenswood;* Rosenblum, *Copper Crucible.*
61. Jane McAlevey with Bob Ostertag, *Raising Expectations (and Raising Hell): My Decade Fighting for the Labor Movement* (London: Verso, 2012).
62. Kate Bronfenbrenner and Tom Juravich, "The Evolution of Strategic and Coordinated Bargaining Campaigns in the 1990s: The Steelworkers' Experience," in Lowell Turner, Harry C. Katz, and Richard W. Hurd (eds.), *Rekindling the Movement: Labor's Quest for Relevance in the Twenty-First Century* (Ithaca, NY: ILR Press, 2001), pp. 211–37; La Botz, *A Troublemaker's Handbook.*
63. Thomas J. DiLorenzo, "The Corporate Campaign against Food Lion: A Study of Media Manipulation," *Journal of Labor Research* 17 (Summer 1996), pp. 359–75; Herbert R. Northrup, "Expanding Union Power by Comprehensive Corporate Campaigns and Manipulation of the Regulatory Process," in Bruce E. Kaufman (ed.), *Government Regulation of the Employment Relationship* (Madison, WI: Industrial Relations Research Association, 1997), pp. 533–46.
64. James J. Brudney, "Collateral Conflict: Employer Claims of RICO Extortion against Union Comprehensive Campaigns," *Southern California Law Review* 83 (May 2010), pp. 731–96.
65. *Edward J. DeBartolo Corp. v. Florida Gulf Coast Building and Construction Trades Council,* 485 U.S. 568 (1988).
66. Victor G. Devinatz and John W. Budd, "Third Party Dispute Resolution—Interest Disputes," in David Lewin, Daniel J. B. Mitchell, and Mahmood A. Zaidi (eds.), *The Human Resource Management Handbook Part II* (Greenwich, CT: JAI Press, 1997), pp. 95–135; Roy J. Lewicki, Stephen E. Weiss, and David Lewin, "Models of Conflict, Negotiation and Third Party Intervention: A Review and Synthesis," *Journal of Organizational Behavior* 13 (May 1992), pp. 209–52.
67. Mario F. Bognanno and Charles J. Coleman (eds.), *Labor Arbitration in America: The Profession and Practice* (New York: Praeger, 1992).
68. Lawrence Susskind and Jeffrey Cruikshank, *Breaking the Impasse: Consensual Approaches to Resolving Public Disputes* (New York: Basic Books, 1987).
69. Christopher W. Moore, *The Mediation Process: Practical Strategies for Resolving Conflict,* 2nd ed. (San Francisco: Jossey-Bass, 1996); Dean G. Pruitt et al., "The Process of Mediation: Caucusing, Control,

and Problem Solving," in M. Afzalur Rahim (ed.), *Managing Conflict: An Interdisciplinary Approach* (New York: Praeger, 1989), pp. 201–8.

70. Stephen B. Goldberg, "The Secrets of Successful Mediators," *Negotiation Journal* 21 (July 2005), pp. 365–76.
71. Devinatz and Budd, "Third Party Dispute Resolution—Interest Disputes"; Ahmid Karim and Richard Pegnetter, "Mediator Strategies and Qualities and Mediation Effectiveness," *Industrial Relations* 22 (Winter 1983), pp. 105–14; James A. Wall and Timothy C. Dunne, "Mediation Research: A Current Review," *Negotiation Journal* 28 (April 2012), pp. 217–44.
72. Deborah M. Kolb, *The Mediators* (Cambridge, MA: MIT Press, 1983).
73. Paul F. Gerhart and John E. Drotning, "Dispute Settlement and the Intensity of Mediation," *Industrial Relations* 19 (Fall 1980), pp. 352–59; Thomas A. Kochan and Todd Jick, "The Public Sector Mediation Process: A Theory and Empirical Examination," *Journal of Conflict Resolution* 22 (June 1978), pp. 209–38; Kolb, *The Mediators;* Gary L. Welton and Dean G. Pruitt, "The Mediation Process: The Effects of Mediator Bias and Disputant Power," *Personality and Social Psychology Bulletin* 13 (March 1987), pp. 123–33.
74. Kearney and Mareschal, *Labor Relations in the Public Sector.*
75. Hebdon, "Public Sector Dispute Resolution in Transition."
76. Carol A. Vendrillo, "Collective Bargaining in California's Public Sector," in Joyce M. Najita and James L. Stern (eds.), *Collective Bargaining in the Public Sector: The Experience of Eight States* (Armonk, NY: M. E. Sharpe, 2001), pp. 137–60.
77. George W. Taylor, *Government Regulation of Industrial Relations* (Englewood Cliffs, NJ: Prentice Hall, 1948); John W. Budd, Aaron J. Sojourner, and Jaewoo Jung, "Are Voluntary Agreements Better? Evidence from Baseball Arbitration," *Industrial and Labor Relations Review* (forthcoming).
78. Frederic C. Champlin and Mario F. Bognanno, "A Model of Arbitration and the Incentive to Bargain," in David B. Lipsky and David Lewin (eds.), *Advances in Industrial and Labor Relations* (Greenwich, CT: JAI Press, 1986), pp. 153–90; Henry S. Farber and Harry C. Katz, "Interest Arbitration, Outcomes, and the Incentive to Bargain," *Industrial and Labor Relations Review* 33 (October 1979), pp. 55–63.
79. Peter Feuille, "Final Offer Arbitration and the Chilling Effect," *Industrial Relations* 14 (October 1975), pp. 302–10; Thomas Kochan, et al., "The Long Haul Effects of Interest Arbitration: The Case of New York State's Taylor Law," *Industrial and Labor Relations Review* 63 (July 2010), pp. 565–84.
80. Carl M. Stevens, "Is Compulsory Arbitration Compatible with Bargaining?" *Industrial Relations* 5 (February 1966), pp. 38–52.
81. Henry S. Farber, "Splitting the Difference in Interest Arbitration," *Industrial and Labor Relations Review* 35 (October 1981), pp. 70–77.
82. Orley Ashenfelter and David E. Bloom, "Models of Arbitrator Behavior: Theory and Evidence," *American Economic Review* 74 (March 1984), pp. 111–24; Frederic C. Champlin and Mario F. Bognanno, "'Chilling' under Arbitration and Mixed Strike–Arbitration Regimes," *Journal of Labor Research* 6 (Fall 1985), pp. 375–87; Devinatz and Budd, "Third Party Dispute Resolution—Interest Disputes"; Hebdon, "Public Sector Dispute Resolution in Transition"; Craig A. Olson, "Final Offer versus Conventional Arbitration Revisited: Preliminary Results from the Lab" (unpublished paper, University of Wisconsin–Madison, 1994).
83. Brian P. McCall, "Interest Arbitration and the Incentive to Bargain: A Principal–Agent Approach," *Journal of Conflict Resolution* 34 (March 1990), pp. 151–67.
84. Richard J. Butler and Ronald G. Ehrenberg, "Estimating the Narcotic Effect of Public Sector Impasse Procedures," *Industrial and Labor Relations Review* 35 (October 1981), pp. 3–20; James R. Chelius and Marian M. Extejt, "The Narcotic Effect of Impasse Resolution Procedures," *Industrial and Labor Relations Review* 38 (July 1985), pp. 629–38; Janet Currie, "Who Uses Interest Arbitration? The Case of British Columbia's Teachers, 1947–1981," *Industrial and Labor Relations Review* (April 1989), pp. 363–79; Kochan, et al., "The Long Haul Effects of Interest Arbitration."
85. Harry C. Katz, John Paul MacDuffie, and Frits K. Pil, "Crisis and Recovery in the U.S. Auto Industry: Tumultuous Times for a Collective Bargaining Pacesetter," in Howard R. Stanger, Paul F. Clark, and Ann C. Frost (eds.), *Collective Bargaining under Duress: Case Studies of Major North American Industries* (Champaign, IL: Labor and Employment Relations Association, 2013), pp. 45–79.
86. Peter Feuille, "Dispute Resolution Frontiers in the Unionized Workplace," in Sandra E. Gleason (ed.), *Workplace Dispute Resolution: Directions for the Twenty-First Century* (East Lansing: Michigan State University Press, 1997), pp. 17–55.
87. Hebdon, "Public Sector Dispute Resolution in Transition"; Lund and Maranto, "Public Sector Labor Law."
88. Richard A. Lester, *Labor Arbitration in State and Local Government* (Princeton, NJ: Princeton University Industrial Relations Section, 1984); Joyce M. Najita and James L. Stern (eds.), *Collective Bargaining in the Public Sector: The Experience of Eight States* (Armonk, NY: M. E. Sharpe, 2001).

89. Janet Currie and Sheena McConnell, "Collective Bargaining in the Public Sector: The Effect of Legal Structure on Dispute Costs and Wages," *American Economic Review* 81 (December 1991), pp. 693–718; Casey Ichniowski, "Arbitration and Police Bargaining: Prescriptions for the Blue Flu," *Industrial Relations* 21 (Spring 1982), pp. 149–66.
90. Devinatz and Budd, "Third Party Dispute Resolution—Interest Disputes"; Lester, *Labor Arbitration in State and Local Government*.
91. David A. Dilts and William J. Walsh, *Collective Bargaining and Impasse Resolution in the Public Sector* (New York: Quorum Books, 1988).
92. Kearney and Mareschal, *Labor Relations in the Public Sector,* p. 293.
93. W. Meagher, "New Frontiers in Dispute Resolution: Skills and Techniques," in Howard J. Anderson (ed.), *New Techniques in Labor Dispute Resolution* (Washington, DC: Bureau of National Affairs, 1976), pp. 166–77.
94. Dilts and Walsh, *Collective Bargaining and Impasse Resolution in the Public Sector.*
95. Devinatz and Budd, "Third Party Dispute Resolution—Interest Disputes"; Hebdon, "Public Sector Dispute Resolution in Transition"; Arnold M. Zack, "Improving Mediation and Fact-Finding in the Public Sector," *Labor Law Journal* 21 (May 1970), pp. 259–73.
96. Rehmus, "Emergency Strikes Revisited."
97. Kearney and Mareschal, *Labor Relations in the Public Sector*; Lund and Maranto, "Public Sector Labor Law."
98. Feuille, "Dispute Resolution Frontiers in the Unionized Workplace."
99. Hebdon and Stern, "Do Public Sector Strike Bans Really Prevent Conflict?"
100. Devinatz and Budd, "Third Party Dispute Resolution—Interest Disputes"; Feuille, "Dispute Resolution Frontiers in the Unionized Workplace."
101. Devinatz and Budd, "Third Party Dispute Resolution—Interest Disputes."
102. Hirsch and Addison, *The Economic Analysis of Unions.*
103. Hicks, *The Theory of Wages.*
104. Bruce E. Kaufman, "Bargaining Theory, Inflation, and Cyclical Strike Activity in Manufacturing," *Industrial and Labor Relations Review* 34 (April 1981), pp. 333–55.
105. Jean-Michel Cousineau and Robert Lacroix, "Imperfect Information and Strikes: An Analysis of Canadian Experience, 1967–82," *Industrial and Labor Relations Review* 39 (April 1986), pp. 377–87; Gramm, Hendricks, and Kahn, "Inflation Uncertainty and Strike Activity"; W. Stanley Siebert and John T. Addison, "Are Strikes Accidental?" *Economic Journal* 91 (June 1981), pp. 389–404.
106. David Card, "Strikes and Wages: A Test of an Asymmetric Information Model," *Quarterly Journal of Economics* 105 (1990), pp. 625–59; Beth Hayes, "Unions and Strikes with Asymmetric Information," *Journal of Labor Economics* 2 (January 1984), pp. 57–83; Sheena McConnell, "Strikes, Wages, and Private Information," *American Economic Review* 79 (September 1989), pp. 801–15.
107. John Kennan, "Pareto Optimality and the Economics of Strike Duration," *Journal of Labor Research* 1 (Spring 1980), pp. 77–94; Melvin W. Reder and George R. Neumann, "Conflict and Contract: The Case of Strikes," *Journal of Political Economy* 88 (October 1980), pp. 867–86.
108. Orley Ashenfelter and George E. Johnson, "Bargaining Theory, Trade Unions, and Industrial Strike Activity," *American Economic Review* 59 (March 1969), pp. 35–49.
109. John Kelly, *Rethinking Industrial Relations: Mobilization, Collectivism and Long Waves* (London: Routledge, 1998).
110. Godard, "Strikes as Collective Voice"; Lambert, *"If the Workers Took a Notion."*
111. Mario F. Bognanno, John W. Budd, and Young-Myon Lee, "Institutional Turmoil and Strike Activity in Korea," *Journal of Industrial Relations* 36 (September 1994), pp. 353–69; Arthur M. Ross and Paul T. Hartman, *Changing Patterns of Industrial Conflict* (New York: John Wiley and Sons, 1960).
112. Ralph Darlington, "The Agitator 'Theory' of Strikes Re-evaluated," *Labor History* 47 (November 2006), pp. 485–509.
113. Stephen D. Bluen, "The Psychology of Strikes," in Cary L. Cooper and Ivan T. Robertson (eds.), *International Review of Industrial and Organizational Psychology, 1994,* Volume 9 (Chichester, England: John Wiley and Sons, 1994), pp. 113–35; Ross Stagner and Hjalmar Rosen, *Psychology of Union–Management Relations* (Belmont, CA: Wadsworth, 1965).
114. Hoyt N. Wheeler, *Industrial Conflict: An Integrative Theory* (Columbia: University of South Carolina Press, 1985).
115. Hicks, *The Theory of Wages,* p. 146.
116. Kaufman, "Research on Strike Models and Outcomes in the 1980s."

Chapter Nine

Contract Clauses and Their Administration

Advance Organizer

The primary objective of most U.S. unions is to negotiate contracts with employers that specify wages, hours, and other terms and conditions of employment. The labor relations processes described in the previous chapters—union organizing, bargaining, and dispute resolution—largely lead the parties to such a contract. This chapter describes the types of clauses that are frequently found in union contracts and also how disputes (grievances) over the application of these clauses are resolved.

Learning Objectives

By the end of this chapter, you should be able to

1. **Understand** the nature of U.S. union contracts.
2. **Explain** important contractual provisions that attach rights and obligations to employees, jobs, unions, and employers.
3. **Outline** how grievances are resolved—that is, how contracts are administered.
4. **Discuss** the importance of grievance arbitration in U.S. labor relations.
5. **Analyze** the pressures for changing the nature of U.S. union contracts and how they are administered.

Contents

The centerpiece of U.S. labor relations has long been union contracts that specify the rights and responsibilities of employees (including wages and other terms and conditions of employment), jobs, unions, and employers. Contracts come in a wide variety of sizes, shapes, formats, and colors: Some are slim, whereas others have grown into thick, multi-volume documents (recall Figure 1.3); some are pocket-sized bound booklets, and others are contained in three-ring binders. But in whatever form and for better or worse, the U.S. labor relations system revolves around these contracts, more so than in most other countries. Employees form unions (Chapter 6) to pursue collective bargaining (Chapter 7), perhaps assisted by mediation or resolved by arbitration (Chapter 8), in order to obtain contracts. The first part of this chapter therefore explores the major elements of U.S. union contracts.

Despite the detailed nature of many contract clauses, they can never anticipate or remove every ambiguity for all scenarios that will arise during the life of the contract. For example, to prevent an employer from repeatedly sending employees home for lack of work, suppose a contract indicates that all employees who report to work will be paid for at least four hours. What happens if employees are sent home because of a bomb scare? Are they entitled to four hours of pay? Alternatively, a contract might specify that promotions are based on seniority and ability. How are the two factors weighted for comparing two specific individuals? Nearly all contracts limit employee terminations to cases in which there is just cause. Is one unexcused absence just cause? How about sending a personal e-mail message from an office computer? In short, conflicts over the interpretation, application, and enforcement of contracts inevitably occur. The process of interpreting, applying, and resolving conflicts regarding collective bargaining agreements is called **contract administration.** In unionized workplaces, contract administration is likely the most frequently used of the major labor relations processes, and may even occur every day.

Contract administration involves rights disputes. Recall from the previous chapter the two broad categories of disputes in labor relations: interest disputes and rights disputes. Interest disputes are conflicts of interest—such as over wage rates, benefit packages, or personnel policies—that are the focus of contract negotiations (Chapters 7 and 8). Once a union contract is in place, **rights disputes** are disagreements over whether someone's rights as specified in the contract have been violated. In other words, rights disputes are grievances—conflicts over the administration (i.e., the application and interpretation) of the contract. The second part of this chapter describes how union contracts are administered and rights disputes resolved.

Contracts are central to U.S. labor relations because of the belief that workplace justice and efficiency are best achieved through written workplace rules enforced by a private system of workplace dispute resolution. Under the employment-at-will doctrine, employers are generally free to establish whatever terms and conditions of employment they desire and to discharge workers at any time (and employees are free to quit at any time). Unions have long sought to protect workers by restricting this absolute authority: "Whether carved on stone by an ancient monarch or written in a Magna Charta [sic] by a King John, or embodied in collective agreement between a union and employer; the intent is the same, to subject the ruler to definite laws to which subjects or citizens may hold him when he attempts to exercise arbitrary power."[1] The result is detailed, legally enforceable union contracts enforced by grievance arbitration.

However, before we proceed, note that this bureaucratic model has critics. From a managerial perspective rules-based contracts and the system of grievance arbitration that relies heavily on past practices and precedents are viewed as inhibiting flexibility and innovation; these important concerns will be addressed in detail in the next chapter. Among some labor activists the bureaucratic system of representation is criticized for achieving stability at the expense of rank-and-file involvement and activism (recall the debate between the servicing and organizing models of union representation from Chapter 5). Mobilizing worker power through grassroots activism (recall the inside-the-workplace pressure tactics from Chapter 8) is an alternative path for protecting workers' rights not typically chosen by U.S. unions.[2] Alternative forms of unionism will be discussed in Chapters 12 and 13. This chapter focuses on the path traditionally favored in U.S. labor relations: striking a balance between efficiency, equity, and voice through specific rules laid out in union contracts that are enforced through formal quasilegal grievance procedures (i.e., a servicing model of representation).

U.S. UNION CONTRACTS

As workers fought for workplace justice in the early decades of the 1900s, they frequently tried to force their employers to follow impartial rules: wages that were based on jobs rather than unfair manipulation of piece rates; promotions and layoffs based on seniority rather than managerial favoritism and discrimination.[3] This was a way of "introducing civil rights into industry—that is, of requiring that management be conducted by rule rather than by arbitrary decision."[4] An alternative quest for workplace justice focused on shop floor militancy and union control of work standards backed up by spontaneous strikes and slowdowns. Many union and corporate leaders preferred the rules-based approach, which supported management's desire for stability and discipline and also fulfilled union leaders' needs for countering managerial authority without having to resort to wildcat strikes that could undermine their own leadership positions.[5] Thus by 1930 the Amalgamated Clothing Workers union had negotiated numerous contracts in the garment industry that replaced the militancy of small work groups with the discipline of "responsible" union leaders.[6] Both workers and managers had to follow the negotiated work rules, performance standards, and disciplinary procedures that were enforced through a grievance procedure culminating with the rulings of impartial arbitrators. In 1940, General Motors agreed to a contract with the United Auto Workers that provided for an impartial umpire to settle disagreements over seniority rights, discipline, and other contractual standards that were not resolved through the first steps of the grievance procedure.[7]

Governmental pressures for industrial peace to promote war production during World War II further spread the use of grievance procedures and umpires/arbitrators rather than wildcat strikes to resolve grievances.[8] The contracts that followed the end of World War II, especially the UAW's agreement with General Motors (Chapter 3), established that unions would negotiate for higher wages, better benefits, and favorable seniority provisions and work rules, but would not be involved in business decisions. Section 301 of the Taft–Hartley amendments to the National Labor Relations Act (NLRA) in 1947 made these collective bargaining agreements enforceable in federal court.[9] Lastly, the Supreme Court confirmed that this enforceability applied to agreements to submit unresolved grievances to binding arbitration.[10] The postwar model of workplace self-government—complete with the law of the workplace (the contract and previous arbitration rulings), defense attorneys (union stewards), and court of appeals (the grievance procedure)—was thus cemented.[11] Note carefully that U.S. labor relations are therefore rooted in contract clauses and their administration through grievance procedures—an administration that is legalistic and orderly (not based on strike power) and private (relying on arbitrators, not court judges).

Today's union contracts, therefore, are legally enforceable documents that specify the laws of the workplace, often in great detail. UAW contracts with the major automakers are hundreds of pages long, contracts with the U.S. Postal Service exceed 300 pages, the collective bargaining agreement between the National Football League and the players' union is over 250 pages long, and the University of Minnesota clerical employees' contract approaches 150 pages. Many shorter contracts are between 25 and 50 pages long. Most contracts have a duration of three years.[12] Some include a reopener clause by which the parties can reopen the contract during its life to negotiate wage or benefit adjustments, but most are renegotiated upon expiration. The following five sections discuss the types of clauses that are frequently found in U.S. contracts—clauses that give rights to employees, jobs, unions, and managers and that govern the resolution of conflicts that arise (see Table 9.1).

EMPLOYEE RIGHTS AND OBLIGATIONS

Four types of employee rights are frequently granted in union contracts: just cause discipline and discharge, seniority rights, compensation, and grievance procedures. In return for these various rights, employees are obligated to follow the employer's work rules and supervisor's directions and to abide by the provisions of the contract (such as not striking over grievances). Over 90 percent of private sector union contracts specify that employees

TABLE 9.1 The Major Components of Traditional U.S. Union Contracts

Rights	Obligations
Employee Rights. . .	**. . . and Obligations**
• Just cause discipline and discharge. • Seniority rights in layoffs, promotions, etc. • Compensation (benefits, call-in pay, etc.). • Fair hearing through the grievance procedure.	• Obey work rules. • Follow supervisor's orders. • Abide by the contract. • Accept arbitrators' awards.
Job Rights . . .	**. . . and Obligations**
• Job holders entitled to a certain wage rate. • Specific tasks must be done within the bargaining unit and by certain jobs.	• Fulfill job standards.
Union Rights . . .	**. . . and Obligations**
• Exclusive bargaining agent. • Union leader access to the workplace. • Union bulletin board in the workplace. • Shop stewards. • Union security and dues checkoff clauses.	• Abide by the contract, including not striking over grievances. • Accept arbitrators' awards.
Management Rights . . .	**. . . and Obligations**
• Hire and fire (with just cause). • Determine job content and workforce size. • Establish production standards and rules of conduct. • Decide what to produce and how and where to make it.	• Abide by the contract, including not making unilateral changes. • Just cause discipline and discharge. • Safety standards. • Accept arbitrators' awards.
Grievance Procedure	
• Employees, the union, and management meet to resolve disputes over the application and enforcement of the contract. • Typically a multistep procedure in which unresolved grievances are appealed to higher levels in the organization. • In most contracts, the final step of the grievance procedure is arbitration.	
Other	
• Contracts are legally enforceable (in the United States). • Contracts are usually several years in duration.	

can be disciplined and discharged only for "cause" or "just cause." Public sector contracts frequently contain this same language. As such, employees have the right to insist that there be valid, job-related reasons for discipline or dismissal. This is of obvious importance for both employees and employers; it is also a significant departure from the employment-at-will doctrine and will therefore be discussed in more detail toward the end of this chapter.

A second category of employee rights pertains to **seniority.** A traditional union objective is to replace arbitrary or discriminatory treatment of workers with an objective standard to prevent favoritism, manipulation, and abuse. But how many truly objective standards exist in the employment relationship? Merit and ability, in particular, are often largely subjective. Seniority—length of employment with the employer—is objective (count the number of days since being hired) and also resonates with basic ideas of fairness.[13] Seniority is therefore widely used in union contracts as a criterion for allocating employment opportunities. Seniority is at least partly a factor (sometimes the only factor) in nearly 90 percent of private sector contracts and can also be found in a variety of public sector contracts. Layoffs are therefore frequently done by inverse seniority—workers with lower seniority are laid off before those with more ("last hired, first fired"). Bumping rights further grant more senior employees the right to bump less senior workers out of their positions during layoffs. Seniority is also a factor in promotions (two-thirds of private sector contracts) and transfers (more than half of private sector contracts) with more senior employees having priority (at least partial) over less senior ones. More senior employees usually receive more vacation days and in some cases get the first opportunities at overtime (though most contracts specify that overtime should be allocated equally).

In allocating employment opportunities, seniority is typically a sole, determining, or secondary factor (see Table 9.2). Consider the case of several workers who all ask to be promoted into a single job that opens up. When seniority is the sole factor, the worker with the longest length of service receives the promotion. If seniority is the determining factor, then among the workers who are minimally qualified for the job, the worker with greatest seniority receives the promotion. When seniority is a secondary factor, the worker with greatest seniority among those with relatively equal ability receives the promotion. Seniority is more likely to be the sole factor for layoffs than for promotions or transfers. As such, promotions and transfers are fertile areas for grievances: Individuals vying for promotions have differing perspectives on the ambiguous nature of "minimal qualifications" and "equal ability," and unions and employers have different views of the relative weight to be accorded to seniority and ability.[14]

A third category of employee rights frequently granted by union contracts is compensation. Unionized workers are significantly more likely than nonunion employees to receive

TABLE 9.2
Seniority Provisions Governing Layoffs

Seniority as the Sole Factor

"The Company will give forty-eight (48) hours notice of layoffs caused by reduction in production schedules. Probationary employees shall be laid off first. Should the reduction of force be such that the layoff of regular employees becomes necessary, the regular employees with the least seniority shall be laid off first." [From a contract at an auto parts company]

Seniority as the Determining Factor

"When it is necessary, because of a lack of work, to reduce the number of persons within a classification, the employees within that classification with the least amount of seniority shall be cut back, provided those employees remaining in that classification possess the skills required to do the work. Cutback employees shall exercise seniority held in another classification(s) than the one from which they are cut back, in the reverse order of their job ladder progression, provided they are able to perform the work without further training other than the normal 'break in' period. . . . Cutback employees who do not possess sufficient seniority to remain in the plant will be laid off." [From a contract at a chemical plant]

Seniority as a Secondary Factor

"When, in the judgment of Board of Education, decline in enrollment, reduction of program, or any other reason requires reduction in staff, the administration shall attempt to accomplish same by attrition. In the event necessary reduction in staff cannot be adequately accomplished by attrition, the administration shall base its decision as to resulting contract renewals on the relative skill, ability, competence, and qualifications of available staff to do the available work. If a choice must be made between two or more staff members of equal skill, ability, competence, and qualifications to do the available work, contract renewals will be given to the staff member with the greater full-time continuous length of service in the school district." [From a contract covering public school teachers] benefits such as health insurance, pensions, life insurance, and the like.[15] Numerous collective bargaining agreements contain provisions pertaining to overtime compensation, premium pay for weekends, rest periods, severance pay, supplemental unemployment benefits, and holidays. A majority of private sector contracts also give employees the right to reporting pay and call-in pay. Reporting pay guarantees that employees will be paid for a certain number of hours (typically four) if they report for work as scheduled but the employer doesn't have sufficient work. Call-in pay is similar but pertains to situations in which employees are called in to work by the employer.

Finally, nearly every U.S. union contract contains a grievance procedure in which employees are entitled to challenge managerial actions that they feel violate their rights under the contract. The final step of the grievance procedure is almost always binding arbitration. Although only a small fraction of grievances reach the final arbitration step, the possibility of arbitration by a third-party neutral can promote fair consideration of employee grievances at lower levels.[16] Through the grievance procedure, union contracts grant employees the right to a fair hearing when there is a workplace problem. In return, employees are obligated to seek orderly resolutions to their grievances through specified channels and not to use strikes or other economic weapons to pressure management for settlements. This bureaucratic approach to justice restricts grievances to specific contractual violations; this restriction, in turn, significantly limits worker influence over day-to-day work issues.[17] Because of the importance of the grievance procedure to workplace labor relations in the United States, we revisit this topic later in the chapter.

JOB RIGHTS AND OBLIGATIONS

Union contracts can also convey rights and obligations to jobs. Unions representing blue-collar workers frequently negotiate wage rates that are tied to specific jobs, not individuals.[18] In other words, holders of a specific job are entitled to a certain wage rate irrespective of their individual characteristics. A food processing plant might have a single pay rate for bulk unloaders, one for machine operators, another for janitors, and one for machine repairers; and you can read them all in the contract. This is not universally true—salaries for community college professors might be a function of each faculty member's educational credentials and years of teaching experience, whereas professional athletes typically negotiate their salaries individually within the parameters determined by a union contract. But tying wages to jobs rather than individuals is a significant component of the traditional U.S. union contract for blue-collar workers.

Another aspect of job rights pertains to work assignments: Certain jobs are entitled to perform certain tasks.[19] Unions seek such job rights because of a concern that the employer might whittle away the union-represented jobs by having supervisors expand their duties. Some contracts therefore explicitly prohibit supervisors from doing bargaining unit work (with some exceptions such as training new employees or emergencies). Subcontracting and outsourcing restrictions try to prevent the loss of union jobs by limiting the farming out of work to other employers. Another fear that underlies union pursuit of job rights is that management might try to replace higher-skilled jobs with lower-skilled, and therefore lower-paying, jobs. Some contracts therefore include general language requiring that a job's usual tasks be assigned to those jobs: "The Company agrees that, to the extent practicable, such work assignments will be made consistent with the principal job duties and skills of an employee's classification" (this example is from a chemical plant contract). This concern is particularly sharp among skilled workers because they face the greatest risk of having their jobs diluted and even deleted, so contractual language for job rights is frequently most explicit in guaranteeing certain tasks for skilled job classifications (see Table 9.3). In

TABLE 9.3
Contract Clauses That Protect the Job Rights of Skilled Positions

Auto Industry Examples

"Operators will remove their drill heads when there is a change in operation or going from one part to another as part of their normal setup. . . . The appropriate [skilled] Tradesman will be responsible for the removal of drill heads that are being removed for the sole purpose of being repaired. When repairs are completed, it will be the duties of the Tradesman to replace drill heads and make necessary alignment."

"When a Skilled Tradesman is assigned a job, he will be able to remove switches, guards, hydraulic lines, air lines, etc., in order to perform his work. He will not repair any portion of the job that is not in his classification. If any wires have to be disconnected, this will be done by electricians. In the event a piece of equipment is either dismantled for moving or a new machine is set up, the appropriate [skilled] Tradesman will be utilized."

Grocery Store Examples

"Meat helpers' work is limited to marking, weighing, labeling, wrapping, cleaning cases, stocking and displaying of smoked meats, stocking and displaying of luncheon meats, and cleaning any and all tools. Meat helpers may wait upon customers and use the knife or slicers when necessary to finish a product already supplied by the [skilled] meat cutters as in the sale to an individual customer. . . . There must be a minimum of one (1) journeyman meat cutter on duty any time a meat helper is on duty."

"Food Handler's work includes marking, stocking, displaying, and weighing of all preprocessed, fresh, frozen, and smoked meat, poultry, and fish, including receiving of meat products, fresh and frozen, the storage of all the above mentioned products, and the cleaning of cases. These employees shall not be allowed to work in the processing areas of the meat department including wrapping or service cases."

return for these various categories of job rights, the holders of these jobs must fulfill the performance standards for these jobs.

UNION RIGHTS AND OBLIGATIONS

A third category of clauses frequently found in collective bargaining agreements gives unions rights and obligations. It is probably universal for one of the first sections of the contract to include a recognition clause in which the employer recognizes the union as the exclusive bargaining agent for the bargaining unit and affirms the union's right to represent the employees. A broadly written recognition clause can help unions maintain their strength by including new occupations within the bargaining unit, such as when new positions are created when traditional media companies expand into online ventures.[20] Unions are also concerned with maintaining recognition rights if a business is sold or if a public sector operation is privatized. Under favorable conditions, various legal rulings indicate that a successor employer must recognize and bargain with the union; but to cement this continued recognition, some unions negotiate a successorship clause into their contracts.[21] Such a clause requires a successor employer to recognize and bargain with the existing union; a strong successorship clause further obligates the successor employer to abide by the union contract.

To facilitate communication between a union and the employees, unions traditionally negotiate rights for union leaders to use a bulletin board on company premises and to enter the workplace to meet with employees (without interfering with their work); unions are now trying to supplement this with rights to use company intranet and e-mail systems to communicate with employees. To help the union effectively represent the workers, unions also negotiate for workplace systems of shop stewards. Stewards are employees who are elected by the rank and file or appointed by the union leadership to be the first line of advocates for the workers in ensuring that the contract is not violated. For most workers, stewards are the personification of the union—when there is a problem, employees typically contact their steward.[22] Contracts frequently include clauses in which employers recognize the right of stewards to investigate grievances, and some contracts further specify the number of stewards, grant them special seniority rights ("superseniority"), and indicate that the company will pay the stewards for their time conducting legitimate union business.

Union Security Clauses

The most controversial clauses within the category of union rights pertain to issues of dues and mandatory membership. Recall from Chapter 4 that there are three types of **union security clauses:** (1) a closed shop, requiring the employer to hire only union members, (2) a union shop, requiring employees to become union members after hired in order to keep their jobs, and (3) an agency shop, requiring employees to pay union dues after hired in order to keep their jobs. The NLRA outlaws the closed shop; right-to-work laws outlaw union and agency shops. But in the 24 states that do not have right-to-work laws, unions are allowed to negotiate union or agency shop provisions into their contracts with employers. The controversial nature of union shop clauses is underscored by the fact that employees can petition the NLRB to hold a special deauthorization poll (not to be confused with a decertification election; see Chapter 6) in which the employees can vote to revoke a union shop clause. In 2015 there were 30 such polls.[23]

The Supreme Court has further determined that union shop clauses are enforceable only as agency shops—workers can be forced to pay dues but not to join the union.[24] In other words, when a union shop or agency shop clause is included in the collective bargaining agreement, a worker can be fired for failing to pay dues but not for refusing to join the union. Furthermore, workers need to pay only the amount of dues that goes toward collective bargaining and contract administration. This right to pay less than full union dues is called ***Beck* rights**—named after the 1988 Supreme Court case that established this right (see the accompanying "Ethics in Action" box).[25] In principle this sounds straightforward, but in practice it is complex. Some union expenses are clearly germane to bargaining and administering contracts—salaries for union staff who negotiate contracts or arbitrator fees, for example—and some are not—such as union publications, social activities, and political lobbying. But what about organizing new members? This does not directly support bargaining and contract administration for existing union members, but it supports these activities indirectly by increasing union power. Whether organizing expenses can be charged to employees who exercise their *Beck* rights has been intensely debated. The NLRB has ruled that organizing expenses for employees in the same competitive market are allowed, whereas the courts have not allowed general organizing expenses.[26] This also raises significant practical issues—especially whether calculating the amount of allowable expenses can be done at the national union level or must be done separately for each local.[27]

Union and agency shop clauses are frequently used in conjunction with a dues checkoff provision in which employees can agree to have their union dues automatically deducted from their paychecks and deposited directly with the union. This gives the union a predictable revenue stream and saves union leaders valuable dues-collecting time and energy—though this individual contact might develop stronger linkages between union leaders and rank-and-file workers and prevent the leadership from becoming detached from the membership.[28]

Unions typically try to negotiate union shop or agency shop clauses (in non–right-to-work states) to counter the free-rider problem of bargaining unit members benefiting from the union without paying for it. As we will discuss shortly, labor law requires that unions fulfill a duty of fair representation by representing *all* employees—members and nonmembers alike—so unions argue that it is unfair to allow free riders to benefit from

Ethics in Action Union Shops and *Beck* Rights

Except in right-to-work states, it is common for unions to negotiate union shop clauses into their collective bargaining agreements. However, the Supreme Court has interpreted the NLRA to require only the payment of dues: Union membership is "whittled down to its financial core" [*NLRB v. General Motors Corp.*, 373 U.S. 734, 742 (1963)]. Workers can thus satisfy a union shop requirement by paying dues; they do not need to formally join the union. This might seem like a distinction without a difference, but consider two points:

- Nonmembers cannot vote in union elections or to ratify contracts.
- Nonmembers do not have to pay full union dues.

With respect to this last point, the courts have determined that nonmembers need to pay only dues that go toward collective bargaining and contract administration (*Beck* rights). As such, nonmembers might only pay 75 percent of the amount of full union dues (the actual amount varies from union to union).

QUESTIONS

1. Union shop clauses are legal, but a court will enforce them only as equivalent to agency shop clauses. Is it ethical for a union steward to show the contract's union shop clause to new employees to get them to join the union? Before you jump to a quick answer, remember that contracts are ratified by majority votes.
2. Should a union steward have a legal obligation to inform employees of their *Beck* rights?
3. Should employers have a legal obligation to inform employees of their rights under the NLRA, such as being able to discuss wages and working conditions with their coworkers?

union representation without sharing the costs by paying dues. Majority rule is also a basic feature of democratic institutions, and any dues-paying requirements are subject to majority approval. On the other hand, right-to-work advocates label this "compulsory unionism" and argue that it violates individual freedoms by depriving workers of their "right to work"—that is, the right to freely choose whether to become union members and pay union dues. The public sector has more restrictions on union security clauses—in other words, there are more right-to-work laws for the public sector (including the federal sector) than the private sector.[29] However, a few states such as Minnesota and Hawaii mandate the agency shop. Agency shop payments in the public sector are frequently called fair share payments, and various states have legislated processes for determining their amount.[30]

In 2016, public sector unions were anticipating a Supreme Court ruling in *Friedrichs v. California Teachers Association* that would have prohibited agency fee arrangements and thus made the entire public sector a "right-to-work" sector; Justice Antonin Scalia's sudden death, however, left the Court split and the legality of public sector agency fees survived, at least for the time being.

Union Obligations

In return for the various rights that a union might be granted by contract clauses, it is obligated to live up to the terms of the complete contract. In particular, unions usually give up the right to strike over grievances and instead must pursue orderly resolution of disputes over the application of the contract through the grievance procedure. This includes respecting the terms of any arbitration awards. Unions can be sued for violating a collective bargaining agreement.

Another union obligation, and a central issue in contract administration for labor unions, is the **duty of fair representation.**[31] Recall from Chapter 4 that under the NLRA a union that wins an NLRB election becomes the *exclusive* bargaining agent for that bargaining unit. Similar principles apply under the Railway Labor Act and public sector bargaining laws. As early as 1944, the Supreme Court ruled that in return for this privilege of being the exclusive representative, unions have an obligation to fairly and without discrimination represent all bargaining unit employees.[32] This obligation applies to both contract negotiation and administration, though it is frequently discussed in terms of administration. In particular, a union "may not arbitrarily ignore a meritorious grievance or process it in a perfunctory fashion" in a discriminatory or bad faith manner.[33] As specific examples, unions cannot ignore the grievances of African American workers because of racial discrimination, advocate less strenuously for nonmembers because they haven't joined the union, or ignore the grievance of a member who is an outspoken political opponent of the union leadership. This does not mean unions have to pursue every grievance all the way to arbitration, but it does mean that unions must have valid reasons for not pursuing a grievance (in particular, that the grievance truly lacks merit). Because the duty of fair representation is rooted in Supreme Court applications of labor law, this obligation is universal and does not depend on the presence of specific clauses in a union contract.

MANAGEMENT RIGHTS AND OBLIGATIONS

Labor relations are frequently concerned with balancing competing interests of various stakeholders, so it should be unsurprising that union contracts also provide rights to management—especially through conveniently named **management rights clauses.** Management rights clauses embody management's longstanding insistence on maintaining sole authority over traditional management functions such as hiring, firing, assigning work, determining job content, and deciding what to produce and how and where to make it.[34] Such clauses are found in 80 percent of private sector contracts. In the public sector, management rights clauses are also frequently found in union contracts, and they are even specified by law in the federal sector by the Civil Service Reform Act and in the state and local sectors by some state bargaining laws.

Two examples are shown in Table 9.4; note the close similarities even though one covers unskilled workers in the private sector and the other covers skilled professional workers in the

TABLE 9.4
Examples of Management Rights Clauses

Private Sector Hotel Contract

"The Employer and the Union specifically agree that management shall have the right to direct the workforce and to determine the policies and methods of operating its Hotel, except as expressly limited by the specific provisions of this Agreement and longstanding custom and past practice. Such management rights and responsibilities shall include, but not be limited to, the following: the right to select the employees it will hire; the right to establish or revise work schedules; to determine the size and composition of its working force; to determine the number and type of equipment, material, products and supplies to be used or operated; to discipline or discharge employees for just cause; to maintain efficiency of employees; to determine assignments of work; to discontinue all or any part of its business operations; to expand, reduce, alter, combine or transfer, assign, or cease any job, department, or operation for business purposes; to introduce new, different, or improved methods and procedures in its operations; and to otherwise generally manage the Hotel, except as expressly restricted by the provisions of this Agreement."

Public Sector Community College Faculty Contract

"It is recognized that except as expressly stated herein the Employer shall retain whatever rights and authority are necessary for it to operate and direct the affairs of the colleges in all of their various aspects, including, but not limited to, the educational policies of the colleges; the right to select, direct, and assign faculty members; to schedule working hours; to determine whether goods or services should be made or purchased; and to make and enforce reasonable rules and regulations affecting terms and conditions of employment that are uniformly applied and enforced in accordance with the provisions of the rules or regulations. Any term or condition of employment not specifically established by this Contract shall remain solely within the discretion of the Employer to modify, establish, or eliminate."

public sector. It is common to trace management rights clauses all the way back to the UAW's strike against General Motors in 1945–1946. Even after 113 days of being struck, General Motors refused to relinquish its right to manage strategic decisions in the corporate boardroom and daily issues on the factory floor. This established the postwar pattern of union negotiations over wages, benefits, and work rules, but not managerial decisions. Management rights clauses are now deeply ingrained in U.S. labor relations.[35] In fact, management rights clauses are even found in collective bargaining agreements in which the employer is a union and the workers are regular employees of that union (in such situations the employees are represented by a different union, such as the Office and Professional Employees International Union).

Consider again the two management rights clauses in Table 9.4. In the hotel contract, "management shall have the right to direct the workforce and to determine the policies and methods of operating its Hotel, *except as expressly limited by the specific provisions of this Agreement*" (emphasis added). In the community college contract, "Any term or condition of employment *not specifically established by this Contract* shall remain solely within the discretion of the Employer to modify, establish, or eliminate" (emphasis added). These two provisions capture the **reserved rights doctrine** of management rights (also called the residual rights doctrine): All management rights not explicitly limited, restricted, or modified by the union contract are reserved by management. Many arbitrators uphold the reserved rights doctrine even if this specific language is not in the contract.[36] The detailed work rules often found in traditional union contracts are a natural reaction by organized labor to this doctrine. If management retains authority over all issues that are not limited, restricted, or modified, then of course unions will seek to explicitly limit, restrict, and modify managerial authority where it serves workers' interests.

These limitations, restrictions, and modifications largely represent management's obligations under union contracts. Many of these have already been mentioned in the previous sections: disciplining and discharging workers only for just cause, using seniority as a factor in layoffs and promotions, assigning work to specific job classes, providing call-in pay, allowing shop stewards to investigate grievances, and the like. Union contracts also frequently specify safety standards that management must fulfill. And as with employees and unions, employers are obligated to resolve grievances peacefully through the grievance procedure and to abide by the terms specified not only by the contract but also by arbitration awards.

There are thousands of union contracts in the U.S. private and public sectors, and many elements of these contracts are similar. This is true across all four categories of contract clauses discussed so far: employee rights and obligations, job rights and obligations, union rights and obligations, and management rights and obligations. But these contracts are not identical. Distinctive provisions are frequently specific to various bargaining units depending on industry, occupation, location, history, and the like. Several examples of unique contract clauses are shown in Table 9.5.

Online Exploration Exercise: Search for collective bargaining agreements online and find at least two from different industries or occupations. In each, find the prominent clauses discussed in this chapter. How similar are these clauses across the different contracts? Also, find some unique clauses and think about why they likely arose. Lastly, how do various clauses serve efficiency, equity, and/or voice?

GRIEVANCE PROCEDURES

The elements of union contracts discussed in the previous sections often contain ambiguities and are open to varying interpretations. Does maternity leave include adoption? Is swearing at a supervisor just cause for being fired? How is it determined whether two

TABLE 9.5
Unique Contract Clauses

1. "There will be no contact work (e.g., "live" blocking, tackling, pass rushing, bump-and-run) or use of pads (helmets permitted) at minicamps." [Professional football]
2. "The Local Safety and Health Committee shall promote the cause of safety and health by . . . 5. Reviewing local dog bite prevention efforts." [Post Office]
3. "In the exercise of academic freedom, the faculty member may, without limitation, discuss her/his own subject in the classroom, but s/he should not introduce into his/her teaching controversial matter which is not related to her/his subject. . . . There is an obligation to respect the dignity of others, to acknowledge their right to express differing opinions, and to foster and defend intellectual honesty, freedom of inquiry, and instruction. A faculty member must follow course outlines as developed by and with her/his colleagues in the department(s)." [Community college]
4. "The loss of any employee's property resulting from a hold-up, robbery, accident, violence, or riot, which occurs while the employee is on duty, shall be reimbursed by the Employer. Such reimbursement shall be paid upon submission of replacement receipt, or laundry or dry cleaning expense. Property shall mean: regulation watch (not to exceed $100 in value), prescription eyeglasses, regulation uniform at Employer cost; and any other equipment issued by the Employer in the performance of the employee's duties shall be replaced." [Bus company]
5. "Reporters may be assigned to use multi-media tools to collect video and audio content as part of their primary duty to report and write stories." [Newspaper]
6. "When a pilot is assigned by the Company to deadhead to a station for the purpose of being scheduled out of that station as a pilot, or from a station having flown into that station as a pilot, such deadhead time shall be credited for pay time and credit time purposes at the rate of full pay time and credit time for each hour of such deadhead time." [Commercial airline]
7. "Following a job-related exposure to blood or body fluids, the Hospital will provide, upon request of and without cost to the affected nurse, screening for AIDS. Such screening will be done by a reputable independent laboratory and confidential results will be provided to the nurse. Results shall not be a part of the nurse's personnel or employee health record." [Hospital]
8. "The Employer/Producer agrees to notify the Union if smoke, fog, and/or pyrotechnics are scheduled to be used.... If the Union requests a meeting, it will be scheduled within a reasonable time and shall include representative(s) of the Union and the Employer/Producer at which meeting the parties will discuss any planned special effects such as smoke/fog and/or pyrotechnics and/or any other health and safety problem that either party feels might arise in the production." [Theatrical production association]

individuals have equal ability for a promotion? Do management's traditional powers allow it to create new job categories, or does the inclusion of job classifications in the union contract make this an issue to be negotiated? Conflicts over the interpretation, application, and enforcement of contracts inevitably occur, and contract administration to settle these rights disputes ("grievances") is a key process in U.S. labor relations.

Rejecting Unilateral Grievance Resolution Methods

Consider possible methods for settling grievances. Perhaps one party might unilaterally control how grievances are resolved, whether it be an employer, a union, or a judge. Other options replace unilateral control with dispute resolution procedures that allow multiple parties to participate in grievance resolution. Rejection of the unilateral approach is nearly universal in contemporary U.S. labor relations. Management is unwilling to concede control to unions, and vice versa. In fact, unilateral management control undermines the whole point of collective bargaining: Without a balanced dispute resolution procedure for grievances, workers and workplace justice are at the mercy of employers and markets, which is exactly the situation that the NLRA and public sector bargaining laws seek to improve upon. And resorting to economic weapons to challenge unilateral decisions destroys the goal of industrial peace. In particular, the advantage to employers of signing union contracts is to achieve stability and predictability through employee and union adherence to negotiated rules. This advantage is lost if strikes frequently erupt over these rules. And relying on courts also has significant drawbacks—it is costly, slow, largely beyond the parties' control, and generally lacking in labor or business expertise.

As a result, the nearly universal method for resolving grievances over the interpretation, application, and enforcement of union contracts in U.S. labor relations is through a **grievance procedure** that is negotiated into a contract. Although grievance procedures could occasionally be found in the 1800s, the explosion of their adoption came during World War II when the U.S. government leaned heavily on labor and management to resolve disputes through grievance procedures, not strikes, so as not to interrupt vital war production.[37] Today nearly every union contract in the United States in both the private and public sectors contains a grievance procedure to resolve allegations by employees or the union that the employer has violated the contract.[38] Note that employees and unions react to managerial actions and raise complaints by filing grievances if they think contractual violations have occurred—in other words, "management acts and the union grieves."

The Typical Unionized Grievance Procedure

An example of a typical four-step grievance procedure is shown in Table 9.6. The first step involves discussions between the employee who has a grievance (the grievant) and his or her supervisor. The supervisor can either propose a solution that corrects the alleged contractual violation or reject the grievance. For example, if an employee believes she was entitled to call-in pay, the supervisor might realize that an error was made and agree to provide the call-in pay. Or the supervisor might continue to believe that no call-in pay was warranted and reject the grievance. In either case, if the employee accepts the supervisor's decision, the grievance is settled and the grievance procedure ends.

However, if the grievant is not satisfied with the outcome of step 1, the grievance can be appealed to step 2. During step 2, a union representative, typically a shop steward, and a management official, such as a human resources representative or a department manager, try to settle the dispute. The union representative is responsible for collecting evidence to show that the contract was violated by the managerial action in question, though management will typically also want to conduct its own investigation in order to better understand the issue. It is important to investigate the Five Ws (who, what, when, where, and why) as well as the broader ramifications of the issue.[39] After meeting with the grievant and the union representative, the management official will either reject the grievance or propose a solution. The employee can further appeal the results of the second step to step 3, which is like step 2 but involves higher-level union and management officials. Finally, the union can appeal the step 3 resolution to step 4 which is binding arbitration.

The numbers of steps vary across union contracts, but multistep procedures with between two and four steps are the norm. The example in Table 9.6 provides for a verbal grievance at first; other grievance procedures might require an initial written grievance. Most grievances are settled in the early steps.[40] Note that during the grievance process, unions have dual roles as both advocates and processors. As advocates, unions provide assistance and expertise to help grievants win their cases. As processors, unions determine how far to pursue grievances. In particular, unions (not grievants) decide whether to appeal grievances to arbitration, subject to their duty of fair representation. Every grievance must be filed or appealed to the next step within the time limits specified in the grievance procedure, or it is considered settled.

TABLE 9.6
A Police Contract's Grievance Procedure

Purpose
A grievance is a good faith complaint of one or a group of employees, or a dispute between the City and the Police Officers Association involving the interpretation, application, or enforcement of the express terms of this Agreement. The purposes of this procedure are (a) to resolve grievances informally at the lowest possible level and (b) to provide an orderly procedure for reviewing and resolving grievances promptly.

Step One
An employee who believes he/she has cause for grievance may contact his/her supervisor alone or with his/her union representative. If after discussions with the supervisor, the employee does not feel the grievance has been properly adjusted, the grievance shall be reduced to a written grievance statement that includes (a) the nature of the grievance, (b) the facts on which it is based, (c) the article(s) and section(s) of this Agreement allegedly violated, and (d) the remedy or correction requested of the City. The grieving employee's Deputy Chief shall assign the first-level review to the employee's supervisor and will give his/her answer to the grievance in writing within five (5) standard workdays from the time he/she receives the grievance in writing. Any grievance not appealed in writing to Step 2 within five (5) standard workdays shall be considered waived. No matter shall be considered as a grievance under this Article unless it is presented in writing within thirty (30) calendar days after occurrence of the events on which the grievance was based.

Step Two
An appeal to the second step shall be made within five (5) standard workdays. The hearing of the grievances will be held within five (5) standard workdays of the second-step appeal. The Association representative and designated Department representative will meet in an effort to settle the matter. The City's answer will be made five (5) standard workdays after the hearing is held. The employee has five (5) standard workdays to determine whether or not to appeal the grievance to the third step. Any grievance not appealed in writing to step 3 within five (5) standard workdays shall be considered waived.

Step Three
The Association's representative and the designated representative of the City will meet to hear grievances appealed to the third step. A grievance appealed to the third step of the grievance procedure shall be heard within ten (10) standard workdays after the appeal to the third step of the grievance procedure. A written answer will be made within ten (10) standard workdays after the hearing, stating the City's position.

Step Four: Arbitration

a. If the third-step answer is not satisfactory to the employee, the Association may appeal the grievance to arbitration. The request for arbitration must be given in writing to the designated City representative by the Association within ten (10) standard workdays from the date of the third step answer. Any grievance not appealed in writing to Step 4 within ten (10) standard workdays shall be considered waived.
b. An arbitrator may be selected by mutual agreement between the Association's representative and the City's representative. Should the representatives fail to mutually agree on an arbitrator, they shall make a joint request to the State Mediation and Conciliation Service or the American Arbitration Association for a list of five (5) qualified arbitrators. The parties shall each strike two (2) names from the list and the remaining person shall be accepted as the arbitrator. The first party to strike will be determined by the flip of a coin.
c. It is understood that the arbitrator will only interpret this Agreement and will in no instance add to, delete from, or amend any part thereof. The arbitrator's decision shall be final and binding on the City, the Association, and the employee.
d. All fees and expenses for the arbitrator will be borne equally by the Association and the City.

The Uses of the Grievance Procedure

The grievance procedure provides a fair, orderly, and generally efficient method for resolving rights disputes and enforcing union contracts and is therefore relatively unique in U.S. labor relations in that it receives broad approval from scholars, policymakers, and labor and management practitioners. Employers benefit from an institutionalized system of conflict resolution that avoids strikes and other disruptions. Both employers and unions benefit from continuity, consistency, and a prescribed channel of communication. And employees benefit from due process—the right to have a hearing, be assisted by an advocate if desired, and present evidence in their defense. In other words, the unionized grievance procedure incorporates accepted standards of justice into the workplace. Nonunion grievance procedures—such as open-door policies, peer review panels, or ombudspersons—typically lack due process protections.[41]

The average grievance filing rate in unionized workplaces is perhaps 10–15 grievances per 100 employees per year, but there are large variations in this rate across workplaces and industries—in other words, "formal grievance disputes may be inevitable in unionized workplaces, but the rate at which they emerge certainly is not."[42] Individual and organizational characteristics appear to partly determine whether grievances are initiated—for example, grievance filers are on average younger than employees who do not file grievances, and grievances are more likely to be filed when employees interact with aggressive supervisors and union stewards and when employees perceive that their power is higher.[43] Grievances are also more likely just before contract negotiations begin.[44] This last fact suggests that the grievance procedure not only provides employees with due process but also gives unions an avenue for pressuring management to further their bargaining goals. Lastly, the grievance procedure appears to contain an element of organizational discipline and punishment. On average, grievance filers and their supervisors experience lower performance ratings and fewer promotion opportunities as well as increased job turnover relative to nonfilers and their supervisors after their grievances are settled. Moreover, grievance activity can reflect management's monitoring of worker effort, and slight increases in grievance activity can be associated with increased productivity.[45]

GRIEVANCE ARBITRATION

The grievance procedure is intended to provide an orderly, fair dispute resolution method. But suppose management ignores a union's arguments and evidence at each step of the procedure. What can ensure that the process is fair and respects workers' rights? The answer is **rights arbitration**—also called grievance arbitration. Like interest arbitration, rights arbitration involves a hearing before a third-party neutral (the arbitrator), who issues a decision that is binding on the parties. Unlike interest arbitration, rights arbitration focuses on rights disputes—grievances. An interest arbitrator is a contract writer who establishes new terms and conditions of employment; a rights arbitrator is a contract reader who interprets the existing terms and conditions of employment.

Nearly all contracts in both the private and public sectors include binding rights arbitration as the last step of the grievance procedure, and a few states even require it for public sector contracts. In return for management's acceptance of binding arbitration, most unions waive the right to strike during the life of a contract by agreeing to a no strike clause. At each step of the grievance procedure, the threat of a binding decision by a neutral third party gives labor and management incentives to try to settle grievances fairly and to respect due process.

The Legal Support for Grievance Arbitration

Important Supreme Court rulings have cemented the importance of grievance arbitration in U.S. labor relations.[46] In 1957 the Court ruled that if a union contract contains binding arbitration as the final grievance procedure step, the employer is legally bound to adhere to this agreement and submit unresolved grievances to arbitration.[47] And in 1960 the Court issued three decisions on the same day all involving the United Steelworkers of America; these decisions are collectively referred to as the ***Steelworkers Trilogy.*** The first two cases dealt with employers who refused to submit unresolved grievances to binding arbitration—even though this was in their union contracts—by claiming either that the grievance had no merit or that the subject of the particular grievance was not covered by the arbitration provision. In the first case the Court ruled that in deciding whether a grievance is subject to arbitration, the courts should not look at the merits of the arbitration case—that is the role of the arbitrator.[48] In the second case the Court ruled that unless a subject is explicitly excluded from arbitration by a contract, it is subject to arbitration.[49] Both decisions support the importance of grievance arbitration by making it difficult for management to refuse to arbitrate a grievance when arbitration is specified in a union contract. The third case pertained to a different issue: Can an arbitrator's decision be reviewed and overturned by the courts? The Supreme Court ruled that it is not the role of the courts to second-guess arbitrators; specifically, a judge cannot override an arbitrator's ruling as long as it "draws its essence from the collective bargaining contract."[50]

Taken together, the three decisions of the *Steelworkers Trilogy* provide strong legal support for the grievance arbitration process and are frequently cited as being directly responsible for the centrality of grievance arbitration in U.S. labor relations.[51] The standards established by the *Trilogy* cases have also been adopted in a number of states for public sector labor relations.[52] Roughly 10,000 arbitration awards are now issued each year.[53] But the supremacy of grievance arbitration is clouded when the grievance overlaps with employment laws and public policies. For example, the scope for reviewing an arbitration award is significantly greater if the grievance alleges racial discrimination that violates not only a union contract but also the antidiscrimination provisions of the Civil Rights Act.[54] Somewhat in reverse, the use of arbitration is expanding into the nonunion sector, where it is being used instead of the courts to resolve employment law claims—though this trend is controversial because of potential imbalances between employers and individual nonunion employees.[55] Nonunion employment arbitration will be discussed later in this chapter.

The Quasijudicial Nature of Grievance Arbitration

In practical rather than legal terms, as grievance arbitration was developing in the 1950s, a major debate was whether arbitration should have a problem-solving or judicial character; this debate is often referred to as the Taylor–Braden debate after the leading proponents of each perspective.[56] If grievance arbitration is an exercise in problem solving, the arbitrator can be creative in methods (such as using mediation tactics) and solutions (such as adapting the union contract to fit current problems). If grievance arbitration is a judicial activity, the arbitrator's sole job is to interpret, not adapt or modify, the contract (just as a judge interprets the law). The latter concept won; today grievance arbitration is a formal, quasijudicial process. Note that the sample grievance procedure in Table 9.6 explicitly states, "It is understood that the arbitrator will only interpret this Agreement and will in no instance add to, delete from, or amend any part thereof." Such contract language is common in the private and public sectors, and in the public sector it is occasionally specified by law.

An arbitration hearing is therefore like a courtroom hearing, and extensive preparation by both labor and management advocates is important.[57] The union and the employer make opening statements; the moving party (typically the employer in discipline and discharge cases because it has the burden of proving just cause, and the union in other cases because it has the burden of proving the contract was violated) presents witnesses and evidence, and these witnesses are cross-examined; the other party presents witnesses and evidence, and these witnesses are cross-examined; and each side presents a closing statement. The traditional legal rules of evidence are not strictly applied—for example, circumstantial evidence might be allowed—but arbitrators nevertheless need to determine the credibility and persuasiveness of the evidence presented.[58] Two to three months after the hearing, the arbitrator issues a written decision upholding or denying the grievance in whole or in part. If the grievance is upheld, a remedy that partially or fully corrects the contractual violation is also awarded. For example, an unfairly discharged employee might be reinstated, an inappropriate suspension reduced, or a denied promotion granted. The arbitrator's decision is binding on all the parties.

Interpreting Ambiguous Contract Language

In making a decision, the arbitrator's task is to interpret the contract and apply it to the situation at hand. Disputes for which the contract is clear are likely to be settled early in the grievance procedure, so arbitrators frequently confront difficult and ambiguous matters of interpretation. Suppose a contract reads, "Employees who are unable to work because of being on jury duty will be reimbursed the difference between jury duty pay and their regular earnings."[59] An employee who works the day shift is obviously "unable to work because of being on jury duty"; but what about an employee who works a night shift? A night shift employee might claim that she or he is "unable to work" because of physical and mental exhaustion that would result from having eight hours of jury duty and then eight hours of work in the same day. The employer might argue that "unable to work" applies strictly to direct scheduling conflicts and therefore does not apply to night shift employees. The arbitrator's task is to interpret "unable to work" and apply it to this particular situation.

To interpret a contract, arbitrators use three elements: contractual language, intent, and past practices.[60] In looking at contractual language, arbitrators try to use ordinary and popular meanings of words and place more weight on specific clauses than on general ones. If this fails to resolve ambiguous language, arbitrators look to intent: What meaning did the parties intend when they negotiated a clause? For example, suppose the jury duty clause used to read "unable to report to work" but was changed in the last negotiation to read "unable to work." This might indicate an intent to broaden the jury duty clause and apply it to night shift employees. Sometimes notes from previous negotiating sessions might be used to determine intent. Lastly, past practice is important in determining how to interpret contract clauses. For the jury duty dispute, how have other night shift employees been treated? Have employees worked double shifts in the past (indicating that employees are able to work after eight hours of jury duty)? In sum, arbitrators' decisions are based on the **common law of the workplace**—the written rules and unwritten customs developed in each workplace by the union contract, intent of the negotiators, and past practices.[61]

Criticisms of Grievance Arbitration

Although grievance arbitration can incorporate accepted standards of justice into workplace dispute resolution, it has also been criticized along several dimensions. As noted in the introduction to this chapter, the bureaucratic nature of traditional grievance procedures and the importance of stewards, union officials, and attorneys rather than individual workers are attacked by labor activists for stifling rank-and-file involvement in unions.[62] Some unions are instead trying to create an organizing rather than servicing model of unionism by involving workers more in their own grievance resolution (see Chapter 13). A second criticism of grievance arbitration that comes from all parties is that it can be lengthy (perhaps a year from grievance filing to arbitrator decision) and costly.[63] The costs of an arbitrator are split equally between the union and the employer and might amount to $1,600

HR Strategy Grievance Handling and Preparing for Arbitration

Handling grievances and preparing for arbitration hearings involve largely the same tasks for both labor and management officials:

- Understanding the Five Ws of the initial incident: Who is involved (grievant(s), witnesses, managers). What happened? When? Where? Why did the incident occur and why is it a grievance?
- Gathering evidence: This might include interviewing potential witnesses, collecting information from personnel files, and reviewing past practices, previous grievances, other arbitration awards that might serve as precedents, the contract, and the bargaining history of any relevant clauses.
- Collecting facts: This includes evaluating the reliability, credibility, and consistency of the evidence to determine the facts that come from the evidence.
- Constructing arguments from the facts: Rarely do "the facts speak for themselves." Rather, they need to be carefully assembled and sequenced into a logical argument describing how the contract was violated or not.
- Preparing questions for witnesses: This includes determining the best way to present the case and also cross-examine the other side's witnesses.
- Anticipating evidentiary issues: Will the other side challenge the credibility or admissibility of the evidence? Is the other side's evidence credible and reliable? If not, how can this be demonstrated?

QUESTIONS

1. Which of these tasks apply to all grievances, and which are specific to arbitration hearings?
2. How can successful completion of these tasks help prevent grievances from getting to arbitration?
3. Are these tasks backward- or forward-looking? In other words, do they support the use of the grievance procedure and arbitration for problem solving or for litigating contractual disputes?

References: Charles S. Loughran, *How to Prepare and Present a Labor Arbitration Case: Strategy and Tactics for Advocates,* 2nd ed. (Washington, DC: Bureau of National Affairs, 2006); Mark I. Lurie, "The Eight Essential Steps in Grievance Processing," *Dispute Resolution Journal* 54 (November 1999), pp. 61–65.

each, assuming an average arbitrator rate of $800 per day for four days. Attorney's fees are frequently more than this, so a typical arbitration hearing might cost $10,000 or more. In response, some bargaining pairs have experimented with grievance mediation, typically as a step in the grievance procedure just before arbitration. This process appears successful, and it remains a puzzle why more parties do not adopt this method.[64]

Finally, grievance procedures in general, and arbitration in particular, are also criticized as excessively legal, formal, and reactive. (Reactive means the grievance procedure looks backward at what happened to determine whether the contract was violated.)[65] Grievance arbitration is a quasijudicial process focused on determining the "guilt" or "innocence" of managerial actions that have already occurred; the process is not a forward-looking, problem-solving venue. As such, traditional grievance procedures are potentially inconsistent with recent efforts to involve workers in workplace decision making through high-performance work practices such as teams or quality circles. Reactive grievance processing needs to be complemented with proactive problem solving.[66]

EMPLOYEE DISCIPLINE

One of the most important areas of contract administration is employee discipline and discharge. Employers particularly want to be able to discipline and terminate employees who are substandard performers, and employees do not want to lose their jobs, especially unfairly. In fact, more grievance arbitration hearings pertain to discipline and discharge than to any other topic by a wide margin in both the private and public sectors.[67] Recall that from Chapter 1, under the employment-at-will doctrine that governs the U.S. employment relationship in the absence of specific statutory restrictions (such as antidiscrimination statutes), employees can be discharged at any time for any reason: "for good cause, for no cause, or even for cause morally wrong."[68] In a sharp departure from the employment-at-will doctrine, however, over 90 percent of private sector union contracts, and many public sector ones as well, specify that employees can be disciplined and discharged only for "cause" or "just cause."

Just cause is therefore an important concept in labor relations. In short, the requirement that employees be disciplined or discharged only when there is just cause means that there must be valid, supportable reasons for being disciplined or fired. The quasijudicial nature of grievance arbitration means that there is now an extensive system of published arbitration awards that serve as precedents guiding labor and management thinking about just cause (and numerous other issues).[69] But what do arbitrators use to decide whether the standards of just cause have been fulfilled?

One common method is to apply the seven tests that Arbitrator Carroll Daugherty set forth in a frequently cited 1966 arbitration decision (see Table 9.7).[70] First, did the disciplined or discharged worker know the consequences of certain conduct? Some forms of conduct are so obvious and severe that it is assumed that workers will know the consequences—violence, theft, or vandalism, for example. But for many other actions, it does not seem fair to impose discipline for something the employee does not know is against company policy—leaving work during a break, leaving a workstation without a supervisor's permission, or using a company e-mail system to send a personal message, to name just a few. Second, was the workplace rule, management order, or performance standard that the employee violated reasonably related to (a) the orderly, efficient, and safe operation of the employer's business and (b) the performance that the employer should properly expect of the employee? In other words, just cause discipline requires legitimate and sensible reasons.

The next three of the seven tests pertain to the extent to which management's investigation surrounding the discipline or discharge of an employee provided due process. Was the alleged violation thoroughly investigated *before* the discipline was imposed? Was the investigation fair and objective? Did the investigation reveal convincing proof of guilt? Negative answers to any of these questions undermine due process and just cause. Investigating an employee after imposing discipline looks like an attempt to find evidence to support a predetermined desire to discipline the employee. Investigations that are not fair

TABLE 9.7
The Seven Tests of Just Cause

1. Was the worker given advance warning of the consequences of his or her conduct?
2. Was the rule, order, or standard reasonably related to the orderly, efficient, and safe operation of the employer's business?
3. Was the alleged violation thoroughly investigated before discipline?
4. Was the investigation fair and objective?
5. Did the investigation reveal convincing proof of guilt?
6. Was the employer's discipline nondiscriminatory?
7. Was the discipline reasonably related to the worker's record and the severity of the conduct?

Source: Arbitrator Carroll Daugherty, *Enterprise Wire Company*, 46 LA 359 (1966).

and that do not reveal proof of guilt also cannot be used to support just cause discipline and discharge. Rather, clear, convincing, objective, and credible evidence is needed.

The final two of the seven tests of just cause focus on whether the employer's disciplinary action was appropriate under the circumstances. Was the employer's discipline nondiscriminatory? Was the disciplinary action reasonably related to the worker's record, the severity of the conduct, and any mitigating or extenuating circumstances? The first of these two underscores the importance of past practice. If other employees have not been disciplined in the past for the same misconduct, how is it justified to discipline the current offender? Such discipline is discriminatory. The last test emphasizes the importance of progressive or corrective discipline. Arbitrators do not look favorably upon punitive penalties. Rather, progressive or corrective discipline provides the opportunity for employees to remedy their poor behavior by having penalties that increase as misconduct is repeated or gets more severe. As such, issues such as absenteeism might first be addressed with a warning. If the problem continues, a suspension should be given; and if it persists, discharge is appropriate. Severe issues like violence, theft, vandalism, and gross insubordination might warrant immediate discharge without the need for progressive or corrective discipline. When arbitrators decide discharge cases, three possible outcomes are typical: The discharge is upheld as being consistent with just cause; the employee is exonerated and reinstated with full back pay; or an intermediate option is awarded in which the employee is reinstated but without full back pay (in effect reducing the discharge to an unpaid suspension).

These seven tests provide an important framework for thinking about just cause, though the extent to which they are applied to specific cases varies from arbitrator to arbitrator.[71] In particular, not all arbitrators insist that strict due process be present in management's investigation (tests 3, 4, and 5); rather, some arbitrators see the arbitration hearing as the source of due process and are willing to find that just cause was present if some mistakes were made and the other tests (or something comparable) are fulfilled.[72] Due process should nevertheless be a concern among managers because prejudicial investigations are unlikely to be seen by arbitrators as fulfilling the just cause standard.[73] Regardless of the specific tests used to determine just cause, the major elements are a sensible reason, a fair investigation, reliable evidence, and appropriate discipline.

With the proliferation of unjust dismissal lawsuits in the nonunion sector, these are important issues for managers and employees in nonunion as well as unionized situations. In other words, nonunion managers would do well to use the seven tests of just cause as guidelines for how they handle cases of employee discipline even though they are not bound by a unionized grievance procedure. Additionally, along with the duty of fair representation, the seven tests can shed light on a popular criticism of unions—that they help undeserving workers keep their jobs. Because of the duty of fair representation, unions have an obligation to represent all workers fairly, and thus unions are sometimes put in the awkward role of advocating on behalf of a poorly performing worker—but this is their legal obligation. Moreover, based on the seven tests, if the union can help a poorly performing worker keep a job, management must not be fulfilling the standards of just cause—perhaps the performance has not been documented adequately, or the appropriate corrective steps have not been taken.

A final important issue for the topic of employee discipline is an employee's right to representation. The Supreme Court has interpreted the right of employees to engage in concerted activity for mutual protection (as provided by Section 7 of the NLRA) to mean that an employee who believes that discipline will result from a meeting with management can insist that a union representative be present.[74] This is called an employee's ***Weingarten* rights** after the name of the key 1975 Supreme Court decision.[75] The union representative is entitled to assist the employee but not to obstruct reasonable questioning by the employer. An ongoing controversy is whether nonunion employees have a similar right to have a coworker present when they expect discipline—after all, Section 7 does not pertain solely to unionized situations. During the administration of President Clinton, the NLRB extended *Weingarten* rights to nonunion workers,[76] but this extension was overturned by the more conservative Bush-era NLRB in 2004.[77] A future NLRB might restore the Clinton-era approach, but until that happens only union workers are entitled to *Weingarten* rights.

Online Exploration Exercise: Search for multiple examples of grievance filing forms. Do some of them make it easier to capture all of the relevant information? How important is this for the effective resolution of a grievance? If you were a manager or a shop steward, is there anything more you'd like to know beyond what's asked for on the forms? Why?

DO THESE CONTRACT CLAUSES MATTER?

An important question in labor relations that swirls around contract clauses and their administration is their effect on the employment relationship. As we discussed in Chapter 2, research on the effects of unions generally estimates that wages of union-represented workers are approximately 15 percent higher than those of similar nonunion workers; this is called the union wage premium.[78] Unions also frequently compress the wage structure within a workplace by narrowing the differentials between lower- and higher-paid workers.[79] Unionized workers are significantly more likely than comparable nonunion workers to receive health insurance, pensions, and other employee benefits.[80] Unions are also estimated to increase the likelihood of seniority rights and just cause discipline and discharge provisions.[81] These types of contractual provisions certainly matter, though whether these effects are interpreted as the unfortunate product of monopoly power or as the fairness-enhancing result of a more balanced employment relationship depends on the intellectual lens used to analyze the employment relationship (Chapter 2).

Unions also bring grievance procedures that end in binding arbitration to the employment relationship. The basic statistics of these grievance procedures show that they provide due process protections to employees: The grievance procedure is widely used for diverse issues, grievants are assisted by union officials, neutral arbitrators are used to resolve the most difficult conflicts, employees win a significant fraction of grievances, unfairly dismissed workers are reinstated, and all parties usually accept the results of the grievance procedure.[82] On the other hand, analyses of what happens to individual grievants and their supervisors are less favorable. After grievances are resolved, grievance filers and their supervisors receive lower performance ratings and are more likely to quit (grievants) or be fired (their supervisors).[83] Unfortunately we cannot know what would have happened to these individuals if their issues had occurred under an alternative system (such as no grievance procedure in a nonunion situation), so we do not know whether a grievance procedure makes the best of a bad situation or makes a bad situation worse.

In any case, a major consequence of union representation and the traditional contract provisions is reduced job turnover. This likely stems from the value that workers place on higher wages, better benefits, and objective seniority rights as well as the ability to address problems through grievance procedures. Nonunion workers who lack grievance procedures have more limited options for addressing problems—namely quitting.[84] In fact, unionized workers with stronger grievance procedures are less likely to quit than unionized workers with weaker grievance procedures.[85] Taking into account differences in working conditions and workplace climate between union and nonunion workplaces, there does not appear to be a significant union–nonunion difference in job satisfaction.[86]

Another important effect of unions and union contracts is organizational performance. Many aspects of union contracts are predicted to reduce productivity: Seniority rights can reduce an employer's ability to allocate jobs on the basis of merit, requirements that certain tasks be assigned to skilled workers and other restrictive work rules can reduce flexibility, time spent resolving grievances is time away from production, and the like.[87] In fact, the **control gap** (the difference between restricted managerial control in unionized workplaces and complete unilateral control in nonunion workplaces) might be more important than the wage gap (the difference between union and nonunion wages and benefits) in explaining employer opposition to unions.[88] On the other hand, grievance procedures, seniority provisions, just cause discipline requirements, and other provisions that promote fair treatment, increase morale, and reduce turnover can improve productivity. So what happens in practice? The evidence is mixed. Some studies find that unions increase productivity, and others find the opposite.[89] The effect of unionism on productivity appears to be determined by the specifics of each situation—including whether managers are accommodating or confrontational—rather than the nature of U.S. unionism and contract clauses in general.[90] But because many elements of union contracts increase labor costs—especially higher wages and more generous benefits—even when productivity increases, the increase is not sufficient to offset the increased labor costs; in other words, unions reduce profits.[91]

NONUNION WORKPLACE DISPUTE RESOLUTION

A critical difference between union and nonunion U.S. workplaces is the nature of dispute resolution. Unionized grievance procedures that embrace union representation and assistance for grievants as well as final hearings (if needed) before neutral arbitrators create systems of workplace justice that provide due process to individual employees. Such systems can also benefit employers by avoiding strikes and excessive employee turnover and by providing a channel of communication between employees and employers. But conflicts in *all* workplaces—union and nonunion—are inevitable: Employees might feel unfairly treated, harassed, cheated out of vacation days, overlooked for promotions, or deserving of a raise. Thus methods of conflict resolution are needed in both union and nonunion workplaces.

Nonunion workplaces have traditionally lacked formal dispute resolution systems, and therefore by default they have relied heavily on managerial control. Employees discuss their concerns and complaints with their managers. Employees who are dissatisfied by the managers' responses are free to quit. This type of dispute resolution system is often labeled an open-door policy because the manager's door is open for employees who want to discuss their concerns. But the other open door should not be overlooked: the exit door for those who are dissatisfied. Note that this open-door system is efficient because it is quick and avoids potentially cumbersome decision-making processes; but it lacks guarantees of equity (fairness) and voice (employee participation in resolving the dispute). So although many nonunion workplaces still rely on open-door policies to resolve workplace disputes, there has been significant growth in formal policies that trade off, to varying degrees, reduced efficiency for enhanced equity and voice.[92] By some estimates, perhaps as many as half of nonunion companies have a formal workplace dispute resolution procedure.[93]

The basic element of formal nonunion dispute resolution procedures is an open-door policy that is formalized by specifying a process for appealing the decision of the worker's immediate manager. This appeal process typically consists of appealing the grievance to higher levels of management with the final decision being issued by senior management, such as the vice president of human resources or an appeal board of managers. This type of grievance procedure lacks many elements of due process.[94] In particular, employees generally lack representation or assistance in presenting their grievances, and the decision makers are all members of management. Other elements are sometimes added to this basic nonunion grievance procedure: ombudspersons, peer review panels, and arbitration.

An ombudsperson is a neutral facilitator between employees and managers who helps them resolve workplace disputes. An ombudsperson might investigate disputes, but almost always informally and with the goal of helping employees resolve their complaints. In other words, the ombudsperson is much more of a mediator than arbitrator or fact finder.[95] Note, however, that the ombudsperson is an employee of the company, and therefore this type of nonunion dispute resolution runs the risk of favoring the company's interests over neutrality, confidentiality, and due process. Ombudspersons might also help grievants prepare their cases, but because they are paid by the company, this advocacy role is limited. So while there is somewhat greater neutrality than in standalone open-door policies, employee representation in processing grievances is limited in ombudsperson systems.[96]

Some nonunion procedures add a peer review panel to the appeal process. In this system grievances can be appealed to a review panel in which employees (not managers) comprise the majority of the panel members—hence the name *peer* review panel. Peer review panels are established to counter perceptions that dispute resolution systems in which managers make the final decisions are unfair.[97] In fact, nonunion systems that include a nonmanagerial decision maker have higher grievance filing rates than nonunion systems in which decisions are made by managers, which suggests that employees are more accepting of nonunion grievance procedures in which managers do not make the final decisions.[98] In some instances arbitration is the final step of a nonunion workplace dispute resolution system, but this is the exception, not the norm.[99] Moreover, nonunion arbitration of grievances might still provide less due process to employees than unionized grievance arbitration if there are limitations on discovery (how much information the grievant can collect from the company), if the use of outside advocates such as attorneys is restricted, if employees cannot afford several thousand dollars of arbitration expenses, and if arbitrators favor management to increase their chances of getting selected for future cases (because individual employees are less likely than companies to know an arbitrator's reputation).[100]

Another use of nonunion arbitration is increasing and is also controversial: The use of mandatory arbitration instead of the courts to resolve employment law claims (see the accompanying box). A significant problem is that there is great variation in how companies structure their mandatory arbitration policies and procedures.[101] Quality standards for nonunion employment arbitration have therefore been proposed that include making arbitration agreements voluntary once a claim arises (rather than mandatory in advance of any disputes), ensuring employee access to relevant information, sharing expenses in a fair and affordable way, preserving a full range of remedies such as punitive damage awards, and allowing judicial review of arbitrators' decisions.[102]

There are three possible explanations for the increased adoption of nonunion workplace dispute resolution systems in recent years.[103] First, formal dispute resolution procedures can be part of a human resource management strategy to increase organizational commitment and performance by treating employees fairly and identifying problem areas. Second, these procedures might be implemented to try to avoid costly lawsuits. Third, because grievance procedures are a major feature of unionized workplaces, implementation of a grievance procedure in a nonunion workplace might be part of a union substitution strategy to prevent unionization (Chapter 5). Research supports all three explanations, with peer

Nonunion Application Nonunion Arbitration of Employment Law Claims

No company wants to be sued for discrimination, harassment, or other violations of employment law. Legal fees, negative publicity, and the potential for huge monetary damages awarded by unpredictable juries can all harm a company's reputation and economic performance. An employee who seeks redress in the court system faces lengthy delays and significant lawyer's fees. In an attempt to reduce these delays and expenses in all kinds of court cases (not just employment law), since the 1970s the legal system has been promoting ADR—alternative dispute resolution. ADR includes mediation, arbitration, and other methods of avoiding court trials. As part of this movement, Congress amended the Civil Rights Act in 1991 to encourage the use of arbitration to resolve discrimination lawsuits (though not necessarily through compulsory arbitration).

Some employers have reacted to these developments by requiring their employees to sign agreements to arbitrate rather than litigate (that is, not sue in court) any alleged violations of employment law. Such agreements have generally been enforced by the courts, including by the Supreme Court in *Gilmer v. Interstate/Johnson Lane Corp.* (1991) and *Circuit City Stores, Inc. v. Adams* (2001). Note that these are compulsory agreements to arbitrate future disputes—these are not situations in which an employer and employee who have an existing dispute voluntarily agree that they would both prefer to use arbitration rather than a lengthy, costly jury trial. As such, compulsory arbitration agreements are the subject of intense debate.

Because these compulsory arbitration agreements are required as a condition of employment, some fear that employers can abuse their power to force unfair arbitration procedures on employees. There are examples of one-sided arbitration agreements in which employees are required to waive their rights to discovery (which is essential to gather evidence) and to some remedies (such as reinstatement). Other one-sided examples include agreements in which employers unilaterally select arbitrators and impose significant expenses (such as arbitration fees) on low-paid workers. The courts have refused to enforce some of the most blatantly unfair arbitration procedures; but if the courts need to review significant numbers of cases, then the goal of resolving disputes out of court will be undone.

Arbitrating rather than litigating employment law disputes can be beneficial in terms of speed, cost, and specialized expertise, but a balance must be found between these benefits and the potential destruction of employees' rights if the compulsory arbitration process unfairly favors employers.

Reference: Alexander J.S. Colvin, "Mandatory Arbitration and Inequality of Justice in Employment," *Berkeley Journal of Employment and Labor Law* 35 (2014), pp. 71–90; Richard A. Bales, *Compulsory Arbitration: The Grand Experiment in Employment* (Ithaca, NY: ILR Press, 1997).

review systems being linked with human resources and union substitution strategies, and with employment arbitration being linked with a desire to avoid costly lawsuits. As such, formal dispute resolution systems in nonunion workplaces are not always implemented to enhance employee due process: "The impetus for the adoption of these procedures is the protection of the firm against institutional pressures from outside the organization. Like walls around a citadel, these procedures help prevent intrusion by outside actors—notably, in this case, unions and the courts."[104]

A DIFFERENT APPROACH TO CONTRACT ADMINISTRATION

This chapter has described the major elements of traditional union contracts in U.S. labor relations, including the grievance procedure that is used to administer contracts by enforcing and resolving disputes over clauses in the rest of the contract. By increasing compensation and benefits, using seniority as at least one factor in many personnel decisions, limiting employee discipline and discharge to situations of just cause, placing restrictions on work assignments, and providing for orderly and fair resolution of disputes, union contracts clearly affect employees, organizational performance, and the employment relationship. Whether one evaluates these effects positively or negatively depends to a large degree on the intellectual framework used to analyze the employment relationship—mainstream economics, human resource management, pluralist industrial relations, or critical industrial relations (Chapter 2).

Moreover, the traditional emphasis of U.S. labor relations on detailed, legally enforceable contracts is criticized by both business advocates (for preventing organizational flexibility) and worker advocates (for lacking worker involvement). Therefore, even though union grievance procedures promote workplace justice through due process protections, new forms of contract administration might be necessary if the nature of union contracts changes. More flexible contracts will likely require more flexible methods of administration. To stimulate thinking in this direction, this chapter closes with an alternative example that involves a different type of union contract and contract administration process.

Rather than using traditional job classifications and a strict supervisory hierarchy, this chemical plant is operated by six self-directed work teams that are empowered to make the necessary daily operating decisions, including work assignment. Instead of a single traditional union contract, three agreements are negotiated between the company and union: a philosophy statement, a collective bargaining agreement, and a "good works practices handbook."[105] The philosophy statement defines the basic principles of the plant, such as extensive communication, commitment, employee discretion, and collaborative problem solving. The collective bargaining agreement, which is less than 20 pages long, outlines the basic issues such as shift premiums and the number of vacation days. Administration of these items, however, is not pursued through the contract as is typical with traditional union contracts. Rather, a separate good works practices handbook is used to administer the contract and provides general guidelines for the teams to follow when implementing the contractual provisions.

Note the distinction between the contract and the good works practices handbook. The contract specifies the fundamental rights of each party, which are often stable and involve conflicts of interest (distributive conflicts)—such as the number of vacation days. Implementation of these rights is typically a more flexible process and involves potential for mutual gain (integrative conflicts)—such as scheduling vacation. As such, separating the contract and the handbook can facilitate joint problem solving during administration without the necessity of interpreting the contract in a quasijudicial, formal fashion. In fact, the handbook is continually modified to suit the needs of labor and management; this is possible only by separating administration of rights from the collective bargaining agreement. This continuous updating does not threaten the union's gains in compensation, benefits, and fundamental rights because the contract is a separate document.

In sum, a traditional union contract is the typical outcome of the New Deal industrial relations system. The major processes of this system, which are the focus of Part Two of this book—organizing, bargaining, and contract administration—all lead to the implementation of such contracts and, in this way, strive to balance efficiency, equity, and voice. But as discussed next in Part Three, this system and these processes are under severe pressures in the global economic environment of the 21st century. These pressures for flexible and empowered workplaces, however, do not alter the fundamental objective of the labor relations system: striking a balance. Understanding the existing labor relations processes and traditional union contracts is important not only for knowing how the current system works but also for providing a foundation for thinking about how to strike a new balance in the global economic environment of the 21st century.

Key Terms

contract administration, *310*
rights disputes, *310*
seniority, *312*
union security clauses, *316*
Beck rights, *316*
duty of fair representation, *317*
management rights clause, *318*
reserved rights doctrine, *319*
grievance procedure, *321*
rights arbitration, *323*
Steelworkers Trilogy, *324*
common law of the workplace, *325*
just cause, *327*
Weingarten rights, *328*
control gap, *330*

Reflection Questions

1. Seniority is central in many private and public sector union contracts in the United States. What are the advantages to both employers and employees of using seniority to allocate employment opportunities? What are the disadvantages? How can a balance be struck between the interests of employers and employees?
2. What are the advantages and disadvantages of having the workplace governed by a legally enforceable contract supported by rights arbitration? Is this a good model for the workplace of the 21st century?
3. *Nonunion Application:* Assume you are a manager in a nonunion workplace. Develop a set of guidelines for how you should handle employee discipline and discharge. Do you use all of the seven tests? Why or why not?
4. There is significantly more research on grievance initiation (e.g., trying to identify the circumstances under which grievances are filed) than on the effectiveness of unionized grievance procedures. What are some different ways of defining the effectiveness of a grievance procedure? How would you research these issues? Is grievance procedure effectiveness an issue for policymakers, or is it strictly a private affair between employees, their unions, and their employers?
5. For each of the grievance discussion cases that follow, develop supporting arguments for the grievant and the employer. As an arbitrator, how would you rule? Why?

Grievance Discussion Case 1: Is an Adoptive Mother Entitled to Maternity Leave?

BACKGROUND

Carol Fern has been employed by Bainbridge Borough for 18 years as a tax clerk. The tax clerk position in Bainbridge Borough is part of the bargaining unit represented by Local 10 of the American Federation of State, County, and Municipal Employees (AFSCME).

When Carol Fern and her husband found out that she was unable to conceive, they decided to adopt a child. The Ferns were notified on April 22 that a three-month-old baby girl was available and they could adopt her in three days. However, Carol Fern told the adoption agency that she thought it was unfair to leave Bainbridge Borough on such short notice because April was a busy tax month. Adoption was therefore delayed until May 2.

On April 27 Fern requested two weeks of paid vacation for May 2 to May 17. This request was granted. The day before she was to return from her paid vacation, Fern asked for six months of unpaid maternity leave. This request had to be approved by the Bainbridge Borough Council, which rejected the request by a 4–3 vote. However, the council did offer Fern two successive 90-day reasonable purpose leaves (amounting to six months of leave). On June 1 the following grievance was filed:

> According to Article X, Section 4.A—Unpaid Leaves 5. Maternity on page 13 of the final agreement between Bainbridge Borough and Local Union 10—Maternity leaves not to exceed six months shall be granted at the request of an employee. Maternity leaves shall, upon the request of the employee, be extended or renewed for a period not to exceed six months. Relief or remedy sought: Granting of the just and deserved leave requested.

POTENTIALLY RELEVANT CONTRACT PROVISIONS

ARTICLE X. LEAVES OF ABSENCE

Section 4.A: Unpaid Leaves

1. *Reasonable Purpose*
    a. Leaves of absence for a limited period without pay—not to exceed ninety days—shall be granted for any reasonable purpose. Extension to be granted with approval of Borough Council.
    b. Reasonable purpose in each case shall be agreed upon by the union and the borough.

. . .

5. *Maternity*
    a. Maternity leaves—not to exceed six months—shall be granted at the request of the employee. Maternity leaves shall, upon the request of the employee, be extended or renewed for a period not to exceed six months.

QUESTIONS

1. As an attorney for Bainbridge Borough, develop a case to support the council's rejection of Carol Fern's unpaid maternity leave request.
2. As an attorney for AFSCME Local 10, develop an argument to support your client's contention that the council's rejection of Carol Fern's unpaid maternity leave request violated the collective bargaining agreement.
3. As an arbitrator, how would you rule? Why?

Grievance Discussion Case 2: Full Consideration of Seniority and Ability

BACKGROUND

The Picasso Company's paint gun factory includes three shifts of machinists who are represented by Lodge 821 of the International Association of Machinists and Aerospace Workers (IAM). Historically, the day shift did not have a leader position, unlike the second and third shifts. However, a group of first shift (day) employees presented management with a petition calling for a first shift leader. The employees also developed a list of qualifications for the job. After some investigation, the factory manager, Sharon Murphy, decided that this was a good idea and began the process of selecting an employee for first shift leader.

Murphy first developed her own list of qualifications for the position, which turned out to be quite similar to the employees' list. In particular, it was felt that the position required "a knowledgeable employee to whom others could turn for help and who would troubleshoot and offer suggestions, or do whatever else was necessary to make the operation run more smoothly and efficiently." Moreover, Murphy thought the position needed "a self-starter who did not need to be told what to do."

When the position was posted, there were two applicants: Machinist First Class Robert Elder (seniority date March 10, 1987) and Machinist Second Class Mary Younger (seniority date July 6, 1991). Younger was rated as qualified for machinist first class but had not received a promotion because of a lack of vacancies. Elder was a second and third shift leader for five years until he voluntarily resigned as leader to bump into a day shift position so that he could spend more time with his family. There was a $0.93 per hour pay differential between machinist first class and second class. Leaders received $0.43 per hour above the machinist first class rate. In the past, the second and third shift leader positions were awarded to the senior applicant the majority of the time. No grievances were ever filed when the less senior person was selected. There was no record of a second class machinist ever being promoted to leader.

Murphy interviewed both individuals and also discussed the candidates with a supervisor, Rick Hatch. In the interviews Murphy asked questions regarding initiative, communication skills, decision-making abilities, and scheduling flexibility. Supervisor Hatch evaluated Younger higher than Elder: He felt Younger had better interpersonal skills and greater initiative (Younger would take it upon herself to act whereas Elder would wait to be asked).

Hatch also indicated some flexibility and communication concerns stemming from when Elder had been third shift leader. In particular, Hatch wanted Elder to arrive early enough to discuss instructions and problems with the second shift leader, but Elder rarely was able to because he was in a carpool. Elder never arrived late. In fact, Elder had never been disciplined and had achieved nearly perfect attendance. Hatch also communicated to Murphy that he encouraged Elder to operate a machine with a longer cycle time (in fact the same machine Younger used) when he was third shift leader so he could spend more time with other employees. Elder, however, felt it would be unfair to the other employees if he didn't rotate machines like everyone else. As the third shift leader, Elder was in possession of the building keys and alarm codes after the supervisor clocked out each night.

After her interviews with Elder and Younger and her conversations with Hatch, Murphy selected Younger for the first shift leader position. Her decision was based on "her assessment of Younger as having the edge in interpersonal skills, communication skills, initiative, and attitude in that Younger seemed to enjoy doing the kinds of things that would be required of a leader." She also felt "employees would be more comfortable going to Younger with their questions" and stated that "she considered seniority in making the decision."

Subsequently, Elder filed a grievance claiming the company violated the collective bargaining agreement by failing to give full consideration to Elder's seniority and qualifications and by promoting the more junior employee.

POTENTIALLY RELEVANT CONTRACT PROVISIONS

Section 20.1. Awarding a Job Bid. When job openings occur or there are vacancies in classifications covered by this agreement, excluding leader classifications, the corporation shall post on its bulletin boards a notice of such opening or vacancy, indicating the rate of pay for a period of three (3) days, in order to afford employees an opportunity to qualify for such opening or vacancy on the basis of seniority and ability to perform the available work. The corporation shall not be required to consider the bid of a probationary employee. At the end of the third (3rd) day, the job opening or vacancy shall be filled by the employee who qualifies as soon as possible, but not to exceed ten (10) working days.

. . .

Section 20.4. The provisions of this section, however, shall not be construed to prevent the corporation from immediately filling vacancies in order to maintain scheduled production requirements, subject to the posting

Continued

Continued

provisions of this section. In filling vacancies in leader positions covered by this agreement, the corporation agrees to give full consideration to seniority and the qualifications of employees in filling such vacancies.

QUESTIONS

1. As the president of IAM Lodge 821, how would you try to convince an arbitrator that the selection of Mary Younger violated the collective bargaining agreement?
2. As the human resources manager, develop a case for your contention that the selection of Mary Younger did not violate the contract.
3. As an arbitrator, how would you rule? Why?

Grievance Discussion Case 3: Safety Gloves Discharge, with Just Cause?

BARRERA RECYCLING COMPANY
LOS ANGELES RECLAMATION

REGLAS DE SEGURIDAD

11. Zapatos de seguridad y lentes deben ser usados todo el tiempo. Otras de seguridad deben ser usadas si lo indica el supervisor.

BACKGROUND

This notice was posted on the lunch room bulletin board of the Los Angeles Reclamation facility of the Barrera Recycling Company. Rafael Gomez was the general manager of this facility, and Erin McNamara was an employee with approximately 20 years of seniority and was represented by Local 37 of the United Paperworkers International Union.

McNamara's usual task was handling bundles of newsprint that were bound with plastic straps. McNamara cut the plastic straps and placed the newsprint into a baling machine. The plastic straps were tight, so it was difficult to slide a hand under the strap to lift the bundle and cut the strap. Consequently, McNamara and other employees would not wear the company's bulky safety gloves when lifting the bundles and cutting the straps. Occasionally, and not on a fixed schedule, McNamara would be required to sort loose paper, tin cans, and bottles which arrived in 30-gallon plastic bags. Many of the bottles arrived broken, and the tin cans contained sharp edges, so it was important to wear safety gloves. McNamara ate her lunch in her pickup truck and had never been to the lunch room. She did not speak or read Spanish.

McNamara was transferred to this facility from a Long Beach facility in January and in October was given a disciplinary three-day suspension by Gomez. Prior to this suspension, Gomez had six or seven conversations, which he considered verbal reprimands, with McNamara over work performance and safety issues. One (according to McNamara) or two (according to Gomez) of these conversations dealt with McNamara sleeping through safety meetings. Two others pertained to McNamara's failure to wear safety gloves, another the failure to wear a hard hat (McNamara had accidentally left it in her truck), and still another the failure to wear appropriate safety glasses. McNamara had been issued safety glasses without side panels at the Long Beach facility, but Gomez insisted on glasses with side panels. The company, however, paid for

Continued

Continued

one set of eyeglasses per year, and upon being informed of this benefit, McNamara obtained the appropriate eyewear. The seventh and final conversation before the suspension occurred on October 26 when Gomez noticed McNamara reading *Sports Illustrated* during working hours. On October 28 McNamara was suspended for three days, and her disciplinary notice contained the following warning:

> Should you violate any Barrera rules or regulations during the next 12 months, you will be immediately discharged from Barrera employment.

No grievance was filed protesting this suspension.

December 9 began like nearly every day for McNamara: lifting the bundles of newsprint, cutting the plastic straps, and putting the paper into the baler—not wearing safety gloves because it was more efficient. However, a little while later an unexpected delivery of 30-gallon plastic bags arrived, and McNamara and several other employees had to sort the paper, tin cans, and bottles. The other employees donned their safety gloves for this task, but McNamara had left hers in her pickup truck because the delivery was not expected. Thirty minutes later Gomez wandered by and observed McNamara sorting the materials without safety gloves. After explaining that they were in her pickup truck, she was ordered to go get them. Three minutes later she returned with the gloves and continued sorting—this time with the safety gloves.

Gomez, however, felt that discipline was appropriate and fired her. Consequently, Local 37 filed a grievance protesting the discharge on the grounds that the company did not have just cause.

POTENTIALLY RELEVANT CONTRACT PROVISIONS

Article I—General Purpose of Agreement

The general purpose of this agreement is, in the mutual interest of the plants and the employees, to provide for the operation of the plants hereinafter mentioned under methods which shall further to the fullest extent possible, the safety of the employees, economy of operations, cleanliness of plants, and protection of property. It is recognized by this agreement to be the duty of the plants and the employees to cooperate fully, individually, and collectively for the advancement of said conditions.

Article XIX—Nondiscrimination

Neither the company nor the union shall discriminate against any employee because of race, color, religion, sex, age, handicap, or national origin. The parties further agree that they shall not discriminate against qualified handicapped individuals, qualified disabled veterans, or qualified veterans of the Vietnam Era.

Article XX—Causes for Immediate Discharge

Section 1. Causes for immediate discharge are as follows:

1. Bringing intoxicants into or consuming intoxicants in the plants or on plant premises.
2. Reporting for duty under the influence of liquor.
3. Disobedience.
4. Smoking in prohibited areas.
5. Deliberate destruction or removal of plant or another person's property.
6. Neglect of duty.
7. Refusal to comply with plant rules, provided that such rules shall be posted in each department where they may be read by all employees and further, that no changes in present rules or no additional rules shall be made that are inconsistent with this agreement, and further provided that any existing or new rules or changes in rules may be the subject of discussion between the standing committee and the local plant manager and in case of disagreement, the procedure for other grievances shall apply.
8. Disorderly conduct.
9. Dishonesty.
10. Sleeping on duty.
11. Giving or taking a bribe of any nature as an inducement to obtaining work or retaining a position.
12. Reading books, magazines, or newspapers while on duty, except where required in line of duty.
13. Failure to report for duty without bona fide reasons.
14. Reporting to work under the influence of any drug, marijuana, alcoholic beverage, or any other mind-altering substances; or the possession or use, thereof during work, on work premises or in plant-owned/leased vehicles.

Section 2. Discharge or suspension of an employee (not including a temporary layoff) shall be based on just and sufficient cause with a full explanation given to the employee.

Article XXI—Adjustment of Complaints

Section 5.

a. It is recognized and understood that management's right to discipline shall include the right to reprimand or warn an employee. The receipt of a written reprimand or warning shall be subject to the grievance procedure as set forth herein.

b. Provided further, all written reprimands of which a record is kept will be stricken from the plant's files and the employee's work record after a period of one (1) year in which the employee received no reprimands.

Continued

QUESTIONS

1. As the person responsible for labor relations at Barrera Recycling Company, articulate a case to support your contention that there was just cause for the discharge of Erin McNamara.
2. As the chief steward for Local 37, how would you substantiate your allegation that the dismissal violated the collective bargaining agreement?
3. As an arbitrator, how would you rule? Why?

Grievance Discussion Case 4: Concealment of Education on a Job Application

BACKGROUND

Jim Norbuck was born in rural central Pennsylvania and graduated from high school in the same town. He subsequently attended Bucknell University for two years and then transferred to the University of Illinois. He graduated from Illinois with a B.A. degree with an English major and a philosophy minor. Norbuck then attended the University of Wisconsin, where he received a master of arts degree. Norbuck started working on a Ph.D. but decided that he was tired of school and wanted to work. Consequently, he moved back to Pennsylvania, where he was a substitute high school teacher and taught as an instructor at a local college. Much to his dismay, the pay was quite poor and he needed a higher-paying job.

On August 7, Norbuck applied for a job at the nearby Leech Industries plant. From some friends Norbuck had learned that Leech Industries' policy was not to hire people with a college education for blue-collar jobs (because management believed that college-educated individuals became bored faster in blue-collar jobs, which increased the cost of production). As part of the job application process Norbuck filled out a written job application. In the education section Norbuck circled the number 12 next to the heading "Highest Grade Completed" and left the block pertaining to college blank. In the experience section of the application, Norbuck did not mention his prior teaching experience. The company did not verify any of his answers. On October 22, Norbuck was hired by Leech Industries and commenced work as a utility person in the tube plating department working the third shift from 11:00 P.M. to 7:00 A.M. After 30 days his wage was increased because he had successfully completed the probationary period for new employees.

The steel industry experienced a business slowdown, however, and Norbuck was laid off in December. On January 3, he was recalled to work as a labor pool person in the foundry department. On January 9, he was recalled to his original position as a third shift utility person in the plating department. All these positions were part of a bargaining unit represented by the United Steelworkers.

Meanwhile, the collective bargaining agreement between the United Steelworkers of America Local 55 and Leech Industries expired on January 18. The negotiators were unable to reach an agreement, and the union went out on strike. During the strike Norbuck was actively involved in supporting the union and wrote several pamphlets. These pamphlets, distributed to striking workers, urged them to maintain solidarity so that the union would be successful in winning new contract gains for the bargaining unit.

Susan Napoli, assistant director of human resources at the plant, noticed these pamphlets and heard rumors that Norbuck was college-educated. Thus, Napoli initiated an investigation into Norbuck's background—both his previous employment and his education. Norbuck was the only employee for whom Napoli conducted such an investigation.

The strike ended at the end of February, and Norbuck was recalled back to work on March 8 as a labor pool person in the foundry department (business was slow so there

Continued

Continued

were no openings in the plating department). On April 17, Napoli, Local 55's grievance committee chairperson, and Norbuck discussed Napoli's investigation and her findings about his previous education and work experience. Norbuck was subsequently terminated for falsifying his employment application. After two additional meetings failed to resolve the dispute, the union filed the following grievance:

> Grievance No. 35. The aggrieved charges the company with discharging him on April 17 without just cause. The union is hereby requesting the company to reinstate Mr. Jim Norbuck with full seniority, and all lost wages and other benefits spelled out in the agreement.

POTENTIALLY RELEVANT CONTRACT PROVISIONS

Article VIII. Suspension and Discharge.

Section 1. Procedure. Suspensions, discharges, and disciplinary actions shall be first discussed with the shop steward and/or grievance committee before being put into effect. Failure to discuss will result in rescinding any action taken.

Section 2. Differences. Any difference of opinion between the parties as to the facts and/or judgment shall result in a formal meeting between the parties and if not resolved to the satisfaction of both parties, it shall be referred to an impartial arbitrator for a final and binding decision. . . .

Article XI. Seniority.

Section 1. Basis of Seniority. (a) Plant seniority is defined as the length of continuous service with the company and shall continue until terminated for reasons set forth under paragraph (b) of this section. . . .

(b) Plant seniority shall be terminated for the following reasons:

1. Dismissal for cause . . .

(d) New employees shall be required to serve a probationary period of thirty (30) calendar days. Such probationary period may be extended by mutual agreement between the parties for a period not to exceed fifteen (15) calendar days. During this time the company shall judge the fitness of such employees and will be free to discharge or lay off such employees without regard to seniority. After completion of their probationary period the employee's plant seniority shall start from the first day worked. . . .

Article XII.

Section 1. Management Rights. (a) The right to hire and maintain order and efficiency is the sole responsibility of the management.

(b) The right to promote, and the right to discipline and discharge for just cause, are likewise the sole responsibility of the management.

POTENTIALLY RELEVANT PENNSYLVANIA LEGAL DEFINITION

Under Pennsylvania law deceit is interpreted to consist of a fraudulent misrepresentation of material facts in a business transaction that is calculated to induce reliance, and that actually causes reasonable and justifiable reliance, to the detriment of the reliant. Note: The arbitrator's authority is derived from the collective bargaining agreement, and his or her job is to interpret the agreement. The arbitrator's job is not to enforce legal statutes, but often an arbitrator looks to statutes, and their interpretation, to aid in the interpretation of the collective bargaining agreement.

QUESTIONS

1. Assume the role of Susan Napoli. How would you try to convince an arbitrator that the dismissal was legitimate?
2. Assume the role of Local 55's grievance committee chairperson. How would you try to convince an arbitrator that the dismissal violated the collective bargaining agreement?
3. As an arbitrator, how would you rule? Why?

Grievance Discussion Case 5: Inability to Report to Police Work Due to Child Care Problems

BACKGROUND

Lisa Vincent had been employed as a police officer by the Town of Stevenson for four years. The police officers at the Stevenson Police Department were represented by the American Federation of State, County, and Municipal Employees (AFSCME) Local 7.

Article 3 of the collective bargaining agreement specified that there should be eight police cars on each shift. If for whatever reason there were not enough officers to staff a certain shift, officers would be called on a voluntary basis; this was known as a "callback." If the callback method failed to obtain sufficient personnel for the shift in question, police officers were ordered back to work; this was called an "orderback." In orderback situations the department was first required to order officers scheduled to work the next shift in early.

On May 29, the police department was understaffed for the second shift. The voluntary callback procedure did not yield sufficient personnel, so the department started an orderback. Officer Vincent was scheduled to work the third shift at 3:00 P.M. However, under the orderback Officer Vincent was ordered to report to work at 11:00 A.M. instead of 3:00 P.M. Officer Vincent had previously arranged for a babysitter to care for her three children during her regularly scheduled shift beginning at 3:00 P.M., but she was unable to find anyone on such short notice to care for them between 11:00 A.M. and 3:00 P.M. She was thus unable to report for the orderback, but instead reported to work for her scheduled shift at 3:00 P.M.

Because Officer Vincent did not report when ordered in, the town suspended her without pay for five days. The union subsequently filed a grievance stating that Officer Vincent's failure to report for the orderback was not insubordination, but rather was analogous to the situation in which an officer is unable to report due to sickness.

POTENTIALLY RELEVANT CONTRACT PROVISIONS

ARTICLE 3: HOURS OF WORK

Section 2. The shift hours of the patrol division, dispatchers, and corporals shall be as follows, except in a justifiable emergency:

Shift #1. 11:00 P.M. to 7:00 A.M.

Shift #2. 7:00 A.M. to 3:00 P.M.

Shift #3. 3:00 P.M. to 11:00 P.M.

On shift #1, there shall be eight (8) cars; on shift #2, there shall be eight (8) cars; and on shift #3, there shall be eight (8) cars. The number of cars assigned to each subshift shall be determined by the chief.

ARTICLE 8: SICK LEAVE AND HOSPITALIZATION BENEFIT

Section A. Sick Leave Policy and Procedures

1. Sick leave shall be provided for police officers as insurance against loss of income when a police officer is unable to perform assigned duties because of illness or injury.
2. Police officers shall be entitled to 96 hours of sick leave each calendar year.
3. Police officers absent from work on account of illness or injury shall report intended absence to their division head or supervisor as soon as practical, but no later than fifteen (15) minutes after commencement of the police officer's duty shift unless justified by emergency circumstances.
4. Sick leave in excess of 16 hours for any one illness shall be documented by a written certification from a licensed practicing and attending physician, that during the period of leave, the police officer was prevented by illness from discharging the duties required by his or her office or position of employment. Such certification shall also be required of any police officer claiming sick leave benefits for an absence not reported in compliance with subsection (3) hereof or at such other times at which verification is requested by a supervisor or department head.

QUESTIONS

1. As an attorney for the Town of Stevenson, develop a case to support the department's just cause in suspending Officer Vincent.
2. As an attorney for AFSCME Local 7, develop an argument to support your client's contention that just cause does not exist for suspending Lisa Vincent.
3. As an arbitrator, how would you rule? Why?

Grievance Discussion Case 6: Work Requirements for Holiday Pay

BACKGROUND

John Arnett was a truck driver for Saga Food Services. He was part of a bargaining unit represented by Teamsters Local 444. Arnett's normal workweek consisted of four 10-hour workdays, Tuesday through Friday. The Labor Day holiday fell on a Monday, and as was past practice, employees who were normally not scheduled to work Monday observed the holiday on Tuesday.

Thus Arnett's Labor Day holiday was actually scheduled for Tuesday. At 11:00 P.M. on Tuesday night Arnett called the company and informed the clerk on duty that he was not coming to work on the following day because he was taking a personal leave day. Arnett did not receive permission from his shift manager or any supervisor to take Wednesday as a personal leave day. However, as established by past practice, the company did not refuse a personal leave day if the leave was requested an hour and a half or more before a worker's schedule shift starting time.

In sum, Labor Day was on a Monday, but Arnett was not scheduled to work Mondays so his Labor Day holiday was on Tuesday. Arnett then took a personal leave day on Wednesday. The company subsequently refused to pay Arnett for his holiday (Tuesday), claiming that he did not fulfill the requirements of the collective bargaining agreement.

The union filed a grievance requesting that Arnett be paid his holiday pay because he fulfilled the requirement for holiday pay computation set forth in the collective bargaining agreement.

POTENTIALLY RELEVANT CONTRACT PROVISIONS

Article 7: Holidays

Section 7.03. Holiday pay allowances will be given subject to the following terms and conditions:

. . .

(B) The employee shall have worked his full scheduled work day immediately before and immediately after the holiday except for proven sickness or injury. The shift manager may offer to waive this rule in advance of the holiday, and acceptance thereof by an employee or employees shall be on a seniority basis.

Article 23: Leaves of Absence

Section 23.06. Each present employee will be entitled to four (4) days of personal leave per contract year. Said personal leave will be noncumulative, and said personal days will be paid if not used.

QUESTIONS

1. Assume the role of director of human resources for Saga Food Services. How would you present your case that John Arnett is not entitled to his holiday pay for Labor Day?
2. As a business agent for Local 444, how would you argue that John Arnett is due his holiday pay?
3. As an arbitrator, how would you rule? Why?

Grievance Discussion Case 7: Insubordination or Unreasonable Assignment?

BACKGROUND

Local 4417 was the authorized bargaining agent for all employees, except clerical, supervisory, and security employees, at the Tiger Oil Mill in Mississippi. On January 5 an electric motor broke, causing the mill to shut down. Shortly thereafter mill superintendent Frank Tempest assigned Bob White and Michael Johnson to clean the mill's cyclone. This assignment required the two employees to go up on the mill roof 50 feet above the ground, each holding onto the cyclone with one hand and cleaning the cyclone with the other hand. There was no railing or catwalk surrounding the cyclone. The temperature was 24°F, and there were strong winds.

White and Johnson worked on cleaning the cyclone for approximately 20 minutes but then returned to the mill. The superintendent asked if the cyclone had been cleaned and, upon learning that it had not been, asked for an explanation. The employees responded that the severe cold combined with slippery conditions made the job unsafe. Tempest ordered the two employees to return to the roof and clean the cyclone.

Consequently, White and Johnson returned to the cyclone but found that they could not clean the cyclone due to the hazardous conditions. Upon returning to the mill the second time, the employees were again confronted by the superintendent. Tempest ordered them to "clean the damn cyclone."

What happened next was unclear (even after testimony). A "cursing tirade" between Tempest and White ensued, but it was not clear who initiated it. The course of this conversation was disputed: Tempest claimed that White voluntarily quit by saying he was going home instead of going up on the roof in that weather. White claimed that Tempest ordered him off company premises because of his refusal to obey a clear directive to clean the cyclone. White further claimed that he asked for another job assignment. There was no doubt that White used profanity toward his supervisor.

The end result was that White left work, and his employment at the Tiger Oil Mill ceased (but it was unclear whether he quit or was discharged—even after testimony and cross-examination). Subsequently, the union filed a grievance on behalf of White claiming the company violated the collective bargaining agreement by discharging White without just cause.

POTENTIALLY RELEVANT CONTRACT PROVISIONS

Article XI—Miscellaneous

(A) The company will discipline and discharge employees only for just cause.

. . .

(J) In addition to the grounds for temporary suspension or permanent discharge hereinbefore in this section enumerated, employees guilty of the following activities shall be the subject of permanent dismissal or other disciplinary action at the discretion of the employer: (1) insubordination, (2) using materials or machinery contrary to instructions, (3) inefficiency, spoilage, or negligent waste of materials, (4) throwing materials about the plant or out of windows, (5) boisterous talk, profanity, or horseplay, (6) gambling on employer's premises, (7) theft of employer's or private property, (8) smoking anywhere inside the plant fence or in any of the employer's departments, (9) drunkenness, obscenity, or immorality, (10) bringing intoxicating liquors on employer's property, (11) interference with production by slowdown or sitdown, (12) violations of plant or department rules or regulations, or (13) padding pay reports or any other form of dishonesty.

POTENTIALLY RELEVANT ARBITRATION PRECEDENT

Standard arbitrator practice is that safety and health reasons are potentially valid reasons for not carrying out a work assignment. The following portion of an arbitration award sums up the accepted standard:

> An employee may refuse to carry out a particular work assignment if, at the time he is given the work assignment, he reasonably believes that by carrying out such work assignment he will endanger his safety or health. In such an instance the employee has the duty, not only of stating that he believes there is a risk to his safety or health, and has the reason for believing so, but he also has the burden, if called upon, of showing by appropriate evidence that he had a reasonable basis for his belief. In the case of dispute, . . . the question to be decided is not whether he actually would have suffered injury but whether he had a reasonable basis for believing so. [*Laclead Gas Co.*, 39 LA 833 (1962)]

QUESTIONS

1. As the labor relations representative for the Tiger Oil Mill, develop a case for your contention that the discharge of Bob White was proper.
2. As the chief steward for Local 4417, how would you try to convince an arbitrator that the dismissal violated the collective bargaining agreement?
3. As an arbitrator, how would you rule? Why?

(*Hint:* Pay careful attention to issues of burden of proof.)

Grievance Discussion Case 8: Is Purchasing Parts from a Catalog Subcontracting?

BACKGROUND

The Bangs Manufacturing Company made heavy equipment used primarily for rock crushing and asphalt paving. Although this business was seasonal and cyclical, the company normally employed approximately 850 production and maintenance employees (on two shifts) at its production facility. These production and maintenance employees were represented by the International Association of Machinists and Aerospace Workers Lodge 138. Due to the cyclical and seasonal nature of the industry and the fear of job loss, the union fought hard to win contract provisions pertaining to subcontracting.

All of the heavy equipment the company manufactured used belt conveyors, which were supported by a wide variety of wing pulleys. The company had made these pulleys itself for many years. In fact, making and painting these pulleys were the primary jobs of several employees. The pulleys were traditionally painted orange.

During the fall a salesman from The Pulley Place made an unsolicited visit to the company's director of procurement, Harold Hill. The Pulley Place made nothing but pulleys. The salesman showed Hill a variety of pulleys in The Pulley Place catalog that could be used directly on the machinery made by the Bangs Manufacturing Company without any necessary alterations.

Intrigued by the idea, Hill had some others in the company verify that the pulleys in The Pulley Place catalog could be used in the manufacturing process without any alterations or modifications. Although the pulleys were a slightly different size, the results showed that the pulleys could be used without modification at an estimated savings of 30–60 percent. Thus, the company subsequently ordered pulleys directly from The Pulley Place catalog. No specifications were given to The Pulley Place, and the pulleys were ordered by catalog number. To help avoid confusion, the traditional (Bangs Manufacturing Company) part numbers were affixed to the pulleys by The Pulley Place. The ordered pulleys were gray.

Earlier in the year 295 bargaining unit employees had been laid off due to economic conditions. Several months later a substantial number had been recalled, but there were still many employees on layoff. At that time the workers started noticing that the pulleys they were using to assemble the heavy equipment were gray, not orange. Upon further investigation, the union discovered that the pulleys were being shipped in. The union subsequently filed the following grievance:

> By utilizing pulleys made elsewhere, the company is in violation of the collective bargaining agreement because work customarily performed by bargaining unit employees is being performed by outside sources while bargaining unit employees are laid off. Further, the work is to be returned to the bargaining unit employees and all affected employees are to be fully reimbursed for lost rewards stemming from this violation.

POTENTIALLY RELEVANT CONTRACT PROVISIONS

Article XVII. Grievance Procedure.

Step 6. . . . The arbitrator shall conduct a hearing on the grievance within a reasonable time and shall be empowered to rule on all disputes concerning the effect, interpretation, and application of this agreement. However, he shall have no power to add to, subtract from, or modify any of the terms of this agreement or any other agreement made supplementary hereto.

Article XXVII. Subcontract.

During the periods of layoff the company will not have any work that is normally done by Bangs Manufacturing performed by any outside source, either in or outside the plant except:

1. There is no machine or plant capacity at Bangs Manufacturing.
2. Where we do have machine or plant capacity and the provisions of the contract have been followed and additional employees are needed, the company will ask the laid-off employees senioritywise if they would return to work on said jobs, which would be voluntary. If they accepted, the regular provision of the contract would apply. This would apply only when subcontracting is involved.
3. No employees laid off from development are involved.
4. Any work farmed out will be returned to the company within 48 hours from the date the layoff notice goes out, except per paragraph 5 below.
5. The following items are made at Bangs Steel and Iron Works at any time—truck frames, elevating wheels, bins, columns, hoppers, feed chutes, drier drums, bolsters, lifting flights, dust collectors, elevator housings, cyclones, smoke boxes, exhaust washers, feeder frames.

POTENTIALLY RELEVANT UNITED STATES LEGAL DEFINITION

"A contract for the sale of articles then existing, or such as the seller in the ordinary course of his business manufactures or procures for the general market, whether on hand at the time or not, is a contract for the sale of goods to which the statute applies; but if the goods are to be

Continued

manufactured for the buyer on his special order, and not for the general market, it is not a contract of sale" [but rather a contract for work, labor, and materials] *(American Jurisprudence,* Section 250). *Note:* The arbitrator's authority is derived from the collective bargaining agreement, and his or her job is to interpret the agreement. The arbitrator's job is not to enforce legal statutes, but often an arbitrator looks to statutes, and their interpretation, to aid in the interpretation of a collective bargaining agreement.

QUESTIONS

1. Develop an argument supporting the company's right to use pulleys from The Pulley Place.
2. Assume the role of Lodge 138's grievance committee chairperson. How would you try to convince an arbitrator that the company's action violated the collective bargaining agreement?
3. As an arbitrator, how would you rule? Why?

Grievance Discussion Case 9: Is Upward Bumping an Unauthorized Promotion?

BACKGROUND

A plant manufactured approximately 1,200 different aluminum shapes. About 450 of the shapes were anodized by attaching the aluminum shapes to a rack and then dipping the rack into an anodizing tank. Anodizing was done by teams of two rackers each. Each racker had to do a careful job of securing the aluminum to the rack. Aluminum pieces that were not racked properly could be ruined, causing significant financial loss to the company.

Local 491 of the International Chemical Workers Union was the authorized bargaining agent for the production workers of this plant. Christine Hinds was hired by the company on September 15, 1990, and at the time of the grievance she was working as an anodyne racker. Ray Davies was hired on July 30, 1990, and was the grievant.

While employed by the company, Davies had been classified as a packer helper, saw helper, head sawer (which is the same job grade as racker), fork truck operator, and die cleanup, but never as a racker. On December 3, Davies was laid off by the company due to economic reasons. Thus, he filed a grievance claiming that the company violated the collective bargaining agreement by retaining a worker with less seniority (namely Hinds, who was a racker). At the time of the grievance filing Davies was employed as a saw helper, which was two job grades below racker.

TESTIMONY AT THE ARBITRATION HEARING

At the grievance hearing Davies testified that although he never was actually classified as a racker, he learned racking while working as a second shift forklift operator. He stated that he learned how to be a racker by filling in for 15 or 20 minutes at a time and also by observing rackers at other times. He further testified that he had become a "jack-of-all-trades" and could have satisfactorily performed the duties of a racker if paired with an experienced racker.

At the grievance hearing the plant manager also testified regarding several points. First, had Davies been retained as a racker, he would have been paired with a regular racker. Second, Davies was a willing and cooperative worker and would be able to do any job after training. Third, in the plant manager's estimation, Davies would probably have required 30 days' training to become as efficient as a normal racker. Fourth, four men bumped into being rackers during the layoffs—one of them was a rack maker who had acquired some experience being a racker by filling in during lunch breaks.

POTENTIALLY RELEVANT CONTRACT PROVISIONS

ARTICLE IX.

Section 1: Seniority shall be on a plantwide basis.

Section 2: In all matters of promotion, demotion, transfer, job training, shift preference, layoff, and recall, the following will be the determining factors:

a. Seniority.
b. Ability to do the work required.

QUESTIONS

1. As the labor relations manager for the company, how would you argue a case supporting your client's actions?
2. Assume the role of Local 491 chief steward. How would you support your contention that the company violated the collective bargaining agreement?
3. As an arbitrator, how would you rule? Why?

Grievance Discussion Case 10: Are Special Skills the Same as Merit?

BACKGROUND

Nearly 90 percent of the residents of the south Florida city of Ditchburn were Hispanic, and many residents spoke only Spanish. Many of the city's civil service jobs, including the fire dispatcher, comprised the bargaining unit represented by the American Federation of State, County, and Municipal Employees (AFSCME) Local 3.

Jose Obradors was a fire dispatcher for the City of Ditchburn on the 7:00 A.M. to 3:00 P.M. shift. A regular dispatcher on the 11:00 P.M. to 7:00 A.M. shift started maternity leave on November 23, which caused a temporary (six-month) vacancy on this shift. To temporarily fill this vacancy until a six-month replacement could be found, Fire Chief Dave Franz transferred Obradors to the 11:00 P.M. to 7:00 A.M. shift because Obradors was bilingual.

The chief then posted a vacancy notice for a temporary dispatcher for the 11:00 P.M. to 7:00 A.M. shift and stated that the dispatcher must be bilingual. However, no one volunteered, so the chief transferred Obradors to fill the position until the prior dispatcher returned from maternity leave six months later. While Obradors was the most junior bilingual dispatcher, he was not the most junior dispatcher. In fact, Obradors had enough seniority to work a shift other than 11:00 P.M. to 7:00 A.M., and the transfer was made despite his objection. The city freely admitted that Obradors was transferred because of his ability to speak Spanish.

Obradors, however, did not want to work the 11:00 P.M. to 7:00 A.M. shift and thus filed a grievance requesting to be transferred back to his day shift immediately because the city violated the collective bargaining agreement.

TESTIMONY AT THE ARBITRATION HEARING

At the grievance hearing the city's personnel director testified that the city had considered language ability as a factor in establishing schedules for the last 10 years, especially for the fire dispatcher and police complaint officer positions. In fact, the city's schedules specified the number of bilingual workers required per shift. Consequently, shift assignments were based not solely on seniority but also on language ability. Examples could be cited of junior employees who were promoted instead of more senior employees because of language ability. Finally, the city's recently enacted hiring policy required all new fire dispatchers to be bilingual.

Both parties agreed that Jose Obradors' transfer was based on his language ability and that he had the seniority to work a different shift.

POTENTIALLY RELEVANT CONTRACT PROVISIONS

ARTICLE 6: MANAGEMENT RIGHTS

Section 1. The union agrees that the city has and will continue to retain, whether exercised or not, the right to operate and manage its affairs in all respects; that the powers or authority which the city has not officially abridged, deleted, or modified by the express provisions of this agreement are retained by the city. The rights of the city, through its management officials, shall include, but shall not be limited to, the right to determine the organization of city government; to determine the purpose of each of its constituent departments; to exercise control and discretion over the organization and efficiency of operations of the city; to set standards for service to be offered to the public; to direct the employees of the city, including the right to assign work and overtime, to hire, examine, classify, promote, train, transfer, assign, and schedule employees in positions with the city; to suspend, demote, discharge, or take other disciplinary action against employees for proper cause; to increase, reduce, change, modify, or alter the composition and size of the workforce, including the right to relieve employees from duties because of lack of work or funds; to determine the location, methods, means, and personnel by which operations are to be conducted, including the right to determine whether goods or services are to be made or purchased; to establish, modify, combine or abolish job pay positions; to change or eliminate existing methods of operations, equipment, or facilities; to determine the methods, means, and number of personnel needed or desirable for carrying out the city's mission and to direct the workforce.

. . .

Section 5. Delivery of municipal services in the most efficient, effective, and courteous manner is of paramount importance to the City of Ditchburn. Such achievement is recognized to be a mutual obligation of both parties in their respective roles and responsibilities.

ARTICLE 10: NO DISCRIMINATION

Section 1. The city and the union agree that the provisions of the agreement shall be applied equally to all employees in the bargaining unit without discrimination as to age, sex, marital status, race, color, creed, national origin, or political affiliation.

ARTICLE 30: LAYOFF AND RECALL

Section 2. Recall

Continued

Continued

A. Employees shall be called back from layoff according to the same criteria for layoff (i.e., the most senior person will be recalled) unless in the city's judgment special skills are required.

ARTICLE 31: SENIORITY

Section 1. All provisions within this article shall constitute the basis for establishing a uniform procedure of seniority for vacations, shift transfers, days off preference, and overtime.

. . .

Section 4. It is recognized that the principle of merit must be given consideration in any "efficiency conscious" organization; therefore, the department/division heads reserve the right to final determination regarding employee transfer, shift assignment, days off, and vacation time.

QUESTIONS

1. As the City of Ditchburn personnel director, how would you present your case that the transfer of Jose Obradors did not violate the agreement?
2. As a local union official, how would you argue that the City's action regarding Jose Obradors' transfer violated the contract?
3. As an arbitrator, how would you rule? Why?

End Notes

1. William M. Leiserson, "Constitutional Government in American Industries," *American Economic Review* 12 (May 1922), pp. 58–79 at 75.
2. Victor G. Devinatz, "An Alternative Strategy: Lessons from the UAW Local 6 and the FE, 1946-52," in Cyrus Bina, Laurie Clements, and Chuck Davis (eds.), *Beyond Survival: Wage Labor in the Late Twentieth Century* (Armonk, NY: M. E. Sharpe, 1996), pp. 145–60.
3. David Brody, "Workplace Contractualism in Comparative Perspective," in Nelson Lichtenstein and Howell John Harris (eds.), *Industrial Democracy in America: The Ambiguous Promise* (Washington, DC: Woodrow Wilson Center Press, 1993), pp. 176–205.
4. Sumner H. Slichter, *Unions Policies and Industrial Management* (Washington, DC: Brookings Institution, 1941), p. 1.
5. Charles C. Heckscher, *The New Unionism: Employee Involvement in the Changing Corporation* (New York: Basic Books, 1988); Nelson Lichtenstein, "Great Expectations: The Promise of Industrial Jurisprudence and its Demise, 1930–1960," in Nelson Lichtenstein and Howell John Harris (eds.), *Industrial Democracy in America: The Ambiguous Promise* (Washington, DC: Woodrow Wilson Center Press, 1993), pp. 113–41.
6. Steve Fraser, "Dress Rehearsal for the New Deal: Shop-Floor Insurgents, Political Elites, and Industrial Democracy in the Amalgamated Clothing Workers," in Michael H. Frisch and Daniel J. Walkowitz (eds.), *Working-Class America: Essays on Labor, Community, and American Society* (Urbana: University of Illinois Press, 1983), pp. 212–55.
7. Lichtenstein, "Great Expectations."
8. James B. Atleson, *Labor and the Wartime State: Labor Relations and Law during World War II* (Urbana: University of Illinois Press, 1998); Nelson Lichtenstein, *Labor's War at Home: The CIO in World War II* (Cambridge, England: Cambridge University Press, 1982).
9. Bruce S. Feldacker, *Labor Guide to Labor Law,* 4th ed. (Upper Saddle River, NJ: Prentice Hall, 2000).
10. *Textile Workers Union of America v. Lincoln Mills,* 353 U.S. 448 (1957).
11. Brody, "Workplace Contractualism in Comparative Perspective"; David E. Feller, "A General Theory of the Collective Bargaining Agreement," *California Law Review* 61 (May 1973), pp. 663–856; Lichtenstein, "Great Expectations"; Katherine V.W. Stone, "The Post-War Paradigm in American Labor Law," *Yale Law Journal* 90 (June 1981), pp. 1509–80.
12. Unless otherwise noted, in this chapter the statistics on the frequency of union clauses in private sector agreements are from *Basic Patterns in Union Contracts,* 14th ed. (Washington, DC: Bureau of National Affairs, 1995).
13. Barry Bluestone and Irving Bluestone, *Negotiating the Future: A Labor Perspective on American Business* (New York: Basic Books, 1992); Sumner H. Slichter, James J. Healy, and E. Robert Livernash, *The Impact of Collective Bargaining on Management* (Washington, DC: Brookings, 1960).
14. Karen L. Ertel, *Grievance Guide,* 13th ed. (Washington, DC: Bloomberg BNA, 2012); Kenneth May (ed.), *Elkouri and Elkouri: How Arbitration Works,* 7th ed. (Washington, DC: Bloomberg BNA, 2012).
15. John W. Budd, "The Effect of Unions on Employee Benefits and Non-Wage Compensation: Monopoly Power, Collective Voice, and Facilitation," in James T. Bennett and Bruce E. Kaufman (eds.), *What Do Unions Do? A Twenty-Year Perspective* (New Brunswick, NJ: Transaction Publishers, 2007), pp. 160–92; Richard B. Freeman and James L. Medoff, *What Do Unions Do?* (New York: Basic Books, 1984).
16. Trevor Bain, "Third Party Dispute Resolution—Rights Disputes," in David Lewin, Daniel J.B. Mitchell, and Mahmood A. Zaidi (eds.), *The Human Resource Management Handbook Part II* (Greenwich, CT: JAI Press, 1997), pp. 219–44; Peter Feuille, "Dispute Resolution Frontiers in the Unionized Workplace," in Sandra E. Gleason (ed.), *Workplace Dispute Resolution: Directions for the Twenty-First Century* (East Lansing: Michigan State University Press, 1997), pp. 17–55.
17. David Fairris, *Shopfloor Matters: Labor—Management Relations in Twentieth-Century American Manufacturing* (London: Routledge, 1997).
18. Harry C. Katz, *Shifting Gears: Changing Labor Relations in the U.S. Automobile Industry* (Cambridge, MA: MIT Press, 1985); Slichter, Healy, and Livernash, *The Impact of Collective Bargaining on Management.*
19. Slichter, Healy, and Livernash, *The Impact of Collective Bargaining on Management.*
20. Howard R. Stanger, "Newspapers: Collective Bargaining Decline amidst Technological Change," in Paul F. Clark, John T. Delaney, and Ann C. Frost (eds.), *Collective Bargaining in the Private Sector* (Champaign, IL: Industrial Relations Research Association, 2002), pp. 179–215.
21. Thomas Benjamin Huggett, "Successor Clauses: What They Are and Why Every Union Should Have One," *Catholic University Law Review* 46 (Spring 1997), pp. 835–905.

22. David Prosten, *The Union Steward's Complete Guide* (Annapolis, MD: Union Communication Services, 1997); Robert M. Schwartz, *The Legal Rights of Union Stewards,* 4th ed. (Cambridge, MA: Work Rights Press, 2006).
23. National Labor Relations Board, Election Reports, available at www.nlrb.gov/reports-guidance/reports/election-reports.
24. *NLRB v. General Motors,* 373 U.S. 734 (1963).
25. *Communication Workers of America v. Beck,* 487 U.S. 735 (1988).
26. *Food and Commercial Workers Locals 951, 1036, and 7 (Meijer, Inc.),* 329 NLRB No. 69 (1999); Christopher David Ruiz Cameron, "The Wages of Syntax: Why the Cost of Organizing a Union Firm's Non-Union Competition Should Be Charged to 'Financial Core' Employees," *Catholic University Law Review* 47 (Spring 1998), pp. 979–1003.
27. Jeff Canfield, "What a Sham(e): The Broken *Beck* Rights System in the Real World Workplace," *Wayne Law Review* 47 (Fall 2001), pp. 1049–74.
28. Rick Fantasia and Kim Voss, *Hard Work: Remaking the American Labor Movement* (Berkeley: University of California Press, 2004).
29. B.V.H. Schneider, "Public Sector Labor Legislation–An Evolutionary Analysis," in Benjamin Aaron, Joyce M. Najita, and James L. Stern (eds.), *Public Sector Bargaining,* 2nd ed. (Washington, DC: Bureau of National Affairs, 1988), pp. 189–228.
30. John Lund and Cheryl L. Maranto, "Public Sector Labor Law: An Update," in Dale Belman, Morley Gunderson, and Douglas Hyatt (eds.), *Public Sector Employment in a Time of Transition* (Madison, WI: Industrial Relations Research Association, 1996), pp. 21–57.
31. Jean T. McKelvey (ed.), *The Changing Law of Fair Representation* (Ithaca, NY: ILR Press, 1985); Benjamin J. Taylor and Fred Witney, *Labor Relations Law,* 7th ed. (Englewood Cliffs, NJ: Prentice Hall, 1996).
32. *Steele v. Louisville and Nashville Railroad,* 323 U.S. 192 (1944); *Wallace Corporation v. NLRB,* 323 U.S. 248 (1944); *Ford Motor Co. v. Huffman,* 345 U.S. 330 (1953); Deborah C. Malamud, "The Story of *Steele v. Louisville and Nashville Railroad*: White Unions, Black Unions, and the Struggle for Racial Justice on the Rails," in Laura J. Cooper and Catherine L. Fisk (eds.), *Labor Law Stories* (New York: Foundation Press, 2005), pp. 55–105.
33. *Vaca v. Sipes,* 386 U.S. 171, 191 (1967).
34. Howell John Harris, *The Right to Manage: Industrial Relations Policies of American Business in the 1940s* (Madison: University of Wisconsin Press, 1982).
35. Bluestone and Bluestone, *Negotiating the Future.*
36. May, *Elkouri and Elkouri.*
37. Atleson, *Labor and the Wartime State*; Lichtenstein, *Labor's War at Home.*
38. Bain, "Third Party Dispute Resolution–Rights Disputes"; *Basic Patterns in Union Contracts*; Jill Kriesky, "Trends in Dispute Resolution in the Public Sector," in Adrienne E. Eaton and Jeffrey H. Keefe (eds.), *Employment Dispute Resolution and Worker Rights in the Changing Workplace* (Champaign, IL: Industrial Relations Research Association, 1999), pp. 247–72.
39. Prosten, *The Union Steward's Complete Guide*.
40. David Lewin, "Theoretical and Empirical Research on the Grievance Procedure and Arbitration: A Critical Review," in Adrienne E. Eaton and Jeffrey H. Keefe (eds.), *Employment Dispute Resolution and Worker Rights in the Changing Workplace* (Champaign, IL: Industrial Relations Research Association, 1999), pp. 137–86; David Lewin, "Collective Bargaining and Grievance Procedures," in William K. Roche, Paul Teague, and Alexander J.S. Colvin, eds., *The Oxford Handbook of Conflict Management in Organizations* (Oxford: Oxford University Press, 2014), pp. 116–34.
41. Alexander J.S. Colvin, "The Relationship between Employment Arbitration and Workplace Dispute Resolution Procedures," *Ohio State Journal on Dispute Resolution* 16 (2001), pp. 643–68.
42. Feuille, "Dispute Resolution Frontiers in the Unionized Workplace," p. 31.
43. Brian Bemmels, "The Determinants of Grievance Initiation," *Industrial and Labor Relations Review* 47 (January 1994), pp. 285–301; Lewin, "Theoretical and Empirical Research on the Grievance Procedure and Arbitration"; Samuel Bacharach and Peter Bamberger, "The Power of Labor to Grieve: The Impact of the Workplace, Labor Market, and Power Dependence on Employee Grievance Filing," *Industrial and Labor Relations Review* 57 (July 2004), pp. 518–39.
44. Lewin, "Collective Bargaining and Grievance Procedures."
45. David Lewin and Richard B. Peterson, "Behavioral Outcomes of Grievance Activity," *Industrial Relations* 38 (October 1999), pp. 554–76; Morris M. Kleiner, Gerald Nickelsburg, and Adam Pilarski, "Monitoring, Grievances, and Plant Performance," *Industrial Relations* 34 (April 1995), pp. 169–89.

46. Theodore J. St. Antoine, "The Law of Arbitration," in James L. Stern and Joyce M. Najita (eds.), *Labor Arbitration under Fire* (Ithaca, NY: ILR Press, 1997), pp. 1–41; Douglas E. Ray, Calvin William Sharpe, and Robert N. Strassfield, *Understanding Labor Law* (New York: Mathew Bender, 1999); Taylor and Witney, *Labor Relations Law*; May, *Elkouri and Elkouri*.
47. *Textile Workers Union of America v. Lincoln Mills,* 353 U.S. 448 (1957).
48. *United Steelworkers of America v. American Manufacturing Co.,* 363 U.S. 564 (1960).
49. *United Steelworkers of America v. Warrior and Gulf Navigation Co.,* 363 U.S. 574 (1960).
50. *United Steelworkers of America v. Enterprise Wheel and Car Corp.,* 363 U.S. 593 (1960).
51. Feuille, "Dispute Resolution Frontiers in the Unionized Workplace"; Katherine V.W. Stone, "The *Steelworkers' Trilogy:* The Evolution of Labor Arbitration," in Laura J. Cooper and Catherine L. Fisk (eds.), *Labor Law Stories* (New York: Foundation Press, 2005), pp. 149–89.
52. Harry Graham, "Grievance Arbitration in State and Local Government in the 1990s and Beyond," in James L. Stern and Joyce M. Najita (eds.), *Labor Arbitration under Fire* (Ithaca, NY: ILR Press, 1997), pp. 72–87.
53. Dennis R. Nolan and Roger I. Abrams, "Trends in Private Sector Grievance Arbitration," in James L. Stern and Joyce M. Najita (eds.), *Labor Arbitration under Fire* (Ithaca, NY: ILR Press, 1997), pp. 42–71.
54. *Alexander v. Gardner-Denver,* 415 U.S. 36 (1974).
55. Alexander J.S. Colvin, "Mandatory Arbitration and Inequality of Justice in Employment," *Berkeley Journal of Employment and Labor Law* 35 (2014), pp. 71–90.
56. Nolan and Abrams, "Trends in Private Sector Grievance Arbitration."
57. Charles S. Loughran, *How to Prepare and Present a Labor Arbitration Case: Strategy and Tactics for Advocates,* 2nd ed. (Washington, DC: Bureau of National Affairs, 2006); Nolan and Abrams, "Trends in Private Sector Grievance Arbitration"; May, *Elkouri and Elkouri*.
58. Edwin R. Render, "The Rules of Evidence in Labor Arbitration," *Loyola Law Review* 54 (Summer 2008), pp. 297–351.
59. Arnold M. Zack, *Grievance Arbitration: Issues on the Merits in Discipline, Discharge, and Contract Interpretation* (Lexington, MA: Lexington Books, 1989), p. 154.
60. Carlton J. Snow, "Contract Interpretation," in Theodore J. St. Antoine (ed.), *The Common Law of the Workplace: The View of Arbitrators,* 2nd ed. (Washington, DC: Bureau of National Affairs, 2005), pp. 67–97; May, *Elkouri and Elkouri*.
61. Theodore J. St. Antoine (ed.), *The Common Law of the Workplace: The View of Arbitrators,* 2nd ed. (Washington, DC: Bureau of National Affairs, 2005).
62. Karl E. Klare, "Workplace Democracy and Market Reconstruction: An Agenda for Legal Reform," *Catholic University Law Review* 38 (Fall 1988), pp. 1–68; Kim Moody, *An Injury to All: The Decline of American Unionism* (London: Verso, 1988); Stone, "The Post-War Paradigm in American Labor Law"; Fantasia and Voss, *Hard Work*.
63. Peter Feuille, "Grievance Mediation," in Adrienne E. Eaton and Jeffrey H. Keefe (eds.), *Employment Dispute Resolution and Worker Rights in the Changing Workplace* (Champaign, IL: Industrial Relations Research Association, 1999), pp. 187–217; Nolan and Abrams, "Trends in Private Sector Grievance Arbitration."
64. Feuille, "Grievance Mediation."
65. Lewin, "Theoretical and Empirical Research on the Grievance Procedure and Arbitration."
66. Michelle Kaminski, "New Forms of Organization and Their Impact on the Grievance Procedure," in Adrienne E. Eaton and Jeffrey H. Keefe (eds.), *Employment Dispute Resolution and Worker Rights in the Changing Workplace* (Champaign, IL: Industrial Relations Research Association, 1999), pp. 219–46.
67. Graham, "Grievance Arbitration in State and Local Government in the 1990s and Beyond"; Nolan and Abrams, "Trends in Private Sector Grievance Arbitration."
68. *Payne v. Western and Atlantic R.R. Co.,* 81 Tenn. 507, 519–20 (1884), overruled on other grounds; *Hutton v. Watters,* 179 S.W. 134, 138 (Tenn. 1915).
69. Adolph Koven, Susan L. Smith, and Kenneth May, *Just Cause: The Seven Tests,* 3rd ed. (Washington, DC: Bureau of National Affairs, 2006); St. Antoine, *The Common Law of the Workplace*; May, *Elkouri and Elkouri*.
70. *Enterprise Wire Company,* 46 LA 359 (1966); Koven, Smith, and May, *Just Cause*.
71. Koven, Smith, and May, *Just Cause*.

72. John E. Dunsford, "Arbitral Discretion: The Tests of Just Cause," in Gladys W. Gruenberg (ed.), *Proceedings of the 42nd Annual Meeting, National Academy of Arbitrators* (Washington, DC: BNA Books, 1989), pp. 23–50.
73. Norman Brand, Patricia Thomas Bittel, and Henry G. Stewart, *Discipline and Discharge in Arbitration*, 3rd ed. (Washington, DC: BNA Books, 1998).
74. Feldacker, *Labor Guide to Labor Law.*
75. *NLRB v. J. Weingarten, Inc.*, 420 U.S. 251 (1975).
76. *Epilepsy Foundation of Northeast Ohio*, 331 NLRB No. 92 (2000).
77. *IBM Corp.*, 341 NLRB No. 148 (2004); Christine Neylon O'Brien, "The NLRB Waffling on *Weingarten* Rights," *Loyola University Chicago Law Journal* 37 (Fall 2005), pp. 111–46.
78. Alison L. Booth, *The Economics of the Trade Union* (Cambridge, England: Cambridge University Press, 1995); H. Gregg Lewis, *Union Relative Wage Effects: A Survey* (Chicago: University of Chicago Press, 1986); Barry T. Hirsch, "Reconsidering Union Wage Effects: Surveying New Evidence on an Old Topic," *Journal of Labor Research* 25 (Spring 2004), pp. 233–66; David G. Blanchflower and Alex Bryson, "What Effect Do Unions Have on Wages Now and Would Freeman and Medoff Be Surprised?" in James T. Bennett and Bruce E. Kaufman (eds.), *What Do Unions Do? A Twenty-Year Perspective* (New Brunswick, NJ: Transaction Publishers, 2007), pp. 79–113.
79. Richard B. Freeman, "Union Wage Practices and Wage Dispersion Within Establishments." *Industrial and Labor Relations Review* 36 (October 1982), pp. 3–21; Freeman and Medoff, *What Do Unions Do?*; David Card, Thomas Lemieux, and W. Craig Riddell, "Unions and Wage Inequality," in James T. Bennett and Bruce E. Kaufman (eds.), *What Do Unions Do? A Twenty-Year Perspective* (New Brunswick, NJ: Transaction Publishers, 2007). pp. 114–59.
80. Thomas C. Buchmueller, John DiNardo, and Robert G. Valletta, "Union Effects on Health Insurance Provision and Coverage in the United States," *Industrial and Labor Relations Review* 55 (July 2002), pp. 610–27; Budd, "The Effect of Unions on Employee Benefits and Non-Wage Compensation"; Richard B. Freeman, "The Effect of Unionism on Fringe Benefits," *Industrial and Labor Relations Review* 34 (July 1981), pp. 489–509; Richard B. Freeman, "Unions, Pensions, and Union Pension Funds," in David A. Wise (ed.), *Pensions, Labor, and Individual Choice* (Chicago: University of Chicago Press, 1985), pp. 89–121; Freeman and Medoff, *What Do Unions Do?*
81. Richard B. Freeman and Morris M. Kleiner, "The Impact of New Unionization on Wages and Working Conditions," *Journal of Labor Economics* 8 (January 1990), pp. S8–S25; Tom Juravich, Kate Bronfenbrenner, and Robert Hickey, "Significant Victories: An Analysis of Union First Contracts," in Richard N. Block, et al. (eds.) *Justice on the Job: Perspectives on the Erosion of Collective Bargaining in the United States* (Kalamazoo, MI: Upjohn, 2006), pp. 87–114.
82. Lewin, "Theoretical and Empirical Research on the Grievance Procedure and Arbitration."
83. Lewin and Peterson, "Behavioral Outcomes of Grievance Activity."
84. Richard B. Freeman, "The Exit-Voice Tradeoff in the Labor Market: Unionism, Job Tenure, Quits, and Separations," *Quarterly Journal of Economics* 94 (June 1980), pp. 643–73; Tove Helland Hammer and Ariel Avgar, "The Impact of Unions on Job Satisfaction, Organizational Commitment, and Turnover," in James T. Bennett and Bruce E. Kaufman (eds.), *What Do Unions Do? A Twenty-Year Perspective* (New Brunswick, NJ: Transaction Publishers, 2007), pp. 346–72.
85. Daniel I. Rees, "Grievance Procedure Strength and Teacher Quits," *Industrial and Labor Relations Review* 45 (October 1991), pp. 31–43.
86. Jeffrey Pfeffer and Alison Davis-Blake, "Unions and Job Satisfaction: An Alternative View," *Work and Occupations* 17 (August 1990), pp. 259–83; Michael E. Gordon and Angelo S. DeNisi, "A Re-Examination of the Relationship between Union Membership and Job Satisfaction," *Industrial and Labor Relations Review* 48 (January 1995), pp. 226–36; Keith A. Bender and Peter J. Sloane, "Job Satisfaction, Trade Unions, and Exit-Voice Revisited," *Industrial and Labor Relations Review* 51 (January 1998), pp. 222–40; Alex Bryson, Lorenzo Cappellari, and Claudio Lucifora, "Does Union Membership Really Reduce Job Satisfaction?" *British Journal of Industrial Relations* 42 (September 2004), pp. 439–59.
87. Anil Verma, "What Do Unions Do to the Workplace? Union Effects on Management and HRM Policies," in James T. Bennett and Bruce E. Kaufman (eds.), *What Do Unions Do? A Twenty-Year Perspective* (New Brunswick, NJ: Transaction Publishers, 2007), pp. 275–312.
88. John Logan, "The Union Avoidance Industry in the United States," *British Journal of Industrial Relations* 44 (December 2006), pp. 651–75.
89. Freeman and Medoff, *What Do Unions Do*?; Barry T. Hirsch, "What Do Unions Do for Economic Performance?" in James T. Bennett and Bruce E. Kaufman (eds.), *What Do Unions Do? A Twenty-Year*

Perspective (New Brunswick, NJ: Transaction Publishers, 2007), pp. 193–237; Christos Doucouliagos and Patrice LaRoche, "What Do Unions Do to Productivity? A Meta-Analysis," *Industrial Relations* 42 (October 2003), pp. 650–91; Aaron J. Sojourner, et al., "Impacts of Unionization on Quality and Productivity: Regression Discontinuity Evidence from Nursing Homes," *Industrial and Labor Relations Review* 68 (August 2015), pp. 771–806; Cassandra M.D. Hart and Aaron J. Sojourner, "Unionization and Productivity: Evidence from Charter Schools," *Industrial Relations* 55 (July 2015), pp. 422–48.

90. Dionne Pohler and Andrew Luchak, "Are Unions Good or Bad for Organizations? The Moderating Role of Management's Response," *British Journal of Industrial Relations* 53 (September 2015), pp. 423–459; Joel Cutcher-Gershenfeld, Dan Brooks, and Martin Mulloy, *Inside the Ford-UAW Transformation: Pivotal Events in Valuing Work and Delivering Results* (Cambridge: MIT Press, 2015).
91. Hirsch, "What Do Unions Do for Economic Performance?"; Christos Doucouliagos and Patrice LaRoche, "Unions and Profits: A Meta-Analysis," *Industrial Relations* 48 (January 2009), pp. 146–84.
92. John W. Budd and Alexander J.S. Colvin, "Improved Metrics for Workplace Dispute Resolution Procedures: Efficiency, Equity, and Voice," *Industrial Relations* 47 (July 2008), pp. 460–79; Alexander J.S. Colvin, "Grievance Procedures in Non-Union Firms," in William K. Roche, Paul Teague, and Alexander J.S. Colvin, eds., *The Oxford Handbook of Conflict Management in Organizations* (Oxford: Oxford University Press, 2014), pp. 168–89.
93. Colvin, "The Relationship between Employment Arbitration and Workplace Dispute Resolution Procedures"; David Lewin, "Resolving Conflict," in Paul Blyton et al. (eds.), *Sage Handbook of Industrial Relations* (London: Sage, 2008), pp. 447–67.
94. Colvin, "The Relationship between Employment Arbitration and Workplace Dispute Resolution Procedures."
95. Mary Rowe and Howard Gadlin, "The Organizational Ombudsman," in William K. Roche, Paul Teague, and Alexander J.S. Colvin, eds., *The Oxford Handbook of Conflict Management in Organizations* (Oxford: Oxford University Press, 2014), pp. 210–232.
96. David Lewin, "Workplace Dispute Resolution," in David Lewin, Daniel J.B. Mitchell, and Mahmood A. Zaidi (eds.), *The Human Resource Management Handbook Part II* (Greenwich, CT: JAI Press, 1997), pp. 197–218.
97. Colvin, "The Relationship between Employment Arbitration and Workplace Dispute Resolution Procedures."
98. Alexander J.S. Colvin, "The Dual Transformation of Workplace Dispute Resolution," *Industrial Relations* 42 (October 2003), pp. 712–35.
99. Joseph F. Gentile, "The Structure and Workings of Employer-Promulgated Grievance Procedures and Arbitration Agreements," in James L. Stern and Joyce M. Najita (eds.), *Labor Arbitration under Fire* (Ithaca, NY: ILR Press, 1997), pp. 136–61.
100. John L. Zalusky, "A Union View of Nonrepresented Employees' Grievance Systems," in James L. Stern and Joyce M. Najita (eds.), *Labor Arbitration under Fire* (Ithaca, NY: ILR Press, 1997), pp. 182–207.
101. Colvin, "Mandatory Arbitration and Inequality of Justice in Employment."
102. Richard A. Bales, "The Laissez-Faire Arbitration Market and the Need for a Uniform Federal Standard Governing Employment and Consumer Arbitration," *Kansas Law Review* 52 (2004), pp. 583–603; Martin H. Malin, "Due Process in Employment Arbitration: The State of the Law and the Need for Self-Regulation," *Employee Rights and Employment Policy Journal* 11 (2007), pp. 363–403; Jeffrey W. Stempel, "Mandating Minimal Quality in Mass Arbitration," *University of Cincinnati Law Review* 76 (Winter 2008), pp. 383–445.
103. Alexander J.S. Colvin, "Institutional Pressures, Human Resource Strategies, and the Rise of Nonunion Dispute Resolution Procedures," *Industrial and Labor Relations Review* 56 (April 2003), pp. 375–92; Colvin, "Grievance Procedures in Non-Union Firms."
104. Colvin, "Institutional Pressures, Human Resource Strategies, and the Rise of Nonunion Dispute Resolution Procedures," p. 377.
105. Tom Rankin, *New Forms of Work Organization: The Challenge for North American Unions* (Toronto: University of Toronto Press, 1990).

Part **Three**

Issues for the 21st Century

Part Two examined contemporary U.S. labor relations with an emphasis on the development of the New Deal industrial relations system and the operation of its four key processes—organizing, bargaining, dispute resolution, and contract administration. But intense competitive challenges have put U.S. labor relations in the 21st century under great pressure. The next two chapters explore the central challenges that now confront labor and management: the drive for increased workplace flexibility, employee empowerment, and labor–management partnerships (Chapter 10) combined with intense globalization and financialization (Chapter 11).

Chapter Ten

Flexibility, Empowerment, and Partnership

Advance Organizer

When successful, the processes described in the previous chapters result in a union contract. Typically these contracts are detailed and reinforce bureaucratic forms of work organization. Contrast that with what you've probably heard about today's workplace and business demands for achieving cost competitiveness through flexibility, employee empowerment, and labor–management partnerships. This chapter discusses how these pressures conflict with traditional U.S. labor relations practices and the controversies that result.

Learning Objectives

By the end of this chapter, you should be able to

1. **Identify** the importance of the structure of work for labor relations.
2. **Explain** the pressures for increased workplace flexibility, employee empowerment, and labor–management partnerships in the contemporary employment relationship, and strategies for implementation.
3. **Compare** the conflicts between workplace flexibility, employee empowerment, and labor–management partnerships on the one hand, and the traditional U.S. model of job control unionism on the other.
4. **Understand** the debates over new forms of participatory work: whether these are methods for empowering workers and enhancing competitiveness, or for making employees work harder for less.
5. **Understand** the debates over nonunion employee representation: whether this is a vehicle of legitimate employee voice or an attempt to prevent unionism.

Contents

Many of the central policies and practices of contemporary U.S. labor relations date back to earlier eras. The major provisions of labor law were enacted in 1935 and 1947. A pragmatic business unionism focus on improving wages and working conditions has been emphasized by U.S. unions since the early days of the American Federation of Labor in the late 1800s. Managerial insistence on retaining the right to manage with unchallenged authority to make business decisions was formalized in the 1940s. Multiyear contracts that are renegotiated with great formality only upon expiration began in the 1950s, and the importance of grievance arbitration was cemented during World War II in the early 1940s.

But consider the changes in the global economic system, business practices, labor force education levels, and technology that have occurred since these earlier eras. From the end of World War II up to the oil crisis in 1974, U.S. manufacturers dominated both the U.S. and world economies.[1] Monopoly profits were often captured by a handful of large firms in each industry. After the oil crisis, increased domestic and international competition ended this dominance and put downward pressure on profits, employment, and wages. The strong U.S. economic growth between the 1940s and 1970s was based on a stable system of mass manufacturing with narrowly defined, routine jobs in which economies of scale created falling labor costs and increases in productivity.[2] But in the 21st century, routine jobs can be shifted to low-cost countries. U.S. companies can no longer be competitive in the global marketplace using traditional mass manufacturing methods.

Rather, for U.S. companies to create a competitive advantage, they must now produce high-quality goods and services that respond to quickly changing consumer tastes.[3] At a minimum, this requires replacing the traditional and bureaucratic mass manufacturing methods with more flexible employment systems. Moreover, because the U.S. workforce is more highly educated than in previous generations and because technology is more sophisticated, many advocate not only for increased flexibility but also for greater levels of employee empowerment in workplace decision making.[4] Compared to hierarchical work systems, participatory systems are believed to better harness employee skills, create loyal and motivated employees, and produce higher-quality products. Lastly, competitive pressures have caused some to call for unions to be less adversarial and more receptive to forming labor–management partnerships. The push for flexibility, employee empowerment, and labor–management partnerships, however, clashes with longstanding roles, practices, and expectations in U.S. labor relations. This chapter explores the need for these changes, and why these changes are so difficult in 21st-century labor relations.

POSTWAR WORK ORGANIZATION, POSTWAR UNIONISM

Labor unions rarely determine how work is organized. But they must design strategies for representing workers that fit with how businesses organize work. Table 10.1 summarizes the development of the major trends in work organization—from early craft-based production systems, to mass manufacturing systems based on specialized division of labor, to flexible and participatory workplaces that require teamwork and employee involvement. This evolution provides an important foundation for understanding the development of traditional labor–management relationships, and contemporary pressures for change.

20th-Century Mass Production Methods

The dominant paradigm for how to structure work in much of the 20th century was **scientific management.** Expanding on the logic of the famous economist Adam Smith, who praised the efficiency benefits of using 18 distinct steps to make a single pin in 1776, Frederick Winslow Taylor and others developed scientific management (or "Taylorism") in the early 20th century to maximize efficiency through carefully studying work tasks and scientifically determining the one best way of completing a task.[5] Time and motion studies were used to reduce jobs into their most basic components, stopwatches were used to calculate the optimal time required for each task, and instruction cards listed each specific operation—sometimes to the fraction of a second (see Figure 10.1). This specialization of work serves efficiency by allowing workers to become proficient through repetition; standardization further promotes efficiency through the use of carefully determined processes and the ease of training unskilled workers in rote tasks. Taylor assumed that workers were motivated by pay, and once the time standards were established, differential piecework

TABLE 10.1
Work Organization Time Line

18th century	Industrial Revolution—the rise of factories, mills, and mines.
19th century	Dominance of skilled crafts in production.
1911	Frederick Winslow Taylor publishes *The Principles of Scientific Management;* scientific management (or Taylorism) comes to dominate 20th-century thinking.
1913	Henry Ford starts producing cars on an assembly line (Taylorism + assembly line = Fordism); skilled crafts are replaced by unskilled mass production workers.
1920s	The rise of welfare capitalism, including employee representation plans (company unions).
1935	Section 8(a)(2) of the National Labor Relations Act (NLRA) bans company-dominated employee representation plans.
1946	UAW strike at General Motors fails to win employee input into managerial decisions; management's right to manage is cemented.
1950s	Institutionalization of job control unionism—emphasis on stability, predictability, and seniority.
	Two Americans, W. Edwards Deming and Joseph Juran, launch the quality movement in Japan.
1972	General Motors Lordstown strike reflects the blue-collar blues and worker alienation; first-generation quality of working life (QWL) programs start to spread.
1980s	Total quality management (TQM) returns to the United States with increased efforts at using quality circles and other initiatives.
	Japanese auto manufacturers open U.S. plants using lean production techniques.
1981	Desktop computing era begins with the launch of the IBM personal computer.
1990	Production starts at Saturn based on extensive employee involvement in production and business decisions, highlighting a new model of high-performance work systems.
1992	The *Electromation* ruling finds some forms of labor–management committees to be illegally dominated employee representation plans under Section 8(a)(2) of the NLRA.
1993	The first hypertext browser is released, paving the way for the World Wide Web and the internet age.
	Reengineering the Corporation: A Manifesto for Business Revolution advocates an end to Taylorism.
1996	The TEAM Act to amend Section 8(a)(2) is vetoed by President Bill Clinton.
21st century	Emphasis on flexibility, pay for performance, employee involvement, and continuous change.

wage rates—perhaps to three decimal places—could encourage high production. Taylor saw this as a win–win situation: Productivity and profits would increase, employees would earn more, and labor unrest would disappear.

On the other hand, critics saw scientific management as degrading work through extreme specialization of jobs, competition between workers, speeding up of the work pace, and hostility toward labor unions.[6] Note that as scientifically trained managers determine each job's "one best way," Taylorism creates a divide between management and labor: Management determines job content and optimal job processes and does the planning; labor provides

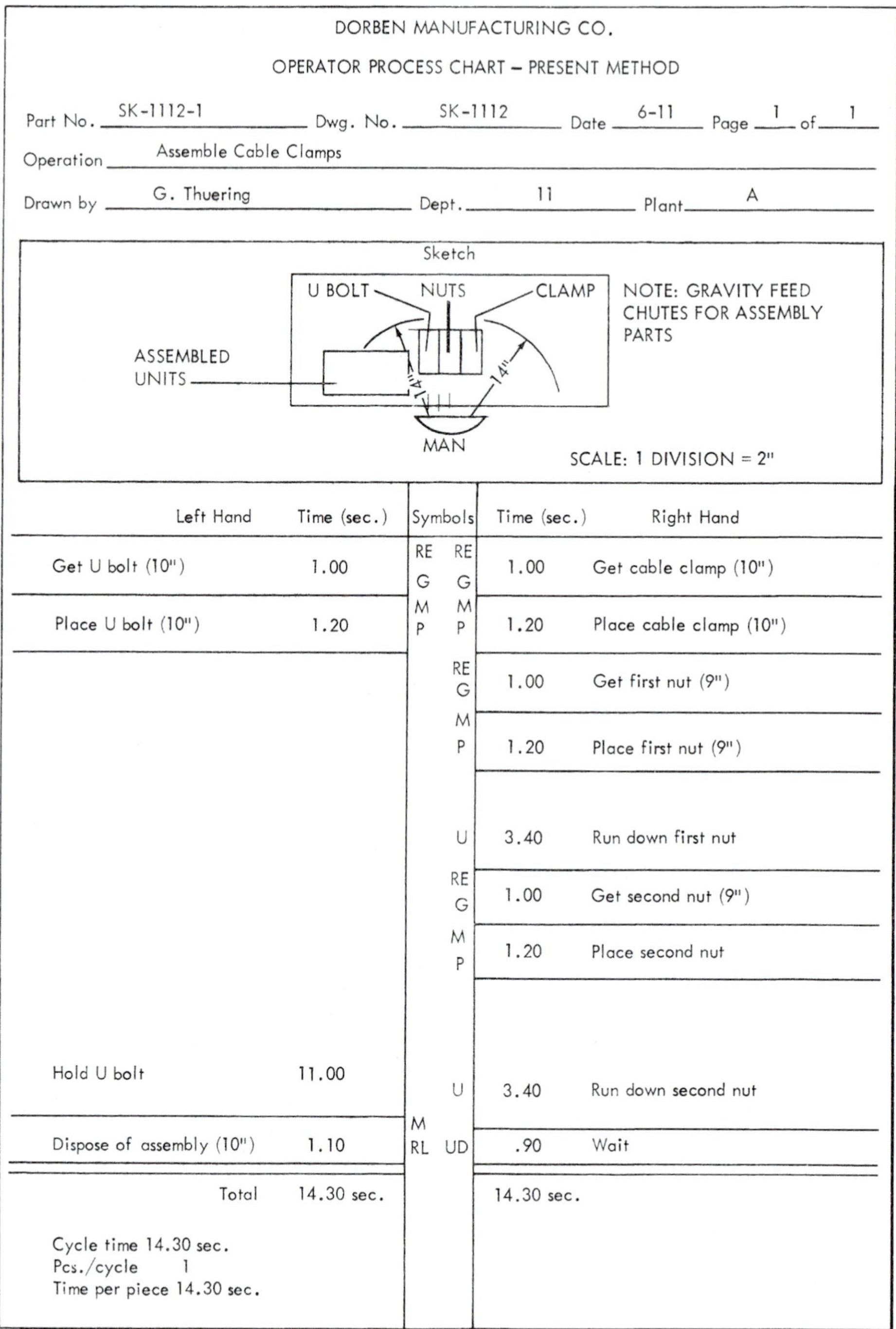

DORBEN MANUFACTURING CO.

OPERATOR PROCESS CHART – PRESENT METHOD

Part No. SK-1112-1 Dwg. No. SK-1112 Date 6-11 Page 1 of 1

Operation Assemble Cable Clamps

Drawn by G. Thuering Dept. 11 Plant A

Sketch

U BOLT
NUTS
CLAMP
NOTE: GRAVITY FEED CHUTES FOR ASSEMBLY PARTS
ASSEMBLED UNITS
14"
14"
MAN
SCALE: 1 DIVISION = 2"

Left Hand	Time (sec.)	Symbols		Time (sec.)	Right Hand
Get U bolt (10")	1.00	RE G	RE G	1.00	Get cable clamp (10")
Place U bolt (10")	1.20	M P	M P	1.20	Place cable clamp (10")
			RE G	1.00	Get first nut (9")
			M P	1.20	Place first nut (9")
			U	3.40	Run down first nut
			RE G	1.00	Get second nut (9")
			M P	1.20	Place second nut
Hold U bolt	11.00		U	3.40	Run down second nut
Dispose of assembly (10")	1.10	M RL	UD	.90	Wait
Total	14.30 sec.			14.30 sec.	

Cycle time 14.30 sec.
Pcs./cycle 1
Time per piece 14.30 sec.

FIGURE 10.1
Standardizing Workers' Actions
The left column specifies that the worker's left hand should spend one second getting a U bolt, 1.20 seconds putting this bolt in place, and 11 seconds holding it in place, while the right column provides similarly narrow directions for the worker's right hand to the tenth of a second.

Source: Benjamin W. Niebel, *Motion and Time Study,* 7th ed. p. 160 Copyright © 1982. Reprinted by permission of The McGraw-Hill Companies.

the muscle to implement management's directions but is not expected to think. To the craft unions of the AFL, the time study engineer with a stopwatch was therefore seen as an affront to the judgment, freedom, and dignity of skilled craft workers, and strikes against time studies and incentive pay plans resulted.[7]

In 1913 Henry Ford also broke jobs down into their basic components while adding another innovation—assembly line production. This method of mass manufacturing using very narrowly defined jobs combined with assembly lines became known as Fordism. But

FIGURE 10.2
"At last, a perfect soldier." And under scientific management for much of the 20th century, a perfect worker.

Taylorism is not limited to manufacturing or assembly lines—banks, credit card processing centers, and other service-oriented workplaces were traditionally organized on the basis of repetitive, specialized tasks. Time and motion studies can be applied to making beds in a hotel, and McDonald's hamburgers are a classic example of a standardized product.[8] The cartoon from the time of Frederick Winslow Taylor and Henry Ford shown in Figure 10.2 portrays the ideal early 20th-century army recruit—all muscle and no brains. Because of the dominance of Taylorism and Fordism, this also portrays management's vision of the ideal worker for much of the 20th century.

Job Control Unionism

Managers, not union leaders, determined this vision of the ideal worker who labored without thought in narrow job classifications for much of the 20th century; but unions had to design their representation strategies accordingly. Specifically, unions had to contend with two deeply ingrained managerial practices that descended from the principles of scientific management: (1) the insistence on preserving management rights by maintaining sole authority over traditional management functions such as hiring, firing, assigning work, determining job content, and deciding what to produce and how and where to make it, and (2) narrow job classifications with minimal employee decision making.[9] The pursuit of equity and voice in the postwar period was therefore necessarily limited to negotiating wages, benefits, and fair employment policies that fit into the Taylorist systems of work with minimal on-the-job thinking and narrow job classifications.

The resulting postwar pattern of traditional unionized practices and policies is called **job control unionism.**[10] In short, job control unionism seeks to protect workers against favoritism and other potential forms of managerial abuse by controlling the rewards and allocation of jobs using objective measures. Seniority is therefore embraced as the primary method for determining layoffs, promotions, and transfers. Similarly, subjectivity is removed from wage outcomes by closely linking wage rates to job classifications rather than to perceptions of individual performance.

Detailed work rules further control how work is performed and allocated. These work rules are the union response to the reserved rights (or residual rights) doctrine of management rights. Recall from Chapter 9 that the reserved rights doctrine means that all management rights not explicitly limited, restricted, or modified by the union contract are

FIGURE 10.3
A Traditional Seniority Ladder in a Truck Assembly Plant

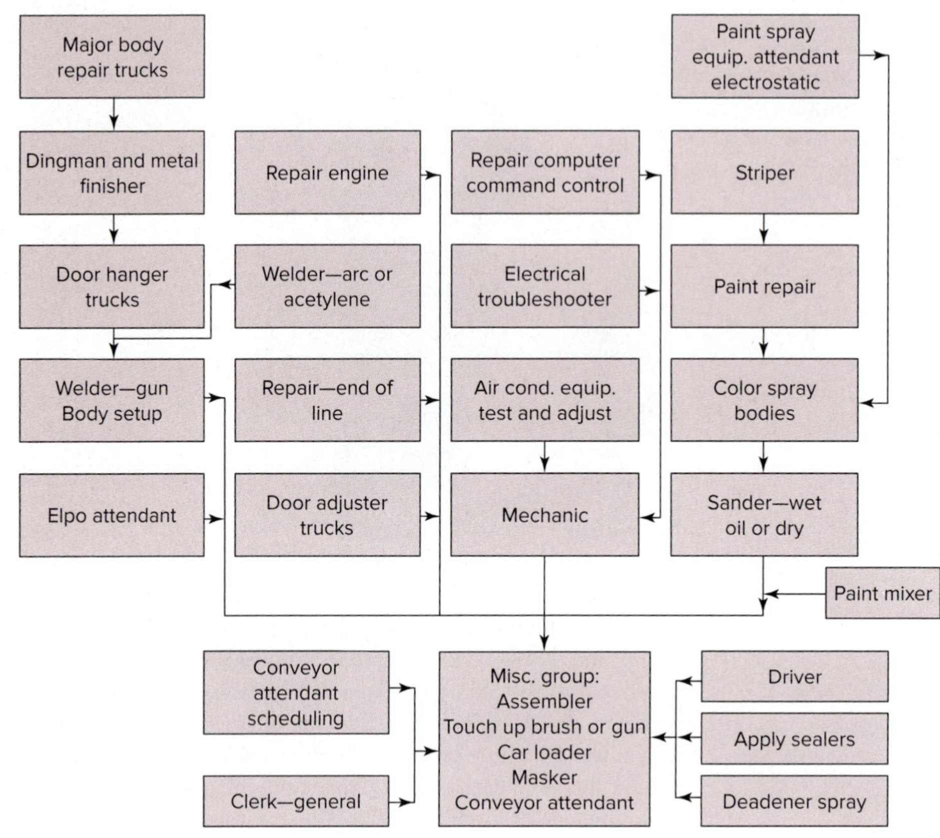

Note: Arrows denote bumping sequence during layoffs. For example, if the number of employees in the "major body repair trucks" classification is reduced, those with the least seniority move down to the "dingman and metal finisher" classification, and so forth. The miscellaneous group including assemblers is at the bottom of the seniority ladder.

reserved by management; management therefore has sole authority over all unmodified managerial issues.[11] As a result, unions have sought to explicitly limit, restrict, and modify managerial authority where this is perceived to serve workers' interests. Examples include requirements that discipline and discharge be based on just cause, restrictions on subcontracting work, limitations on work speed, and specifications of the job duties that must be done by union-represented workers. Detailed rules also specify how seniority systems operate; some auto industry contracts contain 50 pages or more of such rules. Complex flow charts sometimes delineate seniority ladders that employees can climb up and down through promotions or layoffs (see Figure 10.3).

The traditional U.S. union contract within job control unionism is a lengthy, detailed, legalistic document. Disputes over the contract's provisions are resolved through a formal grievance procedure (see Chapter 9). Over time, arbitration awards and past practices establish precedents and create a common law of the workplace that further reinforces the legalistic nature of job control unionism. This system of job control unionism became widespread in the postwar U.S. industrial relations system because it serves both management and union needs. It supports the mass manufacturing requirements for stable and predictable production while also fulfilling union leaders' needs for countering managerial authority without having to resort to wildcat strikes that could undermine their own leadership positions.[12] Efficiency and equity are served through the peaceful, quasilegal application of workplace rules and contracts that fulfill industrial justice; voice is provided through collective bargaining.[13]

Job control unionism, therefore, is more than just convenient: It embodies a strong sense of workplace justice through wages that are based on jobs rather than the possibility of unfair manipulation of piece rates, through promotions and layoffs based on seniority rather than the possibility of managerial favoritism, and through quasilegal interpretation of contractual rules rather than the possibility of arbitrary decisions.[14] Justice is bureaucratic, however, and worker influence over day-to-day work issues is not part of the bargain. Moreover, there is a certain amount of adversarialism built into this system—unions seek to check unilaterial managerial decision making, and managers push back as they try to maintain their control over the production process; clashes are inevitable at the bargaining table and in grievance meetings.[15]

THE CHANGING NATURE OF WORK

The Breakdown of the Mass Production Business Model

The bureaucratic control of scientific management and the complementary system of job control unionism are well suited to the mass production of standardized goods and services in a stable economy. Unstable economic markets in the 1970s, however, challenged the dominance of mass manufacturing methods because companies could no longer sell massive quantities of identical products and could not react quickly to changing consumer demands.[16] Moreover, simple, repetitive job tasks can cause boredom, alienation, and mental and physical fatigue. A focus on monetary motivation ignores intrinsic motivators such as satisfaction from achievement, interest in a task, and responsibility. These factors can cause absenteeism, turnover, shirking, and low-quality output. All these issues—both the macro-level economic shocks and the micro-level issues with employee satisfaction—caused a competitive crisis in U.S. business in the 1970s and launched efforts at changing forms of work organization, human resources practices, and more generally, business strategies (see Table 10.1).

In 1972 workers at the General Motors plant in Lordstown, Ohio, went on strike over the exhausting pace of work, confrontational methods of discipline, harassment, and a backlog of over 10,000 grievances.[17] This strike became symbolic of the blue-collar blues—worker dissatisfaction resulting from repetitive and exceptionally narrow (in other words, boring) jobs that leads to absenteeism, poor quality, and even sabotage. Concern with this growing issue of worker dissatisfaction led to experimentation with **quality of working life (QWL) programs** in the 1970s. These programs focused on improving the work environment—such as through improved ventilation—and the nature of employee–supervisor relations. Although there was some experimentation with team-based production, most QWL programs were simply added on top of the existing structure of scientific management and job control unionism.[18] The underlying principle was that if working conditions were made more humane, job satisfaction and product quality would increase; absenteeism and grievances—the blue-collar blues—would decrease.[19] In the 21st century similar ideas are embodied in employee assistance programs and family-friendly benefits. Because the first-generation QWL programs did not change the underlying structure of work organization, their success was limited.

Since the 1970s, competitive pressures on business have intensified. In fact, globalization and technology have resulted in what some have labeled market chaos and hypercompetition:

> Since any element in a company's value chain can be produced by an independent external party specializing in that activity, companies no longer compete just with other companies in their "industries." They must compete laterally with the best-in-world producer of that activity, wherever that producer may be. Everyone is competing with everyone else.... To deal with this, wholly new strategies—focusing on core

> competencies, strategic outsourcing, alliances, and highly disaggregated organizations—now link enterprises and nations in new ways. All center on developing, managing, and leveraging intellectual capabilities much more effectively.[20]

Strategies for corporate reform have therefore included continuous improvement and reengineering. Continuous process improvement is often associated with a Japanese management style (*kaizen*) and focuses on creating a corporate culture of constant change and small improvements. Total quality management (TQM) is an example of a continuous process improvement strategy in which statistical methods to measure defects guide efforts at constantly improving the quality of manufactured products and customer service.[21]

Whereas continuous process improvement emphasizes gradual change, reengineering targets large, one-time improvements in business processes:

> To reinvent their companies, American managers must throw out their old notions about how businesses should be organized and run. They must abandon the organizational and operational principles and procedures they are now using and create entirely new ones.... For two hundred years people have founded and built companies around Adam Smith's brilliant discovery that industrial work should be broken down into its simplest and most basic *tasks*. In the postindustrial business age we are now entering, corporations will be founded and built around the idea of reunifying those tasks into coherent business *processes*.[22]

Replacing narrowly focused order fulfillment, engineering, or compensation specialists with generalist customer service, product design, or human resource teams are examples of reunifying tasks into processes that contain value for the organization.

The 21st-Century Organization of Work

These strategies for reforming corporate structures, processes, and strategies have tremendous implications for human resources practices and the organization of work. Scientific management forms of work organization are being replaced with flatter, team-oriented work structures that serve flexible specialization and employee involvement rather than mass manufacturing. Narrowly defined jobs are being replaced by job rotation, cross-training, and job enrichment. Wage rates are becoming less tied to job classifications and more tied to individual and organizational performance. Intrinsic as well as extrinsic motivators are recognized as important determinants of employee behavior and performance. Once looked at as simply muscle, workers are now asked to provide input into process improvements, and perhaps granted authority to make decisions such as in self-directed work teams.

Business today therefore emphasizes the need for flexibility. More ambitiously, some organizations strive to implement high-performance work systems—coherent systems of mutually supporting human resource practices that combine flexibility with employee involvement in decision making. Others argue that traditional adversarial labor–management relationships prevent the cooperation needed to be competitive in a global economy, and therefore call for labor–management partnerships. All of these strategies—flexibility, employee empowerment, and labor–management partnerships—place significant pressure on the established labor relations practices embodied by job control unionism. In short, job control unionism is under fire in the 21st century (see Table 10.2).

FLEXIBILITY

Flexibility has multiple elements—from the ability to easily adjust employment and compensation levels to the ability to easily shift workers between tasks and alter production methods (see Table 10.3).[23] The traditional model of job control unionism, however, is

TABLE 10.2
Job Control Unionism under Fire

Elements of Job Control Unionism . . .	. . . and Why They Do Not Fit Today's Business Needs
Wages are tied to jobs, not individuals.	Runs counter to paying for performance—cannot reward individual merit, productivity, skills, or organizational performance.
Jobs are narrowly defined.	Difficult to deploy workers to different tasks. Problems with employee boredom and alienation. Workers are not responsible for monitoring their own quality. Teamwork is absent.
Seniority is a major determinant of promotions, layoffs, and transfers through seniority ladders.	Hard to promote the best performers or lay off the worst performers. Extensive bumping results in disruptive adjustment to changes in labor demand.
Extensive work rules.	Flexibility to move workers around, change job definitions, and adjust production methods is restricted. Layoffs and subcontracting might also be restricted.
Union contracts are detailed and legalistic. Grievance procedures provide a quasilegal forum for resolving disputes.	Difficult to break with past practices. Change is slow. Innovation is stifled.
No employee involvement in business and production decision making; these are *management* rights.	Opportunities for harnessing workers' ideas for productivity improvements are limited. Innovation is stifled.
Employee voice is limited to the grievance procedure and periodic collective bargaining.	Change is slow. Issues are solved only through formalized procedures. Problems accumulate until the next round of bargaining.
Labor–management relationships are frequently adversarial.	Adversarialism breeds conflict. Cooperation and partnership are needed to be competitive.

antithetical to these forms of flexibility that are so strongly emphasized by business in the 21st century. Standardized wages tied to jobs that are independent of both individual merit and company ability-to-pay prevent wage flexibility and pay-for-performance. Detailed systems of narrow job classifications are a barrier to functional flexibility because it is difficult to reassign workers to different tasks in response to shifts in market demand. Restrictive work rules similarly limit functional flexibility and may also restrict employment flexibility through limitations on the use of part-time or temporary workers, subcontracting, or layoffs. Seniority-based procedures make it difficult to transfer and promote workers on the basis of skills and merit. Extensive bumping rights make frequent changes in deploying labor cumbersome. This longstanding focus on seniority rather than skills also hampers training and other developmental opportunities. Detailed, lengthy, and legalistic union contracts that are renegotiated every few years inhibit procedural flexibility and stifle innovation. The system of grievance arbitration and its continued reliance on past precedents similarly make change and innovation difficult. The sharp divisions between labor that provides the brawn and management that provides the brains limit the benefits that business can reap from listening to its employees' ideas for process improvement.

So why don't unions simply move away from representing workers through job control unionism? As will be described, many are. By saving jobs, enhancing employee autonomy, and promoting improved work–family balance, for example, flexibility can be beneficial.

TABLE 10.3
Employment Relationship Flexibility

Goals	Examples	Employee Concerns
Employment Flexibility		
Change labor utilization through varying work hours or number of employees.	Part-time employment; temporary employment; seasonal employment; outsourcing.	Lack of sufficient hours to earn enough income to take care of basic needs and raise a family; uncertainty; periods of unemployment; stress.
Pay Flexibility		
Make compensation responsive to changes in competitive pressures and organizational performance.	Pay for performance; profit sharing; no wage indexation.	Risky. Compensation is uncertain and may decrease; potential for managerial abuse; organizational performance beyond individual or work group control; stress.
Functional Flexibility		
Easily shift workers into different jobs in response to changing customer demands and production needs.	Job enrichment; work teams; cross-training.	Potential for replacing high-wage, skilled employees with low-wage, unskilled employees; disguised old-fashioned work speed-up; stress.
Procedural Flexibility		
Change production methods, technology, and work organization.	Unilateral management authority to restructure the workplace.	Lack of a voice in the absence of unions or work councils; stress.

References: Muneto Ozaki (ed.), *Negotiating Flexibility: The Role of the Social Partners and the State* (Geneva: International Labour Office, 1999); Nick Wailes and Russell D. Lansbury, "Collective Bargaining and Flexibility: Australia," LEG/REL Working Paper (Geneva: International Labour Office, 1999).

But flexibility can also have a dark side (see the third column of Table 10.3). A hyperflexible culture can have deep psychological and social effects:

> "Who needs me?" is a question which suffers a radical challenge in modern capitalism. The system radiates indifference. It does so in terms of the outcomes of human striving, as in winner-take-all markets, where there is little connection between risk and reward. It radiates indifference in the organization of absence of trust, where there is no reason to be needed. And it does so through reengineering of institutions in which people are treated as disposable. Such practices obviously and brutally diminish the sense of mattering as a person, of being necessary to others.[24]

Downsizing, restructuring, asset sales, and the use of contingent employees not only bring stress to individual workers but also increase economic and social inequality. Excessive flexibility risks breaking the longstanding social compact or psychological contract in which employees have come to expect that their hard work and loyalty should be rewarded by economic security (see the "Ethics in Action" feature at the end of this chapter).[25] Weakening union-won protections such as seniority rights can increase opportunities for managerial abuse. Contingent forms of compensation make it difficult for individuals to manage their household budgets.

It is these types of risks that job control unionism was designed to lessen. So while some union leaders are not opposed to moving away from job control unionism, they have reservations about giving away what they see as their hard-won gains on terms that are unfavorable to workers. The greatest resistance is probably in the area of employment flexibility. For the other dimensions of flexibility, there are more examples where labor and management have experimented with moving beyond traditional job control unionism. The UAW contracts with Ford, General Motors, and Chrysler now include a profit-sharing plan in which hourly workers can receive an annual profit-sharing bonus based on overall company profitability.[26] Skill-based pay has been successfully introduced in a variety of unionized settings.[27] There are significant examples of quality circles, self-managed work teams, labor representatives on corporate boards of directors, and other initiatives to involve workers in business decision making in unionized establishments.[28] But labor-endorsed models of work organization move beyond a simple focus on flexibility by requiring employee involvement in decision making, and treating unions as an equal partner to management (see the accompanying "Labor Relations Application" box). As described in the next two sections, these changes to make organizations more productive and more democratic are not easy to achieve, and they are criticized by some for weakening labor unions.

Online Exploration Exercise: The International Association of Machinists (IAM) takes a proactive approach to support high-performance work organizations (HPWO). Review their materials for local union leaders at *www.goiam.org/departments/headquarters/hpwo-partnerships*. Does this seem like a good approach? What elements might a business leader object to? Why?

EMPLOYEE EMPOWERMENT

In the 1940s, two staff members of the United Steelworkers union, Clinton Golden and Harold Ruttenberg, developed principles for getting employees more involved in their work.[29] The basic idea is simple: Workers perform their job tasks over and over and therefore often have good ideas for improving productivity, increasing quality, and lowering costs. Moreover, employees' discretion in their work might increase job satisfaction and make them better employees. Golden also predicted—accurately and coming from a union leader, ironically—that management's insistence on retaining the right to manage and the accompanying scientific management distinction between management's thinking and labor's action "might well restrict the flexibility so necessary to efficient operation."[30] Although other countries such as Germany and Japan have longer traditions of involving employees in decision making (see Chapter 12), U.S. management categorically rejected this thinking for much of the 20th century.

As noted earlier, the competitive crisis in the 1970s challenged this wisdom of treating workers as unthinking cogs in a machine. But the resulting quality of working life initiatives brought limited changes because they left the organization of work unchanged. Intensified competitive pressures in the 1980s caused a redoubling of corporate efforts at restructuring the workplace for a competitive edge. Since then, unions and companies have experimented with various forms of employee involvement. The extent to which employees are actively involved in decision making varies widely. In gainsharing programs such as a Scanlon plan or a Rucker plan, workers make suggestions for process improvement, and a portion of the gains (reduced labor and nonlabor costs) are shared with the workers through an explicit formula. **Quality circles** provide a forum for workers to make suggestions about how to improve productivity and quality through regular group meetings with supervisors. Quality circles are a frequent component of continuous improvement programs such as total quality management. Other types of joint labor–management committees might be formed to address ad hoc issues or establishmentwide issues such as increasing trust between labor and management. These initiatives, however, do not necessarily change the underlying scientific management system of work organization.

Labor Relations Application The AFL–CIO's Five Principles for a New Model of Work Organization

- First, the model begins by rejecting the traditional dichotomy between thinking and doing, conception and execution.
- Second, in the new model, jobs are redesigned to include a greater variety of skills and tasks and, more importantly, greater responsibility for the ultimate output of the organization.
- Third, this new model of work organization substitutes for the traditional, multilayered hierarchy a flatter management structure.
- Fourth, the new model goes beyond the workplace level to insist that workers, through their unions, are entitled to a decision-making role at all levels of the enterprise.
- Fifth and finally, the new model of work organization calls for the rewards realized from transforming the work organization to be distributed on equitable terms agreed upon through negotiations between labor and management.

Source: AFL–CIO Committee on the Evolution of Work, *The New American Workplace: A Labor Perspective* (Washington, DC: American Federation of Labor–Congress of Industrial Organizations, 1994), pp. 8–9. The full document was reprinted in Bruce Nissen (ed.), *Unions and Workplace Reorganization* (Detroit: Wayne State University Press, 1997).

High-Performance Work Systems

The most extensive efforts to restructure the workplace involve not only increasing employee involvement in decision making but also changing how work is organized. In other words, these efforts try to create high-performance work systems—systems of mutually supporting human resources practices that combine flexibility with employee involvement in decision making. Two forms of team-oriented, high-performance work systems have received the greatest attention in U.S. labor relations. First, **lean production** is generally regarded as the Japanese approach to mass manufacturing—and because the traditional U.S. assembly-line system is referred to as "Fordism," lean production is sometimes referred to as "Toyotism" or the "Toyota production system." Lean production emphasizes just-in-time inventories, the smooth flow of materials, teamwork, and off-line quality circles to deliver continuous process improvement. Second, the sociotechnical systems approach is structured around **self-directed work teams**—autonomous groups of employees who are responsible for a set of job tasks as well as routine maintenance tasks. In lean production, work teams have little authority and are managed by a supervisor; self-directed work teams in a sociotechnical system are empowered to manage their internal affairs without a supervisor, and the teams can make their own decisions regarding job pacing, task assignment, and quality control.

The effects of high-performance work systems are the focus of many academic debates. Surveys reveal that various elements of high-performance work systems—quality circles, job rotation, teams, total quality management, and the like—are becoming more prevalent.[31] But are they good for firms? Or for workers? Systems or bundles of human resources practices (but perhaps not individual practices) have been found to reduce employee turnover and increase productivity.[32] But such findings are not universal and also do not necessarily translate into improved corporate profitability.[33] Adopting high-performance work practices does not necessarily yield higher wages or reduced layoffs.[34] Moderate adoption of such practices appears to increase employee satisfaction, esteem, and commitment, but extensive adoption can reduce employee well-being because of higher levels of stress.[35] When implementing high-performance work systems, the presence of a union can lessen the negative effects on worker well-being.[36] Research has also linked the use of quality circles, work teams, and job rotation to higher levels of cumulative trauma disorders such as carpal tunnel injuries.[37] As such, some research supports the promise of high-performance work systems, but other research reveals possible pitfalls and therefore questions whether these promises are overstated.[38] These debates provide the backdrop for a more detailed consideration of the labor relations issues stemming from lean production and self-directed work teams.

Labor Relations Debates over Lean Production

Lean production has been popularized in the United States through the spread of total quality management (TQM) and the opening of Japanese auto plants in the United States—Honda in Ohio, Nissan in Tennessee, Subaru in Indiana, Toyota in Kentucky, and a now-defunct joint General Motors–Toyota venture in California (NUMMI). Lean production is associated with TQM because workers participate in quality circles to make suggestions for continuous improvement (*kaizen*). The American version of lean production, however, is often quite centralized with management still tightly in control of decision making.[39] As such this model is often not well received by the U.S. labor movement, which questions how much workers are involved or empowered in lean production systems. In fact, critics have labeled lean production as "management by stress"; this label comes from lean production's constant pressure to reduce inefficiencies such as idle time and from the peer pressure created by teams that must cover for absent workers:

> Work standards are constantly *kaizened* upward so that team members work 57 out of 60 seconds; buffers are eliminated so that workers cannot pace themselves and create a break; relief personnel are reduced or eliminated and absent workers are not replaced; responsibility for handling these disruptions is forced downward; the supervisor is therefore pressured to fill out more papers and take on more tasks; he protects himself by holding out the team leader for production breakdowns, which means team members cannot get bathroom relief when they need it. The result that management desires is for workers to pressure each other to reduce absenteeism and bathroom breaks.[40]

This view clashes sharply with supporters of lean production, who see team members as empowered to make decisions over their work and who highlight the quality and productivity advantages—especially the quality and labor hour differences between the U.S. and Japanese auto manufacturers.[41] There is no easy way to resolve these conflicting perspectives, but they reveal why labor unions are hesistant to embrace lean production methods as the solution to competitive pressures.

Labor Relations Debates over Self-Directed Work Teams

Turning to the sociotechnical systems approach, the most widely discussed U.S. example of the extensive use of self-directed work teams is the Spring Hill, Tennessee, plant of the former Saturn subsidiary of General Motors.[42] Saturn developed in the mid-1980s out of a joint labor–management study of worldwide auto manufacturing practices that resulted in a new partnership embracing team-based production and comanaged decision making by Saturn and the UAW (see Table 10.4). A series of formal joint labor–management committees, called decision rings, were empowered with decision-making authority over extensive issues. The UAW was further recognized as a legitimate stakeholder and therefore participated in business decisions about technology, supplier selection, pricing, business planning, training, business systems development, budgeting, quality systems, productivity improvement, job design, new product development, recruitment and hiring, maintenance, and engineering. In terms of production, roughly 600 self-directed work teams of 6–15 employees were responsible for their parts of the production process. These teams were further empowered to make decisions regarding work pace, planning and scheduling, vacation approvals, and training and were responsible for safety and health, inventory, quality and scrap control, repair, maintenance, and other issues.

TABLE 10.4
The (Former) Structure of Work at Saturn

Work unit member: An individual Saturn employee.

Work unit: An integrated team of 6–15 work unit members. The work unit was self-directed with the authority to, *inter alia,* assign jobs, approve vacations, undertake scrap control and supply acquisition, keep records, handle absenteeism, select new members, and elect its own leader. There were approximately 600 teams at Saturn.

Work unit module: A grouping of work units that were interrelated by geography, product, process, or technology that had two (jointly selected) advisers (one from the represented [i.e., union] workforce, one not). Each work unit module had a weekly decision ring consisting of the work unit module advisers and work unit leaders.

Business unit: An integration of work unit modules according to the business area (body systems, powertrain, or vehicle systems) with various common advisers. Each business unit had a weekly decision ring consisting of the work unit module advisers and representatives of Saturn and the union.

Manufacturing action council (MAC): A weekly decision ring of business unit advisers and representatives of Saturn and the union. This council focused primarily on internal issues and decisions (e.g., manufacturing problems).

Strategic action council (SAC): A weekly decision ring of representatives of Saturn and the union. This was the top executive management of Saturn that was responsible for long-range objectives and planning and focused primarily on external issues (e.g., pricing, advertising, dealers).

Just as the structure of work at Saturn differed from the traditional scientific management workplace, so too were labor relations at Saturn different from the traditional model of job control unionism. Most visibly, the union contract at Saturn had considerably fewer pages than usual union contracts in the United States. Teams and decision rings were empowered to make numerous decisions, so detailed work rules and a management rights clause were not necessary. But because the decision-making processes were negotiated between the UAW and Saturn, supporters believed that protections were built into the structure and the union could ensure that employees received support and due process. In particular, formal grievances were allowed, and during contract renegotiations the union could strike.

Extensive employee empowerment as well as union comanagement of business operations presented numerous challenges for the operation of the local union.[43] To match the participatory nature of employee involvement in workplace decision making, the local union created participatory structures to promote employee involvement in union decision making. These structures included town hall meetings, rap sessions, and a twice-a-month congress meetings involving 450 union leaders and were supplemented by an extensive annual membership survey. Nevertheless, conflicts persisted between the union's dual functions of comanagement and representation—that is, between being a strategic business partner and an advocate for the workers. First, note that "while union leaders need to add value to the firm through their roles in the governance or management process, if this is all they do, they are undifferentiated from other competent managers."[44] Second, union leaders must be careful that their efforts at adding value do not come at the expense of representing individual employees.[45]

To put this more bluntly, some in the labor movement see this form of strategic business partnership as selling out. In this view, when unions are concerned with business decisions, they are no longer looking out for employee interests to the fullest extent possible: "At Saturn, the union has made meeting the needs of the business *its* business. This means that there are two parties looking after management's interests (or one and a half), and only half a party looking after the [union] members' interests."[46] Moreover, it is argued that this form of unionism fails to develop a power base independent of the company and is therefore too weak to challenge management on a sustained basis.[47] What some see as a slimmer union contract that promotes flexibility and increased employee discretion, others see as a lack of well-defined standards that can be exploited by managers. In fact, the Saturn experiment failed—in 2003 the Spring Hill workers voted to return to the UAW master contract with General Motors, and in 2010 General Motors discontinued the Saturn brand. The reasons for this failure are complex and involve business as well as labor issues, but a resistance to change from the traditional model among UAW leaders is part of the story.[48] As with the debates over lean production, there are no easy answers to questions about whether the system of union representation at Saturn represented an advance or retreat from the traditional system of job control unionism; but these questions are vital for U.S. labor relations in the 21st century.

Although Saturn was a particularly extensive example of employee empowerment, other examples can be found in many industries and locations. A municipality in Washington reorganized its maintenance department into four self-directed work teams that are complemented by a joint labor–management group for problem solving.[49] Xerox completely redesigned its manufacturing methods around autonomous work teams and business area work groups that incorporated both employee and union involvement in decision making.[50] Some nurses are covered by contractual provision allowing them to temporarily close units to new patient admissions if they are understaffed and unable to handle additional patients. Within a framework negotiated through collective bargaining—that therefore gave nurses certain rights and protections—individual employees were empowered to make business decisions. This is a limited example of employee empowerment because it is confined to a single issue, but it illustrates the possibilities of moving away from a narrow model of job control unionism. These examples reinforce the need for unions to continue challenging the parts of systems of work organization that workers view as exploitative while strengthening the aspects that are empowering.

LABOR–MANAGEMENT PARTNERSHIPS

In responding to competitive pressures, managers in unionized businesses can try to reduce labor costs, achieve greater flexibility, and redesign the work to empower employees by using **escape, force, or foster change strategies.**[51] Escape here means escaping from the company's bargaining obligation by relocating operations to a nonunion site—perhaps in another country—or by subcontracting work or decertifying the union. Engaging in surface bargaining to prompt a strike, using permanent strike replacements to replace the striking union members, and winning a decertification election are escape strategies—albeit ones that violate U.S. labor law and that might be risky and costly for other reasons.[52] In a unionized situation, forcing change means pressuring the union and employees to accept changes—often wage and work rule concessions that reduce labor costs and provide greater flexibility—through hard bargaining. This strategy might require taking a strike to convince the employees to accept concessions, but this is not a strike to break a union as in the escape strategy.

Fostering Improved Labor–Management Relationships

The escape and force strategies reinforce the adversarialism that has traditionally characterized labor–management relationships. In contrast, the fostering change strategy seeks to create a more cooperative labor–management relationship. A fostering change strategy might involve the bargaining process, and result in a set of trade-offs in which wage and work rule concessions are granted in return for gains for workers.[53] For example, job security provisions such as no layoff guarantees have been won by unions in return for agreeing to wage restraints (or cuts), reductions in job classifications, or significant weakening of existing work rules in many industries. Some of these bargains even put a labor representative on a corporation's board of directors, though this is often short-lived.

But a successful fostering change strategy typically involves much more than negotiating changes at the bargaining table, and more than creating quality circles or self-directed work teams. In the terminology of Chapter 7, a fostering change strategy requires not only distributive and integrative bargaining to change the specific terms and conditions of employment but also attitudinal structuring to shape the attitudinal climate of the labor–management relationship. In fact, an examination of labor relations in the airline industry indicates that to improve organizational performance, improving the quality of labor–management relationships is more important than changing structural factors such as reducing wages or adding labor representatives to a company's board of directors.[54] A key element of the fostering change strategy therefore focuses on developing new labor–management partnerships based on recognition of both labor and management goals and the opportunities for mutual gain.

Labor–Management Partnerships in Practice

A **labor–management partnership** is a formal initiative in which workers and union leaders participate in organizational decision making beyond the daily work-related decisions of employee empowerment and beyond the usual collective bargaining subjects.[55] As an example from the public sector, in 2009 President Obama mandated labor-management forums for federal government agencies and created the National Council on Federal Labor-Management Relations to support partnership efforts (*www.lmrcouncil.gov*). Research on an earlier federal sector partnership initiative indicates that they were successful in creating a better labor–management climate, reducing disputes, and improving targeted performance outcomes such as customer service.[56] Indeed, at various levels of the public sector, labor-management collaboration has found efficiencies, improved or maintained customer service in the face budgetary challenges, reduced health-care costs, improved training, and proactively addressed major policy shifts such as hospital operational changes brought on by the Affordable Care Act.[57] In the private sector, in addition to the now-defunct Saturn partnership, Ford and motorcycle manufacturer Harley-Davidson are often-cited examples of successful labor–management partnerships in which workers and union leaders are involved in business decision making.[58]

The most ambitious labor–management partnership is the Kaiser Permanente Labor–Management Partnership, which covers over 80,000 health care employees in eight states represented by over 30 different local unions from 10 national unions. This partnership was formed in the 1990s at the suggestion of some unions at Kaiser Permanente as an alternative to escalating the conflicts with Kaiser Permanente that had resulted from hard bargaining, strikes, and layoffs as the health care giant sought to reduce its labor costs. The partnership was formalized by the negotiation of a labor–management partnership agreement that specified the goals and structure of the partnership. The partnership has evolved into a multilevel structure with a high-level committee of company and union senior leaders at the top, business unit steering committees in the middle, and work unit teams at the lowest level. In this way, labor and management partner to tackle a wide range of issues, and employees at all organization levels can participate. The Kaiser Permanente labor–management partnership has successfully changed the nature of labor–management relationships—as witnessed by the successful adoption of interest-based bargaining in contract negotiations—while improving employee job satisfaction, patient access to health care, and Kaiser Permanente's cost structure.[59] These gains have not been easy to achieve; building and sustaining this partnership requires a significant amount of work, extensive training, and a deep commitment from business and union leaders, and the partnership continually faces significant challenges (such as strained resources and distributive conflicts). But it nevertheless stands out "as a beacon in American labor relations" for businesses and labor unions who are seeking improved relationships for mutual gain.[60]

The logo of the Kaiser Permanente labor–management partnership emphasizing the power of labor–management partnerships

(L+M)P ©

The Power of Partnership

Online Exploration Exercise: Explore the Kaiser Permanente labor–management partnership site at *www.lmpartnership.org*. Is there anything surprising about this site? Now find the contracts. How do the contracts differ from traditional union contracts? What other supports (skills, practices, training, and the like) are used to support this partnership arrangement?

Challenges for Unions

Labor–management partnerships bring considerable challenges for unions.[61] To be successful, union leaders need to develop new skills to effectively guide partnership programs and make wise business decisions. Under partnership arrangements, union leaders must continue to fulfill their traditional roles (like communicating with members, increasing rank-and-file participation in union affairs, and processing grievances) but must also find time to take on new roles (such as leading decision-making teams). And perhaps the most fundamental challenge for labor unions is figuring out how to be effective business partners without excessively weakening their fundamental purpose of representing worker interests. In fact, within the labor movement and academic research circles there are ongoing debates about whether labor–management partnerships benefit or harm labor unions. The evidence indicates that partnerships can be good for unions, but they must be strongly perceived by workers as able to represent their interests and deliver tangible benefits.[62]

Thus, although it is common for business leaders to advocate "labor–management cooperation," union leaders reject the "cooperation" label in favor of "involvement," "participation," or "partnership." To labor leaders this is more than semantics. When managers emphasize cooperation, unions often interpret this as a push for unions and workers to quietly go along with management-driven initiatives. In effect, cooperation is seen by labor leaders as a corporate strategy to weaken unions. As such, to the extent that it requires abandoning its advocacy role, unions are opposed to cooperation. Rather, unions want substantive changes in work organization and decision-making authority. Instead of cooperation, labor is looking for worker empowerment through involvement and for union empowerment through true partnerships.

EMPLOYEE REPRESENTATION: ARE UNIONS REQUIRED?

Many corporate strategies to improve competitiveness and quality explicitly include some form of employee voice. An ongoing debate is whether the presence of a labor union increases the effectiveness of these voice mechanisms. Some research suggests workers participate more freely in these initiatives when a union is present to provide protections such as job security or just cause discipline and discharge provisions, and thus employee involvement efforts are more successful when a union is present.[63] This is an interesting and important question, but there is no well-accepted consensus on the extent to which unions increase the effectiveness of high-performance work practices.

Employer-Dominated Nonunion Committees

There is also a deeper question of whether nonunion voice mechanisms truly benefit workers. Consider the following scenario from a nonunion workplace:

> An employer wants to try to accommodate working parents by allowing more flexible scheduling. However, the employer does not know which employees want a more flexible schedule or how to make a series of flexible schedules fit the organization's daily work requirements. A committee of employees and managers is formed and charged to discuss the matter with coworkers and develop a new scheduling plan. The committee eventually produces a plan that the employer considers and implements with some modifications.[64]

While this type of employee representation through nonunion committees might seem like a win-win situation for employers and employees, it can potentially be used as a management weapon for suppressing unionization and true employee voice. In some situations, then, nonunion committees are prohibited by U.S. labor law (see "Labor Law Discussion Case 8" at the end of this chapter). In the example just described, note that although the committee did not engage in formal bargaining, it acted as a union by representing other employees (the committee members were not simply expressing individual opinions but were also speaking for their coworkers) in dealing with management over terms and conditions of employment. But unlike a union, management unilaterally determined the committee's structure, the issues covered, the extent of the plan's authority, and its continued existence. Such a committee has the possibility of being manipulated by managers so that employees think they are receiving the benefits of a union, but it is really a sham union (a "company union") because management is firmly in control. For example, managers might appoint loyal employees to the committee, limit the agenda to noncontroversial issues, and shut down the committee if the employer's authority is challenged. To prevent workers from thinking they need a union, managers might mollify the workers by occasionally giving a committee or representation plan a victory without truly granting the employees any power. If there is an organizing drive, management might portray this as a choice between an adversarial outside union and a cooperative committee (see "Labor Law Discussion Case 9" at the end of this chapter).

This manipulation of nonunion employee representation plans to prevent unionization is what Senator Wagner witnessed in the early 1930s (recall Chapter 4). And thus Section 8(a)(2) of the National Labor Relations Act (NLRA) prohibits employer domination of committees and representation plans that deal with employers over terms and conditions of employment. This was a controversial issue in the 1990s. In 1989 Electromation, a small manufacturing company, established several committees with a handful of employees and two managers to discuss working conditions and policies. These committees were formed to better understand the employees' concerns and to improve the company's policies where feasible; there was no evidence that these committees were established because of a union organizing drive. However, in its 1992 ***Electromation*** decision, the National Labor Relations Board (NLRB) ruled that these committees were illegally dominated labor organizations because they dealt with management over terms and conditions of employment, but management controlled their structure (such as how many employees would serve and how they would be selected), the issues, and their continued existence.[65] In other words, labor law can be viewed as a truth-in-advertising requirement that seeks to prevent employee representation plans that look like unions but really are not. So by appearing to be legitimate alternatives to a union when they really are not, committees or nonunion representation plans like the ones at Electromation are illegal.

The *Electromation* case caused an uproar in the business community because it seemed that labor law was preventing businesses from creating participatory structures to engage their employees, improve job satisfaction, and enhance competitiveness. Thus the Teamwork for Employees and Managers (TEAM) act was introduced in Congress in 1995 to modify Section 8(a)(2) to explicitly exclude labor–management committees that do not seek to negotiate collective bargaining agreements. The TEAM act was passed by Congress but vetoed by President Clinton in 1996, and it subsequently faded as an important legislative concern for business.

Legal versus Illegal Committees and Representation Plans

A closer look at the distinctions between legal and illegal employee involvement and representation plans helps illustrate why the TEAM act is no longer a major business concern. First, remember that one concern of labor law is the illusion of a true bilateral, give-and-take relationship between labor and management. Thus, plans that are obviously one-way are legal. For example, brainstorming sessions in which employees provide ideas to management or information-sharing sessions in which employers share information with employees are legal.[66] These situations offer no give-and-take; in the legal language of Section 2(5) of the NLRA, there is no "dealing with" in these situations. Second, recall that the NLRA focuses on concerted—that is, group—activity. Employee involvement plans in which employees speak for themselves as individuals, not as representatives of their coworkers, do not violate U.S. labor law.[67] Third, the NLRA also focuses on wages, hours, and terms and conditions of employment. Nonunion plans that are primarily concerned with business issues such as quality and productivity are therefore outside the domain of the NLRA and are legal.[68] Lastly, Section 8(a)(2) bans management domination, not involvement. Plans in which employees have some control over structure and function are acceptable.[69] Therefore, because employers can engage employees as individuals (rather than as representatives of coworkers) and can deal with business issues (rather than terms and conditions of employment) in any way they see fit, their concerns with the *Electromation* controversy are not nearly as prominent as they were in the 1990s. On a more

Employee Empowerment Isn't Always Empowering Because of Managerial Dominance

Source: TeddGoff.com. Copyright © Ted Goff. All rights reserved. Used with permission.

"Before we start this round of wide-open brainstorming, I'd just like to remind you that all ideas that are not mine must be rejected."

pragmatic level, the risk of facing an 8(a)(2) unfair labor practice charge is low because not many complaints are lodged, especially in the absence of an organizing drive, and the only penalty for violating 8(a)(2) is abandonment of the representation plan.[70]

Labor advocates, however, continue to believe that only freely selected and independent employee representatives—that is, labor unions—have the true power and legitimacy to make collective voice meaningful.[71] The NLRA does not go quite this far, but it does prohibit false empowerment. If a company wants to engage its employees collectively over wages and working conditions in the absence of a union, it should make sure employees have sufficient power in the process to shape the structure of participation, the agenda, and the like. Or a company can go all the way and give employees the final decision-making authority, as in the case of self-directed work teams or some grievance committees.[72]

Nonunion Application: What Happens in Practice?

Nonunion employee representation plans can be found in many forms in many countries.[73] In fact, nonunion employee representation plans are not illegal under the Railway Labor Act or in Canada, despite the strong similarities of these laws to the NLRA framework in other key respects. Under the Railway Labor Act, Delta Airlines, for example, has a nonunion employee representation plan for its flight attendants.[74] At Imperial Oil in Canada—Canada's premier oil and gas company that is owned by ExxonMobil—a system of joint industrial councils has been in operation since 1919. The joint industrial councils have equal numbers of management and employee representatives, and the employee representatives are elected every two years. Local councils meet monthly to discuss local workplace issues; local councils also send delegates to a district-level joint industrial council that discusses issues affecting multiple work sites. An extensive case study of these joint industrial councils found that they are neither manipulative management schemes to prevent unionization nor perfect participatory vehicles to create labor–management harmony.[75] The councils are clearly weaker than unions: Management ensures that each item is treated individually and evaluated against the company's business needs, some employees fear reprisal for speaking out, and the higher-level corporate office ultimately makes important decisions unilaterally. Moreover, the councils have helped management prevent unionization by providing information about employee dissatisfaction and by socializing workers to focus their voice into the councils rather than a union. At the same time, employees have a voice in decision making that is not completely powerless. The joint industrial councils receive more information than many unions, the district councils let workers from multiple work sites share information and work together, and the threat of unionization provides an incentive for management to ensure that the workers see tangible gains from the councils. Interestingly, in some respects the workers have a greater voice than if they were unionized because of the broad issues that are tackled by the joint industrial councils—issues that are typically considered management rights and therefore not relinquished in collective bargaining.

There are therefore three major views of nonunion employee representation—good, better than nothing, and bad. Only from the last perspectives are unions absolutely necessary for nonunion voice to be beneficial for employees. Disputes over these views split the field of human resources and industrial relations in the 1930s and are again dividing the field in the 21st century.[76] There are no easy answers here. But returning to the framework presented in Part One of this book, the avenue to understanding these debates is twofold: (1) recognizing the divisions as competing visions for the delivery of efficiency, equity, and voice, and (2) recognizing that the roots of these competing visions lie in different beliefs over the nature of the employment relationship as captured by the human resource management and pluralist industrial relations schools of thought.

OVERCOMING RESISTANCE TO CHANGE

An organization that wants to increase its flexibility, deepen its level of employee empowerment, or build a labor–management partnership faces the tough task of implementing and executing a new workplace strategy. This task is challenging in any organization, and many of the issues are similar in both unionized and nonunion situations—communicating change, building competencies, establishing supportive policies and cultures, and providing incentives and leadership (see the accompanying "HR Strategy" box).[77] But certain aspects of unionized employment relationships make change efforts different—not *always* better or worse, easier or more difficult, but definitely different. In particular, as emphasized in Part Two, when employees are represented by a certified union, management has an obligation to bargain over wages, hours, and terms and conditions of employment. Recall further that effects bargaining requires companies to negotiate the effects of many managerial actions even if the actions themselves are business rather than employment issues that do not require bargaining. An organization therefore cannot unilaterally impose whatever changes it wants in a unionized setting.[78] Additionally, the presence of a union introduces another institution into the change process. Relative to a nonunion setting, the presence of a union can either add a layer of resistance to change or provide opportunities for improving the quality of change.[79]

This chapter has described a number of reasons why union leaders and employees might resist changing from traditional ways of representing employees. Not only might increased flexibility or stress-inducing empowerment make workers worse off; efforts to increase flexibility, employee involvement, and cooperation might also result in co-optation—these changes might intentionally or unintentionally reduce the union to an irrelevant and powerless outsider.[80] The initial union reaction to proposed changes is therefore likely to be resistance. How can managers overcome this resistance to change?

Common strategies for overcoming resistance to change are described in Table 10.5. The first three are consistent with the forcing change approach described in this chapter. In short, labor union resistance to change is overcome by superior bargaining power and the threat of layoffs, bankruptcies, or other adverse consequences. In contrast, a fostering change approach requires that managers take the necessary steps to ensure that the union is a positive force rather than an additional source of resistance. This can be pursued through a combination of the last three strategies in Table 10.5. In this way, unions should be given full information, be involved in training, and participate in designing and implementing changes. In other words, unions should be recognized as legitimate full partners by being fully incorporated into the decision-making process, and not relegated to junior partners by marginalizing their participation and influence—"if the union is a junior partner, it will generally become a high-profile partner in blame and silent partner in success."[81] Also, unions should be allowed to participate in the evaluation of ongoing efforts. In this way unions will feel that by being involved in workplace change, "they are an extension of union advocacy, not sellouts."[82] Fulfilling these requirements often rests on a multipronged strategy that involves training, communication, formal and informal participation structures, interest-based bargaining, joint monitoring arrangements, pay for performance or other incentive programs, extensive information sharing, and ethical leadership by both corporate and union leaders.[83] These are significantly different behaviors than those that dominated the traditional New Deal industrial relations system; they reflect the competitive pressures in a global economy that make flexibility, employee empowerment, and labor–management partnerships such important issues in contemporary labor relations.

HR Strategy Fundamental Strategy-Implementing Tasks

1. Building an organization with the competencies, capabilities, and resource strengths to carry out strategies successfully.
2. Developing budgets to steer ample resources into the value chain activities that are critical to strategic success.
3. Establishing strategy-supportive policies and procedures.
4. Instituting best practices and pushing for continuous improvement in how value chain activities are performed.
5. Installing information, communication, e-commerce, and operating systems that enable company personnel to carry out their strategic roles successfully.
6. Tying rewards and incentives to the achievement of performance objectives and good strategy execution.
7. Creating a strategy-supportive work environment and corporate culture.
8. Exerting the internal leadership needed to drive implementation forward and keep improving on how the strategy is being executed.

QUESTIONS

1. How do these tasks apply to the specific context of moving from a traditional scientific management work organization system to a flexible, team-based production system with high degrees of employee empowerment?
2. In a unionized environment, should these tasks be pursued by management alone or jointly with the union? What is the role of the collective bargaining process?

Reference: Arthur Thompson, Jr., and A.J. Strickland, III, *Strategic Management: Concepts and Cases*, 12th ed. (Boston: McGraw-Hill, 2001), p. 347.

TABLE 10.5 Dealing with Resistance to Change

Strategy	Used When Resistance Stems from ...	Example	Advantages	Disadvantages
Manipulation and co-optation	. . . any source (but be careful!).	Superficially involve a popular leader in the change.	Quick and inexpensive.	Loss of cooperation if people feel manipulated.
Explicit and implicit coercion	. . . any source, and if the initiators have power (but be careful!).	Threaten with job loss or demotion.	Quick and effective (in the short run).	Sharpened resistance if people feel threatened or get angry.
Negotiation and agreement	. . . being made worse off by the change.	Increase wages in return for implementing a change.	Can buy out resistance; also see education and participation.	Potentially expensive, especially if it sets a precedent.
Education and communication	. . . inaccurate or incomplete information about the change.	Make presentations about the proposed change.	People will be more cooperative after being persuaded.	Can be slow and cumbersome.
Participation and involvement	. . . power to resist.	Create a team to design and implement the change.	People will be more committed and can share their knowledge and skills.	Can be slow and cumbersome; loss of control.
Facilitation and support	. . . difficulties of adjusting to the change.	Provide training or counseling.	Effective for addressing adjustment problems.	Time-consuming and potentially expensive and ineffective.

Reference: John P. Kotter and Leonard A. Schlesinger, "Choosing Strategies for Change," *Harvard Business Review* 57 (March–April 1979), pp. 106–14.

Key Terms

scientific management, *356*
job control unionism, *359*
quality of working life program, *361*
quality circle, *365*
lean production, *366*
self-directed work team, *366*
escape, force, or foster change strategies, *369*
labor–management partnership, *370*
Electromation, 372

Reflection Questions

1. What are the major strengths of job control unionism? The major weaknesses? Has job control unionism outlived its usefulness?
2. Full-fledged labor–management partnerships are rare. Why? In your answer, do not blame only labor unions. In other words, be sure to identify reasons why a variety of stakeholders (shareholders, managers, employees, and union leaders) might resist the formation of labor–management partnerships.
3. Suppose you are the HR manager at a small unionized manufacturer of auto parts located in a small town in the South. The production work is repetitive and routine, and there are no particular skill or educational requirements for the production employees. Nearly all the parts produced are sold to one major automaker. This automaker demands a 10 percent price cut. To reduce labor costs, do you use an escape, forcing, or fostering strategy with the union? Why? Now suppose instead that you are the HR manager for a local school district where the teachers are unionized. To balance the state budget, the school district's budget is cut by 10 percent. Do you take the same approach as in the auto parts scenario? Why or why not?
4. Recall the pluralist industrial relations and unitarist human resource management schools of thought from Chapter 2. Assume that labor leaders adhere to the pluralist industrial relations school of thought and that management adheres to the human resource management school of thought. How does the contrast between these two schools help increase the understanding of management's emphasis on cooperation versus labor's emphasis on partnership? How do the two schools help increase the understanding of different perspectives on nonunion employee representation and the *Electromation* controversy?
5. While not sharing its concern for psychological motivators and rewards, Frederick Winslow Taylor's views illustrate the human resource management school's perspectives on employment relationship conflict and labor unions. Explain.

Ethics in Action Breaking the Psychological Contract

Many, if not all, portions of the contract or bond between employer and employee are unwritten, and many are probably never explicitly discussed. Rather, employees work hard for an employer because they *perceive* that they will be rewarded. This is a psychological contract; the perceptions are shaped through personal experience and long-standing practices. In the postwar period the dominant psychological contract in the U.S. employment relationship has consisted of employees' expectations that their hard work, loyalty, and investments in firm-specific skills will be rewarded with increased compensation, promotions, and job stability.

By many accounts this psychological contract has now been unilaterally broken by private- and public-sector employers in pursuit of flexibility. Employers no longer expect that they will provide stable, near-lifetime employment security to loyal workers. Compensation, promotions, and job security are now a function of short-term market or budgetary pressures, not longer-term psychological commitments. Individual employees, not organizations, are responsible for career management and skill acquisition.

QUESTIONS

1. Is this breaking of the psychological contract ethically acceptable? *Hint:* Use the ethical analysis template from Chapter 5. If not, what would you have management do to remedy the situation?
2. An employee who is frustrated with a broken psychological contract might react by directing negative behaviors toward the organization, toward co-workers, and/or toward customers. Evaluate whether each of these possible reactions is ethical.

References: Niall Cullinane and Tony Dundon, "The Psychological Contract: A Critical Review," *International Journal of Management Reviews* 8 (June 2006), pp. 113–29; Neil Conway et al., "Doing More With Less? Employee Reactions to Psychological Contract Breach Via Target Similarity or Spillover During Public Sector Organizational Change," *British Journal of Management* 25 (October 2014), pp. 737–54.

Labor Law Discussion Case 8: Are Issue Committees Dominated Labor Organizations?

BACKGROUND

Tratelemonioc is a manufacturer of electrical components located in Elkhart, Indiana, and employs approximately 200 employees. None of the employees are represented by a union. The company was experiencing severe financial losses and decided that changes were needed to keep the company viable. To reduce costs, the company decided not to give a wage increase for the year, but instead paid employees a lump-sum bonus that depended on length of service. Additionally, the existing employee attendance bonus policy was dropped. In early January, 68 employees signed a petition expressing dissatisfaction with the new attendance policy. In response, the company decided to meet directly with the employees.

On January 11, the company met with a group of eight randomly chosen employees and discussed a wide range of issues, including wages, bonuses, incentive pay, attendance programs, and the leave policy. After this meeting, the company president concluded

> it was very unlikely that further unilateral management action to resolve the problems was going to come anywhere near making everybody happy . . . and we thought the best course of action would be to involve the employees in coming up with solutions to these issues.

The company decided that the employees' concerns could be divided into five categories (absenteeism/ infractions, no smoking policy, communications, pay progression for premium positions, attendance bonus program). Thus the company's management decided to form five "issues committees" to involve the employees in trying to resolve these problems.

A week later, the eight employees were informed of the proposal to create five issues committees of six employees and two managers each. The employees were told by the company president that the committees would meet to try to find solutions to problems and that if the company believed the solutions "were within budget concerns and they generally felt would be acceptable to the employees, that we would implement these suggestions or proposals." It was agreed that the issues committee employees would not be chosen at random. After the meeting, management drafted the goals and responsibilities of the committees.

On January 19, Tratelemonioc sent a memo to each employee announcing the formation of five issues committees. Also, sign-up sheets were posted for each committee. The sign-up sheets contained the goals and responsibilities of each committee. The company determined the number of employees who were allowed to sign up for the committees and restricted several employees to serve on only one committee. From the sign-up sheets management was to select the members of the committee, although this proved unnecessary.

Tratelemonioc's employee benefits manager, Elaine Nixon, served as coordinator of the committees, was the discussion facilitator in the committee meetings, and was "in charge of the issues committee program." The issues committees began weekly meetings in late January in a company conference room with the employees being paid for their time and with supplies being provided by the company. The employees were informed that they were expected to "kind of talk back and forth" with the other employees in the plant to get their ideas.

On February 13, the International Brotherhood of Teamsters, Chauffeurs, Warehousemen, and Helpers of America Local 1049 requested that Tratelemonioc recognize them as the authorized bargaining agent of the employees. There is no evidence that the company was aware of the Teamsters' organizing drive. Subsequently, Nixon informed each issues committee that management could no longer participate, but that the employees could keep meeting if they wanted. Three committees decided to keep meeting on company premises and on company time. The attendance bonus committee devised a proposed solution that was rejected by the company's controller because it was too expensive. Subsequently, the employees met again and drafted a second proposal. The company controller accepted this proposal, but it was never presented to the company president because of the union organizing drive.

On March 15, the company president informed employees that because of the Teamsters' organizing drive, the company "would be unable to participate in the committee meetings and could not continue to work with the committees until after the election." A representation election was scheduled for March 31.

QUESTIONS

1. Do the issues committees constitute a labor organization?
2. Assuming that the issues committees are a labor organization, do they violate the NLRA?
3. If Tratelemonioc violated the NLRA, what is the appropriate remedy?
4. If Tratelemonioc violated the NLRA, does this ruling mean that labor law needs to be reformed to allow for employee participation plans?

Quoted in David Twomey, *Labor and Employment Law: Text & Cases*, Cengage Learning, Febuary 2012.

Labor Law Discussion Case 9: Is a Plant Council a Dominated Labor Organization?

BACKGROUND

On February 13, employees at Webcor Packaging's corrugated box plant in Burton, Michigan, received a memo from the plant superintendent establishing the Webcor Plant Council. As outlined in this memo, the plant council would "consist of five hourly employees who will be elected by the hourly workforce" and three management employees and would "function as a policy development body . . . involved with the development of plant policies, the employee handbooks, the creation of a grievance procedure that will involve council member representation, and with the process of hourly compensation and benefits." The memo further stated that "all matters of plant policy, procedure, and compensation will be jointly reviewed prior to implementation by the plant council and management." The hourly employees were notified that an election would be held in a week, and each employee was to vote for five of the hourly employees who would serve on the council for a year (unless promoted to management).

When the election was held on February 22, 18 of the 28 ballots were blank and four of the five people with the most votes refused to serve. Robert Sikorsky, vice president for operations and an owner of Webcor, then ordered that the plant council process be suspended. In early May a second vote was held. This time employees were asked to volunteer, and employees voted for five of the volunteers. This election was successful in choosing five hourly employees for the plant council.

Sikorsky was a self-described employee involvement apostle. Before arriving at Webcor the previous year, Sikorsky had been a manager at a different box plant where he was convinced that employee involvement generated quality levels higher than at Webcor. He believed that "quality and low cost [could be achieved] by involving all the people in our operation . . . not checking their brains at the door, but thinking about and participating in how we are going to get better at what we do." Consequently, upon arrival at Webcor Sikorsky established an employee involvement steering committee composed of three hourly employees (chosen randomly from volunteers) and two managers. This committee was to focus on quality, waste reduction, housekeeping, and productivity.

The employee involvement steering committee began weekly meetings in January, and employees submitted items for discussion. For example, overtime issues, being paid for lunch breaks, vacation pay, and reimbursement for safety shoes were brought up for discussion. Because these issues were not directly concerned with quality or productivity, Sikorsky decided to create the plant council to handle policy issues.

After the successful plant council election in May, it began holding regular meetings. Webcor provided necessary supplies and paid members for their time. A different member of the council chaired each meeting, and decisions were typically made by consensus. A suggestion box was created and placed in the plant for workers who were not on the council to submit concerns. After reaching agreement, policies of a "substantive nature" would be taken "very seriously" by management and approved or rejected. Policies dealing with "lesser issues" were implemented by the council.

Since its inception, the plant council had drafted policies regarding company purchase of employee tools and overtime equalization. In the latter case, the policy developed by the plant council specified that overtime would be allocated by first offering overtime hours to the employee in the relevant job category with the lowest amount of overtime, then offering the extra hours to the employee with the second lowest amount, and so on, irrespective of seniority. Additionally, the council had reviewed parts of Webcor's attendance policy and proposed increasing the safety shoe reimbursement from one pair per year to two. In reviewing the attendance policy, the council circulated a proposed revision to all employees and asked them to respond with comments. The council also discussed whether employees should be granted paid bereavement leave after a grandparent's death. The tools, overtime equalization, and safety shoes policies were approved by management and implemented.

None of the employees at Webcor were represented by a union.

QUESTIONS

1. Did the employee involvement steering committee violate the NLRA? *Hint:* Remember to consider both Section 2(5) and Section 8(a)(2).
2. Did the plant council violate the NLRA? *Hint:* Remember to consider both Section 2(5) and Section 8(a)(2).

AFTER CONSIDERING THESE QUESTIONS, READ ON

In late January, some Webcor employees approached Local 332 of the International Brotherhood of Teamsters, Chauffeurs, Warehousemen, and Helpers of America about organizing the Webcor plant. A petition for a certification election was filed with the National Labor Relations Board (NLRB) on February 19, and an election was scheduled for April 18.

Continued

Continued

During March, Webcor management distributed the following campaign literature to the hourly employees (these exhibits contain actual statements but are not exact replicas):

IF THE UNION WINS THE ELECTION

- All wages are subject to change.
- All benefits are subject to change.
- Policies, rules, etc. are subject to change.

There is NO guarantee that those items will be as good as they are now.

IF THE UNION LOSES THE ELECTION:

As we stated prior to this organizing drive, We, the owners of Webcor:
GUARANTEE:

- The Employee handbook will not be changed unless it is changed through the Employee Involvement/Plant Council Process.

Dear Valued Employee:

An NLRB election will be held on April 18 to determine whether you will be unionized by the Teamsters. You are a valuable employee and it is unnecessary to let a third party disrupt our relationship. There are many reasons why you should vote against the Teamsters. Reason No. 1 is our commitment to Employee Involvement. Reason No. 2 is the implementation of the Plant Council.

The choice you will make on election day is a simple one. Either you will choose to hire Teamsters #332 as the sole and exclusive agent. Or you will choose to continue a relationship with Webcor based on Employee Involvement.

Bob

The results of the April 18 NLRB election were as follows:

Teamsters Local 332	14
No union	21

QUESTION

3. Do the organizing drive events change your answers to the previous questions?

End Notes

1. Barry Bluestone and Irving Bluestone, *Negotiating the Future: A Labor Perspective on American Business* (New York: Basic Books, 1992); Edward E. Potter and Judith A. Youngman, *Keeping America Competitive: Employment Policy for the Twenty-First Century* (Lakewood, CO: Glenbridge Publishing, 1995).
2. Eileen Appelbaum and Rosemary Batt, *The New American Workplace: Transforming Work Systems in the United States* (Ithaca, NY: ILR Press, 1994).
3. Michael J. Piore and Charles F. Sabel, *The Second Industrial Divide: Possibilities for Prosperity* (New York: Basic Books, 1984).
4. Appelbaum and Batt, *The New American Workplace*; Bluestone and Bluestone, *Negotiating the Future;* David I. Levine, *Reinventing the Workplace: How Business and Employees Can Both Win* (Washington, DC: Brookings, 1995); James O'Toole and Edward E. Lawler III, *The New American Workplace* (New York: Palgrave Macmillan, 2006).
5. Robert Kanigel, *The One Best Way: Frederick Winslow Taylor and the Enigma of Efficiency* (New York, Penguin, 1997); Frederick Winslow Taylor, *The Principles of Scientific Management* (New York: Harper and Brothers, 1911).
6. Kanigel, *The One Best Way;* Daniel Nelson, "Scientific Management in Retrospect," in Daniel Nelson (ed.), *A Mental Revolution: Scientific Management since Taylor* (Columbus: Ohio State University Press, 1992), pp. 5–39.
7. David Montgomery, *Workers' Control in America: Studies in the History of Work, Technology, and Labor Struggles* (Cambridge, England: Cambridge University Press, 1979); Clayton Sinyai, *Schools of Democracy: A Political History of the American Labor Movement* (Ithaca, NY: Cornell University Press, 2006).
8. Kanigel, *The One Best Way.*
9. Howell John Harris, *The Right to Manage: Industrial Relations Policies of American Business in the 1940s* (Madison: University of Wisconsin Press, 1982).
10. Harry C. Katz, *Shifting Gears: Changing Labor Relations in the U.S. Automobile Industry* (Cambridge, MA: MIT Press, 1985); Thomas A. Kochan, Harry C. Katz, and Robert B. McKersie, *The Transformation of American Industrial Relations* (New York: Basic Books, 1986).
11. Kenneth May (ed.), *Elkouri and Elkouri: How Arbitration Works,* 6th ed. (Washington, DC: Bloomberg BNA, 2012).
12. Charles C. Heckscher, *The New Unionism: Employee Involvement in the Changing Corporation* (New York: Basic Books, 1988); Nelson Lichtenstein, "Great Expectations: The Promise of Industrial Jurisprudence and its Demise, 1930–1960," in Nelson Lichtenstein and Howell John Harris (eds.), *Industrial Democracy in America: The Ambiguous Promise* (Washington, DC: Woodrow Wilson Center Press, 1993), pp. 113–41.
13. John W. Budd, *Employment with a Human Face: Balancing Efficiency, Equity, and Voice* (Ithaca, NY: Cornell University Press, 2004).
14. David Brody, "Workplace Contractualism in Comparative Perspective," in Nelson Lichtenstein and Howell John Harris (eds.), *Industrial Democracy in America: The Ambiguous Promise* (Washington, DC: Woodrow Wilson Center Press, 1993), pp. 176–205.
15. David Fairris, *Shopfloor Matters: Labor–Management Relations in Twentieth-Century American Manufacturing* (London: Routledge, 1997).
16. Piore and Sabel, *The Second Industrial Divide.*
17. John Russo, "Lordstown, Ohio, Strike of 1972," in Ronald L. Filippelli (ed.), *Labor Conflict in the United States: An Encyclopedia* (New York: Garland Publishing, 1990), pp. 283–86.
18. Katz, *Shifting Gears.*
19. Bruce Nissen, "Unions and Workplace Reorganization," in Bruce Nissen (ed.), *Unions and Workplace Reorganization* (Detroit: Wayne State University Press, 1997), pp. 9–33.
20. James Brian Quinn, Jordan J. Baruch, and Karen Anne Zein, *Innovation Explosion: Using Intellect and Software to Revolutionize Growth Strategies* (New York: Free Press, 1997), pp. 32–33; Richard A. D'Aveni, *Hypercompetitive Rivalries: Competing in Highly Dynamic Environments* (New York: Free Press, 1994).
21. John S. Oakland, *Total Quality Management: The Route to Improving Performance,* 2nd ed. (East Brunswick, NJ: Nichols Publishing, 1993).
22. Michael Hammer and James Champy, *Reengineering the Corporation: A Manifesto for Business Revolution* (New York: HarperBusiness, 1993), pp. 1–2 (emphasis in original).
23. Muneto Ozaki (ed.), *Negotiating Flexibility: The Role of the Social Partners and the State* (Geneva: International Labour Office, 1999); Nick Wailes and Russell D. Lansbury, "Collective Bargaining and Flexibility: Australia," LEG/REL Working Paper (Geneva: International Labour Office, 1999).

24. Richard Sennett, *The Corrosion of Character: The Personal Consequences of Work in the New Capitalism* (New York: Norton, 1998), p. 146.

25. Peter Cappelli, *The New Deal at Work: Managing the Market-Driven Workforce* (Boston: Harvard Business School Press, 1999).

26. Harry C. Katz, John Paul MacDuffie, and Frits K. Pil, "Crisis and Recovery in the U.S. Auto Industry: Tumultuous Times for a Collective Bargaining Pacesetter," in Howard R. Stanger, Paul F. Clark, and Ann C. Frost (eds.), *Collective Bargaining under Duress: Case Studies of Major North American Industries* (Champaign, IL: Labor and Employment Relations Association, 2013), pp. 45–79.

27. Kenneth Mericle and Dong-One Kim, "From Job-Based Pay to Skill-Based Pay in Unionized Establishments: A Three-Plant Comparative Analysis," *Relations Industrielles* 54 (Summer 1999), pp. 549–78.

28. Appelbaum and Batt, *The New American Workplace;* Bluestone and Bluestone, *Negotiating the Future*; Thomas A. Kochan et al., *Healing Together: The Labor-Management Partnership at Kaiser Permanente* (Ithaca, NY: Cornell University Press, 2009); Joel Cutcher-Gershenfeld, Dan Brooks, and Martin Mulloy, *Inside the Ford-UAW Transformation: Pivotal Events in Valuing Work and Delivering Results* (Cambridge: MIT Press, 2015).

29. Clinton S. Golden and Harold J. Ruttenberg, *The Dynamics of Industrial Democracy* (New York: Harper and Brothers, 1942); John P. Hoerr, *And the Wolf Finally Came: The Decline of the American Steel Industry* (Pittsburgh: University of Pittsburgh, 1988).

30. Hoerr, *And the Wolf Finally Came*, p. 280.

31. Casey Ichniowski and Kathryn Shaw, "Beyond Incentive Pay: Insiders' Estimates of the Value of Complementary Human Resource Management Practices," *Journal of Economic Perspectives* 17 (Winter 2003), pp. 155–80; Paul Osterman, "Work Reorganization in an Era of Restructuring: Trends in Diffusion and Effects on Employee Welfare," *Industrial and Labor Relations Review* 53 (January 2000), pp. 179–96.

32. Rosemary Batt, "Work Organization, Technology, and Performance in Customer Service and Sales," *Industrial and Labor Relations Review* 52 (July 1999), pp. 539–64; Mark A. Huselid, "The Impact of Human Resource Management Practices on Turnover, Productivity, and Corporate Financial Performance," *Academy of Management Journal* 38 (June 1995), pp. 635–72; Ichniowski and Shaw, "Beyond Incentive Pay"; Olga Tregaskis et al., "High Performance Work Practices and Firm Performance: A Longitudinal Case Study," *British Journal of Management* 24 (June 2013), pp. 225–44.

33. Peter Cappelli and David Neumark, "Do 'High-Performance' Work Practices Improve Establishment-Level Outcomes?" *Industrial and Labor Relations Review* 54 (July 2001), pp. 737–75; John Godard, "A Critical Assessment of the High-Performance Paradigm," *British Journal of Industrial Relations* 42 (June 2004), pp. 349–78.

34. Osterman, "Work Reorganization in an Era of Restructuring"; Sandra E. Black, Lisa M. Lynch, and Anya Krivelyova, "How Workers Fare When Employers Innovate," *Industrial Relations* 43 (January 2004), pp. 44–66; Michael J. Handel and Maury Gittleman, "Is There a Wage Payoff to Innovative Work Practices?" *Industrial Relations* 43 (January 2004), pp. 67–97.

35. John Godard, "High Performance *and* the Transformation of Work? The Implications of Alternative Work Practices for the Experiences and Outcomes of Work," *Industrial and Labor Relations Review* 54 (July 2001), pp. 776–805; Tregaskis et al., "High Performance Work Practices and Firm Performance."

36. Alex Bryson, Erling Barth, and Harald Dale-Olsen, "The Effects of Organizational Change on Worker Well-Being and the Moderating Role of Trade Unions," *Industrial and Labor Relations Review* 66 (July 2013), pp. 989–1011; Dionne M. Pohler and Andrew A. Luchak, "Balancing Efficiency, Equity, and Voice: The Impact of Unions and High-Involvement Work Practices on Work Outcomes," *Industrial and Labor Relations Review* 67 (October 2014), pp. 1063–94.

37. Mark D. Brenner, David Fairris, and John Ruser, "'Flexible' Work Practices and Occupational Safety and Health: Exploring the Relationship between Cumulative Trauma Disorders and Workplace Transformation," *Industrial Relations* 43 (January 2004), pp. 242–66.

38. Godard, "A Critical Assessment of the High-Performance Paradigm"; John Godard, "What Is Best for Workers? The Implications of Workplace and Human Resource Management Practices Revisited," *Industrial Relations* 49 (July 2010), pp. 466–88; Bill Harley, "High Performance Work Systems and Employee Voice," in Adrian Wilkinson et al. (eds.), *The Handbook of Research on Employee Voice* (Northampton, MA: Edward Elgar, 2014), pp. 82–96; Bernd J. Frick, Ute Goetzen, and Robert Simmons, "The Hidden Costs of High-Performance Work Practices: Evidence from a Large German Steel Company," *Industrial and Labor Relations Review* 66 (January 2013), pp. 198–224.

39. Appelbaum and Batt, *The New American Workplace;* Steve Babson (ed.), *Lean Work: Empowerment and Exploitation in the Global Auto Industry* (Detroit: Wayne State University Press, 1995); Fairris, *Shopfloor Matters.*

40. Mike Parker and Jane Slaughter, *Choosing Sides: Unions and the Team Concept* (Boston: South End Press, 1988); Mike Parker and Jane Slaughter, "Unions and Management by Stress," in Steve Babson (ed.), *Lean Work: Empowerment and Exploitation in the Global Auto Industry* (Detroit: Wayne State University Press, 1995), pp. 41–53. Quote is from pp. 45–46.
41. James Womack, Daniel Jones, and Daniel Roos, *The Machine That Changed the World* (New York: Rawson Associates, 1990).
42. Bluestone and Bluestone, *Negotiating the Future;* Heckscher, *The New Unionism*; Saul A. Rubinstein and Thomas A. Kochan, *Learning from Saturn: Possibilities for Corporate Governance and Employee Relations* (Ithaca, NY: ILR Press, 2001).
43. Saul A. Rubinstein, "A Different Kind of Union: Balancing Co-Management and Representation," *Industrial Relations* 40 (April 2001), pp. 163–203; Rubinstein and Kochan, *Learning from Saturn.*
44. Rubinstein, "A Different Kind of Union," p. 195.
45. Rubinstein, "A Different Kind of Union."
46. Mike Parker and Jane Slaughter, "Advancing Unionism on the New Terrain," in Bruce Nissen (ed.), *Unions and Workplace Reorganization* (Detroit: Wayne State University Press, 1997), pp. 208–25 at 218.
47. Parker and Slaughter, "Advancing Unionism on the New Terrain."
48. Paul Ingrassia, "Saturn Was Supposed to Save GM," *Newsweek* (April 13, 2009).
49. U.S. Department of Labor, *Working Together for Public Service* (Washington, DC: Government Printing Office, 1996).
50. Joel Cutcher-Gershenfeld, "The Impact on Economic Performance of a Transformation in Workplace Relations," *Industrial and Labor Relations Review* 44 (January 1991), pp. 241–60.
51. Richard E. Walton, Joel E. Cutcher-Gershenfeld, and Robert B. McKersie, *Strategic Negotiations: A Theory of Change in Labor–Management Relations* (Boston: Harvard Business School Press, 1994).
52. Jonathan D. Rosenblum, *Copper Crucible: How the Arizona Miners Strike of 1983 Recast Labor–Management Relations in America,* 2nd ed. (Ithaca, NY: ILR Press, 1998); Rick Fantasia and Kim Voss, *Hard Work: Remaking the American Labor Movement* (Berkeley: University of California Press, 2004).
53. Ozaki, *Negotiating Flexibility.*
54. Jody Hoffer Gittell, Andrew von Nordenflycht, and Thomas A. Kochan, "Mutual Gains or Zero Sum? Labor Relations and Firm Performance in the Airline Industry," *Industrial and Labor Relations Review* 57 (January 2004), pp. 163–80; Greg J. Bamber et al., *Up in the Air: How Airlines Can Improve Performance by Engaging Their Employees* (Ithaca, NY: Cornell University Press, 2009).
55. Thomas A. Kochan et al., "The Potential and Precariousness of Partnership: The Case of the Kaiser Permanente Labor–Management Partnership," *Industrial Relations* 47 (January 2008), pp. 36–65; Kochan et al., *Healing Together*; Stewart Johnstone, "The Case for Workplace Partnership," in Stewart Johnstone and Peter Ackers (eds.), *Finding a Voice at Work: New Perspectives on Employment Relations* (Oxford: Oxford University Press, 2015), pp. 153–76.
56. Marick F. Masters, Robert R. Albright, and David Eplion, "What Did Partnerships Do? Evidence from the Federal Sector," *Industrial and Labor Relations Review* 59 (April 2006), pp. 367–85.
57. Erin Johansson, "Improving Government Through Labor-Management Collaboration and Employee Ingenuity" (Jobs with Justice Education Fund, 2014).
58. Eileen Appelbaum and Larry W. Hunter, "Union Participation in Strategic Decisions of Corporations," in Richard B. Freeman, Joni Hersch, and Lawrence Mishel (eds.), *Emerging Labor Market Institutions for the Twenty-First Century* (Chicago: University of Chicago Press, 2005), pp. 265–91; Cutcher-Gershenfeld, Brooks, and Mulloy, *Inside the Ford-UAW Transformation*.
59. Kochan et al., *Healing Together.*
60. Kochan et al., "The Kaiser Permanente Labor Management Partnership," p. 6.
61. Adrienne E. Eaton, Saul A. Rubinstein, and Thomas A. Kochan, "Balancing Acts: Dynamics of a Union Coalition in a Labor Management Partnership," *Industrial Relations* 47 (January 2008), pp. 10–35; Gregor Gall, "Labour Union Responses to Participation in Employing Organizations," in Adrian Wilkinson et al. (eds.), *The Oxford Handbook of Participation in Organizations* (Oxford: Oxford University Press, 2010), pp. 361–82; Cutcher-Gershenfeld, Brooks, and Mulloy, *Inside the Ford-UAW Transformation*; Melanie Simms, "Union Organizing as an Alternative to Partnership. Or What to Do When Employers Can't Keep Their Side of the Bargain," in Stewart Johnstone and Peter Ackers (eds.), *Finding a Voice at Work: New Perspectives on Employment Relations* (Oxford: Oxford University Press, 2015), pp. 127–52.

62. John Geary, "Do Unions Benefit from Working in Partnership with Employers? Evidence from Ireland," *Industrial Relations* 47 (October 2008), pp. 530–68.
63. Pohler and Luchak, "Balancing Efficiency, Equity, and Voice"; Saul R. Rubinstein, "The Impact of Co-Management on Quality Performance: The Case of the Saturn Corporation," *Industrial and Labor Relations Review* 53 (January 2000), pp. 197–218; Godard, "What Is Best for Workers?"
64. Michael H. LeRoy, "Employee Participation in the New Millennium: Redefining a Labor Organization under Section 8(a)(2) of the NLRA," *Southern California Law Review* 72 (September 1999), pp. 1651–723 at 1657.
65. *Electromation, Inc. and International Brotherhood of Teamsters, Local Union No. 1049, AFL–CIO,* 309 NLRB 990 (1992), enforced 35 F.3d 1148 (7th Cir. 1994); Robert S. Moberly, "The Story of *Electromation:* Are Employee Participation Programs a Competitive Necessity or a Wolf in Sheep's Clothing?" in Laura J. Cooper and Catherine L. Fisk (eds.), *Labor Law Stories* (New York: Foundation Press, 2005), pp. 315–51.
66. *Sears, Roebuck and Co.,* 274 NLRB 230 (1985); *E.I. du Pont and Co.,* 311 NLRB 893 (1993).
67. *E.I. du Pont and Co.,* 311 NLRB 893 (1993).
68. Webcor Packaging, Inc. and Local 332, International Brotherhood of Teamsters, 319 NLRB No. 142 (1995).
69. *Chicago Rawhide Mfg. Co. v. NLRB,* 221 F.2d 165 (7th Cir. 1955).
70. Michael H. Leroy, "What Do NLRB Cases Reveal About Non-Union Employee Representation Groups? A Typology from Post-*Electromation* Cases," in Paul J. Gollan et al. (eds.), *Voice and Involvement at Work: Experience with Nonunion Representation* (London: Routledge, 2014), pp. 366–93.
71. Patricia A. Greenfield and Robert J. Pleasure, "Representatives of Their Own Choosing: Finding Workers' Voice in the Legitimacy and Power of Their Unions," in Bruce E. Kaufman and Morris M. Kleiner (eds.), *Employee Representation: Alternatives and Future Directions* (Madison, WI: Industrial Relations Research Association, 1993), pp. 169–96.
72. *Crown Cork and Seal,* 334 NLRB No. 92 (2001); *General Foods,* 231 NLRB 1232 (1977); *John Ascuaga's Nugget,* 210 NLRB 275 (1977); *Mercy Memorial Hospital,* 231 NLRB 1108 (1977).
73. Paul Gollan, *Employee Representation in Non-Union Firms* (London: Sage, 2007); Paul J. Gollan, Bruce E. Kaufman, Daphne Taras, and Adrian Wilkinson (eds.), *Voice and Involvement at Work: Experience with Nonunion Representation* (London: Routledge, 2014).
74. Bruce E. Kaufman, "Keeping the Commitment Model in the Air during Turbulent Times: Employee Involvement at Delta Air Lines." *Industrial Relations* 52 (January 2013), pp. 343–77.
75. Daphne Gottlieb Taras, "A Century of Employee Representation at Imperial Oil," in Paul J. Gollan et al. (eds.), *Voice and Involvement at Work: Experience with Nonunion Representation* (London: Routledge, 2014), pp. 197–226.
76. Bruce E. Kaufman, "Experience with Company Unions and Their Treatment under the Wagner Act: A Four Frames of Reference Analysis," *Industrial Relations* 55 (January 2016), pp. 3–39; Michele Campolieti, Rafael Gomez, and Morley Gunderson, "Does Non-Union Employee Representation Act as a Complement or Substitute to Union Voice? Evidence from Canada and the United States," *Industrial Relations* 52 (January 2013), pp. 378–96.
77. Jay A. Conger, Gretchen M. Spreitzer, and Edward E. Lawler III (eds.), *The Leader's Change Handbook: An Essential Guide to Setting Direction and Taking Action* (San Francisco: Jossey-Bass, 1999); John P. Kotter, *Leading Change* (Boston: Harvard Business School Press, 1996); Arthur A. Thompson and A.J. Strickland, *Strategic Management: Concepts and Cases,* 12th ed. (Boston: McGraw-Hill/Irwin, 2001).
78. Kirk Blackard, *Managing Change in a Unionized Workplace: Countervailing Collaboration* (Westport, CT: Quorum Books, 2000).
79. Blackard, *Managing Change in a Unionized Workplace.*
80. Edward Cohen-Rosenthal and Cynthia E. Burton, *Mutual Gains: A Guide to Union–Management Cooperation,* 2nd ed. (Ithaca, NY: ILR Press, 1993).
81. Cohen-Rosenthal and Burton, *Mutual Gains,* p. 30.
82. Cohen-Rosenthal and Burton, *Mutual Gains,* p. 30.
83. Blackard, *Managing Change in a Unionized Workplace;* Cohen-Rosenthal and Burton, *Mutual Gains*; U.S. Department of Labor, *Working Together for Public Service;* Walton, Cutcher-Gershenfeld, and McKersie, *Strategic Negotiations.*

Chapter Eleven

Globalization and Financialization

Advance Organizer

The New Deal industrial relations system developed when U.S. corporations dominated world markets and did not face significant international competition. But as trade barriers fall and capital mobility increases, the global economy becomes more integrated. Additionally, financial motives and institutions have become more important. Globalization and financialization therefore create pressures that are putting great strain on the New Deal industrial relations system and its participants.

Learning Objectives

By the end of this chapter, you should be able to

1. **Discuss** the key elements of globalization and how they affect the employment relationship and labor relations.
2. **Outline** alternative institutional arrangements for governing the global workplace and the implications of each for labor relations.
3. **Explain** various strategies for representing workers in a global economy.
4. **Understand** the labor relations challenges for managers in multinational companies.
5. **Identify** the dimensions of financialization and how they affect the employment relationship and labor relations.

Contents

Globalization: The term is frequently used—often negatively—but what does it mean? And what does it have to do with labor relations? Financialization: Maybe that's a term you haven't heard. What does it mean, and what does it have to do with labor relations? In brief, globalization is increased economic integration among countries, whereas financialization is the increased importance of financial markets, motives, results, and institutions relative to the production and delivery of goods and services. Globalization and financialization are intertwined. They are facilitated by free-market public policies and advances in information technology. Globalization opens up greater financial opportunities while adding competition that can reduce financial returns; financialization deepens global integration while increasing the pressure on organizations to search globally for ways to generate the highest financial returns, which in turn pushes them to lobby for free trade agreements and other instruments of globalization.

Globalization and financialization are each a bundle of interrelated structural changes that "have similar consequences in the distribution of power, income, and wealth, and in the pattern of economic growth."[1] Consequently, both are important pressures on labor relations—and employment more generally—in the United States and around the world in the 21st century. Increasing foreign trade puts competitive pressures on, and opens up new opportunities for, companies and workers. Expanding multinational corporations undermine nationally focused labor unions and government regulations while also demanding new skills and knowledge for managers. Increasing capital mobility makes it easier to move jobs around the globe. In the labor relations environment, globalization both decreases the demand for unskilled labor in the United States and makes labor easier to replace. In other words, globalization reduces labor's bargaining power. U.S. unions are therefore struggling to preserve the legitimacy of collective bargaining in the face of the pressures of globalization. This has been a painful process in industries such as steel and textiles that have collapsed and reduced manufacturing communities in the northeastern and midwestern United States to a rustbelt. Financialization magnifies these pressures.

Globalization and financialization also raise broader issues. Deepening economic and financial integration brings increased social and political integration that threatens local cultures, standards, and ways of life. Options for foreign subsidiaries, outsourcing, joint ventures, and the like bring both opportunities and challenges for managers and labor leaders. These options are shaped by various international institutional arrangements such as the World Trade Organization (WTO) and the European Union—or free trade agreements such as the North American Free Trade Agreement (NAFTA)—and by the responses of organized labor and other groups that push for enforceable international labor standards, antisweatshop codes of conduct for corporations, and transnational collective bargaining. Similarly, financialization is driven by institutional arrangements related to corporate governance, private equity, and banking regulations. As these subjects are presented in more detail in this chapter, note how the institutional arrangements enhance or undermine the viability of traditional collective bargaining. Moreover, looking at institutional arrangements reveals a range of alternatives for governing the global workplace to balance efficiency, equity, and voice. Understanding globalization and financialization is therefore important not only for labor relations but also for broader employment, business, and social issues.

THE DEBATE OVER GLOBALIZATION

Globalization increases economic integration along four major dimensions: international trade, foreign direct investment, international investment portfolios, and immigration (see Table 11.1).[2] To varying degrees, all four dimensions have been linked in theory to

TABLE 11.1
The Dimensions of Globalization

International trade	Cross-border flow of goods and services; exports and imports.
Foreign direct investment (FDI)	Cross-border flow of multinational corporation investment; purchasing or establishing foreign subsidiaries and joint ventures.
International investment portfolios	Cross-border flow of investment securities; investing in foreign stocks and bonds (but no control over the foreign enterprise in contrast to FDI).
Immigration	Cross-border flow of people; migrating from one country to another.

employment opportunities, working conditions, living standards, income inequality, consumer choices, prices, life expectancy, child mortality, educational attainment, cultural diversity, endangered species and biodiversity, deforestation, pollution, crime, democracy, peace, and human rights.[3] In fact, increased globalization has been accused of both improving *and* worsening all these critical elements of human life. Moreover, with the collapse of state socialism and communism in the former Soviet Union and Eastern Europe by the early 1990s, and with China trying to increase foreign investment and trade, capitalism, international investment, and multinational corporations have penetrated virtually every corner of the globe. In fact, the world can now be characterized as flat—because of information technology, "it is now possible for more people than ever to collaborate and compete in real time with more other people on more different kinds of work from more different corners of the planet and on a more equal footing than at any previous time in the history of the world"; as "the global competitive playing field [is] being leveled . . . the world [is] being flattened."[4] Globalization is therefore the subject of intense debates (see Table 11.2).

TABLE 11.2
Globalization: The Good, the Bad, and the Unequal

Sources: Douglas A. Irwin, *Free Trade under Fire*, 4th ed. (Princeton, NJ: Princeton University Press, 2015); and various issues of United Nations Development Programme, *Human Development Report* (New York).

The Good

Trade promotes increased economic growth and income through the more efficient use of scarce resources and opportunities for increasing returns to scale. Trade also lowers prices and increases choices through competition.

Foreign direct investment boosts technology, infrastructure, and productivity.

Foreign portfolio investment provides capital for entrepreneurs and financing for government debt.

Improving property rights, reducing subsidies, and increasing wealth can lead to practices that conserve the environment.

Since 1990, the number of countries characterized by a low level of human development has fallen from 62 to 43, and the population in that group decreased by 2 billion.

The Bad

Low-cost competition from countries that violate labor rights causes domestic job losses and erosion of income and working conditions.

Foreign multinational companies exploit workers and the environment in poor countries that are desperate for any investment and income. Low-income countries and families cannot afford to protect the environment.

Volatile flows of foreign portfolio investment destabilize fragile developing country banking systems and economies.

Economic integration with concentrated economic power undermines democracy, national sovereignty, and indigenous cultures.

More than a billion people have to live on less than $1.25 a day. Nearly 40 percent of the world's population has to live on less than $2.50 a day.

The world's largest corporations are bigger than the economies of many countries.

The Unequal

The world's 85 richest people have the same wealth as the poorest 3.5 billion. The richest 1 percent receive nearly 15 percent of world income.

Developed countries have policies to attract skilled immigrants while limiting unskilled immigrants. More than 50 million primary school–age children do not attend school, and over half of them are in Sub-Saharan Africa.

Child mortality rates in the least developed countries are 10 times higher than in high-income developed countries.

International Trade

The first dimension of globalization is international trade: the cross-border flow of goods and services—in other words, imports and exports. The benefits of international trade are clearly revealed in textbook economic models as well as in Adam Smith's 1776 classic *The Wealth of Nations.*[5] In short, free trade across countries allows consumers and producers to benefit from specialization. If one country has a comparative advantage in producing one product, such as computer software because of an educated population, and another has a comparative advantage in something else, such as clothing, then both countries are better off by specializing in what they are best at and trading for the other goods. Scarce resources are used more efficiently, productivity is higher, and greater income is produced. Additional benefits from free trade arise from increasing the size of markets (so that companies can take advantage of increased economies of scale) and by reducing the monopoly power of domestic companies (so that domestic companies become more efficient). Countries benefit from increased growth and income while consumers enjoy lower prices and greater choices. Increased wealth can also be used to conserve the environment, promote public health, and improve education.

However, if there are market imperfections, the benefits and costs of international trade are distributed unevenly, resulting in winners and losers.[6] Recall the fundamental industrial relations assumption of unequal bargaining power between corporations and individual employees (especially those lacking savings, education, and a social safety net). With unequal bargaining power, the benefits of trade flow disproportionately toward shareholders; some employees are left with low wages, long hours, and dangerous working conditions, others can see their jobs outsourced to low-cost foreign competition. Globally, just as the United States struggled with the labor problem of worker exploitation in the early 20th century, developing countries are now struggling with similar labor problems in the 21st century.

Consequently, it is important not to gloss over the human and social costs of job loss. With the decline of the U.S. steel industry, for example, single cities saw the disappearance of thousands of high-paying jobs and resulting sharp increases in unemployment, small business failure, and crime. The loss of 40,000 manufacturing jobs in the Youngstown, Ohio, area triggered the closing of 400 local businesses, the loss of $414 million in personal income, and significant reductions in tax revenues for public schools (as much as 75 percent in some cases).[7] As for the personal costs, consider the recollection of one ex-steelworker in Homestead, Pennsylvania:

> When [the steel mill] shut down, and when guys did lose their jobs—people with fifteen, twenty, thirty years on the job—the psychological and social damage was a hundred times more than the economic. . . . Within four years of the place shutting down, I had eighty-one guys that I knew of personally—not just knew of, but knew personally—who died of strokes, cancer, heart attacks—including seven suicides—within a period of three-and-a-half years after the mill shut down. All under the age of sixty.[8]

Similar stories have been repeated elsewhere with the decline of autos, textiles, and other industries. Images of the decline of Flint, Michigan, in particular were starkly captured by the film *Roger and Me.*

Disparities across countries raise concerns with **social dumping.** In international trade, dumping occurs when a foreign competitor is able to unfairly sell something at a lower price than domestic producers, where *unfairly* means because of a subsidy, not because of greater efficiencies. In such a case, the low-priced goods are seen as being "dumped" into the domestic market. Social dumping occurs when a foreign competitor is able to unfairly sell something at a lower price because of lower labor or environmental standards—for example, no minimum wage floors, lack of safety regulations, or absence of pollution standards—and thereby "dump" social problems of low wages and poor working conditions on another country or location. As an example of the vast labor cost differentials between countries that give rise to fears of social dumping, monthly wages for garment workers are $48 in Bangladesh, $100 in Vietnam, $235 in China, and $1,440 in Oklahoma.[9] Social dumping can be a problem if it undermines the tighter labor and environmental standards of the domestic country by making it difficult for companies to remain competitive while respecting these standards. As we will soon discuss, labor and environmental groups in the United States and Europe therefore continue to push for fair trade rather than free trade—that is, the addition of labor and environmental standards for international trade.

Foreign Direct Investment

A second component of globalization is foreign direct investment (FDI), which consists of cross-border flows of investment by multinational corporations to establish partial or full ownership in foreign businesses. Examples of FDI include opening a new factory, call center, or other operation in another country, purchasing a foreign-owned company, or entering into a joint venture with a foreign enterprise; the global reach of many companies is further extended by global networks of suppliers (see Table 11.3). In 2015, global FDI exceeded $1.8 trillion.[10]

Companies may invest in other countries for many reasons.[11] By investing in Chinese factories, U.S. companies can, for example, lower their labor costs, diversify a company's labor pool and talent base, avoid independent unions, have an authoritarian state limit worker protest, take advantage of tax breaks, provide access to raw materials, reduce transportation costs to some destinations, open up new markets, and help win contracts to sell products to Chinese businesses and the government. The benefits of FDI for the host country include new capital for investment, higher-paying jobs, new technology, more products and competition, and opportunities to learn new management practices and share in research and development activities. Indeed, FDI has been instrumental in some success stories of such developing countries as Singapore and Malaysia.[12]

However, there is also the potential for FDI to threaten domestic workers with job loss or plant closings unless concessions are made. Indeed, the jobs that can now be done by anyone from anywhere in the world are seemingly limitless.[13] Many technical jobs have been moved to India—including software programmers, computer engineers, financial analysts, and even the saying of special intentions (requests by individuals for a priest to pray for a family member or friend). So the threat of job loss is real.

Moreover, FDI can further exploit workers with no alternatives and degrade the environment in the absence of protections or incentives. These problems are especially acute in export processing zones, which are special areas of developing countries dedicated to attracting and supporting multinational investment and production.[14] Developing countries hope these zones create employment, bring in foreign exchange, and stimulate economic development. Export processing zones typically include explicit incentives such as duty-free importing and exporting, reduced taxes, and publicly provided infrastructure. Critics

TABLE 11.3
Global Design and Production of Boeing Airplanes

Boeing works with over 15,000 suppliers in more than 80 countries:	
Tail sections and miscellaneous components	China
Aircraft doors	France
Cabin lighting	Germany
Landing gears	Japan
Wing tips	Korea
Engineering	Russia, Spain

Labor Relations Application The Maquiladora Program

The *maquiladora* program started in 1965 as the Border Industrialization Program, under which U.S. parts assembled in the northern part of Mexico along the border with the United States shipped back into the United States would be nearly free of duties or tariffs. Mexican factories that assemble U.S. components for export to the United States are called *maquiladoras*. The program is no longer limited to the border region, but the term *maquiladoras* is popularly associated with factories close to the border in Tijuana, Nogales, Ciudad Juárez, Matamoros, and other cities.

With an explicit emphasis on assembly of premade parts, the early *maquiladora* workforce was mostly young, single women doing simple assembly tasks and largely managed by American managers and engineers. A typical early example was apparel. However, assembly methods have become more complex, the workforce is less dominated by women, and the managerial staffs include many more Mexican managers and engineers. Typical recent examples are now autos and electronics. Some *maquiladora* plants use flexible, team-based production methods, and some include sophisticated technology. Employee turnover is high, and bonus systems are used to reduce absenteeism.

The *maquiladora* program started as a way to provide jobs to Mexican workers who were no longer allowed to work in the U.S. agricultural industry—and as a way for U.S. companies to take advantage of low labor costs—but has since expanded into a major economic development strategy for Mexico. Because of the pressures to attract foreign investment for economic development, *maquiladoran* labor relations are controversial. In particular, critics assert that government control and suppression of unions are used to keep labor costs low at the expense of workers and their families. Unions appear to be weaker or more tightly controlled in the western areas than in the eastern ones. In the eastern area (bordering Texas) there is a stronger tradition of powerful unions in the petroleum industry, and unions in *maquiladoras* appear stronger. In this region pay has been higher and workweeks shorter. In the western region interunion conflict in Tijuana undermines union power, and yellow unionism (government-controlled unions) is frequent in Nogales. A yellow union might accept conditions lower than the minimums specified by law, and its presence can be used to keep out more aggressive unions.

As *maquiladoras* compete with U.S. factories and increasingly with Mexican factories as well, government control of wages and benefits affects workers throughout the United States and Mexico. But the *maquiladora* sector is also struggling with the pressures of globalization. The North American Free Trade Agreement (NAFTA) phased out the *maquiladoras'* duty-free status, wages have been rising, and corporate tax subsidies have been reduced. Consequently, some production moved out of Mexico to lower-cost countries in the early 2000s. For example, Sanyo moved some TV production to China and Indonesia, Canon moved ink-jet printer production to Vietnam, and others have moved to Guatemala. But after the oil price spike in 2008, some U.S. companies increased their investment in Mexico because of the transportation cost savings of being close to the U.S. market. An improved education system in parts of Mexico, the ability of U.S. managers to commute daily to factories in Mexico from places like El Paso and San Diego, and a greater understanding of business difficulties in China such as intellectual property piracy, communication problems, and requirements to work with government-linked partners are also renewing the attractiveness of Mexico.

Sources: Altha J. Cravey, *Women and Work in Mexico's Maquiladoras* (Lanham, MD: Rowman and Littlefield, 1998); Alfredo Hualde, "Industrial Relations in the *Maquiladora* Industry: Management's Search for Participation and Quality," in Maria Lorena Cook and Harry C. Katz (eds.), *Regional Integration and Industrial Relations in North America* (Ithaca, NY: Institute of Collective Bargaining, Cornell University, 1994), pp. 207–17; Kathryn Kopinak, *Desert Capitalism: Maquiladoras in North America's Western Industrial Corridor* (Tucson: University of Arizona Press, 1996); Geri Smith, "The Decline of the *Maquiladora*," *BusinessWeek* (April 29, 2002); Pete Engardio and Geri Smith, "Mexico: Business Is Standing Its Ground," *BusinessWeek* (April 20, 2009).

believe that some areas also include under-the-table inducements like lax enforcement of labor laws and government assistance in keeping out independent unions. An example of an export processing zone is the *maquiladora* sector in Mexico along the U.S. border (see the accompanying "Labor Relations Application" box).

International Investment Portfolios

International investment portfolios—cross-border flows of investment securities like stocks and bonds—are a third dimension of globalization. In contrast with FDI, this is foreign indirect investment and unlike FDI, this form of global investing occurs by institutional and individual investors who own foreign stocks and bonds or invest in international mutual funds. Shareholder activism, especially by large institutional investors such as union pension funds, might therefore seek to influence perceived problems with labor and environmental exploitation, such as concerns with the working conditions faced by workers making iPhones and iPads in China.

International investment can be beneficial: It provides working capital for local companies and financing for foreign government operations, improves risk sharing across borders, and allows investments to find their most productive uses.[15] But a large segment of international investing involves hedge funds and other professional investors engaging in currency speculation. This speculative, short-term focus causes high volatility in the foreign exchange markets that handle $5 trillion of transactions *each day*.[16] Such volatility destabilizes fragile developing country economies and can have severe negative effects on wages, job opportunities, and living standards.

Immigration

The fourth and final dimension of globalization is immigration, the cross-border flow of people. More than 240 million people live outside their countries of birth.[17] Like the other dimensions of globalization, immigration can be beneficial. As FDI and international portfolio flows allow capital to seek its highest rate of return, immigration gives labor the same opportunity. In other words, immigration provides an avenue for people to escape persecution and find a better life in a new country. By taking jobs that no one else wants or is qualified for, both unskilled and skilled immigrants can benefit the destination country if labor demand exceeds supply. Immigrants also bring new cultures, foods, and ideas.

But like the other dimensions of globalization, immigration is controversial because it has disadvantages and can create winners and losers. In particular, most immigrants to the United States are low-skilled. This does not negatively affect most U.S. workers, but it appears to provide additional competition for low-skilled workers, especially high school dropouts.[18] These workers therefore suffer from lower wages while employers and consumers benefit from lower labor costs and prices. Because of language barriers, fears of reprisal, cultural differences, and other factors, immigrant workforces also bring challenges and opportunities for union organizing.[19]

The United States has restricted the number of immigrants allowed to enter legally and work in the country since the 1920s because of a variety of complex fears including perceived threats to jobs, wages, social services, and national security. U.S. immigration law favors family reunification, and this is the basis for most legal immigration to the United States.[20] There are also a limited number of work visas available for skilled workers. Some argue that this program should be expanded in order to enhance the skill base and entrepreneurial activity of the economy while others fear that this would undermine the employment opportunities for existing skilled workers.[21] Undocumented immigration is also a very controversial topic, and U.S. employers are legally obligated to verify that each employee is eligible to work in the United States.[22]

GOVERNING THE GLOBAL WORKPLACE

Globalization can be regulated in various ways by diverse institutions. The primary U.S. policy is to promote free trade by reducing tariffs and other barriers to trade. The United States therefore negotiates free trade agreements with specific countries, such as the North American Free Trade Agreement (NAFTA) with Canada and Mexico, and participates in the multilateral global trading system administered by the World Trade Organization (WTO). Going even further in economic integration, the European Union is a free trade area that also includes free capital and labor mobility as well as common monetary and fiscal policies (see Table 11.4).

TABLE 11.4 Economic Integration Arrangements

	Reciprocal Trade Liberalization	Free Trade within Area	Common External Tariffs	Free Capital and Labor Mobility within Area	Common Monetary and Fiscal Policy	Examples
International Trading System	✓					World Trade Organization
Free Trade Area	✓	✓				NAFTA
Customs Union	✓	✓	✓			
Common Market	✓	✓	✓	✓		European Union ↓
Economic Union	✓	✓	✓	✓	✓	

Source: Adapted from Ali M. El-Agraa, *Economic Integration Worldwide* (New York: St. Martin's Press, 1997).

But how can workplaces be governed in these global systems? The alternatives parallel the alternatives for workplace governance discussed in a national context in Chapter 2. The free trade emphasis of U.S. policy is a free market mechanism for global workplace governance. Critics of unbridled free trade, however, believe that institutional intervention is necessary to protect workers (and the natural environment) from suffering the negative effects of social dumping and other pressures of globalization. Protections for workers can be pursued through the creation and enforcement of explicit international labor standards, increased enforcement of national laws, transnational employee representation or unionism, or voluntary corporate codes of conduct.

Enforceable labor standards are analogous to using government regulation to govern the global workplace. Two options are discussed here: worldwide standards through the International Labor Organization (ILO) and increased compliance with existing national laws through provisions attached to free trade agreements, such as NAFTA's labor side agreement. Using corporate codes of conduct to establish labor standards in the global arena is similar to relying on human resource policies to establish standards in the domestic arena—in both cases compliance is voluntary and relies on education and self-interest. Lastly, transnational employee representation is analogous to unionization and other forms of employee representation in the domestic context. Two alternatives are presented here: European Works Councils in the European Union and various attempts at transnational collective bargaining and labor solidarity.

Because of the importance of globalization for labor relations and business, these institutions are each important in their own right. But the WTO, ILO core labor standards, NAFTA and its side agreement, the European Union and its European Works Councils, examples of transnational collective bargaining, and corporate codes of conduct should also be considered as a set of alternatives for governing the global workplace.

FREE TRADE VIA THE WTO

The dominant institution for reducing trade barriers and pursuing free trade on a global scale is the **World Trade Organization (WTO).** The WTO is an international organization of over 160 member countries that provides a forum for negotiating and enforcing global trade agreements. The WTO promotes free trade through reduction of trade barriers. The most obvious trade barrier is a tariff (a tax on imports), but there are numerous others. Nontariff trade barriers include quotas (numerical restrictions on imported units), domestic subsidies (which make it more difficult for foreign firms to compete with a subsidized domestic firm), discriminatory government procurement policies (which also favor domestic producers), and regulations such as import licensing and product standards, which can be manipulated to favor domestic companies. The WTO seeks to reduce all these trade barriers. Additional factors that affect international trade, such as transportation costs, language barriers, and exchange rate risk, are beyond the scope of the WTO.

The WTO Supports Free Trade, Not Fair Trade

A key ongoing controversy is the difference between free trade and fair trade. Free trade is the removal of all trade barriers. **Fair trade** is the incorporation of labor, environmental, public health, and other standards into trade agreements and the ability to impose trade sanctions on countries that violate these standards. This is labeled fair trade because it is believed that adding these social clauses to trade agreements can prevent social dumping and avoid a "race to the bottom" in wages and working conditions. In other words, promoters of fair trade distinguish between legitimate and illegitimate (socially unacceptable) sources of comparative or competitive advantage.[23] An abundance of natural resources or differences in worker productivity are legitimate, but what about slavery? Should a country enjoy a comparative advantage because it uses slaves? This debate can extend to other possibly illegitimate practices: Child labor? Racial discrimination? Suppression of unions? Abuse of the environment? To date, many countries have opposed the inclusion of such standards in the WTO's free trade system. Opposition is particularly strong among the leaders of developing countries because they see labor standards as depriving their countries of their low labor costs comparative advantage.[24] So attempts to add labor and environmental standards to the overall WTO framework have failed.

Note, however, that the WTO system allows individual countries to establish standards that are "necessary to protect public morals [or] ... human, animal, or plant life or health" or conserve "exhaustible natural resources" as long as such standards are not trade barriers. As an example, the United States established the requirement that all tuna be caught with nets that are safe for dolphins. Labor activists would like to see the United States and other countries refuse to import goods from a country that violates basic labor standards or environmental standards.[25] Some countries, however, claim that such requirements are disguised trade barriers. The WTO has the authority to resolve trade disputes over these issues, and a country found in violation must change its trade policy or pay damages. Refusal to do so can result in trade sanctions.

Those who emphasize the efficiency gains of free markets (recall the mainstream economics school from Chapter 2) see free trade as optimal and therefore think national standards like dolphin-safe nets should be invalidated by the WTO as illegal trade barriers.[26] For those who question the fairness of free markets (recall the industrial relations school from Chapter 2), the push for free trade looks more like a way to satisfy the "desires of transnational corporations in search of lower cost labor and freer regulatory environments."[27] For those in this camp, then, fair trade with basic labor and environmental standards is needed, not unfettered free trade. This can be achieved through a broader interpretation of the WTO allowance of standards that are "necessary to protect human, animal, or plant life or health," but this has not yet happened on a widespread basis; rather, WTO rulings in trade disputes generally support free trade and the removal of national standards.[28]

INTERNATIONAL LABOR STANDARDS VIA THE ILO

The **International Labor Organization (ILO)** is a specialized agency of the United Nations focused on promoting social justice and internationally recognized human and labor rights. The ILO was created in 1919 as part of the peace settlement that ended World War I; it became the United Nations' first specialized agency at the end of World War II. Most countries now belong to the ILO, which has a unique tripartite structure: Each country sends two government representatives plus a worker representative and an employer representative. The ILO is the undisputed chief international authority on labor standards, and its primary activity is adopting and promoting conventions that specify minimum labor standards on particular issues. Nearly 200 conventions have been adopted to date. Technical assistance to help implement these standards is also provided.[29]

Against a backdrop of growing concern with labor issues and globalization, the ILO adopted the Declaration on Fundamental Principles and Rights at Work in 1998. This declaration establishes a set of **core labor standards:** freedom of association and collective bargaining, the abolition of forced labor, no discrimination in employment and pay, and the elimination of child labor, which are all declared to be "fundamental to the rights of human beings at work." However, labor standards—core or otherwise—are not legally enforceable. The ILO relies on publicity, diplomacy, and technical assistance, not legal or economic punishment, to encourage compliance with its labor standards.[30]

Consequently, supporters of the ILO labor standards try to work with international bodies to increase the visibility of the standards, and ideally to make them enforceable. This has resulted in the World Bank requiring companies that borrow money from its International Finance Corporation to agree to follow the ILO's core labor standards.[31] For a more comprehensive approach, note again that unlike the ILO, the WTO has the authority to issue rulings and impose trade sanctions. Consequently, a commonly-proposed way to establish universal, enforceable global labor standards would be to marry the expertise of the ILO with the power of the WTO.[32] Adding a social clause to global trade agreements that would require countries to adhere to the ILO's core labor standards would let the WTO impose trade sanctions on countries that violate these standards (as is currently the case for countries that establish illegal trade barriers such as tariffs). But as noted above, leaders of developing countries and free trade economists see labor standards as protectionist trade measures to protect developed country jobs. So efforts to link ILO labor standards to WTO trade regulations have yet to be successful.

Even though enforceable global labor standards do not exist on a broad scale, it is still an important issue to understand. Note further that this approach is essentially a government regulation model of governing the workplace (recall Chapter 2) on a global scale. A uniform set of rules and standards is established, and violations can be punished. The debates over enforceable labor standards therefore parallel debates over the wisdom of government regulation—especially the difficulty of establishing universally applicable laws and the negative efficiency consequences of interfering in free markets. This is true whether the standards are established globally, or among specific sets of countries, such as the United States, Canada, and Mexico.

DOMESTIC LEGAL COMPLIANCE VIA NAFTA AND OTHER U.S. FREE TRADE AGREEMENTS

In addition to being part of the WTO, the United States has negotiated its own free trade agreements with some countries, such as Australia, Jordan, and Korea, with more agreements currently in the process of being negotiated or implemented, namely the Trans-Pacific Partnership and the Transatlantic Trade and Investment Partnership. The most visible is the 1992 North American Free Trade Agreement (NAFTA) among the United States, Canada, and Mexico. NAFTA eliminated tariff and nontariff trade barriers among the three countries, allowed companies based in any of the three countries to invest, sell services, and bid on government contracts in all three countries, and protected intellectual property rights. Also important are detailed rules of origin specifying that products must contain a minimum amount of North American content—for example, 62.5 percent for automobiles—to be part of the North American free trade zone. Note, however, an important asymmetry in NAFTA that is also common in other free trade arrangements: Companies are free to invest in all three NAFTA countries, but individuals are not free to work outside their home countries. In other words, NAFTA and other free trade agreements allow capital mobility but not labor mobility.

NAFTA's Labor Side Agreement

NAFTA includes a side agreement, the **North American Agreement on Labor Cooperation (NAALC),** to address labor's fears that low Mexican wages might undercut U.S. competitiveness, put downward pressure on U.S. wages and working conditions, and cause widespread plant closings. In other words, the NAALC is intended to prevent social dumping; a separate side agreement similarly seeks to protect the environment. The NAALC provides 11 guiding principles that the three countries commit to promote—including union activity, nondiscrimination, equal pay, minimum wages, and workplace safety—but these are not uniform standards and are not enforced through trade sanctions (see Table 11.5). Rather, the explicit emphasis in the NAALC is on cooperation to promote compliance with existing domestic laws. No new laws are required, nor are there restrictions on future laws. Article 2, for example, explicitly recognizes "the right of each [country] to establish its own domestic labor standards," and the NAALC's intent is to ensure that those domestic labor standards—whatever they may be—are enforced. Each country was required to establish a national administrative office (NAO) to collect information. If people think that a domestic labor law is not being enforced, they can file a complaint with that country's NAO. If the NAO believes a labor law violation has occurred, it can recommend that the relevant secretaries of labor consult with one another. There are also complex provisions for additional hearings and even arbitration with penalties if consultation fails to resolve certain complaints, but these provisions are full of limitations and restrictions.[33] As such, the NAALC dispute resolution procedures are best thought of as public consultation without significant enforcement powers.[34] Compliance depends on the "sunshine factor"—adverse publicity that stems from the public NAALC proceedings—or in other words, the "naming and shaming" of violators.[35]

As of mid-2016, thirty-nine NAO submissions have been filed alleging a violation of domestic labor law.[36] Most complaints have named multinational companies as the violators, but some have alleged violations by one of the three governments as a public sector employer. The U.S. NAO has received the most complaints (23), followed by Mexico (10) and Canada (6). Fewer than half the complaints have reached the ministerial consultation stage, and no submissions have advanced past this consultation stage. Evaluation of the NAALC cases fails to reveal a strong pattern of victories for organized labor and workers' rights advocates.[37] One success story appears to be a complaint about pre- and postemployment discrimination against pregnant women in Mexico's *maquiladora* sector (U.S. NAO case 9701). Although preemployment discrimination against pregnant women is legal in Mexico, postemployment discrimination is not; and as a result of the publicity generated by this NAALC case, the Mexican government has increased inspections and education on this issue.

On the other hand, in cases involving freedom of association and collective bargaining, violations do not appear to have been remedied. Workers fired for union activity, for

TABLE 11.5
NAFTA's Labor Side Agreement

Excerpts from the North American Agreement on Labor Cooperation (1993):

Article 1: Objectives
The objectives of this Agreement are to:

1. improve working conditions and living standards in each Party's territory;
2. promote, to the maximum extent possible, the labor principles set out in Annex 1;
3. encourage cooperation to promote innovation and rising levels of productivity and quality;
4. encourage publication and exchange of information, data development and coordination, and joint studies to enhance mutually beneficial understanding of the laws and institutions governing labor in each Party's territory;
5. pursue cooperative labor-related activities on the basis of mutual benefit;
6. promote compliance with, and effective enforcement by each Party of, its labor law; and
7. foster transparency in the administration of labor law.

Article 2: Levels of Protection
Affirming full respect for each Party's constitution, and recognizing the right of each Party to establish its own domestic labor standards, and to adopt or modify accordingly its labor laws and regulations, each Party shall ensure that its labor laws and regulations provide for high labor standards, consistent with high-quality and -productivity workplaces, and shall continue to strive to improve those standards in that light.

Article 3: Government Enforcement Action

1. Each Party shall promote compliance with and effectively enforce its labor law through appropriate government action . . .

. . .

Annex 1: Labor Principles
The following are guiding principles that the Parties are committed to promote, subject to each Party's domestic law, but do not establish common minimum standards for their domestic law. They indicate broad areas of concern where the Parties have developed, each in its own way, laws, regulations, procedures, and practices that protect the rights and interests of their respective workforces.

1. **Freedom of association and protection of the right to organize**
   The right of workers exercised freely and without impediment to establish and join organizations of their own choosing to further and defend their interests.
2. **The right to bargain collectively**
   The protection of the right of organized workers to freely engage in collective bargaining on matters concerning the terms and conditions of employment.
3. **The right to strike**
   The protection of the right of workers to strike in order to defend their collective interests.
4. **Prohibition of forced labor**
   The prohibition and suppression of all forms of forced or compulsory labor, except for types of compulsory work generally considered acceptable by the Parties, such as compulsory military service, certain civic obligations, prison labor not for private purposes, and work exacted in cases of emergency.
5. **Labor protections for children and young persons**
   The establishment of restrictions on the employment of children and young persons that may vary taking into consideration relevant factors likely to jeopardize the full physical, mental, and moral development of young persons, including schooling and safety requirements.

(continued)

TABLE 11.5
(Continued)

6. Minimum employment standards
The establishment of minimum employment standards, such as minimum wages and overtime pay, for wage earners, including those not covered by collective agreements.

7. Elimination of employment discrimination
Elimination of employment discrimination on such grounds as race, religion, age, sex, or other grounds, subject to certain reasonable exceptions, such as, where applicable, *bona fide* occupational requirements or qualifications and established practices or rules governing retirement ages, and special measures of protection or assistance for particular groups designed to take into account the effects of discrimination.

8. Equal pay for women and men
Equal wages for women and men by applying the principle of equal pay for equal work in the same establishment.

9. Prevention of occupational injuries and illnesses
Prescribing and implementing standards to minimize the causes of occupational injuries and illnesses.

10. Compensation in cases of occupational injuries and illnesses
The establishment of a system providing benefits and compensation to workers or their dependents in cases of occupational injuries, accidents, or fatalities arising out of, linked with, or occurring in the course of employment.

11. Protection of migrant workers
Providing migrant workers in a Party's territory with the same legal protection as the Party's nationals in respect of working conditions.

. . .

Note: The full text is available at www.naalc.org.

example, are not reinstated; and independent unions in Mexico that challenge state- or company-dominated unions have yet to gain recognition. Instead workshops and academic studies have been the frequent product of ministerial consultations (see the "Labor Relations Application" box describing the Sony NAALC case).

Despite this poor track record, some remain optimistic that the NAALC can promote the 11 principles outlined in Table 11.5.[38] This optimism stems from at least three factors. First, the NAALC partners have been successful in educational activities and in increasing cross-border understanding. Perhaps this provides a foundation for greater protection of rights in the future. Second, the sunshine aspect of the NAALC procedures provides the opportunity to generate public concern over trade and labor issues. Although the existing process does not work perfectly, it might be a starting point for building stronger public forums to examine trade–labor linkages. And third, the submission process also provides the opportunity for greater cross-border cooperation among unions.

Indeed, it is this last element that seems to have generated the most lasting effects. Specifically, unlike protests against the WTO in which labor is an outsider, the NAALC-NAO machinery provides a legitimate mechanism for labor to express and seek resolution of grievances, and also specifies procedural rules that require cross-border contact. This provides the basis for unions in the three countries to cooperate in repeated, concrete ways, which in turn has created some enduring, transnational union relationships.[39] Moreover, led by the Canadian labor movement, NAFTA caused a shift in the attitudes of the Canadian and U.S. labor movements that went from seeing Mexican workers as "foreign workers" who are the problem—attitudes often tinged with racist stereotypes—to seeing them as partners in their struggle.[40] These attitudinal changes go beyond NAFTA—the U.S. labor

Labor Relations Application The Sony NAALC Case

A Sony subsidiary in Mexico's *maquiladora* sector was the subject of an early case under the North American Agreement on Labor Cooperation (NAALC), which was added to NAFTA to facilitate enforcement of existing domestic labor laws. On paper, Mexican labor law is quite favorable to workers—much more favorable than U.S. labor law; but in reality, unions are frequently weak, state-controlled extensions of the government's economic development strategy. Such unions are often affiliated with the *Confederación de Trabajadores México* (CTM, Confederation of Mexican Workers) and are used to prevent the formation of more aggressive, independent unions.

At Sony, workers were frustrated with the CTM- affiliated union's acquiescence to management demands, and they therefore tried to form an independent union. The CTM union held a fraudulent election to prevent dissidents from winning any leadership positions, and police broke up a resulting peaceful protest. The Mexican Conciliation and Arbitration Board (CAB) rejected a petition for a decertification election on a technicality. Dissident workers who were involved in the organizing drive were threatened and fired. By many accounts Sony, the government-controlled CTM union, and the government's CAB conspired to prevent the formation of an independent union.

Within the NAALC procedures, two human rights organizations from Mexico and two from the United States filed a complaint with the U.S. National Administrative Office (NAO) alleging that these actions violated Mexican labor law (NAO Submission No. 940003, 1994). After a hearing, the NAO report found sufficient questions about the enforcement of Mexican law with respect to unjust dismissals and the union registration process in this case that it recommended ministerial consultations.

Subsequently, the U.S. Secretary of Labor and the Mexican Secretary of Labour consulted with each other and agreed to a program of workshops, seminars, and studies to improve understanding of the union registration procedures. Mexican government officials also agreed to meet with employees, Sony management, and local CAB officials to discuss the case. A follow-up report by the NAO six months later found that the discharged workers had not been reinstated and no election for the independent union had been held.

References: Norman Caulfield, *NAFTA and Labor in North America* (Urbana: University of Illinois Press, 2010); George Tsogas, *Labor Regulation in a Global Economy* (Armonk, NY: M. E. Sharpe, 2001).

movement now openly embraces organizing immigrant workers and the AFL-CIO supports comprehensive immigration reform that includes a pathway to citizenship for undocumented workers. So while the NAALC machinery is limited, it appears to have been the surprising catalyst for other changes.

Extending the NAALC Model

With both its pitfalls and potential, the NAALC framework illustrates another alternative for trying to balance efficiency, equity, and voice in the global workplace. In fact, the United States has extended this NAALC model to bilateral and regional trade agreements negotiated after NAFTA, such as those with Jordan (2000), Central American countries (CAFTA, 2004), Australia (2005), and Korea (2012). In each of these, the signatory countries pledged to respect the core ILO labor standards through enforcement of their respective domestic labor laws. Though the dispute resolution mechanisms vary across these free trade agreements, none of them require changes to the countries' existing labor laws, even if they appear inadequate.[41] For some, this bilateral or regional approach is better than a universal approach as would be the case under the WTO not only because it's politically more feasible but also because agreements can be better tailored to specific situations, and non-governmental actors like unions and human rights groups can be better incorporated into monitoring and enforcement.[42] For others, however, bilateralism and regionalism run the risk of creating fragmented standards with unequal enforcement, uneven application, and uncertain legal status.[43] This is similar to other debates over the appropriate level of government regulation, for example federal or state.

TRANSNATIONAL EMPLOYEE CONSULTATION IN THE EUROPEAN UNION

Part of the rationale for creating a North American free trade zone through NAFTA was to counter the expanding European Union (EU). The EU is an integrated community of over 25 European nations. As evidenced by the debates over Britain's vote in 2016 to leave, the EU is more integrated than a simple free trade area like the one created by NAFTA (recall Table 11.4). Rather, the EU includes common external tariffs, extensive capital mobility across the member countries, elements of common monetary and fiscal policies, a common currency (the euro), legislative powers, and attempts to coordinate foreign policies. Unlike free trade arrangements under the WTO and NAFTA, residents of the EU are allowed to freely work in any EU country. This free movement has allowed workers, especially those from eastern Europe, to seek better employment opportunities elsewhere in Europe, but has also caused controversies as construction firms and other companies from lower-wage European countries have established operations in higher-wage countries using low-paid workers who are "posted" from their home countries.[44] Indeed, against a backdrop of fear over the effects of mass migration on income, jobs, services like the national health system, public safety, and national identity, the key factor in Britain's vote to leave the EU was concern with the difficulty of limiting migration into Britain while in the EU.

Policymaking in the European Union

Though the main impetus for European unification has been preventing additional European wars, noninflationary economic growth (not labor and social standards) is a priority of the EU. So economic concerns prevail over labor and social concerns (as in the WTO and NAFTA). In other words, the EU has long embraced the "reasoning that the social caboose would be pulled by the economic locomotive."[45] Nevertheless, there has been concern with labor standards because of respect for basic human dignity and fears of social dumping from member countries with lower standards and labor costs—such as Portugal—to countries with more generous standards and higher labor costs—such as Germany.[46]

As a result, the Charter of Fundamental Rights of the European Union specifies a number of workers' rights, including freedom of movement, equal treatment and compensation for men and women, health and safety protections, annual leave, access to training, guarantees of information and consultation, the freedom of association to join labor unions, and the right to engage in collective bargaining and to strike.[47] And because the EU is more than simply a free trade zone, the EU-level political institutions can issue follow-up laws that enact specific sections of the charter. A number of binding directives has been passed by the European Council of Ministers that obligates the EU-member countries to achieve specific results.[48] For example, a 2008 directive mandates equal pay and working conditions between temporary workers and regular employees. However, the commitment to a "European Social Model" has been called into question by (a) recent trends toward the use of nonbinding "soft law" recommendations and social dialogue instead of enforceable "hard law" directives, and (2) European Court of Justice rulings that favor the free movement of goods and services over workers' rights.[49]

European Works Councils: Definition and Operation

The EU policy that is of particular interest to the subject of labor relations and employee representation is the directive "on the establishment of a European Works Council or a procedure in community-scale undertakings and community-scale groups of undertakings for the purposes of informing and consulting employees" (generally referred to as the "European Works Council directive").[50] This is also important to consider in the context of globalization because European Works Councils represent another approach to addressing workers' concerns in a global context—that is, through information sharing and consultation between multinational corporations and their multinational workforces.

For companies with significant operations in at least two EU countries, a **European Works Council** is a transnational, company-level committee of employees from these different operations that has consultation and information rights on issues that affect workers in more than one country. Because EU directives allow individual countries to determine implementation details, the European Works Council directive specifies minimum standards: Councils must meet with management at least once a year, must be informed and consulted regarding the "progress of the business," and

> The meeting shall relate in particular to the structure, economic and financial situation, the probable development of the business and of production and sales, the situation and probable trend of employment, investments, and substantial changes concerning organization, introduction of new working methods or production processes, transfers of production, mergers, cutbacks or closures of undertakings, establishments or important parts thereof, and collective redundancies (Annex 2).

A company's European Works Council can also request a meeting with management when there are exceptional circumstances, such as a plant closing. Expenses are paid by the company. Additional details such as the council's size, allocation of members, location and duration of meetings, and procedure for consultation are left up to individual companies and their employees. The requirements for what information must be provided and whether employee representatives are elected by the employees or appointed by elected union officials are determined by the national law of the country in which the company is headquartered.[51]

The rationale for this directive is to enhance employees' rights to consultation and information that pertains to their company and employment situation. Note carefully that this does not grant workers the right to bargain: Specific terms and conditions of employment such as wages are not negotiated by European Works Councils (though within each country, some workers might be represented in collective bargaining by national unions). Rather, a European Works Council lets employees learn about their company's financial health and future plans (the information aspect) and have a voice in providing feedback and ideas about these plans (the consultation aspect). These are viewed as important workers' rights, but the EU directive also states the belief that "harmonious" development of economic activities will be aided by informing and consulting with employees. Rather than creating a bargaining relationship, the European Works Council directive is intended to create a cooperative dialogue between labor and management.

European Works Councils in Practice

In practice, European Works Councils can be divided into four categories: symbolic, service, project-oriented, and participative.[52] Symbolic European Works Councils are passive and fulfill the minimum requirements of the directive by a single annual meeting in which management provides limited information and the representatives do not try to engage in a dialogue. A service European Works Council has a more active information flow but primarily services national unions by passing along the information received by the council. Project-oriented European Works Councils build their own internal capabilities and pursue projects—such as comparing employment conditions across plants in the company—beyond the scope of the required meetings with management. A participative European Works Council is the most advanced form and includes active consultation and perhaps joint projects with management.

Although symbolic European Works Councils contribute little toward employee representation, the other forms have greater potential. At BMW, the activities of the European

Works Council have been modest, but they provided a mechanism for British and German union leaders to develop communication and trust—which was important when the British union leaders engaged in traditional negotiations with BMW management.[53] The European Works Council at Nestlé is an example of a participative council. The works council and management established a consultation procedure for discussing plant closures and for implementing equal opportunity policies.[54] At Unilever, the European Works Council has actively pursued activities outside the annual meeting with management. The top two officials meet monthly, and this European Works Council has developed a system to integrate information received by the European-level council and the workplace-level works councils in each country. A handbook of guidelines for corporate restructuring has also been developed, and the European Works Council has been actively involved with management in implementing Unilever's restructuring initiatives.

A common thread in many success stories, however, is the presence of strong national unions. The BMW, Nestlé, and Unilever examples all include union leaders as council members. The General Motors European Works Council similarly has had strong union participation and linkages, albeit not strong enough to always overcome local interests to save jobs (see the "Labor Relations Application" box discussing the General Motors European Works Council). In contrast, McDonald's has been successful in marginalizing a union presence in its European Works Council, and in fact a majority of the council members are salaried managers even though 90 percent of McDonald's employees are hourly workers; the council is therefore merely symbolic.[55] That individual council members come from very different national systems (Chapter 12) not only raises language issues and the reality of national over European identity but also means that there are challenges resulting from very different expectations about what employee voice should consist of (e.g., bargaining or social dialogue) and the fact that those from countries with stronger unions might see that as a better route for influence.[56] European Works Councils are an intriguing option for representing employee interests in a global economy, but the exact route to making them effective is difficult.

TRANSNATIONAL COLLECTIVE BARGAINING

With increased globalization and multinational corporate activity, labor unions are under pressure to collaborate across international borders.[57] This transnational collaboration ranges from simple messages of solidarity to sympathy strikes, from sharing information to conducting coordinated lobbying or public pressure campaigns, and from helping establish unions in developing countries to coordinating collective bargaining. Corporate global initiatives are facilitated by free trade arrangements such as the WTO and NAFTA, but international labor union activities rarely are. In fact, laws restricting sympathy strikes, secondary boycotts, and affiliations of labor unions with international federations all hamper transnational collaboration.[58] The NAALC procedures under NAFTA pushed some unions to work together across borders, and another exception is the European Works Council directive because unions can use European Works Councils to develop networks and alliances with other unions (recall the Labor Relations Application on the General Motors European Works Council).[59] But more generally, unions cannot rely on international treaties or public policies to facilitate transnational collaboration, and the labor movement has instead created its own institutions for international solidarity.

Institutions for Fostering International Labor Solidarity

The apex of international labor organizations is the **International Trade Union Confederation (ITUC).**[60] The ITUC is a worldwide federation of national union federations

Labor Relations Application The European Works Council and Union Solidarity at General Motors Europe

Throughout the first decade of the 21st century, General Motors (GM) Europe has struggled with profitability and has therefore attempted numerous restructuring plans. GM is required to consult with its European Works Council before implementing major restructuring plans, but the European Works Council, which calls itself the European Employees' Forum, often feels that GM takes action without such consultations. With strong leadership and active trade union participation, the GM European Works Council has aggressively challenged this lack of consultation. Most notably, several European Days of Action have pressured GM Europe to negotiate its restructuring plans.

On January 25, 2001, for example, more than 40,000 workers, including 7,000 in Belgium, 16,000 in Germany, 11,000 in Great Britain, 1,000 in Portugal, and 5,000 in Spain, stopped working for a day and caused GM to negotiate a framework agreement with its European Works Council. This framework agreement specified important principles to guide GM's restructuring. National unions were involved in administering this agreement in each country and in making sure the principles were followed. Work was also stopped at various European GM plants for an hour or more on similar Days of Action in between 2004 and 2009.

Also, to prevent GM workers in different countries from competing against each other, GM's European Works Council helped the unions involved agree to a solidarity pact that presents a unified front to GM and combats whipsawing. With these activities, the GM European Works Council were not been able to stop GM's restructuring and prevent job cuts, but it helped employee voices be heard during the drafting and implementation of GM's restructuring efforts. In 2012, however, unions in Poland and the UK struck their own deals with GM to keep plants open, undermining earlier years of cross-national cooperation.

Reference: Magdalena Bernaciak, "Labour Solidarity in Crisis? Lessons from General Motors," *Industrial Relations Journal* 44 (March 2013), pp. 139–53.

such as the AFL–CIO (United States), Trades Union Congress (Great Britain), *Deutscher Gewerkschaftsbund* (DGB, German Trade Union Confederation), and over 300 others from more than 160 countries representing 180 million union members around the world. The ITUC resulted from the merger of two longstanding federations, the western-oriented International Confederation of Free Trade Unions and the leftist World Federation of Trade Unions, to try to strengthen international union solidarity and have more influence in the global sociopolitical–economic system.

The ITUC's main objectives are to facilitate consultation, communication, and cooperation among unions. To pursue these objectives, the ITUC collects and publishes information and research to keep unions abreast of developments in other countries. The ITUC also provides education and training to union leaders and financial assistance to emerging labor movements. In the international arena, the ITUC is an important advocate for organized labor, especially when lobbying transnational organizations such as the World Trade Organization. The ITUC is also pushing for multinational corporations to adopt codes of conduct that respect basic workers' rights (discussed in the next section).

The ITUC cooperates closely with 11 global union federations (see *www.global-unions.org*). Global union federations are "international associations of national trade unions representing workers in specific industries, industry groups, occupations, professions, or other sectors of employment such as the public services."[61] For example, the International Transport Workers' Federation (ITF) includes more than 600 unions from over 140 countries that represent 4.5 million workers in various transportation industries such as railroads, trucking, airlines, shipping, and longshoring. Although these are international federations like the ITUC, the global union federations are composed of national unions, not national union federations (see Figure 11.1). The global union federations promote transnational collaboration through information exchange, publicity, education, and various solidarity actions.[62]

FIGURE 11.1
The Structure of the International Labor Movement

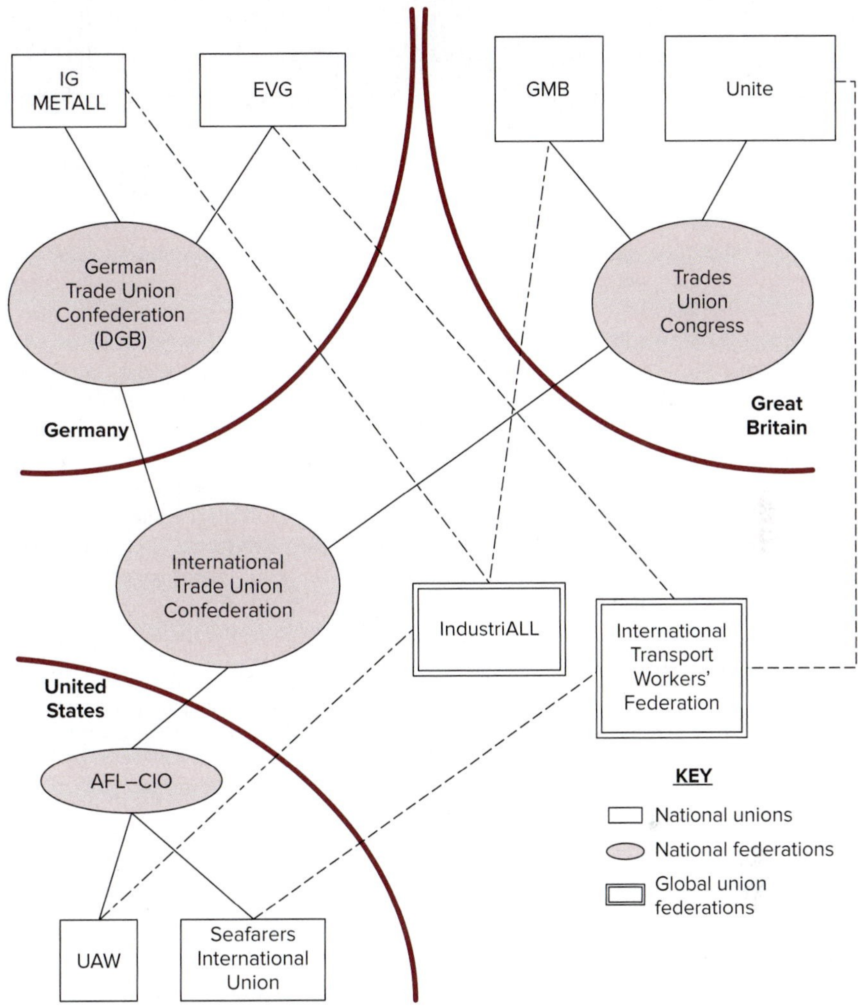

International Labor Solidarity in Practice

There are significant barriers to transnational labor collaboration: in addition to being expensive, there can be language barriers, cultural, religious, and ideological differences, a lack of interconnected social networks, fears of losing domestic autonomy, legal constraints, differences in union structures and goals, and employer resistance.[63] Consequently, the starting point for building transnational collaboration is through international solidarity actions in support of organizing campaigns or bargaining disputes in one country.[64] The ITF has led campaigns supporting global delivery workers for over two decades (see the accompanying "Labor Relations Application" box). During a United Mine Workers of America coal strike, unions in Australia, Colombia, and South Africa conducted 24-hour sympathy strikes at mines and factories owned by the same multinational parent corporation.[65] Screenwriters in Britain, Ireland, Germany, France, Australia, and elsewhere conducted coordinated demonstrations to support the Hollywood writers' strike in 2007; Cooper Tire workers in Serbia and the United Kingdom rallied in support of locked-out U.S. Cooper Tire workers in 2011; in 2016, workers from various European countries participated in coordinated protests against a GE restructuring plan.

Labor Relations Application International Labor Solidarity in the Global Delivery Business

The Teamsters' strike against UPS in 1997 has been widely cited as an example of how organized labor can succeed by mobilizing greater rank-and-file participation and by emphasizing issues that resonate with the public—in this case, the plight of part-time workers. However, the UPS strike also involved significant actions of international labor solidarity by UPS unions in other countries. Before the strike, the International Transport Workers' Federation (ITF) created the ITF World Council of UPS Unions which provided a forum for unions from 11 countries to share information about UPS business strategies as well as working conditions, including common concerns with part-time workers and lifting injuries.

The council subsequently led a UPS World Action Day in May 1997 that included actions at 150 locations around the world. Most actions were demonstrations or information distribution efforts, but half-day strikes occurred in Spain and Italy. In August, 185,000 U.S. UPS workers went on strike for 15 days. During the strike, British workers engaged in a sick-out (a "brown flu" because of the color of their uniforms), workers in Belgium struck to resolve outstanding health and safety issues, and demonstrations in Spain and the Philippines temporarily disrupted package deliveries. These actions also raised the public profile of issues pertaining to safety and part-time workers in many countries, which furthered empowered workers to address those issues.

The ITF subsequently created a global delivery network to exchange information and build solidarity among unions and workers in the world's largest delivery companies, such as DHL, FedEx, and UPS. In 2010, a Global Action Day to support fired union activists at UPS in Turkey included solidarity actions in numerous countries, including Germany, Japan, Korea, Thailand, South Africa, India, Argentina, and the United States. The workers' reinstatement and recognition of their union in 2011 was largely credited to this and related international support actions. In 2016, actions in Poland, Australia, Korea, India, and elsewhere were conducted to pressure DHL to correct abuses in Chile, Colombia, and Peru.

Sources: Andrew Banks and John Russo, "The Development of International Campaign-Based Network Structures: A Case Study of the IBT and ITF World Council of UPS Unions," *Comparative Labor Law and Policy Journal* 20 (Summer 1999), pp. 543–68; http://www.itfglobal.org/en/cross-sectoral-work/supply-chain-logistics/.

In addition to these international solidarity campaigns, global union federations are being increasingly successful in getting multinational corporations to sign international framework agreements in which the corporations pledge to respect workers' rights such as organizing labor unions and having safe workplaces. Some agreements go further; for example, the services industry global union federation Uni negotiated a framework agreements with G4S, the world's largest security firm, that provides for union access to workers, employer neutrality, and a dispute resolution procedure in addition to a pledge to respect the ILO's core conventions, while Uni pledges to help prevent unauthorized work stoppages. The implementation of framework agreements is left to unions in each country.[66] The GS4 agreement paved the way for union organizing success in South Africa and several other countries, but unions in India did not have success.[67] Indeed, if unions have little leverage, these framework agreements are reduced to voluntary corporate codes of conduct.

Whether these international solidarity campaigns and international framework agreements give domestic unions sufficient leverage to confront the pressures of globalization, or whether these efforts need to develop into true transnational collective bargaining alliances is an open question. In the meantime, true transnational collective bargaining—in which unions in more than one country negotiate jointly with the same company over wages and other economic items—is rare. U.S. and Canadian Chrysler workers were covered by a single UAW contract in the 1970s, but the U.S. and Canadian situations were so similar that one can question whether this was truly international bargaining. Some transnational collective bargaining occurs in flag-of-convenience shipping—shipping companies who are granted flags from developing countries for a small fee. Without a real attachment to these countries, these companies are effectively unregulated by national laws. The ITF has negotiated roughly 150 contracts with shipping companies that have been able to dodge national unions. These agreements, however, must be enforced by national unions at their local ports—for example, by refusing to unload a ship if it does not demonstrate compliance with the negotiated standards for wages and hours.[68] As with the other forms of international labor solidarity, then, the effectiveness of transnational labor collaboration crucially depends on the strength of domestic labor unions in their home countries.

Online Exploration Exercise: Explore the sites or tweets of the International Trade Union Confederation (*www.ituc-csi.org*) or of a global union federation such as Education International (*www.ei-ie.org*) or the International Transport Workers' Federation (*www.itfglobal.org*). What are some of the current campaigns? What campaigns can you find that pertain to collective bargaining? Is there a transnational aspect to this collective bargaining situation?

CORPORATE CODES OF CONDUCT

A **corporate code of conduct** is a written statement of standards that a company pledges to follow in its business activities often as part of a corporate social responsibility (CSR) initiative. The codes can be created by transnational governmental organizations (such as the ILO) or by national and local governments, but they are more frequently established by labor unions and other allied organizations or by individual corporations on their own. A code of conduct can touch on many subjects, including corporate governance, human rights, sustainability, and labor standards.[69] Codes that include labor issues commonly include outcome standards, such as minimum work age, minimum wages, maximum hours, health and safety standards, and nondiscrimination, as well as process standards, including the right to freedom of association (to form unions) and collective bargaining.[70] These codes are almost always voluntary which means that compliance cannot be legally enforced; one emerging, possible exception is when an entity makes these standards part of a procurement agreement, such as a university contracting with an apparel maker for logoed sweatshirts.[71]

Why Corporate Codes of Conduct?

In the 1970s and 1980s, U.S. multinationals were pressured to follow the antiapartheid Sullivan Principles by desegregating their South African workplaces and promoting advancement opportunities for black South Africans. And then in the 1990s, an antisweatshop movement grew out of very visible examples of labor abuses in the supplier networks of Nike and other apparel brands.[72] To counter bad publicity and damage to their brands, apparel companies starting adopting voluntary codes of conduct. Fast forward to today and codes of conduct are widespread for companies and their suppliers. Wal-Mart's supplier code of conduct is shown in the accompanying "Labor Relations Application" box and is meant to be displayed in the language of the employees in a common area in the workplaces of all suppliers along with a way to confidentially report violations.

Wal-Mart's approach is an example of a code developed and monitored by the company. Also common in the apparel industry are codes developed and monitored by non-profit workers' rights groups. One such group is the Fair Labor Association (*www.fairlabor.org*), a collaborative effort of universities, civil society organizations, and over 50 companies

Labor Relations Application Wal-Mart's Standards for Suppliers

1. COMPLIANCE WITH LAWS

Suppliers and their designated manufacturing facilities ("Suppliers") must fully comply with all applicable national and/or local laws and regulations, including but not limited to those related to labor, immigration, health and safety, and the environment.

2. VOLUNTARY LABOR

All labor must be voluntary. Slave, child, underage, forced, bonded, or indentured labor will not be tolerated. Suppliers shall not engage in or support trafficking in human beings. Suppliers shall certify that they have implemented procedures to manage the materials, including all labor related processes, incorporated into their products to ensure they comply with laws on slavery and human trafficking. Workers must be allowed to maintain control over their identity documents.

3. LABOR HOURS

Suppliers must provide workers with rest days and must ensure that working hours are consistent with the law and not excessive.

4. HIRING AND EMPLOYMENT PRACTICES

Suppliers must implement hiring practices that accurately verify workers' age and legal right to work in the country prior to employment. All terms and conditions of employment including, but not limited to, hiring, pay, training, promotion, termination, and retirement must be based on an individual's ability and willingness to do the job.

5. COMPENSATION

Suppliers must compensate all workers with wages, overtime premiums, and benefits that meet or exceed legal standards or collective agreements, whichever are higher. Suppliers are encouraged to provide wages that meet local industry standards. Suppliers are encouraged to provide wages and benefits that are sufficient to meet workers' basic needs and provide some discretionary income for workers and their families.

6. FREEDOM OF ASSOCIATION AND COLLECTIVE BARGAINING

Suppliers must respect the right of workers to choose whether to lawfully and peacefully form or join trade unions of their choosing and to bargain collectively.

7. HEALTH AND SAFETY

Suppliers must provide workers with a safe and healthy work environment. Suppliers must take proactive measures to prevent workplace hazards.

8. DORMITORIES AND CANTEEN

Suppliers who provide residential and dining facilities for their workers must provide safe, healthy and sanitary facilities.

9. ENVIRONMENT

Suppliers should ensure that every manufacturing facility complies with environmental laws, including all laws related to waste disposal, air emissions, discharges, toxic substances and hazardous waste disposal. Suppliers must validate that all input materials and components were obtained from permissible harvests consistent with international treaties and protocols in addition to local laws and regulations.

10. GIFTS AND ENTERTAINMENT

Suppliers must not offer gifts or entertainment to Walmart associates.

11. CONFLICTS OF INTEREST

Suppliers must not enter into transactions with Walmart associates that create a conflict of interest.

12. ANTI-CORRUPTION

Suppliers must not tolerate, permit, or engage in bribery, corruption, or unethical practices whether in dealings with public officials or individuals in the private sector.

13. FINANCIAL INTEGRITY

Suppliers must keep accurate records of all matters related to their business with Walmart in accordance with standard accounting practices such as Generally Accepted Accounting Principles (GAAP) or International Financial Reporting Standards (IFRS).

Source: corporate.walmart.com/sourcing-standards-resources

and suppliers, including adidas, Apple, Nestlé, Nike, and Under Armour.[73] Its code of conduct requires adherence to national laws and specifies requirements for nondiscrimination, freedom of association and collective bargaining, health and safety, environmental mitigation, and compensation fulfilling workers' basic needs, along with prohibitions against forced and child labor, excessive work hours, and all forms of harassment or abuse.

The code is monitored by the Fair Labor Association, which requires that employees be informed of the standards and given opportunities to report noncompliance, and accredited external monitors also conduct inspections. Companies can use product labels to demonstrate their compliance. Spurred by college student activism against sweatshops, over 150 colleges and universities require the producers of their licensed apparel to adhere to the Fair Labor Association standards. The Fair Labor Association is funded primarily by the companies and while it is not a corporate-controlled program, it is heavily corporate influenced.[74] Other similar initiatives includes the ILO's Better Work program and Worldwide Responsible Accredited Production ("WRAP").

Corporate codes of conduct are more visible in apparel, retailing, and other similar industries partly because of the value of maintaining a good consumer brand. But this form of worker activism is also connected to the nature of the supply chain.[75] These industries have a buyer-driven global supply chain consisting of very decentralized production that requires low capital investment. Production is outsourced on the basis of low labor costs; turnover is high, the workforce is vulnerable, and production can easily shift to new locations. These conditions are not conducive to traditional union campaigns focused on mobilizing worker power directed at the company. Rather, labor protest flares up organically, the workers' basic human rights grievances have the potential to resonate with the public, and alliances of diverse groups, such as worker activists, human rights groups, and college students, are needed to generate publicity. Under these conditions, efforts to monitor corporate codes of conduct have taken root more than traditional union organizing. In producer-driven global supply chains, as in automobiles, with centralized production decisions in stable locations due to high investment requirements, unions are better able to build stable membership bases and alliances across multiple locations; and with worker concerns like job security that do not garner as much public sympathy, pressure is directed at the company in traditional ways, such as job actions. So the nature of the global supply chain is important when thinking about why or why not corporate codes of conduct are important in different segments of the global economy.[76]

Do Corporate Codes of Conduct Work?

For the reasons just described, corporate codes of conduct are particularly relied upon in the apparel and footwear industries, in which brand-conscious retailers such as Reebok, Nike, Levi Strauss, Liz Claiborne, and Polo Ralph Lauren utilize extensive contractors, subcontractors, and suppliers in Indonesia, Thailand, China, Mexico, and other low-wage developing countries. But debates continue as to how effective these efforts are at improving workers' conditions. With sufficient public and consumer pressure, these codes have the potential to address some of the worst abuses.[77] In 2009, for example, Cornell, Georgetown, the University of Michigan, and other universities terminated their licensing agreements with apparel company Russell Athletic after a monitoring report revealed that Russell Athletic closed a factory in Honduras when workers there formed a union. In 2012, extensive negative publicity about the working conditions in the Chinese factories making iPhones and iPads caused Apple to allow the Fair Labor Association to audit those factories, and the audit resulted in an agreement to enforce stricter standards, especially pertaining to overtime and health and safety. Publicity may also increase government enforcement of existing laws, and when the codes of conduct protect freedom of association, they can also spur unionization (see the "Labor Relations Application" box discussing the Nike code of conduct).[78]

With that said, there are also serious doubts about the widespread effectiveness of the voluntary, self-governing nature of corporate codes of conduct.[79] There are still factory disasters that claim significant lives, such as the Rana Plaza factory tragedy in Bangladesh that killed over 1,000 workers in 2013.[80] The number of factories, their geographical

Labor Relations Application A Nike Code of Conduct Fosters a *Maquiladora* Union

The Mexmode *maquiladora* factory in Atlixco, Mexico, is owned by the South Korea–based Kukdong International and makes licensed college apparel for Nike, including sweatshirts for the Universities of Arizona, California–Berkeley, Connecticut, Illinois, Michigan, North Carolina, and Wisconsin as well as Boston College, Northwestern, and Stanford. Mexmode had signed a collective bargaining agreement with the Revolutionary Confederation of Workers and Peasants Union (ironically abbreviated "CROC") that did not contain any wage or benefit provisions above the legal minimums. In 2001, the 800 Mexmode workers—many of them young single mothers—tried to form an independent union to fight sexual harassment, long hours, unhealthful plant cafeteria food, and low wages (less than $40 per week). The workers first boycotted the cafeteria and then went on strike when the boycott leaders were fired. Mexican police broke up the strike.

Nike's code of conduct, however, pledges to respect workers' rights to freedom of association and collective bargaining. Moreover, Nike is a member of the Fair Labor Association, and its Workplace Code of Conduct also recognizes the right to collective bargaining. Consequently, the antisweatshop group the Workers Rights Consortium, several U.S. labor unions, and other organizations launched an investigation and a global solidarity campaign that resulted in 6,000 letters of protest to Nike urging the company to follow its own corporate code of conduct. Nike relented and pressured Mexmode to recognize a new independent union. In September, the fired workers were reinstated and the new union was recognized. In April 2002, wages and benefits were improved, and an attendance program with significant bonuses was introduced.

In 2008, CROC reappeared and tried to oust the leaders of the independent union using intimidation and violence. CROC's local government allies then tried to illegally conduct a new union election without a secret ballot election. Mexmode management and Nike fully cooperated with an investigation by the U.S.-based Worker Rights Consortium and were not found responsible for these events.

Source: Worker Rights Consortium, "Worker Rights Consortium Assessment re Mexmode, S.A. de C.V. (Mexico): Findings and Rrecommendations" (Washington, DC, July 3, 2008).

dispersion, and the complicated tiers of subcontracting make it very difficult to monitor and inspect all of the work sites.[81] When codes are self-monitored, inspections might only happen after a factory's managers are given advance notice of the inspection. But research has found that surprise inspections and off-site, confidential interviewing of workers is critical.[82] Monitoring also needs to be complemented by technical assistance to help managers improve their production processes.[83] Lastly, research finds that inspections are significantly more likely to identity health and safety and wages, benefits, and hours of work violations than freedom of association violations.[84] So while the inclusion of freedom of association standards in corporate codes of conduct is now quite widespread, this still appears to be window dressing. In other words, companies seem to be trying to balance the legitimacy of the corporate social responsibility efforts with maintaining control over their global supply chain, and unionization and collective bargaining are perceived as giving up too much control.[85] Indeed, companies continue to favor China and Vietnam as production locations because their authoritarian political regimes keep labor protest in check.[86]

In the global arena, the use of corporate codes of conduct to address labor issues is analogous to the use of human resource management to govern the workplace (recall Chapter 2). Like human resource management, the use of corporate codes of conduct admits that working conditions are not entirely dictated by market forces; companies have choices, and establishing conditions more favorable to workers than the market minimums can mutually benefit the company and workers. Before it was acquired by adidas, Reebok's code stated, "We believe that the incorporation of internationally recognized human rights standards into our business practice improves worker morale and results in a higher-quality working environment and higher-quality products." This is similar to the human resource management philosophy that treating workers with respect increases morale and effectiveness. In other words, the use of corporate codes of conduct rejects the market-oriented conception of labor as a commodity and also the assumption of perfect competition that protects employees from abuse; it is based on the unitarist belief of shared interests between labor and management—just like the philosophy of human resource management (recall Chapter 2). But as is also true in human resource management, corporate codes of conduct are ultimately a unilateral mechanism for establishing employment conditions that lacks a rigorous set of minimum standards and an external enforcement mechanism. Many companies might be entrusted to this voluntary mechanism, but with the potential for abuse, it is reasonable to question whether the global workplace should rely entirely on corporate codes of conduct to balance efficiency, equity, and voice.

Online Exploration Exercise: Explore the sites for the Fair Labor Association (*www.fairlabor.org*) and the Worker Rights Consortium (*www.workersrights.org*), including looking at some inspection reports. Is this an effective method for combating sweatshops in developing countries? Or is it a public relations scheme? Find the lists of participating colleges and universities. Does your school participate in either of these antisweatshop organizations? Should it?

NONUNION APPLICATION: INTERNATIONAL MANAGEMENT

The intensified competition resulting from globalization is widely associated with pressures to restrain wage and benefit costs and to increase employment flexibility (recall Chapter 10). But globalization adds significant complexities to managing multinational corporations. A multinational corporation's global strategy has two central dimensions: configuration and coordination.[87] Configuration involves the location of various activities, such as whether production is concentrated in one country and exported to other markets or production is globalized into various countries through foreign direct investment. The location of suppliers and subcontractors is another element of configuration. Note that configuration decisions are not limited to production but also include research and product development, marketing, and other functions. The coordination dimension consists of the degree to which activities in different countries are harmonized or autonomous. The extent to which human resource management strategies and production techniques are required to follow one consistent model throughout the local operations of a multinational corporation is a key element of this coordination dimension.

The configuration dimension affects labor relations through its effects on relative bargaining power between corporations and employees. The threat of moving production to a lower-wage country reduces labor's bargaining power.[88] Multiple production locations make it more difficult for a strike to place significant financial pressure on a company. Transfer pricing—the terms at which goods and services are exchanged within a company—can hide the true profitability of specific operations from labor unions.[89] Complex international joint ventures or subcontracting arrangements can also make it more difficult for unions to discern the true state of a company's operations and financial situation.

The coordination dimension of global strategy and international management represents an important conflict in multinational corporations between centralization that serves global integration and efficiency, on one hand, and decentralization that serves local responsiveness and autonomy on the other. A significant task of international managers is balancing this tension—it is not a case of choosing one or the other but rather of finding the appropriate mix of both sides of this centralization–decentralization or global integration–local responsiveness duality.[90] An organization in which all units are fully autonomous lacks a source of global competitive advantage such as standardized products, economies of scale, or organizational learning. In other words, where is the global synergy if all units act independently? On the other hand, a multinational corporation in which all decisions are centralized and all practices follow global uniform policies lacks the ability to capitalize on local differences and opportunities. In other words, there is little respect for diversity and a lessened sense of accountability, participation, and entrepreneurial activity. The task of international management is to find the appropriate balance between integration and autonomy. The difficulty in seeking this balance, however, is magnified by the complexity of communication within multinational corporations.[91] Communication gaps can result not only from distance but also from differences in language and culture.

For labor relations, the tension between integration and autonomy manifests itself in the extent to which local labor relations practices and strategies are shaped by local managers and environmental conditions versus being determined by corporatewide policies and strategies. The general international management prescription of "organize one way, manage the other way" is equally valid for labor relations in multinational corporations.[92] If formal labor relations processes and structures are centralized, local managers should strive for ways to incorporate local responsiveness and problem solving. If labor relations processes are decentralized, local managers should build networks across the organization to facilitate coordination and learning.

Globalization also brings particular legal challenges for international managers. On one hand are difficult questions about whether corporate actions that occur outside the United States are subject to U.S. laws (examine this yourself with the "Labor Law Discussion Case" at the end of this chapter). On the other hand is the fact that some amount of national responsiveness by managers is required because of international differences in relevant laws. For example, the U.S. Family and Medical Leave Act requires companies to provide employees 12 weeks of unpaid leave to care for newborn children and for other family and medical purposes. In the European Union, however, parental leave laws typically require 14 to 16 weeks of leave, and some laws also require at least partial compensation. Ensuring compliance with these different national standards is an important challenge for multinational corporations.[93] The legal and institutional differences in labor relations across different countries—such as the British system of voluntary recognition of unions and labor contracts or the tightly specified German system that provides specific codetermination rights to employees—are presented in the next chapter. These differences must be appreciated by successful international managers and union leaders.

FINANCIALIZATION

The pressures on labor relations, and on employment more generally, brought on by globalization are magnified by another multidimensional process called **financialization** in which financial markets, motives, results, and institutions become more important than the production and delivery of goods and services. Financialization is like globalization in that they both consist of a bundle of interrelated structural changes in the economy, and they both affect economic and political power.[94] Note that ideally, money is simply a medium of exchange and financial institutions are neutral sources of financing, but with financialization, financial motives and institutions become active players that strongly influence corporate decision-making and challenge governmental sovereignty, and thereby affect workers and all parties to the labor relations process.[95] Four key dimensions of financialization are presented here (see Table 11.6). Note how these trends not only put pressure on workers and labor union leaders, but on human resource managers, too.

TABLE 11.6
The Dimensions of Financialization

Share Price Maximization	Cost-cutting to boost financial returns rather than productive competitiveness. Stock repurchases rather than reinvestment.
Profits via Financial Transactions	Pursuing profits through financial transactions rather than the production and delivery of goods and services. Increasing importance of the financial sector and the financial activities of nonfinancial firms.
Private Equity	Leveraged buyouts to buy and then sell companies after cost-cutting and asset-stripping
Public Sector Budget Austerity	National economies subjected to international financial requirements. State and local governments focused on budget reduction.

Share Price Maximization

After seeing corporations become bloated conglomerates with low financial returns in the 1970s, the 1980s ushered in the shareholder-value movement.[96] Principal-agent problems were seen as responsible for poor corporate performance as self-interested managers were able to make decisions that benefited themselves at the expense of passive shareholders, rather than the managers acting as the agents of the principals. New corporate governance structures were therefore implemented with outside directors and incentives for executives, buttressed by shareholder-friendly laws, activist shareholders, and deregulated financial institutions. Shareholders were recognized as the key owners of the corporation, with managers obligated to act the best interests of the shareholders.[97] This was

> a fundamental shift in the concept of the American corporation—from of a view of it as a productive enterprise and stable institution serving the needs of a broad spectrum of stakeholders to a view of it as a bundle of assets to be bought and sold with an exclusive goal of maximizing shareholder value.[98]

So the **shareholder value model** is today's approach to corporate governance, maximizing shareholder value is the corporate and investment mantra, executives are largely rewarded through stock options, and monitoring stock prices is the focal activity of executives and investors.

This has important implications for workers and labor relations. In response to Japanese production methods, U.S. industry rationalized its operations in the 1980s (recall Chapter 10); with the rise of digital technology, employment has been increasingly marketetized; and in response to globalization, employment has been globalized.[99] Each of these trends were initially driven by corporate strategies to restore competitiveness by restructuring the productive capacity of their workforce in the face of changing technology and competition. But under the pressure of maximizing shareholder value, these efforts can turn into cost-cutting exercises for the sake of increasing short-term profitability and driving up stock prices. Workers and unions are thus faced with demands for wage and benefit concessions, layoffs, and stressful restructurings, all while being asked to invest more of themselves but denied a role in corporate governance.

These issues are magnified by stock repurchases. Rather than retaining and reinvesting cost savings and earnings back into the business as was the norm before the shareholder-value movement, cost savings and earnings are increasingly being used to repurchase shares of the company's stock. This "downsize and distribute" strategy drives up the stock price which not only benefits investors but also top executives because of their sizable stock options.[100] A lack of investment back in the business places further strain on the employment relationship as employees are working in outdated stores or with outdated technologies that reduce their competitiveness, leading to corporate demands for further concessions. For example, after technology outages at Southwest Airlines caused massive flight delays and cancellations in 2016, unions at Southwest Airlines publicly criticized the CEO for spending millions of dollars on stock buybacks rather than updating the airline's aging computer system.

Moreover, advances in information technology have enabled the rise of the networked firm with the potential for extensive outsourcing and splintering of the supply chain.[101] Corporations, therefore, have become collections of "semi-autonomous units with responsibility for maximizing labor productivity," and these units are in competition with each other for investment from the corporate parent on the basis of financial returns.[102] So human resource managers in these units disconnected from the parent might be unable to invest in high performance work practices (Chapter 10) and reward employees even when they earn it, because the managers are unable to secure the financing from corporate leaders focused on short-term financial metrics.[103] Rather, cost-control, work intensification, and other pressures that strain labor relations are predicted to occur.[104]

Profits via Financial Transactions

A second dimension of financialization is an increased emphasis on pursuing profits through financial transactions rather than the production and delivery of goods and services. This has two elements.[105] One element is the increasing importance of the financial sector. Deregulation of the financial sector allowed commercial banks to become more like investment banks and led to industry consolidation so that the small number of key financial firms are "too big to fail." Moreover, information technology has allowed sophisticated financial investments to be priced and traded.[106] These changes have created a concentration of wealth in the financial sector, widens inequalities between Wall Street and Main Street, and further reinforces the primacy of financial investment over productive investment.[107] This concentration of wealth also reallocates political influence in ways that do not favor labor unions.

The other element of this dimension of financialization is the increased importance of financial activities of nonfinancial firms, such as the Ford Credit arm of Ford. From 1970 to just before the financial crisis in 2008, the fraction of profits earned from financial transactions in nonfinancial firms doubled, and in manufacturing it tripled.[108] This is associated with reduced employment and overall economic growth, presumably as funds are diverted away from research and development and productivity-enhancing investment.[109] This leads back to the same labor relations challenges as in the previous section, such as human resources managers in nonfinancial units not having the resources to invest in and reward employees. Firms can also strategically choose its financial strategies to provide leverage in contract negotiations with its unions, for example by converting cash to debt.[110]

Private Equity

Perhaps the most visible and aggressive examples of wringing profits out of companies is the third dimension of financialization—private equity funds that use leveraged buyouts to take over companies that are seen as underperforming, install their own cost-cutting leadership teams, strip off assets, and then sell the pieces at a significant profit. This pushes the shareholder value ethos to the extreme by seeing companies solely as assets to be traded for maximum profit, and the private equity structure allows private equity firms to do this using financial engineering strategies that are much riskier and involve a lot more debt than public corporations are able to do, or find it prudent to do.[111]

Some private equity interventions create jobs, some destroy them. On net, the evidence seems to suggest that more jobs are lost than created.[112] With respect to labor relations specifically, the attitudes of private equity firms vary, just as attitudes of public corporations vary.[113] At Spirit Aerosystems which resulted from purchasing a division from Boeing, management's relationship with the International Association of Machinists (IAM) improved, whereas the private equity owners of Stella D'Oro Biscuits immediately demanded significant concessions, hired replacement workers during the resulting strike, closed the plant temporarily, and then sold it to another anti-union private equity firm. The way in which private equity firms seem uniformly different from public corporations, however, is "their determination to extract higher-than-average returns" from the business, and "for union workers, this often means giving up wages and benefits that they have fought hard to win."[114] The sophisticated financial engineering and debt strategies involved in private equity buyouts also means that unions need to be equally sophisticated in their understanding of these financial strategies, though the information can be hard to obtain, especially with workers and unions left out of corporate governance.[115]

Public Sector Budget Austerity

Aspects of financialization are affecting public sector employment and labor relations, too. At a national level, this is clearest in the case of countries with high levels of public debt where national sovereignty has been challenged by the international lending requirements of financial institutions. In Greece, for example, financial institutions like the International Monetary Fund (IMF) and the European Central Bank have become active parties in labor relations.[116] Specifically, in return for loans, the Greek government enacted various changes, including cutting public sector wages and decentralizing private sector collective bargaining.[117] A second loan agreement stipulated cutting minimum wages by 22 percent.

In the United States, efforts to restrain or remove bargaining rights for public sector workers in Wisconsin, Ohio, and elsewhere starting in 2010 have consistently been justified by citing the need for budget austerity, including Wisconsin's "Budget Repair Bill."[118] This can be seen as an extension of financialization because fiscal concerns are being prioritized over service delivery, and because budget deficits and public sector pension shortfalls were at least partly a result of the financial crisis. So public sector labor relations are not immune to the pressures of financialization. As with the other dimensions of financialization, increases in the importance of financial markets, motives, results, and institutions are putting significant pressures on all of those involved in labor relations, including workers, union leaders, and managers. Financialization is therefore important to understand.

GLOBALIZATION AND FINANCIALIZATION: ECONOMICS AND ETHICS

It is easy to reduce globalization and financialization to purely economic phenomena dominated by discussions of trade statistics, trade barriers, foreign direct investment, and financial returns. In the textbook economics model, increased economic integration, free trade, and international capital mobility improve aggregate welfare in the long run, and short-run issues are dismissed as "adjustment costs." The economics of globalization are certainly important and should not be overlooked, but it is also critical to not overlook the broader effects of globalization on individuals, unions, communities, cultures, the environment, and nations. Globalization has brought many benefits to people around the world but has also closed U.S. factories, hollowed out entire communities, brought sweatshops to other countries, and placed great strains on the environment. Financialization, too, brings about winners and losers. Globalization and financialization, therefore, raise important ethical

Ethics in Action Putting Factories on a Barge?

Jack Welch, the legendary ex-CEO of General Electric (GE), was interviewed by business journalist Lou Dobbs on CNN's *Moneyline* during his tenure as GE's CEO:

> **Dobbs:** . . . Jack, the—no one—very few people, I should say have as—certainly as widespread, as diverse a set of businesses and assets as does GE, as do you. Give us your sense about the economy in the year going forward and where you'd expect to see pressures, your outlook.
>
> **Welch:** Well, it's clear that the deflationary pressures continue, whether it's copper hitting new lows, oil hitting new lows. Almost every key raw material hitting new lows. There's clearly a mood of deflation in the air, excess capacity in all global markets, price compression in financial services offerings, margin squeezes. So there's real competitive pressure, and yet there are enormous opportunities at the same time. Japan is opening up its financial markets. We've made a number of moves, have a number more on the drawing board. We've never had a better opportunity to source in joint ventures around the globe, to be more competitive.
>
> Ideally, you'd have every plant you own on a barge to move with currencies and changes in the economy. You can't do that, but the job of a company is to be agile, and to capitalize on these things. But it's a tough economy.

***

General Electric has been an unabashed champion of globalization: "Globalization is not only striving to grow revenues by selling goods and services in global markets. It also means globalizing every activity of the company, including the sourcing of raw materials, components, and products. Globalization especially means finding and attracting the unlimited pool of intellectual capital—the very best people—from all around the globe." GE has also been very successful financially. Its operating margin is close to 20 percent, and its operating profit is around $15 billion annually. Its stock price consistently outperforms the broader market.

According to *BusinessWeek*, "GE's U.S. workforce has been shrinking for more than a decade as Welch has cut costs by shifting production and investment to lower-wage countries." In recent years, non-U.S. employment nearly doubled while U.S. employment fell by almost 50 percent. Moreover, U.S. unionized employment at GE is only one-third of its early 1980s level while GE has expanded in Mexico, India, and other low-wage countries. There is also evidence that GE has pressured its suppliers to relocate to Mexico and other areas. All of the GE gas ranges and most of the electric stoves and side-by-side refrigerators sold in the United States are now produced in Mexico. However, production of minibar refrigerators was moved from Mexico to China in search of lower labor costs.

QUESTIONS

1. Use the ethical analysis template from Chapter 5 to analyze the ethical content of putting factories on a barge to find the best labor costs around the world.
2. What is the role of ethics for managers in the global economy? For union leaders?

Sources: Cable News Network Financial, *Money Week* (December 13, 1998, Transcript # 98121300V35), www.ge.com/en/company/companyinfo (accessed July 12, 2006); Aaron Bernstein, "Welch's March to the South," *BusinessWeek* (December 6, 1999); Geri Smith, "Is the Magic Starting to Fade for Manufacturing in Mexico?" *BusinessWeek* (August 6, 2001).

issues.[119] It can further be argued that everyone—including corporations and consumers—has a moral obligation to do their fair share in addressing these ethical challenges and in improving well-being around the world.[120]

With respect to labor relations, private sector unions are struggling to maintain the viability of collective bargaining in the face of intertwined globalization and financialization pressures. The threat of moving production to low-wage countries has labor on the defensive and undermines labor standards; financialization has widened inequality and diverted investment away from the shop floor. Traditional industrial unions like the United Steelworkers and United Auto Workers have lost thousands of members in their core industries and are now general unions with very diverse memberships. With the New Deal industrial relations system under fire from globalization and financialization, it is important to consider alternative institutional mechanisms for governing the global workplace. Some of these arrangements, especially enforceable international labor standards and transnational collective bargaining, have the potential to support domestic-level collective bargaining, while a continued emphasis on free trade and financial returns rather than fair trade and broadly shared prosperity is likely to keep labor on the defensive in many countries. Sharp disagreements persist as to which institutional arrangements will best provide efficiency, equity, and voice in the 21st century. The key to understanding these disagreements lies in appreciating the different models of the employment relationship—mainstream economics, human resource management, pluralist industrial relations, and critical industrial relations.

Key Terms

globalization, *388*
social dumping, *390*
World Trade Organization, *394*
fair trade, *395*
International Labor Organization (ILO), *396*
core labor standards, *396*
North American Agreement on Labor Cooperation (NAALC), *397*
European Works Council, *402*
International Trade Union Confederation (ITUC), *403*
corporate code of conduct, *407*
financialization, *412*
shareholder value model, *413*

Reflection Questions

1. In a concise paragraph, paraphrase what you have learned about globalization to explain to a policymaker why globalization has profound implications for domestic employment issues. Based on these implications, should enforceable labor standards (a social clause) be added to free trade agreements? If so, what should the standards be and how should they be enforced?
2. Is coordinated, transnational collective bargaining a good idea for unions and workers? If so, how should it be promoted? What are the potential drawbacks?
3. How do globalization and financialization affect U.S. managers, labor leaders, and workers in a unionized workplace? Does labor law need to be reformed because of these effects? If so, how?
4. *Nonunion Application:* How do globalization and financialization affect human resource management in nonunion companies? What pressures do they place on managers? What opportunities does this present?
5. The ethics of globalization and financialization should not be overlooked. For many, the push for free trade and deregulation of financial laws is based on the belief that "the social caboose [is] pulled by the economic locomotive."[121] Which ethical frameworks in Chapter 5 are consistent with this belief? How would the remaining ethical frameworks challenge this belief?

Labor Law Discussion Case 10: Do Threats in Mexico Violate U.S. Labor Law?

BACKGROUND

Southwest Propane Transport, Inc., was a U.S. company that transported propane from Arizona, Texas, New Mexico, and California to customer distribution sites in Mexico. Its main employees were therefore truck drivers who drove propane from these southwestern states to cities in Mexico such as Tijuana, Nogales, and Juarez. These truck drivers were U.S. citizens, the majority of their working time was spent in the United States, and they were clearly the employees of a U.S. company (Southwest Propane Transport, hereafter called SPT).

For several years the SPT truck drivers were allowed to sell whatever diesel fuel was left over from their runs. This typically amounted to between $50 and $100 per week, and the drivers viewed this as meal money. In fact, when some employees asked for meal money, they were told that if they wanted something to eat, they should watch their fuel consumption and sell the extra to buy something to eat. But when a new operations manager, Oscar Silva, took over, he stopped the practice of allowing drivers to sell their extra fuel. The drivers were already concerned with the safety of the trucks; their frustrations were magnified by this abrupt cut in their compensation, and they collectively went to talk with Silva about these issues. When he refused to listen to their concerns, the Arizona-based truck drivers talked with a union organizer. Shortly thereafter the union received signed authorization cards from 16 of the 19 Arizona-based drivers and filed a petition with the NLRB for a representation election. During the election campaign, SPT had numerous small group meetings to try to convince the employees not to vote for the union in the upcoming election.

Two of the most vocal union supporters were drivers Maria Meraz and Rogelio Delgado. During this period of campaigning, Meraz and Delgado had several conversations with Gabriel Acosta. Acosta frequently assigned routes to the truck drivers and could discipline them. In other words, he was seen by the SPT drivers as a supervisor. Acosta indicated that the drivers would get a raise if they voted against the union, and they would be "showed the door" if they voted the union in. Moreover, Acosta told Meraz and Delgado that after they were "showed the door," he would be sure to badmouth them to other gas companies so they could not get new jobs.

QUESTIONS

1. As a review of earlier chapters, explain how Acosta's actions violated the National Labor Relations Act (NLRA).
2. Interestingly, the conversations between Acosta, Meraz, and Delgado occurred at the Nogales distribution center in Mexico, not in the United States. Moreover, Acosta was a Mexican citizen who worked in Mexico for a Mexican company. Acosta was not employed by SPT but instead worked for SPT's major customer in Mexico. Nevertheless, Acosta frequently assigned routes to the truck drivers for their return to the United States and sometimes disciplined them. He was seen by the SPT drivers not only as a supervisor but as the voice and authority of SPT in Mexico. In Silva's words, Acosta was his "eyes and ears" in Nogales. Do you still think Acos-ta'a actions violated American labor law (the NLRA)?
3. Did Acosta's actions violate any human rights standards? If so, should there be any consequences or remedies for this violation?

End Notes

1. Ronald Dore, "Financialization of the Global Economy," *Industrial and Corporate Change* 17 (December 2008), pp. 1097–112 at 1097.
2. Kenneth F. Scheve and Matthew J. Slaughter, *Globalization and the Perception of American Workers* (Washington, DC: Institute for International Economics, 2001).
3. United Nations Development Programme, *Human Development Report* (New York: Oxford University Press, various years).
4. Thomas L. Friedman, *The World Is Flat: A Brief History of the Twenty-First Century* (New York: Farrar, Straus, and Giroux, 2006), p. 8.
5. Douglas A. Irwin, *Free Trade under Fire*, 4th ed. (Princeton, NJ: Princeton University Press, 2015).
6. Dani Rodrik, *Has Globalization Gone Too Far?* (Washington, DC: Institute for International Economics, 1997).
7. Robert Bruno, *Steelworker Alley: How Class Works in Youngstown* (Ithaca, NY: Cornell University Press, 1999), p. 149.
8. Steve Mellon, *After the Smoke Clears: Struggling to Get By in Rustbelt America* (Pittsburgh: University of Pittsburgh Press, 2002), pp. 14–15.
9. Mehul Srivastava, "Perilous Arithmetic for Bangladesh's Factories," *BusinessWeek* (June 10, 2013).
10. United Nations Conference on Trade and Development, *World Investment Report 2016* (Geneva: United Nations, 2016).
11. Mario F. Bognanno, Michael P. Keane, and Donghoon Yang, "The Influence of Wages and Industrial Relations Environments on the Production Location Decisions of U.S. Multinational Corporations," *Industrial and Labor Relations Review* 58 (January 2005), pp. 171–200; Mark Anner, "Labor Control Regimes and Worker Resistance in Global Supply Chains," *Labor History* 56 (2015), pp. 292–307.
12. Joseph E. Stiglitz, *Globalization and Its Discontents* (New York: W.W. Norton, 2002).
13. Friedman, *The World Is Flat.*
14. Michael E. Gordon, "Export Processing Zones," in Michael E. Gordon and Lowell Turner (eds.), *Transnational Cooperation among Labor Unions* (Ithaca, NY: ILR Press, 2000), pp. 60–78; Samanthi Gunawardana, "Struggle, Perseverance, and Organization in Sri Lanka's Export Processing Zones," in Kate Bronfenbrenner (ed.), *Global Unions: Challenging Transnational Capital through Cross-Border Campaigns* (Ithaca, NY: Cornell University Press, 2007), pp. 78–98; Mark S. Anner, *Solidarity Transformed: Labor Responses to Globalization and Crisis in Latin America* (Ithaca, NY: Cornell University Press, 2011).
15. Maurice Obstfeld, "The Global Capital Market: Benefactor or Menace?" *Journal of Economic Perspectives* 12 (Fall 1998), pp. 9–30.
16. Bank for International Settlements, "Triennial Central Bank Survey" (Basel, 2013).
17. United Nations, Department of Economic and Social Affairs, Population Division.
18. George J. Borjas, *Heaven's Door: Immigration Policy and the American Economy* (Princeton, NJ: Princeton University Press, 1999); Gordon H. Hanson, "Challenges for U.S. Immigration Policy," in C. Fred Bergsten (ed.), *The United States and the World Economy: Foreign Economic Policy in the Next Decade* (Washington, DC: Institute for International Economics, 2005), pp. 343–72; Philip L. Martin, "Immigration and the U.S. Labor Market," in Charles J. Whalen (ed.), *Human Resource Economics and Public Policy: Essays in Honor of Vernon M. Briggs, Jr.* (Kalamazoo, MI: Upjohn, 2010), pp. 49–78.
19. Ruth Milkman and Ed Ott (eds.), *New Labor in New York: Precarious Worker Organizing and the Future of Unionism* (Ithaca, NY: Cornell University Press, 2014); Immanuel Ness, *Immigrants, Unions, and the New U.S. Labor Market* (Philadelphia: Temple University Press, 2005).
20. Marie Weisenberger, "Broken Families: A Call for Consideration of the Family of Illegal Immigrants in U.S. Immigration Enforcement Efforts," *Capital University Law Review* 39 (Spring 2011), pp. 495–533.
21. Ajay Malshe, "From Obsolete to Essential: How Reforming Our Immigration Laws Can Stimulate and Strengthen the United States Economy," *Albany Government Law Review* 3 (2010), pp. 358–90; Peter H. Schuck and John E. Tyler, "Making the Case for Changing U.S. Policy Regarding Highly Skilled Immigrants," *Fordham Urban Law Journal* 38 (November 2010), pp. 327–62.
22. David Bacon and Bill Ong Hing, "The Rise and Fall of Employer Sanctions," *Fordham Urban Law Journal* 38 (November 2010), pp. 77–105.
23. Rodrik, *Has Globalization Gone Too Far?*; Clyde W. Summers, "The Battle in Seattle: Free Trade, Labor Rights, and Societal Values," *University of Pennsylvania Journal of International Economic Law* 22 (Spring 2001), pp. 61–90.
24. Kevin Kolben, "The WTO Distraction," *Stanford Law and Policy Review* 21 (June 2010), pp. 461–92.
25. Micah Globerson, "Using Border Trade Adjustments to Address Labor Rights Concerns under the WTO," *American University Labor and Employment Law Forum* 3 (2013), pp. 48–87.

26. Irwin, *Free Trade under Fire*; Drusilla K. Brown, "Labor Standards: Where Do They Belong on the International Trade Agenda?" *Journal of Economic Perspectives* 15 (Summer 2001), pp. 89–112.
27. Sara Dillon, "Opportunism and Trade Law Revisited: The Pseudo-Constitution of the WTO," *Boston College International and Comparative Law Review* 36 (2013), pp. 1005–36 at 1019.
28. Joshua M. Kagan, "Making Free Trade Fair: How the WTO Could Incorporate Labor Rights and Why It Should," *Georgetown Journal of International Law* 43 (September 2011), pp. 196–224; Michael J. Trebilcock and Robert Howse, "Trade Policy and Labor Standards," *Minnesota Journal of Global Trade* 14 (Summer 2005), pp. 261–300; Rachel Harris and Gillian Moon, "GATT Article XX and Human Rights: What Do We Know from the First 20 Years?" *Melbourne Journal of International Law* 16 (December 2015), pp. 432–483.
29. Gerry Rodgers et al., *The International Labour Organization and the Quest for Social Justice, 1919–2009* (Ithaca, NY: Cornell University Press, 2009).
30. Daniel S. Ehrenberg, "From Intention to Action: An ILO–GATT/WTO Enforcement Regime for International Labor Rights," in Lance A. Compa and Stephen F. Diamond (eds.), *Human Rights, Labor Rights, and International Trade* (Philadelphia: University of Pennsylvania Press, 1996), pp. 163–80.
31. Hannah Murphy, "The World Bank and Core Labour Standards: Between Flexibility and Regulation," *Review of International Political Economy* 21 (2014), pp. 399–431.
32. Kimberly A. Elliott, "Getting Beyond No . . . ! Promoting Worker Rights and Trade," in Jeffrey J. Schott (ed.), *The WTO after Seattle* (Washington, DC: Institute for International Economics, 2000), pp. 187–204; Robert Howse, "The World Trade Organization and the Protection of Workers' Rights," *Journal of Small and Emerging Business Law* 3 (Summer 1999), pp. 131–72; Summers, "The Battle in Seattle."
33. Roy J. Adams and Parbudyal Singh, "Early Experience with NAFTA's Labour Side Accord," *Comparative Labor Law Journal* 18 (Winter 1997), pp. 161–81; Mario F. Bognanno and Jiangfeng Lu, "NAFTA's Labor Side Agreement: Withering as an Effective Labor Law Enforcement and MNC Compliance Strategy?" in William N. Cooke (ed.), *Multinational Companies and Global Human Resource Strategies* (Westport, CT: Quorum Books, 2003), pp. 369–401.
34. Edward Mazey, "Grieving through the NAALC and the Social Charter: A Comparative Analysis of Their Procedural Effectiveness," *Journal of International Law* 10 (Summer 2001), pp. 239–79.
35. Bognanno and Lu, "NAFTA's Labor Side Agreement"; George Tsogas, *Labor Regulation in a Global Economy* (Armonk, NY: M. E. Sharpe, 2001), p. 164.
36. U.S. Department of Labor, Bureau of International Labor Affairs, Submissions under the NAALC, *www.dol.gov/ilab/trade/agreements/naalc.htm.*
37. Bognanno and Lu, "NAFTA's Labor Side Agreement"; Norman Caulfield, *NAFTA and Labor in North America* (Urbana: University of Illinois Press, 2010).
38. Adams and Singh, "Early Experience with NAFTA's Labour Side Accord"; Tsogas, *Labor Regulation in a Global Economy.*
39. Tamara Kay, *NAFTA and the Politics of Labor Transnationalism* (New York: Cambridge University Press, 2011); Daniel Ozarow, "Pitching For Each Others' Team: The North American Free Trade Agreement and Labor Transnationalism," *Labor History* 54 (2013), pp. 512–26.
40. Kay, *NAFTA and the Politics of Labor Transnationalism.*
41. Stacie E. Martin, "Labor Obligations in the U.S.–Chile Free Trade Agreement," *Comparative Labor Law and Policy Journal* 25 (Winter 2004), pp. 201–26; Marisa Pagnattaro, "Leveling the Playing Field: Labor Provisions in CAFTA," *Fordham International Law Journal* 29 (January 2006), pp. 386–431.
42. Kolben, "The WTO Distraction."
43. Jordi Agusti-Panareda, Franz Christian Ebert, and Desiree LeClercq, "ILO Labor Standards and Trade Agreements: A Case for Consistency," *Comparative Labor Law and Policy Journal* 36 (Spring 2015), pp. 347–80.
44. Guglielmo Meardi, *Social Failures of EU Enlargement: A Case of Workers Voting with Their Feet* (New York: Routledge, 2012); Jon Erik D lvik and Jelle Visser, "Free Movement, Equal Treatment and Workers' Rights: Can the European Union Solve Its Trilemma of Fundamental Principles?" *Industrial Relations Journal* 40 (November 2009), pp. 491–509.
45. Roger Blanpain, *European Labour Law,* 6th ed. (The Hague: Kluwer, 1999), p. 91.
46. Christopher L. Erickson and Sarosh Kuruvilla, "Labor Costs and the Social Dumping Debate in the New European Union," *Industrial and Labor Relations Review* 48 (October 1994), pp. 27–47; Jimmy Donaghey and Paul Teague, "The Free Movement of Workers and Social Europe: Maintaining the European Ideal," *Industrial Relations Journal* 37 (November 2006), pp. 652–66; Magdalena Bernaciak (ed.), *Market Expansion and Social Dumping in Europe* (London: Routledge, 2015).

47. Valeria Bonavita, "The EU Charter of Fundamental Rights and the Social Dimension of International Trade," in Giacomo Di Federico (ed.), *The EU Charter of Fundamental Rights: From Declaration to Binding Instrument* (Dordrecht: Springer, 2011), pp. 241–64; Csilla Kollonay-Lehoczky, Klaus Lörcher, and Isabelle Schömann, "The Lisbon Treaty and the Charter of Fundamental Rights of the European Union," in Niklas Bruun, Klaus Lörcher, and Isabelle Schömann (eds.), *The Lisbon Treaty and Social Europe* (Oxford: Hart Publishing, 2012), pp. 61–104.
48. W. Stanley Siebert, "Labour Market Regulation in the EU-15: Causes and Consequences," in Peter Bernholz and Roland Vaubel (eds.), *Political Competition and Economic Regulation* (New York: Routledge, 2007), pp. 113–36. Gregor Thüsing, *European Labour Law* (Munich: C.H. Beck, 2013).
49. Meardi, *Social Failures of EU Enlargement*; Sabrina Weber, "Sectoral Social Dialogue at EU Level—Recent Results and Implementation Challenges," *Transfer: European Review of Labour and Research* 16 (November 2010), pp. 489–507; Dølvik and Visser, "Free Movement, Equal Treatment and Workers' Rights"; Daniel Vaughan-Whitehead (ed.), *The European Social Model In Crisis: Is Europe Losing Its Soul?* (Cheltenham, UK: Elgar, 2015).
50. Janice R. Bellace, "The European Works Council Directive: Transnational Information and Consultation in the European Union," *Comparative Labor Law Journal* 18 (Spring 1997), pp. 325–61; Michael Gold, "Employee Participation in the EU: The Long and Winding Road to Legislation," *Economic and Industrial Democracy* 31 (November 2010), pp. 9–23; Andrew Timming and Michael Whittall, "The Promise of European Works Councils: 20 years of Statutory Employee Voice," in Stewart Johnstone and Peter Ackers (eds.), *Finding a Voice at Work: New Perspectives on Employment Relations* (Oxford: Oxford University Press, 2015), pp. 218–38.
51. Jeremy Waddington, *European Works Councils: A Transnational Industrial Relations Institution in the Making* (New York: Routledge, 2011).
52. Wolfgang Lecher, Hans-Wolfgang Platzer, Stefan Rüb, and Klaus-Peter Weiner, *European Works Councils: Developments, Types, and Networking* (Aldershot, Hampshire, UK: Gower, 2001).
53. Michael Whittall, "The BMW European Works Council: A Cause for European Industrial Relations Optimism?" *European Journal of Industrial Relations* 6 (March 2000), pp. 61–83.
54. Lecher, Platzer, Rüb, and Weiner, *European Works Councils.*
55. Tony Royle, "Where's the Beef? McDonald's and Its European Works Council," *European Journal of Industrial Relations* 5 (November 1999), pp. 327–47.
56. Timming and Whittall, "The Promise of European Works Councils."
57. Michael E. Gordon and Lowell Turner, "Going Global," in Michael E. Gordon and Lowell Turner (eds.), *Transnational Cooperation among Labor Unions* (Ithaca, NY: ILR Press, 2000), pp. 3–25; Jamie K. McCallum, *Global Unions, Local Power: The New Spirit of Transnational Labor Organizing* (Ithaca, NY: Cornell University Press, 2013).
58. Jean-Michel Servais, "Labor Law and Cross-Border Cooperation among Unions," in Michael E. Gordon and Lowell Turner (eds.), *Transnational Cooperation among Labor Unions* (Ithaca, NY: ILR Press, 2000), pp. 44–59.
59. Kay, *NAFTA and the Politics of Labor Transnationalism*; Ian Greer and Marco Hauptmeier, "Political Entrepreneurs and Co-Managers: Labour Transnationalism at Four Multinational Auto Companies," *British Journal of Industrial Relations* 46 (March 2008), pp. 76–97; Magdalena Bernaciak, "Labour Solidarity in Crisis? Lessons from General Motors," *Industrial Relations Journal* 44 (March 2013), pp. 139–53.
60. Elizabeth Cotton and Rebecca Gumbrell-McCormick, "Global Unions as Imperfect Multilateral Organizations: An International Relations Perspective," *Economic and Industrial Democracy* 33 (November 2012), pp. 707–28; Michael E. Gordon, "The International Confederation of Free Trade Unions: Bread, Freedom, and Peace," in Michael E. Gordon and Lowell Turner (eds.), *Transnational Cooperation among Labor Unions* (Ithaca, NY: ILR Press, 2000), pp. 81–101.
61. John P. Windmuller, "The International Trade Secretariats," in Michael E. Gordon and Lowell Turner (eds.), *Transnational Cooperation among Labor Unions* (Ithaca, NY: ILR Press, 2000), pp. 102–19 at 102.
62. Richard Croucher and Elizabeth Cotton, *Global Unions, Global Business: Global Union Federations and International Business* (London: Middlesex University Press, 2009); Cotton and Gumbrell-McCormick, "Global Unions as Imperfect Multilateral Organizations."
63. Cotton and Gumbrell-McCormick, "Global Unions as Imperfect Multilateral Organizations"; Gordon and Turner, "Going Global"; Meardi, *Social Failures of EU Enlargement*; McCallum, *Global Unions, Local Power*.
64. Kate Bronfenbrenner (ed.), *Global Unions: Challenging Transnational Capital through Cross-Border Campaigns* (Ithaca, NY: Cornell University Press, 2007); Verena Schmidt (ed.), *Trade Union*

Responses to Globalization: A Review by the Global Union Research Network (Geneva: International Labour Office, 2007).

65. Kenneth S. Zinn, "Solidarity across Borders: The UMWA's Corporate Campaign against Peabody and Hanson PLC," in Michael E. Gordon and Lowell Turner (eds.), *Transnational Cooperation among Labor Unions* (Ithaca, NY: ILR Press, 2000), pp. 223–37.
66. Lone Riisgaard, "International Framework Agreements: A New Model for Securing Workers Rights?" *Industrial Relations* 44 (October 2005), pp. 707–37; Konstantinos Papadakis, "Globalizing Industrial Relations: What Role for International Framework Agreements," in Susan Hayter (ed.), *The Role of Collective Bargaining in the Global Economy: Negotiating for Social Justice* (Cheltenham, UK: Elgar, 2011), pp. 277–304; Croucher and Cotton, *Global Unions, Global Business*.
67. McCallum, *Global Unions, Local Power*.
68. Sigrid Koch-Baumgarten, "Trade Union Regime Formation under the Conditions of Globalization in the Transport Sector: Attempts at Transnational Trade Union Regulation of Flag-of-Convenience Shipping," *International Review of Social History* 43 (December 1998), pp. 369–402; Nathan Lillie, "Global Collective Bargaining on Flag of Convenience Shipping," *British Journal of Industrial Relations* 42 (March 2004), pp. 47–67.
69. Deborah Leipziger, *The Corporate Responsibility Code Book*, 3rd ed. (Sheffield: Greenleaf, 2016).
70. Mark Anner, "Corporate Social Responsibility and Freedom of Association Rights: The Precarious Quest for Legitimacy and Control in Global Supply Chains," *Politics & Society* 40 (December 2012), pp. 609–44; Niklas Egels-Zandén and Jeroen Merk, "Private Regulation and Trade Union Rights: Why Codes of Conduct Have Limited Impact on Trade Union Rights," *Journal of Business Ethics* 123 (September 2014), pp. 461–73.
71. Jill Esbenshade, "Corporate Social Responsibility: Moving from Checklist Monitoring to Contractual Obligation?" in Richard Appelbaum and Nelson Lichtenstein (eds.), *Achieving Workers' Rights in the Global Economy* (Ithaca, NY: Cornell University Press, 2016), pp. 51–69.
72. Richard P. Appelbaum, "From Public Regulation to Private Enforcement: How CSR Became Managerial Orthodoxy" in Richard Appelbaum and Nelson Lichtenstein (eds.), *Achieving Workers' Rights in the Global Economy* (Ithaca, NY: Cornell University Press, 2016), pp. 32–50.
73. Anner, "Corporate Social Responsibility and Freedom of Association Rights"; Kate McDonald, "The Fair Labor Association," in David Held and Thomas Hale (eds.), *Handbook of Transnational Governance Innovation* (Cambridge: Polity Press, 2011), pp. 243–51.
74. Appelbaum, "From Public Regulation to Private Enforcement"; Anner, "Corporate Social Responsibility and Freedom of Association Rights."
75. Anner, *Solidarity Transformed*.
76. Anner, *Solidarity Transformed*.
77. Lance Compa, "Corporate Social Responsibility and Workers' Rights," *Comparative Labor Law and Policy Journal* 30 (Fall 2008), pp. 1–10.
78. Robert J. Liubicic, "Corporate Codes of Conduct and Product Labeling Schemes: The Limits and Possibilities of Promoting International Labor Rights through Private Initiatives," *Law and Policy in International Business* 30 (Fall 1998), pp. 111–58.
79. Richard Appelbaum and Nelson Lichtenstein (eds.), *Achieving Workers' Rights in the Global Economy* (Ithaca, NY: Cornell University Press, 2016).
80. Robert J. S. Ross, "The Twilight of CSR: Life and Death Illuminated by Fire," in Richard Appelbaum and Nelson Lichtenstein (eds.), *Achieving Workers' Rights in the Global Economy* (Ithaca, NY: Cornell University Press, 2016), pp. 70–92.
81. Appelbaum, "From Public Regulation to Private Enforcement."
82. Esbenshade, "Corporate Social Responsibility."
83. Richard M. Locke, Fei Qin, and Alberto Brause, "Does Monitoring Improve Labor Standards? Lessons from Nike," *Industrial and Labor Relations Review* 61 (October 2007), pp. 3–31.
84. Anner, "Corporate Social Responsibility and Freedom of Association Rights"; Egels-Zandén and Merk, "Private Regulation and Trade Union Rights."
85. Anner, "Corporate Social Responsibility and Freedom of Association Rights."
86. Anner, "Labor Control Regimes and Worker Resistance in Global Supply Chains."
87. Michael E. Porter, *The Competitive Advantage of Nations* (New York: Free Press, 1990).
88. Jefferson Cowie, *Capital Moves: RCA's Seventy-Year Quest for Cheap Labor* (Ithaca, NY: Cornell University Press, 1999); Gordon and Turner, "Going Global."

89. Harvie Ramsay and Nigel Haworth, "Managing the Multinationals: The Emerging Theory of the Multinational Enterprise and Its Implications for Labour Resistance," in Stewart R. Clegg (ed.), *Organization Theory and Class Analysis: New Approaches and New Issues* (Berlin: Walter de Gruyter, 1990), pp. 275–97.

90. Paul Evans, Vladimir Pucik, and Ingmar Bjorkman *The Global Challenge: International Human Resource Management* (Boston: McGraw-Hill/Irwin, 2011).

91. Harvie Ramsay, "Know Thy Enemy: Understanding Multinational Corporations as a Requirement for Strategic International Laborism," in Michael E. Gordon and Lowell Turner (eds.), *Transnational Cooperation among Labor Unions* (Ithaca, NY: ILR Press, 2000), pp. 26–43.

92. Evans, Pucik, and Bjorkman, *The Global Challenge,* p. 449.

93. Kathryn L. Morris, "A Matter of Compliance: How Do U.S. Multinational Corporations Deal with the Discrepancies in the Family and Medical Leave Act of 1993 and the European Union Directive on Parental Leave; Is an International Standard Practical or Appropriate in This Area of Law?" *The Georgia Journal of International and Comparative Law* 30 (Spring 2002), pp. 543–68.

94. Dore, "Financialization of the Global Economy"; Natascha van der Zwan, "Making Sense of Financialization," *Socio-Economic Review* 12 (January 2014), pp. 99–129.

95. Joel Cutcher-Gershenfeld et al., "Financialization, Collective Bargaining, and the Public Interest," in Christian E. Weller (ed.), *Inequality, Uncertainty, and Opportunity: The Varied and Growing Role of Finance in Labor Relations* (Champaign, IL: Labor and Employment Relations Association, 2015), pp. 31–56; van der Zwan, "Making Sense of Financialization."

96. Gerald F. Davis, *Managed by the Markets: How Finance Reshaped America* (New York: Oxford University Press, 2009); Eileen Appelbaum and Rosemary Batt, *Private Equity at Work: When Wall Street Manages Main Street* (New York: Russell Sage Foundation, 2014).

97. C.A. Harwell Wells, "The Cycles of Corporate Social Responsibility: An Historical Retrospective for the Twenty-first Century," *Kansas Law Review* 51 (November 2002), pp. 77–140.

98. Appelbaum and Batt, *Private Equity at Work*, p. 15.

99. William Lazonick, "Labor in the Twenty-First Century: The Top 0.1% and the Disappearing Middle-Class," in Christian E. Weller (ed.), *Inequality, Uncertainty, and Opportunity: The Varied and Growing Role of Finance in Labor Relations* (Champaign, IL: Labor and Employment Relations Association, 2015), pp. 143–95.

100. William Lazonick, *Sustainable Prosperity in the New Economy? Business Organization and High-Tech Employment in the United States* (Kalamazoo, MI: Upjohn Institute, 2009); Lazonick, "Labor in the Twenty-First Century."

101. Davis, *Managed by the Markets*.

102. Melanie Simms, "Union Organizing as an Alternative to Partnership. Or What to do when Employers Can't Keep Their Side of the Bargain," in Stewart Johnstone and Peter Ackers (eds.), *Finding a Voice at Work: New Perspectives on Employment Relations* (Oxford: Oxford University Press, 2015), pp. 127–52 at 132.

103. Paul Thompson, "The Trouble with HRM," *Human Resource Management Journal* 21 (November 2011), pp. 355–67; Simms, "Union Organizing as an Alternative to Partnership."

104. Jean Cushen and Paul Thompson, "Financialization and Value: Why Labour and the Labour Process Still Matter," *Work Employment & Society* 30 (April 2016), pp. 352–65.

105. Donald Tomaskovic-Devey and Ken-Hou Lin, "Financialization: Causes, Inequality Consequences, and Policy Implications," *North Carolina Banking Institute* 18 (November 2013), pp. 167–94.

106. Davis, *Managed by the Markets*.

107. Tomaskovic-Devey and Lin, "Financialization."

108. Tomaskovic-Devey and Lin, "Financialization."

109. Donald Tomaskovic-Devey, Ken-Hou Lin, and Nathan Meyers, "Did Financialization Reduce Economic Growth?" *Socio-Economic Review* 13 (July 2015), pp. 525–48.

110. David A. Matsa, "Capital Structure as a Strategic Variable: Evidence from Collective Bargaining," *Journal of Finance* 65 (June 2010), pp. 1197–232.

111. Appelbaum and Batt, *Private Equity at Work*.

112. Appelbaum and Batt, *Private Equity at Work*.

113. Appelbaum and Batt, *Private Equity at Work*.

114. Appelbaum and Batt, *Private Equity at Work*, p. 11.

115. Ron Blum and Peter Rossman, "Leveraged Buyouts, Restructuring and Collective Bargaining," *International Journal of Labour Research* 1 (2009), pp. 159–770.

116. Cutcher-Gershenfeld et al., “Financialization, Collective Bargaining, and the Public Interest.”
117. Aristea Koukiadaki and Lefteris Kretsos, “Opening Pandora’s Box: The Sovereign Debt Crisis and Labour Market Regulation in Greece,” *Industrial Law Journal* 41 (September 2012), pp. 276–304.
118. Cutcher-Gershenfeld et al., “Financialization, Collective Bargaining, and the Public Interest”; Robert Hebdon, Joseph E. Slater, and Marick F. Masters, “Public Sector Collective Bargaining: Tumultuous Times,” in Howard R. Stanger, Paul F. Clark, and Ann C. Frost (eds.), *Collective Bargaining under Duress: Case Studies of Major North American Industries* (Champaign, IL: Labor and Employment Relations Association, 2013), pp. 255–95.
119. Hoyt N. Wheeler, “Globalization and Business Ethics in Employment Relations,” in John W. Budd and James G. Scoville (eds.), *The Ethics of Human Resources and Industrial Relations* (Champaign, IL: Labor and Employment Relations Association, 2005), pp. 115–40.
120. Michael A. Santoro, *Profits and Principles: Global Capitalism and Human Rights in China* (Ithaca, NY: Cornell University Press, 2000).
121. Blanpain, *European Labour Law*, p. 91.

Part **Four**

Reflection

The previous parts of this book have provided an intellectual framework for studying labor relations, a description of how the U.S. New Deal industrial relations system works, and an overview of the intense contemporary pressures on this system. The final two chapters explore labor relations systems in other countries and possibilities for the future of the U.S. labor relations system. This provides the opportunity to reflect upon where the U.S. labor relations system has been and where it should go in the future.

Chapter Twelve

Comparative Labor Relations

Advance Organizer

The previous chapters of this book presented the U.S. labor relations system in detail, but labor relations in other countries can be quite different. The scope of bargaining, the extent of legal protection, and the nature of labor unions vary from country to country. Studying labor relations in other countries provides a richer understanding of the subject, can present ideas for reforming the U.S. system, and is also important for professionals working in a global economy.

Learning Objectives

By the end of this chapter, you should be able to

1. **Compare** the basic features of labor relations systems in the major industrialized, democratic countries around the world.
2. **Identify** the basic features of labor relations systems in the transitional and less developed economies of eastern Europe and Asia.
3. **Understand** various options in labor relations systems for reacting to the pressures of globalization, decentralization, and flexibility while trying to balance efficiency, equity, and voice.
4. **Analyze** the extent to which the labor relations experiences of other countries can provide ideas and lessons for reforming the U.S. labor relations system.

Contents

Comparative labor relations is the study of labor relations systems in different countries, and the goal of this chapter is to compare the U.S. labor relations system to other systems. A comparative perspective on labor relations is important for three reasons. The analytical reason is that considering labor relations in multiple countries provides a rich basis for thinking broadly about the underlying problem of balancing efficiency, equity, and voice and for obtaining a stronger understanding of the primary issues in labor relations. The public policy reason is that comparative analyses of labor relations can provide ideas for reforming the U.S. system. Aspects of labor relations in Canada, Germany, and Japan have all been championed as proposals for reforming U.S. labor relations. The practical reason is that if you work for an organization that does business in another country or for a labor union that has strategic alliances with labor unions in another country, it is important to

TABLE 12.1 Labor Relations around the World: A Snapshot

	Union Density	Bargaining Level	Key Features	Current Questions
United States	11%; falling.	Mostly workplace or company.	Exclusive representation; business unionism; detailed contracts.	How to protect workers with low union density and promote efficiency with bureaucratic unionism?
Mexico	15%	Government control.	Detailed contracts; strong constitutional protections, but weak, tightly controlled unions.	How to manage tension between state control, emerging independent labor unions, and competitiveness?
Great Britain	25%; falling.	Mostly workplace or company.	Voluntarism; wildcat strikes; Labour Party.	Does voluntarism yield unpredictable labor relations and harm competitiveness?
Ireland	30%; falling.	National-level social partnerships and workplace bargaining.	Social partnership; voluntarism.	How to sustain social partnerships and extend them to the workplace?
Germany	20% (55% coverage); falling.	Industry.	Codetermination; extension of agreements to entire industry; many mandated benefits.	Generous benefits and extensive consultation, but is it flexible enough?
Australia	15%; falling.	Occupational awards; workplace negotiations.	Arbitration awards; craft or occupation unions; wildcat strikes.	Are decentralization and deregulation the answers to international competition?
Japan	15%; falling.	Company.	Enterprise unions; cooperative relationships; Spring Labor Offensive.	Flexibility and cooperation, or management domination?
China	Estimates vary.	Bargaining is not a key union role.	Official unions as extensions of the state.	How to manage tension between state control and independent worker protests?

understand that country's labor relations framework. This chapter, therefore, outlines the major features of labor relations in Canada, Great Britain, Ireland, France, Germany, Sweden, Australia, New Zealand, and Japan (see Table 12.1). These countries are representative of the types of labor relations systems found in industrialized, democratic countries. The labor relations systems in Mexico, eastern Europe, and selected less developed Asian countries are also discussed.

In thinking about these various labor relations systems, it is useful to remember that labor relations in each of these countries take place within a labor relations environment that includes legal, economic, sociopolitical, and institutional dimensions that can vary from country to country (recall Chapter 5). Along many of these dimensions, a traditional claim is that U.S. labor relations are exceptional. Low levels of support for unionization,

TABLE 12.2
Labor Relations around the Globe: Union Membership ≠ Contract Coverage

Source: Jelle Visser, ICTWSS Data base, version 5.0 (Amsterdam: Amsterdam Institute for Advanced Labour Studies AIAS, 2015).

Country	Bargaining Coverage	Union Density
Korea	11%	10%
United States	12	11
Japan	15+	18
Canada	29	29
United Kingdom	30	25
South Africa	33	30
Germany	54	18
Australia	60	17
Brazil	60	25
Spain	70	17
Sweden	90	68
France	90+	8
Finland	90+	69
Belgium	95	55
Austria	95+	27

Notes: Figures are circa 2012–2014. + indicates a lower-bound estimate.

lack of a socialist movement, legal protection of individuals rather than unions, and intense employer resistance to unions are all claimed to be relatively unique to the United States among industrialized, democratic countries; in other words, support for unionization, a socialist movement, legal rights for unions, and low employer resistance to unions are widely present in industrialized, democratic countries *except* the United States.[1] In this vein, when considering the labor relations systems of other countries, note the sometimes great differences with the U.S. system—exclusive representation is not always present, contracts are not always legally enforceable, and business unionism is not always the dominant philosophy. Moreover, not only are unions often organized differently but so too are employers. In many countries outside North America, employers' associations rather than individual companies dominate collective bargaining. Table 12.2 shows that in many other countries, union membership is not as closely associated with being covered by a union contract as it is in the United States. In Spain and France over 70 percent of employees are covered by a collective bargaining agreement, yet union density is less than 20 percent—and is not even 10 percent in France.

At the same time, labor relations around the globe are similar in other respects. The contemporary pressures on labor, management, and government are universal: globalization, financialization, decentralization, and flexibility. Moreover, the fundamental issues of labor relations are constant across all countries. The objectives of the employment relationship are efficiency, equity, and voice; there is a need to balance labor rights and property rights; and labor relations outcomes are determined by the environment and individual decision making. The U.S. New Deal labor relations system is one possible method of pursuing these objectives, but the comparative study of labor relations in other countries reveals many alternative possibilities. Therefore, this chapter outlines the labor relations systems of a number of representative countries. There are innumerable ways to order these countries, so to avoid confusion the tour here proceeds geographically from North America to Europe to Asia. The chapter concludes by revisiting the question of globalization: In an integrated world economy, is it possible to have unique national labor relations systems, or does integration force convergence of national institutions?

CANADA

In broad terms, Canada and the United States have similar economic, institutional, and legal features, comparable demographic, occupational, and industrial structures, interdependent product markets, and many of the same corporations. Labor unions in the two countries have similar structures, many Canadian workers are represented by U.S. unions, and Canadian labor law is patterned after the U.S. Wagner Act (but not the Taft–Hartley Act).[2] Exclusive representation, bargaining structures and strategies, and the resulting union contracts are therefore similar.[3] However, some cultural and small yet important legal differences have caused Canadian outcomes to diverge from those in the United States.

Canadian labor law is not centralized as it is in the United States. The provinces have similar yet unique laws that govern labor relations. Although these laws are largely modeled after the U.S. National Labor Relations Act (NLRA), there are some important differences between the provincial laws and the NLRA (see Table 12.3).[4] First, Canadian labor law makes it easier to establish and maintain a union. In contrast to the sometimes lengthy National Labor Relations Board certification election procedure in the United States, some Canadian provinces provide for card check recognition (certification based on authorization cards without a secret ballot election) and instant elections that occur within a couple of

TABLE 12.3 U.S. and Canadian Labor Law: Small Differences That Matter?

Topic	United States	Canada
Legal jurisdiction	Centralized: private sector governed by federal law.	Decentralized: governed by provincial laws.
Union certification	National Labor Relations Board election procedure. Employers can campaign and use delay tactics.	Some provinces allow card check certification or instant elections.
First contract arbitration	No.	Provided in some provinces.
Decertification elections	Strike replacements can vote and permanently replaced strikers can only vote for 12 months.	Some provinces exclude replacement workers from voting or prohibit decertification petitions during a strike.
Nonunion representation	Illegal.	Company domination and interference with organizing are illegal; otherwise legal.
Union security	Right-to-work laws in 26 states forbid union and agency shops.	No right-to-work laws. Unions are guaranteed at least an agency shop in many provinces.
Technological change	Not a mandatory bargaining item.	Equivalent of a mandatory bargaining item in some provinces.
Strike replacements	Except in unfair labor practice strikes, permanent and temporary replacements are allowed.	Most provinces ban the use of permanent replacements. Two provinces ban all replacements.

Sources: See text.

days of filing the election petition. These quick processes reduce the scope for contentious campaigning and antiunion managerial tactics, and when newly organized unions fail to reach a first contract, some Canadian provinces provide for arbitration to establish a contract.[5] Canadian labor relations also lack right-to-work laws banning union security agreements, and in fact the larger provinces require at least an agency shop, which strengthens the financial base of Canadian unions.[6] Second, Canadian labor law makes it more difficult for employers to break an existing union. Some provinces do not allow decertification elections during a strike; and where they are allowed, strike replacements are often not considered part of the bargaining unit and therefore are not allowed to vote. Moreover, most provinces ban permanent strike replacements or provide striking workers with immediate reinstatement rights; in Quebec and British Columbia, even temporary replacements are prohibited.[7]

Relative to the processes in the rest of the world, Canadian labor relations processes are similar to those in the United States; but subtle legal differences and some cultural factors appear to support a more stable labor relations system in Canada.[8] Union density has remained more stable, though Canada also has a larger public sector that accounts for at least some of this difference with the United States. During the concession bargaining period of the 1980s, Canadian unions fared better in wage bargaining than their U.S. counterparts.[9] In contrast to the U.S. business unionism philosophy, Canadian unions are moving toward a social unionism philosophy in which labor has a more militant, social activist role. For advocates of a stronger labor movement and greater employee representation in the workplace, the small legal differences pertaining to union organizing and strike replacements form the basis for proposals to reform U.S. labor law.

MEXICO

The increasing economic integration of the United States, Canada, and Mexico via the North American Free Trade Agreement (NAFTA) has focused greater attention on the labor relations system of Mexico. The Mexican system is important in its own right, but it is also presented here as broadly representative of labor relations in developing countries. In essence, the primary theme is appearance versus reality: On paper Mexican law provides strong protections for workers and unions, but the extent of enforcement is questionable.[10] Moreover, labor negotiations and unions have traditionally been controlled by the government as part of a larger economic development strategy. As in many other developing countries, this results in sharp clashes between the government and independent labor unions because of the government's focus on competitiveness and foreign investment at the expense of democracy and working conditions.

Quite strikingly, social and economic rights for workers are written directly into Mexico's constitution of 1917. In fact, this was the first constitution or basic national charter anywhere to explicitly include workers' rights.[11] Article 123 guarantees the right to organize unions, bargain collectively, and strike; provides protections against unjust dismissal and dangerous working conditions; and mandates minimum wages, overtime pay, profit sharing, an eight-hour day, a six-day workweek, and pregnancy and childbirth leave. Under Mexican labor law, a union must have at least 20 employees and can be an industrial union, craft union, or enterprise union (representing workers at only one company). In rural areas where there is difficulty meeting the 20-worker minimum, general unions are also allowed. To have legal rights, unions must register with the government as one of these types. A union does not need to represent a majority of employees to engage in collective bargaining, but it does need this to legally strike. All contracts automatically include the minimum provisions mandated by the constitution. Once approved by the government, contracts are legally enforceable.

There is no explicit obligation for management to bargain; rather, this is enforced through the strike-related aspects of labor law. Once the legal standards for a strike are fulfilled and mediation fails, a strike can occur. Red and black flags are flown at the entrances to the workplace, and all employees must stop working except those necessary to protect raw materials and equipment.[12] Interestingly, the union is legally responsible for protecting the company's materials and equipment. The employer must cease operations, and permanent strike replacements are prohibited. As such, the legal protections for workers and unions are much greater in Mexico than in the United States—at least on paper.[13]

In practice there are questions about the effectiveness of these protections. For 50 years the most influential union federation was the *Confederación de Trabajadores México* (CTM, Confederation of Mexican Workers). The CTM was closely connected to the long-time ruling party—the *Partido Revolucionario Institucional* (PRI, Institutional Revolutionary Party)—and was therefore frequently criticized as making the labor movement subservient to the government.[14] CTM-affiliated union leaders have been portrayed as being more loyal to the PRI than to their unions. Similarly, collective bargaining agreements are alleged to be more a function of the government's overall economic development strategy than the product of independent collective bargaining. To wit, as the government privatized industries and embraced free trade, union density fell from 30 percent to 20 percent from 1984 to 2000.[15]

Government control of labor unions is facilitated by Mexican labor law. Government agencies play significant roles in approving union registrations, determining the legality of strikes, and approving contracts. These seemingly administrative requirements allow for abuse. Of particular concern are "protection contracts" in which a "ghost union" and an employer agree to a collective bargaining agreement that does not grant workers any benefits or rights. The government is complicit in this by approving the registration of this sham union (even if the registrant is the company's lawyer), by using the existence of this sham contract to prevent workers from switching to an alternative, independent union, and by denying approval to strikes not supported by the ghost union. By some estimates, these sham ghost unions and protection contracts are widespread.[16] The independence, and therefore legitimacy, of the Mexican labor movement has been a concern nationwide. Such concerns are particularly acute in the *maquiladora* industry because of the need to attract foreign investment (recall Chapter 11). At the same time, the rank and file are not universally passive, and struggles for democratic unions and free collective bargaining occur within and outside the official (government-approved) labor movement (see the accompanying "Labor Relations Application" box).[17]

Such struggles sharpened in the first decade of the 21st century. After seven decades in power, the PRI was ousted by the conservative *Partido Acción Nacional* (PAN, National Action Party) with the election of Vicente Fox to Mexico's presidency in 2000. Fox was elected on a platform of government reform and transparency, and he was supported by independent unions who saw these reforms as ending the government's control of the labor movement. But after taking office, Fox and his successor Felipe Calderón pushed a pro-business agenda of privatization, budget cuts, and labor law reform.[18] Indeed, in 2012 unions from 35 countries participated in a global solidarity effort to pressure the Mexican government to stop its repression of independent labor unions. The PRI returned to power in 2013, but has not been friendly to the independent labor movement in Mexico, and labor conflict has continued in mining, education, and other sectors.[19] As such, Mexico continues to be broadly representative of labor relations in developing countries: strong labor rights on paper, but in reality a high degree of state control (although not as repressive as in some regimes) that creates conflicts with independent labor movements.

Labor Relations Application Struggles for a Democratic Teachers' Union in Mexico

The teachers' union in Mexico illustrates the tension between rank-and-file union members, union leaders, and the government in Mexico—and other countries in which the government tries to control the labor movement. The *Sindicato Nacional de Trabajadores de la Educación* (SNTE, National Union of Education Workers) was formed in 1943 and is now the largest union in Mexico with more than a million members. Similar to the private sector unions affiliated with the *Confederación de Trabajadores México* (CTM, Confederation of Mexican Workers), the SNTE has traditionally been a typical "official" union—a centralized structure with leaders who are closely connected to the government and the ruling party, especially the *Partido Revolucionario Institucional* (PRI, Institutional Revolutionary Party) before 2000.

SNTE leaders generally were more interested in pleasing the PRI than the union's members: If they could keep the rank-and-file teachers tranquil, they would be rewarded by the PRI, and movement into government positions was common. But over time, relations between union leaders and the government shifted, alliances changed, and priorities varied so that new accommodations and compromises were often pursued. Moreover, the rank-and-file teachers were not always passive, and at various times their discontent pressured the SNTE leadership and the government.

The first decades of the SNTE were characterized by the government-aided repression of important dissident movements that reflected grassroots frustration with declining real wages and the SNTE's undemocratic practices. A 29-day strike against the government and the national SNTE in the southern state of Chiapas in 1979 led to the founding of the *Coordinadora Nacional de Trabajadores de la Educación* (CNTE, National Coordinating Committee of Education Workers). The CNTE's major objective was to work within the structure of the SNTE to instill greater democracy. In the early 1980s, local branches of the CNTE were active in several states in leading strikes and other forms of protest against the government's working conditions and the SNTE's unresponsiveness or repression. Marches to state and federal government offices were common and sometimes were accompanied by a takeover of the office or violence against the marchers. CNTE groups were successfully elected to leadership positions in Chiapas and Oaxaca, but the SNTE effectively repressed the dissident movement elsewhere. Moreover, in the mid-1980s the national SNTE frustrated the Chiapas and Oaxaca locals through delays in authorizing local elections to renew the authority of the CNTE-supported leaders.

A fresh national struggle for democracy within the SNTE followed the controversial election of Carlos Salinas to the presidency of Mexico in 1988. Led by the CNTE and fueled again by frustration with declining real wages and with the lack of democracy in the SNTE, numerous strikes, marches, and hunger strikes erupted in 1989, and the government ousted the head of the SNTE. Under the new leadership, reforms were enacted that included secret ballot elections and official disaffiliation with the PRI.

The PRI was replaced in 2000 by the conservative *Partido Acción Nacional* (PAN, National Action Party) when Vicente Fox was elected president of Mexico. Nevertheless, dissidents continued to push for democratic reforms, and the SNTE continued to be embroiled in national and regional politics. A strike by teachers in Oaxaca in 2006 for higher pay turned violent when police tried to clear the strikers from town plazas; subsequently huge demonstrations of more than 100,000 protesters called for the resignation of the provincial governor. Another massive strike by dissident teachers in 2008 aimed at the Mexican government and the head of the SNTE also turned violent. The PRI returned to power in 2013 and immediately enacted educational reforms backed by a business group, triggering more teacher protests. In 2014, 43 teachers' college students were kidnapped before a protest, which launched further demonstrations. In 2016, police killed 9 people clearing a highway blockade erected by the CNTE. As such, the tense relationship between unions and the government in Mexican labor relations are exemplified by the teachers' union, as are the recurring struggles not only between the union and the government, but also between the rank and file and their leaders.

References: Maria Lorena Cook, *Organizing Dissent: Unions, the State, and the Democratic Teachers' Movement in Mexico* (University Park: The Pennsylvania State University Press, 1996); updated using Mexican Labor News and Analysis (www.ueinternational.org/MLNA/index.php).

GREAT BRITAIN

The labor relations system in Great Britain illustrates the important concept of **voluntarism.** Unlike U.S. and Canadian labor relations, in which the law requires unions and companies to negotiate if the union represents a majority of the workers, in Great Britain collective bargaining has traditionally occurred only if the parties voluntarily agreed. Voluntary refers to the absence of legal force—labor and management use their economic power, not legal rights, to get the other side to do something, especially to bargain or abide by a contract. When management voluntarily agrees to bargain, for example, it is because the economic costs of refusing to bargain, such as strikes or poor morale, are greater than the costs of bargaining. Representation questions have traditionally been settled through economic force, not elections as in the U.S. system. Management recognizes a union when the union is powerful enough to make it costly for the firm to refuse. The Employment Relations Act (1999) modified the voluntaristic approach by providing for statutory recognition of a union under specified majority demonstration provisions, but voluntary recognition is still encouraged.[20] Another major component of British voluntarism is that contracts are not legally enforceable. Labor and management voluntarily agree to abide by the contract—as long as the costs of following the contract are smaller than the costs of breaking it. Contracts are thus enforced by economic force, not the legal system.

British voluntarism can be traced back to the late 19th century. At that time production was largely craft-based, and skilled workers could shape workplace practices through formal and informal negotiations in individual workplaces using the scarcity of their skills as bargaining leverage.[21] Based on this tradition of unregulated bargaining, both labor and management feared unfavorable, restrictive government involvement—unions did not want restrictions on strikes and boycotts while management did not want restrictions on the freedom to manage. Thus, a voluntarism system emerged and has essentially been maintained. This does not mean, however, that British labor relations are not regulated. The Trades Disputes Act facilitates voluntarism by making labor unions immune from being sued for breach of contract and for striking. Moreover, various pieces of legislation passed by the Conservative government of Margaret Thatcher in the 1980s restrict labor's ability to conduct secondary boycotts, outlaw the closed shop, and require unions to follow certain democratic procedures for electing officers and determining membership support for a strike.[22] Legislation enacted in 2016 further tightened the rules for strike ballots and strike notice, and required unions to get members to opt-in before collecting money for union political funds. Voluntarism in labor relations is therefore a relative term, not an absolute one: British labor relations are voluntaristic relative to labor relations in many other countries that have more extensive legal regulation of labor relations, but they are not free of all regulation.

As a result of its craft origins, the British labor movement historically consisted of numerous occupationally focused unions. Recent mergers have created more general unions. Relative to the United States, there are still many unions, and the largest are UNISON (representing public sector workers), Unite, and the General, Municipal, and Boilermakers' Union (GMB).[23] Many unionized workplaces have multiple unions. There is one union federation, the Trades Union Congress (TUC), and its role in British labor relations is similar to the AFL–CIO's role in the United States: political lobbying, education, and union coordination, but not collective bargaining. Another notable feature of the British labor movement is its close association with the Labour Party, which was founded in 1900 by British unions and the TUC to increase labor's legislative representation in the House of Commons.[24] Although the Labour Party has tried to distance itself from the unions recently, before the 1980s there were periods in which Labour governments worked closely with the labor movement—for example, in linking wage restraint to industrial relations reform.[25]

Labor Relations Application The British Miners' Strike of 1984–1985

The singular watershed event in U.S. labor relations in the last 50 years was arguably the illegal Professional Air Traffic Controllers Organization (PATCO) strike in 1981 (Chapter 3). President Ronald Reagan's firing of the 11,000 striking air traffic controllers is often cited as the event that made it acceptable for private sector companies to aggressively fight unions in organizing drives, at the bargaining table, and by using replacement workers for strikers. In Great Britain, the analogous watershed event was the National Union of Mineworkers (NUM) 12-month strike against the government-run National Coal Board (NCB) in 1984–1985, now often referred to simply as the Great Strike.

By many accounts, the roots of the 1984–1985 NUM strike go back to large coal strikes in 1972 and 1974, which were at least partly responsible for the downfall of the Conservative government of Edward Heath. When Conservative leader Margaret Thatcher was elected in 1979, she was determined not to let this happen again—and perhaps also to extract some revenge. An equally aggressive personality with opposite political views became leader of the NUM in 1981: the militant socialist Arthur Scargill. Adding to the mix of strong personalities was Thatcher's 1983 appointment to head the NCB: Ian MacGregor, who had already shed thousands of jobs at the nationalized (and unprofitable) British Steel. For NUM, this was a sign that Thatcher wanted a confrontation.

The strike was triggered by the NCB's March 1984 announcement that it was closing a mining pit in Yorkshire and by its unilateral insistence that a total of 20 pits be closed—in violation of earlier promises and agreements. Although the coal board claimed that most of the 20,000 lost jobs would come through attrition, NUM was prepared to fight unilateral pit closures to protect both jobs and communities, and the union went on strike without a strike vote. At the height of the strike 150,000 miners were on strike, but 25,000 miners in Nottinghamshire refused to strike until a strike vote was taken. Their later strike vote rejected striking. With this large division within its own ranks, NUM garnered little support from the rest of the British labor movement. The lack of an initial strike vote also came back to haunt NUM as the strike was declared illegal because NUM's constitution required a strike vote, and its funds were sequestered.

The primary issue of the strike was pit closings—the government's right to unilaterally close mining pits versus the destruction of jobs and rural mining communities. With such a difficult issue dividing them, both NUM and the NCB took a hard line in negotiations. Depending on which side is believed, these hard-line bargaining stances were backed up by violent miners on the picket lines or by overly aggressive police supported by complicit judges. There were numerous violent clashes between miners and police, and it is estimated that 1,700 injuries and a couple of deaths resulted. Nearly 10,000 striking miners were arrested. A warm winter, some domestic mining, and increased imports of coal and oil generally offset the loss of coal production due to the strike. With no end in sight and more miners returning to work, the miners voted to end the strike without a collective bargaining agreement after 51 weeks.

Politically, the strike was extremely divisive. It highlighted north (poor) versus south (rich) divisions within Britain, created fissures within the labor movement and the Labour Party, and questioned the fabric of British society. Thatcher's opposition was so intense that she labeled the miners "the enemy within." It was later revealed that MI5, Britain's domestic CIA, led a widespread surveillance effort that included infiltration of NUM, bugging restaurants frequented by NUM leaders, and tapping the phone of every NUM branch. At the end of the strike Thatcher remained concerned about future strikes, and in 1990 NUM leader Scargill was accused in the media of using donations from Libya and the Soviet Union for his personal gain rather than helping striking miners. The accusations proved to be false, and evidence points toward an MI5 conspiracy to plant these false accusations in the media.

As in the PATCO strike in the United States, the NUM strike of 1984–1985 arguably established a climate in Britain of aggressive antiunionism. British union density has continued to decline, and the Labour Party continues to distance itself from the labor movement that founded it. And all the pit mines have been closed.

Ironically, however, for many miners' wives and other women the strike was an empowering event. In stories that parallel the Women's Emergency Brigade in the General Motors sit-down strike in 1936–1937 or the women's auxiliary in the Phelps Dodge strike in 1983 in the United States, women became actively involved in the NUM strike by running soup kitchens, speaking to groups around Great Britain to develop support for the strike, and picketing. The following two quotes from participants in the strike are revealing:

> "The NUM, as far as I can see, put all its eggs in the picketing basket, as they traditionally have, and made no particular provision for dealing with destitution amongst the families. So the women began to see that as well as campaigning there was a need to support the families. That meant going far beyond the traditional housewife role of the mining women. There has been large-scale catering, feeding five

(Continued)

(*Continued*)

and six hundred people in a day; having to raise the money for that, learning to argue for it, to earn it in all sorts of ways, by speaking at meetings and rallies, by collecting on the streets. What they did was to set up an alternative welfare system, and an effective one at that. And these women who had never done anything outside the home before, learning to speak on public platforms to enormous audiences. The change in those women is tremendous." (A daughter, mother, and ex-wife of miners in South Yorkshire)

"The strike has brought me out of my shell. I am not a quiet person, but I am not particularly outgoing. Now, if I thought something was wrong, or if someone needed my support, I would do it. I'm glad it happened, because we got up and shook ourselves." (A self-described "little simple housewife" before the strike, and a miner's wife in southeastern Wales)

References: Teresa Ghilarducci, "When Management Strikes: PATCO and the British Miners," *Industrial Relations Journal* 17 (Summer 1986), pp. 115–28; Ian MacGregor, *The Enemies Within: The Story of the Miners' Strike, 1984–1985* (London: Collins, 1986); Seamas Milne, *The Enemy Within: MI5, Maxwell, and the Scargill Affair* (London: Verso, 1994); Vicky Seddon (ed.), *The Cutting Edge: Women and the Pit Strike* (London: Lawrence and Wishart, 1986). The two quotes are from Seddon, *The Cutting Edge*, pp. 29 and 229.

Additional viewing: The movies *Billy Elliot* and *Pride* are set against the backdrop of the 1984–1985.

The current issues facing British unions are similar to those in the United States. The biggest issue is probably the decline in union density. Although the British decline began much later (1979) than that in the United States (mid-1950s), since 1980 British union membership has fallen by more than 5 million members, and union membership as a fraction of the labor force (union density) has plummeted from 50 percent to 25 percent. This decline appears to stem from structural changes in the economy, labor market weakness, and the previously mentioned Conservative government legal changes enacted in the 1980s.[26] Similar to what happened in the United States, this has caused the British labor movement to increasingly emphasize organizing.[27] A second issue for unions in Great Britain is the challenge of employer demands for flexibility and partnership. As in the United States, diverse and widespread changes in workplace practices present a great challenge for unions.[28] A third issue is the future course of public policy. As its power has waned with the legal reforms of the Conservative government, British labor is looking more toward the European Union (EU) as a method for achieving labor regulations that favor workers and their representatives.[29] For example, the European Works Council directive discussed in the previous chapter was enacted by the British government in 1999 and the EU's Information and Consultation Directive in 2004. Under the latter, an employer must consult with employees about business changes that might affect employment if 10 percent of the employees request consultation. Movement toward a European type of representation, however, entails significant change from the voluntaristic and adversarial traditions of British labor, and uncertainty looms after the 2016 vote to leave the EU.

The balance among efficiency, equity, and voice in a voluntaristic system to a large extent depends on markets and the economic leverage of the two parties. In the early 1960s low unemployment gave workplace shop stewards significant leverage, and many strikes were called to win grievances and other gains—recall that contracts are enforced by economic force, not legal procedures.[30] As a result, British labor relations developed a reputation of being adversarial and turbulent and therefore harmful to efficiency and competitiveness (see the accompanying "Labor Relations Application" box). When unemployment is higher, management has the upper hand and efficiency-enhancing policies dominate equity and voice concerns.

Because a voluntaristic system lacks legal standards for representation and bargaining, strong employer leverage can result in representation mechanisms that are illegal elsewhere. As a graphic example, consider Nissan and Toyota's recognition of the Amalgamated Engineering and Electrical Union (now Unite) at their British plants. Because of their economic leverage, the companies were able to insist that broad managerial prerogatives remain the sole function of management. In addition to production methods and standards, these prerogatives include core labor issues such as employee communications, transfers, and promotions. Moreover, wages and terms and conditions of employment are established not through bargaining but through a joint employee–management company council in which the union has no formal role, strikes are not allowed, and the company retains final decision-making authority.[31] This essentially nonunion form of employee representation is illegal in the United States because of restrictions on company-dominated unions and obligations to bargain over wages and terms and conditions of employment; but voluntarism allows any arrangement that is mutually acceptable, where the definition of acceptable is determined by bargaining power.

IRELAND

Labor relations in Ireland are an interesting contrast with the British system. At their core, Irish labor relations are similar to British labor relations. When Ireland gained independence from Great Britain in 1922, the existing British laws for labor relations continued under the new Irish government. Consequently, the British system of voluntarism and labor union immunity from common law liabilities underlies Irish as well as British labor relations.[32] Collective bargaining was therefore also traditionally adversarial and produced restrictive work rules, and until 1980 Ireland was perceived as one of the most strike-prone countries in Europe.[33] The Industrial Relations Act of 1990 implemented reforms similar to the British changes in labor law initiated in the 1980s by the Thatcher government—restrictions on secondary activity and picketing plus requirements for secret ballot strike votes—but the basic labor relations framework remains voluntarism. As in many other countries, union density declined after 1980 and now stands at approximately 30 percent.

The striking contrast with British labor relations was the Irish inclusion of **social partnership** on top of its voluntaristic labor relations system between 1987 and 2009. Social partnership can mean various things, but here the term is used in a corporatist sense: a social partnership of labor, business, and the government that results in a series of peak-level agreements on social and economic issues.[34] Peak-level organizations are the highest national groups representing the public, employees, and employers. For the public this is the government; for labor it is the major labor union federation; and for employers it is the major employers' association. In a corporatist political system, these key peak-level organizations are integrated into the political decision-making process. This stands in contrast to a pluralist political system (as in the United States) in which interest groups such as the labor movement and employers' associations compete for influence by pressuring and lobbying lawmakers, but are not formally incorporated into the decision-making process.

The Irish peak-level organizations include the major union federation—the Irish Congress of Trade Unions (ICTU)—and the Irish Business and Employers' Confederation (IBEC) representing employers. Prompted by a growing economic crisis in the 1980s—including stagnant personal income and sharply increasing unemployment and government debt—the government, the ICTU, and the IBEC negotiated a social partnership agreement called the Programme for National Recovery (PNR) in 1987. The goal of the PNR was to create a fiscal and monetary climate that was conducive to economic growth and a reduction in government debt. This included changes in the tax system, increased employment opportunities, and private sector pay guidelines (a six-month pay freeze followed by 2.5 percent annual increases). This three-year social partnership agreement was followed by six additional agreements (see Table 12.4). In a break from the earlier agreements, the seventh partnership agreement, "Towards 2016," negotiated in 2006, was designed to last for 10 years except for the wage agreement, which covered only the first 27 months. A new wage agreement was negotiated in 2008, but this agreement, and the social partnership process more generally, broke down when the government implemented a pay freeze during the recession in 2009.

TABLE 12.4
Social Partnership Agreements in Ireland

The Programme for National Recovery (PNR), 1987–1990

Objectives: Creation of a fiscal and monetary climate that is conducive to economic growth and a reduction in government debt.

Provisions: Changes in the tax system, increased employment opportunities, and private sector pay guidelines (a six-month pay freeze followed by 2.5 percent annual increases).

The Programme for Economic and Social Progress (PESP), 1990–1994

Objectives: Sustained economic growth, increased employment, development of greater social rights (education, health, and housing), worker participation, women's rights, and consumer rights.

Provisions: Pay guidelines and a pledge by labor and management to maintain industrial harmony and to resolve bargaining differences through formal dispute resolution machinery (such as the Labour Court).

The Programme for Competitiveness and Work (PCW), 1994–1997

Objectives: Pay stability and creation of a climate for growth (similar to the PNR).

Provisions: Primarily pay guidelines, but also employment and training programs and tax reform.

Partnership 2000 for Inclusion, Employment, and Competitiveness, 1997–2000

Objectives: Continued development of an efficient, internationally competitive economy, employment growth, and social inclusion.

Provisions: Tax relief, government debt reduction targets, creation of a national framework for creating labor–management partnerships at the enterprise level, attempts at tackling social exclusion, a framework for resolving union recognition questions, and pay guidelines.*

The Programme for Prosperity and Fairness, 2001–2003

Objectives: Promote competitiveness, further economic prosperity, improvements in the quality of life and living standards for all, and a fairer and more inclusive Ireland.

Operational frameworks: Living standards and workplace environment (including pay standards, workplace partnerships, and flexibility), prosperity and economic inclusion, social inclusion and equality, successful adaptation to continuing change, and renewing partnership.

Sustaining Progress, 2003–2005

Objectives: To continue progress toward economic inclusion (based on full employment, consistent economic development that is socially and environmentally sustainable, social inclusion and a commitment to social justice, and continuing adaptation to change) by sustaining economic growth and high levels of employment while strengthening the economy's competitiveness.

Provisions: Pay guidelines with strengthened enforcement mechanisms, a commitment to seek specific labor law reforms, enhanced severance pay, and affordable housing targets.

Towards 2016, 2006–2015

Objectives: Fulfill a longer-term vision for Ireland that links social policy and economic prosperity, develops a vibrant knowledge-based economy, increases the integration of the island of Ireland, and successfully handles diversity.

Provisions: Pay guidelines, increased penalties for employment law violators, social welfare payments linked to average wage level, increased provision of affordable housing, child care, and health care, infrastructure spending targets, greater investments in education.

Social exclusion captures the idea that those in poverty are often excluded not only from jobs but also from political rights, health care, and education. This might stem from racism, religious discrimination, lack of education, being an immigrant, or other reasons.

On one level these social partnership agreements reflect a system of centralized bargaining. Each of the agreements established pay guidelines for the Irish economy, and while some local bargaining occurred, collective bargaining for wages was essentially done by the one major union federation and employers' association on an economywide basis. But this was more than just centralized collective bargaining. In addition to labor and management, the government participated as a third pillar, and in the 1990s a fourth pillar of community groups was added to the partnership process.[35] The later social partnership talks therefore included representatives from organizations such as the Irish Farmers Association, the Irish National Organization of the Unemployed, and the Conference of Religious of Ireland; the resulting agreements reflected a *social* partnership much broader than a limited economic or workplace agreement. Far-ranging economic and social issues were tackled in these agreements: government spending and taxation, unemployment, housing, access to health care, poverty and social exclusion, and education and lifelong learning. Moreover, although the agreements were not legally binding contracts, they provided a public framework to which the parties generally tried to adhere. The resulting stability and predictability—for the aggregate economy as well as workplace labor relations—was widely credited with laying the foundation for Ireland's exceptional economic performance during the 1990s and early 2000s.[36] How thoroughly this climate of partnership extended to the workplace, however, can be questioned.[37] Moreover, in the 2000s, the Irish economy shifted to being driven by a housing bubble induced by financialization, and this pressured the social partnership away from moderation. The global financial crisis burst the housing bubble, collapsed the Irish economy collapsed, and revealed that social partnership was no longer serving its earlier economic purpose. The government then made unilateral changes to public sector pay and conditions, and social partnership ended.[38]

Various forms of social partnerships or corporatism have been prevalent, albeit not continuously, in smaller European countries such as Austria, Belgium, Denmark, the Netherlands, Norway, and Switzerland.[39] The benefits of the participation of labor, business, government, and other groups in developing a national plan for both economic and social development are inclusion, stability, predictability, and a climate of consensus rather than conflict. Government policy can also be depoliticized because labor and business are involved in establishing economic and social policy. For unions, a social partnership arrangement provides greater social relevance as the voice for all workers, and perhaps for consumers and taxpayers as well. This voice is on a national level, however, not in the workplace, and unions need to be careful not to lose their workplace voice. Echoing the workplace-level debates over unions and high-performance work systems (Chapter 10), there can be a fine line for unions in a social partnership arrangement between collaboration and "selling out."[40] Lastly, although social partnerships can promote stability and consensus, the centralized nature of this form of labor relations is under pressure at the workplace level as management seeks greater flexibility, increased prevalence of pay for performance, and other decentralized, efficiency-enhancing human resource management innovations.

FRANCE

Labor relations in France consist of an interesting mixture of militant, often politically oriented unions but weak collective bargaining, very low union density, very high contract coverage by industry-level agreements, and several mechanisms for workplace-level representation.[41] As Table 12.5 shows, there are eight major union federations; recall that the United States (between 1955 and 2005), Britain, and Ireland each had or have one. Unlike the U.S. emphasis on business unionism, the French union federations often have distinct political or ideological perspectives. The CGT has traditionally been

TABLE 12.5
French Union Confederations

Industrial Unions	Membership	National Representation Elections
Confédération générale du travail (CGT)—General Confederation of Labor *Traditionally communist though moving away from Marxist orthodoxy.*	710,000	25.6%
Confédération française democratique du travail (CFDT)—French Democratic Confederation of Labor *Radical support of worker control in 1960s, but recently a more moderate focus on union adaptation to economic change.*	875,000	23.8
Force ouvriére (FO)—Workers' Strength *Anti-communist and militant.*	300,000	16.9
Confédération française des travailleurs chrétiens (CFTC)—French Confederation of Christian Workers *Christian orientation, anti–class struggle, pro–collective bargaining.*	160,000	7.3
Solidaires Unitaires Démocratiques (SUD)–Solidarity, Unity, Democracy *Militant, left-wing, and anti-globalization orientation*	100,000	4.6
Occupational Unions		
Union nationale des syndicats autonomes (USNA)—National Federation of Independent Unions *Mostly public sector workers, especially teachers.*	200,000	6.3
Confédération française de l'encadrement–Confédération générale des cadres (CFE–CGC)—French Confederation of Professional and Managerial Staff–General Confederation of Managerial Staffs *Focus on economic issues for engineers, technicians, supervisors, sales representatives, and others.*	140,000	7.2
Fédération syndicale unitaire (FSU)—Unitary Union Federation *Primarily teachers with more of a left-wing orientation than those affiliated with the USNA.*	162,000	2.8

communist and therefore has conveyed Communist Party priorities to the working class, though it is moving away from this platform. While also becoming more pragmatic in recent years, the FO and CFDT have traditionally been associated with socialist ideals of worker control; the CFTC has a Christian orientation. The CFTC supports collective bargaining—but note that in general terms, communist and socialist unions have not always supported collective bargaining because signing a contract limits worker freedom and legitimizes capitalism.[42] With such sharp ideological differences between unions, and between labor and employers, a stable social partnership arrangement is nearly impossible to achieve. Rather, political mobilization and political strikes motivated by each union's ideological focus have been as important as, if not more important than, collective bargaining in French labor relations. As such, France is an example of political or **ideological unionism.** This could be labeled "mass and class unionism" because of the emphasis in using class struggle ideology to create large-scale protests.[43] In 2016, for example, there were (again!) repeated demonstrations in multiple cities to protest the government's consideration (again!) of reforms that would make it easier for companies to fire workers, increase working hours, and reduce pay. Other southern European countries such as Italy and Spain are broadly similar in this regard. Moreover, this is a pluralist model of political unionism rather than a corporatist model: Unlike in the Irish social partnerships, the French unions (as "outsiders") pressure the government to enact policies favorable to the unions' agendas rather than participating directly in policymaking (as "insiders").

Continuing competitive and economic problems led to government initiatives to regularize French labor relations, and since the 1980s collective bargaining and workplace representation have increased in importance. Bargaining takes place on three levels: multi-industry, industry, and company. The multi-industry and industry agreements provide the broad parameters and minimum standards for individual companies to follow regarding flexibility and working time (multi-industry) and pay (industry). Company-level agreements implement specific pay and working conditions provisions. Note that there is no exclusive representation: French law mandates company-level bargaining regardless of whether a majority of employees authorize a single union as their representative. Thus, an employer may negotiate with a committee composed of individuals from various unions as long as they represent at least 30 percent of the workforce, and any single union has official representation status if at least 10 percent of the workers support it in a periodic election. These elections are held nationwide every few years, and the most recent aggregate results are shown in Table 12.5. Moreover, as is true in a number of other European countries, French law allows industry agreements to be extended to all companies within the same industry irrespective of the number of union members (if any) at a specific company. Thus, while union density is low, the fraction of workers covered by collective bargaining agreements is high. On the other hand, collective bargaining agreements in France are weak by U.S. standards—though this is perhaps offset by national legislation that often favors workers, such as a 35-hour workweek.

Lastly, French law provides for several forms of workplace-level employee representation separate from labor unions. Employee delegates are required to handle grievances and to monitor the enforcement of both labor laws and collective bargaining agreements. Works committees are entitled to information and consultation on workplace and companywide decisions (see the discussion of German codetermination in the next section). Employee delegates and works committee representatives are elected via secret ballot by all workers. A single works committee likely has members of different unions. French labor law also guarantees workers a right of expression, so workers are entitled to voice their opinions regarding the nature of their work. How French law struggles with trying to balance efficiency, equity, and voice is captured by this description of earlier reforms: "The Auroux laws were intended to foster a mutual learning process within the enterprise, with employers becoming more aware of their social employment responsibilities and unions more attentive to the firm's economic constraints."[44]

GERMANY

The labor relations system of Germany is best known for its system of codetermination, but this important feature must be understood in conjunction with a second major feature, sector bargaining. In contrast to France, there is one dominant union federation, *Deutscher Gewerkschaftsbund* (DGB, German Trade Union Confederation), that accounts for over 80 percent of German union membership and has eight affiliated unions, each of which represents a specific industry. Employer federations are also organized by industry. As such, each major industry or sector has a dominant employer association and union, and these two bodies engage in **sector bargaining**—industrywide bargaining that produces a contract for the entire sector.

Sector bargaining often takes place at a regional level, but it is tightly coordinated by the national organizations, and the first regional agreement sets a strong pattern for the other regions. For example, a regional branch of *Gesamtmetall,* the metal and electrical industry employers' association, and the regional branch of *IG Metall,* the metal and electrical industry union, will negotiate basic agreements on wages, pay structures, working time, and working conditions under the direction of their parent organizations. These agreements establish minimum labor standards that apply to *all* members of the employers' association—the number of union members at each company is unimportant. Moreover, to promote a level playing field and "take wages out of competition," an agreement can be legally extended by the government to cover other companies, as is the case in a majority of European countries.[45] As such, the contract coverage rate (approximately 50–60 percent) is much higher than the union membership rate (approximately 20 percent). Strikes are illegal during the life of an agreement. A company cannot invalidate the contract by leaving the employers' association, so it is difficult to become nonunion in Germany.[46] As in many other countries, competitive forces are pressuring the German collective bargaining system to become more decentralized. Thus, local exceptions to the industry standards are increasing, and some companies have negotiated independently rather than through their employers' association—Volkswagen is a prominent example; but because of strong traditions and institutions, such deviations are still exceptional.[47] Increased outsourcing to subcontractors that fall outside the sectoral bargaining agreements is another threat to the stability of the traditional sector bargaining system.[48] Like labor movements elsewhere, then, German unions are under pressure to develop new strategies for maintaining their strength and influence.[49]

Centralized collective bargaining in Germany is complemented in the workplace by **codetermination**—an institutionalized system of employee voice in which employees are entitled to participate in workplace decision making. German codetermination has two components: works councils and employee representation on corporate supervisory boards. A **works council** is a workplace-level committee of employees elected to represent all the workers (except senior executives)—skilled and unskilled, blue- and white-collar, union members and nonmembers—in dealings with management. Works councils in various forms are also found in France, Spain, the Netherlands, Austria, Italy, and Belgium, but the German example is perhaps the best known.[50] German law entitles all workers in companies with at least five employees to form a works council if some employees wish; generally only 5 percent of the employees need to sign a list of candidates to trigger an election of employee representatives to a works council (or a minimum of two employees in very small establishments and a maximum of 50 in large workplaces). Do not confuse this with a drawn-out and sharply contested NLRB representation election as in the United States (Chapter 6)—"once the procedure is initiated by employees, the election of a works council is to all intents and purposes automatic."[51] Nearly 90 percent of establishments with at least 500 employees have works councils, but fewer than 10 percent of small establishments do; changes to the German Works Constitution Act in 2001 therefore further simplified the election process in small establishments.[52]

German works councils have codetermination, consultation, and information rights regarding various workplace issues and are legally distinct from unions—their existence does not depend on a local union presence. Nevertheless, in practice union members are likely to be active in the works councils and unions help provide training and expertise; in return, unions can use the rights granted to works councils to strengthen their influence within the workplace.[53] The size of works councils varies with the size of the workforce: A 500-person establishment has an 11-member works council (including one full-time member), whereas a 5,000-person establishment has a 29-person works council (including seven full-time members). The works council must meet with the employer at least once a month, and the company pays for the works council's expenses. Companies with multiple establishments must also establish companywide works councils. The law mandates that "the employer and the works councils shall work together in a spirit of mutual trust . . . for the good of the employees and of the establishment." A works council cannot strike, but it can sue if the employer does not fulfill its legal obligations of codetermination, consultation, and information provision.

Granting codetermination rights to works councils means that a company must jointly determine with the works council issues pertaining to work rules and discipline, daily working hours, leave schedules, performance-based pay and bonuses, overtime, safety and health, training, and personnel selection methods (see Table 12.6). In other words, on these matters the employer cannot take action without the agreement of the works council. Negotiated agreements on codetermined issues are incorporated into works agreements. The second set of rights granted to works councils are consultation rights—the works council must be consulted before an employer changes the nature of its work. And third, a firm's works council must be given financial information about the firm's balance sheet, investment and marketing plans, and other corporate intentions (see Table 12.6).

Remember that industrywide collective bargaining agreements specify minimum standards and other broad parameters for the workplace. As such, works councils are left to work out specific details, especially pertaining to implementation issues, for each workplace.[54] Moreover, when the labor market is strong, some works councils are able to negotiate extra wage increases; conversely, when a firm's financial health is weak, some works councils agree to concessions below the collective bargaining agreement's standards ("wildcat cooperation").[55] Works councils are also viewed as generally supportive of workplace changes and the implementation of new processes and technologies if the company and its workforce will be strengthened, and management can utilize works councils to help implement such changes.[56] German companies are introducing the same types of flexible work systems as in other countries, but the legal rights of works councils give them the power to ensure that employee interests are represented when these changes are implemented.[57] Research on works councils fails to consistently uncover significant effects on economic efficiency; in other words, it is difficult to conclude that works councils either improve or harm productivity, employee turnover, investment, and the like.[58] Supporters of works councils, however, see them as mechanisms for providing equity and especially voice, but not efficiency.

Complementing works councils is the other major component of German codetermination: employee representation on corporate supervisory boards. German corporations have two boards for managing the company: A management board controls the daily management of the firm and reports to the higher-level supervisory board, which sets strategic

TABLE 12.6
Excerpts from the German Works Constitution Act

74. **Principles of collaboration**
(1) The employer and the works council shall meet together at least once a month for joint conferences. They shall discuss the matters at issue with an earnest desire to reach agreement and make suggestions for settling their differences.
(2) Industrial action between the employer and the works council shall be unlawful; the foregoing shall not apply to industrial action between collective bargaining parties. The employer and the works council shall refrain from activities that interfere with operations or imperil the peace in the establishment.

85. **Works council's role in dealing with grievances**
(1) The works council shall hear employees' grievances and, if they appear justified, induce the employer to remedy them.

Social Matters
87. **Right of codetermination**
(1) The works council shall have a right of codetermination in the following matters insofar as they are not prescribed by legislation or collective agreement:

1. Matters relating to the order by operation of the establishment and the conduct of employees in the establishment.
2. The commencement and termination of the daily working hours, including breaks and the distribution of working hours among the days of the week.
3. Any temporary reduction or extension of the hours normally worked in the establishment.
4. The time and place for and the form of payment of remuneration.
5. The establishment of general principles for leave arrangements and the preparation of the leave schedule as well as fixing the time at which the leave is to be taken by individual employees, if no agreement is reached between the employer and the employees concerned.
6. The introduction and use of technical devices designed to monitor the behavior or performance of the employees.
7. Arrangements for the prevention of employment accidents and occupational diseases and for the protection of health on the basis of legislation or safety regulations.
8. The form, structuring, and administration of social services whose scope is limited to the establishment, company, or combine.
9. The assignment of and notice to vacate accommodation that is rented to employees in view of their employment relationship as well as the general fixing of the conditions for the use of such accommodation.
10. Questions related to remuneration arrangements in the establishment, including in particular the establishment of principles of remuneration and the introduction and application of new remuneration methods or modification of existing methods.
11. The fixing of job and bonus rates and comparable performance-related remuneration including cash coefficients.
12. Principles for suggestion schemes in the establishment.
13. Principles governing the performance of group work; group work within the meaning of this provision is defined as a group of employees performing a complex task within the establishment's workflows, which has been assigned to it and is executed in a largely autonomous way.

Structuring, Organization, and Design of Jobs, Operations, and the Working Environment
90. **Information and consultation rights**
(1) The employer shall inform the works council in due time of any plans concerning

1. the construction, alteration, or extension of works, offices, and other premises belonging to the establishment;
2. technical plants;

TABLE 12.6
(*Continued*)

3. working procedures and operations or
4. jobs

and submit the necessary documents.
(2) The employer shall consult the works council in good time on the action envisaged and its effects on the employees, taking particular account of its impact on the nature of their work and the resultant demands on the employees so that suggestions and objections on the part of the works council can be taken into account in the plans.

91. **Right of codetermination**
Where a special burden is imposed on the employees as a result of changes in jobs, operations, or the working environment that are in obvious contradiction to the established findings of ergonomics relating to the tailoring of jobs to meet human requirements, the works council may request appropriate action to obviate, relieve, or compensate for the additional stress thus imposed.

92. **Manpower planning**
(1) The employer shall inform the works council in full and in good time of matters relating to manpower planning including in particular present and future manpower needs and the resulting staff movements and vocational training measures and supply the relevant documentation. He shall consult the works council on the nature and extent of the action required and means of avoiding hardship.

95. **Guidelines for selection**
(1) Guidelines for the selection of employees for recruitment, transfer, regrading, and dismissal shall require the approval of the works council.

98. **Implementation of vocational training in the establishment**
(1) The works council shall participate in the decisions relating to the implementation of vocational training programs in the establishment.

102. **Codetermination in the case of dismissal**
(1) The works council shall be consulted before every dismissal. The employer shall indicate to the works council the reasons for dismissal. Any notice of dismissal that is given without consulting the works council shall be null and void.

Financial Matters
106. **Finance committee**
(1) A finance committee shall be established in all companies that normally have more than 100 permanent employees. It shall be the duty of the finance committee to consult with the employer on financial matters and report to the works council.
(2) The employer shall inform the finance committee in full and in good time of the financial affairs of the company and supply the relevant documentation insofar as there is no risk of disclosing the trade or business secrets of the company and demonstrate the implications for manpower planning.

111. **Alterations**
In establishments that normally have more than 20 employees with voting rights the employer shall inform the works council in full and in good time of any proposed alterations which may entail substantial prejudice to the staff or a large sector thereof and consult the works council on the proposed alterations.

policies and appoints upper-level managers. The supervisory board generally meets four times per year. Depending on the size of the company, one-third to one-half of the supervisory board members are representatives of the employees. German supervisory boards are less powerful than U.S. boards of directors, but employee representation nevertheless gives workers a voice in strategic decisions.[59] In the United States unions occasionally obtain a single board seat, often as part of a significant package of employee wage and work rule concessions; but significant board-level representation is mandated by law in Germany.

Finally, note that because union membership is not linked to industry-level collective agreements, workplace-level works council representation, or supervisory board representation, the decision to join a union is different than in the United States. In Europe "joining a trade union is as much an act of political commitment as it is a step to support collective bargaining. It is more an act of solidarity than simply a means to secure personal gains."[60] Similarly, European unions traditionally have not focused solely on winning economic improvements for their members. Rather, advocacy of broad working-class interests—either within capitalism or in opposition to it—and integration of workers into broader political movements have been as important as, and frequently more important than, collective bargaining.[61]

SWEDEN

The major dimensions of labor relations in Sweden and the other Nordic countries appear broadly similar to those in Germany: A high contract coverage rate and a dual representation structure with centralized, industrywide collective bargaining and strong workplace representation.[62] An important difference, however, is that while workplace representation in Germany is institutionalized by law in the form of works councils that are technically independent of labor unions, until recently workplace representation in Sweden has been institutionalized by culture and tradition in the form of strong workplace-level unions. Like the United States, workplace representation in Sweden relies on unions; unlike the United States, union density in Sweden is high (close to 70 percent), so workplace representation is widespread. As in other countries around the world, economic pressures are causing greater decentralization in bargaining: Peak-level negotiations have been sporadic since 1980, industrywide agreements have become less detailed, and local agreements have become both more important and more diverse albeit with significant coordination within a sector.[63] The traditional goal of the Swedish labor movement was a "solidaristic wage policy" that consisted of equal pay for equal work across companies (making company ability to pay unimportant) and a compression of wage outcomes within an establishment. New forms of work organization, however, have reoriented this objective more toward a "solidaristic work policy" in which unions are involved in transforming work to ensure that workers as well as companies benefit from these changes.[64] In particular, the solidaristic work policy advocates self-directed work teams, training, job and skill development, and compensation for skills and responsibilities. The extent to which U.S. unions might also be less resistant to workplace change if they had the institutional and cultural security of Swedish unions is a thought-provoking question.

Online Exploration Exercise: Explore the sites of employers' associations that engage in collective bargaining (e.g., Gesamtmetall at *www.gesamtmetall.de* or the Korean Employers Federation at *www.kefplaza.com*). What themes are emphasized by these associations? Why are employers' associations less likely to be important actors in U.S. collective bargaining relative to some other countries? What are some advantages to greater participation in collective bargaining by employers' associations?

EASTERN EUROPE

After World War II, labor relations in the Soviet Union and the communist countries of eastern Europe were characterized by **Stalinist unionism,** named for the Soviet dictator Joseph Stalin.[65] In centrally planned Stalinist economies, managers of state-owned enterprises and unions were both controlled by the government (the Communist Party). Unions were a critical part of this economic and political system, primarily to transmit the Communist Party's agenda to the working class (the common phrase is that unions are the Party's "transmission belt"). In the workplace, unions in a Stalinist system had dual roles: to facilitate the state's production goals (such as through maintaining discipline) and to protect individual workers from abusive managers (such as by refusing to approve employee dismissals).[66] As transmission belts of the Communist Party, unions emphasized the first role much more than the second. Unions also administered the government's various social benefits, such as housing and recreational programs, and therefore membership rates were very high (approaching 100 percent). There was no collective bargaining because wages and other terms of employment were determined by central planners—"the official trade unions in the Soviet Union were never designed to represent workers' interests, since official ideology held that there could be no conflict of interests between the working class and its vanguard that ran the economy, the Communist Party."[67] As such, strikes and independent unions were illegal. Unions were tightly controlled by the Communist Party, typically structured along industry lines, and, following the model of the Communist Party, very centralized.

There were some deviations from this strict model during the Cold War—for example in Hungary and most visibly in Poland. Led by electrician Lech Walesa, 17,000 workers conducted a sit-down strike at the Lenin Shipyards in Gdansk, Poland, in 1980.[68] The most important demand of the strikers was the right to form free labor unions independent of the Communist Party, and thus the Solidarity union (*Solidarność*) was born. The strike was a major victory, and Solidarity's membership jumped to 10 million workers. In 1981 additional strikes were used to pressure the Polish government for free elections. However, under pressure from the Soviet Union, the Polish government imposed martial law in December 1981, outlawed Solidarity, and jailed its leaders. Strikes in 1988 again pressured the government to legalize Solidarity, and it was allowed to participate in free elections in 1989. Solidarity was very successful in these elections and was able to form a coalition government. Walesa won the Nobel Peace Prize in 1983 and in 1990 became Poland's first popularly elected president.

In addition to the Solidarity movement in Poland, the fall of the Berlin Wall in 1989 marked the end of communist East Germany; by the end of that year, communism was collapsing throughout eastern Europe. In 1991, the Soviet Union dissolved into Russia and a number of independent states. These events were triggered by the Solidarity movement, which underscores the power of collective action and the need for independent labor movements in society. All of these countries, however, have been struggling with the transition to capitalist, free market economies, and democratic, pluralistic political systems since that time. Stable systems of labor relations have yet to emerge, and unions have struggled to find their most effective roles in the new transitional economies.[69] Are they workplace advocates, or independent political representatives of the working class in a pluralist political system, or part of governing coalitions responsible for shaping new economic and political institutions?

Collective bargaining, economic strikes, and independent labor unions have been legalized in eastern Europe. The emergence of independent unions has resulted in significant interunion competition, though in many countries the largest unions continue as reformed versions of the earlier communist unions.[70] Because of the traditional importance of the government in economic affairs in these countries before the collapse of communism, the governments of many postcommunist countries remain actively involved in economic activities generally and in labor relations specifically. Tripartite bodies involving unions, employers' associations, and the government have therefore been used in Bulgaria, Hungary, and elsewhere.[71] As in other social partnerships (recall the earlier discussion of Ireland), such arrangements have dealt with establishing wage guidelines, reforming labor law, and dispute resolution. These accomplishments might be more symbolic than real, however, and political and economic instability, interunion competition, and a legacy of dependence on management and the state undermine the prospects for successful social partnerships.[72]

The Stalinist model left behind a legacy of weak unions at the enterprise and workplace levels with no experience in collective bargaining and with little rank-and-file involvement. Thus bargaining is still often conducted with the government, and wage settlements reflect political power and maneuvering rather than economic conditions and bargaining tactics. Enterprise-level collective bargaining therefore remains weak.[73] Works councils have been implemented in Hungary, but elsewhere they either were not legislated or were enacted and then repealed; and unions are struggling to develop influence in the workplace. Unions have frequently been marginalized in industries that have been privatized and turned over to private ownership. It will be interesting to watch what types of employment systems emerge when the eastern European economies develop greater economic and political stability and to see whether unions have a significant role to play. Will existing Western systems be adopted, or will new methods for balancing efficiency, equity, and voice be created?

AUSTRALIA AND NEW ZEALAND

Whereas unions in Germany and Sweden are organized primarily along industry lines, unions in Australia were traditionally organized mostly on a craft or occupational basis. Unions typically had members in more than one industry, and managers often had to deal with multiple unions—in the 1980s the average number of unions per Australian firm was 12.[74] Union density, however, has declined sharply since the mid-1970s from above 50 percent to less than 20 percent.[75] Consequently, since the late 1980s the Australian labor movement has actively pursued union mergers and amalgamations to transform a relatively large number of small unions into a smaller number of industry-based or general unions. By 1995 nearly all union members belonged to one of 20 unions. This strategy unsuccessfully attempted to counter the decline in union density by increasing the number of services that larger, industry-focused unions can provide to potential members.[76] Such merger activity, however, raises the same issue that faces the U.S. labor movement: how to balance union strength with responsiveness to the needs of individual workers and workplaces.

The drive to increase the power of Australian unions through rationalization along industry lines also stems from the trend toward decentralization of Australian labor relations. A main feature of labor relations in Australia has traditionally been a centralized system of arbitration awards. In this **awards system** a federal or state arbitration commission (or tribunal) issues an award that specifies the minimum standards for pay and working conditions, often for an occupation. This arbitration system dates back to the early 1900s and was devised to prevent strikes. For a number of years the basic federal award established a minimum wage for unskilled workers to fulfill "the normal needs of an average employee, regarded as a human being living in a civilized community" based on a family of five. Wage differentials for skilled occupations were established relative to this basic wage award. The federal awards established the pattern for state and industry-level awards. In tight labor markets unions were successful in using collective bargaining with individual employers to negotiate "over-award" pay more generous than the arbitration awards. Working conditions were established separately from the arbitration awards through workplace-level bargaining, often informally and with high levels of wildcat strikes. But because of the importance of the national and regional awards, overall this was a very centralized system of labor relations in which arbitration, not collective bargaining, was the centerpiece.[77]

In the late 1980s, Australian labor relations pushed away from centralized awards toward greater decentralization and enterprise-level bargaining. This effort was the product of both the government (due to macroeconomic problems such as an exchange rate crisis) and employers (to improve labor–management cooperation, flexibility, and responsiveness to firm-specific conditions). In other words, Australia has also struggled with globalization, decentralization, and flexibility. In the 1990s, the role of the federal arbitration commission shifted away from issuing awards to ensuring that union and nonunion enterprise-level agreements met a few minimum standards.

Opposition to these trends, however, led to the defeat of the conservative government in 2007, and many of the changes were rolled back. A new system now includes (i) 10 minimum national employment standards for all workers, including maximum weekly hours of work, parental and other leaves, and public holidays; (ii) "modern awards" on minimum wages and other issues that will be tailored to the needs of particular industries or occupations; (iii) enterprise-level collective bargaining, including a legal obligation for companies and unions to bargain in good faith; and (iv) a national agency (Fair Work Australia) to oversee the modern awards, facilitate bargaining, and resolve disputes.[78] These changes reflect a desire to restore some of the equity and voice that were sacrificed in the pursuit of efficiency between 1987 and 2007—that is, to strike a new balance among efficiency, equity, and voice.

Labor relations in New Zealand exhibit a similar trend, albeit with even more radical reforms.[79] New Zealand's arbitration system dated back to 1894 and operated much like Australia's. A federal arbitration commission issued awards for minimum conditions while collective bargaining, often on a multiemployer basis, established above-award terms. Moreover, an employer could unilaterally establish terms and conditions of employment as long as they exceeded the minimum provisions established by the relevant arbitration award. Unlike the 1987–2007 Australian initiative to decentralize labor relations by weakening the arbitration awards system, New Zealand has pursued decentralization by abolishing its award system. The 1991 Employment Contracts Act replaced the awards system with voluntarism (recall Great Britain's system described earlier in this chapter). The Employment Contracts Act created a voluntaristic system, so it did not require bargaining of any type—unions could negotiate collective contracts, but only if they had explicit authorization from each worker and if the employer wanted to bargain; otherwise, individual nonunion contracts were used. The Employment Relations Act of 2000 moved New Zealand industrial relations away from a pure voluntarism system. Individual employment contracts are still allowed, but employers have an obligation to bargain in good faith with a union if a group of employees requests it. It is also illegal for employers to pressure or discriminate against employees in order to encourage or discourage union membership.

In 2010, New Zealand was swept up in an interesting labor controversy when several actors unions, including the U.S. Screen Actors Guild and American Federation of Television and Radio Artists, urged their members to not work on *The Hobbit* movies being produced by Peter Jackson because the production company would not agree to a union agreement for the filming that was likely to occur in New Zealand. After Warner Brothers publicly threatened to move filming to a different country, the New Zealand government gave the filmmakers $25 million in additional subsidies and took only a single day to amend the Employment Relations Act to clearly exclude anyone involved in making a film, thus excluding them from any labor law protections.[80] Filmed in New Zealand, the three *Hobbit* movies would become worldwide blockbusters.

JAPAN

The primary institutional feature of Japanese labor relations is enterprise unionism. An **enterprise union,** such as the Hitachi Workers' Union, represents only workers in a single company (enterprise). The dominant type of enterprise union in Japan represents *all* regular (not temporary or part-time) employees in a single company, including white-collar workers except higher-level managers. At some companies, however, several enterprise unions coexist and compete; but even in these cases, each union represents only workers within the one enterprise.[81] As such, while union density is approximately 20 percent, there are more than 50,000 labor unions.[82] In addition to a close alignment between enterprises and unions, there are also close ties between management and the union leadership. Supervisors are generally part of the enterprise union, and union leaders are often career-type employees who continue their promotions within the enterprise through the management ranks after being union leaders.

This system of enterprise unionism is embedded in a broader system of human resource management structured around lifetime employment, seniority and firm-based wages, and broad job classifications. These features are not universal, but they have traditionally been central for core employees in large firms. Lifetime employment is an arrangement in which employees normally are never laid off and stay with a single firm until retirement. Cyclical and seasonal burdens are shifted to temporary workers who are not covered by this implicit—not contractual—lifetime employment tradition (and are usually not covered by the union either). Wages for regular employees are generally based on seniority plus a large annual bonus that partly reflects firm or industry profitability. Japanese firms also often use broad job classifications, and workers are rotated across jobs to increase their skills. All these features mean that employees identify with an enterprise—its internal labor market and financial performance—not a specific job.

Enterprise unionism fits well with this strong enterprise identification among employees, and Japanese labor relations are often characterized as cooperative or consensual.[83] Enterprise unions are very concerned with the company's performance and tailor demands and agreements accordingly. A number of companies also have joint labor–management consultation bodies in which information about the firm is shared with employees, and employees are consulted about personnel matters and working conditions. Although enterprise unions are entitled to bargain over wages and working conditions, some argue that a more cooperative and less adversarial relationship can develop if these issues are settled through a consensual approach in a joint consultation committee. By some accounts, joint consultation is therefore more important than collective bargaining in Japanese labor relations.[84] Enterprise-level consultation and bargaining are complemented by an annual wage negotiation process called *Shunto*. Traditionally the Japanese labor movement was successful in using the *Shunto* negotiations to obtain uniform wage increases across companies, but this uniformity hasn't been as strong in the 2000s as companies have successfully increased the linkages between pay and company performance.

The Japanese system is an important contrast to U.S. labor relations. The two countries share a broadly similar labor law framework. In fact, Japanese labor law was established by the U.S. occupation authorities at the end of World War II and is based on the U.S. model of using unfair labor practices to support employee rights to organize and bargain collectively. There is limited use of exclusive representation and majority rule, however.[85] Also, enterprise unions are not mandated by law—there are isolated examples of industrial and other forms of unions in Japan—and have essentially developed within a Wagner Act framework. Because of the economic success of Japan in recent decades, the cooperative model of Japanese labor relations, with high levels of employee participation and union concern for firm profitability, is often advocated as a model for U.S. labor relations. As discussed in Chapter 10, it is often argued that U.S. unions should be more cooperative and do more to enhance productivity and quality. These arguments are frequently rooted in an idealized view of a cooperative and productive Japanese labor relations system of enterprise unionism. On the other hand, what some view as cooperative enterprise unions, others see as management-dominated sham unions. This is a major debate in both countries. For example, the prevalence of enterprise unions in Japan is characterized by some as stemming from worker concern for an efficient enterprise and by others as resulting from management and state suppression of industrial unions in the 1950s.[86] Lastly, note that in a system of enterprise unionism, existing unions have little incentive to organize new unions at other establishments, and overall labor movement solidarity is low.

Online Exploration Exercise: Search online for union sites in other countries. How are they different and/or similar to union sites in the United States?

ASIAN DEVELOPING COUNTRIES

The history of labor relations in the developing countries of Asia parallels the major concerns in other countries. As emphasized in Parts Two and Three of this book, the U.S. labor relations system has evolved from a mid-20th-century emphasis on economic growth through industrial peace to a 21st-century struggle with competitiveness through flexibility. Asian industrial relations are undergoing this same evolution: Earlier policies emphasized industrial peace to promote industrial development, whereas contemporary policies focus on achieving global competitiveness through flexibility.[87] The developing countries of Asia have taken different approaches in designing specific labor systems to promote similar objectives. By this point in the chapter the types of systems found in Asia should be familiar: a high-level tripartite or corporatist model (Singapore—recall Ireland), a pluralist model with varying combinations of political representation and collective bargaining (the Philippines and India—recall Germany, France, Canada, and the United States), and a government control model (Malaysia and Indonesia—recall Mexico), as well as systems that are in flux (China and South Korea—recall eastern Europe).[88]

Within these developing countries, however, the government frequently exercises tighter control over unions and labor relations than in developed countries. In Singapore's tripartite system, unions appear to participate with the government and employers at high levels to craft wage guidelines and various social policies, but the tightly controlled unions are not an equal partner in this tripartite system. Moreover, government control over workplace-level labor relations is exercised through restrictions on bargaining items, limitations on strikes, and government approval of collective bargaining agreements (agreements not deemed consistent with Singapore's economic development interests can be rejected).[89] In the Philippines, legacies of earlier authoritarian regimes persist with very weak unions (less than one percent of workers are covered by a collective bargaining agreement), and a dominant federation that continues to be focused more on pleasing the government than organizing workers.[90] Government control over labor relations is more explicit in Malaysia and Indonesia. In Malaysia, for example, the government controls the structure and size of unions by selectively approving or rejecting the required union registration applications and has used this administrative power to force Japanese-style enterprise unions rather than industrial unions.[91] In the export-focused electronics industry in particular, the government has used the registration requirements to keep unions weak.[92]

An important underlying thread in all these developing country models of labor relations is the subservience of labor relations to the country's industrial development strategy.[93]

When the Philippines was pursuing an import substitution strategy in which domestic industries were protected from foreign competition, a pluralist labor relations model was allowed because international cost competitiveness was not critical. But when the industrial development strategy switched to an emphasis on exports, the government stepped in with greater control over labor relations to keep costs low and attract foreign investment. The supremacy of industrial development strategies underlies another theme in developing country labor relations: appearance versus reality. Malaysian law, for example, might appear to allow collective bargaining, but in reality government control of union registration can be manipulated to keep unions weak, as we also discussed for Mexico earlier in this chapter. Labor union subservience to governmental political regimes and developmental policies is also a common theme in African labor relations.[94]

Finally, several Asian developing countries are experiencing significant economic or political transitions similar to the situation in eastern Europe. Perhaps most notably, the Republic of Korea (South Korea) became a democracy in 1987, and China's economic system has been moving from state socialism to a mixed economy with elements of private ownership and competition. In Korea, political democratization loosened the government's previously tight grip on labor relations—unions were given greater freedoms to strike, and collective bargaining became more important. Note, however, that a second labor federation that challenged the longtime government-recognized federation was not legalized until 1999. Since that time, there has been an unusual trend away from enterprise unionism toward industrial unionism, and increased levels of labor–management conflict. In 2011, a long-awaited law allowing multiple unions to coexist in a single workplace came into effect, though whether this encourages more enterprise unionism or industrial unionism remains to be seen. Works councils for consultation and communication are required in companies with more than 30 employees, and there have been recent attempts at high-level tripartite social dialogue as well. Another challenge for the Korea labor relations system is a sharp increase in the number of contingent and nonstandard workers who lack benefits and earn only half the pay of regular employees. Korean labor relations are therefore still in transition.[95]

China

The People's Republic of China is a single-party state ruled by the Communist Party of China that legally recognizes only one umbrella labor union organization—the All-China Federation of Trade Unions (ACFTU). Before the late 1980s, labor relations were similar to the eastern European Stalinist model, and the ACFTU union structure served as a transmission belt for the Communist Party. Remember that communism and socialism are seen as solving capitalism's deep-seated conflict between capital and labor; in other words, the official ideology of communist and socialist states insists that communism and socialism achieve a unitarist employment relationship (recall Chapter 2) where the interests of workers, managers, and the state are aligned. Thus, the ACFTU's function was not to represent workers' interests in opposition to employers' interests as in a pluralist employment relationship. Rather, the ACFTU's traditional responsibilities focused on promoting the common, national good and social harmony through enterprise unions that maintained labor discipline and administered state-sponsored housing and other social benefits programs.[96] These widespread enterprise unions were also generally dependent on and integrated with management. Indeed, by Western standards, the ACFTU has not been the world's largest labor union, but instead has been a quasi-government organ controlled by and subordinate to the Communist Party.[97]

Since the late 1980s, China's economic system has been transitioning from socialism to a socialist market economy. The Communist Party has weakened its control over economic activities while allowing the growth of private ownership and market mechanisms, but it has not relaxed its control over the political system. Labor relations changes have therefore been driven by economic rather than political change, and a mixed picture continues to emerge. On paper, a number of legal changes have intended to benefit workers.[98] New labor laws were enacted in the mid-1990s to promote collective bargaining, though to be more consistent with the conflict avoidance ethos of Chinese culture and unitarism, this is called "collective consultation."[99] The Labor Contracts Law (2008) requires written employment contracts for individuals that meet certain protective standards, and the Labor Mediation and Arbitration Law (2008) provides for improved dispute resolution procedures. Enforcement of these laws, however, depends on complex dynamics between local union officials, managers, and local government officials, and is typically weak.[100] The high number of worker suicides at Foxconn in 2010–11 is one graphic indicator of the extent to which abusive working conditions persist.

Moreover, workers lack a true freedom of association because the ACFTU remains the only legally approved union organization and continues to be closely intertwined with the Communist Party. Many union leaders are appointed by Party leaders rather than elected by workers. Independent union representation is also undermined by the emphasis in Chinese labor law on regulating outcomes rather than promoting true collective bargaining, which would require the Communist Party to give up some control; indeed, strikes are still illegal. Nevertheless, workers have been able to use protest methods to win some gains. This includes grassroots strikes not led by the official ACFTU leaders, such as those at a number of Honda auto factories during 2010. Adding to this complicated mixed picture is that even though it is highly dependent on the Communist Party, the ACFTU has pushed for stronger labor legislation at a national level and has undertaken some local-level reforms, such as limited elections of local leaders, in response to grassroots activism; otherwise, the ACFTU risks losing further legitimacy among workers struggling to improve their conditions.[101] In spite of its limitations, then, the ACFTU is not strictly a paper tiger, and there are some signs that the ACFTU is experimenting with a type of collective bargaining that uses state power to win (modest) gains for workers.[102] But significant pressures remain in the quest to develop a labor relations system with Chinese characteristics that balances economic competitiveness with improved living and working standards for millions of Chinese workers; in the meantime, labor protest and accommodation will continue, and the economic and political landscape surrounding Chinese labor relations will be important to watch.

Briefly and in broad terms, the situation in Vietnam is similar to that in China—a Communist state with party-controlled labor unions, wildcat strikes that cannot be ignored, and attempts to make some adjustments to labor law and the practice of collective bargaining to pacify the workers without allowing for a truly independent labor movement.[103]

BARGAINING OR LEGISLATING LABOR STANDARDS?

From these descriptions of labor relations systems in different countries, it is apparent that there are numerous possibilities for structuring labor relations (see Table 12.7). The U.S. emphasis on exclusive representation and majority support is often absent outside North America. Consultation between labor and management through peak-level organizations at a national level and through works councils at a workplace level occurs throughout Europe, and in some Asian countries. Some countries have centralized industrywide bargaining arrangements while others focus on enterprise-level unions. Moreover, while U.S. union contracts are highly complex, legally enforceable documents that specify a wide range of employment terms, in many other countries union agreements provide more of a skeletal specification of minimum terms. In some countries, union contracts are not legally enforceable.

TABLE 12.7 Common Dimensions of Industrialized Labor Relations Systems around the Globe

Dimension	Features	Examples
Centralized		
Social partnership	Peak-level labor, business, and government agreements on broad economic and social issues.	Austria, Finland, Ireland (1987–2009), Sweden.
Sector bargaining	Collective bargaining with employers' associations to produce industrywide contracts.	France, Germany, Sweden.
Centralized awards	Occupational or industrial arbitration awards.	Australia, New Zealand (pre-1991).
Decentralized		
Enterprise unionism	Unions limited to one company.	Japan.
Exclusive representation/ majority rule*	Representation and bargaining only if a union represents a majority of the employees.	Canada, United States.
Codetermination	Workplace-level shared decision making including works councils and board-level representation.	France, Germany, Sweden.
Voluntarism*	Representation and bargaining based on economic power, not legal backing.	Great Britain, Ireland, New Zealand (1991–2000).

*Bargaining in a system of exclusive representation or voluntarism can be centralized or decentralized depending on the parties, but it is commonly decentralized.

The political activities of the labor movement in many countries outside the United States are also at least as important as their workplace activities, if not more so. Rather than the U.S. labor movement's philosophy of business unionism, European labor movements often embrace social movement unionism. Gains for workers are won through social and political activism as well as through bargaining with employers, and unions are often closely aligned with left-wing political parties. In Great Britain, the Trades Union Congress founded the Labour Party. One of the major parties that sometimes rules Australia is the Australian Labor Party. In Sweden and Germany, the labor movement is closely aligned with social democratic parties. French and Italian unions are closely connected with communist and socialist political parties, and political strikes to win gains for workers are common. Advocates of a stronger U.S. labor movement see this type of political and social activism as the avenue to more power.[104] Such activism can bolster the labor movement's voice in the political arena and can result in laws supporting union activities.

Nonunion Application: Universally Mandated Benefits and Protections

Political strength can also result in labor standards that are legislated for all workers rather than confined to workers covered by collective bargaining. Outside the United States, many employment conditions, especially employee benefits, are established by government regulations. For example, while the United States does not mandate any vacation days, workers in many European countries are entitled to at least four weeks of paid vacation each year. The importance of legislated rather than negotiated labor standards is further demonstrated by job security protections. U.S. workers are subject to the employment-at-will doctrine

FIGURE 12.1
Employees Covered by Unjust Dismissal Protections

Source: See text.

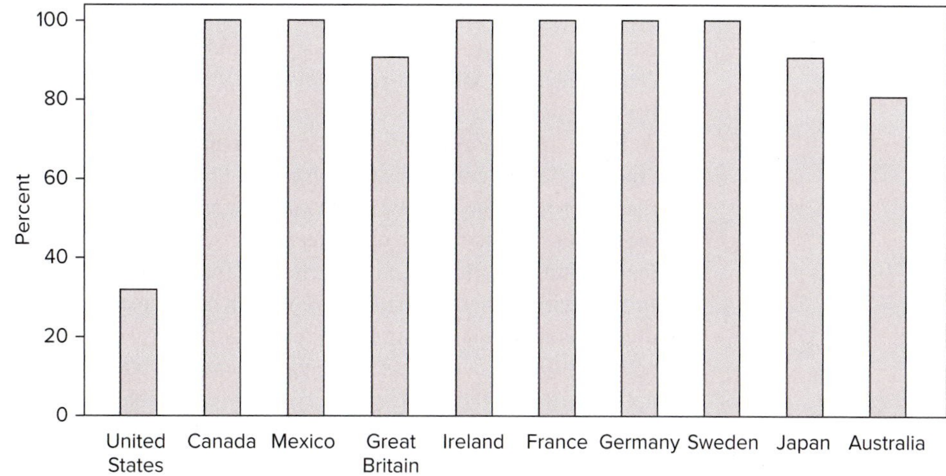

and can therefore be laid off or fired at any time. In addition to legislative restrictions against discriminatory discharge, the major exceptions to this doctrine are just cause provisions in union contracts and unjust dismissal protections in some public sector civil service systems. Thus, only about one-third of U.S. workers are protected against dismissals except for valid reasons related to job performance or economic conditions.[105] This contrasts starkly with the widespread unjust dismissal protections granted by national legislation in much of the rest of the industrialized democratic world. Legislation in many countries also limits employers' abilities to lay off workers.

In Germany, for example, after a six-month probationary period, only "socially justified" employee discharges are legal. In other words, employees can be dismissed only with just cause due to poor performance or economic necessity; discharge must be justified by "the conduct of the employee or by pressing reasons connected with the enterprise." Note that in contrast to the United States, this protection is provided by law and does not depend on union representation. Disputes are resolved by a federal labor court, and coverage is nearly universal. Belgium, France, Great Britain (except for part-time or temporary workers), Italy, and Spain all have legislative protections similar to those found in Germany.[106] In Mexico, after a 30-day probationary period, employees may be laid off for economic reasons or dismissed only for just cause—and these protections are written into Mexico's constitution.[107] In Japan, the doctrine of abusive dismissal protects workers against unjust dismissal. This doctrine has been extended to all employees with the exception of short-term, contract employees who have not yet had their initial contracts renewed.[108] Even in Canada, employees must either be dismissed for just cause or given several weeks of advance notice.[109] In other words, the United States stands alone with its low level of protection against unjust dismissal (see Figure 12.1). But in many countries, such protection was obtained through the legislative rather than the bargaining process. This political aspect of comparative labor relations should not be overlooked, and an important question for the future is whether labor standards should be negotiated or legislated (or neither).

GLOBALIZATION RECONSIDERED

Analyzing national labor relations systems from around the world is important. A comparative approach provides rich material for thinking broadly about the underlying labor relations problem of balancing efficiency, equity, and voice. Examining the pros and cons of other countries' policies and practices can aid efforts to reform law and practice in the United States to better strike this balance. And understanding how labor relations work in other countries is vital for managers and union leaders whose professional activities involve other countries.

But recall from the previous chapter that a major feature of the labor relations environment in nearly every country is globalization. Globalization raises a key question for comparative labor relations in the 21st century: In an integrated world economy, is it possible to have unique national labor relations systems, or does integration force convergence of national institutions? In a competitive world, free trade should harmonize labor standards if countries with higher standards have higher labor costs and are unable to compete with lower-cost countries. If certain labor relations practices are more productive than others, competitive pressures are expected to cause others to adopt those practices—such as U.S. attempts to emulate the more cooperative style of Japanese labor relations. More ambitious efforts at political and legal as well as economic integration, such as in the European Union, should further weaken national differences as common standards and policies are enacted. The **convergence thesis** predicts that labor relations practices and policies across countries will converge to a common set of practices and policies, and national differences will disappear.

The evidence, however, does not support this convergence thesis.[110] In particular, arguably the most important effects of globalization on labor relations across many countries are declining union strength and intense corporate pressures for increased workplace flexibility (Chapter 10). These factors have caused increased decentralization of labor relations activities in many countries.[111] Even though collective bargaining in Germany, for example, has traditionally been much more centralized than in the United States, the bargaining structure in both countries has become more decentralized than in earlier years. This decentralization is key: Increasing decentralization gives rise to *divergent* local labor relations practices because of attempts to tailor employment practices to the specific needs and constraints of individual workplaces, and because local practices are the outcome of bargaining processes in which firms, unions, and other institutions such as work councils have varying degrees of influence.[112] Uniform convergence, therefore, is not occurring. However, several standard models appear to be followed across workplaces, such as an antiunion, low-wage approach, a traditional human resource management approach, and a high-performance work systems approach. Thus, labor relations practices within countries are becoming more diverse but are simultaneously embracing several common patterns. In other words, rather than a strict convergence, there appears to be "converging divergences."[113]

Increased divergence on a local level as well as convergence can undermine the importance of national-level labor relations systems. So in the face of globalization and decentralization, does it continue to make sense to discuss *national* labor relations systems? In a word, yes. The laws and institutions that characterize the labor relations systems of different countries shape the choices faced by companies and unions as they confront competitive pressures. National-level institutions are therefore still important determinants of labor relations practices and employment outcomes.[114] Even in the European Union (EU), the greatest convergence toward uniformity has been in minimum standards through European-wide directives for health and safety requirements, gender equity, and other labor standards.[115] With the limited exception of the European Works Councils mandate (Chapter 11), EU policies have not erased national differences in the labor relations processes in individual countries; instead, employment relationships in Europe and elsewhere are increasingly characterized by a multilevel system of governance with important institutions and outcomes embedded in the workplace, company, sector, national, *and* supranational levels.[116]

In sum, globalization is causing converging divergences of labor relations practices across countries through pressures for decentralization and flexibility. National-level institutions nevertheless remain important for shaping the responses of companies and unions to these pressures. Studying labor relations in different countries is therefore still an important component of understanding labor relations. Moreover, these local practices and national institutions can be evaluated against the objectives of efficiency, equity, and voice.[117] Comparative labor relations therefore reveals numerous labor relations possibilities for tackling the challenges of the 21st-century employment relationship and striking an effective balance between the objectives of employers and workers.

Key Terms

voluntarism, *434*
social partnership, *437*
ideological unionism, *441*
sector bargaining, *442*
codetermination, *442*
works council, *442*
Stalinist unionism, *447*
awards system, *448*
enterprise union, *450*
convergence thesis, *456*

Reflection Questions

1. In moments of frustration, some U.S. labor leaders have claimed that U.S. unions would be better off with a deregulation of labor law and a return to the "law of the jungle." How would a return to voluntarism affect U.S. unions? Workers? Employers?
2. In 2013, Volkswagen said that it would welcome a works council at its Chattanooga, Tennessee, plant. Why do you think Volkswagen would do this? More generally, what might be the pros and cons of adopting the German system of mandatory works councils in the United States?
3. Are Japanese-style enterprise unions effective vehicles of voice that align worker interests with firm interests, or are they weak, company-dominated, sham unions? Explain your response.
4. Describe what a non-Chinese manager working for a U.S. company in China should know about the Chinese labor relations system. Also, what are the arguments for and against multinational corporations taking advantage of weak labor law enforcement and weak labor unions in China and elsewhere?
5. Labor unions can be important players in three different political systems: pluralism, corporatism, and communism. Give examples of each and describe the key roles of unions. What are the pros and cons of pluralism and corporatism for both organized labor and employers? Should U.S. unions play a stronger role in U.S. politics?

End Notes

1. Larry G. Gerber, "Shifting Perspectives on American Exceptionalism: Recent Literature on American Labor Relations and Labor Politics," *Journal of American Studies* 31 (August 1997), pp. 253–74; Sanford M. Jacoby, "American Exceptionalism Revisited: The Importance of Management," in Sanford M. Jacoby (ed.), *Masters to Managers: Historical and Comparative Perspectives on American Employers* (New York: Columbia University Press, 1991), pp. 173–200; Kim Voss, *The Making of American Exceptionalism: The Knights of Labor and Class Formation in the Nineteenth Century* (Ithaca: Cornell University Press, 1993).
2. Joseph B. Rose, "Union Organising and Union Revitalisation in Canada," in Gregor Gall (ed.), *Union Revitalisation in Advanced Economies: Assessing the Contribution of Union Organising* (Basingstoke, UK: Palgrave Macmillan, 2009), pp. 175–90; Daphne Gottlieb Taras, "Collective Bargaining Regulation in Canada and the United States: Divergent Cultures, Divergent Outcomes," in Bruce E. Kaufman (ed.), *Government Regulation of the Employment Relationship* (Madison, WI: Industrial Relations Research Association, 1997), pp. 295–341.
3. John Godard, *Industrial Relations, the Economy, and Society,* 3rd ed. (Concord, Ontario: Captus Press, 2005); Mark Thompson and Daphne G. Taras, "Employment Relations in Canada," in Greg J. Bamber, Russell D. Lansbury, and Nick Wailes (eds.), *International and Comparative Employment Relations: Globalisation and Change* (London: Sage, 2011), pp. 88–116.
4. Steven E. Abraham, "The Relevance of Canadian Labour Law to U.S. Firms Operating in Canada," *International Journal of Manpower* 18 (October 1997), pp. 662–74.
5. Paul Weiler, "Promises to Keep: Securing Workers' Rights to Self-Organization under the NLRA," *Harvard Law Review* 96 (June 1983), pp. 1769–827; Chris Riddell, "Union Certification Success under Voting versus Card-Check Procedures: Evidence from British Columbia, 1978–1998," *Industrial and Labor Relations Review* 57 (July 2004), pp. 493–517; Chris Riddell, "Labor Law and Reaching a First Collective Agreement: Evidence From a Quasi-Experimental Set of Reforms in Ontario," *Industrial Relations* 52 (July 2013), pp. 702–36.
6. Daphne Gottlieb Taras and Allen Ponak, "Mandatory Agency Shop Laws as an Explanation of Canada–U.S. Union Density Divergence," *Journal of Labor Research* 22 (Summer 2001), pp. 541–68.
7. John W. Budd, "Canadian Strike Replacement Legislation and Collective Bargaining: Lessons for the United States," *Industrial Relations* 35 (April 1996), pp. 245–60.
8. Taras, "Collective Bargaining Regulation in Canada and the United States"; Thompson and Taras, "Employment Relations in Canada"; Seymour Martin Lipset and Noah M. Meltz, with Rafael Gomez and Ivan Katchanovski, *The Paradox of American Unionism: Why Americans Like Unions More Than Canadians Do but Join Much Less* (Ithaca, NY: Cornell University Press, 2004).
9. John W. Budd, "Union Wage Determination in Canadian and U.S. Manufacturing, 1964–1990: A Comparative Analysis," *Industrial and Labor Relations Review* 49 (July 1996), pp. 673–89.
10. Stephen F. Befort and Virginia E. Cornett, "Beyond the Rhetoric of the NAFTA Treaty Debate: A Comparative Analysis of Labor and Employment Law in Mexico and the United States," *Comparative Labor Law Journal* 17 (Winter 1996), pp. 269–313; María Cristina Bayón, "Persistence of an Exclusionary Model: Inequality and Segmentation in Mexican Society," *International Labour Review* 148 (September 2009), pp. 301–15.
11. Commission for Labor Cooperation, *Labor Relations Law in North America* (Washington, DC, 2000).
12. Commission for Labor Cooperation, *Labor Relations Law in North America.*
13. Befort and Cornett, "Beyond the Rhetoric of the NAFTA Treaty Debate."
14. Altha J. Cravey, *Women and Work in Mexico's Maquiladoras* (Lanham, MD: Rowman and Littlefield, 1998); Richard A. Morales, "Mexico," in Miriam Rothman, Dennis R. Briscoe, and Raoul C. D. Nacamulli (eds.), *Industrial Relations around the World: Labor Relations for Multinational Companies* (Berlin: Walter de Gruyter, 1992), pp. 285–95; Alberto Aziz Nassif, "The Mexican Dual Transition: State, Unionism, and the Political System," in Maria Lorena Cook and Harry C. Katz (eds.), *Regional Integration and Industrial Relations in North America* (Ithaca, NY: Institute of Collective Bargaining, Cornell University, 1994), pp. 132–41.
15. David Fairris and Edward Levine, "Declining Union Density in Mexico, 1984–2000," *Monthly Labor Review* 127 (September 2004), pp. 10–17.
16. Dan La Botz, "Mexico's Labor Movement in Transition," *Monthly Review* 57 (June 2005), pp. 62–72; Chris Tilly, "Beyond 'contratos de protección': Strong and Weak Unionism in Mexican Retail Enterprises" (UCLA Institute for Research on Labor and Employment, 2009).
17. Maria Lorena Cook, *Organizing Dissent: Unions, the State, and the Democratic Teachers' Movement in Mexico* (University Park: The Pennsylvania State University Press, 1996); La Botz, "Mexico's Labor Movement in Transition."

18. La Botz, "Mexico's Labor Movement in Transition"; Norman Caulfield, *NAFTA and Labor in North America* (Urbana: University of Illinois Press, 2010).
19. www.ueinternational.org/MLNA/index.php.
20. Gregor Gall (ed.), *Union Organizing: Campaigning for Trade Union Recognition* (London: Routledge, 2003); Nancy Peters, "The United Kingdom Recalibrates the U.S. National Labor Relations Act: Possible Lessons for the United States," *Comparative Labor Law and Policy Journal* 25 (Winter 2004), pp. 227–56.
21. Paul Edwards et al., "Great Britain: From Partial Collectivism to Neo-Liberalism to Where?" in Anthony Ferner and Richard Hyman (eds.), *Changing Industrial Relations in Europe* (Oxford: Blackwell Publishers, 1998), pp. 1–54.
22. Edwards et al., "Great Britain"; Chris Howell, *Trade Unions and the State: The Construction of Industrial Relations Institutions in Britain*, 1890–2000 (Princeton, NJ: Princeton University Press, 2005); Mick Marchington, Jeremy Waddington, and Andrew Timming, "Employment Relations in Britain," in Greg J. Bamber, Russell D. Lansbury, and Nick Wailes (eds.), *International and Comparative Employment Relations: Globalisation and Change* (London: Sage, 2011), pp. 36–61.
23. Melanie Simms and Andy Charlwood, "Trade Unions: Power and Influence in a Changed Context," in Trevor Colling and Mike Terry (eds.), *Industrial Relations: Theory and Practice*, 3rd ed. (Oxford: Wiley-Blackwell, 2010), pp. 125–48.
24. Robert Taylor, "Out of the Bowels of the Movement: The Trade Unions and the Origins of the Labour Party 1900–18," in Brian Brivati and Richard Heffernan (eds.), *The Labour Party: A Centenary History* (London: Macmillan Press, 2000), pp. 8–49.
25. Brian Brivati and Richard Heffernan (eds.), *The Labour Party: A Centenary History* (London: Macmillan Press, 2000).
26. Brian Towers, *The Representation Gap: Change and Reform in the British and American Workplace* (Oxford: Oxford University Press, 1997).
27. Melanie Simms, Jane Holgate, and Edmund Heery, *Union Voices: Tactics and Tensions in UK Organizing* (Ithaca, NY: Cornell University Press, 2013).
28. Andy Danford et al., "Union Organising and Partnership in Manufacturing, Finance and Public Services in Britain," in Gregor Gall (ed.), *Union Revitalisation in Advanced Economies: Assessing the Contribution of Union Organising* (Basingstoke, UK: Palgrave Macmillan, 2009), pp. 56–82; Stewart Johnstone, Peter Ackers, and Adrian Wilkinson, "Better than Nothing? Is Non-Union Partnership a Contradiction in Terms?" *Journal of Industrial Relations* 52 (April 2010), pp 151–68; Stewart Johnstone and Peter Ackers (eds.), *Finding a Voice at Work: New Perspectives on Employment Relations* (Oxford: Oxford University Press, 2015).
29. Richard Hyman, "British Industrial Relations: The European Dimension," in Trevor Colling and Mike Terry (eds.), *Industrial Relations: Theory and Practice*, 3rd ed. (Oxford: Wiley-Blackwell, 2010), pp. 54–80; Marchington et al., "Employment Relations in Britain."
30. Towers, *The Representation Gap.*
31. Harry C. Katz and Owen Darbishire, *Converging Divergences: Worldwide Changes in Employment Systems* (Ithaca, NY: ILR Press, 2000).
32. Joseph Wallace et al., *Industrial Relations in Ireland: Theory and Practice,* 4th ed. (Dublin: Gill and Macmillan, 2013).
33. Ferdinand von Prondzynski, "Ireland: Corporatism Revived," in Anthony Ferner and Richard Hyman (eds.), *Changing Industrial Relations in Europe* (Oxford: Blackwell Publishers, 1998), pp. 55–73.
34. Hans Slomp, *Between Bargaining and Politics: An Introduction to European Labor Relations* (Westport, CT: Praeger, 1996).
35. William K. Roche, "Social Partnership in Ireland and the New Social Pacts," *Industrial Relations* 46 (July 2007), pp. 395–425; Paul Teague and Jimmy Donaghey, "Why Has Irish Social Partnership Survived?" *British Journal of Industrial Relations* 47 (March 2009), pp. 55–78.
36. Lucio Baccaro and Marco Simoni, "Centralized Wage Bargaining and the 'Celtic Tiger' Phenomenon," *Industrial Relations* 46 (July 2007), pp. 426–55; Teague and Donaghey, "Why Has Irish Social Partnership Survived?"
37. Patrick Gunnigle, "More Rhetoric Than Reality: Enterprise Level Industrial Relations Partnerships in Ireland," *The Economic and Social Review* 28 (October 1997), pp. 179–200; Teague and Donaghey, "Why Has Irish Social Partnership Survived?"
38. Paul Teague and Jimmy Donaghey, "The Life and Death of Irish Social Partnership: Lessons for Social Pacts," *Business History* 57 (2015), pp. 418–37.

39. Anthony Ferner and Richard Hyman (eds.), *Changing Industrial Relations in Europe* (Oxford: Blackwell Publishers, 1998).
40. Richard Hyman, *Understanding European Trade Unionism: Between Market, Class and Society* (London: Sage, 2001); Melanie Simms, "Union Organizing as an Alternative to Partnership. Or What to do when Employers Can't Keep Their Side of the Bargain," in Stewart Johnstone and Peter Ackers (eds.), *Finding a Voice at Work: New Perspectives on Employment Relations* (Oxford: Oxford University Press, 2015), pp. 127–52.
41. Unless otherwise noted, this section draws heavily on these sources: Anthony Daley, "The Hollowing Out of French Unions: Politics and Industrial Relations after 1981," in Andrew Martin and George Ross (eds.), *The Brave New World of European Labor: European Trade Unions at the Millennium* (New York: Berghahn Books, 1999), pp. 167–216; Janine Goetschy, "France: The Limits of Reform," in Anthony Ferner and Richard Hyman (eds.), *Changing Industrial Relations in Europe* (Oxford: Blackwell Publishers, 1998), pp. 357–94; Jérôme Gautié, "France's Social Model: Between Resilience and Erosion," in Daniel Vaughan-Whitehead (ed.), *The European Social Model In Crisis: Is Europe Losing Its Soul?* (Cheltenham, UK: Elgar, 2015), pp. 121–74.
42. Hyman, *Understanding European Trade Unionism.*
43. Heather Connolly, "Trade Union Radicalism in France: The Renewal of Radicalism in the Context of Crisis and Austerity?" in Heather Connolly, Lefteris Kretsos, and Craig Phelan (eds.), *Radical Unions in Europe and the Future of Collective Interest Representation* (Oxford: Peter Lang, 2014), pp. 49–67.
44. Goetschy, "France," p. 379.
45. Thorsten Schulten, "The Meaning of Extension for the Stability of Collective Bargaining in Europe," ETUI Policy Brief No. 4/2016 (Brussels: ETUI, 2016).
46. Katz and Darbishire, *Converging Divergences*; Gerhard Bosch, "The Changing Nature of Collective Bargaining in Germany: Coordinated Decentralization," in Harry C. Katz, Wonduck Lee, and Joohee Lee (eds.), *The New Structure of Labor Relations: Tripartism and Decentralization* (Ithaca, NY: Cornell University Press, 2004), pp. 84–118.
47. Berndt K. Keller and Anja Kirsch, "Employment Relations in Germany," in Greg J. Bamber, Russell D. Lansbury, and Nick Wailes (eds.), *International and Comparative Employment Relations: Globalisation and Change* (London: Sage, 2010), pp. 196–223.
48. Virginia Doellgast and Ian Greer, "Vertical Disintegration and the Disorganization of German Industrial Relations," *British Journal of Industrial Relations* 45 (March 2007), pp. 55–76; Virginia Doellgast, *Disintegrating Democracy at Work: Labor Unions and the Future of Good Jobs in the Service Economy* (Ithaca, NY: Cornell University Press, 2012).
49. Lowell Turner, "Institutions and Activism: Crisis and Opportunity for a German Labor Movement in Decline," *Industrial and Labor Relations Review* 62 (April 2009), pp. 294–312; Stephen J. Silvia, *Holding the Shop Together: German Industrial Relations in the Postwar Era* (Ithaca, NY: Cornell University Press, 2013).
50. Rebecca Gumbrell-McCormick and Richard Hyman, "Works Councils: The European Model of Industrial Democracy?" in Adrian Wilkinson et al. (eds.), *The Oxford Handbook of Participation in Organizations* (Oxford: Oxford University Press, 2010), pp. 286–314; Christine Aumayr et al., *Employee Representation at Establishment Level in Europe*. (Dublin: European Foundation for the Improvement of Living and Working Conditions, 2011); John T. Addison, *The Economics of Codetermination: Lessons from the German Experience* (New York: Palgrave Macmillan, 2009).
51. John T. Addison et al., "The Reform of the German Works Constitution Act: A Critical Assessment," *Industrial Relations* 43 (April 2004), pp. 392–420 at 398.
52. Addison et al., "The Reform of the German Works Constitution Act"; Silvia, *Holding the Shop Together.* Michael Gold and Ingrid Artus, "Employee Participation in Germany: Tensions and Challenges," in Stewart Johnstone and Peter Ackers (eds.), *Finding a Voice at Work: New Perspectives on Employment Relations* (Oxford: Oxford University Press, 2015), pp. 193–217.
53. Doellgast, *Disintegrating Democracy at Work*; Walther Müller-Jentsch, "Germany: From Collective Voice to Co-Management," in Joel Rogers and Wolfgang Streeck (eds.), *Works Councils: Consultation, Representation, and Cooperation in Industrial Relations* (Chicago: University of Chicago Press, 1995), pp. 53–78; Turner, "Institutions and Activism."
54. Müller-Jentsch, "Germany."
55. Doellgast, *Disintegrating Democracy at Work*; Otto Jacobi, Berndt Keller, and Walther Müller-Jentsch, "Germany: Facing New Challenges," in Anthony Ferner and Richard Hyman (eds.), *Changing Industrial Relations in Europe* (Oxford: Blackwell Publishers, 1998), pp. 190–238.

56. Müller-Jentsch, "Germany."
57. Doellgast, *Disintegrating Democracy at Work*; Katz and Darbishire, *Converging Divergences*; Lowell Turner, *Democracy at Work: Changing World Markets and the Future of Labor Unions* (Ithaca, NY: Cornell University Press, 1991).
58. Addison, *The Economics of Codetermination*; Steffen Mueller, "Works Councils and Establishment Productivity," *Industrial and Labor Relations Review* 65 (October 2012), pp. 880–98.
59. Doellgast, *Disintegrating Democracy at Work*; Michael Gold, "'Taken on Board': An Evaluation of the Influence of Employee Board-Level Representatives on Company Decision-Making Across Europe," *European Journal of Industrial Relations* 17 (March 2011), pp. 41–56; Raymond Markey, Nicola Balnave, and Greg Patmore, "Worker Directors and Worker Ownership/Cooperatives," in Adrian Wilkinson et al. (eds.), *The Oxford Handbook of Participation in Organizations* (Oxford: Oxford University Press, 2010), pp. 237–57.
60. Slomp, *Between Bargaining and Politics,* pp. 21–22.
61. Hyman, *Understanding European Trade Unionism*; Slomp, *Between Bargaining and Politics.*
62. Anders Kjellberg, "Sweden: Restoring the Model?" in Anthony Ferner and Richard Hyman (eds.), *Changing Industrial Relations in Europe* (Oxford: Blackwell Publishers, 1998), pp. 74–117.
63. Olle Hammarström, Tony Huzzard, and Tommy Nilsson, "Employment Relations in Sweden," in Greg J. Bamber, Russell D. Lansbury, and Nick Wailes (eds.), *International and Comparative Employment Relations: Globalisation and the Developed Market Economies* (London: Sage, 2004), pp. 254–76; Søren Kaj Andersen et al., "Changes in Wage Policy and Collective Bargaining in the Nordic Countries," in Guy Van Gyes and Thorsten Schulten (eds.), *Wage Bargaining Under the New European Economic Governance: Alternative Strategies for Inclusive Growth* (Brussels: ETUI, 2015), pp. 139–68.
64. Åke Sandberg, "Justice at Work: Solidaristic Work Policy as a Renewal of the Swedish Labor Market Model?" *Social Justice* 21 (Winter 1994), pp. 102–14; Jan Johansson, Lena Abrahamsson, and Stina Johansson, "If You Can't Beat Them, Join Them? The Swedish Trade Union Movement and Lean Production," *Journal of Industrial Relations* 55 (June 2013), pp. 445–60.
65. Simon Clarke and Peter Fairbrother, "Post-Communism and the Emergence of Industrial Relations in the Workplace," in Richard Hyman and Anthony Ferner (eds.), *New Frontiers in European Industrial Relations* (Oxford: Blackwell Publishers, 1994), pp. 368–97; Derek C. Jones, "The Transformation of Labor Unions in Eastern Europe: The Case of Bulgaria," *Industrial and Labor Relations Review* 45 (April 1992), pp. 452–70; Hans Slomp, Jacques van Hoof, and Hans Moerel, "The Transformation of Industrial Relations in Some Central and Eastern European Countries," in Joris Van Ruysseveldt and Jelle Visser (eds.), *Industrial Relations in Europe: Traditions and Transitions* (London: Sage, 1996), pp. 337–57.
66. Robert J. Flanagan, " Institutional Reformation in Eastern Europe," *Industrial Relations* 37 (July 1998), pp. 337–57.
67. Sarah Ashwin, "Social Partnership or a 'Complete Sellout'? Russian Trade Unions' Responses to Conflict," *British Journal of Industrial Relations* 42 (March 2004), pp. 23–46 at 24.
68. Lawrence Goodwyn, *Breaking the Barrier: The Rise of Solidarity in Poland* (New York: Oxford University Press, 1991).
69. Heribert Kohl and Hans-Wolfgang Platzer, *Industrial Relations in Central and Eastern Europe: Transformation and Integration—A Comparison of the Eight New EU Member States* (Pete Burgess, transl.) (Brussels: European Trade Union Institute, 2004); Guglielmo Meardi, "Emerging Systems of Employment Relations in Central Eastern European Countries," in James Arrowsmith and Valeria Pulignano (eds.), *The Transformation of Employment Relations in Europe: Institutions and Outcomes in the Age of Globalization* (New York: Routledge, 2013), pp. 69–87.
70. Flanagan, "Institutional Reformation in Eastern Europe"; Stephen Crowley, "Russia's Labor Legacy: Making Use of the Past," in Teri L. Caraway, Maria Lorena Cook, and Stephen Crowley (eds.), *Working through the Past: Labor and Authoritarian Legacies in Comparative Perspective* (Ithaca, NY: Cornell University Press, 2015), pp. 122–41.
71. Lajos Héthy, "Tripartism in Eastern Europe," in Richard Hyman and Anthony Ferner (eds.), *New Frontiers in European Industrial Relations* (Oxford: Blackwell Publishers, 1994), pp. 312–36.
72. Vadim Borisov and Simon Clarke, "The Rise and Fall of Social Partnership in Postsocialist Europe: The Commonwealth of Independent States," *Industrial Relations Journal* 37 (November 2006), pp. 607–29; Guglielmo Meardi, *Social Failures of EU Enlargement: A Case of Workers Voting with Their Feet* (New York: Routledge, 2012); Meardi, "Emerging Systems of Employment Relations in Central Eastern European Countries."

73. Borisov and Clarke, "The Rise and Fall of Social Partnership in Postsocialist Europe"; Gerd Schienstock, Paul Thompson, and Franz Traxler (eds.), *Industrial Relations between Command and Market: A Comparative Analysis of Eastern Europe and China* (New York: Nova Science Publishers, 1997).
74. John Niland and Dennis Turner, *Control, Consensus, or Chaos? Managers and Industrial Relations Reform* (Sydney: Allen and Unwin, 1985).
75. Russell D. Lansbury and Nick Wailes, "Employment Relations in Australia," in Greg J. Bamber, Russell D. Lansbury, and Nick Wailes (eds.), *International and Comparative Employment Relations: Globalisation and Change* (London: Sage, 2011), pp. 117–37; Rae Cooper and Bradon Ellem, "Trade Unions and Collective Bargaining," in Marion Baird, Keith Hancock, and Joe Isaac (eds.), *Work and Employment Relations: An Era of Change* (Sydney: Federation Press, 2011), pp. 34–50.
76. Lansbury and Wailes, "Employment Relations in Australia."
77. Edward M. Davis and Russell D. Lansbury, "Employment Relations in Australia," in Greg J. Bamber and Russell D. Lansbury (eds.), *International and Comparative Employment Relations: A Study of Industrialised Market Economies* (London: Sage, 1998), pp. 110–43.
78. Lansbury and Wailes, "Employment Relations in Australia"; Ron McCallum, "Legislated Standards: The Australian Approach," in Marion Baird, Keith Hancock, and Joe Isaac (eds.), *Work and Employment Relations: An Era of Change* (Sydney: Federation Press, 2011), pp. 6–16; Mark Bray, "The Distinctiveness of Modern Awards," in Marion Baird, Keith Hancock, and Joe Isaac (eds.), *Work and Employment Relations: An Era of Change* (Sydney: Federation Press, 2011), pp. 17–33; Cooper and Ellem, "Trade Unions and Collective Bargaining."
79. Ellen J. Dannin, *Working Free: The Origins and Impact of New Zealand's Employment Contracts Act* (Auckland: Auckland University Press, 1997); Robyn May and Paul Goulter, "Union Organising in New Zealand: The Near Death Experience," in Gregor Gall (ed.), *Union Revitalisation in Advanced Economies: Assessing the Contribution of Union Organising* (Basingstoke, UK: Palgrave Macmillan, 2009), pp. 191–205.
80. Jonathan Handel, *The New Zealand Hobbit Crisis* (Los Angeles: Hollywood Analytics, 2013).
81. Hirosuke Kawanishi, *Enterprise Unionism in Japan* (London: Keegan Paul International, 1992); Takashi Araki, "Changing Employment Practices, Corporate Governance, and the Role of Labor Law in Japan," *Comparative Labor Law and Policy Journal* 28 (Winter 2007), pp. 251–81.
82. Hiromasa Suzuki and Katsuyuki Kubo, "Employment Relations in Japan," in Greg J. Bamber, Russell D. Lansbury, and Nick Wailes (eds.), *International and Comparative Employment Relations: Globalisation and Change* (London: Sage, 2011), pp. 252–80.
83. Araki, "Changing Employment Practices, Corporate Governance, and the Role of Labor Law in Japan"; Suzuki and Kubo, "Employment Relations in Japan."
84. Takashi Araki, "A Comparative Analysis: Corporate Governance and Labor and Employment Relations in Japan," *Comparative Labor Law and Policy Journal* 22 (Fall 2000), pp. 67–95.
85. William B. Gould, *Japan's Reshaping of American Labor Law* (Cambridge, MA: MIT Press, 1984); Araki, "Changing Employment Practices, Corporate Governance, and the Role of Labor Law in Japan."
86. Araki, "A Comparative Analysis"; Kawanishi, *Enterprise Unionism in Japan*; Dae Yong Jeong and Ruth V. Aguilera, "The Evolution of Enterprise Unionism in Japan: A Sociopolitical Perspective," *British Journal of Industrial Relations* 46 (March 2008), pp. 98–132.
87. Sarosh Kuruvilla and Christopher L. Erickson, "Change and Transformation in Asian Industrial Relations," *Industrial Relations* 41 (April 2002), pp. 171–227.
88. Sarosh Kuruvilla and C.S. Venkataratnam, "Economic Development and Industrial Relations: The Case of South and Southeast Asia," *Industrial Relations Journal* 27 (March 1996), pp. 9–23; Dong-One Kim, "Industrial Relations in Asia: Old Regimes and New Orders," in Michael J. Morley, Patrick Gunnigle, and David G. Collins (eds.), *Global Industrial Relations* (New York: Routledge, 2006), pp. 146–77.
89. Sarosh Kuruvilla, "Linkages between Industrialization Strategies and Industrial Relations/Human Resource Policies: Singapore, Malaysia, the Philippines, and India," *Industrial and Labor Relations Review* 49 (July 1996), pp. 635–57; Kim, "Industrial Relations in Asia."
90. Jane Hutchison, "Authoritarian Legacies and Labor Weakness in the Philippines," in Teri L. Caraway, Maria Lorena Cook, and Stephen Crowley (eds.), *Working through the Past: Labor and Authoritarian Legacies in Comparative Perspective* (Ithaca, NY: Cornell University Press, 2015), pp. 64–81.
91. Stephen J. Frenkel and David Peetz, "Globalization and Industrial Relations in East Asia: A Three-Country Comparison," *Industrial Relations* 37 (July 1998), pp. 282–310; Kim, "Industrial Relations in Asia."

92. Kuruvilla, "Linkages between Industrialization Strategies and Industrial Relations/Human Resource Policies."
93. Sarosh Kuruvilla, "Economic Development Strategies, Industrial Relations Policies, and Workplace IR/HR Practices in Southeast Asia," in Kirsten S. Wever and Lowell Turner (eds.), *The Comparative Political Economy of Industrial Relations* (Madison, WI: Industrial Relations Research Association, 1995), pp. 115–50; Kuruvilla, "Linkages between Industrialization Strategies and Industrial Relations/Human Resource Policies."
94. Frank M. Horwitz, "Industrial Relations in Africa," in Michael J. Morley, Patrick Gunnigle, and David G. Collins (eds.), *Global Industrial Relations* (New York: Routledge, 2006), pp. 178–98; Gérard Kester, *Trade Unions and Workplace Democracy in Africa* (Aldershot, Hampshire, UK: Ashgate, 2007).
95. Byoung-Hoon Lee, "Employment Relations in the Republic of Korea," in Greg J. Bamber, Russell D. Lansbury, and Nick Wailes (eds.), *International and Comparative Employment Relations: Globalisation and Change* (London: Sage, 2011), pp. 281–306; Joohee Lee, "Between Fragmentation and Centralization: South Korean Industrial Relations in Transition," *British Journal of Industrial Relations* 49 (December 2011), pp. 767–91; Jennifer Jihye Chun, *Organizing at the Margins: The Symbolic Politics of Labor in South Korea and the United States* (Ithaca, NY: Cornell University Press, 2009).
96. Simon Clarke, Chang-Hee Lee, and Qi Li, "Collective Consultation and Industrial Relations in China," *British Journal of Industrial Relations* 42 (June 2004), pp. 235–54; Fang Lee Cooke, "Employment Relations in China," in Greg J. Bamber, Russell D. Lansbury, and Nick Wailes (eds.), *International and Comparative Employment Relations: Globalisation and Change* (London: Sage, 2011), pp. 307–29; Tim Pringle, *Trade Unions in China: The Challenge of Labour Unrest* (New York: Routledge, 2011).
97. Bill Taylor, Chang Kai, and Li Qi, *Industrial Relations in China* (Cheltenham: Elgar, 2003); Bill Taylor and Qi Li, "Is the ACFTU a Union and Does It Matter?" *Journal of Industrial Relations* 49 (November 2007), pp. 701–15.
98. Cooke, "Employment Relations in China"; Pringle, *Trade Unions in China*.
99. Cooke, "Employment Relations in China."
100. Sean Cooney, "China's Labour Law, Compliance and Flaws in Implementing Institutions,"*Journal of Industrial Relations* 49 (November 2007), pp. 67386; E. Patrick McDermott, "Industrial Relations in China: Ball of Confusion?" in Keith Townsend and Adrian Wilkinson (eds.), *Research Handbook on the Future of Work and Employment Relations* (Cheltenham, UK: Elgar, 2011), pp. 31941.
101. Pringle, *Trade Unions in China*; Eli Friedman, *Insurgency Trap: Labor Politics in Postsocialist China* (Ithaca, NY: Cornell University Press, 2014).
102. Chang Hee Lee and Mingwei Liu, "Collective Bargaining in Transition: Measuring the Effects of Collective Voice in China," in Susan Hayter (ed.), *The Role of Collective Bargaining in the Global Economy: Negotiating for Social Justice* (Cheltenham, UK: Elgar, 2011), pp. 205–26; Chang-Hee Lee, William Brown, and Xiaoyi Wen, "What Sort of Collective Bargaining Is Emerging in China? *British Journal of Industrial Relations* 54 (March 2016), pp. 214–36; Katie Quan, "One Step Forward: Collective Bargaining Experiments in Vietnam and China," in Anita Chan (ed.), *Chinese Workers in Comparative Perspective* (Ithaca, NY: Cornell University Press, 2015), pp. 174–92.
103. Quan, "One Step Forward"; Mark Anner, "Labor Control Regimes and Worker Resistance in Global Supply Chains," *Labor History* 56 (2015), pp. 292–307; Bernadine Van Gramberg, Julian Teicher, and Tien Nguyen, "Industrial Disputes in Vietnam: The Tale of the Wildcat," *Asia Pacific Journal of Human Resources* 51 (April 2013), pp. 248–68.
104. Gregory Mantsios (ed.), *A New Labor Movement for the New Century* (New York: Garland, 1998); Kim Moody, *An Injury to All: The Decline of American Unionism* (London: Verso, 1988); Ray M. Tillman and Michael S. Cummings (eds.), *The Transformation of U.S. Unions: Voices, Visions, and Strategies from the Grassroots* (Boulder, CO: Lynne Rienner Publishers, 1999); Rick Fantasia and Kim Voss, *Hard Work: Remaking the American Labor Movement* (Berkeley: University of California Press, 2004).
105. J.H. Verkerke, "Discharge," in Kenneth G. Dau-Schmidt, Seth D. Harris, and Orly Lobel (eds.), *Labor and Employment Law and Economics* (Northampton, MA: Elgar, 2009), pp. 447–79.
106. Hoyt N. Wheeler, Brian S. Klaas, and Douglas M. Mahony, *Workplace Justice without Unions* (Kalamazoo, MI: W.E. Upjohn Institute for Employment Research, 2004).
107. Befort and Cornett, "Beyond the Rhetoric of the NAFTA Treaty Debate."
108. Vai Io Lo, "Atypical Employment: A Comparison of Japan and the United States," *Comparative Labor Law Journal* 17 (Spring 1996), pp. 492–525; Kazuo Sugeno, *Japanese Employment and Labor Law*, Leo Kantowitz (trans.) (Durham, NC: Carolina Academic Press, 2002).

109. James C. Oakley, "Employee Duty of Loyalty—A Canadian Perspective," *Comparative Labor Law Journal* 20 (Winter 1999), pp. 185–203; Alexander J.S. Colvin, "Flexibility and Fairness in Liberal Market Economies: The Comparative Impact of the Legal Environment and High-Performance Work Systems," *British Journal of Industrial Relations* 26 (March 2006), pp. 73–97.
110. Stephen Frenkel and Sarosh Kuruvilla, "Logics of Action, Globalization, and Changing Employment Relations in China, India, Malaysia, and the Philippines," *Industrial and Labor Relations Review* 55 (July 2002), pp. 387–412; Katz and Darbishire, *Converging Divergences*; Richard M. Locke, "The Demise of the National Union in Italy: Lessons for Comparative Industrial Relations Theory," *Industrial and Labor Relations Review* 45 (January 1992), pp. 229–49.
111. Harry C. Katz, "The Decentralization of Collective Bargaining: A Literature Review and Comparative Analysis," *Industrial and Labor Relations Review* 47 (October 1993), pp. 3–22; Harry C. Katz, Wonduck Lee, and Joohee Lee (eds.), *The New Structure of Labor Relations: Tripartism and Decentralization* (Ithaca, NY: Cornell University Press, 2004).
112. Doellgast, *Disintegrating Democracy at Work*.
113. Katz and Darbishire, *Converging Divergences;* Paul Marginson and Keith Sisson, *European Integration and Industrial Relations: Multi-Level Governance in the Making* (London: Palgrave/Macmillan, 2004).
114. Doellgast, *Disintegrating Democracy at Work*; Frenkel and Peetz, "Globalization and Industrial Relations in East Asia"; Katz and Darbishire, *Converging Divergences*; Colvin, "Flexibility and Fairness in Liberal Market Economies"; John Godard, "Institutional Environments, Employer Practices, and States in Liberal Market Economies," *Industrial Relations* 41 (April 2002), pp. 249–86.
115. Slomp, *Between Bargaining and Politics*.
116. Marginson and Sisson, *European Integration and Industrial Relations*; Maarten Keune and Paul Marginson, "Transnational Industrial Relations as Multi-Level Governance: Interdependencies in European Social Dialogue," *British Journal of Industrial Relations* 51 (September 2013), pp. 473–97; Barbara Bechter, Bernd Brandl, and Guglielmo Meardi, "Sectors or Countries? Typologies and Levels of Analysis in Comparative Industrial Relations," *European Journal of Industrial Relations* 18 (September 2012), pp. 185–202.
117. John W. Budd, *Employment with a Human Face: Balancing Efficiency, Equity, and Voice* (Ithaca, NY: Cornell University Press, 2004).

Chapter Thirteen

What Should Labor Relations Do?

Advance Organizer

The goal of a labor relations system is to balance efficiency, equity, and voice. The previous chapters analyzed the development and operation of the U.S. labor relations system, the major pressures on this system, and varied international examples. This chapter looks to the future by exploring alternatives for unions, employers, and labor policy for balancing efficiency, equity, and voice in the 21st century.

Learning Objectives

By the end of this chapter, you should be able to

1. **Outline** alternative directions for union strategies in the 21st century.
2. **Describe** alternative directions for corporate behaviors in the 21st century.
3. **Identify** alternative directions for labor relations public policies in the 21st century.
4. **Understand** strategic management and leadership issues pertaining to labor relations for managers and union leaders in the 21st century.

Contents

As highlighted by recent events such as attempts to change public sector bargaining laws, the U.S. labor relations system is under fire from many angles and perspectives. Proponents of free markets and human resource management see unions as interfering with markets and managers. Advocates of employment relationship flexibility criticize union policies as restrictive barriers to competitiveness. Proponents of greater labor–management cooperation and employee involvement attack U.S. labor law as adversarial and overly restrictive. Globalization, financialization, and the need to create high-performance workplaces are placing great strains on the U.S. labor relations system (recall Chapters 10 and 11). The current state of U.S. labor relations is also sharply criticized by proponents of labor unions and workers' rights. Flexible and team-based work systems are attacked as old-fashioned speedups in which workers are forced to work harder for lower pay and less security. Organized labor believes that U.S. labor law is exceptionally weak and fails to prevent antiunion employer actions like firing union supporters or replacing striking workers. Labor activists further criticize the traditional business unionism approach of U.S. unions for failing to develop a vibrant labor movement based on grassroots participation. More generally, the Occupy and Fight for $15 movements have challenged economic inequality and criticized the power of corporations in society. To varying degrees, all these criticisms reflect frustration with the current state of efficiency, equity, and voice in the U.S. employment relationship.

Comparative examples from other countries show that there are many institutional arrangements and behaviors for seeking the common underlying goal of balancing efficiency, equity, and voice (Chapter 12). In other words, if the U.S. system no longer effectively serves its purposes, there are plenty of alternatives. This chapter therefore builds on the preceding chapters to look toward the future. What should unions do in the 21st century? Labor unions have a variety of options such as becoming more militant or cooperative, or changing their structures and strategies. What should companies do? Companies, too, have a variety of options ranging from a continued short-term focus on shareholder returns to broader visions of the importance of embracing stakeholders and corporate responsibility, and there are analogous alternatives in the public sector. What should labor policy do? Labor law can be deregulated, strengthened, loosened, or rewritten from a clean slate to reflect a new environment and set of priorities. Putting these questions together yields the concluding subject for this book's investigation of labor relations: What should labor relations do?

WHAT SHOULD UNIONS DO?

Labor unions are the representatives of workers. As such, unions champion the interests and aspirations of workers, not vice versa. Unions do not determine these aspirations, but rather must shape their strategies and structures to respond to them; the early AFL craft unions, the CIO industrial unions in the 1930s, and the public sector unions in the 1960s created strategies and structures to fit the blossoming needs of skilled craftsmen, mass manufacturing workers, and government employees, respectively.[1] As employment relationships change in response to the pressures of globalization, flexibility, and decentralization, as the nature of work changes in response to new workforce demographics (including ethnicity, gender, and education) and increased employee involvement, and as the U.S. economy experiences shifts in industries and occupations, workers in the 21st century will likely create a unique sense of workplace justice different from earlier eras. Unions will have to adapt to these changes.

As the world and work are changing in diverse ways, there are numerous alternative directions for U.S. unions. U.S. unions can try to become more powerful, or more cooperative; to emphasize greater social activism, or greater individual empowerment; to network like a professional association, or buy firms and become owners (see Figure 13.1). As such, there are various proposals for reforming union strategies and structures. The most important possibilities are summarized in Table 13.1. Before we consider these options in more detail, some cautionary notes are important. First, the categories are presented here as intentionally broad to stimulate wide-ranging reflection and debate. Second, the categories are not necessarily mutually exclusive—some can be complementary. In fact, it is common to argue that reviving U.S. labor unions requires discarding the servicing model by actively engaging individual workers.[2] Most of the options presented here share this theme, albeit in different ways. Moreover, some proposals for a new unionism draw from several of the categories outlined here.[3] Third, even with the broad categories presented here, it is not clear whether one size fits all, or whether various workers, companies, industries, and occupations are best suited to diverse forms of unionism. Fourth, some proposals are consistent with existing U.S. labor law, whereas others require legal changes. And fifth, except for employee ownership unionism, these alternative directions apply to public sector unionism, too.

Solidarity Unionism

Proposals that focus on increasing the traditional bargaining power of U.S. unions can be grouped in a category of **solidarity unionism** because they generally rely on increasing labor power through enhanced solidarity within and across workplaces. Of the options listed in Table 13.1, solidarity unionism is the closest to the existing model of business

FIGURE 13.1
Directions for U.S. Labor Unionism

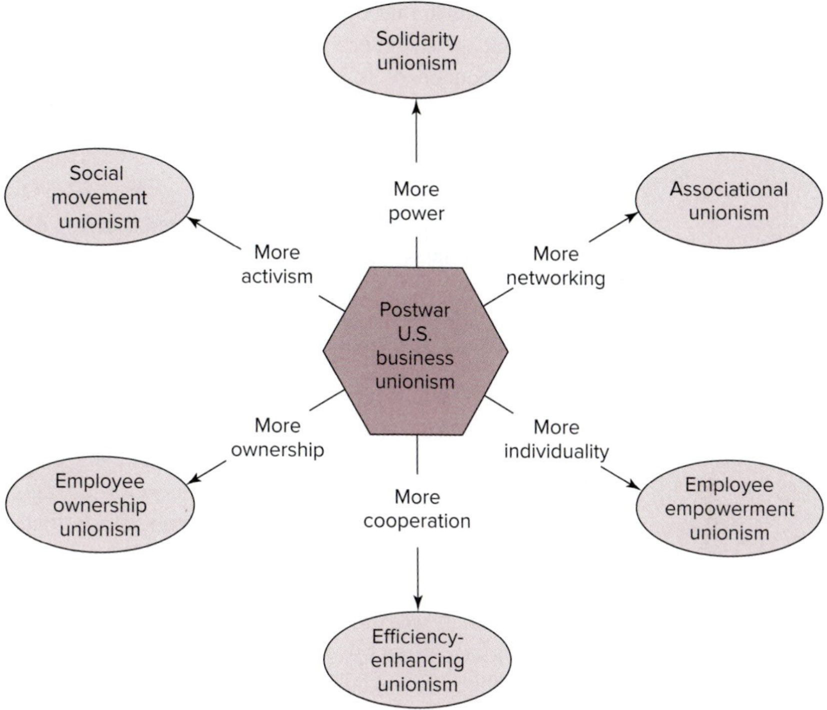

TABLE 13.1 **Possibilities for 21st–Century Labor Unions**

Possibilities	Unions As . . .	Emphases	Concerns
Solidarity unionism	Powerful solidarity alliances.	Strong worker advocacy in the workplace through bargaining backed up by strikes, and solidarity across workplaces.	More adversarial than cooperative; more rules-based than flexible. How to achieve competitiveness and quality?
Social movement unionism	Community and political activists.	Social and political militancy and activism; alliances with community groups.	What about workers' workplace concerns?
Efficiency-enhancing unionism	Productivity and cooperation enhancers.	Concern with establishing participatory structures to serve competitiveness and quality. Rewards based on performance; training initiatives.	What is the source of employee power? Is there solidarity across workplaces? Who's looking out for employee interests?
Employee ownership unionism	Employee owners.	Control over employment conditions through employee ownership of companies.	Is employee ownership efficient? How are business decisions made? Is it too risky for employees when their savings are invested in their company?
Employee empowerment unionism	Individual empowerment supporters.	Bargaining for procedures that empower individual decision making; inclusion of procedural safeguards and minimum standards.	What is the source of employee power? Is there solidarity across workplaces?
Associational unionism	Loose networks of professional associations.	Flexible, multiple forms of representation and networks based on multiple concerns. More than just bargaining. No exclusive representation.	What is the source of employee power?

unionism—as illustrated by solidarity unionism's focus on strengthening collective bargaining. Relative to some proposals that emphasize greater responsiveness to business concerns, proponents of solidarity unionism make no apologies for championing a strong labor movement as the protector of worker interests in opposition to management. Unions are seen as a needed force of worker power and protection; the problem with the current weakness of unions

> is not that most American workers have no representative to develop and to express their views on the business strategies and tactics, or the personnel policies and benefits, chosen by their employers. The problem is that American workers have lost power—power to extract a larger share of the returns of American enterprise and power to protect individual employees from arbitrary, unjust, or discriminatory treatment by their managers.[4]

Proponents of this view advocate more aggressive organizing and bargaining tactics to bolster labor's power.[5] This might include organizing workers outside of the mainstream labor movement. For example, immigrant workers who are segregated into ethnic enclaves in American workplaces and communities develop strong collective bonds through their shared struggles and are ripe for unionization efforts that build on this solidarity.[6] And when necessary, labor advocates argue for the greater use of strikes, sit-ins, civil disobedience, and other militant tactics to mobilize worker power.[7] For example, to try to pressure the Yale University administration to recognize their union, graduate teaching assistants conducted a grade strike by refusing to turn in grades. Workers at a door and window factory outside of Chicago conducted sit-down strikes in 2008 and 2012 to fight plans to close it. More than 100,000 workers and their supporters demonstrated outside the Wisconsin state capitol in 2011 to protest proposed changes in Wisconsin's public sector bargaining law. Fight for $15 strikers in multiple cities have blocked traffic and been arrested for civil disobedience. These efforts to build greater labor power frequently include developing greater solidarity linkages with other workers. The Yale graduate assistants struck at the same time as clerical and food service workers; Fight for $15 action days are coordinated to occur on the same day worldwide in hundreds of cities.

Increased solidarity among rank-and file-members within unions is also emphasized. The development of this solidarity often focuses on harnessing an organizing model of representation.[8] Recall from Chapter 5 that in contrast to the servicing model, an organizing model seeks to create widespread rank-and-file participation in union activities. These efforts are closely related to efforts to increase internal union democracy, thereby creating a vibrant and powerful labor movement through rank-and-file involvement.[9] Some have encouraged negotiating members-only agreements by bargaining on behalf of their supporters in workplaces where majority support has not yet been achieved (see Chapter 4). Such unions would be **nonmajority unions**—that is, unions that have the support of a minority rather than a majority of employees in a workplace. Nonmajority unions can gain a foothold in new workplaces, demonstrate to reluctant workers the benefits of unionism, and ultimately achieve majority support—as often was the case in the 1930s. On the other hand, at least one labor supporter has advocated for a strategy of "fortress unionism" in which the labor movement focuses on maintaining its strength in its traditional areas and existing locals while waiting for nonunion workers to get fed up with the status quo in large numbers as in the 1930s because this "is how massive union growth occurs—workers take matters into their own hands and then unions capture that energy like lightning in a bottle."[10]

Some proposals for increasing labor's power also suggest altering the structure of unions. Unions need to become less bureaucratic while increasing their willingness to lend financial and institutional support to diverse grassroots organizations while promoting their autonomy.[11] Another proposed change in union structure is the call for moving beyond industrial unionism to occupational unionism.[12] This represents a partial return to

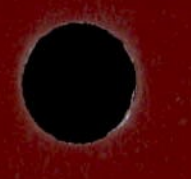

Labor Relations Application Occupational Unionism among Waitresses

Between the 1900s and 1960s, significant numbers of waitresses were represented by the Hotel Employees and Restaurant Employees International Union (HERE). In fact, in the 1940s a majority of waitresses were unionized in New York, Detroit, and San Francisco. Interestingly, the local waitress unions emphasized occupational rather than employer-specific standards. They developed standards for good waitressing and established work boundaries (such as excluding menial cleanup duties). Employment security in the local industry, not at a specific restaurant, was emphasized. Restaurant managers retained broad rights to discharge waitresses except in retaliation for union activity; discharged waitresses would simply return to the local hiring hall to await an opening at another restaurant. And the union would discipline workers for poor performance to maintain the standards of the union and the craft. Benefits were provided through union welfare funds, not by specific employers. Some union contracts specified only minimum wage rates; individual waitresses were free to earn more.

Later restrictions on closed shops in U.S. labor law, however, removed the waitress unions' ability to control their occupation, and with the passage of the Civil Rights Act in 1964, the all-female waitress unions were merged into other hospitality unions and took on a more traditional industrial union flavor. But this model of occupational rather than job-specific unionism—including the provision of training, job opportunities, and occupational standards—might have appeal for today's professional service sector workers.

References: Dorothy Sue Cobble, *Dishing It Out: Waitresses and Their Unions in the Twentieth Century* (Urbana: University of Illinois Press, 1991); Dorothy Sue Cobble, "Organizing the Postindustrial Workforce: Lessons from the History of Waitress Unionism," *Industrial and Labor Relations Review* 44 (April 1991), pp. 419–36.

earlier forms of craft unionism in that occupational unionism emphasizes workers' identification with their occupations rather than their specific employers. It moves beyond craft unionism, however, in not being limited to skilled crafts. Waitresses, flight attendants, and janitors, for example, can have strong occupational interests that are tied more closely to those same occupations at other companies than to other workers at their own companies (see the accompanying "Labor Relations Application" box discussing occupational unionism). These occupational interests are the basis for solidarity across employers. This model might be well suited to the 21st century as the trends toward increased use of contingent workers and increased job switching (rather than stable lifetime employment) continue.

Social Movement Unionism

Social movement unionism rejects the narrow business unionism focus on workplace-based collective bargaining and instead sees labor unions as representatives of the entire working class and as part of a broader social movement of community, social, and political activist groups.[13] Rather than winning gains for workers only through narrow workplace bargaining, social movement unionism involves building strong coalitions with other community groups to achieve social change through social and political channels, and to better integrate workers' workplace, family, and community concerns through a "whole worker" mindset.[14] Social movement unionism can also help revitalize unions as organizations, and thereby strengthen union bargaining power. In other words, advocates of a stronger U.S. labor movement see greater social activism as an important route to achieving more power in society and at the bargaining table.[15] In this way, efforts to increase grassroots participation and mobilization can serve both social movement unionism and solidarity unionism.

A popular example of using community activism and union alliances with social, religious, and political groups to increase labor's effectiveness is the Justice for Janitors campaigns.[16] These campaigns expand the drive to organize janitors from a workplace issue to a community issue. Public demonstrations, strong ties with immigrants' rights and religious groups, and active participation by janitors—not just union leaders—give these campaigns social vibrancy and have won bargaining rights and contracts. For example, during a campaign in Washington, D.C., the Service Employees International Union (SEIU) led multiple mass demonstrations that blocked traffic, marched through city streets, and picketed various locations. But they did not simply demand better wages—the campaign highlighted the social issues revealed by the janitors' conditions. The low pay and sexual harassment of janitors was contrasted with the massive tax breaks granted to the property owners and the resulting decline in school funding and other city services. In the words of one SEIU official,

> Civil disobedience by a cross-section of supporters, including religious and other community leaders, helps draw attention to the janitors' plight. The themes of the campaign play a role here: "Justice" as opposed to "wage" slogans help broaden the appeal of the workers' struggle. The problems of the working poor, mistreatment of minority groups, sexual harassment, and lack of health insurance are issues that will attract a diverse constituency. [The] Justice for Janitors picket line gives sympathizers a vehicle for expressing their diverse concerns.[17]

The Justice for Janitors campaigns reject a narrow business unionism approach and try instead to create a broad social movement in which organized labor champions workers' issues in their social context beyond the confines of individual workplaces.

Also, labor–religious alliances between unions and the Chicago Catholic archdiocese and an interdenominational committee helped organize O'Hare Airport concession workers.[18] There is also increased activism to win gains for nonunion workers through education (e.g., *www.fixmyjob.com*), protest, lobbying, lawsuits, and other means. These efforts are commonly led by worker centers such as the Restaurant Opportunities Center that seek to assist workers in industries and occupations that are difficult to organize because of turnover, employer opposition, or exclusion from the National Labor Relations Act. These community groups have been called "alt-labor" and they are increasingly receiving the support of labor unions.[19] For example, the Fight for $15 movement is supported by a coalition of labor and community groups. Such initiatives also underscore an important aspect of creating a vibrant, socially focused labor movement: unions embracing diversity by reaching out to workers not traditionally included in the labor movement, especially in leadership positions—women, minorities, and immigrant workers.[20]

On a national scale, another significant aspect of increased labor activism is reasserting influence in the political arena. Labor's influence with the Democratic Party fell to an all-time low in the 1970s; since then the AFL–CIO and individual unions have devoted renewed attention to political activities.[21] In recent elections, organized labor has focused on creating vibrant grassroots efforts that involves many rank-and-file workers in campaigning for pro-labor political candidates and in get-out-the-vote efforts. The AFL-CIO also tries to mobilize nonunion workers through its community organization Working America. Nevertheless, organized labor continues to face a hostile political environment. This has been most evident under Republican administrations, but even during the Democratic administrations of Bill Clinton and Barack Obama, few of labor's legislative priorities have been enacted. Some labor supporters have therefore called for the creation of an independent labor party as an additional component of a social movement unionism strategy.[22]

Lastly, note that social movement unionism attempts to move beyond the sole exercise of what is called "structural power" by also changing how the public thinks about certain issues. Structural power is traditional leverage that comes from imposing costs on another party, such as when a strike or a demonstration drives customers away from an employer. But there can also be power that comes from moral legitimacy. So in the face of declining structural power due to globalization and other factors, social movement unionism seeks greater leverage by attempting to change shared meanings and values, and thus altering beliefs about what is considered socially unacceptable.[23] Just as the civil rights movement sought to make racial discrimination morally unacceptable, coalitions of unions and community groups seek to reframe labor issues in ways that give their causes, such as harsh working conditions for migrant farmworkers or low pay for fast food workers, moral legitimacy. This underscores the power of meanings in our society, such as when only certain forms of work are seen as "real work," and thus only certain workers are seen as worthy of certain standards.[24] Campaigns to win better conditions for home-based health care workers, for example, therefore start with efforts to get the public to see these individuals not simply as caregivers but also as legitimate workers.

Efficiency-Enhancing Unionism

Solidarity unionism and social movement unionism include diverse initiatives or proposals that can generally be thought of as militant or activist and that embody a strong need to represent workers' interests *in opposition to* employers' interests. The remaining alternatives in Figure 13.1 and Table 13.1 seek to create new forms of unionism that are not as adversarial or oppositional. Some see these alternatives as more productive, but others see them as weak. The most extreme case of the nonoppositional—that is, cooperative—approach can be labeled **efficiency-enhancing unionism.** Efficiency-enhancing unionism sees labor unions as strategic business partners that can help advance productivity, quality, and competitiveness.

One proposal for this type of unionism argues for replacing the typical detailed union contract with an enterprise compact.[25] Note the cooperative philosophy:

> A *contract* is essentially adversarial in nature, representing a compromise between the separate interests of each party to the agreement. In contrast, a *compact* is fundamentally a cooperative document, providing for a mutual vision and a joint system for achieving common goals that foster the general well-being of all stakeholders in a given endeavor.[26]

Thus an enterprise compact specifies the principles of a labor–management relationship based on union and employee involvement in business decision making in return for greater union commitment to competitiveness, as well as increased sharing by employees in both the risks and rewards of the company. Examples of such principles might include productivity growth targets and prices established jointly by labor and management, guaranteed employment security, base compensation established by productivity growth with added profit sharing, and the replacement of management rights clauses with joint decision making.[27] A leading example of this approach was the automaker Saturn before its reversion to a more traditional system. Recall from Chapter 10 that the union and managers at Saturn used to jointly make strategic business decisions, and that teams of workers were empowered to make daily production and work decisions. Recall further that supporters of this form of unionism view this as a way to serve the company's interests of competitiveness and quality while providing a richer, positive work environment for employees; critics see it as selling out and leaving workers without strong protections against management.[28]

Another approach to efficiency-enhancing unionism is through active union involvement in providing training. For example, the Wisconsin State AFL–CIO has been instrumental in establishing and running the Wisconsin Regional Training Partnership (WRTP).[29] In cooperation with both private sector companies and public sector agencies and technical colleges, the WRTP provides training across the broad spectrum of workforce needs—from basic job and language skills to advanced technical skills. Elsewhere across the country, unions have provided training for hotel, hospital, and child care workers, to name just a few. This cooperative approach can increase workers' incomes while providing a more skilled—and therefore more efficient and competitive—workforce to employers.

Employee Ownership Unionism

Another approach to aligning workers' and employers' interests is through employee ownership.[30] If employees own stock in a company, they may work harder to promote the profitability of their company. More importantly, if ownership comes with voting rights in corporate governance or direct representation on a corporation's board of directors, employees can participate in business decision making at the highest levels of the corporation. Thanks to these channels of influence, companies might weigh employees' interests (such as job security) more heavily when making strategic decisions. **Employee ownership unionism,** therefore, seeks to represent workers by facilitating employee ownership of companies.

Some examples of union involvement in employee ownership efforts include employee stock ownership plans (ESOPs) in the steel, trucking, and airline industries. These ESOPs have usually occurred when the companies were struggling and involved employees trading wage and benefit concessions for stock ownership. To date, organized labor has therefore participated in ESOPs as a defensive rather than a proactive representation strategy. Moreover, the difficulty of using employee ownership to advocate for employee interests is underscored by the fact that only a tiny minority of ESOPs include employee representatives on corporations' boards of directors.[31]

Another potential direction of employee ownership unionism focuses on the investment policies of pension funds. Employee pension funds in the United States have several trillion dollars invested in stocks, bonds, and other instruments—this is labor's capital.[32] Various efforts are underway to use the power of these assets to promote workers' interests by creating "worker–owner" investment objectives that pursue a broader social agenda than simply short-term financial returns. Union pension funds are leading a movement of shareholder activism in which workers use their rights as shareholders to submit shareholder proposals and resolutions to limit executive compensation, ensure the independence of outside board members, and bring about other changes in corporate strategies and governance.[33] These proposals and resolutions are voted on by shareholders; even if they do not pass, their publicity can cause companies to make changes. One potential for employee ownership unionism is expanding shareholder resolutions to encompass employment practices as well as corporate governance issues. A second method is using union pension funds to directly make worker-friendly investments, such as in unionized construction projects, but legal constraints would need to be relaxed before this could happen on a broad scale.[34] The use of labor's capital to promote efficiency, equity, and voice is an important labor relations development to watch in the 21st century.

Employee Empowerment Unionism

A frequent concern with the traditional postwar model of U.S. business unionism is its emphasis on uniformity and standardization through rules.[35] Not only does this job control unionism approach clash with managerial drives for flexibility (Chapter 10), but it is also reasonable to question whether this is what workers want. In **employee empowerment unionism** unions negotiate processes rather than outcomes and thus provide the framework for greater employee autonomy, discretion, and empowerment (Chapter 5).[36] Unlike systems installed unilaterally by employers, negotiated processes can include minimum standards and procedural safeguards (ultimately backed up by a strike threat). Unions can also provide expertise and support to employees as needed.

In professional sports and the entertainment industry, unions typically only negotiate minimum salaries. Within the processes negotiated by the unions, individual players or actors negotiate their own salaries (see the accompanying "Labor Relations Application" box discussing Hollywood unions). As an example among office workers, the clerical workers at Harvard University negotiated joint committees and problem-solving systems

Labor Relations Application Collective and Individual Representation in Hollywood

In the entertainment industry, collective bargaining agreements for the Screen Actors Guild-American Federation of Television and Radio Artists, the Writers Guild of America, and the Directors Guild of America contain a set of sometimes complicated minimum rates, the framework for individual negotiations, and industrywide standards on residual payments. Actors, writers, and directors are explicitly allowed to negotiate their own compensation above the negotiated minimums. Moreover, this model is not limited to superstars: The International Alliance of Theatrical and Stage Employees (IATSE) takes the same approach for craft employees in the television and film industry who handle cameras, sound, lighting, and other production aspects.

Through typical collective bargaining, IATSE negotiates basic agreements with various associations of producers, such as the Alliance of Motion Picture Television Producers or the Association of Independent Commercial Producers, and with production companies, such as Walt Disney or Twentieth Century Fox. The basic agreements are similar to typical union contracts and include union recognition and security clauses, benefits, standards for rest and meal periods, overtime provisions, no strike clauses, and a grievance procedure. The critical differences between these basic agreements and a typical U.S. union contract, however, are that there are no just cause provisions and the wage rates are minimums. Individual IATSE members can negotiate higher rates—often referred to as "better conditions"—on their own. In other words, "IATSE's collective bargaining agreement is simply an umbrella that contains and defines the parameters of embedded individual bargains." This embedded bargaining fits well with IATSE's membership because of their episodic employment patterns. Specific jobs, such as making a commercial or a movie, last only a few days or months, so the self-representation aspect lets producers and employees tailor wages and hours for each project. At the same time the umbrella collective bargaining agreement provides minimum standards and continuity of benefits.

References: Alan Paul and Archie Kleingartner, "The Transformation of Industrial Relations in the Motion Picture and Television Industries: Talent Sector," in Lois S. Gray and Ronald L. Seeber (eds.), *Under the Stars: Essays on Labor Relations in Arts and Entertainment* (Ithaca, NY: ILR Press, 1996), pp. 156–80; Katherine V.W. Stone, "The New Psychological Contract: Implications of the Changing Workplace for Labor and Employment Law," *UCLA Law Review* 48 (February 2001), pp. 519–661; the quote is from p. 635.

instead of rules and a traditional grievance procedure. In this way, individual employees are empowered to participate in determining their working conditions within a union-negotiated framework and with the union's support (see the accompanying "Labor Relations Application" box discussing self-representation at Harvard).[37] Employee empowerment unionism can also overlap with efficiency-enhancing unionism in workplaces run by self-directed work teams, as was the case at Saturn.

Associational Unionism

Another possible direction for employee representation is called **associational unionism.**[38] This perspective is rooted in a contrast with the postwar model of industrial unionism and U.S. labor law. These postwar institutions are premised on a balance of power between (often large) unions and (often large) corporations. In a mass manufacturing economy, this balance was achieved through rules-based contracts; stability was achieved through uniformity of contracts across an industry. In other words, both union representation and production were bureaucratic. Proponents of associational unionism argue that this bureaucratic balance of power no longer matches the need for nimble, flexible, and competitive organizations. Perhaps more importantly, the traditional sharp distinction between labor and management no longer matches large numbers of today's semiprofessional, professional, and knowledge workers. These workers have multiple interests—personal, occupational, industry-specific, and company-specific—and often join professional associations to serve their interests in a flexible, positive, and nonadversarial way, such as through training and establishing

Labor Relations Application Self–Representation at Harvard University

Recall from Chapter 6 that the Harvard Union of Clerical and Technical Workers (HUCTW) successfully unionized clerical and technical workers at Harvard University in the 1980s by emphasizing nontraditional tactics. In particular, the HUCTW relied heavily on building one-to-one relationships with the workers and by trying to create the HUCTW as a vehicle for employee empowerment, not for institutional confrontation with Harvard (recall the slogan "It's not anti-Harvard to be pro-union."). This approach was based on trying to counter the paternalism of Harvard toward the predominantly female clerical workers.

But after the organizing drive succeeded, what then? A standard union contract with narrow work rules and a quasilegal grievance procedure (in the tradition of the servicing model of representation) would be inconsistent with the empowerment philosophy of the HUCTW (an organizing model of representation). In fact, this type of contract would simply replace the paternalism of Harvard with the paternalism of the union. Consequently, using an inclusive and participative bargaining structure, the HUCTW negotiated a nontraditional contract. Rather than restrictive work rules, the contract explicitly recognized that "Each school and administrative unit of Harvard has a unique culture and therefore an employee participation program must be flexible to accommodate the needs of the school or administrative department and its staff."

To support employee participation and flexibility, a two-part system was established: (1) joint committees to discuss and seek consensus on "workplace matters which have a significant impact on staff" and (2) problem-solving teams to resolve problems. The principles guiding these procedures include consensus building, open communication, and developing individual problem-solving skills. If an individual has a workplace problem (a "grievance" in traditional lingo), the first step is employee–supervisor discussions. Employees can rely on the HUCTW for support, but the explicit goal is for employees to resolve their own issues. If the problem is not resolved at this level, it can be referred to a joint problem-solving team and ultimately to mediation. In cases of impasse, a mediator can issue a binding decision.

Clerical and technical workers have thus created a system of self-representation at Harvard. Through joint councils and an individual problem resolution system, individual workers are empowered to participate in determining their conditions of employment, backed up by the expertise and negotiating power of their union.

Reference: John P. Hoerr, *We Can't Eat Prestige: The Women Who Organized Harvard* (Philadelphia: Temple University Press, 1997). The quotes are from pages 155, 183, 197, and 211.

professional standards. But professional associations, such as the Society for Human Resource Management (SHRM), generally lack or even pursue power in the workplace.

Associational unionism attempts to blend the multiple-interest philosophy and services of professional associations with the power of unions to create a new organizational form that is more powerful than an association but more decentralized and flexible than a typical U.S. union. Associational unions (if they existed) could strike, but like a professional association they could also use other tactics such as political pressure and publicity. Such unions could also negotiate contracts with employers; but because of the multiple interests they represent, associational unions would have to become skilled in multilateral negotiations, not just bilateral negotiations with a single employer. In fact, this proposed system is not based on exclusive representation; rather, workers can belong to various associations that reflect their interests and ideals. For example, the Freelancers Union (*www.freelancersunion.org*) is an associational union for independent workers. While it doesn't engage in collective bargaining, it uses collective strength and shared experiences through education, cooperation, political lobbying, and shared identity to improve conditions for independent workers. This includes obtaining group rates for health care insurance and getting a favorable tax change in New York City.[39] In other words, associational unions coordinate employee networking with others who share similar interests.

In sum, there are a number of possible directions for private and public sector labor unions in the 21st century. As shown in Table 13.1, there are pros and cons to all of these directions. These alternatives can also be analyzed against the critical dimensions of the employment relationship: efficiency, equity, and voice. Efficiency is emphasized most strongly by efficiency-enhancing unionism, but employee ownership unionism can also promote efficiency if stock ownership motivates employees or if social investing produces stable companies with high-performance employment systems. Moreover, the flexibility and individual discretion aspects of employee empowerment unionism and associational unionism can also be consistent with increased competitiveness. Equity is stressed most sharply in solidarity unionism and social movement unionism and is pursued through strong bargaining and social power. In contrast, employee empowerment unionism seeks equity through minimum standards and procedural safeguards. Social voice is an important feature of social movement unionism, while workplace voice is delivered in alternative ways in the other models. Employee ownership unionism provides workplace voice through participation in corporate governance, while employee empowerment and associational unionism emphasize a combination of individual and collective voice mechanisms.

Discussions of the future of unionism should not ignore the current weak state of the U.S. labor movement. In particular, can weak unions successfully pursue more cooperative strategies such as efficiency-enhancing or employee empowerment unionism? Cooperative behavior from a position of weakness likely promotes efficiency, but it is unlikely to revive the labor movement or make positive contributions to equity and voice. Moreover, weak unions that feel that their existence is threatened might turn to militant, adversarial strategies to increase their power. As such, the extent to which unions are institutionally secure in the economic, political, and social system of the 21st century can shape in which direction U.S. unions move (see Figure 13.1). Whether unions are secure or threatened depends not only on choices that the labor movement must make but also on corporate behavior and public policies.

Online Exploration Exercise: Browse some union-related sites at random. Can you find examples of the different forms of unionism described in Table 13.1?

WHAT SHOULD EMPLOYERS DO?

Earlier chapters have discussed a variety of labor relations strategies used by employers, and the pressures for change brought on by globalization, the need for flexible work practices, and other trends. Just as the previous section considered deeper questions about future directions for labor unions, in looking toward the future of labor relations, it is also important to consider deeper issues of corporate governance, corporate social responsibility, and public sector values.

Maximizing Shareholder Value

An influential perspective on corporate social responsibility is that business's role in society is to make money:

> The baseline answer to this important (and highly debated) question is to make a profit: Few trends could so thoroughly undermine the very foundations of our free society as the acceptance of corporate officials of a social responsibility other than making as much money for their stockholders as possible. . . . The view has been gaining widespread acceptance that corporate officials . . . have a "social responsibility" that goes beyond serving the interest of their stockholders. . . . This view shows a fundamental misconception of the character and nature of a free economy. In such an economy, there is one and only one social responsibility of business—to use its resources and engage in activities designed to increase profits so long as it stays within the rules of the game, which is to say, engages in open and free competition, without deception or fraud.[40]

This view is rooted in utilitarian and libertarianism ethical views (see Chapter 5), and forms the foundation for the U.S. approach to corporate governance: the shareholder value model (Chapter 11).[41] From this perspective, shareholders are viewed as the key group in the corporation because they invest their money and bear the risk of making a profit or loss. As such, for both economic and legal reasons, shareholders are recognized as the owners of the corporation and managers have a primary legal obligation to act in the best interests of the shareholders.[42] Maximizing shareholder value is therefore the primary mission of U.S. corporations.

The principle of maximizing shareholder value does not have to embrace a short-term perspective, but increasingly this is the norm. In other words, in the United States, maximizing shareholder value has come to mean maximizing short-term stock prices.[43] In this way, the shareholder value model of corporate governance has led to a corporate preoccupation with short-term financial results. Executive compensation plans that include generous stock options can further reinforce this focus because executives directly benefit from increased share prices. As explained in Chapter 11, the sharp increase in emphasis on financial results that has occurred since the 1980s is called financialization.[44] One element of financialization is a direct focus on boosting stock prices to satisfy Wall Street expectations while also increasing the value of executive stock options. Corporations are therefore increasingly using their cash reserves to repurchase shares of their stock, which drives up the share price.[45] Another aspect of financialization is an increased pursuit of profits through financial transactions rather than through the delivery of valuable goods and services. Within the economy, this includes an increase in the importance of financial corporations such as investment banks, and within nonfinancial corporations this includes the increased importance of financing units and the use of financial instruments such as derivatives to generate profits. Financialization also includes leveraged buyouts that seek to buy and sell companies at a profit, typically after implementing cost-cutting strategies.[46]

Shareholder value maximization and financialization have important consequences for employees and for labor relations because short-term financial gains are prioritized over longer-term investments, corporate cash is used to fund financial transactions rather than capital investment, employees are treated as labor costs, and employees and their unions are denied meaningful participation in corporate governance and decisions over investments, mergers, and other major business activities. In other words, the traditional business model of "retain and reinvest" earnings and profits has become a new model of "downsize and distribute" with adverse effects for employees.[47]

Corporate Social Responsibility: A Broader Alternative View

Critics therefore challenge what they see as a narrow view of corporate social responsibility and advocate for rethinking the accompanying short-term focus on shareholder value maximization (see Figure 13.2). There are ethical and legal arguments that can be made in

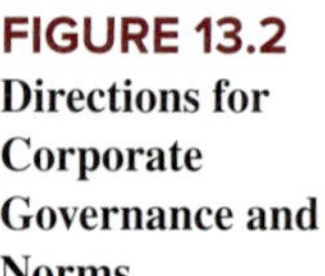

FIGURE 13.2
Directions for Corporate Governance and Norms

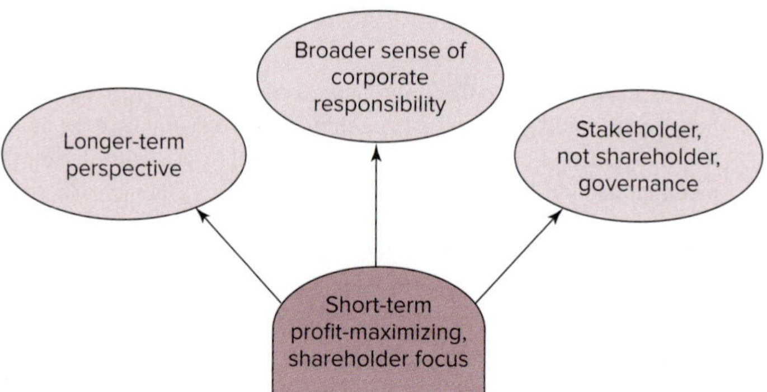

support of a broader view of corporate social responsibility. In ethical terms, recall from Chapter 5 that the ethics of duty (in the tradition of Kant) and virtue (in the tradition of Aristotle) rejects a sole focus on outcomes (such as profit maximization) without regard for actions (such as how people are treated). The ethics of justice further gives weight to the fairness of economic outcomes. From these perspectives, business is viewed as a human activity; seeking profits through efficiency and competitiveness is important but must be balanced with respect for humanity and the corporation's role in society.[48] From a legal perspective, it is argued that stockholders have important rights but that corporations are legally sanctioned by governments and thus shareholder rights are not unlimited. In particular, because of a perceived public interest, the law grants shareholders limited liability (if you own stock in a bankrupt company, creditors cannot take your house); in return, corporations must serve the public interest. In other words, corporations are viewed as social rather than purely private institutions.[49]

From this perspective, corporate social responsibility is seen as encompassing broader concerns than short-term profit maximization. New societal norms for corporate behavior are therefore advocated. At the workplace level, it is argued that employee dignity in daily work requires new norms for management behavior that respect workers' interests and rights.[50] In terms of human resources and industrial relations strategies, for example, high-performance work practices in which employees have decision-making authority can be used instead of confrontational methods of supervision (Chapter 5); in union organizing drives, employers can choose a policy of neutrality instead of union suppression (Chapter 6). Similar arguments about the need to respect workers' interests and rights are made for policies and institutions at the national and international levels.[51] The United Nations is promoting a global compact with business in which corporations agree to voluntarily respect human labor and environmental concerns while in return, the United Nations promotes trade and open markets.[52] The United Nations has also developed a model code of conduct for companies with respect to human rights based partly on the belief that corporate citizenship is good for business and partly on the foundation that "business enterprises have increased their power in the world . . . with power comes responsibility."[53] Broad views of corporate social responsibility also include concerns for environmental sustainability and other issues.

A Stakeholder Model of Corporate Governance

Perspectives that call for a broader conceptualization of corporate social responsibility are closely aligned with views that argue for replacing the shareholder model of corporate governance with a **stakeholder model.** The stakeholder model is rooted in a belief that *all* stakeholders—employees, customers, suppliers, local communities, and others in addition to shareholders or owners—are sufficiently affected by corporate actions to deserve consideration in corporate decision making.[54] In other words, a corporation exists not just for the benefit of shareholders, and it should be operated to benefit all who have a stake in it. In its most extensive form, adopting the stakeholder model requires legal changes in corporate governance, especially mandated representatives of employees and other stakeholders on corporate boards of directors. This is the case in other countries such as Germany (Chapter 12).[55] More commonly, supporters of a stakeholder approach in the United States advocate changing corporate and societal norms and stop short of calling for legal changes.

A stakeholder rather than shareholder approach to labor relations would represent a significant change from past U.S. experiences. High-performance work systems with extensive employee involvement would likely be more widespread (Chapter 10). Employers would probably maintain neutrality in union organizing drives (Chapter 6). Labor–management negotiations would likely have more of an integrative or win–win, problem-solving approach than a distributive and adversarial character (Chapter 7). Grievance resolution would probably be more flexible and informal (Chapter 9). Companies might be less likely to move production to different locations in response to union activity or modest labor cost differentials. Significantly more information would probably be shared with employees and their representatives, and employees would have a voice in strategic decisions. And unions might adopt less militant strategies and structures.

What are the prospects for moving from a shareholder to a stakeholder model of corporate governance? The fallout from the financial scandals at AIG, Bear Stearns, and elsewhere raised the issue of corporate ethics and social responsibility while bringing into question the preoccupation with short-term financial results. Whether the shareholder model will change significantly, however, remains to be seen. Nevertheless, discussions of the future of U.S. labor relations should not overlook questions of corporate governance, responsibility, and business norms.[56]

Alternative Directions for the Public Sector

Similar tensions affect the public sector. Paralleling the private sector and public policy trends emphasizing free markets, financial incentives, and financial results since the 1980s, there has been a "New Public Management" movement to bring free market ideas and private-sector management tools to the public sector, such as decentralization, competition among service providers, privatization, outsourcing, and financial incentives. This puts strains on labor relations as unions seek to preserve wages, benefits, and jobs.[57] The financial crisis in 2008 magnified these strains by creating greater budget deficits in the public sector. Under the banner of fiscal austerity, states with Republican governors tried, and in some cases succeeded (e.g., Wisconsin), limiting bargaining rights for public sector workers.[58] Analogous to a continued emphasis on maximizing shareholder value in the private sector, this fiscal-first approach to government is one direction that public sector management can continue to take, with likely continued pressure on public sector workers and unions.

But some have criticized New Public Management and fiscal austerity for their narrow and short-run economic objectives, and instead advocate for approaches that take a broader view of the role of the public sector in promoting diverse public values—not just efficiency but also values related to democracy.[59] This is similar in spirit to arguments for broadening the private sector emphasis from shareholders to stakeholders because both shifts prioritize a broader set of interests. Embracing a public values approach to public sector management would likely result in a different approach to labor relations—one in which workers and their representatives would not only be seen as partners in the delivery of effective public services but more generally as partners in helping to foster public values around fairness, inclusion, participation, and citizenship.[60] So just as in the private sector, those responsible for shaping, leading, and paying for government services should be thinking about the values and norms that are desired, and the implications for strategy and practice.

Online Exploration Exercise: Try to find a state that is considering changing a public sector bargaining law. What positions can you find online in support and opposed to this change? What types of public values are these positions consistent with? In other words, what are the visions of the appropriate role of government that different positions are founded upon?

THE FUTURE OF U.S. LABOR RELATIONS POLICY

Any discussion of the future of U.S. labor relations is incomplete without considering alternative directions for U.S. public policies pertaining to labor relations—in other words, the

Nonunion Application Who Should Govern the Workplace?

Thinking about labor law reform is not just an issue for labor relations professionals. Rather, this is important for nonunion managers and others, too, because questions about labor law reform cannot be separated from the more fundamental question of who should govern the workplace. Recall from Chapter 2 that the question of workplace governance is who gets to make the rules of the workplace? Is it the invisible hand of the labor market? Or management? What about government policymakers through laws and public policies? How about workers themselves? Or employers and employees (or their representatives) together?

Whoever gets to make the rules governs the workplace. So by determining how these rules are made, a country's system of labor law is a critical determinant of workplace governance. If labor law is weak, managers have greater freedom to establish policies and practices unilaterally, rather than negotiating or consulting with employees. If this is the case, should employment law impose standards for certain things, or should society leave decisions in the hands of managers with markets as the only check? Alternatively, strong laws promoting different forms of labor–management negotiations establish joint mechanisms for rule making, such as traditional collective bargaining, consultation via works councils, or other options. This constrains the ability of managers to make unilateral decisions, which some might find beneficial, and others not (recall the alternative perspectives presented in Chapter 2).

In broad terms then, the issue of whether U.S. labor law needs to be reformed is a question of how the workplace should be governed, with broad ramifications for all managers and workers. So ask yourself, how should the workplace be governed? And how is this best achieved? In considering these questions, don't forget to identify the objectives of the employment relationship that you think are important.

question of labor law reform. This is a tremendously important issue with ramifications that extend far beyond the small fraction of U.S. workplaces that are unionized (see the accompanying "Nonunion Application" box). There is perhaps widespread agreement among proponents and opponents of labor unions that U.S. labor law needs to be reformed. U.S. labor law dates back to the 1930s and 1940s. Think of the drastic changes in technology, demographics, industries and occupations, globalization, financialization, and other areas of economic and social life that have occurred since that time. There is certainly good reason to question whether U.S. labor law—and by extension, the current system of workplace governance—still makes sense more than half a century later. In other words, does the existing labor law system continue to produce the desired combination of efficiency, equity, and voice?[61] Many say that the answer to this question is no, and thus they believe that U.S. labor law needs to be reformed. But because of differing beliefs about how the employment relationship works, there are significant disagreements over how labor law should be revised. It is therefore important to consider four major directions for the future of U.S. labor policy: strengthening, deregulating, loosening, or transforming the National Labor Relations Act (NLRA) system (see Figure 13.3). While the discussion here will be in the context of the NLRA, the same alternative directions apply equally well to public sector labor law.

Strengthening the NLRA

Union membership as a fraction of the U.S. workforce—that is, union density—has been declining in the U.S. private sector since the 1950s (recall Chapter 1). One explanation for this decline is that weaknesses in the law allow employers to suppress unionization efforts. Direct evidence for this contention is difficult to obtain, but proponents of this view cite the existence of a representation gap: Significant numbers of employees say they want more workplace representation than they have.[62] Moreover, the union density rate is much higher in the public sector than in the private sector, and it is commonly believed that public sector employers have fewer opportunities to fight unionization than private sector

FIGURE 13.3
Directions for U.S. Labor Law

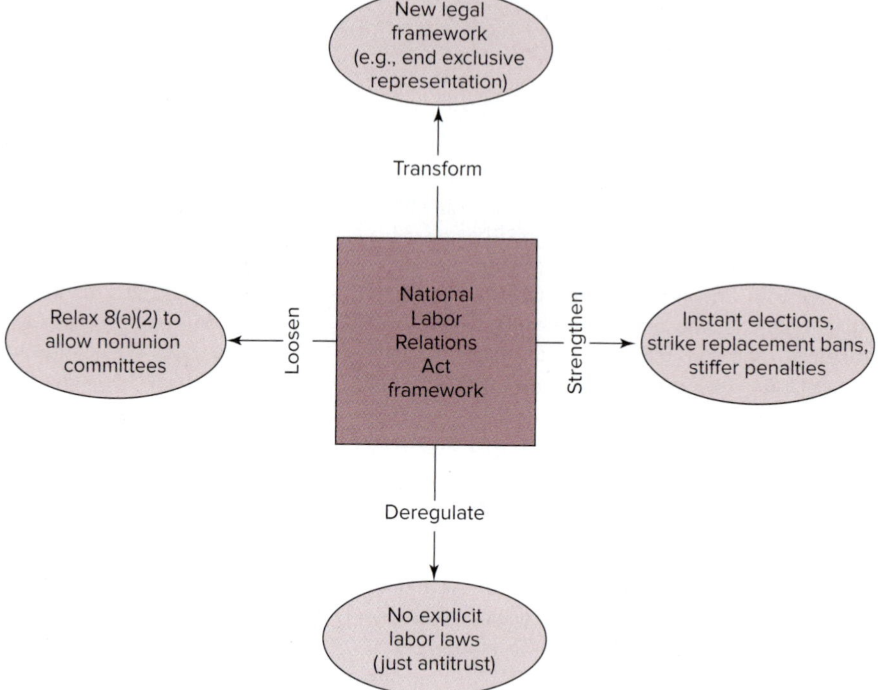

employers—the local board of education cannot threaten to shut down a school and move it to a lower-cost country in response to a union organizing drive. Consequently, organized labor and workers' rights supporters believe that weaknesses in the NLRA are an important cause of the frail health of today's unions. When combined with a pluralist industrial relations view that sees unions as needed counterweights to corporate power, the logical consequence of this thinking is to advocate strengthening the NLRA.

Among those who believe the NLRA needs strengthening, one perspective asserts that the NLRA's weaknesses are the result of decades of unfavorable court decisions that have effectively rewritten the law.[63] In this view, the route to strengthening the NLRA is to educate judges about labor issues and reverse these legal decisions to restore the original intent of the law. More common, however, is the belief that the NLRA's weaknesses stem from management exploitation of the NLRA.[64] In this view, congressional rather than judicial action to revise and amend the NLRA is urgent. Such calls for strengthening the NLRA are increasingly rooted in the argument that the current NLRA framework fails to fulfill international human rights standards pertaining to freedom of association and collective bargaining (recall Chapter 1).[65]

Table 13.2 lists the major options for strengthening the NLRA. It is useful to consider two categories: remedial and substantive changes.[66] Remedial changes include increasing the penalties for violating the NLRA—both monetary penalties and stronger remedial directives such as bargaining orders—and reducing delays in the organizing process that stem from legal challenges. Substantive changes include expanding NLRA coverage to include low-level supervisors, removing restrictions on secondary boycotts, and widening the scope of bargaining items. The two substantive issues that receive the most attention, however, are representation elections and strike replacements.

Criticisms of the election process include problems with delay and the asymmetries between managers and union organizers, especially in access to employees.[67] Recall from Chapter 6 that employers can force employees to listen to their views in captive audience

TABLE 13.2
Strengthening the NLRA: Common Reform Proposals

Remedial Reforms

- *Create strict timetables for unfair labor practice processing* to prevent "justice delayed being justice denied."
- *Penalize violators with fines,* such as triple back pay for illegal firings.
- *Provide immediate reinstatement* of illegally fired workers.
- *Allow bargaining orders* when an employer's illegal actions prevent a union from obtaining majority support.

Substantive Reforms

- *Expand coverage* to include contingent employees, independent contractors, and supervisors.
- *Provide equal access* to employees by unions and managers during organizing drives. Union organizers should be able to give a captive audience speech if management does.
- *Limit management and union campaigning* to prohibit lies and to restrict statements that imply negative consequences (such as a plant closure) will result from supporting a union.
- *Require card check or instant elections* so that certification elections are avoided or occur soon after a petition is filed to remove opportunities for negative campaigning and selective discharges.
- *Require arbitration of first contracts* if bargaining fails to produce a contract for a newly organized unit.
- *Broaden the scope of mandatory bargaining items* to include plant closures, subcontracting, introduction of new technology, and other issues that directly affect working conditions and job security.
- *Ban permanent strike replacements* so that companies can use temporary workers during a strike, but strikers will not lose their jobs. Temporary replacements could also be prohibited from participating in decertification elections.

References: Stephen F. Befort and John W. Budd, *Invisible Hands, Invisible Objectives: Bringing Workplace Law and Public Policy into Focus* (Stanford, CA: Stanford University Press, 2009); Charles B. Craver, *Can Unions Survive? The Rejuvenation of the American Labor Movement* (New York: New York University Press, 1993).

speeches while using private property rights to bar union organizers from the workplace. Union organizers are relegated to trying to contact employees in their homes. Commonly proposed reforms therefore include instant elections or card check recognition procedures that avoid a long and contentious campaigning period, restrictions on management campaigning or equal access to union organizers, punitive damages and immediate reinstatement for illegally discharged union supporters, and first contract arbitration. Many of these reforms have been included in the proposed Employee Free Choice Act, which was organized labor's top legislative priority during the early years of the Obama presidency, but failed to be enacted into law. Others possibilities range from rethinking the legal rules on electronic communication (especially allowing unions to send mass e-mail messages to counter captive audience speeches) to a far-reaching change that would make NLRB elections an automatic, annual occurrence for all workers.[68]

For workers who are already unionized, the biggest perceived weakness in U.S. labor law is the ability of companies to hire permanent replacement workers during a strike (Chapter 8). Because a strike is by far a union's most powerful weapon, critics see the use of permanent replacements as fundamentally stripping the union of its power, thereby reducing collective bargaining to collective begging.[69] The obvious reform proposal from this point of view is to ban the use of permanent strike replacements, though specific proposals vary on whether this ban should be indefinite or for a specific period (such as the first six months of a strike). Note in conclusion that labor law debates over union access and the use of strike replacements involve an important theme in this book: how to balance property rights versus labor rights, and by extension how to balance efficiency, equity, and voice.

Deregulating the NLRA

Directly opposed to the viewpoint that the NLRA should be strengthened is the belief that U.S. labor law should be deregulated—that is, completely repealed or discarded:

> If deregulation in product markets can foster price competition and increase productivity, jobs, and the array of new products and services, why not in [labor] markets too? There are no real intellectual obstacles. It's mostly a matter of superstitions that free labor markets are "different" and exploitative, combined with the familiar tyranny of an entrenched status quo. . . . Whether judged by the criteria of justice, liberty, equality of income, social conflict, or general productivity, the special-interest legislation supporting adversarial unions and compelling employers to deal with them and forcing unwilling workers to be represented by them should be repealed.[70]

This view is strongly rooted in mainstream economics thinking and the closely related philosophy of libertarianism (described in Chapter 5). Recall from Chapter 2 that mainstream economics emphasizes free-market transactions because of the belief that perfect competition maximizes efficiency and aggregate welfare. Monopolies, laws, and other barriers to competition are bad. From this perspective, unions are labor market monopolies that cause harmful economic effects by using strikes to raise wages higher than the competitive market rate.[71] As such, the NLRA reduces aggregate welfare by protecting monopoly unions, forcing unwilling employers to bargain with them, and in some situations making unwilling employees pay union dues.

Rather than strengthening the NLRA, therefore, others support its repeal.[72] Consistent with mainstream economic thought, unions should not be protected by any special legislation. Rather, they should be subject to the same antitrust (antimonopoly) regulations that limit other business organizations from engaging in anticompetitive practices. At the same time, consistent with the libertarian emphasis on individual freedom and liberty, advocates of deregulation generally do not push for legal restrictions on unions beyond antitrust regulations. As long as individuals and unions abide by the common law principles that outlaw fraud, violence, and threats, individuals should be free to *voluntarily* form unions—but not with explicit legal protections. If an employer feels that bargaining with a union is in its best interests, that employer should be free to *voluntarily* bargain. But the law should not compel action because this interferes with free markets and encroaches on individual freedoms. Thus in this viewpoint, the NLRA should be deregulated.

Note that advocates of deregulating labor law interpret the longstanding decline in U.S. union density quite differently than those who support strengthening the NLRA. Whereas the latter group believes that managerial exploitation of NLRA weaknesses is responsible for this decline, deregulation proponents feel that this decline stems from a reduced need and desire for unions among workers. In other words, there has been a decline in the demand for unions.[73] In this view, competitive labor markets force employers to respond to employee needs and to treat them well through human resource management policies. As such, workers are seen as preferring a system of individual rather than collective representation.[74] And if the decline in union density is voluntary (rather than forced by management suppression), there is no need to strengthen the NLRA. In fact, if unions are only monopolies that interfere with competitive markets, then labor law should be deregulated by repealing the NLRA.

Loosening the NLRA

Between two arguments for strengthening or deregulating the NLRA is a compromise position: loosening the NLRA. This view focuses on the NLRA's section 8(a)(2) restriction on company-dominated labor organizations. Recall from Chapter 10 that the NLRA defines labor organizations quite broadly and can include labor–management committees as well as formal unions. In some instances, therefore, workplace committees have been ruled illegal—most notably in the *Electromation* case. To some, these rulings demonstrate that the NLRA needs to be loosened to allow legitimate employee participation mechanisms to give workers a voice and promote cooperation and competitiveness.[75] In other words, labor law is viewed as partially obsolete and no longer in tune with the realities of global competition and flexibility.

The most concrete example of a proposal to loosen the NLRA was the proposed TEAM Act. Though it was never enacted, the TEAM Act sought to modify Section 8(a)(2) to allow labor–management committees that do not seek to negotiate collective bargaining agreements. Critics of a TEAM Act–type loosening of section 8(a)(2) emphasize the ability of employers to manipulate nonunion employee representation plans to prevent the formation of independent unions and therefore label the TEAM Act a "weakening" rather than a "loosening" of labor law.[76] Advocates of reform do not view this as a weakening because of the belief that the NLRA's company union ban unnecessarily restricts some legitimate initiatives that serve both employee and employer interests.[77] With that said, many academic commentators do not want a TEAM Act–type change to undermine workers' abilities to form an independent union when workers prefer this over a nonunion representation plan. It is therefore common for reform proposals for loosening the NLRA by narrowing the scope of Section 8(a)(2) to also include provisions for strengthening the ability of workers to organize a union—such as increased union access to employees, faster representation elections, and steeper penalties for companies that illegally discharge union supporters.[78]

Another possibility is to modify the NLRA to allow for employee committees that monitor employer compliance with employment laws, as is already the case for health and safety committees in numerous states. This would be consistent with trends toward increased corporate self-regulation and self-monitoring, though outside support through an independent monitoring organization might be needed to make these committees effective. If successful, this could provide employees with a platform for participating in employment law compliance tailored to the needs of each workplace; in many companies, this might also grow into a greater voice in shaping broader codes of conduct. Encouragement of these committees could come from providing employers with partial immunity from legal penalties when their compliance program includes effective committees, and from making the establishment of these committees part of a remediation program for employment law violators.[79] This is another example of a labor law reform proposal that would update the NLRA to be more consistent with contemporary trends and would ideally create benefits for employees and employers.

Transforming the NLRA

The fourth possible direction for U.S. labor law is to transform the NLRA into something brand new for the 21st century by completely rewriting labor law. Proponents of this view believe that the New Deal industrial relations system performed admirably in the stable mass manufacturing era immediately following World War II, but that this framework no longer matches the global, competitive environment of the 21st century. Compared to strengthening or loosening the NLRA, the arguments for transforming the NLRA are based on the belief that the NLRA framework is obsolete—a complete overhaul is therefore necessary, and modifications will not suffice. Put differently, transformation proponents believe there is a mismatch between the assumptions of the New Deal industrial relations the world of work in the 21st century. This perspective shares the deregulation camp's desire to repeal the NLRA; but because of their pluralist industrial relations foundation, supporters of a transformation believe new institutions should be created to place checks and balances on free markets. In fact, the strengthening, loosening, and transforming platforms are all rooted in the industrial relations school of thought, but they differ on the form of employee representation that will best provide equity and voice in the environment of the 21st century—traditional unions, a combination of unions and nonunion representation plans, or new forms of unionism, respectively.

Perhaps the primary basis cited for needing to transform the NLRA system into something completely different is **adversarialism,** which is a culture of conflict.[80] In U.S. labor relations, adversarialism is typically equated to traditional distributive negotiations that revolve around a power struggle; every labor–management interaction is a contest of strength, and each side assumes the other is always trying to gain the upper hand. Adversarial U.S. labor relations might stem from inherent conflicts of interest in the employment relationship between labor and management rather than from specific NLRA provisions. But others believe that adversarialism is caused by specific features of U.S. labor law. To these critics, adversarialism is bad for unions and employees because it makes effective representation and job security more difficult to achieve in today's environment; business attacks adversarialism as inimical to developing the level of cooperation needed in a competitive environment.[81] So from this perspective, the adversarial NLRA framework is harmful for both employees and employers in a global economy, and should be discarded and replaced with a completely transformed system.

The NLRA is believed to create a culture of adversarial conflict primarily because of its reliance on exclusive representation and majority support. Because a union must garner the support of a majority of workers to have any workplace rights, the representation process becomes a battle for support between labor and management. To create support for a union, management is attacked as abusive, and an us-versus-them adversarial culture is established. This culture of conflict is perpetuated because existing unions must continue to maintain majority support or be decertified. It is also argued that the NLRA's sharp distinctions between labor and management reinforce an us-versus-them mentality.

As a result, many proposals to transform U.S. labor law would replace or supplement exclusive representation and majority support with alternative arrangements. One option is to provide legal support for nonmajority unions; as noted earlier, these are unions that have the support of a minority rather than a majority of employees in a workplace. This legal support might include full collective bargaining rights for members-only bargaining in which contracts would apply only to members, not the entire bargaining unit. Technically the NLRA might not even need to be reformed because refusing to bargain with a nonmajority union might already be a section 8(a)(1) unfair labor practice (Chapter 4).[82] But explicit legal reform to endorse nonmajority unions is probably necessary to make them a reality. Alternatively, a nonmajority union might be limited to consultation rights; in fact, this arrangement is already in use by U.S. federal government employees (see the accompanying "Labor Relations Application" box discussing consultation rights for federal employees).

A second option is to supplement or replace the certification process with works councils, as are widely found in Europe.[83] The trigger to create a works council is typically significantly less than majority support, and might be quite low—perhaps just a handful of employees wanting a works council would suffice, or they could even be required in all workplaces. Employees would then elect their works councils' representatives from among existing employees; alternatively, workers could be allowed to vote for a variety of representatives—union or professional association leaders, consultants, coworkers, friends, and even managers—and the number of seats on the works council allocated to each type of

Labor Relations Application National Consultation Rights in the U.S. Federal Government

Union representation in the U.S. private sector is an all-or-nothing affair: With majority support, a union is the exclusive representative of all employees and is entitled to bargain over wages, hours, and terms and conditions of employment. But without majority support, unions have few rights. This contrasts sharply with European labor relations in which works councils have codetermination, consultation, and information rights even if only a few workers desire such representation. But for employees of the U.S. federal government, it is possible for a union that represents less than a majority of employees to have consultation rights.

Specifically, the Civil Service Reform Act includes the following:

> Sec. 7113. National consultation rights
>
> (a) If, in connection with any agency, no labor organization has been accorded exclusive recognition on an agency basis, a labor organization which is the exclusive representative of a substantial number of the employees of the agency, as determined in accordance with criteria prescribed by the Authority, shall be granted national consultation rights by the agency. . . .
>
> (b) 1. Any labor organization having national consultation rights in connection with any agency under subsection (a) of this section shall—
>
> (A) be informed of any substantive change in conditions of employment proposed by the agency, and
>
> (B) be permitted reasonable time to present its views and recommendations regarding the changes.
>
> (2) If any views or recommendations are presented under paragraph (1) of this subsection to an agency by any labor organization—
>
> (A) the agency shall consider the views or recommendations before taking final action on any matter with respect to which the views or recommendations are presented; and
>
> (B) the agency shall provide the labor organization a written statement of the reasons for taking the final action.
>
> (C) Nothing in this section shall be construed to limit the right of any agency or exclusive representative to engage in collective bargaining.

The Federal Labor Relations Authority (FLRA) specifies that *substantial number of employees* means at least 3,500 or 10 percent of the civilian employees of a specific government agency (whichever is smaller). Unlike in the U.S. private sector, federal government employees can be represented by a union through consultation if the union represents only 10 percent of the employees.

The U.S. Department of Agriculture (USDA) has consulted with the American Federation of Government Employees (AFGE) and the National Federation of Federal Employees (NFFE) over issues pertaining to equal employment opportunity procedures, reasonable accommodation, telecommuting, mentoring, child care, and tuition subsidies. Other examples of consultation have changed the Veterans Administration's policy of providing nurses with annual wage comparability increases to match the local labor market and a National Guard Bureau's policy allowing National Guard personnel to fill positions previously filled by civilian technicians represented by the National Association of Government Employees (NAGE).

Consultation is not the same as bargaining because management need only consider the union's views; it does not have to reach agreement before acting. Nevertheless, consultation has the potential to provide employee voice when a union does not represent a majority of the employees (as in the U.S. federal sector) or over a broader range of issues than just working conditions (as in Europe).

agent would be proportional to the number of votes received.[84] A works council is typically entitled to jointly determine certain issues and to have information and consultation rights with respect to other issues. In most proposals U.S. works councils would lack the right to strike. The emphasis on joint determination and consultation, rather than bargaining and strikes, underscores the cooperative rather than adversarial aspect of works councils. And giving workers more influence over their work might increase their sense of legitimacy and justice, thereby increasing cooperation and productivity.[85] Before anyone rejects these proposals too quickly, note that some states already require joint labor–management safety and health committees, and in 2013 Volkswagen said that it would welcome a works council at its Chattanooga, Tennessee, plant.

Other elements of a transformation of U.S. labor law might include additional employee rights such as employee free speech, unjust dismissal protections, and the right to workplace information.[86] Transforming U.S. labor law might also involve encouraging employee ownership and representation on corporate boards of directors—for example, through legal changes or tax subsidies.[87] Or it might change the legal conception of bargaining units and items to allow workers from multiple employers in a community to negotiate local standards for wages, portable benefits, and training programs.[88] The most effective transformation will overhaul both employment and labor law to integrate labor relations reform into the broader context of the changing employment relationship—such as the importance of information technologies, flexibility, diversity, work–family conflicts, the growth of contingent employees, and an increased reliance on corporate self-regulation.[89]

All of these same considerations apply to public sector labor law, too. Where it doesn't exist in a particular jurisdiction or for particular employees, should a new law be implemented? If so, in what form? If a public bargaining law exists, is it functioning in desired ways or should it be reformed, and in what ways?

STRATEGIC LABOR RELATIONS AND LEADERSHIP

The previous three sections have an institutional focus: In what directions should labor unions, employer behavior, and labor law move in the future? But questions of future directions for U.S. labor relations also involve individual-level issues for managers and union leaders. Insights from strategic management have been applied to human resource management, and they can be equally useful for management and labor practitioners in private and public sectors labor relations. Human resource managers can be seen as having three roles: builder, change partner, and navigator.[90] The builder assembles the basic components of an organization's human resource management function in a coherent way—staffing, compensation, and the like. The change partner reshapes the human resource functions in response to changes in the external environment, often in partnership with others in the organization. Changing forms of pay and work organization for greater flexibility is a common example. Note that the builder is focused internally on making sure the pieces of the puzzle fit together while the change partner is focused externally on fitting organizational practices with the outside environment. In the third role, the navigator must continuously develop organizational competencies and performance by balancing these internal and external pressures. An effective organization has both flexibility and control, both change and stability, and responsiveness to both the demands of markets and the needs of employees. Each of these contrasts constitutes a duality—a tension that is best managed through balancing rather than choosing one option over the other (as might be the case if either internal or external fit is the sole focus).[91]

This three-part framework is useful for thinking about the roles of labor relations managers and union leaders (see Table 13.3). On the corporate side, managers must build labor relations functions that have high internal fit. Long-term contracts, formalized grievance handling, and adversarial negotiations served mass manufacturing modes of production in which stability and labor costs were important concerns. But as the environment has changed, labor relations managers as change agents must restructure the labor relations function to fit an external environment that demands flexibility and quality in both the private and public sectors. This is a major challenge for contemporary managers. But the third role is the most challenging: Managers must also navigate (or steer) the labor relations function so as to balance the competing internal and external concerns (dualities). It is often difficult to force flexibility onto unionized employees; rather, navigating means negotiating change and creating flexible systems that are also responsive to employee needs. This

TABLE 13.3 The Strategic Roles of Managers and Union Leaders

Role	Major Focus	Labor Relations Managerial Issues	Union Leader Issues
Builder	Internal fit/coherence.	Creating processes for negotiating and administering contracts that fit with other organizational needs.	Building internal competencies like leadership and strategic planning skills to support organizing, bargaining, and other core activities; creating democratic structures.
Change partner	External fit/ responsiveness.	Shaping contracts and labor–management partnerships that promote competitiveness in a global economy.	Creating strategies for representing workers that fit changing demographics, globalization, and other external trends.
Navigator	Balancing competing internal and external pressures (dualities).	Respecting union and employee needs while promoting competitiveness; creating flexibility from union and employee security.	Balancing centralized power with decentralized responsiveness to local needs, control with discretion, and solidarity with individuality.

might require managing the paradox of making unions and employees feel more secure so that they can be more flexible. When making strategic and operational choices, managers should remember that their actions set the tone for the labor-management relationship and thereby help determine whether unionization will be good or bad for the bottom line.[92] So managers should think about the kind of labor-management relationship they want to foster, and appreciate their own role in contributing to this.

Union leaders face these same tasks in managing their own organizations.[93] They must build union structures to fulfill the labor movement's basic functions, such as organizing, bargaining, contract administration, and political lobbying. These structures must be internally consistent; for example, the Justice for Janitors campaigns have emphasized organizing through intense rank-and-file activism, but after bargaining rights have been won, contract negotiations and administration have reverted to traditional methods without significant rank-and-file involvement to the frustration of the workers.[94] These structures must also be consistent with the fact that unions are democratic organizations, and union leaders need to work hard to make sure that they do not become detached from the rank and file. At the same time, unions must build core self-management skills relating to budgeting, strategic planning, and benchmarking.[95]

Union leaders must also be change partners: They must partner with rank-and-file employees to construct new forms of representation that fit changes in the external environment, including greater workforce diversity, higher educational levels, and increased competitive pressures on their employers. The six alternative directions for unions discussed earlier in this chapter are all responses to the external environment.

Finally, union leaders must be navigators to balance the dualities created by internal and external pressures. Important dualities in labor unions include the tension between organizing new members and servicing existing members, between providing guidance and letting workers handle matters, between centralized power and decentralized responsiveness to local conditions, between centralized control and democratic participation, and between solidarity across workplaces and concern for individual needs.

This book can help make you a more effective private or public sector management or union leader by understanding the dualities that need to be navigated. By studying labor relations in a framework that recognizes multiple perspectives or schools of thought on the employment relationship, you can better understand others with whom you may interact in the workplace—managers, union leaders, employees, and government officials. Without needing to agree with all alternative viewpoints, this understanding will make you a better leader. Leadership issues were also discussed in Chapters 7 and 10 in the context of resistance to change and strategies for change in moving to integrative bargaining and to more flexible work systems. Finally, the ethical framework presented in this book has important ramifications for effective leadership (see the "Ethics in Action" case at the end of this chapter).

STRIKING A BALANCE

A major goal of this book has been to present an intellectual framework for understanding labor relations that provides an effective foundation not only for understanding the development and operation of the New Deal industrial relations system and how current U.S. labor relations processes work but also for critically evaluating this system, these processes, and the need for reform. To do this, we need to go beyond an examination of how the processes work (though this is important) and ask what the processes are trying to accomplish. Studying any aspect of the employment relationship, in fact, should be rooted in the objectives of the employment relationship: efficiency, equity, and voice. Efficiency is the effective use of labor to promote competitiveness, cost-effective service delivery, and economic prosperity; equity encompasses fair labor standards in both material outcomes and personal treatment; and voice is the ability to have meaningful input into decisions.

The framework for studying labor relations used in this book is therefore how employee representation—typically through independent labor unions—contributes to the achievement of efficiency, equity, and voice. The goal of the U.S. labor relations system is to balance efficiency, equity, and voice through balancing property rights and labor rights (Part One). Laws, processes, and behaviors should seek to handle employment relationship conflict and power imbalances between employees and employers in ways that promote effective private and public sector organizations, a healthy economy, equitable outcomes, respect for human dignity, and fulfillment of the principles of democracy. In the language of the previous section, labor relations and labor law must navigate a number of critical dualities: tensions between property rights and labor rights, between work rules and flexibility, between bilateral negotiation and unilateral control, and among efficiency, equity, and voice.

Different schools of thought about the nature of the employment relationship have varying beliefs about the best way to fulfill these goals.[96] Mainstream economic thought emphasizes providing the greatest good for the greatest number through free-market exchange; the foundation of this thinking is perfect competition. The human resource management school focuses on management-led policies and practices that can simultaneously benefit employers and employees; this perspective is rooted in unitarist employment relationship conflict. Critical, or Marxist, industrial relations emphasize radically changing capitalist institutions to give workers more control in the workplace and throughout society. The basis for this school of thought is conflict between labor and capital that is pervasive throughout society—not narrow economic conflict limited to the employment relationship. Mainstream U.S. industrial relations focus on adding institutional checks and balances to the employment relationship in the private and public sectors. This perspective is rooted in pluralist employment relationship conflict—conflict that includes some win–win opportunities for mutual gain and some win–lose, zero-sum clashes of interests.

The New Deal industrial relations system is a crucial centerpiece of the pluralist industrial relations system of employment relationship checks and balances. U.S. labor law explicitly protects workers' rights to form unions and collectively bargain because it is believed that these protections balance efficiency, equity, and voice.[97] Efficiency is served through industrial peace and increased consumer purchasing power through increased labor bargaining power. Efficiency is also promoted through the relatively limited incursions of labor law: Employee rights are confined to wages and working conditions, not organizational decision making, and rather than a government bureaucracy imposing specific outcomes, the parties fashion their own agreements to shape their particular circumstances. Equity is fulfilled through collective rather than individual labor power to better equalize corporate bargaining power. This collective power can prevent exploitation (recall the labor problem of the early 20th century from Chapter 2), promote a more equitable distribution of economic rewards, and provide economic security. Voice is achieved by replacing unilateral managerial authority with the requirement that employee issues be negotiated with employee representatives. As such, workers have input into decisions that affect them. Understanding the major processes of the U.S. labor relations system—union organizing, bargaining contracts, resolving conflicts, and administering grievances—was therefore the major goal of Part Two of this book.

But as we discussed in Part Three, the traditional operation of processes such as adversarial negotiations and the typical postwar outcomes such as detailed contracts are under heavy pressure to change in both the private and public sectors because of global competition, financialization, and the need for workplace flexibility, employee involvement, and labor–management partnerships. The New Deal industrial relations system's processes and work rules are not important in their own right—they are important only to the extent that they promote efficiency, equity, and voice. Labor relations processes are means to greater ends, not untouchable ends in themselves. As such, Part Four of this book discussed various alternatives to the traditional New Deal system for promoting efficiency, equity, and voice. Understanding the current system, the role of labor unions, and future systems of employee representation all require appreciation of the same fundamental principle: striking a balance.

The major concluding question of this book is therefore what type of system for governing the workplace—and in particular, what form(s) of employee representation—will best achieve the goals of the employment relationship in the economic, social, technological, and global environment of the 21st century. The Occupy and Fight for $15 movements have drawn attention to the importance of this type of deep question. Creating the ideal system will likely require changing union and corporate strategies, visions of government, social norms, and public policies—changes that will be shaped by the choices that all of us make as workers, managers, consumers, investors, taxpayers, and citizens. With respect to policy, there are four major possible directions for U.S. labor law in the 21st century: The NLRA (and public sector labor law) can be strengthened, deregulated, loosened, or transformed. Note how these different directions imply different systems of workplace governance—a continued reliance on traditional labor unions, a renewed emphasis on free markets, greater forms of nonunion employee representation, or some new model of representation, respectively. As such, labor law reform cannot and should not be separated from the larger question of how employment relationships of the future will be structured.

Furthermore, as described in Chapter 11, international debates over free trade, fair trade, and other issues in the global economy are closely related to issues of governing the global workplace and the viability of domestic unions. And there are also various options for changing corporate governance structures and expectations surrounding corporate social responsibility, or the nature of public value in the public sector. These issues are closely interrelated, and the direction of reforms should be mutually supporting rather than addressed in isolation from each other. Put differently, a free trade model of global governance and the continued primacy of shareholders in corporate governance or of budget austerity in the public sector can potentially undermine systems of workplace governance that seek a balance between employers and employees. These linkages should not be overlooked—workplace practices, labor laws, corporate governance or public value norms, and international treaties must work together to strike a balance.

Finally, in considering the various aspects of what labor relations should do in the future and the various perspectives on the need to potentially reform labor unions, corporate and public sector agency behavior, and labor law, there is the difficult question of law versus behavior. If U.S. labor law is a major determinant of outcomes, the law likely needs to be changed. But if the law provides only the broad skeleton of the system and various outcomes are possible, then perhaps behavior—not the law—needs reforming. To wit, if the union density decline stems from weaknesses in the NLRA or public sector labor law, many argue that legal reform is needed. But if the union density decline reflects a lack of worker demand for unionization, what probably needs reform is union behavior rather than the law. As a second example, does the NLRA or public sector labor law force labor and management into an adversarial relationship with little employee involvement and flexibility? Perhaps. But there are notable examples under the NLRA and public sector labor law of productive labor–management partnerships. As such, is it the law or behavior—of both labor and management—that needs reforming? Like many other things in labor relations, the truth likely lies in the middle, and thus a careful examination of multiple perspectives is required.

Key Terms

solidarity unionism, *466*
nonmajority union, *468*
social movement unionism, *469*
efficiency-enhancing unionism, *471*
employee ownership unionism, *472*
employee empowerment unionism, *472*
associational unionism, *473*
stakeholder model, *477*
adversarialism, *484*

Reflection Questions

1. Employers commonly try to portray unions in a negative light by characterizing them as outside third-party organizations. Is this accurate if unions are composed of employees? Describe how the pluralist industrial relations school of thought sees value in having a union as both an outsider and an insider. In what direction(s) should U.S. labor unions go to serve these roles in the 21st century?
2. What is a corporation's social responsibility? Are there corporate labor relations practices that should be unacceptable? If so, how should these standards be enforced?
3. Many argue that U.S. labor relations are broadly characterized by adversarialism. In what ways is adversarialism the result of U.S. labor law? In what ways is adversarialism caused by the behavior of companies and unions rather than by the legal system?
4. Is it still necessary for laws to promote and protect some form of unionism? If so, outline any needed reforms to U.S. labor law. Does your answer differ if you focus on the private sector or the public sector?

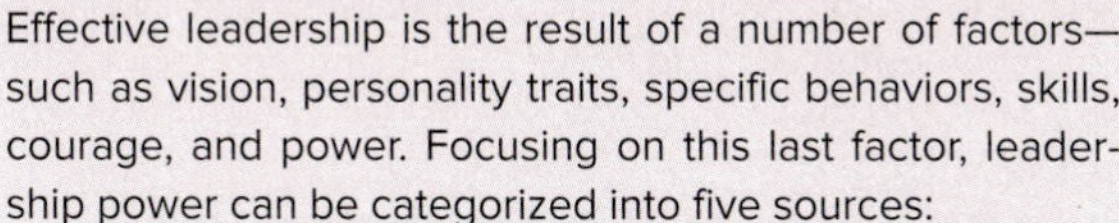

Ethics in Action Leadership in Turbulent Times

Effective leadership is the result of a number of factors—such as vision, personality traits, specific behaviors, skills, courage, and power. Focusing on this last factor, leadership power can be categorized into five sources:

- *Legitimate power:* The authority or right to order someone to do something (followers comply because they have to).
- *Reward power:* Influence that comes from the ability to hand out rewards (followers comply to obtain rewards).
- *Coercive power:* Influence that comes from the ability to hand out punishments (followers comply to avoid punishments).
- *Referent power:* Influence that derives from appealing personal characteristics (followers comply because of admiration or emulation).
- *Expert power:* Influence that stems from knowledge and expertise (followers comply because they believe the action is wise).

Labor relations constrain some of these sources of power. Labor law denies managers and union leaders the legitimate power to order individuals to support or not support a labor union and similarly bans the use of reward and coercive power to influence support for a union. Union contracts often specify limitations on management's legitimate, reward, and coercive power—discipline and discharge must be conducted with just cause, and rewards are often seniority-based.

But these are turbulent times for labor relations. The institutions of labor relations—both labor law and unions—are widely regarded as weak. As such, in many cases these restrictions on a manager's power are more theoretical than real. At the same time, managers are under great pressure in a hypercompetitive global economy.

QUESTIONS

1. Provide labor relations examples of a manager's use of these five types of power that would support good leadership. Provide labor relations examples in which uses of these five types of power would undermine good leadership.
2. It is often argued that integrity is a key component of good leadership and that leaders should adhere to high ethical standards. Why?
3. With weak labor laws and labor unions, is it more or less important that leaders have high ethical standards?

Reference: The five sources of leadership power are from Thomas S. Bateman and Scott A. Snell, *Management: Competing in the New Era,* 5th ed. (Boston: McGraw-Hill/Irwin, 2002).

End Notes

1. David Brody, "Labor's Crisis in Historical Perspective," in George Strauss, Daniel G. Gallagher, and Jack Fiorito (eds.), *The State of the Unions* (Madison, WI: Industrial Relations Research Association, 1991), pp. 277–311; Richard W. Hurd and John Bunge, "Unionization of Professional and Technical Workers: The Labor Market and Institutional Transformation," in Richard Freeman, Joni Hersch, and Lawrence Mishel (eds.), *Emerging Labor Market Institutions for the Twenty-First Century* (Chicago: University of Chicago Press, 2005), pp. 179–206.
2. Samuel Bacharach, Peter Bamberger, and William Sonnenstuhl, *Mutual Aid and Union Renewal: Cycles of Logics of Action* (Ithaca, NY: Cornell University Press, 2001); Jane McAlevey with Bob Ostertag, *Raising Expectations (and Raising Hell): My Decade Fighting for the Labor Movement* (London: Verso, 2012).
3. Thomas A. Kochan, *Restoring the American Dream: A Working Families' Agenda for America* (Cambridge, MA: MIT Press, 2005).
4. Michael C. Harper, "A Framework for the Rejuvenation of the American Labor Movement," *Indiana Law Journal* 76 (Winter 2001), pp. 103–33 at 104.
5. Kate Bronfenbrenner et al. (eds.), *Organizing to Win: New Research on Union Strategies* (Ithaca, NY: ILR Press, 1998); Ray M. Tillman and Michael S. Cummings (eds.), *The Transformation of U.S. Unions: Voices, Visions, and Strategies from the Grassroots* (Boulder, CO: Lynne Rienner Publishers, 1999).
6. Immanuel Ness, *Immigrants, Unions, and the New U.S. Labor Market* (Philadelphia: Temple University Press, 2005); Ruth Milkman and Ed Ott (eds.), *New Labor in New York: Precarious Worker Organizing and the Future of Unionism* (Ithaca, NY: Cornell University Press, 2014).
7. Joe Burns, *Reviving the Strike: How Working People Can Regain Power and Transform America* (Brooklyn: Ig Publishing, 2011); Jane Slaughter (ed.), *A Troublemaker's Handbook 2: How to Fight Back Where You Work—and Win!* (Detroit: Labor Notes, 2005).
8. Andy Banks and Jack Metzgar, "Participating in Management: Union Organizing on a New Terrain," *Labor Research Review* 14 (Fall 1989), pp. 1–55; Bill Fletcher Jr. and Richard W. Hurd, "Beyond the Organizing Model: The Transformation Process in Local Unions," in Kate Bronfenbrenner et al. (eds.), *Organizing to Win: New Research on Union Strategies* (Ithaca, NY: ILR Press, 1998), pp. 37–53.
9. Bill Barry, *Union Strategies for Hard Times*, 2nd ed. (Annapolis: Union Communication Services, 2011); Tillman and Cummings, *The Transformation of U.S. Unions*; Bill Fletcher Jr. and Fernando Gapasin, *Solidarity Divided: The Crisis in Organized Labor and a New Path toward Social Justice* (Berkeley: University of California Press, 2008). Michael Schiavone, *Unions in Crisis? The Future of Organized Labor in America* (Westport, CT: Praeger, 2008); McAlevey, *Raising Expectations (and Raising Hell).*
10. Rich Yeselson, "Fortress Unionism," *Democracy* 29 (Summer 2013).
11. Ness, *Immigrants, Unions, and the New U.S. Labor Market.*
12. Dorothy Sue Cobble, *Dishing It Out: Waitresses and Their Unions in the Twentieth Century* (Urbana: University of Illinois Press, 1991); Dorothy Sue Cobble, "Lost Ways of Unionism: Historical Perspectives on Reinventing the Labor Movement," in Lowell Turner, Harry C. Katz, and Richard W. Hurd (eds.), *Rekindling the Movement: Labor's Quest for Relevance in the Twenty-First Century* (Ithaca, NY: ILR Press, 2001), pp. 82–96.
13. Tillman and Cummings, *The Transformation of U.S. Unions*; Fletcher and Gapasin, *Solidarity Divided*; Schiavone, *Unions in Crisis?*
14. Jo McBride and Ian Greenwood (eds.), *Community Unionism: A Comparative Analysis of Concepts and Contexts* (New York: Palgrave Macmillan, 2009); Amanda Tattersall, *Power in Coalition: Strategies for Strong Unions and Social Change* (Ithaca, NY: Cornell University Press, 2010); McAlevey, *Raising Expectations (and Raising Hell).*
15. Gregory Mantsios (ed.), *A New Labor Movement for the New Century* (New York: Garland, 1998); Kim Moody, *An Injury to All: The Decline of American Unionism* (London: Verso, 1988); Aldon Morris and Dan Clawson, "Lessons of the Civil Rights Movement for Building a Worker Rights Movement," *Working USA* 8 (Winter 2005), pp. 683–704; Tillman and Cummings, *The Transformation of U.S. Unions;* Dan Clawson, *The Next Upsurge: Labor and the New Social Movements* (Ithaca, NY: Cornell University Press, 2003); Rick Fantasia and Kim Voss, *Hard Work: Remaking the American Labor Movement* (Berkeley: University of California Press, 2004); Fletcher and Gapasin, *Solidarity Divided*; Schiavone, *Unions in Crisis?*
16. Stephen Lerner, Jill Hurst, and Glenn Adler, "Fighting and Winning in the Outsourced Economy: Justice for Janitors at the University of Miami," in Annette Bernhardt et al. (eds.), *The Gloves-Off Economy: Workplace Standards at the Bottom of America's Labor Market* (Champaign, IL: Labor and Employment Relations Association, 2008), pp. 243–67; Roger Waldinger et al., "Helots No More: A Case Study of the Justice for Janitors Campaign in Los Angeles," in Kate Bronfenbrenner et al. (eds.),

Organizing to Win: New Research on Union Strategies (Ithaca, NY: ILR Press, 1998), pp. 102–19; Jane Williams, "Restructuring Labor's Identity: The Justice for Janitors Campaign in Washington, D.C.," in Ray M. Tillman and Michael S. Cummings (eds.), *The Transformation of U.S. Unions: Voices, Visions, and Strategies from the Grassroots* (Boulder, CO: Lynne Rienner Publishers, 1999), pp. 203–17.

17. Williams, "Restructuring Labor's Identity," p. 212.
18. Ronald Peters and Theresa Merrill, "Clergy and Religious Persons' Roles in Organizing at O'Hare Airport and St. Joseph Medical Center," in Kate Bronfenbrenner et al. (eds.), *Organizing to Win: New Research on Union Strategies* (Ithaca, NY: ILR Press, 1998), pp. 164–77.
19. Josh Eidelson, "Alt-Labor," *American Prospect* (January 29, 2013); Janice Fine, *Worker Centers: Organizing Communities at the Edge of the Dream* (Ithaca, NY: Cornell University Press, 2006); Janice Fine, "Alternative Labour Protection Movements in the United States: Reshaping Industrial Relations?" *International Labour Review* 154 (March 2015), pp. 15–26.
20. Sharon Kurtz, *Workplace Justice: Organizing Multi-Identity Movements* (Minneapolis: University of Minnesota Press, 2002); José La Luz and Paula Finn, "Getting Serious about Inclusion: A Comprehensive Approach," in Gregory Mantsios (ed.), *A New Labor Movement for the New Century* (New York: Garland, 1998), pp. 197–211; Ruth Milkman (ed.), *Organizing Immigrants: The Challenge for Unions in Contemporary California* (Ithaca, NY: ILR Press, 2000); Ruth Needleman, "Women Workers: Strategies for Inclusion and Rebuilding Unionism," in Gregory Mantsios (ed.), *A New Labor Movement for the New Century* (New York: Garland, 1998), pp. 175–96; Ness, *Immigrants, Unions, and the New U.S. Labor Market.*
21. Taylor E. Dark, *The Unions and the Democrats: An Enduring Alliance* (Ithaca, NY: ILR Press, 2001); Nelson Lichtenstein, *State of the Union: A Century of American Labor* (Princeton, NJ: Princeton University Press); 2013 Robert H. Zieger and Gilbert J. Gall, *American Workers, American Unions: The Twentieth Century,* 3rd ed. (Baltimore: Johns Hopkins Press, 2002).
22. Tony Mazzocchi, "Building a Party of Our Own," in Gregory Mantsios (ed.), *A New Labor Movement for the New Century* (New York: Garland, 1998), pp. 281–93.
23. Jennifer Jihye Chun, *Organizing at the Margins: The Symbolic Politics of Labor in South Korea and the United States* (Ithaca, NY: Cornell University Press, 2009).
24. John W. Budd, *The Thought of Work* (Ithaca, NY: Cornell University Press, 2011).
25. Barry Bluestone and Irving Bluestone, *Negotiating the Future: A Labor Perspective on American Business* (New York: Basic Books, 1992).
26. Bluestone and Bluestone, *Negotiating the Future,* pp. 24–25 (emphases in original).
27. Bluestone and Bluestone, *Negotiating the Future,* p. 26.
28. Peter Lazes and Jane Savage, "New Unionism and the Workplace of the Future," in Bruce Nissen (ed.), *Unions and Workplace Reorganization* (Detroit: Wayne State University Press, 1997), pp. 181–207; Mike Parker and Jane Slaughter, "Advancing Unionism on the New Terrain," in Nissen (ed.), *Unions and Workplace Reorganization,* pp. 208–25.
29. Eric Parker and Joel Rogers, "Building the High Road in Metro Areas: Sectoral Training and Employment Projects," in Lowell Turner, Harry C. Katz, and Richard W. Hurd (eds.), *Rekindling the Movement: Labor's Quest for Relevance in the Twenty-First Century* (Ithaca, NY: ILR Press, 2001), pp. 256–72.
30. Hoyt N. Wheeler, *The Future of the American Labor Movement* (Cambridge, England: Cambridge University Press, 2002). Joseph R. Blasi, Richard B. Freeman, and Douglas L. Kruse, "Employee Stock Ownership and Profit Sharing in the New Era of Financialization and Inequality in the Distribution of Capital Income," in Christian E. Weller (ed.), *Inequality, Uncertainty, and Opportunity: The Varied and Growing Role of Finance in Labor Relations* (Champaign, IL: Labor and Employment Relations Association, 2015), pp. 225–46.
31. Joseph R. Blasi and Douglas L. Kruse, *The New Owners: The Mass Emergence of Employee Ownership in Public Companies and What It Means to American Business* (New York: HarperBusiness, 1991), p. 245.
32. Robin Blackburn, *Banking on Death or Investing in Life: The History and Future of Pensions* (London: Verso, 2002); Archon Fung, Tessa Hebb, and Joel Rogers (eds.), *Working Capital: The Power of Labor's Pensions* (Ithaca, NY: Cornell University Press, 2001).
33. Marleen O'Connor, "Labor's Role in the Shareholder Revolution," in Archon Fung, Tessa Hebb, and Joel Rogers (eds.), *Working Capital: The Power of Labor's Pensions* (Ithaca, NY: Cornell University Press, 2001), pp. 67–92; Andrew K. Prevost, Ramesh P. Rao, and Melissa A. Williams, "Labor Unions as Shareholder Activists: Champions or Detractors?" *Financial Review* 47 (May 2012), pp. 327–49.
34. Michael Calabrese, "Building on Success: Labor-Friendly Investment Vehicles and the Power of Private Equity," in Archon Fung, Tessa Hebb, and Joel Rogers (eds.), *Working Capital: The Power*

of Labor's Pensions (Ithaca, NY: Cornell University Press, 2001), pp. 93–127. Michael A. McCarthy, "Turning Labor into Capital: Pension Funds and the Corporate Control of Finance," *Politics & Society* 42 (December 2014), pp. 455–87.

35. Cobble, "Lost Ways of Unionism"; Charles C. Heckscher, *The New Unionism: Employee Involvement in the Changing Corporation* (New York: Basic Books, 1988).
36. John W. Budd, *Employment with a Human Face: Balancing Efficiency, Equity, and Voice* (Ithaca, NY: Cornell University Press, 2004).
37. John Hoerr, *We Can't Eat Prestige: The Women Who Organized Harvard* (Philadelphia: Temple University Press, 1997).
38. Heckscher, *The New Unionism.*
39. Martha King, "Protecting and Representing Workers in the New Gig Economy: The Case of the Freelancers Union," in Ruth Milkman and Ed Ott (eds.), *New Labor in New York: Precarious Worker Organizing and the Future of Unionism* (Ithaca, NY: Cornell University Press, 2014), pp. 150–70.
40. Milton Friedman, *Capitalism and Freedom* (Chicago: University of Chicago Press, 1962), p. 133.
41. Margaret M. Blair, *Ownership and Control: Rethinking Corporate Governance for the Twenty-First Century* (Washington, DC: Brookings, 1995); Mary O'Sullivan, *Contests for Corporate Control: Corporate Governance and Economic Performance in the United States and Germany* (Oxford: Oxford University Press, 2000); Sanford M. Jacoby, *The Embedded Corporation: Corporate Governance and Employment Relations in Japan and the United States* (Princeton, NJ: Princeton University Press, 2005).
42. C.A. Harwell Wells, "The Cycles of Corporate Social Responsibility: An Historical Retrospective for the Twenty-first Century," *Kansas Law Review* 51 (November 2002), pp. 77–140.
43. Marjorie Kelly, *The Divine Right of Capital: Dethroning the Corporate Aristocracy* (San Francisco: Berrett-Koehler, 2001); William Lazonick and Mary O'Sullivan, "Maximizing Shareholder Value: A New Ideology for Corporate Governance," *Economy and Society* 29 (February 2000), pp. 13–35; O'Sullivan, *Contests for Corporate Control.*
44. Ronald Dore, "Financialization of the Global Economy," *Industrial and Corporate Change* 17 (December 2008), pp. 1097–112; Natascha van der Zwan, "Making Sense of Financialization," *Socio-Economic Review* 12 (January 2014), pp. 99–129; Gerald F. Davis, *Managed by the Markets: How Finance Reshaped America* (New York: Oxford University Press, 2009).
45. William Lazonick, "Labor in the Twenty-First Century: The Top 0.1% and the Disappearing Middle-Class," in Christian E. Weller (ed.), *Inequality, Uncertainty, and Opportunity: The Varied and Growing Role of Finance in Labor Relations* (Champaign, IL: Labor and Employment Relations Association, 2015), pp. 143–95.
46. Ron Blum and Peter Rossman, "Leveraged Buyouts, Restructuring and Collective Bargaining," *International Journal of Labour Research* 1 (2009), pp. 159–770; Eileen Appelbaum and Rosemary Batt, *Private Equity at Work: When Wall Street Manages Main Street* (New York: Russell Sage Foundation, 2014).
47. Lazonick, "Labor in the Twenty-First Century"; O'Sullivan, *Contests for Corporate Control.*
48. Norman E. Bowie, *Business Ethics: A Kantian Perspective* (Malden, MA: Blackwell, 1999); Kelly, *The Divine Right of Capital;* Robert C. Solomon, *Ethics and Excellence: Cooperation and Integrity in Business* (New York: Oxford University Press, 1992); Joel Bakan, *The Corporation: The Pathological Pursuit of Profit and Power* (New York: Free Press, 2004).
49. E. Merrick Dodd Jr., "For Whom Are Corporate Managers Trustees?" *Harvard Law Review* 45 (May 1932), pp. 1145–63.
50. Randy Hodson, *Dignity at Work* (Cambridge: Cambridge University Press, 2001); Frank Koller, *Spark: How Old-Fashioned Values Drive a Twenty-First-Century Corporation* (New York: PublicAffairs, 2010); Michael A. Santoro, *Profits and Principles: Global Capitalism and Human Rights in China* (Ithaca, NY: Cornell University Press, 2000).
51. Budd, *Employment with a Human Face.*
52. http://www.unglobalcompact.org.
53. David Weissbrodt, "Principles Relating to the Human Rights Conduct of Companies," E/CN.4/Sub.2/2000/WG.2/WP.1 (New York: United Nations Commission on Human Rights, 2000), p. 4.
54. Blair, *Ownership and Control*; Thomas Donaldson and Lee E. Preston, "The Stakeholder Theory of the Corporation: Concepts, Evidence, and Implications," *Academy of Management Review* 20 (January 1995), pp. 65–91; R. Edward Freeman, *Strategic Management: A Stakeholder Approach* (Boston: Pitman, 1984).

55. Michael Gold, "'Taken on Board': An Evaluation of the Influence of Employee Board-Level Representatives on Company Decision-Making Across Europe," *European Journal of Industrial Relations* 17 (March 2011), pp. 41–56; Raymond Markey, Nicola Balnave, and Greg Patmore, "Worker Directors and Worker Ownership / Cooperatives," in Adrian Wilkinson et al. (eds.), *The Oxford Handbook of Participation in Organizations* (Oxford: Oxford University Press, 2010), pp. 237–57.
56. Jacoby, *The Embedded Corporation;* Sanford M. Jacoby, "Finance and Labor: Perspectives on Risk, Inequality, and Democracy," *Comparative Labor Law and Policy Journal* 30 (Fall 2008), pp. 17–65.
57. Robert Hebdon, Joseph E. Slater, and Marick F. Masters, "Public Sector Collective Bargaining: Tumultuous Times," in Howard R. Stanger, Paul F. Clark, and Ann C. Frost (eds.), *Collective Bargaining under Duress: Case Studies of Major North American Industries* (Champaign, IL: Labor and Employment Relations Association, 2013), pp. 255–95.
58. Hebdon, Slater, and Masters, "Public Sector Collective Bargaining"; Richard B. Freeman and Eunice Han, "The War Against Public Sector Collective Bargaining in the US," *Journal of Industrial Relations* 54 (June 2012), pp. 386–408.
59. John M. Bryson, Barbara C. Crosby, Laura Bloomberg, "Public Value Governance: Moving Beyond Traditional Public Administration and the New Public Management," *Public Administration Review* 74 (July/August 2014), pp. 445–56.
60. John W. Budd, "Implicit Public Values and the Creation of Publicly Valuable Outcomes: The Importance of Work and the Contested Role of Labor Unions," *Public Administration Review* 74 (July/August 2014), pp. 506–16.
61. Stephen F. Befort and John W. Budd, *Invisible Hands, Invisible Objectives: Bringing Workplace Law and Public Policy into Focus* (Stanford, CA: Stanford University Press, 2009).
62. Richard B. Freeman and Joel Rogers, *What Workers Want*, updated ed. (Ithaca, NY: ILR Press, 2006); Richard B. Freeman and Joel Rogers, "Who Speaks for Us? Employee Representation in a Nonunion Labor Market," in Bruce E. Kaufman and Morris M. Kleiner (eds.), *Employee Representation: Alternatives and Future Directions* (Madison, WI: Industrial Relations Research Association, 1993), pp. 13–80; Seymour Martin Lipset and Noah M. Meltz, with Rafael Gomez and Ivan Katchanovski, *The Paradox of American Unionism: Why Americans Like Unions More Than Canadians Do But Join Much Less* (Ithaca, NY: Cornell University Press, 2004).
63. Ellen Dannin, *Taking Back the Workers' Law: How to Fight the Assault on Labor Rights* (Ithaca, NY: Cornell University Press, 2006).
64. Stephen F. Befort, "Labor and Employment Law at the Millennium: A Historical Review and Critical Assessment," *Boston College Law Review* 43 (March 2002), pp. 351–460; Charles B. Craver, *Can Unions Survive? The Rejuvenation of the American Labor Movement* (New York: New York University Press, 1993); Julius G. Getman, *Restoring the Power of Unions: It Takes a Movement* (New Haven, CT: Yale University Press, 2010).
65. Human Rights Watch, *Unfair Advantage: Workers' Freedom of Association in the United States under International Human Rights Standards* (Washington, DC, 2000); Roy J. Adams, "Collective Bargaining as a Minimum Employment Standard," *Economic and Labour Relations Review* 22 (July 2011), pp. 153–64; James A. Gross, *A Shameful Business: The Case for Human Rights in the American Workplace* (Ithaca, NY: Cornell University Press, 2010).
66. Craver, *Can Unions Survive?*
67. Befort and Budd, *Invisible Hands, Invisible Objectives*; Craver, *Can Unions Survive?*; Cynthia L. Estlund, "Labor, Property, and Sovereignty after *Lechmere*," *Stanford Law Review* 46 (January 1994), pp. 305–59; Getman, *Restoring the Power of Unions*; Paul Weiler, "Promises to Keep: Securing Workers' Rights to Self-Organization under the NLRA," *Harvard Law Review* 96 (June 1983), pp. 1769–827.
68. Jeffrey M. Hirsch, "The Silicon Bullet: Will the Internet Kill the NLRA?" *George Washington Law Review* 76 (February 2008), pp. 262–304; Michael M. Oswalt, "Automatic Elections," *UC Irvine Law Review* 4 (May 2014), pp. 801–56.
69. Craver, *Can Unions Survive*?; Samuel Estreicher, "Collective Bargaining or 'Collective Begging'?: Reflections on Antistrikebreaker Legislation," *Michigan Law Review* 93 (December 1994), pp. 577–608; Befort and Budd, *Invisible Hands, Invisible Objectives*; Getman, *Restoring the Power of Unions*; Paul Weiler, "Striking a New Balance: Freedom of Contract and the Prospects for Union Representation," *Harvard Law Review* 98 (December 1984), pp. 351–420.
70. Morgan Reynolds, "A New Paradigm: Deregulating Labor Relations," *Journal of Labor Research* 17 (Winter 1996), pp. 121–28 at 123.
71. Evergreen Freedom Foundation, "Sweeping the Shop Floor: A New Labor Model for America" (Olympia, WA, 2010); Milton Friedman and Rose Friedman, *Free to Choose: A Personal Statement*

(New York: Harcourt Brace Jovanovich, 1980); Dan C. Heldman, James T. Bennett, and Manuel H. Johnson, *Deregulating Labor Relations* (Dallas: Fisher Institute, 1981); Morgan O. Reynolds, *Power and Privilege: Labor Unions in America* (New York: Universe Books, 1984).

72. Richard A. Epstein, "A Common Law for Labor Relations: A Critique of the New Deal Labor Legislation," *Yale Law Journal* 92 (July 1983), pp. 1357–408; Evergreen Freedom Foundation, "Sweeping the Shop Floor"; Heldman, Bennett, and Johnson, *Deregulating Labor Relations*; Reynolds, *Power and Privilege;* Morgan O. Reynolds, *Making America Poorer: The Cost of Labor Law* (Washington, DC: Cato Institute, 1987); Reynolds, "A New Paradigm."

73. Henry S. Farber and Alan B. Krueger, "Union Membership in the United States: The Decline Continues," in Bruce E. Kaufman and Morris M. Kleiner (eds.), *Employee Representation: Alternatives and Future Directions* (Madison, WI: Industrial Relations Research Association, 1993), pp. 105–34; Robert Flanagan, "Has Management Strangled U.S. Unions?" in James T. Bennett and Bruce E. Kaufman (eds.), *What Do Unions Do? A Twenty-Year Perspective* (New Brunswick, NJ: Transaction Publishers, 2007), pp. 459–91.

74. Leo Troy, *Beyond Unions and Collective Bargaining* (Armonk, NY: M. E. Sharpe, 1999).

75. Edward E. Potter and Judith A. Youngman, *Keeping America Competitive: Employment Policy for the Twenty-First Century* (Lakewood, CO: Glenbridge Publishing, 1995); Karl G. Nelson "Moving Beyond the Zero-Sum Game: Joint Management-Employee Committees in the Twenty-First Century," *Indiana Law Journal* 87 (Winter 2012), pp. 119–122.

76. Jonathan P. Hiatt and Laurence E. Gold, "Employer–Employee Committees: A Union Perspective," in Bruce E. Kaufman and Daphne Gottlieb Taras (eds.), *Nonunion Employee Representation: History, Contemporary Practice, and Policy* (Armonk, NY: M. E. Sharpe, 2000), pp. 498–510.

77. Michael H. LeRoy, "Employee Participation in the New Millennium: Redefining a Labor Organization under Section 8(a)(2) of the NLRA," *Southern California Law Review* 72 (September 1999), pp. 1651–723.

78. Samuel Estreicher, "Labor Law Reform in a World of Competitive Product Markets," *Chicago-Kent Law Review* 69 (1993), pp. 3–46; Samuel Estreicher, "Employee Involvement and the 'Company Union' Prohibition: The Case for Partial Repeal of Section 8(a)(2) of the NLRA," *New York University Law Review* 69 (April 1994), pp. 125–61; Bruce E. Kaufman and Daphne Gottlieb Taras, "Nonunion Employee Representation: Findings and Conclusions," in Bruce E. Kaufman and Daphne Gottlieb Taras (eds.), *Nonunion Employee Representation: History, Contemporary Practice, and Policy* (Armonk, NY: M. E. Sharpe, 2000), pp. 527–58; LeRoy, "Employee Participation in the New Millennium"; Paul C. Weiler, "A Principled Reshaping of Labor Law for the Twenty-First Century," *University of Pennsylvania Journal of Labor and Employment Law* 3 (Winter 2001), pp. 177–206.

79. Cynthia Estlund, *Regoverning the Workplace: From Self-Regulation to Co-Regulation* (New Haven: Yale University Press, 2010).

80. Roy J. Adams, *Industrial Relations under Liberal Democracy: North America in Comparative Perspective* (Columbia: University of South Carolina Press, 1995).

81. Adams, *Industrial Relations under Liberal Democracy*; Heckscher, *The New Unionism*; Potter and Youngman, *Keeping America Competitive*.

82. Charles J. Morris, *The Blue Eagle at Work: Reclaiming Democratic Rights in the American Workplace* (Ithaca, NY: Cornell University Press, 2005); Catherine Fisk and Xenia Tashlitsky, "Imagine a World Where Employers Are Required to Bargain with Minority Unions," *ABA Journal of Labor and Employment Law* 27 (Fall 2011), pp. 1–22.

83. Adams, *Industrial Relations under Liberal Democracy;* Befort and Budd, *Invisible Hands, Invisible Objectives;* Freeman and Rogers, "Who Speaks for Us?"; Paul C. Weiler, *Governing the Workplace: The Future of Labor and Employment Law* (Cambridge, MA: Harvard University Press, 1990).

84. Mark Harcourt and Helen Lam, "Union Certification: A Critical Analysis and Proposed Alternative," *Working USA* 10 (September 2007), pp. 327–45.

85. David Fairris, *Shopfloor Matters: Labor–Management Relations in Twentieth-Century American Manufacturing* (London: Routledge, 1997).

86. Befort and Budd, *Invisible Hands, Invisible Objectives;* Heckscher, *The New Unionism.*

87. Jacoby, "Employee Representation and Corporate Governance"; Kenneth G. Dau-Schmidt, "Promoting Employee Voice in the American Economy: A Call for Comprehensive Reform," *Marquette Law Review* 94 (Spring 2011), pp. 765–836.

88. Katherine V. W. Stone, *From Widgets to Digits: Employment Regulation for the Changing Workplace* (Cambridge: Cambridge University Press, 2004).

89. Befort and Budd, *Invisible Hands, Invisible Objectives*; Paul Osterman, Thomas Kochan, Richard Locke, and Michael J. Piore, *Working in America: A Blueprint for the New Labor Market* (Cambridge, MA: MIT Press, 2001); Kochan, *Restoring the American Dream*; Cynthia Estlund, *Working Together: How Workplace Bonds Strengthen a Diverse Democracy* (Oxford: Oxford University Press, 2003); Estlund, *Regoverning the Workplace*; Stone, *From Widgets to Digits*.
90. Paul Evans, Vladimir Pucik, and Ingmar Bjorkman, *The Global Challenge: International Human Resource Management* (Boston: McGraw-Hill/Irwin, 2011).
91. Evans, Pucik, and Bjorkman, *The Global Challenge*.
92. Dionne Pohler and Andrew Luchak, "Are Unions Good or Bad for Organizations? The Moderating Role of Management's Response," *British Journal of Industrial Relations* 53 (September 2015), pp. 423–59; Joel Cutcher-Gershenfeld, Dan Brooks, and Martin Mulloy, *Inside the Ford-UAW Transformation: Pivotal Events in Valuing Work and Delivering Results* (Cambridge: MIT Press, 2015).
93. John T. Dunlop, *The Management of Labor Unions: Decision Making with Historical Constraints* (Lexington, MA: Lexington Books, 1990).
94. La Luz and Finn, "Getting Serious about Inclusion"; Williams, "Restructuring Labor's Identity."
95. Thomas A. Hannigan, *Managing Tomorrow's High-Performance Unions* (Westport, CT: Quorum Books, 1998); David Weil, *Turning the Tide: Strategic Planning for Labor Unions* (Lexington, MA: Lexington Books, 1994).
96. Befort and Budd, *Invisible Hands, Invisible Objectives;* Budd, *Employment with a Human Face;* John W. Budd and Devasheesh Bhave, "The Employment Relationship," in Adrian Wilkinson et al. (eds.), *Sage Handbook of Human Resource Management* (London: Sage, 2010), pp. 51–70.
97. Budd, *Employment with a Human Face*.

Appendix A

The National Labor Relations Act (1935, as Amended)

Author's note: The most up-to-date version of the National Labor Relations Act (NLRA) can be found in the United States Code at Title 29, Chapter 7. The NLRA was first enacted by the Wagner Act on July 5, 1935. It was significantly amended on June 23, 1947, by the Taft–Hartley Act (the Labor–Management Relations Act). Some further changes were implemented by the Landrum–Griffin Act on September 14, 1959, and other pieces of legislation in various years.

What follows are the separate introductions to the Wagner Act and the Taft–Hartley Act, followed by the current NLRA. The portions of the NLRA that appeared in the Wagner Act are in italics, the Taft–Hartley Act additions are in roman type, and post-1947 additions are underlined. Repealed text is not shown.

THE WAGNER ACT: FINDINGS AND POLICIES

Sec. 1. *The denial by employers of the right of employees to organize and the refusal by employers to accept the procedure of collective bargaining lead to strikes and other forms of industrial strife or unrest, which have the intent or the necessary effect of burdening or obstructing commerce by (a) impairing the efficiency, safety, or operation of the instrumentalities of commerce; (b) occurring in the current of commerce; (c) materially affecting, restraining, or controlling the flow of raw materials or manufactured or processed goods from or into the channels of commerce, or the prices of such materials or goods in commerce; or (d) causing diminution of employment and wages in such volume as substantially to impair or disrupt the market for goods flowing from or into the channels of commerce.*[1]

The inequality of bargaining power between employees who do not possess full freedom of association or actual liberty of contract and employers who are organized in the corporate or other forms of ownership association substantially burdens and affects the flow of commerce, and tends to aggravate recurrent business depressions, by depressing wage rates and the purchasing power of wage earners in industry and by preventing the stabilization of competitive wage rates and working conditions within and between industries.

Experience has proved that protection by law of the right of employees to organize and bargain collectively safeguards commerce from injury, impairment, or interruption, and promotes the flow of commerce by removing certain recognized sources of industrial strife and unrest, by encouraging practices fundamental to the friendly adjustment of industrial disputes arising out of differences as to wages, hours, or other working conditions, and by restoring equality of bargaining power between employers and employees.

It is hereby declared to be the policy of the United States to eliminate the causes of certain substantial obstructions to the free flow of commerce and to mitigate and eliminate these obstructions when they have occurred by encouraging the practice and procedure of collective bargaining and by protecting the exercise by workers of full freedom of association, self-organization, and designation of representatives of their own choosing, for the purpose of negotiating the terms and conditions of their employment or other mutual aid or protection.

THE TAFT–HARTLEY ACT: SHORT TITLE AND DECLARATION OF POLICY

Sec. 1. (a) This Act may be cited as the "Labor Management Relations Act, 1947."

(b) Industrial strife which interferes with the normal flow of commerce and with the full production of articles and commodities for commerce, can be avoided or substantially minimized if employers, employees, and labor organizations each recognize under law one another's legitimate rights in their relations with each other, and above all recognize under law that neither party has any right in its relations with any other to engage in acts or practices which jeopardize the public health, safety, or interest.

It is the purpose and policy of this Act in order to promote the full flow of commerce, to prescribe the legitimate rights of both employees and employers in their relations affecting commerce, to provide orderly and peaceful procedures for preventing the interference by either with the legitimate rights of the other, to protect the rights of individual employees in their relations with labor organizations whose activities affect commerce, to define and proscribe practices on the part of labor and management which affect commerce and are inimical to the general welfare, and to protect the rights of the public in connection with labor disputes affecting commerce.

THE NATIONAL LABOR RELATIONS ACT (AS AMENDED)

Definitions

Sec. 2. *When used in this Act—*

(1) *The term "person" includes one or more individuals, labor organizations, partnerships, associations, corporations, legal representatives, trustees, trustees in bankruptcy, or receivers.*

(2) *The term "employer" includes any person acting as an agent of an employer, directly or indirectly, but shall not include the United States or any wholly owned Government corporation, or any Federal Reserve Bank, or any State or political subdivision thereof, or any person subject to the Railway Labor Act as amended from time to time, or any labor organization (other than when acting as an employer), or anyone acting in the capacity of officer or agent of such labor organization.*

(3) *The term "employee" shall include any employee, and shall not be limited to the employees of a particular employer, unless the Act explicitly states otherwise, and shall include any individual whose work has ceased as a consequence of, or in connection with, any current labor dispute or because of any unfair labor practice, and who has not obtained any other regular and substantially equivalent employment, but shall not include any individual employed as an agricultural laborer, or in the domestic service of any*

family or person at his home, or any individual employed by his parent or spouse, or any individual having the status of an independent contractor, or any individual employed as a supervisor, or any individual employed by an employer subject to the Railway Labor Act, as amended from time to time, or by any other person who is not an employer as herein defined.

(4) *The term "representatives" includes any individual or labor organization.*

(5) *The term "labor organization" means any organization of any kind, or any agency or employee representation committee or plan, in which employees participate and which exists for the purpose, in whole or in part, of dealing with employers concerning grievances, labor disputes, wages, rates of pay, hours of employment, or conditions of work.*

(6) *The term "commerce" means trade, traffic, commerce, transportation, or communication among the several States, or between the District of Columbia or any Territory of the United States and any State or other Territory, or between any foreign country and any State, Territory, or the District of Columbia, or within the District of Columbia or any Territory, or between points in the same State but through any other State or any Territory or the District of Columbia or any foreign country.*

(7) *The term "affecting commerce" means in commerce, or burdening or obstructing commerce or the free flow of commerce, or having led or tending to lead to a labor dispute burdening or obstructing commerce or the free flow of commerce.*

(8) *The term "unfair labor practice" means any unfair labor practice listed in section 8.*

(9) *The term "labor dispute" includes any controversy concerning terms, tenure, or conditions of employment, or concerning the association or representation of persons in negotiating, fixing, maintaining, changing, or seeking to arrange terms or conditions of employment, regardless of whether the disputants stand in the proximate relation of employer and employee.*

(10) *The term "National Labor Relations Board" means the National Labor Relations Board provided for in section 3 of this Act.*

(11) The term "supervisor" means any individual having authority, in the interest of the employer, to hire, transfer, suspend, lay off, recall, promote, discharge, assign, reward, or discipline other employees, or responsibly to direct them, or to adjust their grievances, or effectively to recommend such action, if in connection with the foregoing the exercise of such authority is not of a merely routine or clerical nature, but requires the use of independent judgment.

(12) The term "professional employee" means—

(a) any employee engaged in work (i) predominantly intellectual and varied in character as opposed to routine mental, manual, mechanical, or physical work; (ii) involving the consistent exercise of discretion and judgment in its performance; (iii) of such a character that the output produced or the result accomplished cannot be standardized in relation to a given period of time; (iv) requiring knowledge of an advanced type in a field of science or learning customarily acquired by a prolonged course of specialized intellectual instruction and study in an institution of higher learning or a hospital, as distinguished from a general academic education or from an apprenticeship or from training in the performance of routine mental, manual, or physical processes; or

(b) any employee, who (i) has completed the courses of specialized intellectual instruction and study described in clause (iv) of paragraph (a), and (ii) is performing related work under the supervision of a professional person to qualify himself to become a professional employee as defined in paragraph (a).

(13) In determining whether any person is acting as an "agent" of another person so as to make such other person responsible for his acts, the question of whether the specific acts performed were actually authorized or subsequently ratified shall not be controlling.

(14) The term "health care institution" shall include any hospital, convalescent hospital, health maintenance organization, health clinic, nursing home, extended care facility, or other institution devoted to the care of sick, infirm, or aged persons.

National Labor Relations Board

Sec. 3.

(a) The National Labor Relations Board (hereinafter called the "Board") created by this Act prior to its amendment by the Labor Management Relations Act, 1947, is continued as an agency of the United States, except that the Board shall consist of five instead of three members, appointed by the President by and with the advice and consent of the Senate. Of the two additional members so provided for, one shall be appointed for a term of five years and the other for a term of two years. Their successors, and the successors of the other members, shall be appointed for terms of five years each, excepting that any individual chosen to fill a vacancy shall be appointed only for the unexpired term of the member whom he shall succeed. The President shall designate one member to serve as Chairman of the Board. Any member of the Board may be removed by the President, upon notice and hearing, for neglect of duty or malfeasance in office, but for no other cause.

(b) Board is authorized to delegate to any group of three or more members any or all of the powers, which it may itself exercise. The Board is also authorized to delegate to its regional directors its powers under section 9 to determine the unit appropriate for the purpose of collective bargaining, to investigate and provide for hearings, and determine whether a question of representation exists, and to direct an election or take a secret ballot under subsection (c) or (e) of section 9 and certify the results thereof, except that upon the filing of a request therefore with the Board by any interested person, the Board may review any action of a regional director delegated to him under this paragraph, but such a review shall not, unless specifically ordered by the Board, operate as a stay of any action taken by the regional director. *A vacancy in the Board shall not impair the right of the remaining members to exercise all of the powers of the Board,* and three members of the Board shall, at all times, constitute a quorum of the Board, except that two members shall constitute a quorum of any group designated pursuant to the first sentence hereof. *The Board shall have an official seal, which shall be judicially noticed.*

(c) *The Board shall at the close of each fiscal year make a report in writing to Congress and to the President summarizing significant case activities and operations for that fiscal year.*

(d) There shall be a General Counsel of the Board who shall be appointed by the President, by and with the advice and consent of the Senate, for a term of four years. The General Counsel of the Board shall exercise general supervision over all attorneys employed by the Board (other than administrative law judges and legal assistants to Board members) and over the officers and employees in the regional offices. He shall have final authority, on behalf of the Board, in respect of the investigation of charges and issuance of complaints under section 10, and in respect of the prosecution of such complaints before the Board, and shall have such other duties as the Board may prescribe or as may be provided by law. In case of vacancy in the office of the General Counsel the President is authorized to designate the officer or employee who shall act as General Counsel during such vacancy, but no person or persons so designated shall so act (1) for more than forty days when the Congress is in session unless a nomination to fill such vacancy shall have been submitted to the Senate, or (2) after the adjournment sine die of the session of the Senate in which such nomination was submitted.

Sec. 4. (a) *Each member of the Board and the General Counsel of the Board shall be eligible for reappointment, and shall not engage in any other business, vocation, or employment. The Board shall appoint an executive secretary, and such attorneys, examiners, and regional directors, and such other employees as it may from time to time find necessary for the proper performance of its duties.* The Board may not employ any attorneys for the purpose of reviewing transcripts of hearings or preparing drafts of opinions except that any attorney employed for assignment as a legal assistant to any Board member may for such Board member review such transcripts and prepare such drafts. No administrative law judge's report shall be reviewed, either before or after its publication, by any person other than a member of the Board or his legal assistant, and no administrative law judge shall advise or consult with the Board with respect to exceptions taken to his findings, rulings, or recommendations. *The Board may establish or utilize such regional, local, or other agencies, and utilize such voluntary and uncompensated services, as may from time to time be needed. Attorneys appointed under this section may, at the direction of the Board, appear for and represent the Board in any case in court. Nothing in this Act shall be construed to authorize the Board to appoint individuals for the purpose of conciliation or mediation, or for economic analysis.*

(b) *All of the expenses of the Board, including all necessary traveling and subsistence expenses outside the District of Columbia incurred by the members or employees of the Board under its orders, shall be allowed and paid on the presentation of itemized vouchers therefore approved by the Board or by any individual it designates for that purpose.*

Sec. 5. *The principal office of the Board shall be in the District of Columbia, but it may meet and exercise any or all of its powers at any other place. The Board may, by one or more of its members or by such agents or agencies as it may designate, prosecute any inquiry necessary to its functions in any part of the United States. A member who participates in such an inquiry shall not be disqualified from subsequently participating in a decision of the Board in the same case.*

Sec. 6. *The Board shall have authority from time to time to make, amend, and rescind,* in the manner prescribed by the Administrative Procedure Act, *such rules and regulations as may be necessary to carry out the provisions of this Act.*

Rights of Employees

Sec. 7. *Employees shall have the right to self-organization, to form, join, or assist labor organizations, to bargain collectively through representatives of their own choosing, and to engage in other concerted activities for the purpose of collective bargaining or other mutual aid or protection,* and shall also have the right to refrain from any or all such activities except to the extent that such right may be affected by an agreement requiring membership in a labor organization as a condition of employment as authorized in section 8(a)(3).

Unfair Labor Practices

Sec. 8. (a) *It shall be an unfair labor practice for an employer—*

(1) *to interfere with, restrain, or coerce employees in the exercise of the rights guaranteed in section 7;*

(2) *to dominate or interfere with the formation or administration of any labor organization or contribute financial or other support to it: Provided, That subject to rules and regulations made and published by the Board pursuant to section 6, an employer shall not be prohibited from permitting employees to confer with him during working hours without loss of time or pay;*

(3) *by discrimination in regard to hire or tenure of employment or any term or condition of employment to encourage or discourage membership in any labor organization: Provided, That nothing in this Act, or in any other statute of the United States, shall pre-*

clude an employer from making an agreement with a labor organization (not established, maintained, or assisted by any action defined in section 8(a) of this Act as an unfair labor practice) to require as a condition of employment membership therein on or after the thirtieth day following the beginning of such employment or the effective date of such agreement, whichever is the later, *(i) if such labor organization is the representative of the employees as provided in section 9(a), in the appropriate collective bargaining unit covered by such agreement when made,* and (ii) unless following an election held as provided in section 9(e) within one year preceding the effective date of such agreement, the Board shall have certified that at least a majority of the employees eligible to vote in such election have voted to rescind the authority of such labor organization to make such an agreement: Provided further, That no employer shall justify any discrimination against an employee for nonmembership in a labor organization (A) if he has reasonable grounds for believing that such membership was not available to the employee on the same terms and conditions generally applicable to other members, or (B) if he has reasonable grounds for believing that membership was denied or terminated for reasons other than the failure of the employee to tender the periodic dues and the initiation fees uniformly required as a condition of acquiring or retaining membership;

(4) *To discharge or otherwise discriminate against an employee because he has filed charges or given testimony under this Act;*

(5) *To refuse to bargain collectively with the representatives of his employees, subject to the provisions of section 9(a).*

(b) It shall be an unfair labor practice for a labor organization or its agents—

(1) To restrain or coerce (A) employees in the exercise of the rights guaranteed in section 7: Provided, That this paragraph shall not impair the right of a labor organization to prescribe its own rules with respect to the acquisition or retention of membership therein; or (B) an employer in the selection of his representatives for the purposes of collective bargaining or the adjustment of grievances;

(2) To cause or attempt to cause an employer to discriminate against an employee in violation of subsection (a) (3) or to discriminate against an employee with respect to whom membership in such organization has been denied or terminated on some ground other than his failure to tender the periodic dues and the initiation fees uniformly required as a condition of acquiring or retaining membership;

(3) To refuse to bargain collectively with an employer, provided it is the representative of his employees subject to the provisions of section 9(a);

(4) (i) To engage in, or to induce or encourage any individual employed by any person engaged in commerce or in an industry affecting commerce to engage in, a strike or a refusal in the course of his employment to use, manufacture, process, transport, or otherwise handle or work on any goods, articles, materials, or commodities or to perform any services; or (ii) to threaten, coerce, or restrain any person engaged in commerce or in an industry affecting commerce, where in *either case* an object thereof is—

(A) forcing or requiring any employer or self-employed person to join any labor or employer organization or to enter into any agreement which is prohibited by section 8(e) subsection (e) of this section;

(B) forcing or requiring any person to cease using, selling, handling, transporting, or otherwise dealing in the products of any other producer, processor, or manufacturer, or to cease doing business with any other person, or forcing or requiring any other employer to recognize or bargain with a labor organization as the representative of his employees unless such labor organization has been certified as the representative of such employees under the provisions of section 9: Provided, That nothing contained in this clause (B) shall be construed to make unlawful, where not otherwise unlawful, any primary strike or primary picketing;

(C) forcing or requiring any employer to recognize or bargain with a particular labor organization as the representative of his employees if another labor organization has been certified as the representative of such employees under the provisions of section 9;

(D) forcing or requiring any employer to assign particular work to employees in a particular labor organization or in a particular trade, craft, or class rather than to employees in another labor organization or in another trade, craft, or class, unless such employer is failing to conform to an order or certification of the Board determining the bargaining representative for employees performing such work:

Provided, That nothing contained in this subsection shall be construed to make unlawful a refusal by any person to enter upon the premises of any employer (other than his own employer), if the employees of such employer are engaged in a strike ratified or approved by a representative of such employees whom such employer is required to recognize under this Act: Provided further, That for the purposes of this paragraph (4) only, nothing contained in such paragraph shall be construed to prohibit publicity, other than picketing, for the purpose of truthfully advising the public, including consumers and members of a labor organization, that a product or products are produced by an employer with whom the labor organization has a primary dispute and are distributed by another employer, as long as such publicity does not have an effect of inducing any individual employed by any person other than the primary employer in the course of his employment to refuse to pick up, deliver, or transport any goods, or not to perform any services, at the establishment of the employer engaged in such distribution;

(5) To require of employees covered by an agreement authorized under subsection (a) (3) the payment, as a condition precedent to becoming a member of such organization, of a fee in an amount which the Board finds excessive or discriminatory under all the circumstances. In making such a finding, the Board shall consider, among other relevant factors, the practices and customs of labor organizations in the particular industry, and the wages currently paid to the employees affected;

(6) To cause or attempt to cause an employer to pay or deliver or agree to pay or deliver any money or other thing of value, in the nature of an exaction, for services which are not performed or not to be performed; and

(7) To picket or cause to be picketed, or threaten to picket or cause to be picketed, any employer where an object thereof is forcing or requiring an employer to recognize or bargain with a labor organization as the representative of his employees, or forcing or requiring the employees of an employer to accept or select such labor organization as their collective bargaining representative, unless such labor organization is currently certified as the representative of such employees:

(A) Where the employer has lawfully recognized in accordance with this Act any other labor organization and a question concerning representation may not appropriately be raised under section 9(c) of this Act,

(B) Where within the preceding twelve months a valid election under section 9(c) of this Act has been conducted, or

(C) Where such picketing has been conducted without a petition under section 9(c) being filed within a reasonable period of time not to exceed thirty days from the commencement of such picketing: Provided, That when such a petition has been filed the Board shall forthwith, without regard to the provisions of section 9(c)(1) or the absence of a showing of a substantial interest on the part of the labor organization, direct an election in such unit as the Board finds to be appropriate and shall certify the results thereof: Provided further, That nothing in this subparagraph (C) shall be construed to prohibit any picketing or other publicity for the purpose of truthfully advising the public (including consumers) that an employer does not employ members of, or have a contract with, a labor organization, unless an effect of such picketing is to induce any individual employed by any other person in the course of his employment, not to pick up, deliver or transport any goods or not to perform any services.

Nothing in this paragraph (7) shall be construed to permit any act, which would otherwise be an unfair labor practice under this section 8(b).

(c) The expressing of any views, argument, or opinion, or the dissemination thereof, whether in written, printed, graphic, or visual form, shall not constitute or be evidence of an unfair labor practice under any of the provisions of this Act, if such expression contains no threat of reprisal or force or promise of benefit.

(d) For the purposes of this section, to bargain collectively is the performance of the mutual obligation of the employer and the representative of the employees to meet at reasonable times and confer in good faith with respect to wages, hours, and other terms and conditions of employment, or the negotiation of an agreement or any question arising there under, and the execution of a written contract incorporating any agreement reached if requested by either party, but such obligation does not compel either party to agree to a proposal or require the making of a concession: Provided, That where there is in effect a collective bargaining contract covering employees in an industry affecting commerce, the duty to bargain collectively shall also mean that no party to such contract shall terminate or modify such contract, unless the party desiring such termination or modification—

1. serves a written notice upon the other party to the contract of the proposed termination or modification sixty days prior to the expiration date thereof, or in the event such contract contains no expiration date, sixty days prior to the time it is proposed to make such termination or modification;
2. offers to meet and confer with the other party for the purpose of negotiating a new contract or a contract containing the proposed modifications;
3. notifies the Federal Mediation and Conciliation Service within thirty days after such notice of the existence of a dispute, and simultaneously therewith notifies any State or Territorial agency established to mediate and conciliate disputes within the State or Territory where the dispute occurred, provided no agreement has been reached by that time; and
4. continues in full force and effect, without resorting to strike or lockout, all the terms and conditions of the existing contract for a period of sixty days after such notice is given or until the expiration date of such contract, whichever occurs later.

Whenever the collective bargaining involves employees of a health care institution, the provisions of this section 8(d) shall be modified as follows:

(A) The notice of section 8(d)(1) shall be ninety days; the notice of section 8(d)(3) shall be sixty days; and the contract period of section 8(d)(4) shall be ninety days.

(B) Where the bargaining is for an initial agreement following certification or recognition, at least thirty days' notice of the existence of a dispute shall be given by the labor organization to the agencies set forth in section 8(d)(3).

(C) After notice is given to the Federal Mediation and Conciliation Service under either clause (A) or (B) of this sentence, the Service shall promptly communicate with the parties and use its best efforts, by mediation and conciliation, to bring them to agreement. The parties shall participate fully and promptly in such meetings as may be undertaken by the Service for the purpose of aiding in a settlement of the dispute.

The duties imposed upon employers, employees, and labor organizations by paragraphs (2), (3), and (4) shall become inapplicable upon an intervening certification of the Board, under which the labor organization or individual, which is a party to the contract, has been superseded as or ceased to be the representative of the employees subject to the provisions of section 9(a), and the duties so imposed shall not be construed as requiring either party to discuss or agree to any modification of the terms and conditions contained in a contract for a fixed period, if such modification is to become effective before such terms and conditions can be reopened under the provisions of the contract. Any employee who engages in a strike within any notice period specified in this subsection, or who engages in any strike within the appropriate period specified in subsection (g) of this section, shall lose his status as an employee of the employer engaged in the particular labor dispute, for the purposes of sections 8, 9, and 10 of this Act, but such loss of status for such employee shall terminate if and when he is reemployed by such employer.

(e) It shall be an unfair labor practice for any labor organization and any employer to enter into any contract or agreement, express or implied, whereby such employer ceases or refrains or agrees to cease or refrain from handling, using, selling, transporting, or otherwise dealing in any of the products of any other employer, or cease doing business with any other person, and any contract or agreement entered into heretofore or hereafter containing such an agreement shall be to such extent unenforceable and void: Provided, That nothing in this subsection (e) shall apply to an agreement between a labor organization and an employer in the construction industry relating to the contracting or subcontracting of work to be done at the site of the construction, alteration, painting, or repair of a building, structure, or other work: Provided further, That for the purposes of this subsection (e) and section 8(b)(4)(B) the terms "any employer," "any person engaged in commerce or an industry affecting commerce," and "any person" when used in relation to the terms "any other producer, processor, or manufacturer," "any other employer," or "any other person" shall not include persons in the relation of a jobber, manufacturer, contractor, or subcontractor working on the goods or premises of the jobber or manufacturer or performing parts of an integrated process of production in the apparel and clothing industry: Provided further, That nothing in this Act shall prohibit the enforcement of any agreement which is within the foregoing exception.

(f) It shall not be an unfair labor practice under subsections (a) and (b) of this section for an employer engaged primarily in the building and construction industry to make an agreement covering employees engaged (or who, upon their employment, will be engaged) in the building and construction industry with a labor organization of which building and construction employees are members (not established, maintained, or assisted by any action defined in section 8(a) of this Act as an unfair labor practice) because (1) the majority status of such labor organization has not been established under the provisions of section 9 of this Act prior to the making of such agreement, or (2) such agreement requires as a condition of employment, membership in such labor organization after the seventh day following the beginning of such employment or the effective date of the agreement, whichever is later, or (3) such agreement requires the employer to notify such labor organization of opportunities for employment with such employer, or gives such labor organization an opportunity to refer qualified applicants for such employment, or (4) such agreement specifies minimum training or experience qualifications for employment or provides for priority in opportunities for employment based upon length of service with such employer, in the industry or in the particular geographical area: Provided, That nothing in this subsection shall set aside the final proviso to section 8(a)(3) of this Act: Provided further, That any agreement which would be invalid, but for clause (1) of this subsection, shall not be a bar to a petition filed pursuant to section 9(c) or 9(e).

(g) A labor organization before engaging in any strike, picketing, or other concerted refusal to work at any health care institution shall, not less than ten days prior to such action, notify the institution in writing and the Federal Mediation and Conciliation Service of that intention, except that in the case of bargaining for an initial agreement following certification or recognition the notice required by this subsection shall not be given until the expiration of the period specified in clause (B) of the last sentence of section 8(d) of this Act. The notice shall state the date and time that such action will commence. The notice, once given, may be extended by the written agreement of both parties.

Representatives and Elections

Sec. 9 (a) *Representatives designated or selected for the purposes of collective bargaining by the majority of the employees in a unit appropriate for such purposes, shall be the exclusive representatives of all the employees in such unit for the purposes of collective bargaining in respect to rates of pay, wages, hours of employment, or other conditions of employment: Provided, That any individual employee or a group of employees shall have the right at any time to present grievances to their employer* and to have such grievances adjusted, without the intervention of the bargaining representative, as long as the adjustment is not inconsistent with the terms of a collective bargaining contract or agreement then in effect: Provided further, That the bargaining representative has been given opportunity to be present at such adjustment.

(b) *The Board shall decide in each case whether, in order* to assure to employees the fullest freedom in exercising the rights guaranteed by this Act, the unit appropriate for the purposes of collective bargaining shall be the employer unit, craft unit, plant unit, or subdivision thereof: Provided, That the Board shall not (1) decide that any unit is appropriate for such purposes if such unit includes both professional employees and employees who are not professional employees unless a majority of such professional employees vote for inclusion in such unit; or (2) decide that any craft unit is inappropriate for such purposes on the ground that a different unit has been established by a prior Board determination, unless a majority of the employees in the proposed craft unit votes against separate representation or (3) decide that any unit is appropriate for such purposes if it includes, together with other employees, any individual employed as a guard to enforce against employees and other persons rules to protect property of the employer or to protect the safety of persons on the employer's premises; but no labor organization shall be certified as the representative of employees in a bargaining unit of guards if such organization admits to membership, or is affiliated directly or indirectly with an organization which admits to membership, employees other than guards.

(c)(1) Whenever a petition shall have been filed, in accordance with such regulations as may be prescribed by the Board—

(A) by an employee or group of employees or any individual or labor organization acting in their behalf alleging that a substantial number of employees (i) wish to be represented for collective bargaining and that their employer declines to recognize their representative as the representative defined in section 9(a), or (ii) assert that the individual or labor organization, which has been certified or is being currently recognized by their employer as the bargaining representative, is no longer a representative as defined in section 9(a); or

(B) by an employer, alleging that one or more individuals or labor organizations have presented to him a claim to be recognized as the representative defined in section 9(a); the Board shall investigate such petition and if it has reasonable cause to believe that a question of representation affecting commerce exists shall provide for an appropriate hearing upon due notice. Such hearing may be conducted by an officer or employee of the regional office, who shall not make any recommendations with respect thereto. If the Board finds upon the record of such hearing that such a question of representation exists, it shall direct an election by secret ballot and shall certify the results thereof.

(2) In determining whether or not a question of representation affecting commerce exists, the same regulations and rules of decision shall apply irrespective of the identity of the persons filing the petition or the kind of relief sought, and in no case shall the Board deny a labor organization a place on the ballot by reason of an order with respect to such labor organization or its predecessor not issued in conformity with section 10(c).

(3) No election shall be directed in any bargaining unit or any subdivision within which, in the preceding twelve-month period, a valid election shall have been held. Employees engaged in an economic strike who are not entitled to reinstatement shall be eligible to vote under such regulations as the Board shall find are consistent with the purposes and provisions of this Act in any election conducted within twelve months after the commencement of the strike. In any election where none of the choices on the ballot receives a majority, a runoff shall be conducted, the ballot providing for a selection between the two choices receiving the largest and second largest number of valid votes cast in the election.

(4) Nothing in this section shall be construed to prohibit the waiving of hearings by stipulation for the purpose of a consent election in conformity with regulations and rules of decision of the Board.

(5) In determining whether a unit is appropriate for the purposes specified in subsection (b) the extent to which the employees have organized shall not be controlling.

(d) *Whenever an order of the Board made pursuant to section 10(c) is based in whole or in part upon facts certified following an investigation pursuant to subsection (c) of this section and there is a petition for the enforcement or review of such order, such certification and the record of such investigation shall be included in the transcript of the entire record required to be filed under section 10(e) or 10(f), and thereupon the decree of the court enforcing, modifying, or setting aside in whole or in part the order of the Board shall be made and entered upon the pleadings, testimony, and proceedings set forth in such transcript.*

(e)(1) Upon the filing with the Board, by 30 per centum or more of the employees in a bargaining unit covered by an agreement between their employer and labor organization made pursuant to section 8(a)(3), of a petition alleging they desire that such authorization be rescinded, the Board shall take a secret ballot of the employees in such unit and certify the results thereof to such labor organization and to the employer.

(2) No election shall be conducted pursuant to this subsection in any bargaining unit or any subdivision within which, in the preceding twelve-month period, a valid election shall have been held.

Prevention of Unfair Labor Practices

Sec. 10. (a) *The Board is empowered, as hereinafter provided, to prevent any person from engaging in any unfair labor practice (listed in section 8) affecting commerce. This power shall not be affected by any other means of adjustment or prevention that has been or may be established by agreement, law, or otherwise:* Provided, That the Board is empowered by agreement with any agency of any State or Territory to cede to such agency jurisdiction over any cases in any industry (other than mining, manufacturing, communications, and transportation except where predominantly local in character) even though such cases may involve labor disputes affecting commerce, unless the provision of the State or Territorial statute applicable to the determination of such cases by such agency is inconsistent with the corresponding provision of this Act or has received a construction inconsistent therewith.

(b) *Whenever it is charged that any person has engaged in or is engaging in any such unfair labor practice, the Board, or any agent or agency designated by the Board for such purposes, shall have power to issue and cause to be served upon such person a complaint stating the charges in that respect, and containing a notice of hearing before the Board or a member thereof, or before a designated agent or agency, at a place therein fixed, not less than five days after the serving of said complaint:* Provided, That no complaint shall issue based upon any unfair labor practice occurring more than six months prior to the filing of the charge with the Board and the service of a copy thereof upon the person against whom such charge is made, unless the person aggrieved thereby was prevented from filing such charge by reason of service in the armed forces, in which event the six-month period shall be computed from the day of his discharge. *Any such complaint may be amended by the member, agent, or agency conducting the hearing or the Board in its discretion at any time prior to the issuance of an order based thereon. The person so complained of shall have the right to file an answer to the original or amended complaint and to appear in person or otherwise and give testimony at the place and time fixed in the complaint. In the discretion of the member, agent, or agency conducting the hearing or the Board, any other person may be allowed to intervene in the said proceeding and to present testimony.* Any such proceeding shall, so far as practicable, be conducted in accordance with the rules of evidence applicable in the district courts of the United States under the rules of civil procedure for the district courts of the United States, adopted by the Supreme Court of the United States pursuant to section 2072 of title 28, United States Code.

(c) *The testimony taken by such member, agent, or agency, or the Board shall be reduced to writing and filed with the Board. Thereafter, in its discretion, the Board upon notice may take further testimony or hear argument. If upon the preponderance of the testimony taken the Board shall be of the opinion that any person named in the complaint has engaged in or is engaging in any such unfair labor practice, then the Board shall state its findings of fact and shall issue and cause to be served on such person an order requiring such person to cease and desist from such unfair labor practice, and to take such affirmative action including reinstatement of employees with or without back pay, as will effectuate the policies of this Act:* Provided, That where an order directs reinstatement of an employee, back pay may be required of the employer or labor organization, as the case may be, responsible for the discrimination suffered by him: And provided further, That in determining whether a complaint shall issue alleging a violation of section 8(a)(1) or section 8(a)(2), and in deciding such cases, the same regulations and rules of decision shall apply irrespective of whether or not the labor organization affected is affiliated with a labor organization national or international in scope. *Such order may further require such person to make reports from time to time showing the extent to which it has complied with the order. If upon the preponderance of the testimony taken the Board shall not be of the opinion that the person named in the complaint has engaged in or is engaging in any such unfair labor practice, then the Board shall state its findings of fact and shall issue an order dismissing the said complaint.* No order of the Board shall require the reinstatement of any individual as an employee who has been suspended or discharged, or the payment to him of any back pay, if such individual was suspended or discharged for cause. In case the evidence is presented before a member of the Board, or before an administrative law judge or judges thereof, such member, or such judge or judges, as the case may be, shall issue and cause to be served on the parties to the proceeding a proposed report, together with a recommended order, which shall be filed with the Board, and if no exceptions are filed within twenty days after service thereof upon such parties, or within such further period as the Board may authorize, such recommended order shall become the order of the Board and become affective as therein prescribed.

(d) Until the record in a case shall have been filed in a court, *as hereinafter provided, the Board may at any time, upon reasonable notice and in such manner as it shall deem proper, modify or set aside, in whole or in part, any finding or order made or issued by it.*

(e) *The Board shall have power to petition any court of appeals of the United States, or if all the courts of appeals to which application may be made are in vacation, any district court of the United States, within any circuit or district, respectively, wherein the unfair labor practice in question occurred or wherein such person resides or transacts business, for the enforcement of such order and for appropriate temporary relief or restraining order, and shall file in the court* the record in the proceeding, as provided in section 2112 of title 28, United States Code. *Upon the filing of such petition, the court shall cause notice thereof to be served upon such person, and thereupon shall have jurisdiction of the proceeding and of the question determined therein, and shall have power to grant such temporary relief or restraining order as it deems just and proper, and to make and enter a decree enforcing, modifying and enforcing as so modified, or setting aside in whole or in part the order of the Board. No objection that has not been urged before the Board, its member, agent, or agency, shall be considered by the court, unless the failure or neglect to urge such objection shall be excused because of extraordinary circumstances. The findings of the Board* with respect to questions of fact if supported by substantial evidence on the record considered as a whole shall be conclusive. *If either party shall apply to the court for leave to adduce additional evidence and shall show to the satisfaction of the court that such additional evidence is material and that there were reasonable grounds for the failure to adduce such evidence in the hearing before the Board, its member, agent, or agency, the court may order such additional evidence to be taken before the Board, its member, agent, or agency, and to be made a part of the* record. *The Board may modify its findings as to the facts, or make new findings, by reason of additional evidence so taken and filed, and it shall file such modified or new findings, which findings with respect to question of fact if supported by substantial evidence on the record considered as a whole shall be conclusive, and shall file its recommendations, if any, for the modification or setting aside of its original order.* Upon the filing of the record with it *the jurisdiction of the court shall be exclusive and its judgment and decree shall be final, except that the same shall be subject to review by the appropriate United States court of appeals if application was made to the district court as hereinabove provided, and by the Supreme Court of the United States upon writ of certiorari or certification as provided in section 1254 of title 28.*

(f) *Any person aggrieved by a final order of the Board granting or denying in whole or in part the relief sought may obtain a review of such order in any United States court of appeals in the circuit wherein the unfair labor practice in question was alleged to have been engaged in or wherein such person resides or transacts business, or in the United States Court of Appeals for the District of Columbia, by filing in such court a written petition praying that the order of the Board be modified or set aside. A copy of such petition shall be forthwith* transmitted by the clerk of the court to the Board, *and thereupon the aggrieved party shall file in the court the record in the proceeding, certified by the Board, as provided in section 2112 of title 28, United States Code. Upon the filing of such petition, the court shall proceed in the same manner as in the case of an application by the Board under subsection (e) of this section, and shall have the same jurisdiction to grant to the Board such temporary relief or restraining order as it deems just and proper, and in like manner to make and enter a decree enforcing, modifying and enforcing as so modified, or setting aside in whole or in part the order of the Board;* the findings of the Board with respect to questions of fact if supported by substantial evidence on the record considered as a whole shall in like manner be conclusive.

(g) *The commencement of proceedings under subsection (e) or (f) of this section shall not, unless specifically ordered by the court, operate as a stay of the Board's order.*

(h) *When granting appropriate temporary relief or a restraining order, or making and entering a decree enforcing, modifying and enforcing as so modified, or setting aside in whole or in part an order of the Board, as provided in this section, the jurisdiction of courts sitting in equity shall not be limited by the Norris–LaGuardia Act."*

(i) [Repealed, 1984].

(j) The Board shall have power, upon issuance of a complaint as provided in subsection (b) charging that any person has engaged in or is engaging in an unfair labor practice, to petition any United States district court, within any district wherein the unfair labor practice in question is alleged to have occurred or wherein such person resides or transacts business, for appropriate temporary relief or restraining order. Upon the filing of any such petition the court shall cause notice thereof to be served upon such person, and thereupon shall have jurisdiction to grant to the Board such temporary relief or restraining order as it deems just and proper.

(k) Whenever it is charged that any person has engaged in an unfair labor practice within the meaning of paragraph (4)(D) of section 8(b), the Board is empowered and directed to hear and determine the dispute out of which such unfair labor practice shall have arisen, unless, within ten days after notice that such charge has been filed, the parties to such dispute submit to the Board satisfactory evidence that they have adjusted, or agreed upon methods for the voluntary adjustment of, the dispute. Upon compliance by the parties to the dispute with the decision of the Board or upon such voluntary adjustment of the dispute, such charge shall be dismissed.

(l) Whenever it is charged that any person has engaged in an unfair labor practice within the meaning of paragraph (4)(A), (B), or (C) of section 8(b), or section 8(e) or section 8(b)(7), the preliminary investigation of such charge shall be made forthwith and given priority over all other cases except cases of like character in the office where it is filed or to which it is referred. If, after such investigation, the officer or regional attorney to whom the matter may be referred has reasonable cause to believe such charge is true and that a complaint should issue, he shall, on behalf of the Board, petition any United States district court within any district where the unfair labor practice in question has occurred, is alleged to have occurred, or wherein such person resides or transacts business, for appropriate injunctive relief pending the final adjudication of the Board with respect to such matter. Upon the filing of any such petition the district court shall have jurisdiction to grant such injunctive relief or temporary restraining order as it deems just and proper, notwithstanding any other provision of law: Provided further, That no temporary restraining order shall be issued without notice unless a petition alleges that substantial and irreparable injury to the charging party will be unavoidable and such temporary restraining order shall be effective for no longer than five days and will become void at the expiration of such period: Provided further, That such officer or regional attorney shall not apply for any restraining order under section 8(b)(7) if a charge against the employer under section 8(a)(2) has been filed and after the preliminary investigation, he has reasonable cause to believe that such charge is true and that a complaint should issue. Upon filing of any such petition the courts shall cause notice thereof to be served upon any person involved in the charge and such person, including the charging party, shall be given an opportunity to appear by counsel and present any relevant testimony: Provided further, That for the purposes of this subsection district courts shall be deemed to have jurisdiction of a labor organization (1) in the district in which such organization maintains its principal office, or (2) in any district in which its duly authorized officers or agents are engaged in promoting or protecting the interests of employee members. The service of legal process upon such officer or agent shall constitute service upon the labor organization and make such organization a party to the suit. In situations where such relief is appropriate the procedure specified herein shall apply to charges with respect to section 8(b)(4)(D).

(m) Whenever it is charged that any person has engaged in an unfair labor practice within the meaning of subsection (a)(3) or (b)(2) of section 8, such charge shall be given priority over all other cases except cases of like character in the office where it is filed or to which it is referred and cases given priority under subsection (1).

Investigatory Powers

Sec. 11. *For the purpose of all hearings and investigations, which, in the opinion of the Board, are necessary and proper for the exercise of the powers vested in it by section 9 and section 10—*

(1) *The Board, or its duly authorized agents or agencies, shall at all reasonable times have access to, for the purpose of examination, and the right to copy any evidence of any person being investigated or proceeded against that relates to any matter under investigation or in question.* The Board or any member thereof, shall upon application of any party to such proceedings, forthwith issue to such party subpoenas requiring the attendance and testimony of witnesses or the production of any evidence in such proceeding or investigation requested in such application. Within five days after the service of a subpoena on any person requiring the production of any evidence in his possession or under his control, such person may petition the Board to revoke, and the Board shall revoke, such subpoena if in its opinion the evidence whose production is required does not relate to any matter under investigation, or any matter in question in such proceedings, or if in its opinion such subpoena does not describe with sufficient particularity the evidence whose production is required. *Any member of the Board, or any agent or agency designated by the Board for such purposes, may administer oaths and affirmations, examine witnesses, and receive evidence. Such attendance of witnesses and the production of such evidence may be required from any place in the United States or any Territory or possession thereof, at any designated place of hearing.*

(2) *In case of contumacy or refusal to obey a subpoena issued to any person, any United States district court or the United States courts of any Territory or possession, within the jurisdiction of which the inquiry is carried on or within the jurisdiction of which said person guilty of contumacy or refusal to obey is found or resides or transacts business, upon application by the Board shall have jurisdiction to issue to such person an order requiring such person to appear before the Board, its member, agent, or agency, there to produce evidence if so ordered, or there to give testimony touching the matter under investigation or in question; and any failure to obey such order of the court may be punished by said court as a contempt thereof.*

(3) [Repealed, 1970].

(4) *Complaints, orders, and other process and papers of the Board, its member, agent, or agency, may be served either personally or by registered or certified mail or by telegraph or by leaving a copy thereof at the principal office or place of business of the person required to be served. The verified return by the individual so serving the same setting forth the manner of such service shall be proof of the same, and the return post office receipt or telegraph receipt therefore when registered or certified and mailed or when telegraphed as aforesaid shall be proof of service of the same. Witnesses summoned before the Board, its member, agent, or agency, shall be paid the same fees and mileage that are paid witnesses in the courts of the United States, and witnesses whose depositions are taken and the persons taking the same shall severally be entitled to the same fees as are paid for like services in the courts of the United States.*

(5) *All process of any court to which application may be made under this Act may be served in the judicial district wherein the defendant or other person required to be served resides or may be found.*

(6) *The several departments and agencies of the Government, when directed by the President, shall furnish the Board, upon its request, all records, papers, and information in their possession relating to any matter before the Board.*

Sec. 12. *Any person who shall willfully resist, prevent, impede, or interfere with any member of the Board or any of its agents or agencies in the performance of duties pursuant* *to this Act shall be punished by a fine of not more than $5,000 or by imprisonment for not more than one year, or both.*

Limitations

Sec. 13. *Nothing in this Act,* except as specifically provided for herein, *shall be construed so as either to interfere with or impede or diminish in any way the right to strike* or to affect the limitations or qualifications on that right.

Sec. 14. (a) Nothing herein shall prohibit any individual employed as a supervisor from becoming or remaining a member of a labor organization, but no employer subject to this Act shall be compelled to deem individuals defined herein as supervisors as employees for the purpose of any law, either national or local, relating to collective bargaining.

(b) Nothing in this Act shall be construed as authorizing the execution or application of agreements requiring membership in a labor organization as a condition of employment in any State or Territory in which such execution or application is prohibited by State or Territorial law.

(c)(1) The Board, in its discretion, may, by rule of decision or by published rules adopted pursuant to the Administrative Procedure Act, decline to assert jurisdiction over any labor dispute involving any class or category of employers, where, in the opinion of the Board, the effect of such labor dispute on commerce is not sufficiently substantial to warrant the exercise of its jurisdiction: Provided, That the Board shall not decline to assert jurisdiction over any labor dispute over which it would assert jurisdiction under the standards prevailing upon August 1, 1959.

(2) Nothing in this Act shall be deemed to prevent or bar any agency or the courts of any State or Territory (including the Commonwealth of Puerto Rico, Guam, and the Virgin Islands) from assuming and asserting jurisdiction over labor disputes over which the Board declines, pursuant to paragraph (1) of this subsection, to assert jurisdiction.

Sec. 15. [Obsolete]

Sec. 16. If any provision of this Act, or the application of such provision to any person or circumstances, shall be held invalid, the remainder of this Act, or the application of such provision to persons or circumstances other than those as to which it is held invalid, shall not be affected thereby.

Sec. 17. This Act may be cited as the "National Labor Relations Act."

Sec. 18. [Obsolete]

Individuals with Religious Convictions

Sec. 19. Any employee who is a member of and adheres to established and traditional tenets or teachings of a bona fide religion, body, or sect which has historically held conscientious objections to joining or financially supporting labor organizations shall not be required to join or financially support any labor organization as a condition of employment; except that such employee may be required in a contract between such employee's employer and a labor organization in lieu of periodic dues and initiation fees, to pay sums equal to such dues and initiation fees to a nonreligious, nonlabor organization charitable fund exempt from taxation under section 501(c)(3) of title 26 of the Internal Revenue Code, chosen by such employee from a list of at least three such funds, designated in such contract or if the contract fails to designate such funds, then to any such fund chosen by the employee. If such employee who holds conscientious objections pursuant to this section requests the labor organization to use the grievance arbitration procedure on the employee's behalf, the labor organization is authorized to charge the employee for the reasonable cost of using such procedure.

TITLE II

Conciliation of Labor Disputes in Industries Affecting Commerce: National Emergencies

Sec. 201. It is the policy of the United States that—

(a) sound and stable industrial peace and the advancement of the general welfare, health, and safety of the Nation and of the best interests of employers and employees can most satisfactorily be secured by the settlement of issues between employers and employees through the processes of conference and collective bargaining between employers and the representatives of their employees;

(b) the settlement of issues between employers and employees through collective bargaining may be advanced by making available full and adequate governmental facilities for conciliation, mediation, and voluntary arbitration to aid and encourage employers and the representatives of their employees to reach and maintain agreements concerning rates of pay, hours, and working conditions, and to make all reasonable efforts to settle their differences by mutual agreement reached through conferences and collective bargaining or by such methods as may be provided for in any applicable agreement for the settlement of disputes; and

(c) certain controversies which arise between parties to collective bargaining agreements may be avoided or minimized by making available full and adequate governmental facilities for furnishing assistance to employers and the representatives of their employees in formulating for inclusion within such agreements provision for adequate notice of any proposed changes in the terms of such agreements, for the final adjustment of grievances or questions regarding the application or interpretation of such agreements, and other provisions designed to prevent the subsequent arising of such controversies.

Sec. 202. (a) There is created an independent agency to be known as the Federal Mediation and Conciliation Service (herein referred to as the "Service," except that for sixty days after June 23, 1947, such term shall refer to the Conciliation Service of the Department of Labor). The Service shall be under the direction of a Federal Mediation and Conciliation Director (hereinafter referred to as the "Director"), who shall be appointed by the President by and with the advice and consent of the Senate. The Director shall not engage in any other business, vocation, or employment.

(b) The Director is authorized, subject to the civil service laws, to appoint such clerical and other personnel as may be necessary for the execution of the functions of the Service, and shall fix their compensation in accordance with sections 5101 to 5115 and sections 5331 to 5338 of title 5, United States Code, and may, without regard to the provisions of the civil service laws, appoint such conciliators and mediators as may be necessary to carry out the functions of the Service. The Director is authorized to make such expenditures for supplies, facilities, and services as he deems necessary. Such expenditures shall be allowed and paid upon presentation of itemized vouchers therefore approved by the Director or by any employee designated by him for that purpose.

(c) The principal office of the Service shall be in the District of Columbia, but the Director may establish regional offices convenient to localities in which labor controversies are likely to arise. The Director may by order, subject to revocation at any time, delegate any authority and discretion conferred upon him by this Act to any regional director, or other officer or employee of the Service. The Director may establish suitable procedures for cooperation with State and local mediation agencies. The Director shall make an annual report in writing to Congress at the end of the fiscal year.

(d) All mediation and conciliation functions of the Secretary of Labor or the United States Conciliation Service under section 51 [repealed] of title 29, United States Code, and all functions of the United States Conciliation Service under any other law are transferred to the Federal Mediation and Conciliation Service, together with the personnel and records of the United States Conciliation Service. Such transfer shall take effect upon the sixtieth day after June 23, 1947. Such transfer shall not affect any proceedings pending before the United States Conciliation Service or any certification, order, rule, or regulation theretofore made by it or by the Secretary of Labor. The Director and the Service shall not be subject in any way to the jurisdiction or authority of the Secretary of Labor or any official or division of the Department of Labor.

Functions of the Service

Sec. 203. (a) It shall be the duty of the Service, in order to prevent or minimize interruptions of the free flow of commerce growing out of labor disputes, to assist parties to labor disputes in industries affecting commerce to settle such disputes through conciliation and mediation.

(b) The Service may proffer its services in any labor dispute in any industry affecting commerce, either upon its own motion or upon the request of one or more of the parties to the dispute, whenever in its judgment such dispute threatens to cause a substantial interruption of commerce. The Director and the Service are directed to avoid attempting to mediate disputes which would have only a minor effect on interstate commerce if State or other conciliation services are available to the parties. Whenever the Service does proffer its services in any dispute, it shall be the duty of the Service promptly to put itself in communication with the parties and to use its best efforts, by mediation and conciliation, to bring them to agreement.

(c) If the Director is not able to bring the parties to agreement by conciliation within a reasonable time, he shall seek to induce the parties voluntarily to seek other means of settling the dispute without resort to strike, lockout, or other coercion, including submission to the employees in the bargaining unit of the employer's last offer of settlement for approval or rejection in a secret ballot. The failure or refusal of either party to agree to any procedure suggested by the Director shall not be deemed a violation of any duty or obligation imposed by this Act.

(d) Final adjustment by a method agreed upon by the parties is declared to be the desirable method for settlement of grievance disputes arising over the application or interpretation of an existing collective bargaining agreement. The Service is directed to make its conciliation and mediation services available in the settlement of such grievance disputes only as a last resort and in exceptional cases.

(e) The Service is authorized and directed to encourage and support the establishment and operation of joint labor management activities conducted by plant, area, and industry-wide committees designed to improve labor management relationships, job security, and organizational effectiveness, in accordance with the provisions of section 205A.

(f) The Service may make its services available to Federal agencies to aid in the resolution of disputes under the provisions of subchapter IV of Chapter 5 of title 5, United States Code. Functions performed by the Service may include assisting parties to disputes related to administrative programs, training persons in skills and procedures employed in alternative means of dispute resolution, and furnishing officers and employees of the Service to act as neutrals. Only officers and employees who are qualified in accordance with section 573 of title 5 may be assigned to act as neutrals. The Service shall consult with the agency designated by, or the interagency committee designated or established by, the President under section 573 of title 5 in maintaining rosters of neutrals and arbitrators, and to adopt such procedures and rules as are necessary to carry out the services authorized in this subsection.

Sec. 204. (a) In order to prevent or minimize interruptions of the free flow of commerce growing out of labor disputes, employers and employees and their representatives, in any industry affecting commerce, shall—

1. exert every reasonable effort to make and maintain agreements concerning rates of pay, hours, and working conditions, including provision for adequate notice of any proposed change in the terms of such agreements;
2. whenever a dispute arises over the terms or application of a collective bargaining agreement and a conference is requested by a party or prospective party thereto, arrange promptly for such a conference to be held and endeavor in such conference to settle such dispute expeditiously; and
3. In case such dispute is not settled by conference, participate fully and promptly in such meetings as may be undertaken by the Service under this Act for the purpose of aiding in a settlement of the dispute.

Sec. 205. (a) There is created a National Labor–Management Panel which shall be composed of twelve members appointed by the President, six of whom shall be elected from among persons outstanding in the field of management and six of whom shall be selected from among persons outstanding in the field of labor. Each member shall hold office for a term of three years, except that any member appointed to fill a vacancy occurring prior to the expiration of the term for which his predecessor was appointed shall be appointed for the remainder of such term, and the terms of office of the members first taking office shall expire, as designated by the President at the time of appointment, four at the end of the first year, four at the end of the second year, and four at the end of the third year after the date of appointment. Members of the panel, when serving on business of the panel, shall be paid compensation at the rate of $25 per day, and shall also be entitled to receive an allowance for actual and necessary travel and subsistence expenses while so serving away from their places of residence.

(b) It shall be the duty of the panel, at the request of the Director, to advise in the avoidance of industrial controversies and the manner in which mediation and voluntary adjustment shall be administered, particularly with reference to controversies affecting the general welfare of the country.

Sec. 205A. (a)(1) The Service is authorized and directed to provide assistance in the establishment and operation of plant, area, and industrywide labor management committees which—

A. have been organized jointly by employers and labor organizations representing employees in that plant, area, or industry; and
B. are established for the purpose of improving labor management relationships, job security, organizational effectiveness, enhancing economic development, or involving workers in decisions affecting their jobs including improving communication with respect to subjects of mutual interest and concern.

(2) The Service is authorized and directed to enter into contracts and to make grants, where necessary or appropriate, to fulfill its responsibilities under this section.

(b)(1) No grant may be made, no contract may be entered into, and no other assistance may be provided under the provisions of this section to a plant labor–management committee unless the employees in that plant are represented by a labor organization and there is in effect at that plant a collective bargaining agreement.

(2) No grant may be made, no contract may be entered into, and no other assistance may be provided under the provisions of this section to an area or industrywide labor–management

committee unless its participants include any labor organizations certified or recognized as the representative of the employees of an employer participating in such committee. Nothing in this clause shall prohibit participation in an area or industrywide committee by an employer whose employees are not represented by a labor organization.

(3) No grant may be made under the provisions of this section to any labor–management committee which the Service finds to have as one of its purposes the discouragement of the exercise of rights contained in section 7 of the National Labor Relations Act, or the interference with collective bargaining in any plant or industry.

(c) The Service shall carry out the provisions of this section through an office established for that purpose.

(d) There are authorized to be appropriated to carry out the provisions of this section $10,000,000 for the fiscal year 1979, and such sums as may be necessary thereafter.

National Emergencies

Sec. 206. Whenever in the opinion of the President of the United States, a threatened or actual strike or lockout affecting an entire industry or a substantial part thereof engaged in trade, commerce, transportation, transmission, or communication among the several States or with foreign nations, or engaged in the production of goods for commerce, will, if permitted to occur or to continue, imperil the national health or safety, he may appoint a board of inquiry to inquire into the issues involved in the dispute and to make a written report to him within such time as he shall prescribe. Such report shall include a statement of the facts with respect to the dispute, including each party's statement of its position, but shall not contain any recommendations. The President shall file a copy of such report with the Service and shall make its contents available to the public.

Sec. 207. (a) A board of inquiry shall be composed of a chairman and such other members as the President shall determine, and shall have power to sit and act in any place within the United States and to conduct such hearings either in public or in private, as it may deem necessary or proper, to ascertain the facts with respect to the causes and circumstances of the dispute.

(b) Members of a board of inquiry shall receive compensation at the rate of $50 for each day actually spent by them in the work of the board, together with necessary travel and subsistence expenses.

(c) For the purpose of any hearing or inquiry conducted by any board appointed under this title, the provisions of sections 49 and 50 of title 15, United States Code (relating to the attendance of witnesses and the production of books, papers, and documents) are made applicable to the powers and duties of such board.

Sec. 208. (a) Upon receiving a report from a board of inquiry the President may direct the Attorney General to petition any district court of the United States having jurisdiction of the parties to enjoin such strike or lockout or the continuing thereof, and if the court finds that such threatened or actual strike or lockout—

(i) affects an entire industry or a substantial part thereof engaged in trade, commerce, transportation, transmission, or communication among the several States or with foreign nations, or engaged in the production of goods for commerce; and

(ii) if permitted to occur or to continue, will imperil the national health or safety, it shall have jurisdiction to enjoin any such strike or lockout, or the continuing thereof, and to make such other orders as may be appropriate.

(b) In any case, the provisions of the Norris–LaGuardia Act shall not be applicable.

(c) The order or orders of the court shall be subject to review by the appropriate United States court of appeals and by the Supreme Court upon writ of certiorari or certification as provided in section 1254 of title 28, United States Code.

Sec. 209. (a) Whenever a district court has issued an order under section 208 enjoining acts or practices which imperil or threaten to imperil the national health or safety, it shall be the duty of the parties to the labor dispute giving rise to such order to make every effort to adjust and settle their differences, with the assistance of the Service created by this Act. Neither party shall be under any duty to accept, in whole or in part, any proposal of settlement made by the Service.

(b) Upon the issuance of such order, the President shall reconvene the board of inquiry which has previously reported with respect to the dispute. At the end of a sixty-day period (unless the dispute has been settled by that time), the board of inquiry shall report to the President the current position of the parties and the efforts which have been made for settlement, and shall include a statement by each party of its position and a statement of the employer's last offer of settlement. The President shall make such report available to the public. The National Labor Relations Board, within the succeeding fifteen days, shall take a secret ballot of the employees of each employer involved in the dispute on the question of whether they wish to accept the final offer of settlement made by their employer, as stated by him and shall certify the results thereof to the Attorney General within five days thereafter.

Sec. 210. Upon the certification of the results of such ballot or upon a settlement being reached, whichever happens sooner, the Attorney General shall move the court to discharge the injunction, which motion shall then be granted and the injunction discharged. When such motion is granted, the President shall submit to the Congress a full and comprehensive report of the proceedings, including the findings of the board of inquiry and the ballot taken by the National Labor Relations Board, together with such recommendations as he may see fit to make for consideration and appropriate action.

Compilation of Collective Bargaining Agreements, etc.

Sec. 211. (a) For the guidance and information of interested representatives of employers, employees, and the general public, the Bureau of Labor Statistics of the Department of Labor shall maintain a file of copies of all available collective bargaining agreements and other available agreements and actions there under settling or adjusting labor disputes. Such file shall be open to inspection under appropriate conditions prescribed by the Secretary of Labor, except that no specific information submitted in confidence shall be disclosed.

(b) The Bureau of Labor Statistics in the Department of Labor is authorized to furnish upon request of the Service, or employers, employees, or their representatives, all available data and factual information which may aid in the settlement of any labor dispute, except that no specific information submitted in confidence shall be disclosed.

Exemption of Railway Labor Act

Sec. 212. The provisions of this title shall not be applicable with respect to any matter which is subject to the provisions of the Railway Labor Act, as amended from time to time.

Conciliation of Labor Disputes in the Health Care Industry

Sec. 213. (a) If, in the opinion of the Director of the Federal Mediation and Conciliation Service, a threatened or actual strike or lockout affecting a health care institution will, if permitted to occur or to continue, substantially interrupt the delivery of health care in the locality concerned, the Director may further assist in the resolution of the impasse by establishing within 30 days after the notice to the Federal Mediation and Conciliation Service under clause (A) of the last sentence of section 8(d) (which is required by clause (3) of such section 8(d)), or within 10 days after the notice under clause (B), an impartial Board of Inquiry to investigate the issues involved in the dispute and to make a written report thereon to the parties within fifteen (15) days after the establishment of such a Board. The written report shall contain the findings of fact together with the Board's recommendations for settling the dispute, with the objective of achieving a prompt, peaceful, and just settlement of the dispute. Each such Board shall be composed of such number of individuals as the Director may deem desirable. No member appointed under this section shall have any interest or involvement in the health care institutions or the employee organizations involved in the dispute.

(b)(1) Members of any board established under this section who are otherwise employed by the Federal Government shall serve without compensation but shall be reimbursed for travel, subsistence, and other necessary expenses incurred by them in carrying out its duties under this section.

(2) Members of any board established under this section who are not subject to paragraph (1) shall receive compensation at a rate prescribed by the Director but not to exceed the daily rate prescribed for GS–18 of the General Schedule under section 5332 of title 5, United States Code, including travel for each day they are engaged in the performance of their duties under this section, and shall be entitled to reimbursement for travel, subsistence, and other necessary expenses incurred by them in carrying out their duties under this section.

(c) After the establishment of a board under subsection (a) of this section and for 15 days after any such board has issued its report, no change in the status quo in effect prior to the expiration of the contract in the case of negotiations for a contract renewal, or in effect prior to the time of the impasse in the case of an initial bargaining negotiation, except by agreement, shall be made by the parties to the controversy.

(d) There are authorized to be appropriated such sums as may be necessary to carry out the provisions of this section.

TITLE III

Suits by and against Labor Organizations

Sec. 301. (a) Suits for violation of contracts between an employer and a labor organization representing employees in an industry affecting commerce as defined in this Act or between any such labor organization, may be brought in any district court of the United States having jurisdiction of the parties, without respect to the amount in controversy or without regard to the citizenship of the parties.

(b) Any labor organization which represents employees in an industry affecting commerce as defined in this Act and any employer whose activities affect commerce as defined in this Act shall be bound by the acts of its agents. Any such labor organization may sue or be sued as an entity and in behalf of the employees whom it represents in the courts of the United States. Any money judgment against a labor organization in a district court of the United States shall be enforceable only against the organization as an entity and against its assets, and shall not be enforceable against any individual member or his assets.

(c) For the purposes of actions and proceedings by or against labor organizations in the district courts of the United States, district courts shall be deemed to have jurisdiction of a labor organization (1) in the district in which such organization maintains its principal offices, or (2) in any district in which its duly authorized officers or agents are engaged in representing or acting for employee members.

(d) The service of summons, subpoena, or other legal process of any court of the United States upon an officer or agent of a labor organization, in his capacity as such, shall constitute service upon the labor organization.

(e) For the purposes of this section, in determining whether any person is acting as an "agent" of another person so as to make such other person responsible for his acts, the question of whether the specific acts performed were actually authorized or subsequently ratified shall not be controlling.

Restrictions on Payments to Employee Representatives

Sec. 302. (a) It shall be unlawful for any employer or association of employers or any person who acts as a labor relations expert, adviser, or consultant to an employer or who acts in the interest of an employer to pay, lend, or deliver, or agree to pay, lend, or deliver, any money or other thing of value—

1. to any representative of any of his employees who are employed in an industry affecting commerce; or
2. to any labor organization, or any officer or employee thereof, which represents, seeks to represent, or would admit to membership, any of the employees of such employer who are employed in an industry affecting commerce;
3. to any employee or group or committee of employees of such employer employed in an industry affecting commerce in excess of their normal compensation for the purpose of causing such employee or group or committee directly or indirectly to influence any other employees in the exercise of the right to organize and bargain collectively through representatives of their own choosing; or
4. to any officer or employee of a labor organization engaged in an industry affecting commerce with intent to influence him in respect to any of his actions, decisions, or duties as a representative of employees or as such officer or employee of such labor organization.

(b)(1) It shall be unlawful for any person to request, demand, receive, or accept, or agree to receive or accept, any payment, loan, or delivery of any money or other thing of value prohibited by subsection (a).

(2) It shall be unlawful for any labor organization, or for any person acting as an officer, agent, representative, or employee of such labor organization, to demand or accept from the operator of any motor vehicle (as defined in part II of the Interstate Commerce Act) employed in the transportation of property in commerce, or the employer of any such operator, any money or other thing of value payable to such organization or to an officer, agent, representative, or employee thereof as a fee or charge for the unloading, or in connection with the unloading, of the cargo of such vehicle: Provided, That nothing in this paragraph shall be construed to make unlawful any payment by an employer to any of his employees as compensation for their services as employees.

(c) The provisions of this section shall not be applicable (1) in respect to any money or other thing of value payable by an employer to any of his employees whose established duties include acting openly for such employer in matters of labor relations or personnel administration or to any representative of his employees, or to any officer or employee of a labor organization who is also an employee or former employee of such employer, as compensation for, or by reason of, his service as an employee of such employer; (2) with respect to the payment or delivery of any money or other thing of value in satisfaction of a judgment of any court or a decision or award of an arbitrator or impartial chairman or in compromise, adjustment, settlement, or release of any claim, complaint, grievance, or dispute in the absence of fraud or duress; (3) with respect to the sale or purchase of an article or commodity at the prevailing market price in the regular course of business; (4) with respect to money deducted from the wages of employees in payment of membership dues in a labor organization: Provided, That the employer has received from each employee, on whose account such deductions are made, a written assignment which shall not be irrevocable for a period of more than one year, or beyond the termination date of the applicable collective agreement, whichever occurs sooner; (5) with respect to money or other thing of value paid to a trust fund established by such representative, for the sole and exclusive benefit of the employees of such employer, and their families and dependents (or of such employees, families, and dependents jointly with the employees of other employers making similar payments, and their families and dependents): Provided, That (A) such payments are held in trust for the purpose of paying, either from principal or income or both, for the benefit of employees, their families and dependents, for medical or hospital care, pensions on retirement or death of employees, compensation for injuries or illness resulting from occupational activity or insurance to provide any of the foregoing, or unemployment benefits or life insurance, disability and sickness insurance, or accident insurance; (B) the detailed basis on which such payments are to be made is specified in a written agreement with the employer, and employees and employers are equally represented in the administration of such fund, together with such neutral persons as the representatives of the employers and the representatives of employees may agree upon; and in the event the employer and employee groups deadlock on the administration of such fund and there are no neutral persons empowered to break such deadlock, such agreement provides that the two groups shall agree on an impartial umpire to decide such dispute, or in event of their failure to agree within a reasonable length of time, an impartial umpire to decide such dispute shall, on petition of either group, be appointed by the district court of the United States for the district where the trust fund has its principal office, and shall also contain provisions for an annual audit of the trust fund, a statement of the results of which shall be available for inspection by interested persons at the principal office of the trust fund and at such other places as may be designated in such written agreement; and (C) such payments as are intended to be used for the purpose of providing pensions or annuities for employees are made to a separate trust which provides that the funds held therein cannot be used for any purpose other than paying such pensions or annuities; (6) with respect to money or other thing of value paid by any employer to a trust fund established by such representative for the purpose of pooled vacation, holiday, severance or similar benefits, or defraying costs of apprenticeship or other training programs: Provided, That the requirements of clause (B) of the proviso to clause (5) of this subsection shall apply to such trust funds; (7) with respect to money or other thing of value paid by any employer to a pooled or individual trust fund established by such representative for the purpose of (A) scholarships for the benefit of employees, their families, and dependents for study at educational institutions, (B) child care centers for preschool and school-age dependents of employees, or (C) financial assistance for employee housing: Provided, That no labor organization or employer shall be required to bargain on the establishment of any such trust fund, and refusal to do so shall not constitute an unfair labor practice: Provided further, That the requirements of clause (B) of the proviso to clause (5) of this subsection shall apply to such trust funds; (8) with respect to money or any other thing of value paid by any employer to a trust fund established by such representative for the purpose of defraying the costs of legal services for employees, their families, and dependents for counsel or plan of their choice: Provided, That the requirements of clause (B) of the proviso to clause (5) of this subsection shall apply to such trust funds: Provided further, That no such legal services shall be furnished: (A) to initiate any proceeding directed (i) against any such employer or its officers or agents except in workman's compensation cases, or (ii) against such labor organization, or its parent or subordinate bodies, or their officers or agents, or (iii) against any other employer or labor organization, or their officers or agents, in any matter arising under the National Labor Relations Act, or this Act; and (B) in any proceeding where a labor organization would be prohibited from defraying the costs of legal services by the provisions of the

Labor–Management Reporting and Disclosure Act of 1959; or (9) with respect to money or other things of value paid by an employer to a plant, area, or industrywide labor management committee established for one or more of the purposes set forth in section 5(b) of the Labor Management Cooperation Act of 1978.

(d) Any person who willfully violates any of the provisions of this section shall, upon conviction thereof, be guilty of a misdemeanor and be subject to a fine of not more than $10,000 or to imprisonment for not more than one year, or both.

(e) The district courts of the United States and the United States courts of the Territories and possessions shall have jurisdiction, for cause shown, and subject to the provisions of rule 65 of the Federal Rules of Civil Procedure (relating to notice to opposite party) to restrain violations of this section, without regard to the provisions of the Clayton Act and the Norris–LaGuardia Act.

(f) This section shall not apply to any contract in force on June 23, 1947, until the expiration of such contract, or until July 1, 1948, whichever first occurs.

(g) Compliance with the restrictions contained in subsection (c)(5)(B) upon contributions to trust funds, otherwise lawful, shall not be applicable to contributions to such trust funds established by collective agreement prior to January 1, 1946, nor shall subsection (c)(5)(A) be construed as prohibiting contributions to such trust funds if prior to January 1, 1947, such funds contained provisions for pooled vacation benefits.

Boycotts and Other Unlawful Combinations

Sec. 303. (a) It shall be unlawful, for the purpose of this section only, in an industry or activity affecting commerce, for any labor organization to engage in any activity or conduct defined as an unfair labor practice in section 8(b)(4) of the National Labor Relations Act.

(b) Whoever shall be injured in his business or property by reason of any violation of subsection (a) may sue therefore in any district court of the United States subject to the limitation and provisions of section 301 hereof without respect to the amount in controversy, or in any other court having jurisdiction of the parties, and shall recover the damages by him sustained and the cost of the suit.

TITLE IV

Creation of Joint Committee to Study and Report on Basic Problems Affecting Friendly Labor Relations and Productivity

Secs. 401–407. Omitted.

TITLE V

Definitions

Sec. 501. When used in this Act—

(1) The term "industry affecting commerce" means any industry or activity in commerce or in which a labor dispute would burden or obstruct commerce or tend to burden or obstruct commerce or the free flow of commerce.

(2) The term "strike" includes any strike or other concerted stoppage of work by employees (including a stoppage by reason of the expiration of a collective bargaining agreement) and any concerted slowdown or other concerted interruption of operations by employees.

(3) The terms "commerce," "labor disputes," "employer," "employee," "labor organization," "representative," "person," and "supervisor" shall have the same meaning as when used in the National Labor Relations Act as amended by this Act.

Saving Provision

Sec. 502. Nothing in this Act shall be construed to require an individual employee to render labor or service without his consent, nor shall anything in this Act be construed to make the quitting of his labor by an individual employee an illegal act; nor shall any court issue any process to compel the performance by an individual employee of such labor or service, without his consent; nor shall the quitting of labor by an employee or employees in good faith because of abnormally dangerous conditions for work at the place of employment of such employee or employees be deemed a strike under this Act.

Separability

Sec. 503. If any provision of this Act or the application of such provision to any person or circumstance, shall be held invalid, the remainder of this Act or the application of such provision to persons or circumstances other than those as to which it is held invalid, shall not be affected thereby.

End Note

1. *Author's note:* The Taft-Hartley Act qualified this statement to find that "some employers" (rather than "employers") deny the rights of employees to organize and accept the procedure of collective bargaining, and also added a fourth paragraph:

   Experience has further demonstrated that certain practices by some labor organizations, their officers, and members have the intent or the necessary effect of burdening or obstructing commerce by preventing the free flow of goods in such commerce through strikes and other forms of industrial unrest or through concerted activities which impair the interest of the public in the free flow of such commerce. The elimination of such practices is a necessary condition to the assurance of the rights herein guaranteed.

Appendix B

Universal Declaration of Human Rights (United Nations, 1948)[1]

PREAMBLE

Whereas recognition of the inherent dignity and of the equal and inalienable rights of all members of the human family is the foundation of freedom, justice, and peace in the world,

Whereas disregard and contempt for human rights have resulted in barbarous acts which have outraged the conscience of mankind, and the advent of a world in which human beings shall enjoy freedom of speech and belief and freedom from fear and want has been proclaimed as the highest aspiration of the common people,

Whereas it is essential, if man is not to be compelled to have recourse, as a last resort, to rebellion against tyranny and oppression, that human rights should be protected by the rule of law,

Whereas it is essential to promote the development of friendly relations between nations,

Whereas the peoples of the United Nations have in the Charter reaffirmed their faith in fundamental human rights, in the dignity and worth of the human person, and in the equal rights of men and women and have determined to promote social progress and better standards of life in larger freedom,

Whereas Member States have pledged themselves to achieve, in co-operation with the United Nations, the promotion of universal respect for and observance of human rights and fundamental freedoms,

Whereas a common understanding of these rights and freedoms is of the greatest importance for the full realization of this pledge,

Now, therefore, The General Assembly,

Proclaims this Universal Declaration of Human Rights as a common standard of achievement for all peoples and all nations, to the end that every individual and every organ of society, keeping this Declaration constantly in mind, shall strive by teaching and education to promote respect for these rights and freedoms and by progressive measures, national and international, to secure their universal and effective recognition and observance, both among the peoples of Member States themselves and among the peoples of territories under their jurisdiction.

ARTICLE 1

All human beings are born free and equal in dignity and rights. They are endowed with reason and conscience and should act towards one another in a spirit of brotherhood.

ARTICLE 2

Everyone is entitled to all the rights and freedoms set forth in this Declaration, without distinction of any kind, such as race, color, sex, language, religion, political or other opinion, national or social origin, property, birth, or other status. Furthermore, no distinction shall be made on the basis of the political, jurisdictional, or international status of the country or territory to which a person belongs, whether it be independent, trust, non-self-governing, or under any other limitation of sovereignty.

ARTICLE 3

Everyone has the right to life, liberty, and security of person.

ARTICLE 4

No one shall be held in slavery or servitude; slavery and the slave trade shall be prohibited in all their forms.

ARTICLE 5

No one shall be subjected to torture or to cruel, inhuman, or degrading treatment or punishment.

ARTICLE 6

Everyone has the right to recognition everywhere as a person before the law.

ARTICLE 7

All are equal before the law and are entitled without any discrimination to equal protection of the law. All are entitled to equal protection against any discrimination in violation of this Declaration and against any incitement to such discrimination.

ARTICLE 8

Everyone has the right to an effective remedy by the competent national tribunals for acts violating the fundamental rights granted him by the constitution or by law.

ARTICLE 9

No one shall be subjected to arbitrary arrest, detention, or exile.

ARTICLE 10

Everyone is entitled in full equality to a fair and public hearing by an independent and impartial tribunal, in the determination of his rights and obligations and of any criminal charge against him.

ARTICLE 11

1. Everyone charged with a penal offence has the right to be presumed innocent until proved guilty according to law in a public trial at which he has had all the guarantees necessary for his defense.
2. No one shall be held guilty of any penal offence on account of any act or omission which did not constitute a penal offence, under national or international law, at the time when it was committed. Nor shall a heavier penalty be imposed than the one that was applicable at the time the penal offence was committed.

ARTICLE 12

No one shall be subjected to arbitrary interference with his privacy, family, home, or correspondence, nor to attacks upon his honor and reputation. Everyone has the right to the protection of the law against such interference or attacks.

ARTICLE 13

1. Everyone has the right to freedom of movement and residence within the borders of each state.
2. Everyone has the right to leave any country, including his own, and to return to his country.

ARTICLE 14

1. Everyone has the right to seek and to enjoy in other countries asylum from persecution.
2. This right may not be invoked in the case of prosecutions genuinely arising from nonpolitical crimes or from acts contrary to the purposes and principles of the United Nations.

ARTICLE 15

1. Everyone has the right to a nationality.
2. No one shall be arbitrarily deprived of his nationality nor denied the right to change his nationality.

ARTICLE 16

1. Men and women of full age, without any limitation due to race, nationality, or religion, have the right to marry and to found a family. They are entitled to equal rights as to marriage, during marriage and at its dissolution.
2. Marriage shall be entered into only with the free and full consent of the intending spouses.
3. The family is the natural and fundamental group unit of society and is entitled to protection by society and the State.

ARTICLE 17

1. Everyone has the right to own property alone as well as in association with others.
2. No one shall be arbitrarily deprived of his property.

ARTICLE 18

Everyone has the right to freedom of thought, conscience, and religion; this right includes freedom to change his religion or belief, and freedom, either alone or in community with others and in public or private, to manifest his religion or belief in teaching, practice, worship, and observance.

ARTICLE 19

Everyone has the right to freedom of opinion and expression; this right includes freedom to hold opinions without interference and to seek, receive, and impart information and ideas through any media and regardless of frontiers.

ARTICLE 20

1. Everyone has the right to freedom of peaceful assembly and association.
2. No one may be compelled to belong to an association.

ARTICLE 21

1. Everyone has the right to take part in the government of his country, directly or through freely chosen representatives.
2. Everyone has the right of equal access to public service in his country.
3. The will of the people shall be the basis of the authority of government; this will shall be expressed in periodic and genuine elections which shall be by universal and equal suffrage and shall be held by secret vote or by equivalent free voting procedures.

ARTICLE 22

Everyone, as a member of society, has the right to social security and is entitled to realization, through national effort and international co-operation and in accordance with the organization and resources of each State, of the economic, social, and cultural rights indispensable for his dignity and the free development of his personality.

ARTICLE 23

1. Everyone has the right to work, to free choice of employment, to just and favorable conditions of work, and to protection against unemployment.
2. Everyone, without any discrimination, has the right to equal pay for equal work.
3. Everyone who works has the right to just and favorable remuneration ensuring for himself and his family an existence worthy of human dignity, and supplemented, if necessary, by other means of social protection.
4. Everyone has the right to form and to join trade unions for the protection of his interests.

ARTICLE 24

Everyone has the right to rest and leisure, including reasonable limitation of working hours and periodic holidays with pay.

ARTICLE 25

1. Everyone has the right to a standard of living adequate for the health and well-being of himself and of his family, including food, clothing, housing, and medical care and necessary social services, and the right to security in the event of unemployment, sickness, disability, widowhood, old age, or other lack of livelihood in circumstances beyond his control.
2. Motherhood and childhood are entitled to special care and assistance. All children, whether born in or out of wedlock, shall enjoy the same social protection.

ARTICLE 26

1. Everyone has the right to education. Education shall be free, at least in the elementary and fundamental stages. Elementary education shall be compulsory. Technical and professional education shall be made generally available, and higher education shall be equally accessible to all on the basis of merit.
2. Education shall be directed to the full development of the human personality and to the strengthening of respect for human rights and fundamental freedoms. It shall promote understanding, tolerance, and friendship among all nations, racial or religious groups, and shall further the activities of the United Nations for the maintenance of peace.
3. Parents have a prior right to choose the kind of education that shall be given to their children.

ARTICLE 27

1. Everyone has the right freely to participate in the cultural life of the community, to enjoy the arts, and to share in scientific advancement and its benefits.
2. Everyone has the right to the protection of the moral and material interests resulting from any scientific, literary, or artistic production of which he is the author.

ARTICLE 28

Everyone is entitled to a social and international order in which the rights and freedoms set forth in this Declaration can be fully realized.

ARTICLE 29

1. Everyone has duties to the community in which alone the free and full development of his personality is possible.
2. In the exercise of his rights and freedoms, everyone shall be subject only to such limitations as are determined by law solely for the purpose of securing due recognition and respect for the rights and freedoms of others and of meeting the just requirements of morality, public order, and the general welfare in a democratic society.
3. These rights and freedoms may in no case be exercised contrary to the purposes and principles of the United Nations.

ARTICLE 30

Nothing in this Declaration may be interpreted as implying for any State, group, or person any right to engage in any activity or to perform any act aimed at the destruction of any of the rights and freedoms set forth herein.

End Note

1. Adopted and proclaimed by the General Assembly of the United Nations on December 10, 1948.

Appendix C

A Sample NLRB Decision

Looking at real NLRB decisions can help us understand not only the application of the NLRA but also how the U.S. labor law system operates. The following decision illustrates the common elements of NLRB decisions. By convention, this case can be cited as *News Journal Company,* 331 NLRB No. 117 (2000) or as *News Journal Company,* 331 NLRB 1331 (2000). From these citations, we see that this decision is part of the 331st volume of NLRB decisions and is the 117th decision in this volume and begins on page 1331. Citations for other legal decisions are similar; for example, *NLRB v. Katz,* 369 U.S. 736 (1962) refers to a 1962 U.S. Supreme Court decision in volume 369 that starts on page 736 of that volume. All NLRB decisions are online at *www.nlrb.gov*, and they continue to follow these print-based numbering conventions.

Unfair labor practice cases are first heard by an administrative law judge who issues a written opinion that includes a statement of the issues, a review of the factual background information, a legal analysis, conclusions of law, and if necessary, remedies (see the following example). In the *News Journal Company* case, a union (the Newspaper Guild) accused the employer (The News Journal Company) of violating sections 8(a)(1) and 8(a)(5) by granting wage increases to certain employees without bargaining over them, but the law judge did not agree, so he dismissed the case. This decision was appealed to the NLRB in Washington by the NLRB's general counsel. Three members of the NLRB considered the case and affirmed the judge's dismissal of the case. Note that in the published decisions, the NLRB's decision appears before the administrative law judge's decision, even though chronologically the law judge's decision occurred first.

In *News Journal Company* the NLRB affirmed the law judge's decision without any discussion. In other cases, the NLRB might overturn or expand upon the law judge's decision. This case is presented here because it is concise; most cases are more complicated and have longer descriptions of the facts and more complex legal analyses. Note, however, that even in this case the law judge relied on previous NLRB and court precedents when making his determination.

Gannett Co., Inc., d/b/a The News Journal Company and The Newspaper Guild of Greater Philadelphia, Local No. 10 a/w The Newspaper Guild, AFL–CIO–CLC. Case 4–CA–26797

August 25, 2000

DECISION AND ORDER

BY MEMBERS FOX, LIEBMAN, AND BRAME

On February 18, 2000, Administrative Law Judge Bruce D. Rosenstein issued the attached decision. The General Counsel filed exceptions and a supporting brief which the Charging Party joined. The Respondent filed an answering brief.

The National Labor Relations Board has delegated its authority in this proceeding to a three-member panel.

The Board has considered the record in light of the exceptions and briefs, and has decided to affirm the judge's rulings, findings,[1] and conclusions, and to adopt the recommended Order.

ORDER

The complaint is dismissed.

Margaret M. McGovern, Esq., and *Anne C. Ritterspach, Esq.*, for the General Counsel.

Joyce T. Bailey, Esq., of Arlington, Virginia, for the Respondent Employer.

Laurence M. Goodman, Esq., of Philadelphia, Pennsylvania, for the Charging Party.

[1]The General Counsel and the Charging Party have excepted to some of the judge's credibility findings. The Board's established policy is not to overrule an administrative law judge's credibility resolutions unless the clear preponderance of all the relevant evidence convinces us that they are incorrect. *Standard Dry Wall Products*, 91 NLRB 544 (1950), enfd. 188 F.2d 362 (3d Cir. 1951). We have carefully examined the record and find no basis for reversing the findings.

In affirming the judge's decision, Member Fox and Member Liebman note that significantly more employees with satisfactory ratings at the end of their probationary period received raises from 1993 through September 1997 than received them from October 1997 through 1999. In some cases, a numerical showing is sufficient to establish a discontinuation of past practice and, hence, a violation. *Electrical South, Inc.*, 327 NLRB 270 (1998). Here, however, the Respondent adduced evidence, which was credited by the judge, that the decision to award postprobationary merit wage increases was highly subjective and depended on numerous criteria, including budget, skill, and area of specialty, and the General Counsel failed to show that executive editors who approved those raises prior to October 1997 applied different criteria than current Executive Editor Jane Amari in determining whether to give merit increases.

DECISION

STATEMENT OF THE CASE

Bruce D. Rosenstein, Administrative Law Judge. This case was tried before me on October 27, 1999, in Philadelphia, Pennsylvania, pursuant to a complaint and notice of hearing (the complaint) issued by the Regional Director for Region 4 of the National Labor Relations Board (the Board) on August 27, 1998. The complaint, based on an original and amended charge filed by The Newspaper Guild of Greater Philadelphia, Local 10 a/w The Newspaper Guild, AFL–CIO–CLC (the Charging Party or the Union), alleges that Gannett Co., Inc., d/b/a The News Journal Company (the Respondent or Employer), has engaged in certain violations of Section 8(a)(1) and (5) of the National Relations Act (the Act).[1] The Respondent filed a timely answer to the complaint denying that it had committed any violations of the Act.

ISSUES

The complaint alleges that about July 1997,[2] Respondent discontinued its practice of considering and, when appropriate, granting wage increases to the editorial unit employees on successful completion of their 90-day probationary periods.

On the entire record, including my observation of the demeanor of the witnesses, and after considering the briefs filed by the General Counsel, the Charging Party, and the Respondent, I make the following.

FINDINGS OF FACT

I. JURISDICTION

The Respondent is a corporation engaged in the publishing and distribution of publications, with a place of business in New Castle, Delaware, where it derived gross revenues in excess of $200,000 during the past year and held membership in or subscribed to various interstate news services, including the Associated Press. The Respondent admits, and I find, that it is an employer engaged in commerce within the meaning of

[1]The Regional Director consolidated Case 4–CA–26670 with the subject case. After the opening of the hearing, the parties entered into an informal Board settlement with the posting of a notice, which I approved on the record subject to compliance with its terms and conditions (Jt. Exh. 3). Likewise, I approved the General Counsel's motion to sever that case from the subject case. Therefore, this decision will only address the issues in Case 4–CA–26797.

[2]All dates are in 1997 unless otherwise indicated.

Section 2(2), (6), and (7) of the Act and that the Union is a labor organization within the meaning of Section 2(5) of the Act.

II. ALLEGED UNFAIR LABOR PRACTICES

A. Background

On December 14, 1989, the Union was certified as the exclusive collective bargaining representative of the editorial unit. Since that time, the parties have been operating without a collective bargaining agreement. However, since at least 1995, they have been engaged in negotiations to reach an agreement. Since October 1997, Jane Amari has been Respondent's executive editor and is responsible for all personnel-related decisions of the approximately 150 employees on the editorial staff. This includes all hiring decisions, reviewing performance appraisals written by first-line supervisors, and determining whether employees should receive pay increases after completing their 90-day probationary periods. In order to assist Amari in finalizing performance appraisals and salary decisions, a manager's wage and salary administration guide is followed (R. Exh. 2). It details the procedure for conducting performance appraisals and, at section 4.4, merit increases, states in pertinent part that "Employees should not expect automatic increases and should not expect 12 month increases unless their accomplishments justify it."

B. Discussion and Analysis

The General Counsel asserts in paragraph 6 of the complaint that Respondent maintained a practice that employees who performed at a satisfactory level or higher routinely received wage increases after completion of their 90-day probationary periods. In or about July 1997, the practice was discontinued and a number of employees did not receive a wage increase after the completion of their 90-day probationary periods. The General Counsel opines that the Respondent engaged in this conduct without notice to the Union and without affording the Union an opportunity to bargain with respect to this conduct.

Respondent contends that no firm practice ever existed that editorial employees automatically receive wage increases after completion of their 90-day probationary periods. Rather, it is discretionary, subject to an independent review of the executive editor as to whether individual employees are eligible to receive wage increases.

The evidence discloses that first-line supervisors prepare a performance evaluation after employees complete their first 90 days of employment and award a score from 1 through 5 on the rating system with 3 to 3.5 being average. On occasions, the first-line supervisor will recommend that a wage increase is appropriate. The executive editor then reviews all of the employee performance appraisals and makes an independent decision as to whether a wage increase is warranted. The parties submitted an exhibit that depicts the history of wage increases for employees in the editorial department who completed their 90-day probationary periods from May 1994 to May 1999 (Jt. Exh. 1). That document conclusively shows that three employees, who completed their 90-day probationary periods from May 1994 to the end of June 1997, did not receive a wage increase. Likewise, the document establishes that between July 1997 and May 1999, 17 employees received wage increases while 28 employees did not receive wage increases despite being rated satisfactory or higher after completing their 90-day probationary periods.

Both Executive Editor Amari and former Executive Editor Bennie Ivory (September 1995 to June 1997) credibly testified that the decision to grant wage increases to employees after completion of their 90-day probationary periods is not automatic. Rather, it is within the exclusive discretion of the executive editor, and is based on a number of factors including budget considerations, the evaluation of the employee's performance, the amount of money the employee is currently earning, and whether granting a wage increase might be a factor in retaining an individual on the staff. For example, Amari testified that although employee Hurlock was rated outstanding after completing his 90-day probationary period, he was not given a wage increase because he was a part-time sports clerk. Subsequently, Hurlock was hired as a full-time employee.

The Board previously held in *Oneita Knitting Mills,* 205 NLRB 500 fn. 1 (1973), that "An employer with a past history of a merit increase program neither may discontinue that program . . . nor may he any longer . . . exercise his discretion with respect to such increases, once an exclusive bargaining representative is selected. *NLRB v. Katz,* [369] U.S. 736 (1962). What is required is a maintenance of preexisting practices, i.e., the general outline of the program; however, the implementation of that program (to the extent that discretion has existed in determining the amounts or timing of the increases) becomes a matter as to which the bargaining agent is entitled to be consulted." The

Board further addressed the issue of a respondent discontinuing the practice of granting merit increases to employees after they successfully completed a 90-day probationary period in *Dynatron/Bondo Corp.*, 323 NLRB 1263 (1997). In that case, while finding a violation of the Act when the employer totally discontinued giving merit increases to employees, the Board principally relied on a number of factors including that merit was the sole fixed criterion for granting the raise, the timing of granting the raise was consistent, the amount of the raise fell within a narrow range, the majority of employees received the raises, and the increase had been granted over a significant period of time.

In stark contrast, the merit increases in the subject case have not been totally discontinued. Additionally, other factors beside merit are utilized in determining whether a merit increase is awarded, and the dollar amount of the increase ranges from 100 percent to zero rather than remaining in a narrow range.

Based on the foregoing, I am not convinced that an established practice was in effect that employees automatically received wage increases if they were rated satisfactory or higher after completion of their 90-day probationary periods. Indeed, the evidence establishes that both before and after July 1997, a number of employees did not receive wage increases after completion of their 90-day probationary periods. Likewise, the record discloses that during the same period, a number of employees did receive wage increases after completion of their 90-day probationary periods. Thus, as required under *Oneita Knitting Mills*, the Respondent here maintained its existing practice of using a number of factors including the discretion of the executive editor in determining whether a merit increase was given to employees after completion of the 90-day probationary period. Accordingly, it follows that if there was no change in past practice in July 1997, Respondent was not required to notify or bargain with the Union. Under these circumstances, I find that since there was no change in the practice of granting wage increases to employees after completion of their 90-day probationary periods, Respondent did not violate Section 8(a)(1) and (5) of the Act. See *Selkirk Metalbestos,* 321 NLRB 44 (1996); *Haddon Craftsmen,* 297 NLRB 462 (1989).

CONCLUSIONS OF LAW

1. Respondent is an employer engaged in commerce within the meaning of Section 2(6) and (7) of the Act.
2. The Union is a labor organization within the meaning of Section 2(5) of the Act.
3. Respondent did not engage in violations of Section 8(a)(1) and (5) of the Act by discontinuing its practice of granting wage increases to employees after successful completion of their 90-day probationary periods.

On these findings of fact and conclusions of law and on the entire record, I issue the following recommended[1]

ORDER

The complaint is dismissed.

[1]If no exceptions are filed as provided by Sec. 102.46 of the Board's Rules and Regulations, the findings, conclusions, and recommended Order shall, as provided in Sec. 102.48 of the Rules, be adopted by the Board and all objections to them shall be deemed waived for all purposes.

Appendix D

Collective Bargaining Simulation: The Zinnia and Service Workers Local H–56

Collective bargaining simulations in which student teams representing management and a union negotiate a union contract are a common and important component of many labor relations courses. Unlike other texts, however, the simulation that accompanies *Labor Relations: Striking a Balance* is online. The simulation is titled "The Zinnia and Service Workers Local H-56" and involves a fictitious 300-room hotel in Minneapolis (The Zinnia) and a fictitious local union, Local H-56 of the International Union of Service Workers and Allied Employees. Rather than reading a textbook narrative, students explore the websites of The Zinnia and Local H-56 to learn about the expiring contract, the environment, their priorities, and their constraints. This use of technology and the need for online exploration make for an engaging exercise. As with other simulations, bargaining can take place in person, or if the instructor arranges, via e-mail, chat, or instant messaging. All of the needed materials are on the website at *www.thezinnia.com*, including an Excel spreadsheet for contract costing and Word documents for creating bargaining goals. Additional guidelines for instructors can be found in the online instructor's manual.

www.thezinnia.com

Name Index

(*n* indicates footnotes and source notes)

Subject Index

(*f* indicates a figure; *t* indicates a table)